THE GREEK ALPHABET

	Upper Case	Lower Case
alpha	A	α
beta	B	β
gamma	Γ	γ
delta	Δ	δ
epsilon	E	ϵ
zeta	Z	ζ
eta	H	η
theta	Θ	θ
iota	I	ι
kappa	K	κ
lambda	Λ	λ
mu	M	μ
nu	N	ν
xi	Ξ	ξ
omicron	O	o
pi	Π	π
rho	P	ρ
sigma	Σ	σ
tau	T	τ
upsilon	Υ	υ
phi	Φ	ϕ
chi	X	χ
psi	Ψ	ψ
omega	Ω	ω

Physics

Volume 1

Physics
Volume 1

RICHARD WOLFSON
Middlebury College

JAY M. PASACHOFF
Williams College

LITTLE, BROWN AND COMPANY
Boston   Toronto

Library of Congress Cataloging-in-Publication Data

Wolfson, Richard.
 Physics.

 Includes index.
 1. Physics.   I. Pasachoff, Jay M.   II. Title.
 QC21.2.W65   1987   530   86–21493
 ISBN   0–316–95054–8 (v. 1)
 ISBN   0–316–95055–6 (v. 2)

Library of Congress Catalog Card No. 86–21493

ISBN 0-316-95054-8

9 8 7 6 5 4 3 2 1

KP

Published simultaneously in Canada
by Little, Brown & Company (Canada) Limited

Printed in the United States of America

The cover photo shows a test firing of the Particle Beam Fusion Accelerator II at Sandia
National Laboratories. The electrical discharges are a result of air breakdown at the surface of
the water that covers the pulse-forming section of the PBFA, and are due to extremely high
electromagnetic fields. Photo by Walter Dickenman, courtesy of Sandia National Laboratories.

Credits appear on pages 1065–1070

PREFACE

Physics is fundamental. To understand physics is to understand how the world works, both at the everyday level and on scales of time and space so small and so large as to defy our intuition. This book is meant to provide an understanding of physics for students of science and engineering.

To the student, physics can be at once fascinating, challenging, subtle, and yet simple. Physics fascinates in its myriad applications throughout science and engineering, and in its revelation of unexpected phenomena like superconductivity and black holes. It challenges with its needs for precise thinking and for the application of mathematics in the solution of physical problems. It can be subtle in its interpretation, especially where the phenomena it describes seem at odds with our everyday ways of thinking. Perhaps most important, though, physics is simple. Its few fundamental laws are stated in the simplest of terms, yet they encompass a universe of physical phenomena, both natural and technological.

Students who recognize the simplicity of physics develop a confidence that stems from understanding the physical universe at a fundamental level. Too often, though, students see physics as a complex and forbidding subject that presents a bewildering array of new and seemingly unrelated concepts. These students suffer both in their appreciation of physics and in their ability to apply physical principles in new situations. With this book, we hope to build student competence that is based on a flexible understanding of fundamental principles rather than on rigid memorization of details.

This is a textbook for science and engineering students. It covers the traditional material of a full-year introductory physics course, and does so in the traditional sequence. But within that traditional framework we have made a conscious effort to stress the underlying simplicity and unity of physics, and to make sure that students grasp the full meaning of physical laws as they learn to apply them. We use a variety of techniques to help students achieve a full and coherent understanding of physics. We follow the introduction of new concepts with worked examples that stress different aspects and applications of those concepts, then summarize by showing how these diverse examples are really manifestations of the same underlying concept or principle. Throughout the text, we avoid reinforcing artificial distinctions between phenomena that are really similar. For example, we treat circular motion on a par with all other forms of accelerated motion, stressing that this special case is really the same as any other application of Newton's second law and shunning special terminology that might make circular motion seem somehow different.

This is a calculus-based text designed for students who have had calculus or who are taking their first calculus course concurrently with physics. At the beginning we provide frequent reviews to refresh students' knowledge and to build mathematical confidence. As the text advances, we allow for steady growth in students' mathematical skills. We introduce calculus and vectors not in separate sections but as needed throughout the text. We make frequent references to the mathematical appendices that contain not only equations but also conceptual reviews. Our mathematical expositions stress the intuitive understanding of mathematical concepts, especially in the context of their physical applications. Even students well grounded in calculus should find their understanding of calculus enhanced by its use in this physics book.

The relation between physics and mathematics presents a special challenge. Some students suppose physics to be difficult because it is mathematical. For these students we are careful to distinguish those aspects of problem solving that relate to the concepts of physics from those aspects that are more computational, at the same time building skill in the use of mathematical tools. Other students might be highly skilled in mathematics but find physics difficult because they have trouble casting physics problems in mathematical terms. For these students we stress the relation between the physical and mathematical content of basic principles, making clear how equations are simply more precise renditions of ordinary-language statements. For all students, we refuse to let mathematical derivations go dangling; we ask frequently after the derivation of a new equation or solution of an example problem, "does this result make sense?" We show that it does by appeal to physical insight in easily grasped special cases. And we illustrate the meaning of equations and principles both verbally and through diagrams, making sure that interpretations are conceptually clear as students begin to use the material quantitatively.

We want this to be a book that students can learn from, without professors' needing continually to interpret what we are saying. Our consequent emphasis on careful and thorough explanations of physics and mathematics results in a larger-than-usual ratio of words to equations, but this does not entail any reduction in the level of mathematical sophistication. And our clearer but lengthier explanations often pave the way for examples and end-of-chapter problems involving more sophisticated applications of calculus and vector algebra.

Students in the introductory physics course for scientists and engineers learn most of their physics by working problems. This text contains 2530 end-of-chapter questions and problems. The problems range from simple exercises that familiarize students with basic equations and build confidence, to more complex and realistic problems involving the application of multiple concepts, and finally to physically or mathematically difficult problems that will challenge the best students. The problems for each chapter are grouped to correspond to the major text sections, and within each section they are in roughly increasing order of difficulty. A supplementary section contains problems that extend the ideas of the text, or require more substantial synthesis of concepts from other chapters, or are especially challenging. We have made a special effort to develop new and realistic problems based on contemporary applications in science and technology. With our emphasis on the conceptual understanding of physics, we also include thought-provoking questions intended to foster a deeper understanding of fundamental principles and their applications.

Students have a wide variety of reasons for taking introductory physics. We have tried to capture and maintain the interest of all students through a broad range of examples, applications, and problems drawn from contemporary science and engineering. We have been especially careful to illustrate the principles of classical physics with up-to-date examples from high technology and contemporary scientific research. Thus the student will find, for example, energy storage in capacitors made more lively through its application to laser fusion. The restoration of the Statue of Liberty is used as an example of torque and static equilibrium. In the thermodynamics section, earth's energy balance is discussed in the context of the latest calculations on the climatic effects of nuclear war. Space exploration, communications, biotechnology, geophysics, liquid crystals, computerized automobile braking systems, and jet aircraft technology are among many other applications used to illustrate basic concepts of physics. We integrate these applications directly into the text, where they are most likely to be read by students and to motivate interest in the underlying concepts. The applications incorporate a great many photographs, charts, and diagrams.

We have worked with our publisher to make this text easy to study from. Examples are singled out using color, as are important equations. The many photographs suggest realistic applications of the material. Chapter summaries highlight major ideas and their conceptual relationships. Appendices contain reviews of calculus and trigonometry as well as tables of physical data. Our appendices are referenced throughout the text and problems, to remind students that this background material is readily available. Two levels of subheadings within each chapter provide organizational clarity, and a comprehensive index allows ready access to the material. At the back of the book we also provide answers to most odd-numbered problems. Separate aids include a Student Study Guide by Jeffrey Braun, a manual of worked-out solutions to selected problems by Timothy Halpin-Healy, and an instructor's manual including answers to all problems.

ACKNOWLEDGMENTS

A project of this magnitude is not possible without considerable help and support beyond the authors themselves, and we would like to acknowledge many others whose assistance is greatly appreciated.

From Middlebury, Rich Wolfson would like to thank first all the students in the introductory physics courses Physics 109–110, on whom I have honed the teaching methods that I hope have been captured in this text. Special thanks go to those who went on to become physics majors during the five years this book was in preparation, for their frequent discussions and advice from the student perspective. My colleagues in the sciences at Middlebury have been more than willing to discuss applications in their particular fields and subfields, and many have cheerfully supplied references, data, or illustrations on rather short notice. I am grateful to them all, especially to my immediate colleagues in Physics into whose professional lives this project has made definite intrusions. Bob Prigo, with whom I have alternated teaching the different semesters of the introductory course, gave especially valuable insights into the needs of introductory students, and provided suggestions for many examples and demonstrations. Bob Gould was helpful with material on mechanics, waves, and fluid dynamics, and engaged in vigorous discussion of some more subtle points in electromagnetism. Frank Winkler and Steve Ratcliff supplied astrophysical data and examples, and Jeff Dunham put me in touch with contemporary work in atomic and nuclear physics. Many scientists and engineers at other institutions also supplied information, references, or photographs, often in response to last-minute telephone requests. Several others deserve special thanks. Ann Broughton and Sherry Mahady provided much clerical support. Vijaya Wunnava did much of the research that made possible realistic examples based on data from contemporary applications. The reference staff at Middlebury's Starr Library proved willingly resourceful in tracking down obscure information. Scot Gould, while a Middlebury undergraduate, wrote the software that allowed equations to be set easily in the manuscript. Later, as a graduate student in physics, Scot worked all the nearly 1700 problems and made many helpful suggestions for changes which I have incorporated into the problem sets. Laboratory Supervisor Cris Butler discussed proposed problems and examples, and prepared laboratory demonstrations featured in photographs supplied from Middlebury. Photographer Erik Borg captured those demonstrations on film, and often suggested the best ways for visual presentation. Finally, I am deeply grateful to my wife Artley and daughters Sarah and Carrie for their support and patience during the five long years that it took to bring this project to completion.

From Williams, Jay Pasachoff thanks David Park for his comments on modern physics and on historical aspects, and Stuart B. Crampton, William Wootters, Kevin Jones, Jefferson Strait, and C. Ballard Pierce for useful conversations. I thank also Hugh Kirkpatrick for setting up many lecture demonstrations to be photographed, and Timothy Halpin-Healy for his work on solutions and his contributions to the optics chapters, especially the section on rainbows. My wife, Naomi, and I exchange proofreading on each other's books, and I thank her for her excellent work on this one. Our daughters Eloise and Deborah continue to help me in many ways. The comments of Martine H. Westermann on early drafts of my material were very helpful. Elizabeth Stell has done outstanding work on photographs and other aspects of production.

Both authors would also like to thank a number of individuals without whose professional efforts this book would not have been possible. At Little, Brown and Company, Ian Irvine helped develop the idea of this text, and strongly influenced its direction through his interpretation of initial reviews and survey results. Ron Pullins capably guided the book during most of the years it was in preparation. Garret White supervised the project throughout, while Sally Stickney oversaw the final production. These editors were assisted by Mary Lou Wilshaw, Ann d'Entremont, and Bonnie Wood, who kept track of countless organizational details. We thank Nancy P. Kutner of Rensselaer Polytechnic Institute for preparing the index. Her experience as an indexer and her training in physics and computer science proved helpful in this always-difficult task. Finally, the content, level, and structure of this book were significantly influenced by the many physicists who reviewed the manuscript in its various stages. These reviewers also made a great many valuable suggestions for changes to enhance clarity, to correct conceptual and mathematical errors, and to ensure an authoritative text. We are grateful to them all: Angelo Armenti, Jr., Villanova; F. Todd Baker, University of Georgia; Robert Bearse, University of Kansas; James D. Finley, III, University of New Mexico; A. Lewis Ford, Texas A&M University; Anthony French, MIT; James B. Gerhart, University of Washington; Robert Hallock, University of Massachusetts, Amherst; William M. Hartmann, Michigan State; William H. Ingham, James Madison University; Carl A. Kocher, Oregon State University; Walter H. Kruschwitz, University of South Florida; M. A. K. Lodhi, Texas Tech; David Markowitz, University of Connecticut, Storrs; Terrill W. Mayes, UNC–Charlotte; Howard McAllister, University of Hawaii; Herbert R. Muether, SUNY–Stony Brook; Robert Reynolds, Reed College; John W. Stewart, University of Virginia; Fredrick Thomas, Sinclair Community College; Alan Van Heuvelen, New Mexico State University; and George A. Williams, Utah–SLC.

We have worked to make this book as interesting, as reliable, and as error-free as possible. We would be glad to hear from any readers—faculty, students, and others—with any corrections or suggestions. We are able to make some changes between subsequent printings and would appreciate prompt comments of any sort. We promise a speedy reply to each writer.

Richard Wolfson
Department of Physics
Middlebury College
Middlebury, Vermont 05753

Jay M. Pasachoff
Department of Physics and Astronomy
Williams College
Williamstown, Massachusetts 01267

July, 1986

To the User

Physics, Volume 1 is composed of Chapters 1–19 (pp. 1–509) and the complete Appendices (pp. 1025–1056) from *Physics,* by Richard Wolfson and Jay M. Pasachoff. Cross references, Answers to Odd-Numbered Problems, Credits, and the Index are comprehensive and apply to both volumes of the text.

CONTENTS

1

DOING PHYSICS   1

1.1 Fields of Physics   1
1.2 The Simplicity of Physics   3
1.3 Measurement Systems   4
1.4 Exponential Notation   7
1.5 Estimation   10

2

MOTION IN A STRAIGHT LINE   15

2.1 Distance, Time, Speed, and
    Velocity   15
2.2 Motion in Short Time Intervals   18
2.3 Acceleration   22
2.4 Constant Acceleration   24
2.5 The Constant Acceleration of
    Gravity   29
2.6 Dimensional Analysis   33

3

MOTION IN MORE THAN ONE DIMENSION   40

3.1 The Vector Description of Motion   40

3.2 Constant Acceleration   49
3.3 Projectile Motion   51
3.4 Circular Motion   56
3.5 Motion Is Relative   60

4

DYNAMICS: WHY DO THINGS MOVE?   70

4.1 Finding the Laws of Motion   71
4.2 Force   74
4.3 Newton's Second Law   76
4.4 The Force of Gravity: Mass and
    Weight   80
4.5 Adding Forces   83
4.6 Newton's Third Law   86
4.7 Measuring Force   89

5

USING NEWTON'S LAWS   98

5.1 Using Newton's Second Law   98
5.2 Friction   102
5.3 Circular Motion   112

6

WORK, ENERGY, AND POWER   124

6.1 Work   124
6.2 Work and the Scalar
     Product   126
6.3 A Varying Force   128
6.4 Force and Work in Three
     Dimensions   132
6.5 Kinetic Energy   134
6.6 Energy Units   136
6.7 Power   138

7

CONSERVATION OF ENERGY   148

7.1 Conservative and Nonconservative
     Forces   148
7.2 Potential Energy   151
7.3 Conservation of Mechanical
     Energy   154
7.4 Potential Energy Curves   159
7.5 Force and Potential Energy   162
7.6 Nonconservative Forces   165
7.7 Conservation of Energy and Mass-
     Energy   166

8

GRAVITATION   176

8.1 Toward the Concept of Universal
     Gravitation   177
8.2 The Law of Universal
     Gravitation   178
8.3 Orbital Motion   182
8.4 Gravitational Potential
     Energy   187
8.5 The Superposition
     Principle   193
8.6 The Gravitational Field   198
8.7 Tidal Forces and the Roche
     Limit   200
8.8 Gravity and the General Theory of
     Relativity   203

9

SYSTEMS OF PARTICLES   211

9.1 Center of Mass   211
9.2 Momentum   218
9.3 Kinetic Energy in Many-Particle
     Systems   225

10

COLLISIONS   232

10.1 Impulse and Collisions   232
10.2 Collisions and the Conservation
      Laws   234
10.3 Inelastic Collisions   236
10.4 Elastic Collisions   238

11

TORQUE AND STATIC EQUILIBRIUM   249

11.1 Torque   249
11.2 Static Equilibrium   254
11.3 Center of Gravity   257
11.4 Stability of Static Equilibria   263

12

ROTATIONAL MOTION   274

12.1 Angular Velocity and
      Acceleration   274
12.2 Rotational Inertia and the Analog of
      Newton's Law   279
12.3 Energy and Rotational
      Motion   287
12.4 Angular Momentum   291

13

OSCILLATORY MOTION   308

13.1 Properties of Oscillatory
      Motion   309
13.2 Simple Harmonic Motion   310

13.3 Applications of Simple Harmonic Motion   316

13.4 Simple Harmonic Motion in Two Dimensions   322

13.5 Energy in Simple Harmonic Motion   324

13.6 Damped Harmonic Motion   327

13.7 Driven Oscillations and Resonance   330

14

WAVE MOTION   340

14.1 Properties of Waves   342

14.2 Mathematical Description of Wave Motion   345

14.3 Waves on a String: The Wave Equation   347

14.4 Wave Energy and Intensity   351

14.5 The Superposition Principle and Wave Interference   353

14.6 Wave Reflection   357

14.7 Standing Waves   359

14.8 The Doppler Effect   363

14.9 Shock Waves   365

15

FLUID MOTION   373

15.1 Describing Fluids   374

15.2 Fluids at Rest   376

15.3 Fluid Dynamics   385

15.4 Other Aspects of Fluid Motion   396

16

TEMPERATURE AND HEAT   404

16.1 Macroscopic and Microscopic Descriptions   404

16.2 Temperature and Thermodynamic Equilibrium   405

16.3 Measuring Temperature   406

16.4 Temperature and Heat   408

16.5 Heat Capacity and Specific Heat   410

16.6 Heat Transfer   413

16.7 Thermal Energy Balance   421

17

THE THERMAL BEHAVIOR OF MATTER   431

17.1 The Ideal Gas   431

17.2 Phase Changes   439

17.3 Thermal Expansion   446

18

HEAT, WORK, AND THE FIRST LAW OF THERMODYNAMICS   455

18.1 The First Law of Thermodynamics   455

18.2 Thermodynamic Processes   457

18.3 The Specific Heats of an Ideal Gas   470

19

THE SECOND LAW OF THERMODYNAMICS   481

19.1 Reversibility and Irreversibility   481

19.2 The Second Law of Thermodynamics   483

19.3 Applications of the Second Law of Thermodynamics   490

19.4 The Thermodynamic Temperature Scale   496

19.5 Entropy and the Quality of Energy   496

NOTE Pages 510–1024 (Chapters 20–36) can be found in *Physics, Volume 2.*

APPENDICES

A   Algebra and Trigonometry   1025
B   Calculus   1030
C   The International System of
    Units (SI)   1036
D   Conversion Factors   1042
E   The Elements   1046
F   Astrophysical Data   1049
G   Current Values for Physical Constants   1051
H   Nobel Prizes   1052

*ANSWERS TO ODD-NUMBERED
PROBLEMS*   *1057*

INDEX   *1071*

Physics
Volume 1

1

DOING PHYSICS

When you ride a bicycle, fly in a jet plane, or watch a thunderstorm, you experience physical laws. **Physics** is the science that tells us how and why things work. Knowledge of physics will help you understand both natural phenomena and the technologies that increasingly pervade our lives. In this book, we set forth the basic laws of physics and show how they apply to a myriad of phenomena from atoms and molecules to cars and airplanes, rockets and computers, stars and galaxies.

The dividing line between practical and fanciful applications of physics is eroding. Just a few decades ago, only science fiction writers could suggest that laws conceived by Isaac Newton in the 1600's would be used to guide spacecraft to the planets. Now that is history; exploration of the outer planets by Voyager spacecraft and the rendezvous with Halley's Comet by an international flotilla of spacecraft in 1986 represent triumphs of human ingenuity and of our understanding of the laws of physics (Fig. 1–1).

Fig. 1–1
The European Space Agency's Giotto spacecraft approaches Halley's Comet in March 1986. The spacecraft is an artist's rendition superimposed on an actual photo of the comet.

1.1
FIELDS OF PHYSICS

The branch of physics governing the motion of bodies is called **mechanics.** You use the laws of mechanics when you drive a car, ride a skateboard, build a skyscraper, and many other times each day. Through most of this book, we deal with **classical mechanics,** which applies to objects from molecules to galaxies that are moving at speeds small compared with the speed of light. In later chapters, we will see that classical mechanics is but an approximation to a more comprehensive set of physical laws that includes Einstein's theory of relativity and the theory of quantum mechanics.

In the first eight chapters we deal with the motion of single objects, often called particles. Then, in Chapters 9 to 13, we generalize to the motion of many-particle systems. The wave of standing people that sweeps

physics

mechanics

classical mechanics

1

wave motion

through a football stadium, ocean waves that pound the coastlines, and the sound waves by which we communicate are examples of a special kind of many-particle motion called **wave motion,** which we examine in Chapter 14.

Our earth is five-eighths covered by liquid water, and is surrounded entirely by a gaseous atmosphere. Even the continents on which we live float around on an underlying fluid layer. The cells of our bodies are nurtured by the motion of fluid through our circulatory systems. And the bulk of the matter in the universe—stars and interstellar gas—is in the fluid state. In Chapter 15, we apply the laws of mechanics to fluids.

Nearly all life on earth thrives on a constant supply of energy from the sun, and a delicate balance of energy-transfer processes keeps our planet at a habitable temperature; we worry increasingly that human activity may upset that balance and bring severe climatic changes. For our technological society, we have developed nuclear power plants, gasoline engines, solar collectors, oil and gas furnaces, and a host of other energy sources. Worries about our planet's energy balance, and the operation of our energy technologies, are both concerns of **thermodynamics**—the study of heat and its interaction with matter. We follow our study of mechanics with four chapters on thermodynamics.

thermodynamics

electromagnetism

Following, we deal extensively with another major branch of physics: **electromagnetism.** The Greeks knew something of the electric and magnetic properties of matter; the words electricity and magnetism themselves originate in Greek words for natural materials displaying electric and magnetic effects. The Chinese invention of the magnetic compass resulted by the twelfth century A.D. in widespread use of earth's natural magnetism to aid navigation. In 1800, Alessandro Volta invented the electric battery, paving the way for a series of experiments involving electric current and its magnetic effects. By the late 1800's, application of electromagnetism led to practical technologies including telegraph, telephone, and electric power distribution. In one of the most sweeping syntheses in the history of science, James Clerk Maxwell in the 1860's formulated a complete description of electromagnetism, showing that electricity and magnetism are intimately related. A startling prediction of Maxwell's theory was that light is an electromagnetic wave phenomenon, and that other electromagnetic waves should be possible as well. Radio and television follow directly from that prediction. Today, electromagnetic technology dominates our civilization, as evidenced by our digital watches, video recorders, microwave ovens, and especially computers (Fig. 1–2).

Fig. 1–2
This tiny silicon chip forms the heart of a personal computer. The chip contains the equivalent of over 100,000 electronic parts. Here we see an electron micrograph of an ant carrying the chip.

Electromagnetic theory led directly to many practical technologies, but it also raised bafflingly deep questions about the nature of light, motion, space, and time. With a radically simple statement whose implications seem to violate our common sense, Albert Einstein in 1905 confronted these questions (Fig. 1–3). His **special theory of relativity** gives a surprisingly simple picture of reality, in the context of radically altered notions of space and time. Although relativity provides a more correct description of physical reality than does classical mechanics, the two theories differ significantly only at speeds approaching that of light—seven times around the earth in one second. In our everyday existence we need not worry about relativity. But in particle accelerators probing the basic structure of matter;

special theory of relativity

in studies of exploding supernovas, neutron stars, and the early universe; and even in designing a color television, we must take account of relativity. We explore the theory of relativity in Chapter 33.

optics

The behavior of light is intimately tied to electromagnetism and relativity. In Chapters 34 and 35 we explore the branch of physics called **optics,** building an understanding of light and of optical devices like lenses, prisms, diffraction gratings, and the instruments we build from them—microscopes, telescopes, spectrometers, and the like (Fig. 1–4).

quantum mechanics

But what is light? This question leads to one of the major developments of twentieth-century thought: **quantum mechanics.** Dealing with the smallest objects in the universe, quantum mechanics blurs the distinction between light and matter, giving a description of matter on the atomic scale for which our macroscopic intuition is simply inadequate. We give a brief introduction to quantum mechanics and its philosophical implications in Chapter 36. We also discuss our evolving knowledge of the elementary particles that are the fundamental constituents of matter. Finally, we show how studies of the largest and smallest components of the universe are uniting to give us a picture of the universe only a fraction of a second after its creation.

Fig. 1–3
Albert Einstein at age 26, when he developed the special theory of relativity.

1.2
THE SIMPLICITY OF PHYSICS

Physics is the fundamental science. Its laws and theories describe the workings of the universe at the most basic level. For that reason physics is immensely powerful; the same laws describe the behavior of molecules, of airplanes, and of galaxies. Although no one has done so, most scientists believe in principle that it would be possible to describe the operation of a living cell or organism using only the fundamental laws of physics.

Applying the laws of physics can give rise to challenging problems whose solutions call for clever insight and mathematical agility. The challenge of problem solving is what gives physics some of its intellectual interest and also its reputation as a difficult subject. But if you approach this course thinking that physics presents you with numerous difficult things to learn, you are missing the point. Because it is so fundamental, physics is inherently simple. There are only a few basic laws to learn; if you really understand those laws, you can readily apply them in a wide variety of situations. We wrote this book in a spirit that emphasizes the underlying simplicity of physics by reminding you how diverse examples are really manifestations of the *same* underlying physical laws. You should come to understand the basic laws thoroughly so you can apply them confidently in new situations. As you read the text and work physics problems, remember the simplicity of the underlying physical principles. Ask yourself how each problem you approach is really similar to other problems and to the text examples. And you will find that similarity, because the many problems and examples really do involve only a few underlying laws. So physics is simple—challenging, too—but with an underlying simplicity that reflects the scope and power of this fundamental science.

Fig. 1–4
The Hubble Space Telescope will use optical principles to bring us information about the most remote objects in the universe. Here we see it being assembled; the tube inserted into a central hole in the 2.4-m-diameter main mirror is to block internal stray light.

Fig. 1–5
A standard foot and yard were placed on a wall in the courtyard of the Royal Observatory in Greenwich, England, in the mid-1800's.

1.3
MEASUREMENT SYSTEMS

"A long way" means different things to a sedentary person, to a marathon runner, to a pilot, and to an astronaut. We need to quantify our measurements. In the United States, we still use a unit derived from the length of a person's foot—the foot, a unit that can be traced back through Greek and Roman to Egyptian times. The inch and the yard share that lineage. The Roman mile of 5000 feet was changed by Queen Elizabeth in the late sixteenth century to 5280 feet, or 8 furlongs. But though we think of inches, feet, yards, miles, and pounds as "English units" (Fig. 1–5), they are being phased out even in England. Every country in the world, except the United States, Burma, and Brunei (a sultanate on the island of Borneo), now uses the metric system, in which the unit of length is based on the **meter** (from the Greek word "metron," meaning "a measure"). The meter was first defined at the time of the French Revolution to be one ten-millionth of the distance from the equator to the north pole through Paris. This distance, of course, is not trivial to determine—surveyors sent out at the time to measure a portion of the path were nearly guillotined—and more readily accessible measuring standards proved necessary.

In 1889, a standard meter was carefully made; it is the distance between two lines on a certain bar made of a platinum-iridium alloy when examined at the temperature of the melting point of ice. It is kept in a temperature-controlled room at the Bureau International des Poids et Mesures in Sèvres, France, where the international treaty on measurement signed in 1875 is monitored. Thirty secondary standards were also made from the same ingot of alloy; the United States Bureau of Standards in Washington, D.C., has numbers 21 and 27. (Comparisons over 15 years showed that the standard meters remained the same to within 2 ten-millionths of a meter.) But as new methods developed, even the standard meter was not sufficiently accurate. In 1960, the meter was redefined as 1,650,763.73 wavelengths of orange-red light emitted by the isotope krypton-86.

In recent years, even this standard became insufficient. The speed of light is now one of the most accurately determined quantities (Fig. 1–6). In 1983, the meter was redefined in terms of the speed of light, which, in vacuum, has been measured at 299,792.458 kilometers per second (km/s). The 1983 Conférence Général des Poids et Mesures inverted this result and defined the meter as "the length of the path travelled by light in a vacuum during a time interval of 1/299,792,458 of a second."

In science, we now use the version of the metric system known as SI, for Système International d'Unités (International System of Units). Its basic version was developed in 1960, but it has been modified several times since. Engineers in the United States still often use the English system. If you were in England, though, you would find that bottles labelled with the English unit "1 gallon" actually contain 5 liters, a metric unit. In the United States, the use of the metric system was legalized in 1866, and the yard and the pound have been defined in terms of the meter and the kilogram since 1893. The definitions were changed in 1959 to make 1 yard exactly equal

meter

Fig. 1–6
A helium-neon laser at the National Bureau of Standards laboratory in Boulder, Colorado, is used to make accurate determinations of the speed of light. Here, Kenneth Evenson calibrates the instrument.

to 0.9144 m—slightly less than its previous value of 36/39.37 m—and to make a one-pound mass exactly equal to 0.453 592 37 kg.

SI includes 7 independent base units: the meter (m) for length, the kilogram (kg) for mass, the second (s) for time, the ampere (A) for electric current, the kelvin (K) for temperature, the mole (mol) for the amount of substance, and the candela (cd) for luminosity. Two supplementary units are used to measure angle—the radian (rad) for ordinary angles and the steradian (sr) for solid angles (Fig. 1–7). Units for all other quantities are derived from these base units. In mechanics, we use only the first three of the base units—meter, kilogram, and second—along with measures of angle.

The metric system is a decimal system. Its base units are used with the prefixes listed in Table 1–1 to indicate multiplication by powers of 10. For example, k is the SI symbol for the prefix "kilo-," which means "times 1000." 1 km is thus 1000 m.

When two units are used together, a hyphen appears between them: newton-meter. Each unit has a symbol, such as m for meter or km for kilometer. Since these are symbols, rather than abbreviations, they are not followed by periods. Neither are the plural forms followed by an "s." Symbols are ordinarily lowercase; only those named after people are uppercase (with one exception). Thus the symbol for gram is a lowercase g; the unit "newton" is written with a small "n" but its symbol is a capital N. The only exception is for the volume unit, the liter (spelled "litre" in most other countries), defined as the volume of a cube one-tenth of a meter on each side. Since the lowercase "l" is easily confused with the number one, the symbol for liter is written with a capital L. When two units are multiplied, their symbols are separated by a centered dot: N·m for newton-meter. Division of units is expressed using the slash (/), or by writing the symbol for the denominator unit raised to the −1 power. Thus the SI unit of speed is the meter per second, written m/s or $m \cdot s^{-1}$. When four or more digits are used together, SI recommends the use of spaces to separate groups of three:

$\theta = \dfrac{s}{r}$

$\Omega = \dfrac{A}{r^2}$

Fig. 1–7
SI units of angle. (a) The radian measure of an angle is defined as the ratio of the subtended arc length to the radius. Since the circumference of a circle is $2\pi r$, there are 2π radians in a complete circle. One radian is then equal to $360°/2\pi$ or $57.3°$. (b) The measure of a solid angle is defined as the ratio of the subtended area to the radius squared.

TABLE 1–1

SI Prefixes

Prefix	Symbol	Power	
exa	E	10^{18}	= 1 000 000 000 000 000 000
peta	P	10^{15}	= 1 000 000 000 000 000
tera	T	10^{12}	= 1 000 000 000 000
giga	G	10^{9}	= 1 000 000 000
mega	M	10^{6}	= 1 000 000
kilo	k	10^{3}	= 1 000
hecto	h	10^{2}	= 100
deca	da	10^{1}	= 10
—	—	10^{0}	= 1
deci	d	10^{-1}	= 0.1
centi	c	10^{-2}	= 0.01
milli	m	10^{-3}	= 0.001
micro	μ	10^{-6}	= 0.000 001
nano	n	10^{-9}	= 0.000 000 001
pico	p	10^{-12}	= 0.000 000 000 001
femto	f	10^{-15}	= 0.000 000 000 000 001
atto	a	10^{-18}	= 0.000 000 000 000 000 001

34 365.456 32; we tend to use commas instead of spaces in the United States, though some countries use a comma as we use a period to indicate a decimal point.

The study of the fundamental units is itself an interesting field of physics. There are, for example, at least a half-dozen definitions of units of time, each different. The division of time into hours, minutes, and seconds goes back to the Babylonians. The **second** used to be defined by the earth's rotation, as $1/(24 \times 60 \times 60)$ of a mean solar day, but then it was realized that the earth's rotation is slowing slightly. The second was then redefined as a specific fraction of the year 1900. Later, the second was defined in terms of the vibrations of a certain type of cesium atom (Fig. 1–8); the device used was called an "atomic clock." More recently, devices called hydrogen masers have been used as even more stable time standards. And now some scientists are anticipating that even more accurate time standards will be provided by pulsars—celestial objects that pulse at an extremely steady rate. One pulsar in particular, when its minuscule rate of slowing down is taken into account, can give us time accurate to one-billionth of a second per year. It is a good thing that we have better standards of time than the rotation of the earth; new research in 1984 revealed that the earth's rotation slows down and speeds up slightly as the wind blows. To keep atomic time and earth-spin time in agreement, "leap seconds" are added to our terrestrial clocks when necessary, usually about once a year.

The standard of mass is now the least satisfactory. Unlike the standards of length and time, which are based on measurement procedures that can be repeated by scientists anywhere, the unit of mass is still defined in terms of a particular object—the international prototype **kilogram** kept at the International Bureau of Weights and Measures at Sèvres, France (Fig. 1–9). It is made out of a special platinum-iridium alloy that is very hard, not subject to corrosion, and very dense. Nevertheless, it could conceivably change, and in any event comparison with such a standard is less convenient than a procedural standard that can be checked in a laboratory. So scientists are now working on techniques to measure the spacing of atoms in a crystal of silicon, essentially counting the atoms in a given volume, and therefore to scale up from the mass of a single silicon atom to a new definition of the kilogram.

second

Fig. 1–8
This cesium atomic-beam clock is the primary standard for time in the United States. The SI second is defined as the duration of 9,192,631.770 periods of the waves emitted as the cesium atoms undergo a particular transition.

kilogram

Changing Units

Frequently, we need to change units from one system to another—for example, from English to SI units. Appendix D contains extensive tables for converting among unit systems; you should familiarize yourself with this and the other appendices, and refer to them often.

In changing units, it is helpful to treat the units as algebraic quantities. Then we can derive ratios that are equivalent to 1 and have no dimensions.

Fig. 1–9
In this vault at the International Bureau of Weights and Measures at Sèvres, France, we find on the top shelf the international prototype meter bar of 1889 in its protective case. On the bottom shelf is the international prototype kilogram, its six comparison standards, two thermometers, and a hygrometer. The prototype kilogram has been used only three times: before 1889, in 1939, and in 1946. The standard meter has been superseded by measurement techniques based on the speed of light, but the international prototype kilogram remains the official standard of mass.

Since we can always multiply anything by 1 without changing its value, we can manipulate units in an expression by multiplying by these ratios.

For example, we know that 60 min = 1 h. Dividing both sides of this equation by 1 h, we have

$$\frac{60 \text{ min}}{1 \text{ h}} = 1.$$

Then, if we want to transform 24 hours into minutes, we multiply by this equivalent-to-1 ratio; the h in the denominator of our ratio cancels the h in the top of our original number:

$$(24 \text{ h}) \left(\frac{60 \text{ min}}{1 \text{ h}} \right) = 1440 \text{ min.}$$

We could equally well have divided the equation "60 min = 1 h" by 60 min to get 1 = (1 h)/(60 min), which puts the minutes into the denominator but also gives a ratio equivalent to 1. If we were changing minutes to hours, we would want this alternative form.

This method of changing units can also be used to change between metric and English units. For example, with 1 m = 39.37 in, the 400-inch-diameter mirror of the Keck telescope in Hawaii—to be the world's largest optical telescope—will be

$$(400 \text{ in}) \left(\frac{1 \text{ m}}{39.37 \text{ in}} \right) = 10.2 \text{ m}$$

Fig. 1–10
A model of the Keck Ten-Meter Telescope.

across (see Figure 1–10).

When you change units in some complicated fashion, a chain of such multiplications helps you keep track of units in a mechanical way, and prevents you from carelessly inverting one of the conversion factors.

Example 1–1
Changing Units

Express the United States' 55 mi/h speed limit in meters per second.

Solution

In Appendix D, we find that 1 mi = 1609 m, so we can multiply miles by the ratio 1609 m/mi to get meters. Similarly, we use the conversion factor 3600 s/h to convert hours to seconds. So we have

$$55 \text{ mi/h} = \frac{(55 \text{ mi})(1609 \text{ m/mi})}{(1 \text{ h})(3600 \text{ s/h})} = 24.6 \text{ m/s.}$$

1.4
EXPONENTIAL NOTATION

The range of measured quantities in the universe is enormous; lengths alone range from about 1/1 000 000 000 000 000 m for the radius of the proton to 10 000 000 000 000 000 000 000 m for the size of a galaxy; our telescopes observe to distances 10,000 times farther still. It is easy to lose track with so many zeroes involved. We thus often write numbers as decimals with one digit before the decimal point multiplying 10 to some power.

Fig. 1–11
A galaxy can be 10^{21} m across.

Fig. 1–12
Taken with an electron microscope, this photograph shows both artificial and natural structures on the small scale. Vertical lines are 20-nm-wide strips of polymethyl methacrylate, laid down on a silicon substrate by a process called x-ray lithography. The tailed structure is a T-4 bacteriophage virus, the head of which measures about 100 nm across.

TABLE 1–2
Some Typical Distances

Distance to farthest quasar detected	1×10^{26}	m
Distance to nearest large galaxy (Andromeda)	2×10^{22}	m
Diameter of our galaxy (Milky Way)	8×10^{20}	m
Distance to nearest star (Proxima Centauri)	4×10^{16}	m
Radius of Pluto's orbit	6×10^{12}	m
Radius of earth's orbit	1.5×10^{11}	m
Diameter of earth	1.3×10^{7}	m
Deepest ocean trench (Marianas Trench)	1.1×10^{4}	m
Skyscraper (Sears Tower, Chicago)	4.4×10^{2}	m
Height of person	2	m
Transistor on semiconductor chip	1×10^{-5}	m
Diameter of red blood cell	8×10^{-6}	m
Diameter of virus	1×10^{-7}	m
Smallest human-made structures	2×10^{-9}	m
Atomic diameter (hydrogen)	1×10^{-10}	m
Diameter of proton	2×10^{-15}	m

TABLE 1–3
Some Typical Times

Time since Big Bang	5×10^{17}	s
Age of earth	1.5×10^{17}	s
Time for sun to orbit galactic center	8×10^{15}	s
Existence of human species	6×10^{13}	s
Half-life of plutonium	8×10^{11}	s
Human lifespan	2×10^{9}	s
Orbital period of earth (1 year)	3×10^{7}	s
Rotation period of earth (1 day)	9×10^{4}	s
Flight time of intercontinental missile	1×10^{3}	s
Human heartbeat	1	s
Reaction time of human nervous system	1×10^{-1}	s
Period of highest audible sound	5×10^{-5}	s
Period of AM radio wave	1×10^{-6}	s
Time for fast computer to add two numbers	1×10^{-8}	s
Period of rotation of typical molecule	1×10^{-12}	s
Shortest light pulse produced in laboratory	1×10^{-15}	s
Half-life of neutral pion	2×10^{-16}	s
Time for light to cross a proton	7×10^{-24}	s
Earliest time after Big Bang to which known laws of physics apply	10^{-43}	s

For example, 14 can be written as 1.4×10^{1}, 1687 can be written as 1.687×10^{3}, and 0.023 can be written as 2.3×10^{-2}. (Note that a negative exponent means to take the inverse of the same quantity with a positive exponent, so that $10^{-2} = 1/10^{2} = 0.01$.) This way of writing numbers is called **exponential notation** or **scientific notation.** Exponential notation is often used in computers and calculators, with the letter E for exponential instead of the 10; the numbers above would then be written 1.4E1, 1.687E3, and 2.3E-2, respectively. Tables 1–2, 1–3, and 1–4 list some typical distance, time, and mass measurements in exponential notation (see also Figures 1–11, 1–12, and 1–13).

To add two quantities that have the same exponent, the distributive law of multiplication shows that we simply add the coefficients:

exponential notation
scientific notation

TABLE 1–4
Some Typical Masses

Galaxy (Milky Way)	4×10^{41}	kg
Sun	2×10^{30}	kg
Earth	6×10^{24}	kg
Mountain	2×10^{18}	kg
747 jetliner	4×10^{5}	kg
Compact car	1×10^{3}	kg
Human	65	kg
Raisin	1×10^{-3}	kg
Raindrop	1×10^{-6}	kg
Red blood cell	1×10^{-13}	kg
DNA molecule	2×10^{-18}	kg
Uranium atom	4×10^{-25}	kg
Proton	1.7×10^{-27}	kg
Electron	9.1×10^{-31}	kg

significant figures

Fig. 1–13
A 747 jetliner has a mass of 4×10^5 kg.

$$1.4 \times 10^1 \text{ kg} + 3.8 \times 10^1 \text{ kg} = (1.4 + 3.8) \times 10^1 \text{ kg} = 5.2 \times 10^1 \text{ kg}.$$

As in this example, most numbers we work with in physics represent physical quantities. It is important in working with such quantities to keep the numbers labelled with the appropriate unit symbol; the answer for a physical quantity is meaningful only if its units are specified, and furthermore, attention to units can alert you to mistakes in algebra. In particular, the only quantities that can be added meaningfully are quantities with the same units (adding 5 kilograms to 3 seconds, for example, makes no sense). We discuss the manipulation of units further in Chapter 2.

To add quantities with different exponents, we must first express them with the same exponent. After all, to add 3 pennies to 2 dimes, you would first convert the dimes to their equivalent number of pennies. Similarly,

$$6.8 \times 10^4 \text{ s} + 3.1 \times 10^5 \text{ s} = 6.8 \times 10^4 \text{ s} + 31 \times 10^4 \text{ s} = 37.8 \times 10^4 \text{ s}$$
$$= 3.78 \times 10^5 \text{ s},$$

where we converted 3.1×10^5 s to its equivalent, 31×10^4 s.

How accurate is the answer we just calculated? We only knew two digits of accuracy for each of the original numbers; we say that those numbers are accurate to two **significant figures.** The mere act of calculating cannot add accuracy, so the answer should not have more than two significant figures. We thus round it off to 3.8×10^5 s. Calculators and computers often give us numbers to many figures, but some or even most of those figures may be meaningless. If they are outside the range of accuracy set by our original numbers, they must be discarded.

Exponential notation is particularly useful when we multiply numbers, since then we merely multiply the digits and add the exponents. For example,

$$(3.0 \times 10^8 \text{ m/s})(1.5 \times 10^{-9} \text{ s}) = (3.0)(1.5) \times 10^{8+(-9)} \text{ m}$$
$$= 4.5 \times 10^{-1} \text{ m} = 45 \text{ cm}$$

is the distance that light, moving at 3.0×10^8 m/s, travels in 1.5 ns (nano is the prefix meaning one-billionth, or 10^{-9}; see Table 1.1). Notice in this example how we treated units as algebraic quantities, multiplying meters per second by seconds to get meters.

To raise a number written in exponential form to some power, we raise the digits preceding 10 to that power and multiply the exponent by the power:

$$(3 \times 10^4 \text{ m})^2 = 3^2 \times 10^{(4)(2)} \text{ m}^2 = 9 \times 10^8 \text{ m}^2$$

and

$$\sqrt{64 \times 10^6 \text{ m}^2/\text{s}^2} = (64 \times 10^6 \text{ m}^2/\text{s}^2)^{1/2} = 8.0 \times 10^3 \text{ m/s}.$$

When taking the square root of an odd power, we first convert it to an even power:

$$\sqrt{2.5 \times 10^7} = (25 \times 10^6)^{1/2} = 5.0 \times 10^3.$$

Note that raising a quantity to the one-half power is the same as taking the square root.

1.5

ESTIMATION

Some problems in physics and engineering call for very precise numerical answers. We need to know exactly how long to fire a rocket to put a space probe on course for a distant planet, or exactly what size to cut the tiny quartz crystal whose vibrations set the pulse of a digital watch. But for many other purposes, we need only a rough idea of the size of a given physical effect. Often a rough estimate will tell us that we can ignore a certain effect before we go to the trouble of calculating it exactly. In other cases, an estimate—even though it may be off by a factor of ten or more—may help decide among competing theories. And we can often make a rough estimate to check whether the results of more difficult calculations make sense.

When confronted with any physics problem, especially one involving estimation, think of what you know that might possibly pertain to the problem. Finding such links between what you already know and what the problem requires is more important than looking up formulas in a textbook. Sometimes a little thought will lead you to solutions that you didn't at first think you could achieve.

Example 1-2

Estimation: Is Earth Growing?

(a) Estimate the present mass of the earth. (b) Earth is about 5 billion years old. Micrometeorites, roughly the size of dust grains, rain down on earth at the rate of about 10^6 kg per day (see Figure 1–14). Has this rain of dust contributed significantly to earth's present mass?

Solution

(a) How big is the earth? Maybe you know its diameter, but if you don't, consider how the United States looks on a globe. In its east-west dimension, the United States spans perhaps one-sixth of the globe. From the Atlantic to the Pacific coast is about 3000 miles, a little less than 5000 km. So earth is about 5000 km × 6 $=3 \times 10^4$ km around at the latitude of the United States. At the equator, it is farther around—say about 4×10^4 km. The circumference of a circle is $2\pi r$, so earth's radius is 4×10^4 km$/2\pi$, or about 6×10^3 km. (The actual value, given in Appendix F, is 6.4×10^3 km, so our estimate is quite close.) Now the volume of a sphere is $\frac{4}{3}\pi r^3$, or, since π is close to 3, about $4r^3$. So the volume of the earth is

$$V_e \sim (4)(6 \times 10^6 \text{ m})^3 \sim 8 \times 10^{20} \text{ m}^3,$$

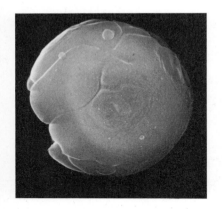

Fig. 1–14
A scanning-electron-microscope image of a micrometeorite.

where we use the sign $\sim$ to indicate a rough approximation. How dense is earth? It is made of rock, which is certainly denser than water. How much denser? Significantly denser, but on the other hand not ten times as dense. Say about twice as dense. Now how dense is water? Maybe you know that 1 cm³ of water has a mass of 1 gram. But if not, maybe you've heard that "a pint's a pound," or maybe you can guess from experience that a gallon of water is around 10 lb, or 5 kg. Let's use the latter estimate. A gallon contains 4 quarts, and a quart is about a liter (look at the label on a 1-quart soda bottle to confirm this!). So a quart of water has a mass of about 5 kg/4, or about 1 kg. A liter is 1000 cm³, or 10^{-3} m³, so the density of water is about 1 kg$/10^{-3}$ m³, or 1×10^3 kg/m³. If rock is twice as dense, the density of rock is 2×10^3 kg/m³. Then, using our value for earth's volume, we can estimate the mass of the earth as

$$M_e = \text{(volume)(density)} = (8 \times 10^{20} \text{ m}^3)(2 \times 10^3 \text{ kg/m}^3) = 1.6 \times 10^{24} \text{ kg}.$$

Appendix F gives the correct value as 5.98×10^{24} kg; our answer is low by a factor of about 4, but is still quite adequate to our purpose of determining whether the rain of micrometeorites is significant. (Part of the reason for our low estimate is the fact that material in the core of the earth is compressed to much higher densities than the rocks with which we are familiar.)

(b) Coming down at the rate of 10^6 kg/day, the total mass of micrometeorites landing on earth in 5×10^9 years is

$$m = (10^6 \text{ kg/day})(365 \text{ days/year})(5 \times 10^9 \text{ years}) = 2 \times 10^{18} \text{ kg}.$$

Since this is far less than our estimate of earth's mass (only about $10^{18}/10^{24}$, or one-millionth), the rain of micrometeorites has made an insignificant contribution to earth's mass.

Our conclusion rests on an important assumption: that micrometeorites have fallen at roughly the same rate for 5 billion years. Actually, the rate was probably higher when the solar system was young. But except for the earliest times, when earth itself was forming from the matter of the primordial solar system, extraterrestrial matter probably has not contributed significantly to earth's mass.

Example 1–3

Estimation: Post Offices

How many post offices are there in the United States?

Solution

Are you tempted to ask for more information? You don't have to! What do you know about post offices? There is at least one in every city, and large cities have several. What is the size of a city that has only one? Let us estimate 20,000. The population of the United States is about 240 million. 240 million divided by 20 thousand is about 10 thousand. So that is one estimate of the number of post offices.

Can we get the answer another way? Consider the area served by a post office. Again, a large city will have several post offices, and small towns separated by 50 km will certainly have separate post offices, so let us estimate an area 25 km × 25 km, say 30 km × 30 km to make the multiplication easier. This is about 1000 square km for a single post office. What is the area of the United States? It is about 3000 miles from coast to coast, and 2000 miles from Maine to Florida. This translates into about (5000 km) (3000 km) = 15×10^6 km². At 1000 km² per post office, this estimate calls for 15×10^6 km²/(1000 km/post office) = 15,000 post offices. This answer is within a factor of 2 of our earlier estimate, which is more consistency than we might expect when estimating.

How about a third method? Zip codes are 5 digits long, so there clearly must be fewer than 99,999 post offices.

What is the right answer? The U.S. Postal Service reports that there are about 30,000 post offices. Our estimates are all within a factor of about 3.

Example 1–4

Estimation: Nuclear-Electric Cars?

(a) Estimate the annual consumption of gasoline by cars in the United States. (b) Burned in a car, a gallon of gasoline is roughly equivalent to 30 kilowatt-hours (kWh) of electricity. If a large nuclear power plant produces electricity at the rate of 10^6 kWh per hour (1000 MW), how many such plants would have to be built if the United States converted to electric cars?

Solution

How far is your family car driven each year? Mine goes about 12,000 miles, or roughly 10^4 mi. A typical car might get 20 miles/gallon, so at 10^4 miles/year, it would use $(10^4$ mi/y$)/(20$ mi/gal$) = 500$ gal/y. How many cars are there in the United States? There are over 200 million people, but certainly not everyone has a car. My family has four people and two cars, so perhaps there are about 100 million, or 10^8 cars. The annual gasoline consumption of all these cars is then $(500$ gal/y/car$)(10^8$ cars$) = 5 \times 10^{10}$ gal/y. (Figures from the U.S. Department of Energy show that the total gasoline consumption in the mid-1980's was somewhat over 10^{11} gal/y, so our estimate is low by only a factor of about 2.)

At 30 kWh/gal, our estimated gasoline consumption is equivalent to $(30$ kWh/gal$)(5 \times 10^{10}$ gal/y$) \sim 10^{12}$ kWh/y. How many power plants would this require if we converted to electric cars? Each plant produces electricity at the rate of 10^6 kWh/h. But there are 24×365 or about 10^4 hours in a year, so each plant produces $(10^6$ kWh/h$)(10^4$ h/y$)$ or 10^{10} kWh/y. We need 10^{12} kWh/y; this requires $(10^{12}$ kWh$)/(10^{10}$ kWh/plant$)$ or 100 new nuclear plants. Since there are about 75 nuclear power plants in the United States, this would represent substantial new construction.

SUMMARY

1. **Physics** is the fundamental science, dealing with the most basic laws governing the behavior of the physical universe. This book deals mainly with **classical physics,** an approximation to the more accurate description provided by **quantum mechanics** and **relativity.** Classical physics is a valid approximation for dealing with all but the smallest systems and the most rapid motion.

2. Physics is a quantitative science. In this book and throughout the scientific community, we use the SI (Système International) of measurement units. Although seven SI base units are defined, the three most central to mechanics are those of length, time, and mass.

   a. The SI unit of length is the **meter,** defined in terms of the distance light travels in a fixed time.

   b. The SI unit of time is the **second,** defined in terms of the vibration period of a certain atom.

   c. The SI unit of mass is the **kilogram,** defined by the international prototype kilogram at the International Bureau of Weights and Measures in France.

3. Some applications call for very precise numerical measurements or calculations; the number of **significant figures** in a number reflects how precisely we know that quantity.

4. In other applications, **estimation** may be all that is required to grasp the significance of a physical phenomenon.

SUGGESTED READINGS

Allen V. Astin, "Standards of Measurement," *Scientific American*, vol. 218, No. 6, p. 50, June 1968.

David T. Goldman and R. J. Bell, eds., "The International System of Units (SI)," NBS Special Publication 330, 1986 edition (U.S. Government Printing Office).

Lewis V. Judson, "Units and Systems of Weights and Measures: Their Origin, Development, and Present Status," U.S. Department of Commerce Letter Circular LC 1035, 1960, revised 1976 by L. E. Barbrow.

Robert A. Nelson, "Foundations of the International System of Units (SI)," *The Physics Teacher*, December 1981, pp. 596–613.

Francis M. Pipkin and Rogers C. Ritter, "Precision Measurements and the Fundamental Constants," *Science*, February 25, 1983, vol. 219, pp. 913–921.

Arthur L. Robinson, "Using Time to Measure Length," *Science*, June 24, 1983, p. 1367.

Margaret L. Silbar, "Measurement to the Limit," *Mosaic*, November/December 1981, pp. 27–32.

_____ **QUESTIONS** _____

1. Explain why measurement standards based on laboratory procedures are preferable to those based on specific objects like the international prototype kilogram.
2. Which measurement standards are now defined procedurally? Which are not?
3. Why is it important that the international prototype kilogram be made from corrosion-resistant material?
4. Given present-day definitions of the fundamental units, is it meaningful to attempt a more accurate measurement of the speed of light?
5. Why are "leap seconds" necessary?
6. When a computer carrying 7 significant figures adds 1.000000 and 2.5E-15, what answer does it display? Why?
7. In what way are the sciences of biology and chemistry based in physics?
8. Why does earth's rotation not provide a suitable standard of time?
9. For which of the two coordinates—latitude or longitude—do navigators need a precise measure of time? Explain.
10. Astronomers distinguish two different measures of the length of a day—solar and sidereal. A solar day is the interval between times when the sun is at its highest position in the sky. A sidereal day is the interval between times when any star other than the sun is at its highest position in the sky. Why are they different? Which is longer?
11. To raise a power of ten to another power, you multiply the exponent by the power. Explain why this works.
12. A scientist and a creationist are arguing about the age of the earth. What facts might the scientist use in estimating this age?
13. How would you determine the length of a curved line?
14. How would you measure the thickness of a sheet of paper?

_____ **PROBLEMS** _____

Section 1.3   Measurement Systems

1. What is your mass in (a) kg; (b) g; (c) Gg; (d) fg?
2. A year is very nearly $\pi \times 10^7$ s. By what percentage is this figure in error?
3. How many cubic centimeters (cm^3) are there in a cubic meter (m^3)?
4. I need a 14-mm wrench to remove the spark plugs in my car, but I have only an English set with sizes that are increments of one-sixteenth of an inch. What size should I use?
5. A gallon of paint covers 350 ft^2. What is its coverage in m^2/L?
6. By what percentage do the 1500-m and 1-mile foot races differ?
7. Superhighways in Canada have speed limits of 100 km/h. Does this exceed the United States' 55 mi/h speed limit? If so, by how much?
8. One m/s is how many km/h?
9. A hydrogen atom is about 0.1 nm in diameter. How many hydrogen atoms lined up side-by-side would make a line 1 cm long?
10. How long a piece of wire would you need to form a circular arc subtending an angle of 1.4 rad, if the radius of the arc is 8.1 cm?

Section 1.4   Exponential Notation

11. Add 3.6×10^5 m and 2.1×10^3 km.
12. The volume of the moon is 2.21×10^{19} m^3. What is its radius?
13. Divide 4.2×10^3 m/s by 0.57 ms, and express your answer in m/s^2.
14. Add 5.1×10^{-2} cm and 6.8×10^3 μm, and multiply the result by 1.8×10^4 N (1 N is the SI unit of force).
15. If there are 100,000 electronic components on a semiconductor chip that measures 5.0 mm by 5.0 mm, (a) how much area does each component occupy? (b) If the individual components are square, how long is each on a side?
16. What is the cube root of 2.7×10^{13}?

Section 1.5   Estimation

17. How many earths would fit inside the sun?
18. Estimate the number of people, standing with outstretched arms touching, needed to form a line from New York to Los Angeles.
19. If you set your watch to be exactly correct now, and if it runs slow by 1 s per month, in how many years would it again read exactly the right time?
20. (a) Estimate the volume of water going over Niagara Falls each second. (b) The falls provides the outlet for Lake Erie; if the falls were shut off, estimate how long it would take Lake Erie to rise 1 m.
21. (a) Estimate the volume of water in earth's oceans. (b) If scientists succeed in harnessing nuclear fusion as an energy source, each gallon of sea water will be equivalent to 400 gallons of gasoline. At our present rate of gasoline consumption (see Example 1–4), how long would the oceans supply our fuel needs?
22. Estimate the number of air molecules in your dormitory room.
23. The density of interstellar space is about 1 atom per cubic cm. Stars in our galaxy are typically a few light-years apart (one light-year is the distance light travels

in one year), and have typical masses of 10^{30} kg. Estimate whether there is more matter in the stars or in the interstellar gas.

24. Solar power roughly equivalent to the light from 10 100-watt light bulbs falls on each square meter of earth's surface. Using the fact that earth is 150 million km from the sun, and that the sun radiates energy equally in all directions, estimate how many 100-watt light bulbs are equivalent to the sun's total power output.

Supplementary Problems

25. A human hair is about 100 μm across. Estimate the number of hairs in a typical braid.
26. The density of bubble gum is about 1 g/cm^3. You blow a 50-g wad of gum into a bubble 10 cm in diameter. What is the thickness of the bubble? *Hint:* think about unrolling the bubble into a flat sheet. The surface area of a sphere is $4\pi r^2$.
27. The moon barely covers the sun at a solar eclipse. Given that the moon is 4×10^5 km from earth and that the sun is 1.5×10^8 km from earth, determine how much bigger the sun's diameter is than the moon's. If the moon's radius is 1800 km, how big is the sun?
28. The semiconductor chip at the heart of a personal computer is a square 4 mm on a side, and contains

10^5 electronic components. (a) If each component is a square, what is the distance across each component? (b) If a calculation requires that electrical impulses traverse 10^4 elements on the chip, each a million times, how many such calculations can the computer perform each second? The maximum speed of an electrical impulse is close to the speed of light, 3×10^8 m/s.
29. Estimate the number of (a) atoms and (b) cells in your body.
30. When we write the number 3.6 as typical of a number with two significant figures, we are saying that the actual value is closer to 3.6 than to 3.5 or 3.7. That is, the actual value lies between 3.55 and 3.65. Show that the percent uncertainty implied by two-significant-figure accuracy varies with the value of the number, being the least for numbers beginning with 9 and most for numbers beginning with 1. In particular, what is the percent uncertainty implied by the numbers (a) 1.1, (b) 5.0, and (c) 9.9?
31. Thermonuclear explosives have about ten million times the explosive power per unit mass of conventional chemical explosives. Estimate the mass of each of the ten 350-kiloton warheads carried on an MX missile. (One kiloton means the equivalent of one thousand tons of chemical explosive.)

2

MOTION IN A STRAIGHT LINE

Electrons swarming around atomic nuclei, cars speeding along a highway, a comet sweeping through the solar system, the galaxies themselves rushing apart in the expanding universe—all these are examples of matter in motion. In physics, the study of motion is called **kinematics** (from the Greek "kinema," motion, as in motion pictures). In this chapter, we deal with the simplest case of motion: a single particle moving along a straight line. Later, we generalize to motion in more dimensions and with more complicated objects. But the basic concepts we develop here remain fundamental to these more complex situations.

kinematics

We define a **particle** as an isolated point of mass, having no size or structure, and incapable of rotation, vibration, or other internal motions. Whether we can treat a real object as a particle depends on the circumstances. We can consider the earth to be a particle when we describe its orbital motion around the sun, for its size and rotation are essentially negligible in that context. But we must consider earth's nonzero size and rotation when we show how the moon gives rise to tides. In later chapters, we will see how the behavior of complicated objects follows from the laws we develop for their constituent particles.

particle

2.1
DISTANCE, TIME, SPEED, AND VELOCITY

average speed

We define the **average speed** of an object as the distance it travels divided by the travel time. The units of speed are therefore length per time, such as m/s (read "meters per second"), km/h, or mi/h (often written mph). For

15

example, a car that goes 7.2 km in 12 min has a speed of

$$\frac{7.2 \text{ km}}{12 \text{ min}} = 0.60 \text{ km/min} = \frac{0.60 \text{ km}}{(1 \text{ min})(1 \text{ h}/60 \text{ min})} = 36 \text{ km/h}.$$

At this speed, the car would go (36 km/h)(2.5 h) = 90 km in 2.5 h. Note how in these calculations we cancelled units just as we multiplied and divided numbers. Had our answers not come out with the correct units, we would have a sure indication of an error in the calculation.

Vectors, Scalars, and Displacement

Suppose you drive 15 minutes to a hamburger stand 10 miles away, grab your food at a drive-through window, and take another 15 minutes to drive home. You've gone a total of 20 miles in half an hour, giving an average speed of 40 mi/h. You certainly have been travelling, as the hamburger proves. But in another sense, you have gone nowhere at all, since you end up back at your starting point.

Physicists distinguish between the distance actually travelled and the overall change in position. This overall change—between the position at which you started and the position at which you finished—we call the *displacement* **displacement.** In our hamburger example, the displacement is zero even though the overall distance travelled is 20 miles.

Starting from Boston, a 400-km displacement to the southwest gets you to Philadelphia. But head north-northwest the same distance and you find yourself in Montreal. Specifying displacement requires not only the overall distance between your final and initial positions, but also the direction you travel. A quantity for which we keep track of direction, like displacement, *vector* is a **vector.** A quantity not associated with a direction, like mass, is a *scalar* **scalar.**

In this book, we write scalars in regular type and vectors in bold type. When handwriting vectors, we often write an arrow over the symbol, as in $\vec{r}$ for the displacement vector. We write the magnitude of the displacement vector **r** as $|\mathbf{r}|$ or simply r. The magnitude of a vector is always greater than or equal to zero (≥ 0).

component We define a **component** of a vector as the projection of the vector onto a given axis. Figure 2–1, for example, graphs our Boston-to-Montreal displacement on coordinate axes x and y that run east-west and north-south. We designate the components of an arbitrary vector **A** by the terms A_x, A_y, and A_z. The components of a vector are simply numbers. As shown in Fig. 2–1, they are the projections of the vector onto the coordinate axes, and can be positive or negative. (We normally define the axes as in Fig. 2–1, with the x-axis horizontal, the y-axis vertical, and the z-axis out of the page. In some circumstances, we will find other orientations more convenient.)

Velocity

In describing motion, we want to know not only the displacement an object undergoes, but also how rapidly that displacement occurs. Accord-
average velocity ingly, we define **average velocity** as displacement divided by time interval.

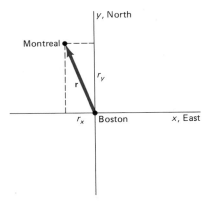

Fig. 2–1
The displacement vector **r** describing a trip from Boston to Montreal. The y-component r_y of the vector is the change in north-south position, while the x-component r_x is the change in the east-west position. With the positive x-direction eastward, the x-component is negative.

(To divide a vector by a scalar, we simply divide the magnitude of the vector by the scalar to get a new vector that lies along the same line as the original vector.) In our hamburger example, our average velocity was zero because our displacement was zero. If our 400-km Boston-to-Montreal trip took 4 hours, then our average velocity was 100 km/h north-northwest. Since displacement is a vector, so is velocity, and we must specify not only its magnitude but also its direction.

To see the relation among velocity, displacement, and time, consider a trip to a town 50 km east of home. If you travel eastward at a constant 50 km/h for 1 hour, your average velocity is 50 km/h eastward. If you paused for an hour in the midst of your trip, then you would have travelled 50 km eastward in 2 hours and your average velocity would have been eastward at 50 km/2 h = 25 km/h. Or suppose you got almost to the town, realized you forgot something, and roared rapidly home and back to the town. If the whole trip again took 2 hours, your average velocity would still be 25 km/h, even though you were actually moving much faster most of the time.

Using symbols, we can write the average velocity as

$$\overline{\mathbf{v}} = \frac{\Delta \mathbf{r}}{\Delta t},$$ (2–1)

where $\Delta \mathbf{r}$ is the vector displacement in the time interval Δt. The bar over the vector **v** indicates an average quantity (and is read "v bar"). We have here introduced the symbol Δ (the Greek capital delta) for "the change in . . . ." The individual components of velocity may be calculated from the components of the displacement; for example, the x-component of the average velocity, $\overline{v}_x$, is

$$\overline{v}_x = \frac{\Delta x}{\Delta t},$$ (2–2)

where Δx is the x-component of the displacement vector $\Delta \mathbf{r}$. In this chapter on one-dimensional motion, we will consider only motion with one non-zero component.

Example 2–1
Flowing Lava

Geologists studying the flow of lava underground often drop a branch of wood in at one hole, and watch downstream a measurable distance away to see how long it takes for the wood to travel that known distance. At a recent volcanic eruption on the island of Hawaii, a branch travelled 100 meters in 12 seconds. What was the magnitude of its average velocity?

Solution

Applying Equation 2–1, we have

$$\overline{v} = \frac{\Delta r}{\Delta t} = \frac{100 \text{ m}}{12 \text{ s}} = 8.3 \text{ m/s}.$$

Since we were interested only in the magnitude, we have not written v or Δr as vectors, or specified a direction.

2.2
MOTION IN SHORT TIME INTERVALS

Although our geologists' experiment told them the average velocity of the lava flow, it did not give them all the details of the motion. For example, did the lava move faster at the beginning of the interval? Was there a region where the flow slowed down significantly? The geologists could answer these questions with a series of observations measuring the lava flow velocity over smaller intervals of time and distance (Fig. 2–2).

As the size of the intervals shrinks, and their number grows, an ever-more-detailed picture of the velocity emerges. In the limit of arbitrarily small time intervals, we achieve a description that gives a value for the velocity at essentially each instant. We call the velocity obtained through this limiting process the **instantaneous velocity, v.** The magnitude of the instantaneous velocity is called the **instantaneous speed.**

instantaneous velocity
instantaneous speed

Physically, we can determine an approximate value for the instantaneous velocity by measuring the average velocity $\Delta r/\Delta t$ over a very small time interval; we will soon see how we can calculate the instantaneous velocity mathematically given displacement as a function of time.

Example 2–2
Average and Instantaneous Velocity

You arrive at Boston's Logan Airport at 2:00 PM to check in for a trip to Detroit. Your plane departs at 3:00 PM and flies westward 1400 km to Chicago at 900 km/h. There, you catch a 5:30 flight to Detroit, which lies 390 km east of Chicago. Your plane lands in Detroit at 6:10. Assuming the planes maintain constant velocity while in the air, what are your instantaneous velocities at 2:30 PM, 4:00 PM, and 6:00 PM? What is your average velocity for the entire trip?

Fig. 2–2
Determining the velocity of a lava flow.
(a) Measuring the time Δt for a branch to go the distance Δx from A to B gives the average flow velocity $\bar{v} = \Delta x/\Delta t$.
(b) A series of measurements over shorter intervals gives a more detailed picture of the flow, by providing values for the velocities $\bar{v}_1 = \Delta x_1/\Delta t_1$, $\bar{v}_2 = \Delta x_2/\Delta t_2$, etc.

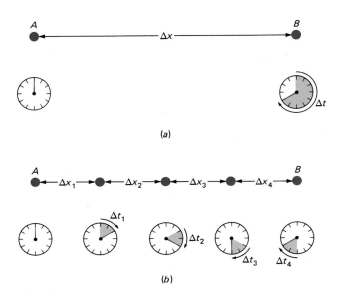

Solution

At 2:30, you are still waiting in Boston, so your instantaneous velocity is zero. At 900 km/h, the 1400-km trip to Chicago will take well over an hour, so that at 4:00 PM you are still en route to Chicago, with instantaneous velocity 900 km/h westward. At 6:00 PM, you are en route to Detroit. Since the 390-km trip from Chicago to Detroit takes 40 min or 0.67 h, the magnitude of your velocity is 390 km/0.67 h = 580 km/h. Because the plane's velocity is constant, your instantaneous velocity at 6:00 PM is also eastward at 580 km/h. The entire trip takes 4 h 10 min, or 4.17 h. Since you travel westward 1400 km, then eastward 390 km, your net displacement is 1400 km − 390 km = 1010 km westward. Then your average velocity is 1010 km/4.17 h = 242 km/h westward.

To make the notion of instantaneous velocity more precise, consider first motion at constant velocity, as shown in Fig. 2–3. The graph is drawn in the usual format for a graph describing motion: time along the horizontal axis and distance along the vertical axis. Note that if we shorten the length of the time interval we consider by any factor, the distance is shortened by the same factor. We get the same value for velocity no matter how short the time interval; thus for this constant-velocity situation, the average and instantaneous velocities are equal. Both velocities are, indeed, given by the slope of the line on the graph—that is, by distance divided by time.

In Fig. 2–4, we plot the motion of an object whose velocity is continually changing. Now as we consider different time intervals, we get different slopes. But if we examine shorter and shorter intervals around one specific time, we find that the part of the curve we are limited to gets closer and closer to a straight line (Fig. 2–5). The average velocity we compute then approaches a single value, which in the limit of arbitrarily small intervals is just the slope of the curve at a single point.

Thus, to compute the instantaneous velocity—the velocity at any given instant—we apply Equation 2–1 or 2–2 as the time interval Δt becomes arbitrarily small. In doing so, we are carrying out the mathematical equivalent of the physical procedure our geologists could have used to discover the detailed motion of their lava flow in Example 2–1. Of course, we cannot take Δt all the way to zero, for then $\Delta x = 0$, and the velocity would be undefined. But the velocity remains perfectly well defined for all nonzero values of Δt, no matter how small. So as we consider ever smaller time intervals, the average velocity we calculate comes ever closer to the instantaneous velocity. We can say this by writing

$$v_x = \lim_{\Delta t \to 0} \frac{\Delta x}{\Delta t}. \qquad (2\text{–}3a)$$

Read this equation as "v_x is the limit as Δt approaches zero of Δx divided by Δt." This statement is true even though the value of $\Delta x/\Delta t$ would be undefined if we evaluated it at $\Delta t = 0$. And it is true even for nonconstant velocity, since a sufficiently short segment of a curve comes arbitrarily close to being straight (Fig. 2–5).

Here physics diverges from mathematics in two significant ways. Mathematically, we can construct position-versus-time graphs including points

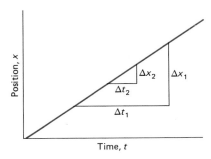

Fig. 2–3
A graph of position versus time for an object moving at constant velocity. Shown are two time intervals Δt and the corresponding displacements Δx. The average velocity over an interval is the ratio $\Delta x/\Delta t$, or the slope of a line connecting the ends of the interval. With constant velocity this slope is the same for all intervals.

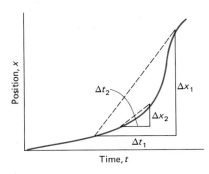

Fig. 2–4
A graph of position versus time for an object whose velocity is continually changing. Dotted lines connect the endpoints of two intervals; since the lines have different slopes, the average velocities $\Delta x/\Delta t$ have different values over the two intervals.

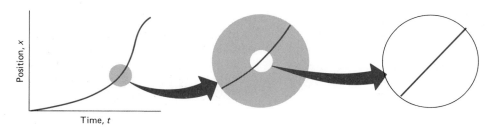

Fig. 2–5
As we examine an ever-smaller segment of the curve, it begins to resemble a straight line. The slope of this line is the magnitude of the instantaneous velocity.

where the limit in Equation 2–3*a* is undefined (Fig. 2–6). But such examples correspond physically to the impossible cases of an abrupt change in velocity or an infinite velocity. So in physics, at least, the limit in Equation 2–3*a* always exists. A second distinction arises because mathematically we take the limiting procedure to arbitrarily small time intervals Δ*t*. But in attempting to measure an instantaneous velocity physically (or for that matter, in calculating such a velocity from position-versus-time data produced by a computer), there is a minimum time interval over which we can obtain accurate data. Our physical determinations of instantaneous velocities are therefore always approximations.

The limiting process we have just described occurs so frequently in physics and mathematics that we give the result a special name and symbol. We define the **derivative** of x with respect to *t* (symbol *dx/dt*) as

derivative

$$\frac{dx}{dt} = \lim_{\Delta t \to 0} \frac{\Delta x}{\Delta t}.$$

infinitesimals

The quantities *dx* and *dt* are called **infinitesimals;** they represent arbitrarily small quantities associated with the limiting process that defines the derivative. We can then write Equation 2–3*a* for the velocity component in the form

$$v_x = \frac{dx}{dt}. \tag{2–3b}$$

We have discussed this limiting procedure for the x-component of the velocity vector—the only component in one-dimensional motion. In the more general case (which we will discuss further in Chapter 3), we write

$$\mathbf{v} = \lim_{\Delta t \to 0} \frac{\Delta \mathbf{r}}{\Delta t} = \frac{d\mathbf{r}}{dt}, \tag{2–4}$$

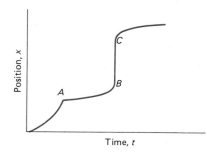

Fig. 2–6
A position-versus-time graph including an abrupt change in velocity (point *A*) and a time when the velocity is infinite (section *BC*). In both these cases, the limit in Equation 2–3*a* is undefined, but both are physically impossible.

where **r** is the displacement vector. Clearly, Equation 2–4 represents the limiting procedure applied to Equation 2–1. More generally, if some variable *y* is a function of some other variable *x*, then the derivative *dy/dx* measures the rate of change of *y* with respect to *x*—that is, the slope of the *y* versus *x* graph. Thus Equation 2–4 says that velocity is the rate of change of position.

Example 2–3

Derivative of a Square Law

The altitude of a space shuttle in the first half minute of its ascent is given approximately by a "square law," that is, $x = bt^2$, where the constant b is 2.9 m/s^2, x is in meters, and t is the time in seconds since lift-off. Using the process of taking limits, derive a general expression for the velocity, and determine its value when $t = 20$ s.

Solution

To find the instantaneous velocity v at some time t, we need to consider a small time interval Δt that includes t. In the limit $\Delta t \rightarrow 0$, the average velocity $\Delta x / \Delta t$ over that interval becomes the instantaneous velocity dx/dt. So consider an interval stretching from t to $t + \Delta t$; then evaluating $x = bt^2$ at $t + \Delta t$ and at t gives

$$v_x = \lim_{\Delta t \rightarrow 0} \frac{\Delta x}{\Delta t} = \lim_{\Delta t \rightarrow 0} \frac{b(t + \Delta t)^2 - bt^2}{\Delta t}$$

$$= \lim_{\Delta t \rightarrow 0} \frac{b(t^2 + 2t\Delta t + \Delta t^2 - t^2)}{\Delta t}$$

$$= \lim_{\Delta t \rightarrow 0} \frac{b(2t\Delta t + \Delta t^2)}{\Delta t} = \lim_{\Delta t \rightarrow 0} (2bt + 2b\Delta t) = 2bt.$$

For $t = 20$ s, $v_x = 2(2.9 \text{ m/s}^2)(20 \text{ s}) = 120$ m/s. Note that the units of b had to be m/s^2 for the expression $x = bt^2$ to be dimensionally correct.

We need not repeat the rather lengthy calculation of Example 2–3 every time we need the derivative of a simple function like t^2. The result of that example—that the derivative of bt^2 is $2bt$—is but a special case of a general rule for derivatives of variables that are raised to a power. We will not prove the general case here; that is usually done in introductory calculus courses. The result is that, for

$$x = bt^n,$$

where b and n are constants, then

$$\frac{dx}{dt} = bnt^{n-1}. \tag{2–5}$$

Equation 2–5 is true for all values of n, including both integer and non-integer values, positive and negative. The equation provides us directly with the result of the limiting process that defines the derivative; using it allows us to bypass the detailed limiting process we did in Example 2–3. You should verify that Equation 2–5, applied to $x = bt^2$, gives the result of Example 2–3. Derivatives of other functions, including trigonometric functions, exponentials, and logarithms, are given in Appendix B (see also Problem 63).

2.3
ACCELERATION

acceleration

In our space shuttle example, the velocity of the shuttle was changing. When velocity changes, an object is said to undergo **acceleration.** Since velocity is a vector, it has both a direction and a magnitude, and either can change. A car starting up from a stoplight is accelerating because the magnitude of its velocity is changing. A car going around a corner at constant speed is also accelerating because the direction of its velocity is changing; we will discuss such two-dimensional motion in the next chapter.

We define acceleration as the rate of change of velocity, just as we defined velocity as the rate of change of position. The average acceleration over a time interval Δt is

$$\bar{\mathbf{a}} = \frac{\Delta \mathbf{v}}{\Delta t},$$

where $\Delta \mathbf{v}$ is the change in velocity and where the bar over the **a** indicates that it is an average value. Since velocity is a vector, so is its rate of change. However, the velocity and acceleration vectors need not have the same direction. In one-dimensional motion, the acceleration is in the same direction as the velocity if the speed is increasing, but is in the opposite direction if the speed is decreasing. Just as we defined instantaneous velocity through a limiting procedure, so we define instantaneous acceleration as

$$\mathbf{a} = \lim_{\Delta t \to 0} \frac{\Delta \mathbf{v}}{\Delta t} = \frac{d\mathbf{v}}{dt}. \tag{2–6}$$

In this chapter, we will always discuss a_x, the component of the acceleration along the x-axis, rather than **a,** the vector acceleration. Clearly, the x-component of Equation 2–6 is

$$a_x = \lim_{\Delta t \to 0} \frac{\Delta v_x}{\Delta t} = \frac{dv_x}{dt}. \tag{2–7}$$

The word "deceleration" is often used to describe a slowing-down—that is, an acceleration whose direction is opposite to the velocity. When solving problems, though, it is usually easier to consider acceleration in one dimension as an algebraic quantity, and to find out whether a solution represents a decrease or increase in speed by comparing the sign of the acceleration with that of the velocity.

Since acceleration is the rate of change of velocity, the units of acceleration must be (unit of velocity) per (unit of time). Since the units of velocity are distance per time, the units of acceleration are (distance/time) per time, which can be written distance/time^2. For example, if you accelerate in such a way that your velocity changes by 5 m/s during each second, your acceleration is 5 (m/s)/s or 5 m/s^2. Sometimes acceleration is specified in mixed units; for example, a car going from 0 to 60 mi/h in 10 seconds has an average acceleration of 6 mi/h/s.

Example 2–4
Average Acceleration

A jetliner rolls down the runway with constant acceleration. From rest, it reaches its takeoff speed of 250 km/h in 1 min. What is its acceleration? Express in km/h².

Solution

The plane undergoes a velocity change Δv_x of 250 km/h in time $\Delta t = 1$ min or 1/60 h. The average acceleration is therefore

$$\bar{a}_x = \frac{\Delta v_x}{\Delta t} = \frac{250 \text{ km/h}}{(1/60 \text{ h})} = 15{,}000 \text{ km/h}^2.$$

Does this huge result make sense? Yes—the jet reaches 250 km/h in only 1 minute, so an increase of 15,000 km/h in 1 hour is not unreasonable. Of course, the plane never reaches such a high speed because it does not accelerate for a full hour.

Example 2–5
Acceleration and Deceleration

Two cars are moving eastward at 20 m/s. At time $t = 0$ both undergo accelerations of magnitude 2 m/s², with one car's acceleration eastward and the other westward. How fast is each car going 5 s later?

Solution

Each car's velocity changes at the rate of 2 m/s², or 2 (m/s)/s, so that in 5 s, each velocity has changed by $(2 \text{ m/s}^2)(5 \text{ s}) = 10$ m/s. (Note how the units work out.) Both cars are *moving* eastward. For the car that is also *accelerating* eastward, this change represents a speeding up to 30 m/s. But for the car that is accelerating westward—opposite to the direction of its velocity—the change represents a slowing down, to 10 m/s.

Just as velocity is the slope of the position-versus-time graph, so acceleration is the slope of the velocity-versus-time graph. Figure 2–7 shows graphs of position, velocity, and acceleration versus time for a particle undergoing one-dimensional motion with position x given by $x = bt^2 - ct^3$, where $b = 4$ m/s² and $c = 1$ m/s³. We obtained the velocity by differentiating the position: $v_x = d(bt^2 - ct^3)/dt = 2bt - 3ct^2$; a second differentiation gives the acceleration: $a_x = d(2bt - 3ct^2)/dt = 2b - 6ct$. Note that where the curve of Fig. 2–7a is steep—where the position x changes rapidly—the magnitude of the velocity in Fig. 2–7b is large. When x is decreasing with time, the velocity is negative. Similarly, where the slope of the velocity graph is greatest, the acceleration has its greatest magnitude. And when the velocity is decreasing—regardless of whether its value is positive or negative—the acceleration is negative. Finally, we have marked on Fig. 2–7 the points where velocity and acceleration are zero. The zero-velocity points appear where the *slope* of the position graph is zero—where that graph is flat. Similarly, the acceleration is zero where the *slope* of the velocity curve is zero.

Notice in Fig. 2–7 that the *value* of the velocity is unrelated to the *value* of the position. We could change all positions by some fixed amount

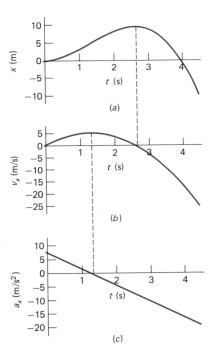

Fig. 2–7
Position, velocity, and acceleration versus time for one-dimensional motion with position given by $x = bt^2 - ct^3$, where $b = 4$ m/s² and $c = 1$ m/s³. Note that zero velocity occurs where the *slope* of the position graph is zero, and zero acceleration where the *slope* of the velocity graph is zero. In general, each graph gives the *slope* of the one above it; there is no particular relation between the actual *values* on one graph and those on a lower graph.

(by simply moving the entire position-versus-time curve up or down on its graph), and this would have no effect on the velocity graph. The velocity is the *slope* of the position curve—and the slope depends on how the position is changing, not on its actual value. Similarly, the value of the acceleration depends only on the rate of change of velocity, not on the velocity itself. In particular, we can have zero velocity and still be accelerating! You can see this in Fig. 2–7, where the point of zero velocity does not correspond to zero acceleration.

How can something be accelerating if it's not moving? If this idea troubles you, remember that we are talking about *instantaneous* values. If the velocity stays zero for any length of time, then the acceleration must also be zero during that time. But if the velocity goes through zero instantaneously—as happens to a ball thrown straight up at the top of its flight—then the acceleration can remain nonzero. Just before the ball was stopped, it was moving upward. Just after it was stopped, it was moving downward. No matter how small a time interval Δt you choose around the instant the ball was stopped, you will find that on one side of that interval the ball was moving upward, and on the other side it was moving downward. There is always a change in velocity, and therefore always an acceleration—even in the limit $\Delta t \rightarrow 0$ that gives the acceleration at the instant the velocity is zero. Graphically, a plot of velocity versus time for the ball shows that the velocity is always changing—even as it passes through zero on its way to negative (downward) values (Fig. 2–8).

Since acceleration is the time derivative (the derivative with respect to time) of velocity and velocity is, in turn, the time derivative of position, we define a **second derivative** as a derivative taken twice. The second derivative of x with respect to t is written d^2x/dt^2; this is a symbol and does not mean that we actually square anything. We then write

second derivative

$$\mathbf{a} = \frac{d\mathbf{v}}{dt} = \frac{d}{dt}\left(\frac{d\mathbf{r}}{dt}\right) = \frac{d^2\mathbf{r}}{dt^2} \tag{2-8}$$

for the acceleration vector and

$$a_x = \frac{dv_x}{dt} = \frac{d}{dt}\left(\frac{dx}{dt}\right) = \frac{d^2x}{dt^2} \tag{2-9}$$

for its x-component.

2.4
CONSTANT ACCELERATION

When the acceleration is constant, the mathematical description of motion takes an especially simple form. In this section, we derive and apply basic equations for the velocity and position of an object undergoing constant acceleration. We do so in two steps, going first from acceleration to velocity and then from velocity to position.

Since $a_x = dv_x/dt$, we must find an expression for v_x which, when differentiated, gives constant a_x. From Equation 2–5, we see that $v_x = a_x t$ is such an expression, since $d(a_x t)/dt = a_x$. If we add a constant to this

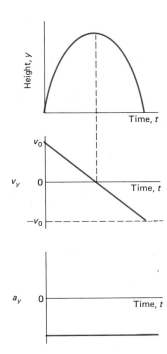

Fig. 2–8
Position, velocity, and acceleration versus time for a ball thrown straight up. At the peak of its flight, the ball is instantaneously at rest ($v=0$). But even at that point, the velocity is in the process of changing—here from upward to downward—so that the acceleration is nonzero. In this case the acceleration is, in fact, constant and downward (i.e., negative).

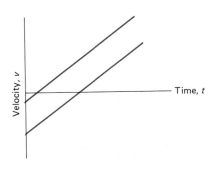

Fig. 2–9
Two velocity-versus-time curves that differ everywhere by the same constant. The two curves have the same slope, and therefore imply the same acceleration.

expression for velocity, the acceleration is still

$$\frac{d}{dt}(a_x t + \text{constant}) = \frac{d(a_x t)}{dt} + \frac{d}{dt}(\text{constant}) = a_x,$$

since the derivative—the rate of change—of a constant is zero. On a graph, adding the constant is equivalent to sliding the entire velocity-versus-time curve up or down by a fixed amount (Fig. 2–9). Such an action does not change the slope, so has no effect on the acceleration.

Evaluating the expression $v_x = a_x t + \text{constant}$ at time $t = 0$ shows that the velocity at time $t = 0$ is equal to the constant. We therefore call this constant v_{x0}, the initial velocity. Thus

$$v_x = v_{x0} + a_x t \tag{2–10}$$

is the general expression for velocity v_x as a function of time when an object undergoes constant acceleration a_x.

Just as we found an expression for velocity that gives constant acceleration, we now seek an expression for position that gives the velocity (Equation 2–10) associated with constant acceleration. Since $v_x = dx/dt$, this means that we want position x as a function of time that when differentiated gives Equation 2–10. We will get the constant term v_{x0} if we start with $v_{x0}t$, since $d(v_{x0}t)/dt = v_{x0}$. As in our reasoning to Equation 2–10, we can in fact start with $v_{x0}t + \text{constant}$ and still get the v_{x0} term when we differentiate. What about the term $a_x t$? Differentiating $a_x t^2$ with respect to t gives $2a_x t$, which is twice what we want, so we must start with $\frac{1}{2}a_x t^2$; again we can add any constant. Combining the two constants gives

$$x = v_{x0}t + \tfrac{1}{2}a_x t^2 + \text{constant}.$$

Evaluating this equation at time $t=0$ shows that the constant is the initial position, which we call x_0. Then

$$x = x_0 + v_{x0}t + \tfrac{1}{2}a_x t^2 \tag{2–11}$$

is the general expression for the position of an object undergoing constant acceleration in one dimension, if its initial position is x_0 and its initial velocity is v_{x0}. The t^2 dependence in Equation 2–11 makes physical sense: with constant acceleration, the longer we travel the faster we go and therefore the more distance we cover in a given time.

We have been working backward, "anti-differentiating," to find the equation for x that would give the result we know we need for $a_x = d^2x/dt^2$. Later, we will use this process, formally known as "integration," more directly.

We can also understand Equation 2–11 by considering the average velocity of an object undergoing constant acceleration. Suppose that at time 0, the velocity is v_{x0}, and at some arbitrary later time t it is v_x. Since the acceleration is constant, the velocity rises steadily with time (Fig. 2–10a). Because the velocity rises steadily, the average velocity $\bar{v}_x$ in the interval from time 0 to time t lies midway between the initial velocity v_{x0} and the final velocity v_x:

$$\bar{v}_x = \tfrac{1}{2}(v_{x0} + v_x). \qquad \text{(constant acceleration)} \tag{2–12}$$

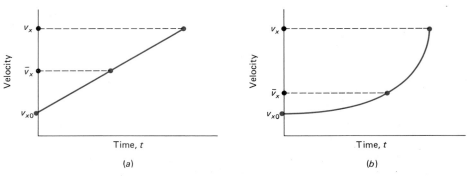

Fig. 2–10
(a) With constant acceleration, the velocity rises steadily, with slope equal to the acceleration. Because the rise is steady, the average velocity lies midway between the initial velocity v_{x0} and the final velocity v_x. (b) When the acceleration is not constant, the velocity-versus-time curve is not a straight line, and the average velocity is not midway between the initial and final velocities.

Note that this result is necessarily true *only* for the case of constant acceleration. When the acceleration varies with time, the velocity-versus-time curve is not straight, and the average velocity will, in general, lie closer to one of the two extremes (Fig. 2–10b).

From Equation 2–2, we know that the average velocity is the displacement divided by time interval, so that in time Δt, we travel a distance $\Delta x = \bar{v}_x \, \Delta t$. Calling x_0 the initial position at time 0, and x the position at time t, we have $\Delta x = x - x_0$. Our time interval Δt is the final time t minus the initial time 0, or simply t. Then we have

$$x - x_0 = \bar{v}_x t.$$

In the case of constant acceleration, we can use Equation 2–12 for the average velocity $\bar{v}_x$, giving

$$x - x_0 = \tfrac{1}{2}(v_{x0} + v_x)t. \tag{2–13}$$

Equation 2–13 is a useful form if we know we have constant acceleration and are given the initial and final velocities but not the acceleration itself. From Equation 2–10, we can write $v_x = v_{x0} + a_x t$, so that Equation 2–13 becomes

$$x - x_0 = \tfrac{1}{2}(v_{x0} + v_{x0} + a_x t)t,$$

or

$$x = x_0 + v_{x0}t + \tfrac{1}{2}a_x t^2,$$

which is Equation 2–11.

In some cases, we want to relate position and velocity directly, without explicit mention of time. To do so, we solve Equation 2–10 for the time t, giving

$$t = \frac{v_x - v_{x0}}{a_x}.$$

Substituting this result for t in Equation 2–13 gives

TABLE 2–1 ▬▬▬▬▬▬▬▬▬▬▬▬▬▬▬▬▬▬▬
Equations of Motion for Constant Acceleration

Equation	Contains	Number
$v_x = v_{x0} + a_x t$	v, a, t; no x	2–10
$x = x_0 + v_{x0}t + \frac{1}{2}a_x t^2$	x, a, t; no v	2–11
$\bar{v}_x = \frac{1}{2}(v_{x0} + v_x)$	Average v	2–12
$x - x_0 = \frac{1}{2}(v_{x0} + v_x)t$	x, v, t; no a	2–13
$v_x{}^2 = v_{x0}{}^2 + 2a_x(x - x_0)$	x, v, a; no t	2–14

$$x - x_0 = \frac{1}{2}\frac{(v_{x0} + v_x)(v_x - v_{x0})}{a_x},$$

or, since $(a + b)(a - b) = a^2 - b^2$,

$$v_x{}^2 = v_{x0}{}^2 + 2a_x(x - x_0). \tag{2–14}$$

Equations 2–10 through 2–14 link all possible combinations of position, velocity, and acceleration for motion with constant acceleration. We summarize these equations in Table 2–1.

You should not memorize these equations. Instead, you will grow familiar with them as you work problems involving one-dimensional motion. As you use the equations, do not regard them as a set of separate laws, but instead see them as complementary descriptions of the same underlying phenomenon—one-dimensional motion with constant acceleration. We stress again that we derived Equations 2–10 to 2–14 under the assumption of *constant acceleration*. They do not hold if the acceleration vector is changing in either magnitude or direction.

Example 2–6
Acceleration from Distance and Velocity

The electron beam in a color TV tube jumps from near zero velocity to 1×10^{10} cm/s in a distance of 4 cm near the back of the tube. What is its acceleration?

Solution

We are given the initial and final velocities, and the distance over which the acceleration occurs. Equation 2–14 links these quantities with the acceleration. Solving for a_x, with $v_{x0} = 0$, we have

$$a_x = \frac{v_x{}^2}{2(x - x_0)} = \frac{(1 \times 10^{10}\ \text{cm/s})^2}{2(4\ \text{cm})} = 1 \times 10^{19}\ \text{cm/s}^2,$$

where we keep only one significant figure in our answer because that is all we were given in the original data. Such a huge acceleration is possible because of the tiny mass of the electron. We will explore the relation between mass and acceleration in Chapter 4.

Example 2–7
Distance from Velocity and Time

I am riding my bicycle at a leisurely 10 km/h, then speed up at a steady rate for 10 s to escape a dog. At the end of that time, I am going at 30 km/h. How far did I go during the 10-s interval?

Solution

We want to link v_x and t, which we know, with x, which we don't know. Equation 2–13 does this. Our answer is the distance $x - x_0$ travelled during the time t:

$$x - x_0 = \tfrac{1}{2}(v_{x0} + v_x)t = \tfrac{1}{2}(10 \text{ km/h} + 30 \text{ km/h})(10 \text{ s})(1 \text{ h/3600 s})$$
$$= 0.028 \text{ km} = 28 \text{ m}.$$

Note that, with our time in seconds and our velocity in km/h, we had to convert seconds to hours for consistency of units.

Occasionally, we are interested in comparing the one-dimensional motions of two different objects, as the example below illustrates.

Example 2–8
Speed Trap

A speeding motorist zooms through a 50 km/h zone at 75 km/h, without noticing a stationary police car by the roadside. The police officer immediately heads after the speeder, accelerating at 9.0 km/h/s. When the officer pulls alongside the speeder, how far down the road are they, and how fast is the police car going?

Solution

In this example, we deal with two different one-dimensional motions, both described by Equation 2–11. We want to know when the two cars are in the same place—that is, when equations for the positions of the two cars give the same value. In working such a problem, it is important to define the initial positions and times consistently for both motions; otherwise a comparison between the two is meaningless.

Let $t=0$ be the time the speeder first passes the police car, and let $x=0$ be the position at which this occurs. Then $x_0=0$ for both cars. For the speeder, we have $v_{s0}=75$ km/h $=21$ m/s and $a_s=0$. For the police car, $v_{p0}=0$ but $a_p=9.0$ km/h/s $=2.5$ m/s^2. (Here we use subscripts s and p for quantities associated with the speeder and police, respectively, and have dropped the subscript x because it is clear we are dealing only with one-dimensional motion.) Then for the two cars Equation 2–11 becomes

$$x_s = v_{s0}t \qquad \text{(speeder)}$$

and

$$x_p = \tfrac{1}{2}a_p t^2. \qquad \text{(police)}$$

Equating these expressions tells when the speeder and police car are at the same place:

$$v_{s0}t = \tfrac{1}{2}a_p t^2,$$

so that $t=0$ or $t=2v_{s0}/a_p$. Why two answers? We asked the equations for *any* times when the two cars were in the same place. Our first answer is just the initial encounter as the speeder passes the stationary police car. The second answer is the one we want—the time when the officer catches up with the speeder. *Where* does this occur? Using the time $2v_{s0}/a_p$ in the speeder equation, we have

$$x = v_{s0}t = v_{s0}\frac{2v_{s0}}{a_p} = \frac{2v_{s0}^2}{a_p} = \frac{(2)(21 \text{ m/s})^2}{2.5 \text{ m/s}^2} = 350 \text{ m}.$$

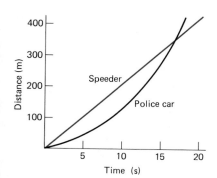

Fig. 2–11
Position versus time for the speeder and police car of Example 2–8.

We can calculate the police car's speed at this time from Equation 2–10, with $v_{p0} = 0$:

$$v_p = a_p t = a_p \frac{2v_{s0}}{a_p} = 2v_{s0} = 150 \text{ km/h}.$$

Does this result make sense? Yes—the police car and the speeder cover the same distance in the same time. Therefore, their average velocities must be the same. The speeder maintains constant velocity, but the police car accelerates from rest. Since the average velocity with constant acceleration is half the sum of the initial and final velocities, the police car must be going twice as fast as the speeder when they meet again. Note that this remains true no matter what the acceleration of the police car.

Figure 2–11 shows both motions plotted on the same graph. Sketching such a graph is often helpful in understanding problems involving two or more one-dimensional motions.

2.5
THE CONSTANT ACCELERATION OF GRAVITY

Gravity is a force with which we are very familiar, so it is suitable to discuss some aspects of it here even though we will not formally define force until Chapter 4, and will study gravity in detail in Chapter 8. Here we concern ourselves only with gravity near the surface of the earth, where its effects do not vary significantly with height.

When you drop an object, it falls at an ever-increasing rate (Fig. 2–12)—that is, it accelerates because the force of gravity is attracting it to the earth. Experimentally, we find that the acceleration remains constant for objects falling near the surface of the earth, and furthermore that this constant acceleration has the same value for all objects, independent of mass or other properties. The rate at which the speed of a falling object increases—the **acceleration of gravity**—is approximately 9.8 m/s^2 near earth's surface. (A more exact value is given in Appendix F, along with other properties of the earth and other planets.)

The acceleration of gravity applies strictly only to objects in **free fall**—that is, objects under the influence of gravity alone. The presence of other forces, in particular air resistance, may alter dramatically the statement that all objects fall with the same constant acceleration. Try dropping a flat piece of paper and a rock, for example. Their behavior is radically different. But if you crumple the paper, lessening its air resistance, it falls with an acceleration closer to that of the rock. An experiment illustrating that all objects fall with the same acceleration was carried out by astronauts on the moon in 1971, when they showed that a feather and a hammer fell together at the airless lunar surface (Fig. 2–13). The acceleration of gravity on the moon is different from that on earth, but the crucial concept is that all objects at the same location experience the same gravitational acceleration.

Galileo is reputed to have shown that all objects fall with the same acceleration by dropping objects off the Leaning Tower of Pisa in about 1600. There is no evidence that the Tower of Pisa played a role, but it is known that Galileo carried out careful experiments by rolling balls down

Fig. 2–12
Strobe photo of a falling apple, with the strobe flashing 30 times per second. Appearances of the apple are farther apart as it falls, showing that the apple is accelerating.

acceleration of gravity

free fall

Fig. 2–13
Apollo 15 astronaut David Scott dropping a feather and a hammer on the moon. Only video images exist, and the objects are hard to see in stills.

TABLE 2–2
A Freely Falling Object

Time (s)	Distance (m)	Speed (m/s)	Acceleration (m/s²)
0	0	0	9.8
1	4.9	9.8	9.8
2	19.6	19.2	9.8
3	44.1	29.4	9.8
4	78.4	39.2	9.8
5	123	49.0	9.8

Fig. 2–14
A graph of distance versus time² for the data of Table 2–2. According to Equation 2–11, a straight-line graph shows that we have constant acceleration whose magnitude is twice the slope.

inclined planes. The gradual inclines "diluted" the effect of gravity, allowing Galileo to make more precise measurements. We now study vertically falling bodies with strobe lights or video cameras, equipment that was not available to Galileo.

That the acceleration of gravity is a constant 9.8 m/s² for objects in free fall near earth's surface means that the downward velocity component increases by 9.8 m/s every second. Table 2–2 gives the position, speed, and acceleration of a freely falling object like that of Fig. 2–12.

We can tell that the data of Table 2–2 represent constant acceleration because the distance increases as the *square* of the time. For example, the total distance after 2 s is 2^2 or 4 times that after 1 s; after 3 s the object has gone 3^2 or 9 times as far as in the first second. According to Equation 2–11, constant acceleration from rest should give distance $= \frac{1}{2}a(\text{time})^2$. Therefore, a graph of distance versus time² should be a straight line with slope $\frac{1}{2}a$. Figure 2–14 shows such a plot for the data of Table 2–2; that the plot is a straight line confirms that we have constant acceleration. The measured slope is 4.9 m/s²; thus the acceleration is 2(4.9 m/s²) or 9.8 m/s². Correspondingly, the velocity increases in direct proportion to the time, adding 9.8 m/s for every second. Although we work in SI units for the most part in this book, it is still worth knowing that the acceleration of gravity in English units is 32 (ft/s)/s, usually written 32 ft/s².

The magnitude of the gravitational acceleration is given the symbol g. Remember that g is relatively constant near earth's surface, but is not fundamentally a constant quantity. If we define the positive y-direction as vertically upward, then the downward acceleration enters Equations 2–10, 2–11, 2–13, and 2–14 with a minus sign, and these equations become

$$v_y = v_{y0} - gt \tag{2–15}$$

$$y = y_0 + v_{y0}t - \tfrac{1}{2}gt^2 \tag{2–16}$$

$$y - y_0 = \tfrac{1}{2}(v_y + v_{y0})t \tag{2–17}$$

$$v_y^2 = v_{y0}^2 - 2g(y - y_0), \tag{2–18}$$

where we have replaced x by y since we are describing motion along the vertical direction. Depending on our measurement system, we use g = 9.8 m/s² or g = 32 ft/s²; the minus signs in the equations take care of the fact that the acceleration is actually downward.

Example 2-9

A High Dive

A stunt diver drops from a 30-m-high platform (Fig. 2–15). At what speed does he enter the water? Give the answer in both m/s and mi/h. How long is he in the air? If a photographer's motor drive can take three frames per second, how many frames cover the dive?

Solution

To find the speed, given the distance, we use Equation 2–18. Since the diver starts from rest, $v_0 = 0$, and the equation becomes

$$v_y^2 = -2g(y - y_0).$$

Calling the water $y = 0$, the initial height is $y_0 = 30$ m. Then we have

$$v_y^2 = (-2)(9.8 \text{ m/s}^2)(0 \text{ m} - 30 \text{ m}) = 590 \text{ m}^2/\text{s}^2.$$

Taking the square root, we find that the speed—the magnitude of the velocity—at impact with the water is 24 m/s. (The actual velocity component v_y is -24 m/s, with the negative sign indicating the diver's downward motion.) Converting this result to mi/h gives

$$v = (24 \text{ m/s})(3600 \text{ s/h})(0.001 \text{ km/m})(0.62 \text{ mi/km}) = 54 \text{ mi/h}.$$

Note how the units cancel. Appendix D is useful for conversions such as this one.

Knowing the initial and final velocities, we can use Equation 2–15 to find out how long the diver is in the air. Solving that equation for time t gives

$$t = \frac{v_{y0} - v_y}{g} = \frac{0 \text{ m/s} - (-24 \text{ m/s})}{9.8 \text{ m/s}^2} = 2.5 \text{ s}.$$

Note here that we were careful to use the negative sign with v_y, indicating a downward velocity. Alternatively, we could have obtained the time from Equation 2–16, knowing the distance and acceleration. Solving for t^2 and setting $y_0 = 30$ m (top of platform), $y = 0$ (water), and $v_{y0} = 0$, we have

$$t^2 = \frac{2(y_0 - y)}{g} = \frac{2(30 \text{ m} - 0 \text{ m})}{9.8 \text{ m/s}^2} = 6.1 \text{ s}^2,$$

so that again, $t = 2.5$ s. At 3 frames per second, the diver will appear on (2.5)(3), or 7, complete frames after the dive starts.

Fig. 2–15
A high dive (Example 2–9).

Example 2-10

A Volcanic Eruption

The fountains of lava at the volcanic eruption shown in Fig. 2–16 are so hot that geologists can't get close. But they can watch a chunk of lava that has been thrown upward, and time its fall. Lava chunks at the peak of the fountain take 5.0 s to fall. How high are the fountains?

Solution

Here we know the time and the acceleration, so we can calculate the distance from Equation 2–16. Let $y_0 = h$, our unknown height at the peak of the fountain, and take $y = 0$ at the ground. With $v_{y0} = 0$ at the peak, Equation 2–15 becomes

$$0 = h - \tfrac{1}{2}gt^2,$$

so that

$$h = \tfrac{1}{2}gt^2 = \tfrac{1}{2}(9.8 \text{ m/s}^2)(5.0 \text{ s})^2 = 120 \text{ m}.$$

Fig. 2–16
Lava fountains at the 1983 eruption of Kilauea volcano in Hawaii.

So far, we have treated only examples of objects that are actually moving downward. In that case, the magnitude of the velocity increases because the acceleration is in the same direction as the velocity. But the acceleration of an object subject only to gravity is 9.8 m/s² *downward* no matter what the direction of its motion. When you throw a ball straight up, for example, it is accelerating *downward* even while moving *upward*. Why? Because its upward velocity is *decreasing*—that is, the *change* in velocity is negative. Equations 2–15 to 2–18 continue to describe the situation no matter what the direction of this initial velocity.

Example 2–11
Upward Initial Velocity

You toss a ball straight up with an initial speed of 7.3 m/s. When it leaves your hand, it is 1.5 m above the floor. Use Equation 2–16 to determine when it hits the floor. Find also the maximum height it reaches and its speed when it passes your hand on the way down.

Solution

If we choose $y = 0$ at the floor, then $y_0 = 1.5$ m and $v_{y0} = +7.3$ m/s. To find out when the ball hits the floor, we must ask of Equation 2–16: At what time t is the ball at $y = 0$? That is, we want t such that

$$0 = y_0 + v_{y0}t - \tfrac{1}{2}gt^2.$$

Using the quadratic formula (see Appendix A), we have

$$t = \frac{v_{y0} \pm \sqrt{v_{y0}^2 + 2y_0g}}{g}.$$

The quantity under the square root is

$$v_{y0}^2 + 2y_0g = (7.3 \text{ m/s})^2 + 2(1.5 \text{ m})(9.8 \text{ m/s}^2) = 82.7 \text{ m}^2/\text{s}^2,$$

so that

$$t = \frac{7.3 \text{ m/s} \pm \sqrt{82.7 \text{ m}^2/\text{s}^2}}{9.8 \text{ m/s}^2} = 1.7 \text{ s or } -0.18 \text{ s}.$$

1.7 s is a reasonable answer, but what about the second answer, -0.18 s? Remember that Equations 2–15 to 2–18 were derived under the assumption that gravity alone provides the acceleration. The equations don't "know" anything about the upward acceleration of your hand or about the ball stopping when it hits the floor; they "assume" that the ball always undergoes a downward acceleration g. Our negative answer means simply this: had our hand not been involved, a ball travelling upward at 7.3 m/s when it was 1.5 m off the floor would have been on the floor 0.18 s *earlier*. Our positive answer, the one we expected, says that the ball will again hit the floor 1.7 s *later*.

At the peak of the ball's flight, its instantaneous velocity is zero since it is moving neither up nor down at that point. Setting $v_y^2 = 0$ in Equation 2–18, we can then solve for the peak height y:

$$0 = v_{y0}^2 - 2g(y - y_0),$$

so that

$$y = \frac{2gy_0 + v_{y0}^2}{2g} = y_0 + \frac{v_{y0}^2}{2g} = 1.5 \text{ m} + \frac{(7.3 \text{ m/s})^2}{(2)(9.8 \text{ m/s}^2)} = 4.2 \text{ m}$$

above the floor.

To determine the speed when the ball reaches 1.5 m on the way down, we can set $y = 1.5$ m in Equation 2–18 and solve for v_y. Since $y_0 = 1.5$ m, the term $y - y_0 = 0$, and Equation 2–18 becomes simply $v_y{}^2 = v_{y0}{}^2$. There are two possibilities: $v_y = v_{y0}$ and $v_y = -v_{y0}$. Again, our formulation of the problem does not really ask only about the downward flight; it simply asks for the velocity whenever the height is 1.5 m. The positive answer corresponds to the initial upward velocity and the negative answer to the velocity on the downward flight. In deriving this result, we have demonstrated the important point that an object thrown upward returns to its initial height with the same speed with which it left that height. (This result is exactly true only in the absence of air resistance.)

2.6
DIMENSIONAL ANALYSIS

We have seen that we can treat units as algebraic quantities, cancelling or multiplying them as needed. Each term of an equation, on either side of the equal sign, must have the same units in order for us to add and compare the terms.

It is often convenient to check the "dimensions" of the terms in an equation, ignoring the particular system of units. The basic dimensions in mechanics are length (L), time (T), and mass (M). Consider, for example, Equation 2–10: $v_x = v_{x0} + a_x t$. Here v_x has the dimensions of L/T. We express this by writing $[v_x] = L/T$, with the square brackets to indicate we are talking only about dimensions, not actual values. How about the term $a_x t$? Acceleration has units of velocity per time, so $[a_x] = (L/T)/T = L/T^2$. Thus $[a_x t] = (L/T^2)(T) = L/T$, matching the other terms in the equation.

Similarly, for Equation 2–11 we see that $[v_{x0} t] = (L/T)(T) = L$ and $[\frac{1}{2} a_x t^2] = (L/T^2)(T^2) = L$, matching the terms $[x]$ and $[x_0]$. Note that numerical constants like $\frac{1}{2}$ have no dimensions.

Dimensional analysis helps physicists and engineers see the form that new equations should take. It is also helpful in checking whether you have made a mistake in working a physics problem. All equations must be dimensionally consistent.

SUMMARY

1. **Kinematics** is the study of motion. In this chapter we limit ourselves to the one-dimensional motion of **particles**—objects that have no extent and therefore cannot rotate or vibrate. Real objects approximate particles to the extent we can ignore their rotation, vibration, or other internal motions.

2. **Displacement** is the net change in an object's position. Both distance and direction are needed to specify displacement, which is therefore a **vector** quantity—one that includes both direction and magnitude. We designate displacement from some fixed origin by the vector **r**.

3. **Velocity** is the rate of change of displacement. The **average velocity** $\bar{\mathbf{v}}$ is the displacement $\Delta\mathbf{r}$ divided by the time interval Δt over which it occurred:

$$\bar{\mathbf{v}} = \frac{\Delta\mathbf{r}}{\Delta t}.$$

Like displacement, velocity is a vector quantity. As with any vector, we can describe velocity in terms of **components**—the projections of the velocity vector onto the coordinate axes. In this chapter on one-dimensional motion, we deal with velocity that has only one nonzero component, for example, v_x. We then write

$$\bar{v}_x = \frac{\Delta x}{\Delta t}$$

for the x-component of the average velocity, where Δx is the x-component of the displacement vector $\Delta\mathbf{r}$.

4. To find the **instantaneous velocity**—the velocity at a specific instant of time—we take the limit of the average velocity as the time interval becomes arbitrarily small. Mathematically, this process defines the **derivative** $d\mathbf{r}/dt$:

$$\mathbf{v} = \lim_{\Delta t \to 0} \frac{\Delta \mathbf{r}}{\Delta t} = \frac{d\mathbf{r}}{dt}.$$

When a component of position can be written in the form $x = bt^n$, the derivative dx/dt, or v_x, is

$$v_x = \frac{dx}{dt} = bnt^{n-1}.$$

Graphically, the instantaneous velocity—the derivative of position with respect to time—is the slope of the position-versus-time curve.

5. **Acceleration** is a vector giving the rate of change of velocity. If $\Delta \mathbf{v}$ is the change in velocity in a time interval Δt, then the **average acceleration** over that interval is

$$\bar{\mathbf{a}} = \frac{\Delta \mathbf{v}}{\Delta t}.$$

Like the instantaneous velocity, the **instantaneous acceleration** is defined as the average acceleration taken in the limit of arbitrarily small time intervals Δt:

$$\mathbf{a} = \lim_{\Delta t \to 0} \frac{\Delta \mathbf{v}}{\Delta t} = \frac{d\mathbf{v}}{dt}.$$

In one dimension, the x-component of acceleration is given by $a_x = dv_x/dt$. The direction of the acceleration in one dimension is the same as that of the velocity when the speed is increasing; when the speed is decreasing, the acceleration is directed opposite to the velocity.

6. For **constant acceleration** (constant in both magnitude and direction), position is a quadratic function of time. The following equations relate displacement, time, velocity, and acceleration in one-dimensional motion with constant acceleration:

$$v_x = v_{x0} + a_x t$$

$$x = x_0 + v_{x0}t + \tfrac{1}{2}at^2$$

$$\bar{v}_x = \tfrac{1}{2}(v_{x0} + v_x)$$

$$x - x_0 = \tfrac{1}{2}(v_{x0} + v_x)t$$

$$v_x^2 = v_{x0}^2 + 2a_x(x - x_0).$$

7. **Gravity** is a force that gives rise to an acceleration that is the same for all objects at the same location. Near the surface of the earth, the acceleration of gravity is directed downward and is essentially constant at 9.8 m/s^2 or 32 ft/s^2.

8. **Dimensional analysis** provides a means of checking equations for consistency. An equation cannot be correct unless all its additive terms have the same dimensions.

QUESTIONS

1. Why can we consider the earth to be a particle in some applications but not in others?
2. Give three common examples of velocity units.
3. What is the difference between your displacement and the total distance you travel between the time you wake up and the time you go back to bed on a typical day?
4. You are driving straight at a steady 80 km/h, but stop a while for a picnic lunch. How does the stop affect your average velocity?
5. Does a speedometer measure speed or velocity?
6. You check your odometer at the beginning of a day's driving, and again at the end. Under what conditions would the difference between the two readings represent the magnitude of your displacement?
7. In the previous question, under what conditions would the difference in odometer readings, divided by the total time, equal the magnitude of your average velocity?
8. Two displacement vectors add to give zero net displacement. How must their magnitudes and their directions compare?
9. Consider two possible definitions of average speed: (a) average speed is the average of the values of the instantaneous speed over a time interval; (b) average speed is the magnitude of the average velocity. Are these definitions equivalent? Give examples to demonstrate your conclusion.
10. Is speed a scalar or a vector?
11. Is the x-component of velocity a scalar or a vector?
12. If your speedometer remains fixed at 55 mi/h, do you know that you are not accelerating?
13. Is it possible to be at the position $x = 0$ and still be moving?
14. Is it possible to have zero velocity and still be accelerating?
15. Is it possible to have zero average velocity over a 10-s interval and still be accelerating during the interval? If so, give an example. If not, why not?
16. Is it possible to have zero instantaneous velocity at all times in a 10-s interval and still be accelerating during the interval? If so, give an example. If not, why not?
17. Suppose your car's brakes provide nearly constant deceleration, independent of speed. If you double your initial speed, what does this do to the time it will take to stop your car? What does it do to the distance the car travels while stopping?

18. Starting from rest, an object undergoes an acceleration given by $a_x = bt$, where t is time and b is a constant. Can you use the expression bt for a_x in Equation 2–11 to predict the object's position as a function of time? Why or why not?

19. In which of the velocity-versus-time graphs shown in Fig. 2–17 would the average velocity over the interval shown equal the average of the velocities at the ends of the interval?

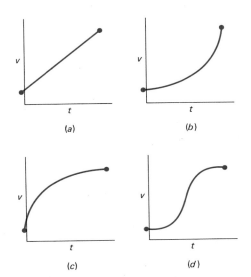

Fig. 2–17   Question 19.

20. What change should be made in Equations 2–15 to 2–18 if the positive y-direction were chosen to be downward?

21. At point A in Fig. 2–6, the slope of the position-versus-time curve changes abruptly. Comment on the velocity and acceleration at that point.

22. What would the third derivative of position signify? (The third derivative is sometimes called the "jerk." It is what can make you sick on an amusement park ride.)

23. What was the advantage in plotting distance versus time² rather than versus time in Fig. 2–14?

24. Standing on a roof, you simultaneously throw one ball straight up and drop another from rest. Which hits the ground first? Which hits the ground moving fastest?

25. Can the height of the lava fountains in Fig. 2–16 be used to estimate the masses of the lava chunks? Why or why not?

26. If you travel in a straight line at 50 km/h for one hour and at 100 km/h for another hour, is your average velocity 75 km/h? If not, is it more or less?

27. If you travel in a straight line at 50 km/h for 50 km, and then at 100 km/h for another 50 km, is your average velocity 75 km/h? If not, is it more or less?

28. (Zeno's paradox) If you try to reach the other side of the room, first you must cross half the distance, then half the remaining distance, then half the distance that still remains, and so forth. At any point, you still have half the distance to go. So it would seem that you can never reach the other side. What is wrong with this reasoning?

29. What relevance does the hammer/feather experiment on the moon have for our understanding of gravity on earth?

30. Why might crumpling a piece of paper make its air resistance less than that of a flat piece?

31. If you drop one rock from rest, and throw another down with velocity v_0, is the difference in their velocities when they hit the ground more than, less than, or equal to v_0? Don't apply any equations here; just think about how long each rock experiences the acceleration of gravity.

─────── **PROLEMS** ───────────
─────── **PROBLEMS** ───────────

Section 2.1   *Distance, Time, and Velocity*

1. The world's record for the 200-m dash is 19.72 s, set by Italy's Pietro Mennea at the 1979 Mexico City Olympics. What was Mennea's average speed?

2. When races in a track meet are timed manually, timers start their watches when they see smoke from the starting gun, rather than when they hear the gun. How much error is introduced in timing a 200-m dash over a straight track if the watch is started on the sound rather than the smoke? The speed of sound is about 340 m/s.

3. The world's fastest marathon was the New York City Marathon of 1981, won by Alberto Salazar. Salazar covered the 26-mi 385-yd course in 2 h 8 min 13.0 s. What was his average speed?

4. Human nerve impulses travel at about 10^2 m/s. Estimate the minimum time that must elapse between the time you perceive a stalled car in front of you and the time you can activate the muscles in your leg to brake your car. (Your actual "reaction time" is much longer than this estimate.) Moving at 90 km/h, how far would your car travel in this time?

5. Starting from home, you bicycle 24 km north in 2.5 h, then turn around and pedal straight home in 1.5 h. What are your (a) displacement at the end of the first 2.5 h, (b) average velocity over the first 2.5 h, (c) average velocity for the homeward leg of the trip, (d) displacement for the entire trip, and (e) average velocity for the entire trip?

6. The European Space Agency's Giotto spacecraft en-

countered Halley's Comet in March 1986, when the comet was 93 million km from earth. How long did it take radio signals (travelling at the speed of light) to reach earth from Giotto?

7. A full-length triathlon is a gruelling event in which contestants first swim 2.4 miles, then bicycle 112 miles, then complete a 26-mile 385-yard marathon on foot. The world's triathlon record for women was set in 1983 by Canada's Sylviane Puntus. She completed the event in 10 h 43 min 36 s. What was her average speed? (Incidentally, her identical twin finished second.)

8. Find values, good to one significant figure, for the speed of light in (a) ft/ns (1 ns = 10^{-9} s) and (b) furlongs per fortnight, where there are 8 furlongs to a mile and 14 days per fortnight.

9. You allow yourself 40 min to drive 25 miles to the airport, but are caught in heavy traffic and average only 20 mi/h for the first 15 min. What must your average speed be on the rest of the trip if you are to get there on time?

10. Taking earth's orbit to be a circle of radius 1.5×10^8 km, determine the speed of earth's orbital motion in (a) m/s and (b) miles per second.

11. What is the conversion factor from m/s to mi/h?

12. If the average American driver goes 5000 miles each year on interstate highways, how much more time does the average driver spend on interstate highways each year as a result of the 1974 change in the speed limit from 70 mi/h to 55 mi/h?

13. A fast base runner can get from first to second base in 3.4 s. If he leaves first base as the pitcher throws a 90-mi/h fastball the 61-ft distance to the catcher, and if the catcher takes 0.45 s to catch and rethrow the ball, how fast does the catcher have to throw the ball to second base to make an out? Home plate to second base is the diagonal of a square 90 ft on a side.

14. Despite the fact that jet airplanes fly at about 600 mi/h, plane schedules and connections are such that the 3000-mi trip from Burlington, Vermont, to San Francisco ends up taking about 11 h. (a) What is the average speed of such a trip? (b) How much time is spent on the ground, assuming that the actual distance covered by the several aircraft involved in connecting flights is 4200 mi and that the planes maintain a steady 600 mi/h in flight?

15. If you drove the 4600 km from coast to coast of the United States at 55 mi/h (88 km/h), stopping an average of 30 min for rest and refueling after every 2 h, (a) how long would it take? (b) What would be your average velocity for the entire trip?

16. I can run 9.0 m/s, 20 per cent faster than my kid brother. How much head start should I give him in order to have a tie race over 100 m?

17. A jetliner leaves San Francisco for New York, 4600 km away. With a strong tailwind, its speed is 1100 km/h. At the same time, a second jet leaves New York for San Francisco. Flying into the wind, it makes only 700 km/h. When and where do the two planes pass each other?

Section 2.2   *Motion in Short Time Intervals*

18. On a single graph, plot distance versus time for the three 50-km trips described on page 17. For each trip, identify graphically the average velocity and the instantaneous velocity for each segment of the trip.

19. By performing the limiting process as in Example 2–3, evaluate the instantaneous velocity as a function of time for an object whose position as a function of time is given by $x = bt^3$. Repeat, using Equation 2–5.

20. For the motion plotted in Fig. 2–18, estimate (a) the greatest velocity in the positive x-direction, (b) the greatest velocity in the negative x-direction, (c) any times when the object is instantaneously at rest, and (d) the average velocity over the interval shown.

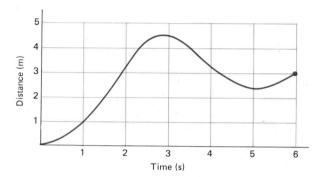

Fig. 2–18 Problem 20.

21. The position of an object is given by $x = bt^3 - ct^2 + dt$, with x in meters and t in seconds. The constants b, c, and d are $b = 3.0$ m/s^3, $c = 8.0$ m/s^2, and $d = 1.0$ m/s. (a) Find all times when the object is at position $x = 0$. (b) Determine a general expression for the instantaneous velocity as a function of time, and from it find (c) the initial velocity and (d) all times when the object is instantaneously at rest. (e) Graph the object's position as a function of time, and identify on the graph the quantities you found in (a) to (d).

22. In a drag race, the position of a car as a function of time is given by $x = bt^2$, with $b = 2.000$ m/s^2. In an attempt to determine the car's velocity midway down a 400-m track, two observers stand 20 m on either side of the 200-m mark and note the time when the car passes them. (a) What value do the two observers compute for the car's velocity? Give your answer to four significant figures. (b) By what percentage does this observed value differ from the actual instantaneous value at $x = 200$ m?

Section 2.3   *Acceleration*

23. A car roars away from a red light. Half a minute later, it screeches to a halt at a second light, one-fourth mile from the first. What is its average acceleration between the times it is stopped at the two lights?

24. The 1986 explosion of the space shuttle Challenger occurred 74 s after lift-off. At that time, mission con-

trol reported a shuttle speed of 2900 ft/s (880 m/s). What was the Challenger's average acceleration during its brief flight? Compare with the acceleration of gravity.

25. Under the influence of a radio wave, an electron in an antenna undergoes back-and-forth motion whose velocity as a function of time is described by Fig. 2–19. From the graph, estimate the electron's maximum acceleration.

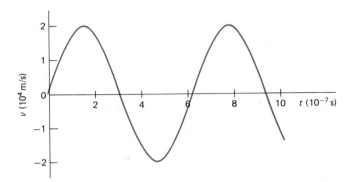

Fig. 2–19 Problem 25.

26. Determine the instantaneous acceleration as a function of time for the motion in Problem 21.
27. The position of an object is given by $x = bt^3$, where x is in meters, t in seconds, and where the constant b is 1.5 m/s³. Determine (a) the instantaneous velocity and (b) the instantaneous acceleration at the end of 2.5 s. Find (c) the average velocity and (d) the average acceleration during the first 2.5 s.

Section 2.4 Constant Acceleration

28. In 1982, drag racer Gary Beck set a new record, travelling a quarter mile from rest in 5.484 s. Assuming constant acceleration, determine (a) Beck's acceleration, (b) the maximum speed achieved, and (c) the time to reach 55 mi/h.
29. Starting from rest, a car accelerates at a constant rate, reaching 88 km/h in 12 s. (a) What is its acceleration? (b) How far does it go in this time?
30. If you are running at 6 m/s and decelerate at 2 m/s², (a) how long will it take you to stop? (b) How far will you go while decelerating?
31. A car moving initially at 50 mi/h begins decelerating at a constant rate 100 ft short of a stoplight. If the car comes to a full stop just at the light, what is the magnitude of its deceleration?
32. In an x-ray tube, electrons are accelerated to a velocity of 10^8 m/s, then slammed into a tungsten target. When they collide with the tungsten atoms, the electrons undergo rapid deceleration, producing x-rays in the process. If the stopping time for an electron is on the order of 10^{-19} s, approximately how far does an electron move while decelerating? Assume constant deceleration.

33. A particle leaves its initial position x_0 at time $t = 0$, moving in the positive x-direction with speed v_0, but undergoing acceleration of magnitude a in the negative x-direction. Find expressions for (a) the time when it returns to the position x_0 and (b) its speed when it passes that point.
34. The Barringer meteor crater in northern Arizona is 180 m deep and 1.2 km in diameter. The fragments of the meteor lie just below the bottom of the crater. If these fragments decelerated at a constant rate of 4×10^5 m/s² as they ploughed through the earth in forming the crater, what was the speed of the meteor's impact at earth's surface?
35. A gazelle accelerates from rest at 4.1 m/s² over a distance of 60 m to outrun a predator. What is its final speed?
36. A frog's tongue flicks out 10 cm in 0.1 s to catch a fly. If it accelerates at a constant rate during this time, what are (a) its average velocity and (b) its acceleration?
37. Amtrak's 20th-Century Limited is en route from Chicago to New York at 110 km/h, when the engineer spots a cow on the track. The train brakes to a halt in 1.2 min with constant deceleration, stopping just in front of the cow. (a) What is the magnitude of the train's acceleration? (b) What is the direction of the acceleration? (c) How far was the train from the cow when the engineer first applied the brakes?
38. A jetliner touches down at 220 km/h, reverses its engines to provide braking, and comes to a halt 29 s later. What is the shortest runway on which this aircraft can land, assuming constant deceleration starting at touchdown?
39. A flea extends its 0.80-mm-long legs, propelling itself 10 cm into the air. Assuming that the legs provide constant acceleration as they extend from completely folded to completely extended, find the magnitude of that acceleration. Compare with the acceleration of gravity at earth's surface.
40. A motorist suddenly notices a stalled car and slams on the brakes, decelerating at the rate of 6.3 m/s². Unfortunately this isn't good enough, and a collision ensues. From the damage sustained, police estimate that the car was moving at 18 km/h at the time of the collision. They also measure skid marks 34 m long. (a) How fast was the motorist going when the brakes were first applied? (b) How much time elapsed from the initial braking to the collision?
41. The maximum acceleration that a human being can survive even for a short time is about 200g. In a highway accident, a car moving at 88 km/h slams into a stalled truck. The front end of the car is squashed by 80 cm on impact. If the deceleration during the collision is constant, will a passenger wearing a seatbelt survive?
42. A racing car undergoing constant acceleration covers 120 m in 2.7 s. (a) If it is moving at 53 m/s at the end of this interval, what was its speed at the beginning of the interval? (b) How far did it travel *from rest* to the end of the 120-m distance?

43. The maximum deceleration of a car on a dry road is about 8 m/s². If two cars are moving head-on toward each other at 88 km/h (55 mi/h), and their drivers apply their brakes when they are 85 m apart, will they collide? If so, at what relative speed? If not, how far apart will they be when they stop? On the same graph, plot distance versus time for both cars.

44. George, a physics student, leaves his dormitory at a speed of 1.2 m/s, heading for the physics building 95 m away. Just as he leaves his dorm, Amy, another physics student, leaves the physics building and heads toward George at a steady 1.6 m/s. George immediately spots her and begins accelerating at 0.075 m/s². Where and when do the two meet? Plot position-versus-time curves for both students on a single graph. *Hint:* Be sure to set the algebraic signs of positions, velocities, and accelerations consistently.

45. After 35 minutes of running, at the 9-km point in a 10-km race, you find yourself 100 m behind the leader and moving at the same speed. What should your acceleration be if you are to catch up by the finish line? Assume that the leader maintains constant speed throughout the entire race.

Section 2.5 *The Constant Acceleration of Gravity*

46. You drop a rock into a deep well, and 2.7 s later hear the splash. How far down is the water? Neglect the travel time of the sound.

47. Your friend is sitting 20 ft above you in a tree branch. How fast should you throw an apple so that it just reaches her?

48. A model rocket leaves the ground, heading straight up at 49 m/s. (*a*) What is its maximum altitude? What are its speed and altitude at (*b*) 1 s; (*c*) 4 s; (*d*) 7 s.

49. A foul ball leaves the bat going straight upward at 23 m/s. (*a*) How high does it rise? (*b*) How long is it in the air? Neglect the distance between the bat and the ground.

50. A Frisbee is lodged in a tree branch, 6.5 m above the ground. A rock thrown from below must be going at least 3 m/s to dislodge the Frisbee. How fast must such a rock be thrown upward, if it leaves the thrower's hand 1.3 m above the ground?

51. Space pirates kidnap an earthling and hold him imprisoned on one of the planets of the solar system. With nothing else to do, the prisoner amuses himself by dropping his watch from eye level (170 cm) to the floor. He observes that the watch takes 0.62 s to fall. On what planet is he being held? *Hint:* Consult Appendix F.

52. The earliest attempts to land instruments on the moon involved Ranger spacecraft that were to release instrument capsules at about 11 km above the lunar surface. After a retrorocket firing, the capsules were to fall freely to the moon. Surrounded by a balsawood sphere, the instrument capsule was designed to withstand an impact speed equivalent to a free fall from 150 m above earth's surface. From what height above the lunar surface could the capsule drop, assuming the retrorocket slowed it to zero speed at that height? (In fact, none of the Ranger instrument packages ever made the intended cushioned landing.)

53. Anders, a physics student, is going to take an exam but has forgotten his calculator. He stops outside the physics building and yells for help. Charlie, another physics student 21 ft above him on the third floor, drops a calculator out the window. A third physics student, Torey, is on the fourth floor, 32 ft above Anders. She throws her calculator down at 15 ft/s at the same time Charlie drops his. Whose calculator reaches Anders first, and by how much?

54. A falling object travels one-fourth of its total distance in the last second of its fall. From what height was it dropped?

55. The defenders of a castle throw rocks down on their attackers from a 15-m-high wall. If the rocks are thrown with an initial speed of 10 m/s, how much faster do they hit the ground than if they were simply dropped?

56. A kingfisher is 30 m above a lake when it accidentally drops the fish it is carrying. A second kingfisher 5 m above the first dives toward the falling fish. What initial speed should it have if it is to reach the fish before the fish hits the water?

57. Two divers jump from a 3.00-m platform. One jumps upward at 1.80 m/s, and the second steps off the platform as the first passes it on the way down. (*a*) What are their speeds as they hit the water? (*b*) Which hits the water first, and by how much?

58. A balloon is rising at 10 m/s when its passenger throws up a ball at 12 m/s. How much later does the passenger catch the ball?

59. A conveyer belt moves horizontally at 80 cm/s, carrying empty shoe boxes. Every 3 s, a pair of shoes is dropped from a chute 1.7 m above the belt. (*a*) How far apart should the boxes be spaced? (*b*) At the instant a pair of shoes drops, where should a box be in relation to a point directly below the chute?

Supplementary Problems

60. A penny dropped from a 90-m-high building embeds itself 3.6 cm into the ground. Compare its average acceleration on stopping with the acceleration of gravity. *Hint:* You need not compute any velocities or times.

61. You see the traffic light ahead of you is about to turn from red to green, so you slow to a steady speed of 10 km/h and cruise to the light, reaching it just as it turns green. You then accelerate to 60 km/h in the next 12 s, then maintain constant speed. At the light, you pass a Corvette that has stopped for the red light. Just as you pass (and the light turns green) the Corvette begins accelerating, reaching 65 km/h in 6.9 s, then maintaining constant speed. (*a*) Plot the motions of both cars on a graph showing the entire minute after the light turns green. (*b*) How long after the light turns green does the Corvette pass you? (*c*) How far are you from the light when the Corvette passes you? (*d*) How far ahead of you is the Corvette 1 min after the light turns green?

62. In the accident of Problem 41, calculate the relative speed with which a passenger not wearing a seatbelt collides with the dashboard. Assume the passenger undergoes no deceleration before striking the dashboard, and that the passenger is initially 1 m from the dashboard.

63. The position of a particle as a function of time is given by $x = x_0 \sin(\omega t)$, where x_0 and ω are constants. Using the limiting procedure as in Example 2–3, show that the instantaneous velocity is given by $v = x_0\omega\cos(\omega t)$. *Hint:* Use the identity for the sine of a sum of angles (see Appendix A), along with appropriate approximations for the sine and cosine of small angles (see Appendix A).

64. A basketball player runs 12 m down court at 4.6 m/s, dribbling the ball so it has an initial downward velocity of 75 cm/s at 90 cm above the floor. How many times does the ball hit the floor during the 12-m run? Neglect any up-and-down motion of the player's hand. *Hint:* The vertical motion of the ball is independent of its horizontal motion.

65. You drop a rock into a well. 2.7 s later, you hear the splash. (*a*) How far down is the water? The speed of sound is 340 m/s. (*b*) What percentage error would be introduced by neglecting the travel time for the sound?

66. The depth of a well is such that an object dropped into the well hits the water going far slower than the speed of sound. Use the binomial theorem (see Appendix A) to show that, under these conditions, the depth of the well is given approximately by

$$d = \tfrac{1}{2}gt^2 \left(1 - \frac{gt}{v_s}\right),$$

where t is the time from when you drop the object until you hear the splash, and v_s is the speed of sound.

67. A student is staring idly out her dormitory window when she sees a water balloon fall past. If the balloon takes 0.22 s to cross the 130-cm-high window, from what height above the top of the window was it dropped?

68. A police radar has an effective range of 1.0 km, while a motorist's radar detector has a range of 1.8 km. The motorist is going 100 km/h in a 70 km/h zone when the radar detector beeps. At what rate must the motorist decelerate to avoid a speeding ticket?

3

MOTION IN MORE THAN ONE DIMENSION

Motion is not limited to moving back and forth along a single railroad track. As we walk, as we drive, as we sail, we move freely about the surface of the earth—that is, in two dimensions. As we fly from city to city, scale a mountain, or are launched into space, we move in a third dimension as well (Fig. 3–1). In this chapter, we formulate laws of motion for two and three dimensions. We show also how vectors provide a relatively simple way to analyze such multidimensional motion.

3.1
THE VECTOR DESCRIPTION OF MOTION

We recognized in the preceding chapter that the quantities characterizing motion—position, velocity, and acceleration—have both magnitude and direction, and are therefore vector quantities. In that chapter, we considered only one-dimensional motion, in which all vectors lie along a single line. Now we generalize to the case of arbitrary motion in two and three dimensions.

Position, Displacement, and Vector Addition

position vector

Motion involves changes of position; we specify position using the **position vector, r** (Fig. 3–2). We can characterize the position vector fully by giving both its length and its direction or, equivalently, by specifying its components—its projections on the coordinate axes (see Fig. 3–2).

What if we move the object in Fig. 3–2 1 m to the right, as shown in Fig. 3–3? The new position is described by a vector $\mathbf{r}_2$; we obtain $\mathbf{r}_2$ by adding to $\mathbf{r}_1$ a vector $\Delta\mathbf{r}$ that is 1 m long and points to the right. To accomplish the addition, we simply place $\Delta\mathbf{r}$ with its tail at the head of $\mathbf{r}_1$; the head of $\Delta\mathbf{r}$ then lies at the head of the sum $\mathbf{r}_1 + \Delta\mathbf{r}$. This procedure defines

Fig. 3–1
Landing at a major airport involves a complex pattern of three-dimensional motion. Here a jetliner passes over an experimental system designed to help pilots avoid dangerous wind shear.

40

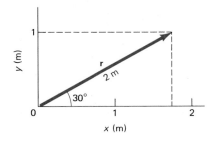

Fig. 3–2
The position vector **r** for an object located 2 m from the origin at 30° to the x-axis. The components of the vector are $x = (2 \text{ m})(\cos 30°) = 1.7$ m and $y = (2 \text{ m})(\sin 30°) = 1.0$ m. These expressions for the components follow from the definitions of sine and cosine as ratios of the opposite and adjacent sides of a right triangle, respectively, to the hypotenuse.

the general rule for adding any two vectors: place the vectors to be added head-to-tail; their vector sum is then a vector from the tail of the first vector to the head of the second. Remember that a vector is specified fully by giving its magnitude and direction. Where the vector starts doesn't matter, which is why we can slide vectors around—as long as we preserve their length and direction—to form vector sums.

In Fig. 3–3, we formed the vector sum $\mathbf{r}_1 + \Delta\mathbf{r}$ graphically; to specify the resultant vector $\mathbf{r}_2$, we could measure its angle and length on our graph. Or we could use the law of cosines to calculate the length of $\mathbf{r}_2$, and the law of sines to determine its angle. (The laws of cosines and of sines are described in Appendix A.) But we will often find it more convenient to handle vector arithmetic in terms of components. In Fig. 3–3, for example, it is obvious that the x-component of $\mathbf{r}_2$ is simply the sum $x_1 + \Delta x$, where x_1 and Δx are the x-components of the vectors $\mathbf{r}_1$ and $\Delta\mathbf{r}$, respectively. Similarly, the y-component of $\mathbf{r}_2$ is the sum of the y-components of $\mathbf{r}_1$ and $\Delta\mathbf{r}$, although in this case Δy, the y-component of $\Delta\mathbf{r}$, is zero.

Since the addition of vector components is commutative and associative, so is vector addition itself. That is, $\mathbf{A} + \mathbf{B} = \mathbf{B} + \mathbf{A}$ and $(\mathbf{A} + \mathbf{B}) + \mathbf{C} = \mathbf{A} + (\mathbf{B} + \mathbf{C})$. You can also see this graphically, as suggested in Fig. 3–4.

Example 3–1 _____
Vector Addition

Determine the vector $\mathbf{r}_2$ in Fig. 3–3 (a) using the laws of cosines and sines and (b) using components.

Solution

The law of cosines (see Appendix A) is like a modified Pythagorean theorem, giving the third side, C, of a triangle in terms of the other two sides A and B and the angle θ between them:

$$C^2 = A^2 + B^2 - 2AB\cos\theta.$$

Applying the law of cosines to the lengths of the vectors in Fig. 3–3, we have

$$r_2{}^2 = r_1{}^2 + (\Delta r)^2 - 2r_1\Delta r \cos\theta.$$

We indicate the lengths—magnitudes—of the vectors by writing their symbols in italic type rather than boldface. Figure 3–5 shows the angle θ is 150°; therefore

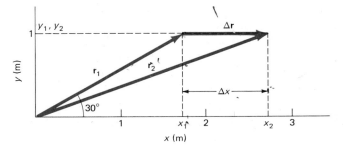

Fig. 3–3
Vector addition. The new position vector $\mathbf{r}_2$ defines the vector sum of the old position vector $\mathbf{r}_1$ and the change $\Delta\mathbf{r}$. Graphically, we sum the vectors by placing them head-to-tail; algebraically, we simply sum their components.

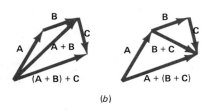

(a)

(b)

Fig. 3–4
(a) Vector addition is commutative; whether we form the sum **A** + **B** or the sum **B** + **A**, we get the same result. (b) Vector addition is also associative; that is, (**A** + **B**) + **C** = **A** + (**B** + **C**).

$$r_2^2 = (2.0 \text{ m})^2 + (1.0 \text{ m})^2 - (2)(2.0 \text{ m})(1.0 \text{ m})\cos 150° = 8.46 \text{ m}^2,$$

so that $r_2 = 2.9$ m. This value is the length of $\mathbf{r}_2$; what about its direction? Applying the law of sines (see Appendix A) to the triangle formed by the vectors $\mathbf{r}_1$, $\Delta\mathbf{r}$, and $\mathbf{r}_2$, we have

$$\frac{\sin\alpha}{\Delta r} = \frac{\sin 150°}{r_2},$$

where α is the angle between $\mathbf{r}_1$ and $\mathbf{r}_2$ (see Fig. 3–5). Then

$$\alpha = \sin^{-1}\left(\frac{\Delta r \sin 150°}{r_2}\right) = \sin^{-1}\left(\frac{(1.0 \text{ m})(0.50)}{2.9 \text{ m}}\right) = 9.9°.$$

Figure 3–5 then shows that $\mathbf{r}_2$ makes an angle $\beta = 30° - \alpha$, or 20°, with the x-axis. The full specification of the vector $\mathbf{r}_2$ includes both its 2.9-m magnitude and its 20° direction.

To determine $\mathbf{r}_2$ using components, we need first the components of $\mathbf{r}_1$ and $\Delta\mathbf{r}$. Using x_1 and y_1 as the components of the 2-m-long vector $\mathbf{r}_1$, we see from Fig. 3–2 that $x_1 = (2 \text{ m})(\cos 30°) = 1.73$ m and $y_1 = (2 \text{ m})(\sin 30°) = 1.0$ m. Since $\Delta\mathbf{r}$ points in the x-direction, only its x-component is nonzero, and is equal to the full 1-m length of the vector. [Formally, we could calculate its components Δx and Δy as we did for $\mathbf{r}_1$: $\Delta x = (1.0 \text{ m})(\cos 0°) = 1.0$ m and $\Delta y = (1.0 \text{ m})(\cos 90°) = 0$.] Adding the components of $\mathbf{r}_1$ and $\Delta\mathbf{r}$ gives the components x_2 and y_2 of $\mathbf{r}_2$:

$$x_2 = x_1 + \Delta x = 1.73 \text{ m} + 1.0 \text{ m} = 2.73 \text{ m}$$

and

$$y_2 = y_1 + \Delta y = 1.0 \text{ m} + 0 \text{ m} = 1.0 \text{ m}.$$

These two numbers give a full description of the vector $\mathbf{r}_2$; alternatively, we could determine the length and direction using the Pythagorean theorem and the definition of tangent as the ratio of the sides of a right triangle (see Fig. 3–5):

$$r_2 = \sqrt{x_2 + y_2} = [(2.73 \text{ m})^2 + (1.0 \text{ m})^2]^{1/2} = 2.9 \text{ m}$$

and

$$\beta = \tan^{-1}\left(\frac{y_2}{x_2}\right) = \tan^{-1}\left(\frac{1.0 \text{ m}}{2.73 \text{ m}}\right) = 20°,$$

in agreement with our graphical method.

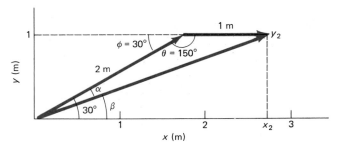

Fig. 3–5
We are given that the angle between $\mathbf{r}_1$ and the x-axis is 30°. Therefore, the angle ϕ is also 30°, so that $\theta = 180° - 30° = 150°$. Knowing θ, we use the law of sines to get the angle α between $\mathbf{r}_1$ and $\mathbf{r}_2$; the angle β between $\mathbf{r}_2$ and the x-axis is $30° - \alpha$.

The two ways of specifying a vector—giving its length and direction or specifying its components—are completely equivalent. Using a vector diagram, the Pythagorean theorem, and definitions of the trig functions, we can always convert from one description to the other. In two dimensions, either description requires specifying two numbers. In three dimensions, we would need an additional angle or the z-component, for a total of three numbers. Whether we work only with length and direction, or only with components, or with some combination of the two, depends on what information we are given and on the form we need for our final answer.

In Example 3–1, we solved for the vector $\mathbf{r}_2$ satisfying the vector equation

$$\mathbf{r}_2 = \mathbf{r}_1 + \Delta\mathbf{r}. \qquad (3\text{–}1)$$

Our second method—using components—involved solving the two scalar equations

$$x_2 = x_1 + \Delta x \qquad (3\text{–}1a)$$
$$y_2 = y_2 + \Delta y \qquad (3\text{–}1b)$$

for the components x_2 and y_2 of the vector $\mathbf{r}_2$. In general, we can think of a vector equation like Equation 3–1 as a shorthand for two (or in three dimensions, three) scalar equations for the vector components. Later in this chapter, we will see how the use of vector equations allows us to express the equations of two- and three-dimensional motion in compact form.

What if we had been given $\mathbf{r}_1$ and $\mathbf{r}_2$, and asked to find what vector $\Delta\mathbf{r}$ must be added to $\mathbf{r}_1$ to give $\mathbf{r}_2$? Then we could solve the vector equation 3–1 for the unknown $\Delta\mathbf{r}$:

$$\Delta\mathbf{r} = \mathbf{r}_2 - \mathbf{r}_1. \qquad (3\text{–}2)$$

This is equivalent to the two scalar equations

$$\Delta x = x_2 - x_1 \qquad (3\text{–}2a)$$

$$\Delta y = y_2 - y_1, \qquad (3\text{–}2b)$$

which give us the two components of the vector $\Delta\mathbf{r}$. Equivalently, we could solve Equation 3–2 graphically by subtracting the vector $\mathbf{r}_1$ from the vector $\mathbf{r}_2$—that is, by adding to $\mathbf{r}_2$ the vector $-\mathbf{r}_1$, whose length is that of $\mathbf{r}_1$ but which points in the opposite direction (Fig. 3–6).

Fig. 3–6
To perform the subtraction $\mathbf{r}_2 - \mathbf{r}_1$, we add to $\mathbf{r}_2$ the vector $-\mathbf{r}_1$—that is, a vector the same length as $\mathbf{r}_1$ but pointing in the opposite direction. The result is the vector difference $\Delta\mathbf{r}$.

It is cumbersome to say "a vector of length 2 m at 30° to the x-axis" or "a vector whose x-component is 1.73 m and whose y-component is 1.0 m." After all, a vector is a mathematical quantity, and we are used to writing mathematical quantities compactly, without a lot of words. We can express arbitrary vectors in compact form using **unit vectors.** We define three such vectors, each of length 1, pointing in the x, y, and z directions. These vectors are called $\hat{\mathbf{i}}$, $\hat{\mathbf{j}}$, and $\hat{\mathbf{k}}$, respectively. They have no dimensions, and serve only to indicate direction.

unit vectors

Before we can use the unit vectors, we must define what it means to multiply a vector by a scalar: the product of a scalar c with a vector $\mathbf{A}$ (written $c\mathbf{A}$) is a vector of length cA (where A is the length of $\mathbf{A}$), pointing in the same direction as $\mathbf{A}$. That is, multiplication by a scalar changes the length of a vector but not its direction (although multiplication by a negative scalar reverses the sense of the vector along the line on which it lies;

Fig. 3–7
Multiplication of a vector by a scalar. The result lies in the same direction as the original vector, although its sense is reversed if the scalar is negative. Note again that where a vector starts doesn't matter; its direction and magnitude fully characterize the vector.

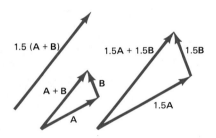

Fig. 3–8
Multiplication of a vector by a scalar is distributive.

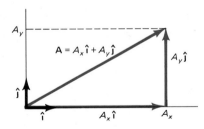

Fig. 3–9
An arbitrary vector expressed in terms of unit vectors $\hat{\imath}$ and $\hat{\jmath}$.

see Fig. 3–7). Multiplication by a scalar is distributive: $c(\mathbf{A} + \mathbf{B}) = c\mathbf{A} + c\mathbf{B}$ (Fig. 3–8).

Using unit vectors, we write an arbitrary vector **A**, whose components are A_x, A_y, and A_z, as the sum of three vectors $A_x\hat{\imath}$, $A_y\hat{\jmath}$, and $A_z\hat{\mathbf{k}}$ that lie along the mutually perpendicular coordinate axes:

$$\mathbf{A} = A_x\hat{\imath} + A_y\hat{\jmath} + A_z\hat{\mathbf{k}}.$$

Figure 3–9 illustrates this process graphically for a vector that lies in the x-y plane. The unit vectors provide us a way of expressing compactly the three perpendicular directions of our coordinate system; weighted by the components along each axis and then summed, they give a full description of an arbitrary vector.

Adding and subtracting vectors expressed in unit vector notation is simple: we just add the individual terms. For example, if $\mathbf{A} = A_x\hat{\imath} + A_y\hat{\jmath} + A_z\hat{\mathbf{k}}$ and $\mathbf{B} = B_x\hat{\imath} + B_y\hat{\jmath} + B_z\hat{\mathbf{k}}$, the sum $\mathbf{A} + \mathbf{B}$ is

$$\mathbf{A} + \mathbf{B} = (A_x\hat{\imath} + A_y\hat{\jmath} + A_z\hat{\mathbf{k}}) + (B_x\hat{\imath} + B_y\hat{\jmath} + B_z\hat{\mathbf{k}})$$
$$= (A_x+B_x)\hat{\imath} + (A_y+B_y)\hat{\jmath} + (A_z+B_z)\hat{\mathbf{k}}. \qquad (3\text{–}3)$$

Example 3–2
Unit Vector Notation

Express the vectors $\mathbf{r}_1$ and $\Delta\mathbf{r}$ of Example 3–1 in unit vector notation, and add them to get $\mathbf{r}_2$.

Solution

In Example 3–1, we found the components of $\mathbf{r}_1$ to be $x_1 = 1.73$ m and $y_1 = 1.0$ m, while those of $\Delta\mathbf{r}$ were $\Delta x = 1.0$ m and $\Delta y = 0$. In unit vector notation, then, these two vectors are

$$\mathbf{r}_1 = 1.73\hat{\imath} + 1.0\hat{\jmath} \text{ m}$$
$$\Delta\mathbf{r} = 1.0\hat{\imath} \text{ m}.$$

Adding these two, we have

$$\mathbf{r}_1 + \Delta\mathbf{r} = (1.73\hat{\imath} + 1.0\hat{\jmath} \text{ m}) + (1.0\hat{\imath} \text{ m}) = 2.73\hat{\imath} + 1.0\hat{\jmath} \text{ m}.$$

Unit vector notation allowed us to carry out this operation neatly and without a lot of words. Our final answer, $2.73\hat{\imath} + 1.0\hat{\jmath}$ m, is a compact and complete description of the vector $\mathbf{r}_2$.

Velocity

In the preceding chapter, we defined average velocity $\overline{\mathbf{v}}$ as the ratio of change in position $\Delta\mathbf{r}$ to the time interval Δt over which that change occurs:

$$\overline{\mathbf{v}} = \frac{\Delta\mathbf{r}}{\Delta t}. \qquad (3\text{–}4)$$

Taking the average velocity in the limit of arbitrarily short time intervals gave us the instantaneous velocity **v**:

$$\mathbf{v} = \lim_{\Delta t \to 0} \frac{\Delta\mathbf{r}}{\Delta t} = \frac{d\mathbf{r}}{dt}, \qquad (3\text{–}5)$$

where the derivative notation $d\mathbf{r}/dt$ is a shorthand way of expressing the result of the limiting process. Since displacement is a vector, so is velocity.

Equation 3–4 shows us that the average velocity $\bar{\mathbf{v}}$ of an object moving between positions $\mathbf{r}_1$ and $\mathbf{r}_2$ in time Δt is given by the vector difference $\Delta\mathbf{r} = \mathbf{r}_2 - \mathbf{r}_1$ divided by the scalar Δt. (Dividing a vector by a scalar means multiplying by the reciprocal of the scalar; we have already defined such multiplication.) Suppose, for example, that the object of Examples 3–1 and 3–2 took 2.0 s to get from $\mathbf{r}_1$ to $\mathbf{r}_2$. We already found the difference $\Delta\mathbf{r}$ between these two vectors is $\Delta\mathbf{r} = 1.0\hat{\mathbf{i}}$ m, so that Equation 3–4 gives

$$\bar{\mathbf{v}} = \frac{\Delta\mathbf{r}}{\Delta t} = \frac{1.0\hat{\mathbf{i}}\text{ m}}{2.0\text{ s}} = 0.50\hat{\mathbf{i}}\text{ m/s.}$$

Here an answer of 0.50 m/s alone would not be enough; velocity is a vector, and its specification requires both direction and magnitude. The answer $0.50\hat{\mathbf{i}}$ m/s includes both.

Example 3–3
LA to Denver via Salt Lake City

You leave Los Angeles on a flight to Denver, with a stop in Salt Lake City. Flying 55° north of east, the plane makes the 970-km trip to Salt Lake City in 72 min. After 40 min on the ground, the plane heads for Denver, which is 600 km away and in a direction 10° south of east. The plane reaches Denver 55 min after leaving Salt Lake City. Determine the average velocity of the plane between Los Angeles and Denver.

Solution

Figure 3–10 shows the situation graphically. The vector displacement $\Delta\mathbf{r}_{LD}$ from Los Angeles to Denver is the sum of the displacement $\Delta\mathbf{r}_{LS}$ from Los Angeles to Salt Lake City and the displacement $\Delta\mathbf{r}_{SD}$ from Salt Lake City to Denver. Choosing coordinate axes x and y running east-west and north-south, respectively, we can compute the components needed to write these vectors in unit vector notation:

$$\Delta\mathbf{r}_{LS} = (970\text{ km})(\cos55°)\hat{\mathbf{i}} + (970\text{ km})(\sin55°)\hat{\mathbf{j}} = 556\hat{\mathbf{i}} + 795\hat{\mathbf{j}}\text{ km}$$

$$\Delta\mathbf{r}_{SD} = (600\text{ km})[\cos(-10°)]\hat{\mathbf{i}} + (600\text{ km})[\sin(-10°)]\hat{\mathbf{j}} = 591\hat{\mathbf{i}} - 104\hat{\mathbf{j}}\text{ km.}$$

Note that the angle associated with the Salt Lake City to Denver displacement is negative, since the direction is south of east. Adding these vectors gives the displacement vector $\Delta\mathbf{r}_{LD}$ from Los Angeles to Denver:

$$\Delta\mathbf{r}_{LD} = \Delta\mathbf{r}_{LS} + \Delta\mathbf{r}_{SD} = (556\hat{\mathbf{i}} + 795\hat{\mathbf{j}}\text{ km}) + (591\hat{\mathbf{i}} - 104\hat{\mathbf{j}}\text{ km}) = 1147\hat{\mathbf{i}} + 691\hat{\mathbf{j}}\text{ km.}$$

The total elapsed time for this trip includes the two flight times and the 40-min ground time, so that $\Delta t = 72$ min + 40 min + 55 min = 167 min or 2.78 h. The average velocity is then

$$\bar{\mathbf{v}} = \frac{\Delta\mathbf{r}_{LD}}{\Delta t} = \frac{1147\hat{\mathbf{i}} + 691\hat{\mathbf{j}}\text{ km}}{2.78\text{ h}} = 413\hat{\mathbf{i}} + 249\hat{\mathbf{j}}\text{ km/h.}$$

The magnitude of this average velocity is given by the Pythagorean theorem:

$$\bar{v} = \sqrt{\bar{v}_x^2 + \bar{v}_y^2} = [(413\text{ km/h})^2 + (249\text{ km/h})^2]^{1/2} = 482\text{ km/h.}$$

Since the actual path is not straight and is therefore longer than the magnitude of the vector $\Delta\mathbf{r}_{LD}$, the average *speed* would be greater than this.

Fig. 3–10
Displacement vectors for a flight from Los Angeles to Denver via Salt Lake City.

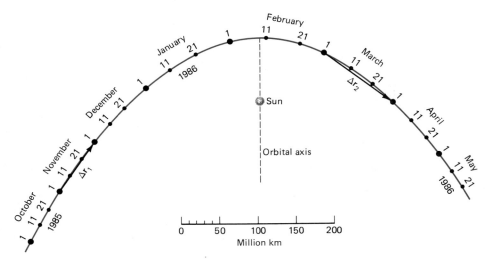

Fig. 3–11
The orbit of Halley's Comet in 1985–86, showing its position at several times each month.

Example 3–4
The Velocity of Halley's Comet

Figure 3–11 shows the orbit of Halley's Comet as it passed through the inner solar system in 1985–86. Determine the average velocity of the comet during November 1985 and again during March 1986.

Solution

On Fig. 3–11 we have drawn the displacement vectors $\Delta\mathbf{r}_1$ and $\Delta\mathbf{r}_2$ for the time intervals of interest. Measuring the length of $\Delta\mathbf{r}_1$ and using the scale factor shown, we find that $\Delta\mathbf{r}_1$ has a magnitude of 80×10^6 km. The time interval Δt_1 over which this displacement occurs is 30 days or 2.6×10^6 s, so that the average velocity $\overline{\mathbf{v}}_1$ over this interval has magnitude

$$\overline{v}_1 = \frac{\Delta r_1}{\Delta t_1} = \frac{80 \times 10^6 \text{ km}}{2.6 \times 10^6 \text{ s}} = 31 \text{ km/s}.$$

The velocity vector points in the same direction as $\Delta\mathbf{r}_1$. A similar analysis gives $\overline{v}_2 = 43$ km/s for the magnitude of the average velocity in March.

Acceleration

In the preceding chapter, we defined average acceleration as change in velocity divided by the time interval involved:

$$\overline{\mathbf{a}} = \frac{\Delta\mathbf{v}}{\Delta t}. \tag{3–6}$$

Taking the limit of arbitrarily small times gives the instantaneous acceleration:

$$\mathbf{a} = \lim_{\Delta t \to 0} \frac{\Delta\mathbf{v}}{\Delta t} = \frac{d\mathbf{v}}{dt}. \tag{3–7}$$

Velocity is a vector, so it can change in either *magnitude* or *direction*. You will understand two- and three-dimensional motion more clearly if you recognize that a change in *either* aspect of velocity necessarily involves acceleration. That's why a car going around a curve at constant speed is accelerating—its speedometer may read 45 mi/h all the while, but the *direction* of its velocity is nevertheless changing. In two and three dimensions, acceleration does not necessarily entail an increase or a decrease in speed. Whether the speed or direction, or both, change depends on the orientation of the acceleration vector relative to the velocity vector, as the examples below suggest.

Example 3–5
The Acceleration of Halley's Comet

Use the result of Example 3–4 to determine the average acceleration of Halley's Comet over the interval from November to March.

Solution

The initial and final velocities over the interval are approximately the average velocities $\bar{\mathbf{v}}_1$ and $\bar{\mathbf{v}}_2$ for November and March that we found in Example 3–4. Figure 3–12 shows a vector diagram of those two velocities and their difference $\Delta\mathbf{v}$. Comparing the length of $\Delta\mathbf{v}$ with that of the 31-km/s vector $\mathbf{v}_1$ shows that $\Delta\mathbf{v}$ represents a 54 km/s change in the magnitude of the velocity. The time interval over which this change occurs is 120 days or 1.04×10^7 s, so that the magnitude of the average acceleration is

$$\bar{a} = \frac{|\Delta\mathbf{v}|}{\Delta t} = \frac{54 \text{ km/s}}{1.04 \times 10^7 \text{ s}} = 5.2 \times 10^{-6} \text{ km/s}^2 = 5.2 \times 10^{-3} \text{ m/s}^2.$$

The direction of $\bar{\mathbf{a}}$ is the same as that of $\Delta\mathbf{v}$, or 162° to the vertical of Fig. 3–11 and Fig. 3–12. In this example the acceleration involves changes in both the magnitude and the direction of the velocity.

As Equation 3–6 suggests, the average acceleration we have calculated is a rough approximation to the instantaneous acceleration near the middle of the November-March interval. Drawing the acceleration vector at the middle of the interval (Fig. 3–13) shows that the acceleration is directed approximately sunward; a more accurate calculation approaching the limit in Equation 3–7 would show that

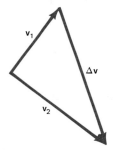

Fig. 3–12
Velocity vector diagram for determining the acceleration of Halley's Comet.

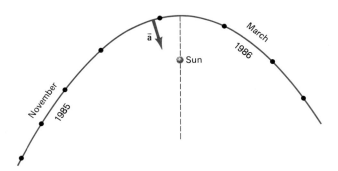

Fig. 3–13
Approximating the instantaneous acceleration at the midpoint of the November-March interval by the average acceleration suggests that the acceleration vector points roughly toward the sun. A more accurate calculation, using an arbitrarily small time interval instead of the 4-month interval of Example 3–5, would show that the acceleration is exactly sunward.

the direction is exactly sunward. This is not surprising, since the sun's gravity is what causes the comet's acceleration. We will explore gravitational acceleration further in Chapter 8.

Example 3–6

Acceleration Parallel and Perpendicular to Velocity

A plane is flying eastward at 250 m/s when it encounters a crosswind that gives it a southward acceleration of 1.2 m/s^2. What are the magnitude and direction of its velocity at the end of 1 minute? Repeat for the case of an eastward acceleration.

Solution

Choosing a coordinate system with the x-axis east-west and the y-axis north-south, the initial eastward velocity is $\mathbf{v}_0 = 250\hat{\imath}$ m/s. Similarly, the southward acceleration is $\mathbf{a} = -1.2\hat{\jmath}$ m/s^2. Using this acceleration in Equation 3–6 gives the change in velocity over the 1-min interval:

$$\Delta\mathbf{v} = \mathbf{a}\Delta t = (-1.2\hat{\jmath} \text{ m/s})(60 \text{ s}) = -72\hat{\jmath} \text{ m/s}.$$

Then the velocity at the end of 1 min is given by

$$\mathbf{v} = \mathbf{v}_0 + \Delta\mathbf{v} = 250\hat{\imath} \text{ m/s} - 72\hat{\jmath} \text{ m/s}.$$

Figure 3–14a shows the vectors $\mathbf{v}_0$, $\Delta\mathbf{v}$, and their sum $\mathbf{v}$. The magnitude of the vector $\mathbf{v}$ is given by the Pythagorean theorem:

$$v = \sqrt{v_x^2 + v_y^2} = [(250 \text{ m/s})^2 + (-72 \text{ m/s})^2]^{1/2} = 260 \text{ m/s},$$

while the tangent of the angle θ that $\mathbf{v}$ makes with the x-axis is the ratio of v_y to v_x:

$$\theta = \tan^{-1}\left(\frac{v_y}{v_x}\right) = \tan^{-1}\left(\frac{-72 \text{ m/s}}{250 \text{ m/s}}\right) = -16°,$$

or 16° south of east. Note that this acceleration—directed initially at right angles to the velocity—has relatively little effect on the magnitude of the velocity. The latter increases by only 10 m/s, even though the acceleration produces a 72 m/s change in the southward component of the velocity. We will find this to be generally true: an acceleration acting always at right angles to the velocity changes only the direction, not the magnitude of the velocity. (Here the acceleration is not always perpendicular to the velocity; as soon as the acceleration starts to act, subsequent velocity vectors are no longer exactly eastward.)

When the acceleration acts eastward, the situation is reduced to a one-dimensional problem. In vector notation, we still have $\mathbf{v}_0 = 250\hat{\imath}$ m/s, but now $\mathbf{a} = 1.2\hat{\imath}$ m/s, so that $\Delta\mathbf{v} = 72\hat{\imath}$ m/s. Then the velocity after 1 min is

$$\mathbf{v} = \mathbf{v}_0 + \Delta\mathbf{v} = 250\hat{\imath} \text{ m/s} + 72\hat{\imath} \text{ m/s} = 322\hat{\imath} \text{ m/s}.$$

(a)   (b)

Fig. 3–14

Velocity vector diagrams for Example 3–6. (a) Eastward initial velocity with southward acceleration. (b) Eastward initial velocity with eastward acceleration. In (a), the acceleration results in a change in direction but only a small change in speed. In (b), the acceleration results in a large change in speed but no change in direction.

Here the acceleration—now in the same direction as the velocity—results in a large change in speed, but no change in direction. This, too, is generally true: an acceleration acting in the direction of the velocity changes only the magnitude, not the direction (an acceleration acting opposite to the velocity can reverse the sense of the velocity, but the new velocity still lies along the same line). Figure 3–14b shows velocity vector diagrams for this case.

3.2
CONSTANT ACCELERATION

When acceleration is constant—no change in either magnitude or direction—then the individual components of the acceleration vector must themselves be constants. The corresponding components of motion in the x- and y-directions are then described by the equations for constant acceleration that we developed in the preceding chapter, written once for each component:

$$v_x = v_{x0} + a_x t \qquad (3\text{--}8a) \qquad\qquad v_y = v_{y0} + a_y t \qquad (3\text{--}8b)$$

$$x = x_0 + v_{x0}t + \tfrac{1}{2}a_x t^2 \qquad (3\text{--}9a) \qquad\qquad y = y_0 + v_{y0}t + \tfrac{1}{2}a_y t^2 \qquad (3\text{--}9b)$$

$$\overline{v}_x = \tfrac{1}{2}(v_{x0} + v_x) \qquad (3\text{--}10a) \qquad\qquad \overline{v}_y = \tfrac{1}{2}(v_{y0} + v_y) \qquad (3\text{--}10b)$$

$$x - x_0 = \tfrac{1}{2}(v_{x0} + v_x)t \qquad (3\text{--}11a) \qquad\qquad y - y_0 = \tfrac{1}{2}(v_{y0} + v_y)t \qquad (3\text{--}11b)$$

$$v_x^2 = v_{x0}^2 + 2a_x(x - x_0) \qquad (3\text{--}12a) \qquad\qquad v_y^2 = v_{y0}^2 + 2a_y(y - y_0) \qquad (3\text{--}12b)$$

For fully three-dimensional motion, we could add a set of equations for constant acceleration in the z-direction. The first four pairs of equations above may be written more compactly in vector notation, using the position vector **r** whose components are the coordinates x and y:

$$\mathbf{v} = \mathbf{v}_0 + \mathbf{a}t \qquad (3\text{--}8)$$

$$\mathbf{r} = \mathbf{r}_0 + \mathbf{v}_0 t + \tfrac{1}{2}\mathbf{a}t^2 \qquad (3\text{--}9)$$

$$\overline{\mathbf{v}} = \tfrac{1}{2}(\mathbf{v}_0 + \mathbf{v}) \qquad (3\text{--}10)$$

$$\mathbf{r} - \mathbf{r}_0 = \tfrac{1}{2}(\mathbf{v}_0 + \mathbf{v})t \qquad (3\text{--}11)$$

Equations 3–8 to 3–11 describe fully the relations among the position, velocity, and acceleration vectors in two-dimensional motion with constant acceleration. Once we choose a coordinate system, we can consider separately the components of Equations 3–8 to 3–11 along our coordinate axes; these component equations are Equations 3–8a,b to 3–11a,b. (Although at this point we cannot combine Equations 3–12a and 3–12b into a single equation, we will later develop a form of vector multiplication that would make such a combination possible.)

Example 3–7
A Spaceship Accelerates

A spaceship is travelling in a straight line at 6.2 km/s, when a rocket is fired that gives it an acceleration of 0.36 km/s² in a direction 60° to its velocity. If the rocket firing lasts 10 s, find the magnitude and direction of the ship's velocity at

Fig. 3–15
The components of the acceleration vector are $a_x = a \cos 60° = 0.18$ km/s^2 and $a_y = a \sin 60° = 0.31$ km/s^2, where $a = 0.36$ km/s^2 is the magnitude of the acceleration vector.

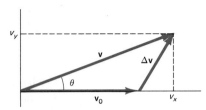

Fig. 3–16
Vector addition diagram for determining the spaceship's velocity after rocket firing. Note that the direction of the new velocity is given by $\tan\theta = v_y/v_x$.

Fig. 3–17
Strobe photo showing one ball dropped and another projected horizontally at the same time. At each instant their vertical positions are identical, showing that the vertical and horizontal motions are independent. The time interval between images is 1/30 s, and the horizontal strings are 15.25 cm apart.

the end of the firing. At the end of the rocket firing, how far is the ship from its initial position?

Solution

Taking the x-axis along the initial direction of motion, the initial velocity is $v_0 = 6.2\hat{i}$ km/s and, as shown in Fig. 3–15, the acceleration is $0.18\hat{i} + 0.31\hat{j}$ km/s^2. To find the velocity after 10 s, we use Equations 3–8a and 3–8b:

$$v_x = v_{x0} + a_x t = 6.2 \text{ km/s} + (0.18 \text{ km/s}^2)(10 \text{ s}) = 8.0 \text{ km/s}$$

$$v_y = v_{y0} + a_y t = 0 \text{ km/s} + (0.31 \text{ km/s}^2)(10 \text{ s}) = 3.1 \text{ km/s},$$

so that the velocity is $v = 8.0\hat{i} + 3.1\hat{j}$ km/s. The magnitude of this vector is given by the Pythagorean theorem:

$$v = \sqrt{v_x{}^2 + v_y{}^2} = [(8.0 \text{ km/s})^2 + (3.1 \text{ km/s})^2]^{1/2} = 8.6 \text{ km/s},$$

while its direction relative to the x-axis is, as shown in Fig. 3–16,

$$\theta = \tan^{-1}\left(\frac{v_y}{v_x}\right) = \tan^{-1}\left(\frac{3.1 \text{ km/s}}{8.0 \text{ km/s}}\right) = 21°.$$

We could also have handled this calculation graphically, as suggested in Fig. 3–16.

To find the change in position Δr, we can use Equation 3–9. If we choose our origin at the point where the rocket is first fired, then $x_0 = y_0 = 0$, and the two components of Equation 3–9 become

$$x = v_{x0}t + \tfrac{1}{2}a_x t^2 = (6.2 \text{ km/s})(10 \text{ s}) + \tfrac{1}{2}(0.18 \text{ km/s}^2)(10 \text{ s})^2 = 71 \text{ km}$$

$$y = \tfrac{1}{2}a_y t^2 = \tfrac{1}{2}(0.31 \text{ km/s}^2)(10 \text{ s})^2 = 16 \text{ km},$$

where in writing the y-equation, we used the fact that $v_{y0} = 0$. The new position vector is then given by $r = x\hat{i} + y\hat{j} = 71\hat{i} + 16\hat{j}$ km, so that the distance from the origin is

$$\Delta r = \sqrt{x^2 + y^2} = [(71 \text{ km})^2 + (16 \text{ km})^2]^{1/2} = 73 \text{ km}.$$

Because we had already calculated the velocity, we could equally well have used Equation 3–11 to determine the new position (see Problem 20).

As Example 3–7 shows, we handle problems of multidimensional motion by breaking them into two or three one-dimensional problems. These individual problems are solved using the methods of Chapter 2, and their solutions are combined to give a full vector description of the motion. Solving each one-dimensional problem separately implies that acceleration and velocity in one direction have no effect on the motion in a perpendicular direction. How do we know that this approach is correct? Ultimately, the answer comes from experiment. Figure 3–17 shows strobe photos of two balls, one dropped and one projected horizontally at the same time. The photos demonstrate that both experience the same downward acceleration, so that their different horizontal motions have no effect on their vertical motions. Similarly, if you toss a ball into the air on a horizontally moving airplane, the time of flight of the ball will be correctly given by the one-dimensional equations of Chapter 2, independent of the plane's horizontal motion.

3.3
PROJECTILE MOTION

projectile

A **projectile** is an object that is launched into the air and then moves predominantly under the influence of gravity. Examples are numerous: baseballs, streams of water, fireworks, missiles, ejecta from volcanoes, drops of ink in an ink-jet computer printer, and leaping dolphins are all projectiles (Fig. 3–18).

To treat projectile motion, we make two simplifying assumptions: (1) we neglect any variation in the direction or magnitude of the gravitational acceleration and (2) we neglect air resistance. Assumption 1 is equivalent to neglecting the curvature of the earth, and is valid for projectiles whose horizontal and vertical motions are small compared with earth's radius. Air resistance has a more variable effect; for dense objects moving relatively slowly, it is completely negligible, but for objects whose ratio of surface area to mass is large—like ping-pong balls and parachutes—or for high-speed objects like meteors entering earth's atmosphere, air resistance may dramatically alter the motion (Fig. 3–19). And the more subtle motions of a baseball—its curves and wobbles—can only be explained by invoking air resistance.

To describe projectile motion, it is usually convenient to choose a coordinate system with the y-axis vertically upward, and the x-axis horizontal and in the direction of the horizontal component of the projectile's initial velocity. Then there is neither velocity nor acceleration in the z-direction, and we have purely two-dimensional motion in the x-y plane. Furthermore, with the only acceleration provided by gravity, $a_x = 0$ and $a_y = -g$, so the components of Equations 3–8 and 3–9 become

Fig. 3–18
The 1986 explosion of a Titan rocket over Vandenburg Air Force Base in California. Each explosion fragment is a projectile, and each describes a parabolic trajectory.

Fig. 3–19
Parachutists descending from New York's Empire State Building. Air resistance has a dominant effect on the motion, and their trajectories are far from parabolic.

$$v_x = v_{x0} \tag{3–13}$$

$$v_y = v_{y0} - gt \tag{3–14}$$

$$x = x_0 + v_{x0}t \tag{3–15}$$

$$y = y_0 + v_{y0}t - \tfrac{1}{2}gt^2. \tag{3–16}$$

With $a_x = 0$, Equation 3–12a is identical to Equation 3–13, while Equation 3–12b is

$$v_y^2 = v_{y0}^2 - 2g(y - y_0). \tag{3–17}$$

In writing Equations 3–13 to 3–17, we take g to be a positive number, as we did in the preceding chapter, and account for the downward direction using minus signs. Equations 3–13 to 3–16 tell us mathematically what Fig. 3–17 tells us physically: that the horizontal motion of a projectile is not affected by gravity, and that the vertical motion is not affected by the horizontal motion.

Example 3–8
Projectile Motion

Standing on the edge of a 120-m-high cliff, you throw a rock horizontally at 14 m/s. How far from the bottom of the cliff does it land? Neglect air resistance (although this assumption is not entirely justified for such a long fall).

Solution

Since there is no component of acceleration in the horizontal direction, the horizontal component of the velocity remains constant at $v_x = 14$ m/s. The answer we seek is the distance the rock travels horizontally; knowing the horizontal component of velocity, we could find this distance if we knew the flight time.

We can find the time by analyzing the vertical motion. Since the rock is thrown horizontally, $v_{y0} = 0$. If we choose our origin at the cliff bottom, then $y_0 = 120$ m. We want to find the time when the rock hits the ground—that is, when $y = 0$. Setting y and v_{y0} to zero in Equation 3–16, and solving for t, we have

$$t = \sqrt{\frac{2y_0}{g}} = \sqrt{\frac{(2)(120 \text{ m})}{9.8 \text{ m/s}^2}} = 4.95 \text{ s}.$$

During this time, the rock drops the 120-m distance to the bottom of the cliff. During the same time, it travels horizontally a distance given by Equation 3–15:

$$x - x_0 = v_{x0}t = (14 \text{ m/s})(4.95 \text{ s}) = 69 \text{ m}.$$

Instead of solving for a numerical value of t, we could have used the expression $t = \sqrt{2y_0/g}$ in Equation 3–15 before substituting numerical values. It is usually easiest to carry calculations as far as possible in symbolic form.

In this example, we were asked only about the horizontal motion of the rock. But to find that, we needed the time—and that required us to analyze the vertical motion. This is a common situation with physics problems involving two dimensions. In such problems, it is often easiest to work backward from the answer, asking what quantities you would need to get that answer, and then formulating and solving other problems that will yield those quantities.

In Example 3–8 we were asked about the rock's horizontal position when it hit the ground. We didn't really care about the time of its flight, although we needed to calculate this time to solve the problem. More generally, we are often interested in describing the path, or **trajectory,** of a projectile without the details of where it is at each instant of time. A look at Fig. 3–18 suggests that objects undergoing projectile motion have similarly shaped trajectories. What is that shape?

Mathematically, we could specify a projectile's trajectory by giving its height y as a function of horizontal position x. To do so, consider a projectile that is launched from the origin ($x_0 = y_0 = 0$) at some angle θ to the horizontal, with initial speed v_0 (Fig. 3–20). As Fig. 3–20 suggests, the components of the initial velocity are $v_{x0} = v_0\cos\theta$ and $v_{y0} = v_0\sin\theta$. Then Equations 3–15 and 3–16 become

$$x = v_0\cos\theta \, t \tag{3–18}$$

and

$$y = v_0\sin\theta \, t - \tfrac{1}{2}gt^2. \tag{3–19}$$

Solving Equation 3–18 for the time t gives

$$t = \frac{x}{v_0\cos\theta};$$

using this result in Equation 3–19, we have

Fig. 3–20
Parabolic trajectory of a projectile.

trajectory

$$y = v_0 \sin\theta \left(\frac{x}{v_0 \cos\theta} \right) - \tfrac{1}{2} g \left(\frac{x}{v_0 \cos\theta} \right)^2,$$

or

$$y = x \tan\theta - \frac{g}{2 v_0^2 \cos^2\theta} x^2. \quad \text{(projectile trajectory)} \quad (3\text{--}20)$$

In Equation 3–20 we have the mathematical description of the projectile's trajectory. Since y is a quadratic function of x, the trajectory is a parabola.

Example 3–9
The Trajectory of a Projectile

A construction worker is standing in a 2.6-m-deep cellar hole, 3.1 m from the side of the hole (Fig. 3–21). He tosses a hammer to a companion outside the hole. If the hammer leaves his hand 1.0 m above the bottom of the hole, at an angle of 35° to the horizontal, what is the minimum speed it must have to clear the edge of the hole, as shown in Fig. 3–21? How far from the edge of the hole does it land?

Solution

If it just clears the edge of the hole, the hammer must be on a trajectory that has $y = 1.6$ m when $x = 3.1$ m, where we take the origin at the point where the hammer leaves his hand, 1.0 m above the bottom of the 2.6-m-deep hole. Solving Equation 3–20 for v_0 and using these x and y values gives

$$v_0 = \left(\frac{g x^2}{2 \cos^2\theta (x \tan\theta - y)} \right)^{1/2}$$

$$= \left(\frac{(9.8 \text{ m/s}^2)(3.1 \text{ m})^2}{(2)(\cos^2 35°)[(3.1 \text{ m})(\tan 35°) - 1.6 \text{ m}]} \right)^{1/2} = 11 \text{ m/s}.$$

To find where the hammer lands on the level ground outside the hole, we need to know the horizontal position when $y = 1.6$ m. Rearranging Equation 3–20 into the standard form $ax^2 + bx + c = 0$ for a quadratic equation for x gives

$$\frac{g}{2 v_0^2 \cos^2\theta} x^2 - (\tan\theta)x + y = 0,$$

so that the coefficients a, b, and c are $a = g/2 v_0^2 \cos^2\theta = 0.0594$ m^{-1}, $b = -\tan\theta = -0.700$, and $c = y = 1.6$ m. Applying the quadratic formula (see Appendix A) then gives

Fig. 3–21
Example 3–9

$$x = \frac{-b \pm \sqrt{b^2 - 4ac}}{2a} = \frac{0.700 \pm [0.700^2 - (4)(0.0594)(1.6)]^{1/2}}{(2)(0.0594)}$$

$$= 3.1 \text{ m or } 8.7 \text{ m},$$

where for clarity we have left off units in the calculation. These two answers give the two horizontal positions where the hammer is at ground level. The first provides a useful check on our work: it is just the horizontal position when the hammer clears the edge of the hole. The second answer is the one we want; it shows that the hammer lands 8.7 m − 3.1 m = 5.6 m to the right of the edge of the hole.

How far will a soccer ball go if I kick it at 12 m/s at 50° to the horizontal? If I can throw a rock at 15 m/s, can I get it across a 30-m-wide pond? At what angle should I throw it for maximum distance? How far off vertical can a rocket's trajectory be and still have it land within 50 km of its launch point? As in these examples, we are frequently interested in the **horizontal range** of a projectile—that is, in how far it moves horizontally over level ground.

horizontal range

Equation 3–20 describes the trajectory—height y versus horizontal position x—for a projectile. For a projectile launched on level ground, we can ask when the projectile will return to the ground by setting $y = 0$ in Equation 3–20:

$$0 = x \tan\theta - \frac{g}{2v_0^2 \cos^2\theta} x^2.$$

Factoring this equation gives

$$x \left(\tan\theta - \frac{gx}{2v_0^2 \cos^2\theta} \right) = 0,$$

so that either $x = 0$, corresponding to the launch point, or

$$x = \frac{2v_0^2}{g} \cos^2\theta \tan\theta = \frac{2v_0^2}{g} \sin\theta \cos\theta.$$

Here we have used $\tan\theta = \sin\theta/\cos\theta$; recalling further that $\sin2\theta = 2\sin\theta\cos\theta$ (see Appendix A), we can write

$$x = \frac{v_0^2}{g} \sin2\theta. \tag{3–21}$$

We emphasize that Equation 3–21 gives the *horizontal* range—the distance a projectile travels horizontally before returning *to its starting height*. From the way it was derived—setting $y = 0$—you can see it does *not* give horizontal distance when the projectile returns to a different height (Fig. 3–22).

Does Equation 3–21 make sense? When $\theta = 0$, the range is zero: a projectile launched horizontally on level ground immediately hits the ground. When $\theta = 90°$, $\sin2\theta = \sin180° = 0$, and again the range is zero. Here the projectile is launched vertically upward, so of course it returns to the same point. When is the range a maximum? The largest value of $\sin2\theta$ is 1, which occurs when $\theta = 45°$. For a given initial speed v_0, then, the maximum range is attained by launching at 45°. Figure 3–23 shows the trajectories of projectiles launched at different angles with the same initial speed. At angles

(a)

(b)

Fig. 3–22
(a) Equation 3–21 gives the horizontal range of a particle that returns to its starting height. (b) It does *not* apply otherwise.

Fig. 3–23
For a given initial speed, the range of a projectile is maximum at a launch angle of 45°. For launch angles equally spaced above and below 45°, the range is the same. Curves are for an initial speed of 50 m/s, with launch angles indicated.

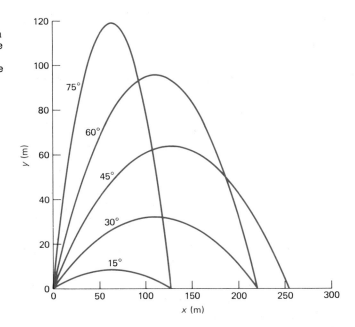

less than 45° the projectile has a greater horizontal component of velocity, but it doesn't get as high and therefore isn't in the air as long as the projectile launched at 45°; the net effect is a shorter range. At angles greater than 45°, the projectile rises higher and is therefore in the air longer, but its horizontal velocity is lower and the net effect is again a shorter range. In fact, as you can prove in Problem 39, the range is the same for angles equally spaced on either side of 45°. (These results are valid only in the absence of air resistance; when air resistance is taken into account, the maximum range angle turns out to be less than 45°.)

Example 3–10
A Sounding Rocket

A sounding rocket is launched from a remote desert site to probe the atmosphere. With a short firing of its engine, the rocket quickly reaches a speed of 4.6 km/s. If the rocket is to land within 50 km of its launch site, what is the maximum allowable deviation from a vertical trajectory? Neglect air resistance.

Solution

Here we neglect the short distance over which the rocket accelerates, considering that it left the ground with its initial speed of 4.6 km/s. Then the answer to the problem is the angle θ for which the range x is 50 km. Solving Equation 3–21 for $\sin 2\theta$ gives

$$\sin 2\theta = \frac{gx}{v_0^2} = \frac{(9.8 \text{ m/s}^2)(50 \times 10^3 \text{ m})}{(4.6 \times 10^3 \text{ m/s})^2} = 0.0232.$$

There are two solutions to this equation, corresponding to $2\theta = \sin^{-1}(0.0232) = 1.33°$ and $2\theta = 180° - 1.33°$. The second solution is the one we want; it represents a nearly vertical launch angle $\theta = 90° - 0.67°$, so that the launch angle must be within 0.67° of vertical.

3.4

CIRCULAR MOTION

uniform circular motion

An important case of accelerated motion in two dimensions is **uniform circular motion**—the motion of an object describing a circular path at constant speed. Although the speed is constant, the motion is accelerated because the *direction* of the velocity is changing. Velocity is a vector, and *any* change in that vector—whether in magnitude or direction or both—implies acceleration.

Examples of uniform circular motion are numerous. Many spacecraft are in circular orbits, and the orbits of the planets and their natural satellites are approximately circular. The earth's daily rotation carries you around in uniform circular motion. Pieces of rotating machinery describe uniform circular motion. In laboratory apparatus and astrophysical objects, electrons undergo uniform circular motion when they encounter magnetic fields. Even with the atom itself, we can gain some insight by picturing electrons in uniform circular motion about the nucleus—although this view is not fully consistent with modern quantum mechanics. Other situations involve uniform circular motion over a limited path. Driving around a curve at constant speed, you temporarily describe a circular arc and are therefore temporarily in uniform circular motion. On a back road in hilly country, you may undergo uniform circular motion as you negotiate valley bottoms and zoom over hillcrests. As you swing a baseball bat, golf club, or hockey stick, you produce motion that is circular and that may be approximately uniform.

In this section, we derive a relation among the acceleration, speed, and radius of uniform circular motion. Consider an object moving with constant speed v around a circle of radius r. Figure 3–24 shows the circular path and some velocity vectors for the object at several points on the path. Note that the velocity vectors are tangent to the circle, indicating the instantaneous direction of motion. Since the speed is constant, the velocity vectors all have the same length. But clearly the object is accelerating; the velocity vector $\mathbf{v}_C$ is not the same as the vector $\mathbf{v}_A$, since their directions differ. In fact, we can find the *average* acceleration between points A and C by dividing the change in velocity by the time interval involved. Figure 3–25 shows the vector $\Delta\mathbf{v}_{AC} = \mathbf{v}_C - \mathbf{v}_A$. This vector has magnitude $\sqrt{2}v$ and points diagonally downward and to the left at 45°. Between A and C, the object moves one-fourth of the way around its circle, or a distance $\frac{1}{2}\pi r$. At speed v, this motion takes a time $\Delta t = \frac{1}{2}\pi r/v$. The average acceleration $\Delta\mathbf{v}/\Delta t$ is then a vector whose magnitude is

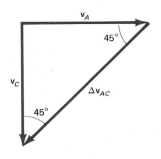

$$\bar{a} = \frac{|\Delta\mathbf{v}|}{\Delta t} = \frac{\sqrt{2}v}{\frac{1}{2}\pi r/v} = \frac{2\sqrt{2}v^2}{\pi r} = \frac{0.90v^2}{r}$$

and which points in the same diagonal direction as $\Delta\mathbf{v}$. Note that we used the magnitude of the *change in velocity*—not the change in speed (which is zero)—to compute the magnitude of the acceleration. We did this calculation in detail to show how to give a meaningful answer for the acceleration even in the case of uniform circular motion in which speed does not change. Clearly we could repeat the calculation for the average acceleration

Fig. 3–24
Uniform circular motion, showing the velocity vectors at several points on the circle.

Fig. 3–25
The change in velocity from point A to point C is the vector $\Delta\mathbf{v}_{AC}$ that must be added to $\mathbf{v}_A$ to make $\mathbf{v}_C$. It has magnitude $\sqrt{2}v$ and points downward and to the left at 45°.

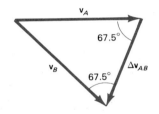

Fig. 3–26
The velocity change Δ**v** from A to B is
a vector of length 0.765v, pointing
downward and to the left at 67.5°. In
going from A to B, the object travels
one-eighth of the circle or a distance
$\frac{1}{4}\pi r$; at speed v, this takes $\Delta t = \frac{1}{4}\pi r/v$.
The acceleration vector then has
magnitude $|\Delta \mathbf{v}|/\Delta t = 0.97v^2/r$ and points
in the same direction as Δ**v**.

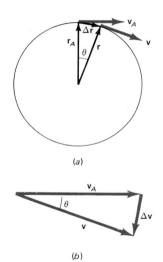

(a)

(b)

Fig. 3–27
(a) Velocity vectors **v**$_A$ and **v** and
(b) their difference Δ**v**. Also shown in
(a) are the associated radius vectors
and their difference Δ**r**. The angle θ in
both figures is the same, so that the
triangles formed by the radius vectors
and their difference in (a) is similar to
the triangle formed by **v**$_A$, **v**, and Δ**v**
in (b).

in the interval AB; analysis of Fig. 3–26 would show that the result is an average acceleration of magnitude $0.97v^2/r$, pointing downward and to the left at an angle of 67.5°.

Now consider the average acceleration over ever shorter time intervals Δt; in the limit Δt→0, this quantity becomes the instantaneous acceleration. Figure 3–27a shows the velocity vector **v**$_A$ and a nearby velocity vector **v**. Now the vectors **v**$_A$ and **r**$_A$ are perpendicular; similarly, **v** and **r** are perpendicular. Therefore, the angle θ between the radii **r**$_A$ and **r** in Fig. 3–27a is the same as the angle θ between the velocity vectors in Fig. 3–27b. Because the radii have the same length, and the velocity vectors have the same magnitude (*speed* is constant), the triangles shown in Fig. 3–27a and Fig. 3–27b are similar. Then we can write

$$\frac{|\Delta \mathbf{v}|}{v} = \frac{|\Delta \mathbf{r}|}{r}.$$

For short time intervals Δt, the angle θ is small, and the length of the vector Δ**r** is approximately that of the circular arc joining the endpoints of the radius vectors. The length of this arc is just the distance travelled by the object in the time interval Δt, or vΔt, so that $|\Delta \mathbf{r}| \approx v\Delta t$. Then we can write

$$\frac{|\Delta \mathbf{v}|}{v} \simeq \frac{v\Delta t}{r}.$$

The magnitude of the average acceleration is then approximately

$$\bar{a} = \frac{|\Delta \mathbf{v}|}{\Delta t} \simeq \frac{v^2}{r}.$$

Taking the limit Δt→0 gives the instantaneous acceleration; in this limit the circular arc and the vector Δ**r** joining the ends of the radius vectors become completely indistinguishable, and the relation $|\Delta \mathbf{r}| \approx v\Delta t$ becomes exact. So we have

$$a = \frac{v^2}{r} \qquad \text{(uniform circular motion)} \qquad (3\text{–}22)$$

for the magnitude of the instantaneous acceleration of an object moving in a circle of radius r at constant speed v. What about the direction of the acceleration vector? As Fig. 3–27b suggests, Δ**v** is very nearly perpendicular to both velocity vectors; in the limit Δt→0, Δ**v** and therefore the acceleration Δ**v**/Δt becomes exactly perpendicular to the velocity. In the limit, then, the direction of the acceleration in Fig. 3–27b is downward—that is, toward the center of the circle.

Although we found the instantaneous acceleration for the point at the top of the circle, the geometrical arguments leading to our result are clearly independent of where the object is on its circular path. (You can rotate the book, for example, and Fig. 3–27 will still lead you to the same result.) We conclude therefore that the acceleration in uniform circular motion has constant magnitude v^2/r, and that it always points toward the center of the circle. Since the direction toward the center changes as the object moves around its circular path, the acceleration vector is not constant, even though its magnitude is. Therefore, uniform circular motion is *not* motion with constant acceleration, and our constant-acceleration equations do not apply. Indeed, we know that constant acceleration in two dimensions gives rise to a parabolic trajectory, not a circle.

Does Equation 3–22 make sense? Yes: an increase in speed v means that the time Δt for a given change in direction of the velocity becomes shorter. Not only that, but the associated change $\Delta \mathbf{v}$ in velocity is larger. These two effects combine to give an acceleration that depends on the *square* of the speed. On the other hand, an increase in radius with a fixed speed simply increases the time Δt associated with a given change in velocity, so that the acceleration is inversely proportional to the radius. Although the form of the acceleration in Equation 3–22 does not look familiar from our work with constant acceleration, we can check that its dimensions are correct:

$$[a] = [v^2]/[r] = (L/T)^2/L = L/T^2,$$

which are indeed the dimensions of acceleration. Incidentally, although we derived Equation 3–22 geometrically, we could have obtained the same results by writing the position in unit vector notation and then differentiating twice to get the acceleration. Problem 60 explores this approach.

Example 3–11

A Space Shuttle Orbit

A space shuttle is in a circular orbit at a height of 250 km, where the acceleration of earth's gravity is 93 per cent of its surface value. What is the period of its orbit? ("Period" means the time to complete one orbit.)

Solution

Here we are given the acceleration and radius and asked to find the period. Our equations for uniform circular motion relate acceleration, radius, and speed. But we can write the speed as the distance travelled in one orbit—the orbital circumference $2\pi r$—divided by the orbital period T:

$$v = \frac{2\pi r}{T}.$$

Using this result in Equation 3–22, we have

$$a = \frac{(2\pi r/T)^2}{r} = \frac{4\pi^2 r}{T^2}. \tag{3–23}$$

This equation is equivalent to Equation 3–22, but relates a, r, and T rather than a, r, and v. Here we are given that $a = 0.93g$ and that the shuttle is 250 km above earth's surface. But the r in Equation 3–23 is the distance to the center of the circular path—that is, to the center of the earth. So $r = R_{\text{earth}} + 250 \text{ km} = 6.6 \times 10^6$ m, where we used $R_{\text{earth}} = 6.37 \times 10^6$ m from Appendix F. Solving Equation 3–23 for the period T then gives

$$T = \left(\frac{4\pi^2 r}{a}\right)^{1/2} = \left(\frac{(4\pi^2)(6.6 \times 10^6 \text{ m})}{(0.93)(9.8 \text{ m/s}^2)}\right)^{1/2} = 5347 \text{ s} = 89 \text{ min,}$$

or about an hour and a half. This value is approximately the orbital period of any object orbiting the earth at altitudes that are small compared with earth's radius. Scientists and engineers have no choice here; the orbital period is fixed by the size and mass of the earth. (At higher altitudes the decrease in the strength of gravity becomes more noticeable, and orbital periods lengthen. The moon, 390,000 km distant, orbits earth with a period of 27 days. We will study gravity and orbits further in Chapter 8.)

Example 3–12

Designing a Road

A flat, horizontal road is being designed for an 80-km/h speed limit. If the maximum acceleration of a car travelling this road at the speed limit is to be 1.5 m/s^2, what is the minimum radius for curves in the road?

Solution

Here we are given speed and acceleration, so we can solve Equation 3–22 for the radius r:

$$r = \frac{v^2}{a} = \frac{[(80 \times 10^3 \text{ m/h})(1 \text{ h/3600 s})]^2}{1.5 \text{ m/s}^2} = 330 \text{ m}.$$

A limit on acceleration is necessary to keep the occupants of a car in their seats, as we will see more clearly in Chapters 4 and 5.

Uniform circular motion represents the special case in which acceleration is always *perpendicular* to velocity. In that case, the acceleration changes only the *direction* of the velocity, and not its magnitude (speed). In this sense, uniform circular motion is the converse of one-dimensional accelerated motion that we examined in Chapter 2; there, acceleration was always *parallel* to velocity, and changed only the *magnitude* of the velocity. The case of constant acceleration in two dimensions lies between these two extremes; in projectile motion, for example, the acceleration is generally neither parallel nor perpendicular to the velocity. Then both the magnitude and direction of the velocity change. Figure 3–28 summarizes these three cases.

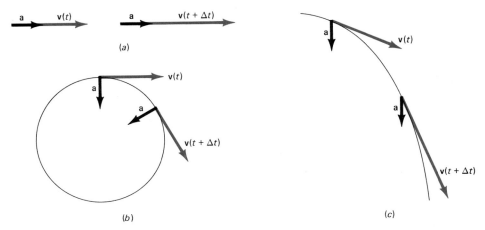

Fig. 3–28
(a) In one-dimensional motion, acceleration is always parallel to velocity and changes only the magnitude of the velocity vector. (b) In uniform circular motion, acceleration is always perpendicular to velocity and changes only the direction of the velocity vector. (c) In the more general case, of which projectile motion is an example, acceleration is neither parallel nor perpendicular to velocity. Then both the magnitude and direction of the velocity vector change.

What about circular motion whose speed changes, like a record turntable spinning up from rest to full speed, or a ball whirling around in a vertical circle (Fig. 3–29)? Since both the direction and magnitude of the velocity are changing, the acceleration cannot be either parallel or perpendicular to the velocity. But we can break the acceleration vector into two components, one perpendicular to the velocity and one parallel. We call the former the **radial acceleration** a_r, since it points radially inward toward the center of the circular path; the latter is the **tangential acceleration** a_t, since it is tangent to the path. The radial acceleration changes only the direction of the velocity; it acts just like the acceleration in uniform circular motion, and therefore has magnitude $a_r = v^2/r$. The tangential acceleration changes only the magnitude of the velocity; it acts just like one-dimensional acceleration, and therefore has magnitude $a_t = dv/dt$. The net acceleration vector can be found by combining these two components, as Example 3–13 illustrates.

radial acceleration

tangential acceleration

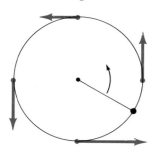

Fig. 3–29
A ball whirled about on a string in a vertical circle undergoes circular motion with nonconstant speed; it moves faster near the bottom and more slowly near the top.

Example 3–13
Radial and Tangential Acceleration

A road makes a 90° bend with a radius of 190 m. A car enters the bend moving at 20 m/s. Finding this too fast, the driver decelerates at 0.92 m/s². Determine the acceleration of the car when its speed rounding the bend has dropped to 15 m/s.

Solution

Since it is rounding a curve, the car has a radial acceleration associated with its changing direction, in addition to the tangential deceleration that changes its speed. We are given that $a_t = 0.92$ m/s²; since the car is slowing down, the tangential acceleration is directed opposite the velocity. The radial acceleration is given by Equation 3–22:

$$a_r = \frac{v^2}{r} = \frac{(15 \text{ m/s})^2}{190 \text{ m}} = 1.2 \text{ m/s}^2.$$

Figure 3–30 shows both components of the acceleration and their vector sum, which is the net acceleration. From the figure, we see that this sum has magnitude

$$a = \sqrt{a_r^2 + a_t^2} = [(1.2 \text{ m/s})^2 + (0.92 \text{ m/s})^2]^{1/2} = 1.5 \text{ m/s}^2$$

and points at an angle

$$\theta = \tan^{-1}\left(\frac{a_r}{a_t}\right) = \tan^{-1}\left(\frac{1.2 \text{ m/s}^2}{0.92 \text{ m/s}^2}\right) = 53°$$

relative to the tangent line to the circle, as shown.

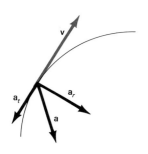

Fig. 3–30
The radial and tangential accelerations add vectorially to give the net acceleration.

3.5
MOTION IS RELATIVE

What does it mean to say that a car is moving at 80 km/h? Usually, it means 80 km/h relative to the earth. But earth is moving at 30 km/s relative to the sun, so that the car's speed relative to the sun is much greater than 80 km/h. Statements about velocity and speed are meaningful only when we have an answer to the question "velocity relative to what?" The object or system with respect to which velocity is measured is called a **frame of reference**; in most of the examples we have considered, the earth is our

frame of reference

frame of reference. But playing tennis on the deck of a moving ship, you would find the ship's frame of reference more appropriate for describing the motion of the tennis ball. Similarly, the motion of a comet or interplanetary space probe is described more simply in the reference frame of the sun rather than of the earth.

Suppose a car is moving at 50 mi/h. Then its speed relative to another car moving in the same direction at 30 mi/h is 50 mi/h − 30 mi/h = 20 mi/h. More generally, if an object is moving at velocity **v** relative to some frame of reference S, and if another frame of reference S′ moves with velocity **V** relative to S, then the velocity **v′** of the object with respect to the frame S′ is given by

$$\mathbf{v'} = \mathbf{v} - \mathbf{V}. \tag{3-25}$$

In our simple example, frame S is the earth, frame S′ is the car moving at 30 mi/h, $v = 50$ mi/h, $V = 30$ mi/h, and $v' = 20$ mi/h. Here all the velocities are in the same direction, so we deal only with their magnitudes. More generally, questions of relative velocity involve vectors, as in the following example.

Example 3-14
Relative Velocity

A jetliner has an airspeed (speed relative to the air) of 600 mi/h. It embarks on a flight from Houston to Omaha, a distance of 800 miles northward. In what direction should it fly if there is a steady 120-mi/h wind from the west at its cruising altitude? What will be its groundspeed?

Solution

Let S be the frame of reference of the ground, and choose x and y axes pointing east and north, respectively. Let S′ be the frame of reference of the air, so that the velocity **V** is 120**î** mi/h. The velocity **v′** of the plane relative to the air has magnitude 600 mi/h, but we don't know its direction. We can write this velocity as

$$\mathbf{v'} = v'\cos\theta\,\mathbf{\hat{i}} + v'\sin\theta\,\mathbf{\hat{j}},$$

where v' is 600 mi/h and θ is the angle **v′** makes with the positive x-axis (see Fig. 3-31). The velocity **v** points northward, so it can be expressed in the form

$$\mathbf{v} = v\mathbf{\hat{j}},$$

where we don't know the magnitude v. We can now write the two components of Equation 3-25:

$$v_x' = v_x - V_x$$
$$v_y' = v_y - V_y.$$

Using our expressions for various velocities, these equations become

$$v'\cos\theta = 0 - V,$$

where $V = 120$ mi/h is the magnitude of **V**, and

$$v'\sin\theta = v - 0.$$

We can solve the first of these equations for θ:

$$\theta = \cos^{-1}\left(\frac{-V}{v'}\right) = \cos^{-1}\left(\frac{-120 \text{ mi/h}}{600 \text{ mi/h}}\right) = 102°.$$

Fig. 3–31
Vector diagram for Example 3–14.

Using this result in the second equation gives

$$v = v' \sin\theta = (600 \text{ mi/h})(\sin 102°) = 590 \text{ mi/h}.$$

So the plane should fly at 102° to the x-axis, or 12° west of north, and its ground-speed will be 590 mi/h. Figure 3–31 is a vector diagram relating the velocities **v'**, **v,** and **V**. Before the advent of sophisticated navigation equipment, pilots routinely carried out such calculations, often using graphical techniques.

What about the acceleration of an object viewed in two different reference frames? Suppose **a** is the acceleration in some frame S; that is, **a** = d**v**/dt, where **v** is the velocity relative to frame S. Equation 3–25 gives the velocity **v'** in a frame S' moving with velocity **V** relative to S. Differentiating this equation then gives the acceleration **a'**:

$$\mathbf{a'} = \frac{d\mathbf{v'}}{dt} = \frac{d\mathbf{v}}{dt} - \frac{d\mathbf{V}}{dt}.$$

We generally consider only reference frames moving with *constant* relative velocity **V**, so that d**V**/dt = 0. Furthermore, d**v**/dt is just the acceleration **a** in the frame S, so that

$$\mathbf{a'} = \mathbf{a}. \tag{3–26}$$

That is, the acceleration of an object is the same in all frames of reference moving at constant velocity relative to one another. This simple result is true because acceleration depends on *changes* in velocity, and the addition of any constant velocity does not alter those changes.

That acceleration does not change from one uniformly moving reference frame to another has a deep significance in physics. Consider the simple experiment of tossing a ball into the air. The experiment will have exactly the same outcome—the ball will go straight up and down in accordance with our equations for one-dimensional motion—both on an airplane moving at a constant 600 mi/h and on the ground. Why? Because in both cases the ball experiences a downward acceleration g, which is unaffected by the uniform motion of the plane relative to the earth.

If you were on a plane flying through perfectly smooth air, there is in fact no experiment involving motion that you could do to tell that the plane was moving. All experiments would come out exactly the same as they would on the ground. This fact is expressed in a simple statement, called the **principle of Galilean relativity:**

principle of Galilean relativity

> The laws of motion are the same in all frames of reference in uniform motion.

What this means is that there is no way of using the laws of motion—the only laws of physics we will consider until Chapter 20—to answer the question "am I moving?" With respect to the laws of motion, the question is meaningless; only *relative motion* matters.

Although our discussion of relative motion and the principle of Galilean relativity may seem almost obvious and straightforward, in fact that discussion rests on deep-seated notions about the nature of time and space.

In Chapter 33, after we have completed our study of electromagnetism, we will see how Albert Einstein was able to extend the principle of Galilean relativity to all of physics; the result is Einstein's special theory of relativity. In the process, Einstein showed that our commonsense notions of space and time are not quite right. As a result, Equations 3–25 and 3–26—and indeed all the equations we develop in Chapters 1 through 19—are really only approximately correct; they work well for our everyday experience, and even for spacecraft probing the solar system, but they break down when relative speeds approach the speed of light.

SUMMARY

1. **Vectors** are used to describe motion in two or three dimensions. Vector quantities have magnitude and direction; we visualize vectors using arrows whose length represents magnitude and whose direction is that of the vector. A vector is described fully by giving its magnitude and direction or, equivalently, its components on a chosen set of coordinate axes.

   a. Vectors may be added: the vector sum $\mathbf{A}+\mathbf{B}$ is formed by placing the tail of vector $\mathbf{B}$ at the head of $\mathbf{A}$; the sum is then a vector from the tail of $\mathbf{A}$ to the head of $\mathbf{B}$. Alternatively, vectors may be added by adding their components to get the components of the sum: the x-component of the vector $\mathbf{A}+\mathbf{B}$, for example, is just A_x+B_x. Vector addition is commutative: $\mathbf{A}+\mathbf{B}=\mathbf{B}+\mathbf{A}$. It is also associative: $(\mathbf{A}+\mathbf{B})+\mathbf{C}=\mathbf{A}+(\mathbf{B}+\mathbf{C})$.

   b. Vector subtraction $\mathbf{A}-\mathbf{B}$ means adding to $\mathbf{A}$ a vector whose magnitude is that of $\mathbf{B}$, but which points in the opposite direction.

   c. A vector may be multiplied by a scalar. If c is a scalar and $\mathbf{A}$ a vector of length A, the vector $c\mathbf{A}$ is a vector of length cA having the same direction as $\mathbf{A}$. Multiplication by a scalar is distributive: $c(\mathbf{A}+\mathbf{B})=c\mathbf{A}+c\mathbf{B}$.

2. **Velocity** is a vector describing the rate of change of position. The average velocity over a time interval Δt is given by the change in position divided by the time interval:

$$\overline{\mathbf{v}} = \frac{\Delta \mathbf{r}}{\Delta t},$$

   where $\Delta \mathbf{r}=\mathbf{r}_2-\mathbf{r}_1$, with $\mathbf{r}_1$ and $\mathbf{r}_2$ the positions at the beginning and end of the time interval Δt. The **instantaneous velocity** is obtained by taking the limit of arbitrarily small time intervals:

$$\mathbf{v} = \lim_{\Delta t \to 0} \frac{\Delta \mathbf{r}}{\Delta t} = \frac{d\mathbf{r}}{dt}.$$

3. **Acceleration** is a vector describing the rate of change of velocity; the average acceleration over a time interval Δt is

$$\overline{\mathbf{a}} = \frac{\Delta \mathbf{v}}{\Delta t},$$

   while the instantaneous acceleration is

$$\mathbf{a} = \lim_{\Delta t \to 0} \frac{\Delta \mathbf{v}}{\Delta t} = \frac{d\mathbf{v}}{dt}.$$

   Since velocity is a vector, it can change in either magnitude or direction or both; any change in velocity represents an acceleration. When the acceleration vector is parallel to the velocity vector, only the magnitude of the velocity changes. When the acceleration vector is perpendicular to the velocity, only the direction of the velocity changes.

4. When an object undergoes **constant acceleration**, its motion is described by the vector equations

$$\mathbf{v} = \mathbf{v}_0 + \mathbf{a}t$$
$$\mathbf{r} = \mathbf{r}_0 + \mathbf{v}_0 t + \tfrac{1}{2}\mathbf{a}t^2.$$

   These equations may be broken into components along any chosen coordinate axes; the result is a set of equations describing independently the components of the motion along the different axes.

5. **Projectile motion** is an important case of motion with constant acceleration. Launched from the origin $(x=y=0)$ with speed v_0 at an angle θ to the horizontal, a projectile follows a parabolic trajectory described by

$$y = x\tan\theta - \frac{g}{2v_0^2\cos^2\theta}x^2.$$

   On level ground, the horizontal range of the projectile is given by

$$x = \frac{v_0^2}{g}\sin2\theta.$$

6. An object moving around a circle of radius r at constant speed v is in **uniform circular motion**. Since the direction of its velocity is changing, it is accelerating. The magnitude of its acceleration is

$$a = \frac{v^2}{r}, \qquad \text{(uniform circular motion)}$$

and the acceleration vector always points toward the center of the circle. When an object moves in a circular path with varying speed, this expression gives the **radial acceleration**—the component of the acceleration perpendicular to the velocity.

7. The concept of velocity is meaningful only in relation to a particular frame of reference; the statement "I am moving" is incomplete unless the answer to the question "moving relative to what?" is understood. Only **relative motion** matters. This idea is summarized in the **principle of Galilean relativity:**

The laws of motion are the same in all frames of reference in uniform motion.

In the context of Galilean relativity, we can determine the velocity $\mathbf{v}'$ of an object relative to some frame of reference S' moving with constant velocity $\mathbf{V}$ relative to a second frame S:

$$\mathbf{v}' = \mathbf{v} - \mathbf{V},$$

where $\mathbf{v}$ is the velocity of the object with respect to the frame S. The acceleration of the object is the same in either frame of reference: $\mathbf{a}' = \mathbf{a}$.

QUESTIONS

1. Under what conditions is the magnitude of the vector sum $\mathbf{A} + \mathbf{B}$ equal to the sum of the magnitudes of the two vectors?
2. Which of the following are valid expressions? Explain. (a) $\mathbf{C} = \mathbf{A} - \mathbf{B}$; (b) $a = \mathbf{B} + c$; (c) $\mathbf{B} = c\mathbf{A}$; (d) $\mathbf{B} = \mathbf{A}/c$; (e) $\mathbf{B} = c/\mathbf{A}$.
3. Can two vectors of equal magnitude sum to zero? Can two vectors of unequal magnitude?
4. Repeat the preceding question for three vectors.
5. One way of adding vectors is to place them tail-to-tail, and then form a parallelogram as shown in Fig. 3–32. The sum of the two vectors is then a vector along the diagonal of the parallelogram. Why is this method equivalent to the head-to-tail method described in the text?

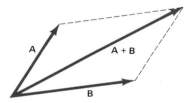

Fig. 3–32 Parallelogram method of adding vectors (Question 5).

6. Can an object have a southward acceleration while moving northward? A westward acceleration while moving northward?
7. Can an object move northward for 10 minutes, all the while having a southward acceleration?
8. Can an object move northward for 10 minutes, all the while having a westward acceleration?
9. Why can we usually use Cartesian coordinates on earth's surface even though earth is round?
10. Is the acceleration of an object in uniform circular motion constant? Explain.
11. A space shuttle completes one full orbit in 89 min. What are its average velocity and average acceleration over this interval? Is its average speed equal to its average velocity?
12. A fly heads west 5 ft, then north 3 ft, then straight up 6 ft. A mosquito starts from the same place, flies straight up 6 ft, west 5 ft, and north 3 ft. Compare their final positions.
13. Is it possible to form the unit vector $\hat{\mathbf{k}}$ from a sum of $\hat{\mathbf{i}}$ and $\hat{\mathbf{j}}$, each multiplied by appropriate scalars? Explain.
14. Is the speed of a projectile constant throughout its parabolic trajectory? Explain.
15. In this chapter, we found that the path of a projectile is a parabola. But what about a projectile launched vertically? It follows a straight up-and-down trajectory, as we described in the preceding chapter. Is there a contradiction here? Explain in terms of limiting cases of near-vertical motion.
16. Three objects are released from the same height, one from rest, one with horizontal velocity component v, and another with horizontal velocity component $2v$. Compare the times each is in the air. Compare the horizontal distances travelled by each.
17. Can there be a true "line drive" in baseball? What is required for the ball to travel a nearly straight horizontal trajectory?
18. Is there any point in the trajectory of a projectile where velocity and acceleration are perpendicular?
19. Explain why the acceleration in uniform circular motion is a vector pointing toward the center of the circle.
20. You are sitting in an airplane cruising at a steady 600 mi/h, and you throw a ball straight up. Describe its trajectory relative to you. Repeat for the case of an airplane accelerating down the runway.
21. A 45° angle maximizes the range of a ground-to-ground projectile. But suppose you are at the base of a slope inclined at some angle to the horizontal. If you want your projectile to land as far as possible up the slope, is 45° with respect to the horizontal still the optimum angle?
22. Why is the statement "I am moving" meaningless?

PROBLEMS

Section 3.1   *The Vector Description of Motion*

1. You walk west 220 m, then turn 45° toward the north and walk another 50 m. How far and in what direction from your starting point do you end up? Solve both with a diagram and by adding vector components.

2. For the vectors shown in Fig. 3–33, evaluate the vectors $\mathbf{A}+\mathbf{B}$, $\mathbf{A}-\mathbf{B}$, $\mathbf{A}+\mathbf{C}$, $\mathbf{A}+\mathbf{B}+\mathbf{C}$.

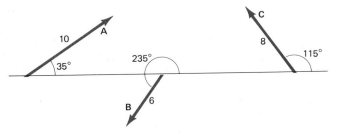

Fig. 3–33   Vectors for Problem 2; lengths are in arbitrary units.

3. A vector $\mathbf{A}$ is 10 units long and points 30° counterclockwise (CCW) from horizontal. What are its x and y components on a coordinate system (a) with the x-axis horizontal and the y-axis vertical; (b) with the x-axis at 45° CCW from horizontal and the y-axis 45° CCW from vertical; and (c) with the x-axis at 30° CCW from horizontal and the y-axis 90° CCW from the x-axis?

4. Express the sum of the unit vectors $\hat{\imath}$, $\hat{\jmath}$, and $\hat{k}$ in unit vector notation, and determine its magnitude.

5. The vector $\mathbf{A}$ is 12 units long and points 30° north of east. The vector $\mathbf{B}$ is 18 units long and points 45° west of north. Find a vector $\mathbf{C}$ such that $\mathbf{A}+\mathbf{B}+\mathbf{C}=0$.

6. In a Hawaiian foot race, runners travel a twisting 58-km path, climbing from the ocean shore to an altitude of 3300 m at the summit of Haleakala volcano. They wind up a horizontal distance 15 km northwest of their starting point. (a) At what angle must someone at the starting line beam a laser to send a signal to someone at the finishing line? (b) Moving at the speed of light, how long does it take the laser beam to go from start to finish line?

7. Let $\mathbf{A}=15\hat{\imath}-40\hat{\jmath}$ and $\mathbf{B}=31\hat{\jmath}+18\hat{k}$. Find a vector $\mathbf{C}$ such that $\mathbf{A}+\mathbf{B}+\mathbf{C}=0$.

8. A mountain expedition starts a base camp at an altitude of 5500 m. Four climbers then establish an advance camp at an altitude of 7400 m; the advance camp is southeast of the base camp, at a horizontal distance of 8.2 km. From the advance camp, two climbers head directly north to a 8900-m summit, a horizontal distance of 2.1 km. Using a coordinate system with the x-axis eastward, the y-axis northward, and the z-axis upward, and with origin at the base camp, express the positions of the advance camp and summit in unit vector notation, and determine the straight-line distance from base camp to summit.

9. An object is moving at 18 m/s at an angle of 220° counterclockwise from the x-axis. What are the x- and y-components of its velocity?

10. A car drives north at 40 mi/h for 10 min, then turns east and goes 5.0 mi at 60 mi/h. Finally, it goes southwest at 30 mi/h for 6.0 min. Draw a vector diagram and determine (a) the car's displacement and (b) its average velocity for this trip.

11. For the car of the preceding problem, determine the average acceleration between the end of the first leg and the beginning of the third leg of the trip.

12. A biologist studying the motion of bacteria notes a bacterium at position $\mathbf{r}_1=2.2\hat{\imath}+3.7\hat{\jmath}-1.2\hat{k}$ μm $(1\ \mu\text{m}=10^{-6}\ \text{m})$. 6.2 s later the bacterium is at $\mathbf{r}_2=4.6\hat{\imath}+1.9\hat{k}$ μm. What is its average velocity? Express in unit vector notation, and calculate the magnitude.

13. A supersonic aircraft is travelling east at 2100 km/h. It then begins to turn southward, emerging from the turn 2.5 min later heading due south at 1800 km/h. What are the magnitude and direction of its average acceleration during the turn?

14. For the preceding problem, write the initial and final velocities in unit vector notation, and from them calculate the average acceleration in unit vector notation. Verify that your result is consistent with the answer to the preceding problem.

15. An object undergoes acceleration of $2.3\hat{\imath}+3.6\hat{\jmath}$ m/s² over a 10-s interval. At the end of this time, its velocity is $33\hat{\imath}+15\hat{\jmath}$ m/s. (a) What was its velocity at the beginning of the 10-s interval? (b) By how much did its speed change? (c) By how much did its direction change? (d) Show that the speed change is *not* given by the magnitude of the acceleration times the time. Why not?

16. An object's position as a function of time is given by $\mathbf{r}=(bt^3+ct)\hat{\imath}+dt^2\hat{\jmath}+(et+f)\hat{k}$, where b, c, d, e, and f are constants. Determine the velocity and acceleration as functions of time.

17. The position of an object is given by $\mathbf{r}=(ct-bt^3)\hat{\imath}+dt^2\hat{\jmath}$, where $c=6.7$ m/s, $b=0.81$ m/s³, and $d=4.5$ m/s². (a) Determine the object's velocity at time $t=0$. (b) How long does it take for the direction of motion to change by 90°? (c) By how much does the speed change during this time?

Section 3.2   *Constant Acceleration*

18. An airplane heads northeastward down a runway, accelerating from rest at the rate of 2.1 m/s². Express the plane's velocity and position at $t=30$ s in unit vector notation, using a coordinate system with x-axis eastward and y-axis northward, and with origin at the start of the plane's take-off roll.

19. A particle leaves the origin with initial velocity $v_0 = 11\hat{i} + 14\hat{j}$ m/s. It undergoes a constant acceleration given by $a = -1.2\hat{i} + 0.26\hat{j}$ m/s².) (a) When does the particle cross the y-axis? (b) What is its y-coordinate at that time? (c) How fast is it moving, and in what direction, at that time?

20. Use Equation 3–11, along with the velocity calculated in the first part of Example 3–7, to determine the final position of the rocket in that example.

21. Figure 3–34 shows a cathode-ray tube, used to display electrical signals in oscilloscopes and other scientific instruments. Electrons are accelerated by the electron gun, then move down the center of the tube at 2.0×10^9 cm/s. In the 4.2-cm-long deflecting region they undergo an acceleration directed perpendicular to the long axis of the tube. The acceleration "steers" them to a particular spot on the screen, where they produce a visible glow. (a) What acceleration is needed to deflect the electrons through 15°, as shown in the figure? (b) What is the shape of an electron's path in the deflecting region?

Fig. 3–34 A cathode-ray tube (Problem 21).

22. A particle starts from the origin with initial velocity $v_0 = v_0\hat{i}$ and constant acceleration $a = a\hat{j}$. Show that the particle's distance from the origin and its direction relative to the x-axis are given by $d = t\sqrt{v_0^2 + \frac{1}{4}a^2t^2}$ and $\theta = \tan^{-1}(at/2v_0)$.

Section 3.3   *Projectile Motion*

23. A carpenter tosses a shingle off a 9.4-m-high roof, giving it an initially horizontal velocity of 7.2 m/s. (a) How long does it take to reach the ground? (b) How far does it move horizontally in this time?

24. You are trying to roll a ball off a 80.0-cm-high table to squash a bug on the floor 50.0 cm from the table's edge. How fast should you roll the ball?

25. Repeat the preceding problem, now with the bug moving away from the table at 30 mm/s and 50.0 cm from the table when the ball leaves the table edge.

26. Mike is standing outside the physics building, 15 ft from the wall. Debbie, at a window 12 ft above, tosses a physics book horizontally. What speed should she give it if it is to reach Mike?

27. You are on the ground 3.0 m from the wall of a building, and want to throw a package from your 1.5-m shoulder level to someone in a second floor window

4.2 m above the ground. At what speed and angle should you throw it so it just barely reaches the window?

28. Derive a general formula for the horizontal distance covered by a projectile launched horizontally at speed v_0 from a height h.

29. A submarine-launched missile has a range of 4500 km. (a) Assuming the missile reaches its full speed within a short distance of the ocean surface, what speed is needed for this range when the missile is launched at a 45° angle? (b) What is the total flight time for the missile? (The shortness of your answer is one reason that your survival in the nuclear age hangs in such precarious balance.) (c) To avoid destruction by space-based antimissile weapons, the missile's trajectory can be "depressed" by giving it a lower launch angle. What is the minimum launch speed needed to give the same 4500-km range if the launch angle is 20°? Neglect air resistance and the curvature of the earth.

30. A rescue airplane is flying horizontally at speed v_0 at an altitude h above the ocean, attempting to drop a package of medical supplies to shipwreck victims in a lifeboat. At what line-of-sight angle α (Fig. 3–35) should the pilot release the package?

Fig. 3–35 Problem 30

31. At a circus, a human cannonball is shot from a cannon at 35 km/h at an angle of 40°. If he leaves the cannon 1.0 m off the ground, and lands in a net 2.0 m off the ground, how long is he in the air?

32. As you stand on the rim of the Grand Canyon, a friend 10 m back from the rim throws you a baseball at 60 km/h and an initial angle of 10°. You miss the ball, and it winds up dropping 500 m below the rim before it hits a trail descending into the canyon. Neglecting air resistance, (a) what horizontal distance from the rim would it travel and (b) at what speed would it hit the trail? (Neglect of air resistance here

is actually not justified; with air resistance, your answers would be quite different.)

33. If you can hit a golf ball 180 m on earth, how far can you hit it on the moon? (Your answer is an underestimate, because the distance on earth is restricted by air resistance as well as by a larger g.)

34. Prove that a projectile launched on level ground reaches its maximum height midway along its trajectory.

35. A projectile launched at an angle θ to the horizontal reaches a maximum height h. Show that its horizontal range is 4h/tanθ.

36. What is the minimum speed for throwing a ball over the house of Fig. 3–36 if the thrower is 15 ft from the wall? Assume the ball is thrown from essentially ground level.

Fig. 3–36 Problem 36

37. A circular fountain has jets of water directed from the circumference inward at an angle of 45°. Each jet reaches a maximum height of 2.2 m. (a) If all the jets converge in the center of the circle and at their initial height, what is the radius of the fountain? (b) If one of the jets is aimed at 10° too low, how far short of the center does it fall?

38. When the Olympics were held in Mexico City in 1968, many sports fans feared that the high altitude would result in poor athletic performances due to reduced oxygen. To their surprise, new records were set in track and field events, probably as a result of lowered air resistance and a decrease in g to 9.786 m/s², both ultimately associated with the high altitude. In particular, Robert Beamon set a new world record of 8.90 m in the long jump. Photographs suggest that Beamon started his jump at a 25° angle to the horizontal. If he had jumped at sea level, where g = 9.81 m/s², at the same angle and initial speed as in Mexico City, how far would Beamon have gone? Neglect air resistance in both cases (although its effect is actually more significant than the change in g).

39. Show that, for a given initial speed, the horizontal range of a projectile is the same for launch angles 45° + α and 45° − α, where α is between 0 and 45°.

40. A typical intercontinental ballistic missile (ICBM) has a range of 10,000 km and reaches a maximum altitude

of 1200 km. Assuming its rocket engine fires for only a short time at the beginning of the flight, determine (a) its launch angle and (b) its flight time. Neglect the curvature of the earth (this is not a particularly good approximation here).

41. A basketball player is 15 ft horizontally from the center of the basket, which is 10 ft off the ground. At what angle should the player aim the ball if it is thrown from a height of 8.2 ft with a speed of 26 ft/s?

Section 3.4 *Circular Motion*

42. How fast would a car have to round a turn 50 m in radius in order for its acceleration to be numerically equal to that of gravity?

43. Estimate the acceleration of the moon, which completes a nearly circular orbit of 390,000 km radius in 27 days.

44. An object is in uniform circular motion. Make a graph of its average acceleration, measured in units of v^2/r, versus angular separation for points on the circular path spaced 40°, 30°, 20°, and 10° apart. Your graph should show the average acceleration approaching the instantaneous value v^2/r as the angular separation decreases.

45. When Apollo astronauts landed on the moon, they left one astronaut behind in a circular orbit around the moon. For the half of each orbit that took him around the back side of the moon, this astronaut was "the loneliest man in the universe," who could neither see earth nor communicate by radio with earth or with his fellow astronauts on the moon. Estimate the duration of this total separation from the rest of humanity, assuming a sufficiently low orbit that you can neglect the distance above the lunar surface (see Appendix F for the acceleration of the moon's gravity).

46. A 10-in-diameter circular saw blade rotates at 3500 revolutions per minute. What is the acceleration of one of the saw teeth? Compare with the acceleration of gravity.

47. A beetle can cling to a phonograph record only if the acceleration is less than 0.25 g. How far from the center of a 33⅓-rpm record can the beetle stand?

48. A jet is diving vertically downward at 1200 km/h (see Fig. 3–37). If the pilot can withstand a maximum ac-

Fig. 3–37 Problem 48

celeration of 5g before losing consciousness, how close to the ground can the plane get before starting a quarter turn to pull out of the dive? Assume the plane's speed remains constant.

49. Electrons in a TV tube are deflected through a 55° angle as shown in Fig. 3–38. During the deflection they move at constant speed in a circular path of radius 4.30 cm. If they experience an acceleration of 3.35×10^{17} m/s^2, how long does the deflection take?

Fig. 3–38   Problem 49

50. How fast would the earth have to be rotating for the radial acceleration of an object on the equator to equal g? Compare with earth's actual rotation rate.

51. A record turntable takes 14 s to reach full speed of $33\frac{1}{3}$ revolutions per minute. With constant tangential acceleration, what are the tangential and radial components of the acceleration of a point on the rim of a 12-in record 10 s after the turntable is turned on?

52. A plane is heading northward when it begins to turn eastward on a circular path of radius 9.10 km. At the instant it begins to turn, its acceleration vector points 22.0° north of east and has magnitude 2.60 m/s^2. (a) What is the plane's speed? (b) At what rate is its speed increasing?

Section 3.5   *Motion Is Relative*

53. A dog paces around the perimeter of a rectangular barge that is headed up a river at 14 km/h relative to the riverbank. The current in the water is at 3.0 km/h. If the dog walks at 4.0 km/h, what are its speeds relative to (a) the shore and (b) the water as it walks around the barge?

54. A jetliner with an airspeed of 1000 km/h sets out on a 1500-km flight due south. To maintain a southward direction, however, the plane must be pointed 15° west of south. If the flight takes 100 min, what is the wind velocity?

55. A car is moving at a constant 19 m/s. Its 72-cm-diameter wheels rotate at 8.4 revolutions per second.

What are the instantaneous velocity and acceleration of (a) the bottom of the wheel, (b) the top of the wheel, and (c) the forward edge of the wheel? Determine these quantities both in the car's frame of reference and in the ground frame of reference.

Supplementary Problems

56. A juggler's hands are 80 cm apart, and the balls being juggled reach a maximum height of 100 cm above the juggler's hands. (a) At what velocity do the balls leave the juggler's hands? (b) If four balls are being juggled, how often must the juggler catch a ball?

57. A monkey is hanging from a branch a distance h above the ground. A hunter stands a horizontal distance d from a point directly below the monkey. The hunter wants to shoot the monkey, but knows that the monkey will let go of the branch at the instant the gun fires. (a) Show that the bullet will hit the falling monkey if the gun is aimed directly at the monkey's initial position. (b) Your result in (a) is independent of the speed of the bullet as it leaves the gun, provided that speed is above a certain minimum value that will ensure the bullet's reaching the monkey before the monkey hits the ground. Show that this minimum value is $\sqrt{(d^2 + h^2)g/2h}$.

58. A child tosses a ball over a flat-roofed house 3.2 m high and 7.4 m wide, so that it just clears the corners on both sides, as shown in Fig. 3–39. If the child stands 2.1 m from the wall, what are the ball's initial speed and launch angle? Assume the ball is launched essentially from ground level.

Fig. 3–39   Problem 58

59. A diver leaves a 3-m board on a trajectory that takes her 2.5 m above the board, and then into the water a horizontal distance of 2.8 m from the end of the board. At what speed and angle did she leave the board?

60. An object moves at constant speed v in the x-y plane, describing a circle of radius r centered at the origin. It is on the positive x-axis at time $t = 0$. Show that the position of the object as a function of time can be written $\mathbf{r} = r[\cos(vt/r)\hat{\mathbf{i}} + \sin(vt/r)\hat{\mathbf{j}}]$, where the argument of the sine and cosine is in radians. Differentiate this expression once to obtain an expression for the velocity and again for the acceleration. Show that the acceleration has magnitude v^2/r and is directed radially inward (that is, opposite to $\mathbf{r}$).

61. In the Olympic hammer throw, contestants whirl a 7.3-kg ball on the end of a 1.2-m-long steel wire before releasing it. In a particular throw, the hammer is released horizontally from a height of 2.4 m and travels 84 m horizontally before hitting the ground. What is its radial acceleration just before release?

62. A projectile is launched at an angle θ to the horizontal, with sufficient speed to give it a horizontal range x. Show that the radius of curvature at the top of its trajectory is given by $r = x/2\tan\theta$.

63. While increasing its speed, a train enters a 90° circular turn of radius r with speed v_0 and with tangential acceleration equal to half its radial acceleration. If its tangential acceleration remains constant, show that when the train leaves the turn its tangential and radial accelerations are related by $a_t = a_r/(2 + \pi)$.

64. A convertible is speeding down the highway at 130 km/h, when the driver spots a police airplane 600 m back at an altitude of 250 m. The driver decelerates at 2.0 km/h/s. If the plane is flying horizontally at a steady 210 km/h, where should the plane be in relation to the car for the police officer to drop a speeding ticket into the car? Assume the ticket is dropped with no initial vertical motion, and it is in a heavy capsule that experiences negligible air resistance. Will the car still be speeding when the ticket reaches it?

65. A space shuttle orbits the earth at 27,000 km/h, while at the equator earth rotates at 1300 km/h. The two motions are in roughly the same direction (west to east), but the shuttle orbit is inclined at 25° to the equator. What is the shuttle's velocity relative to scientists tracking it from the equator?

4

DYNAMICS: WHY DO THINGS MOVE?

Fig. 4–1
This Voyager spacecraft, on its mission to the outermost planets, travels tens of kilometers each second without any need for rocket engines.

A spacecraft moves noiselessly, effortlessly, and smoothly through space. No rocket firing is necessary to maintain its motion (Fig. 4–1). Pioneer and Voyager spacecraft that have visited the outer planets are now on their way out of the solar system, and will continue onward forever—or until they run into something.

Until recent years we had trouble duplicating on earth situations that exist naturally in outer space. If we slide a book across a table top, it soon comes to rest because of friction. If we polish the table top to make it smoother, the book slides farther before friction inevitably stops it. In physics labs, we often use "air tables," in which air forced upward through small holes in the table top supports objects on a nearly frictionless cushion of air (Fig. 4–2). But even here, resistance of the air itself eventually stops the motion.

In this chapter, we seek the fundamental laws of motion, unobscured by the confusing effects of friction and air resistance. In earlier chapters, we studied only **kinematics**—the description of motion without reference to its causes. Here we also want to know *why* things move. The study of motion and its causes is called **dynamics**, from the Greek word "dynami-

kinematics

dynamics

Fig. 4–2
Strobe photo of a puck sliding on a nearly frictionless air table. Time interval between images is the same; since the images are nearly equal distances apart, the puck's speed is essentially constant.

kos,'' meaning force or power. We will see how, building on work of Galileo, Isaac Newton in the seventeenth century laid down basic laws of motion that we still apply today. This chapter describes Newton's laws themselves and their immediate consequences. In the following chapter, we will apply Newton's laws in a variety of practical situations.

4.1
FINDING THE LAWS OF MOTION

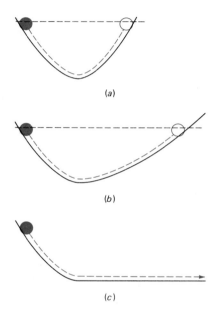

Fig. 4–3
(a) Galileo recognized that a ball rolling down an incline would rise to nearly its starting height on a second incline. *(b)* Making the second incline more gradual would result in the ball's travelling farther in the horizontal direction. *(c)* If the second incline were reduced to a horizontal surface, Galileo reasoned, the ball's motion should continue forever.

What makes things move? For nearly two thousand years following the work of Aristotle (384–322 B.C.), most people believed that a force—a push or a pull—was needed to keep something moving. This idea made a lot of sense: when an ox stopped pulling an ox-cart, for example, the cart quickly came to a stop. Aristotelians extended their thinking to projectiles by saying that an arrow, for instance, could continue moving through the air because air rushed from the front to the back of the arrow to push it forward.

Actually, the very question "what makes things move?" is misleading. In the early 1600's, Galileo Galilei carried out a series of experiments that convinced him that a moving object has an intrinsic "quantity of motion" that needs no cause to maintain itself (Fig. 4–3). Instead of answering the question "what makes things move?" Galileo asserted that the question needs no answer. In doing so, he set the stage for centuries of progress in physics, beginning with the achievements of Isaac Newton.

Newton, son of a modest farming family, attended Trinity College of Cambridge University. Although the Aristotelian theories were taught, advanced students were allowed to explore newer ideas emerging on the European continent. Newton immersed himself in the work of Galileo, Descartes, and others who were breaking with Aristotelian tradition. In 1665–1666, young Isaac Newton (Fig. 4–4) had just graduated from Trinity College, when the plague swept across England and the universities were shut down. Newton returned home to Woolsthorpe in Lincolnshire (Fig. 4–5), where in two years of quiet contemplation he continued to lay the groundwork for much of his later work in physics. During this time Newton also began the development of calculus, a branch of mathematics that was needed for the full application of his laws of gravity and motion. Twenty years later, in completing his work on gravity, Newton formulated his three laws of motion.

Newton's laws of motion are the basis of mechanics. They involve three important concepts: **mass, force,** and **momentum.** Newton thought of mass as a measure of the quantity of matter in an object. Although this description is a valid one, we will see that it is more practical to give an operational definition of mass that arises from Newton's laws. We have an intuitive sense of **force** as a push or a pull, a sense that is consistent with Newton's concept of force. Since pushes and pulls have direction, force is a vector quantity. **Momentum** is a modern word for what Newton called "quantity of motion." Seeking a quantity that reflected both the velocity of a moving object as well as the amount of matter in motion, Newton hit upon the product of mass and velocity as the best measure of the "quantity

mass, force, and momentum

force

momentum

of motion'' or momentum. Thus the momentum of an object of mass m moving with velocity $\mathbf{v}$ is $m\mathbf{v}$; we use the symbol $\mathbf{p}$ for momentum:

$$\mathbf{p} = m\mathbf{v}. \quad \text{(momentum)} \qquad (4\text{--}1)$$

Since velocity is a vector, so is momentum.

We now state Newton's three laws, and then discuss each in detail:

Newton's first law of motion

Newton's first law of motion: A body in motion tends to remain in motion, or to remain stopped if stopped, unless acted on by an outside force.

Newton's second law of motion

Newton's second law of motion: The rate at which a body's momentum changes is equal to the net force acting on the body; mathematically

$$\mathbf{F} = \frac{d\mathbf{p}}{dt}. \quad \text{(Newton's 2nd law)} \qquad (4\text{--}2)$$

When the mass of a body is constant, we can use the definition of momentum, $\mathbf{p} = m\mathbf{v}$, to write

$$\mathbf{F} = \frac{d(m\mathbf{v})}{dt} = m\frac{d\mathbf{v}}{dt}.$$

But $d\mathbf{v}/dt$ is the acceleration, $\mathbf{a}$, so that

$$\mathbf{F} = m\mathbf{a}. \quad \text{(Newton's 2nd law, constant mass)} \qquad (4\text{--}3)$$

Although Newton originally wrote his second law in the form 4–2, which remains the most general form, the form 4–3 is more widely recognized. This form also provides an operational definition of mass: if the same force F is applied to two different objects, then the resulting accelerations are inversely proportional to their masses. Once a standard of mass has been established—like the standard kilogram described in Chapter 1—then this procedure can be used to compare an unknown mass with the standard.

Newton's third law of motion

Newton's third law of motion: For every action there is always an equal and opposite reaction.

Figure 4–6 shows the laws as stated by Newton in the first edition of his book *Philosophiae Naturalis Principia Mathematica* (*The Mathematical Principles of Natural Philosophy*), published in London in 1687. What we now call physical science was then known as natural philosophy.

Fig. 4–4
Isaac Newton at age 47, two years after he published the *Principia*.

Fig. 4–5
Newton's family cottage at Woolsthorpe is still standing. In two years here, he laid the groundwork for his great achievements in science and mathematics.

Newton's First Law and Inertia

Newton's first law is a more precise statement of what Galileo had earlier realized—that, in the absence of external complications like friction or other forces, a moving body will keep moving steadily forward. In other words, its velocity (a vector quantity) will not change in either direction or magnitude. We use the term **inertia** to describe a body's resistance to change in motion. So Newton's first law is equivalent to saying that a body has inertia; for this reason, the first law is also known as the law of inertia.

Fig. 4–6

Newton's three laws as published in his *Principia*. Literally translated, they read: "*Law I.* Every body remains in a state resting or moving uniformly in a straight line, except insofar as forces on it compel it to change its state. *Law II.* The force is proportional to the change of motion, which is in the direction of the force. *Law III.* Opposite actions always have opposite and equal reactions: two actions of a body are always equal and in opposite directions."

We can treat the case of a body at rest as a body with zero velocity. A stationary body's tendency to stay at rest is thus the same as a moving body's tendency to keep moving. Indeed, in Section 3.5, we showed that statements about velocity are meaningful only in the context of a particular frame of reference. A body that is stationary with respect to one frame of reference is moving with respect to another frame. But we also showed that the acceleration of an object is the same in *all* frames of reference that are themselves in uniform motion. So if a body exhibits no acceleration—no change in motion—in one uniformly moving frame of reference, its acceleration must be zero in *all* uniformly moving frames of reference. Newton's first law tells us that a body not subject to outside influences exhibits no change in motion; this statement is therefore true in all frames of reference in uniform motion. Such frames are often called **inertial frames,** since the law of inertia (Newton's first law) is valid in them.

inertial frames

But we do find accelerations; the motions of bodies obviously do change. Newton's first law says that, when motion changes, something must be acting to change it. Whatever is changing the motion is known as a **force.** Newton's first law is not quantitative; it does not assign numerical values to inertia or to forces. Still, it is extremely powerful, for it says that whenever we see the velocity of an object changing, we know that a force must be present. Often, change in velocity is the only visible manifestation of the force. If we see a car slowing, then some force must be acting. If we see a car turning even though its speed remains constant, its velocity is still changing, so again we know that a force must be acting. We observe the moon moving about the earth in a circular path; since the moon's velocity is changing direction, a force must be acting.

force

For Aristotle, the natural state of a body was to be at rest. This is what made meaningful the question "what makes things move?" But for Newton, the natural state of a body is motion at constant velocity. In the context of

Newton's laws, the meaningful question about motion is not "what makes things move?" but "what makes motion change?" The answer, embodied in the first law, is that forces make motion change. In the next few chapters, we will see the power of Newton's new idea, as we calculate the motions of objects from molecules to planets. Much later, in Chapter 33, we will see how the progression from Aristotelian to Newtonian thinking laid the foundation for another scientific revolution: Albert Einstein's theory of relativity.

4.2
FORCE

We are familiar with the forces in our everyday lives, and our usual commonsense notion of force is pretty close to the scientific meaning. We push, pull, or lift objects and thus exert forces on them. We experience the pull of gravity toward the center of the earth. We see objects slow down, and infer the existence of frictional forces. We know that ropes and cables provide forces that can support or accelerate heavy objects. We have used magnets enough to sense that they, too, exert forces. Finally, scientists' nuclear experiments infer the existence of strong forces that bind the atomic nucleus together. In some cases, like your hand pushing a book, the force seems associated with contact between two objects. In other cases, like the earth's gravitational force on the moon or the pull of a magnet, the force

action at a distance seems to act over a great distance. This idea of **action at a distance** has bothered scientists and philosophers over the ages, and it may bother you. How can the moon, way out there, "know" about the earth so far away? Later, in Chapters 8 and 21, we will introduce the concept of a "force field" as an alternative way of describing forces like gravity, electricity, and magnestism that act over long distances. The field concept is a cornerstone of the modern description of matter and its interactions.

The Fundamental Forces

We have already alluded to gravitational forces, contact forces, frictional forces, electrical forces, tension forces, magnetic forces, and nuclear forces. How many kinds of forces are there? New theoretical work of the 1980's indicates that there is probably only one fundamental force, although we do not yet know how to describe it. At present, physicists identify three basic types of forces, each subsuming other forces once thought to be fundamental. The unification of seemingly unrelated forces has been a major theme in the history of physics, and is perhaps the central problem in contemporary physics (Fig. 4–7). Later we will explore one aspect of this unification in detail, as we come to understand how electricity and magnetism are fundamentally related. For now, we merely introduce the three fundamental forces with a brief description of each.

gravitational force We experience the **gravitational force** in our everyday lives. Yet the gravitational force is the weakest of the fundamental forces, and perhaps the least understood theoretically. But though the gravitational force of an individual bit of matter is extremely weak, this force is cumulative. No

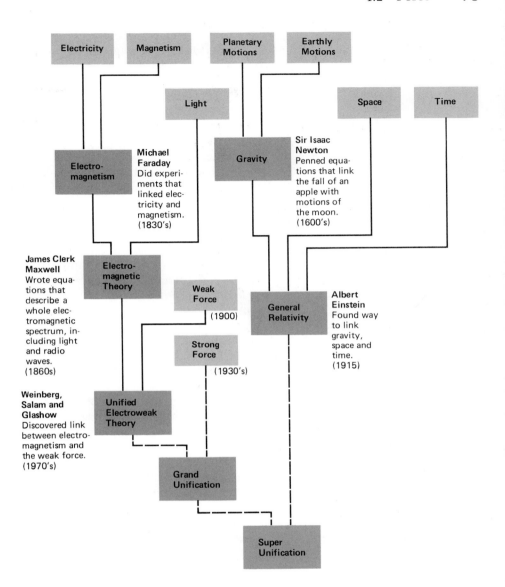

Fig. 4–7
Unification of seemingly unrelated forces has been a major theme in the history of physics.

antigravity is known. So the gravity of a massive object like a star or planet is very large, and on a large scale gravitation is the dominant force in the universe. Our best theory of gravity is now the general theory of relativity, advanced by Albert Einstein in 1916. But physicists have not yet figured out how to combine general relativity with the quantum theory that describes matter on the atomic scale. The lack of a quantum theory of gravity has greatly hindered efforts to unify gravity with the other forces.

electroweak force

The **electroweak force** is also important in our everyday lives. The electroweak force includes the forces of electromagnetism and the so-called weak nuclear force. Just a few years ago, electromagnetism and the weak force were listed separately, and physicists counted four fundamental forces. For their theory linking the weak and electromagnetic forces, Sheldon Glashow, Steven Weinberg, and Abdus Salam received the 1979 Nobel

Fig. 4–8
Carlo Rubbia and Simon van der Meer, who won the 1984 Nobel Prize for Physics for their experimental work that confirmed the unification of electromagnetism and the weak force.

strong force

quark
color force

grand unified force
super unified force
supergravity

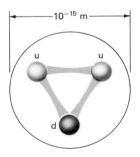

Fig. 4–9
A proton consists of three quarks, two of the so-called "up" variety and one a "down" quark. The quarks are bound by the color force shown symbolically as a link between the quarks. (In a proton, the strength of a color force is about 10,000 lb, or 50,000 N.) Although the quarks are much smaller than the 10^{-15}-m proton diameter, they are in constant motion within that region. The color force actually strengthens with increasing separation, preventing the quarks from escaping the proton volume.

Prize for Physics. That theory was confirmed experimentally in 1983 by a group working under the Italian physicist Carlo Rubbia, a Harvard professor working at CERN, the European Center for Nuclear Research (Fig. 4–8). The 1984 Nobel Prize for Physics went quickly to Rubbia and his Dutch colleague Simon van der Meer. Earlier still, electric and magnetic forces had been considered separate until they were linked by the theory of James Clerk Maxwell in the 1860's. We will study Maxwell's synthesis of electricity and magnetism in Chapters 27 through 32.

Virtually all the nongravitational forces we encounter in everyday life are manifestations of the electroweak force. Contact forces, friction, tension forces, the forces in your muscles, and the forces that hold everyday matter together are all essentially electrical forces. The forces associated with the interaction of light and matter are electromagnetic. Processes involving the weak force occur in the core of the sun and are partially responsible for the generation of solar energy that keeps us alive.

The third basic force of nature, the **strong force,** was advanced in the 1930's to explain how atomic nuclei are held together. Current theories show that the protons and neutrons that make up atomic nuclei are themselves composed of more fundamental particles called **quarks** (Fig. 4–9). The force acting between quarks is known as the **color force.** The color force links the quarks into particles like protons, neutrons, and others, and also links those particles together to form nuclei. What we call the strong force really results from the color force between quarks.

Theories for the gravitational, electroweak, and strong forces are fairly well established. Attempts are being made to unify the electroweak and strong forces, describing them as manifestations of a single **grand unified force.** Further behind are attempts to unify the grand unified force with gravity, to give a **super unified force,** for which a theory called **supergravity** is currently a leading candidate. Such further unifications are tasks for the rest of this century, if not the next. But scientists have realized that unified force theories can be studied by analyzing the earliest fraction of a second of the universe, immediately after the big bang in which the universe was formed. Theory suggests that forces now seemingly distinct would then have had the same strength, and been essentially identical. So studies of the early universe have joined with studies of nuclear physics to probe the fundamental forces of nature. We will look further at unification theories in Chapter 36.

4.3
NEWTON'S SECOND LAW

Why are we so interested in knowing about forces? Because forces cause changes in motion: if we know the force acting on a body, we can use Newton's second law to calculate its acceleration, and thus determine its subsequent motion.

We introduced Newton's second law in Section 4.1; for an object of constant mass, we saw that the law takes the form

$$\mathbf{F} = \mathbf{ma}.$$

(4–3)

Just what does this equation mean? We can think of it in two ways.

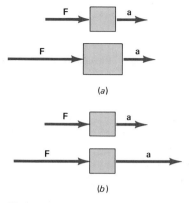

Fig. 4–10
(a) For two objects to have the same acceleration, a greater force must be exerted on the more massive object.
(b) When two objects have the same mass, the one with the greater force experiences the greater acceleration.

First, Equation 4–3 provides a measure of force. If we observe a body of mass m undergoing an acceleration of magnitude a, we know that there is a force of magnitude ma acting on the body. The direction of the force is the same as that of the acceleration. Equation 4–3 shows that the units of force are kg·m/s². If we observe a 2-kg object accelerating at 3 m/s², then we know that a force of (2 kg)(3 m/s²) or 6 kg·m/s² is acting on the object. To honor Isaac Newton, we call one kg·m/s² a newton (symbol N). From Equation 4–3, we see that a force of 1 N will cause a 1-kg mass to accelerate at 1 m/s². Similarly, our 2-kg object accelerating at 3 m/s² experiences a force of 6 N. A 1-N force is about a quarter pound—a fairly small force on the human scale. You readily exert forces of tens to hundreds of newtons on the objects you encounter in everyday life.

Newton's law makes good sense in light of our everyday notions of force. We expect it should take a larger force to produce a given acceleration in a more massive object (Fig. 4–10a). And with a given mass, a larger force should be needed for a larger acceleration (Fig. 4–10b). Newton's second law, with force proportional to the product of mass and acceleration, reflects our intuitive understandings suggested in Fig. 4–10.

Example 4–1

Force, Mass, and Acceleration

A 1200-kg car accelerates from rest to 20 m/s in 7.8 s, moving in a straight line. What force is acting on it? If the car then rounds a bend 85 m in radius at a steady 20 m/s, what force acts on it?

Solution

To calculate the force from Newton's second law, we need to know the acceleration and the mass being accelerated. When the car accelerates from rest to 20 m/s in 7.8 s, it undergoes an acceleration of magnitude

$$a = \frac{\Delta v}{\Delta t} = \frac{20 \text{ m/s}}{7.8 \text{ s}} = 2.6 \text{ m/s}^2.$$

The magnitude of the force causing this acceleration is then

$$F = ma = (1200 \text{ kg})(2.6 \text{ m/s}^2) = 3100 \text{ kg·m/s}^2 = 3100 \text{ N}.$$

Force is a vector, and the full vector form of Newton's second law—$\mathbf{F} = m\mathbf{a}$—shows that the force is in the same direction as the acceleration, which in this case also happens to be in the direction of motion. What is the physical origin of the force? Newton's law does not tell us that; it only tells us the magnitude and direction of the force. *Any* physical mechanism providing the same force on the car would produce the same acceleration. In the case of the accelerating car, the force is in fact provided by friction between tires and road—a force that is ultimately electrical in origin. If the driver tried to accelerate on frictionless ice, the wheels would simply spin and the car would not accelerate.

When the car rounds a circular bend at constant speed, we know from Section 3.4 that it undergoes an acceleration of magnitude v^2/r directed toward the center of the circle. Newton's second law therefore requires a force acting toward the center of the circle; the magnitude of this force is

$$F = ma = \frac{mv^2}{r} = \frac{(1200 \text{ kg})(20 \text{ m/s})^2}{85 \text{ m}} = 5600 \text{ N}.$$

Note that Newton's law does not distinguish between forces that result in a change

Fig. 4–11
Forces acting on the car of Example
4.1. *(a)* Accelerating in straight line.
(b) Rounding a curve. (Only forces in
the horizontal plane are shown; there
are also vertical forces from gravity and
from the road, but these add to zero
and therefore do not accelerate the
car.)

(a)   *(b)*

in speed (car accelerating in a straight line) and those that result in a change in
direction (car accelerating in a circular path at constant speed). Newton's second
law relates force, mass, and acceleration in *all* instances; there is nothing special
about circular or any other form of motion in the eyes of Newton's second law.

What provides the accelerating force in the car's circular motion? Again, it is
the force of friction between tires and road. On an icy road, the car may skid off
the road in a straight line, since the frictional force is virtually absent.

Figure 4–11 shows the force vectors for the two cases in this example.

Example 4–2
Electrons in a TV Tube

Electrons in a TV tube are accelerated essentially from rest to a speed of
8.4×10^7 m/s in the "electron gun" at the back of the tube. If the electron gun is 8.2
cm long and if the acceleration in the gun is constant, what force is exerted on each
electron?

Solution

To calculate the force, we need the acceleration and mass of the electron. Equation 2–14 relates acceleration, velocity, and distance in one-dimensional motion.
With $v_0 = 0$, this equation becomes

$$v^2 = 2a(x - x_0),$$

so that

$$a = \frac{v^2}{2(x - x_0)}.$$

Here $x - x_0$ is the 8.2-cm length of the electron gun and v is the 8.4×10^7 m/s velocity of electrons emerging from the gun. Then Newton's second law gives

$$F = ma = \frac{mv^2}{2(x - x_0)} = \frac{(9.1 \times 10^{-31} \text{ kg})(8.4 \times 10^7 \text{ m/s})^2}{(2)(0.082 \text{ m})} = 3.9 \times 10^{-14} \text{ N},$$

where we found the electron mass in the table of fundamental constants inside the
front cover. That such a small force can accelerate electrons to such high speed in
only a few centimeters is possible because of their minuscule mass. (Our answer in
this case is only approximate because effects of relativity become important.)

Example 4–3
A Variable Force

An object of mass m is observed to move in a straight line with velocity given
by $v_x = bt^2 - ct$, where b and c are positive constants with appropriate units. Find
an expression for the force on the object as a function of time, and find a time when
the force is zero.

Solution

Acceleration is the rate of change of velocity, so that Newton's second law may be written

$$F = ma = m\,\frac{dv}{dt} = m\,\frac{d}{dt}(bt^2 - ct) = 2mbt - mc.$$

The force is zero when $2mbt - mc = 0$, or at time $t = c/2b$.

We have just used Newton's second law as a prescription for measuring forces. Conversely, given the force on an object, we can calculate the object's acceleration and thus predict its motion. It is this use of Newton's law that lets us send a spacecraft to Jupiter, design engines appropriate to a new aircraft, or determine the safe distance between cars on a highway. It also helps us analyze a skyscraper's response to gale-force winds, predict the positions of the planets and the timing of eclipses, and develop better tennis rackets. It is only a slight exaggeration to say that the equation $\mathbf{F} = m\mathbf{a}$ covers all of classical physics.

Example 4–4
An Airport Runway

Fully loaded, a 747 jetliner has a mass of 3.6×10^5 kg. Its four engines provide a total thrust (force) of 7.7×10^5 N. How long a runway is needed for a 747 to achieve takeoff speed of 310 km/h (86 m/s)?

Solution

We are given force and mass, from which we can calculate acceleration using Newton's second law:

$$a = \frac{F}{m}.$$

We need then to relate acceleration to speed and distance; Equation 2–14 provides this relation:

$$v^2 = 2a(x - x_0).$$

Solving for the runway length $x - x_0$ and using $a = F/m$, we have

$$x - x_0 = \frac{v^2}{2a} = \frac{v^2}{2(F/m)} = \frac{mv^2}{2F} = \frac{(3.6 \times 10^5 \text{ kg})(86 \text{ m/s})^2}{(2)(7.7 \times 10^5 \text{ N})} = 1700 \text{ m}.$$

Example 4–5
Predicting Motion Using Newton's Second Law

A 1.2-kg object initially at rest at the origin is acted on by a force $\mathbf{F} = 2.4\hat{\mathbf{i}} + 1.7\hat{\mathbf{j}}$ N. What is the object's acceleration? Where is the object and how fast is it moving 3.5 s after the force is first applied?

Solution

Solving Newton's second law for the acceleration gives

$$\mathbf{a} = \frac{\mathbf{F}}{m} = \frac{2.4\hat{\mathbf{i}} + 1.7\hat{\mathbf{j}} \text{ N}}{1.2 \text{ kg}} = 2.0\hat{\mathbf{i}} + 1.4\hat{\mathbf{j}} \text{ m/s}^2.$$

Given the acceleration, we use methods of the previous chapters to find the position and speed. Equation 3–9 gives the position of an object undergoing constant acceleration:

$$\mathbf{r} = \mathbf{r}_0 + \mathbf{v}_0 t + \tfrac{1}{2}\mathbf{a}t^2 = \tfrac{1}{2}(2.0\hat{\mathbf{i}}+1.4\hat{\mathbf{j}} \text{ m/s}^2)(3.5 \text{ s})^2 = 25\hat{\mathbf{i}}+17\hat{\mathbf{j}} \text{ m}.$$

Here we have set $\mathbf{r}_0$ and $\mathbf{v}_0$ to zero since the object is initially at rest at the origin. The velocity after 3.5 s is given by Equation 3–8:

$$\mathbf{v} = \mathbf{v}_0 + \mathbf{a}t = (2.0\hat{\mathbf{i}}+1.7\hat{\mathbf{j}} \text{ m/s})(3.5 \text{ s}) = 7.0\hat{\mathbf{i}}+6.0\hat{\mathbf{j}} \text{ m/s},$$

so that the speed is

$$v = \sqrt{v_x{}^2+v_y{}^2} = [(7.0 \text{ m/s})^2+(6.0 \text{ m/s})^2]^{1/2} = 9.2 \text{ m/s}.$$

A third use of Newton's law involves determining unknown masses from measured forces and accelerations. This approach is actually used in orbiting spacecraft, where weightlessness (see Section 4.4) precludes more conventional measurements.

Example 4–6
The Mass of an Astronaut

To aid doctors studying the physiological effects of spaceflight, astronauts on the long Skylab missions of the 1970's measured their masses using a chair subject to a known force exerted by a spring (Fig. 4–12). With astronaut Jack Lousma strapped in the chair, the 15-kg chair underwent an acceleration of 2.04×10^{-2} m/s^2 when the spring force was 2.07 N. What was Lousma's mass?

Solution

Solving Newton's second law for mass, we have

$$m = \frac{F}{a} = \frac{2.07 \text{ N}}{2.04\times10^{-2} \text{ m/s}^2} = 101 \text{ kg}.$$

This is the combined mass of the chair and astronaut; subtracting the 15-kg chair mass then gives 86 kg for astronaut Lousma.

Fig. 4–12
Mass-measuring device used on Skylab.

4.4
THE FORCE OF GRAVITY: MASS AND WEIGHT

Newton's second law shows that mass is a measure of a body's resistance to changes in motion—that is, of its inertia. The more massive a body, the greater the force needed to give it a particular acceleration. The mass of a body is an intrinsic property of the body; it doesn't depend on the body's location or other circumstances. If my mass is 65 kg, it is 65 kg whether I am on earth, in an orbiting spacecraft, on the moon, or in the most remote reaches of intergalactic space. That means that no matter where I am, a net force of 65 N is needed to give me an acceleration of 1 m/s^2.

We commonly speak of the weight of a body, using that term in the same way we use the term mass. In physics, though, weight has a very specific meaning that depends on the frame of reference in which the weight is being measured. Before defining weight, we rephrase the defini-

free fall

weight

tion of free fall given in Chapter 2: **free fall** is the state of motion of a body subject only to the gravitational force. The **weight** of a body in a particular reference frame is then defined as that force that, when applied to the body, would give it the same acceleration relative to the reference frame that it would have in free fall. For an object near the surface of the earth, the acceleration in free fall has magnitude g and points downward. In a frame of reference at rest with respect to the earth, the weight of a body has magnitude mg, where m is the body's mass. With my mass of 65 kg, I weigh (65 kg)(9.8 m/s^2) or 640 N. On the moon, the acceleration of gravity is only 1.6 m/s^2; although my mass is everywhere 65 kg, my weight on the moon would be only (65 kg)(1.6 m/s^2) or 100 N. And in the remote reaches of intergalactic space, far from any gravitating object, my weight would be essentially zero.

Example 4–7

Mass and Weight

The two Viking spacecraft that landed on Mars in 1976 had weights of 5880 N on earth. What were their masses on earth and Mars, and their weights on Mars?

Solution

Weight in a planet's frame of reference is the force that would give the local acceleration of gravity: $W = mg$. Solving for m and using the weight on earth and the acceleration of gravity on earth, we have

$$m = \frac{W}{g} = \frac{5880 \text{ N}}{9.8 \text{ m/s}^2} = 600 \text{ kg.}$$

The mass is the same everywhere; on Mars the weight is then given by

$$W = mg_{\text{Mars}} = (600 \text{ kg})(3.74 \text{ m/s}^2) = 2240 \text{ N,}$$

where we obtained the acceleration of gravity on Mars from Appendix F.

What about my weight in a frame of reference that itself is falling freely—like a falling elevator or an orbiting spacecraft? Since all objects experience the same gravitational acceleration, with no force but gravity acting on me I experience no acceleration *relative to the freely falling frame* (Fig. 4–13). In that frame, I am therefore **weightless.** Weightlessness is not a mere mathematical condition; I really *feel* weightless. (The "weight" I experience standing on earth is actually the force of my muscles

weightlessness

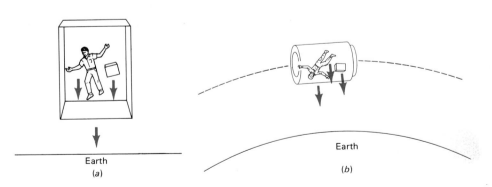

Fig. 4–13
Objects in a freely falling frame of reference are weightless because they experience the same acceleration as the reference frame. Weightlessness would occur in a freely falling elevator near earth's surface just as it does in an orbiting spacecraft. In both cases, the person, book, and elevator or spaceship all have the same acceleration toward earth so that none accelerates relative to its surroundings.

Fig. 4–14
(Left) Astronaut trainees are weightless as the NASA training aircraft executes a parabolic trajectory. *(Right)* Astronauts Richard Truly and Guy Bluford in the space shuttle.

acting to oppose gravity's tendency to accelerate me; in free fall, gravity acts unopposed and my muscles need not exert any force.) If I drop a book in a freely falling elevator, the book stays right next to me as we accelerate downward together; it too is weightless (see Fig. 4–13). If I jump off the floor of the elevator, I do not fall back down to it, but continue in uniform motion relative to the elevator until I hit the ceiling. This weightlessness is identical to that experienced by astronauts in an orbiting spacecraft; the only problem is that my experience of weightlessness would end all too soon when the elevator struck the ground and strong nongravitational forces acted. Weightlessness is not a condition peculiar to outer space; it occurs in any freely falling frame of reference. (Don't be misled by the word "fall." Free fall means that only gravity is acting; a spacecraft in circular orbit is as much in free fall as an elevator actually dropping toward earth's surface.) Practically, though, it is much easier to achieve weightlessness in space, where the absence of air eliminates the nongravitational force of air resistance and permits closed orbits that never intersect the earth. Astronaut training includes flights on aircraft that describe trajectories approximating the parabolas of projectiles moving under the influence of gravity alone; on these parabolic flights, astronauts are every bit as weightless as they are in orbit (Fig. 4–14).

Weightlessness does *not* imply the absence of gravitational force. The acceleration of gravity in low orbit is nearly the same as at earth's surface, so that the gravitational force on an orbiting astronaut is nearly the astronaut's surface weight mg. This had better be the case! It is the gravitational force that keeps the astronaut in orbit around the earth. If the gravitational force were zero, astronaut and spacecraft would obey Newton's first law and move in a straight line, quickly leaving earth's vicinity. Weight depends on frame of reference, and the astronaut is weightless only in the freely falling reference frame of the spacecraft; in a frame of reference at rest with respect to earth, the astronaut is not at all weightless.

The concepts of weight and mass are further confused by the common use of the SI unit kilogram to describe "weight." At the doctor's office, you may be told that you "weigh" 55 kg. Strictly speaking, this is not correct; the kilogram is the unit of mass, not of force or weight. A one-kilogram mass actually has a weight mg at earth's surface of $(1 \text{ kg})(9.8 \text{ m/s}^2) = 9.8$ N, and your 55-kg "weight" is really the mass associated with a weight of $(55 \text{ kg})(9.8 \text{ m/s}^2) = 540$ N. In the English system, in contrast, we customarily give weights in pounds. This is correct; the pound, like the newton, is a unit of force and therefore of weight. One pound is equivalent to 4.448 N. The English unit for mass is the **slug**, which is rarely used. On earth, the relation between mass in slugs and weight in pounds is again $W = mg$, where g in the English system is 32 ft/s² near earth's surface.

slug

In the reference frame of the earth, objects' weights are proportional to their masses. It is this proportionality that allows us to use the words "weight" and "mass" interchangeably in our everyday lives. But in physics, weight and mass mean very different things. Mass measures an object's resistance to acceleration, without any reference to gravity. Weight measures the force needed to give the acceleration of free fall. That we confuse them at all is the result of the remarkable fact that the free-fall acceleration of all objects at a given location is the same. This means that the *weight* of an object—a property defined in terms of free fall and gravity—is proportional to its *mass*—a property that seems to have nothing to do with gravitation. First inferred by Galileo in his experiments with falling bodies, this relation between gravitation and inertia seemed a coincidence until the early twentieth century. Finally, in his general theory of relativity, Albert Einstein showed how that simple relation reflects the underlying geometry of space and time in a way that links intimately the phenomena of accelerated motion and gravitation.

Fig. 4–15
When two people push a stalled car, the force they exert is the vector sum of their individual forces.

4.5
ADDING FORCES

In our previous examples, we considered only one force acting on an object. But often we can identify several forces acting (Fig. 4–15). The flight of a jet involves the forces associated with engine thrust, the force of air on the wings and body of the plane, and the force of gravity (Fig. 4–16). Indeed, for any object near earth, gravity is always among the forces acting.

Fig. 4–16
Forces on a jet include the force of the engines, the force of the air that provides both lift and drag, and the force of gravity. When the plane moves with constant velocity, these forces sum to zero.

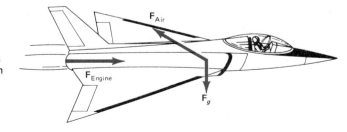

How are we to apply Newton's law in these multiple-force cases? The answer is given ultimately by experiment: we add vectorially the individual forces to find the **net force** on an object. Newton's second law then relates the object's mass and acceleration to this net force.

The *net force* is all-important! It is only the *net force* that matters in Newton's second law. There may be all sorts of forces acting on a body, but if they sum to zero, then the net force is zero and the body is not accelerating (Fig. 4–17). More generally, when the net force on a body is not zero, then that body must be accelerating with acceleration given by Newton's second law: $\mathbf{a} = \mathbf{F}_{net}/m$.

net force

Fig. 4–17
A seated person is not accelerating, so that the net force on the person must be zero. Since the gravitational force $\mathbf{F}_g$ acts, there must be another force to counteract gravity and make zero net force. That force is the upward contact force $\mathbf{F}_c$ from the chair. (Ultimately, this contact force arises from electrical interactions between the molecules of the person and the chair.)

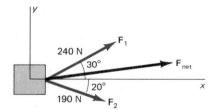

Fig. 4–18
Example 4–8. (View is from above; both x- and y-axes are in horizontal plane.)

Example 4–8
The Net Force

Two fishermen are pulling a 260-kg ice-fishing shanty on essentially frictionless runners, with forces shown in Fig. 4–18. What is the net force on the shanty? What is its acceleration?

Solution

The net force is the vector sum of all the forces acting. In the coordinate system shown in Fig. 4–18, we can write

$$F_{x1} = (240 \text{ N})(\cos 30°) = 208 \text{ N},$$

$$F_{y1} = (240 \text{ N})(\sin 30°) = 120 \text{ N},$$

$$F_{x2} = (190 \text{ N})[\cos(-20°)] = 179 \text{ N},$$

$$F_{y2} = (190 \text{ N})[\sin(-20°)] = -65 \text{ N},$$

where the negative sign shows that $\mathbf{F}_2$ lies clockwise from the x-axis. Then the net force may be written

$$\mathbf{F} = (208 \text{ N} + 179 \text{ N})\hat{\imath} + (120 \text{ N} - 65 \text{ N})\hat{\jmath} = 387\hat{\imath} + 55\hat{\jmath} \text{ N}.$$

This is a vector of magnitude

$$F = \sqrt{F_x^2 + F_y^2} = [(387 \text{ N})^2 + (55 \text{ N})^2]^{1/2} = 391 \text{ N}$$

that points at an angle

$$\theta = \tan^{-1}\left(\frac{F_y}{F_x}\right) = \tan^{-1}\left(\frac{55 \text{ N}}{387 \text{ N}}\right) = 8.1°$$

to the x-axis. The acceleration then has magnitude

$$a = \frac{F}{m} = \frac{391 \text{ N}}{260 \text{ kg}} = 1.5 \text{ m/s}^2,$$

and points in the same direction as the force.

Have we accounted for all forces in this example? Not quite: there are also a downward gravitational force and an upward contact force from the ice. But the shanty is not accelerating in the vertical direction, so that these two forces sum to zero. The force we have calculated is then the true net force on the shanty.

Example 4–9
An Elevator

A 740-kg elevator is accelerating upward at 1.1 m/s², pulled by a cable of negligible mass, as shown in Fig. 4–19. What is the tension force in the elevator cable?

Fig. 4–19
Forces on the elevator include the cable tension **T** and the gravitational force **F**$_g$; the net force is their vector sum. Since the elevator is accelerating upward, this net force must be upward.

Solution

This is an important example, and understanding it thoroughly will help you apply Newton's second law correctly in more complicated situations. We are given the acceleration and mass and asked for the force in the cable. Can't we just write **F** = m**a** for that force? No! **F** = m**a** is true only for the *net force*, and here the cable tension is not the only force acting. There is also the force of gravity which has magnitude mg and points downward. An important step in working a Newton's law problem is to identify *all* the forces acting on the object of interest. It's a good idea to draw all the force vectors so you can picture all the forces contributing to the net force. Here only the two forces of tension and gravity are acting; we have shown them in Fig. 4–19. Calling the tension force **T** and the gravitational force **F**$_g$, Newton's second law becomes

$$\mathbf{F} = \mathbf{T} + \mathbf{F}_g = m\mathbf{a}. \qquad (4\text{--}4)$$

You might be tempted to put minus signs in Equation 4–4 because the forces point in opposite directions. But not yet! Equation 4–4 is a *vector* equation stating that the *vector sum* of the forces acting is equal to the mass times the acceleration. Skipping the step of writing Newton's law in vector form will often get you into trouble with signs; that's why it's always best to write the full vector equation first. And in writing the vector equation, you don't need to worry about signs—they're built into the directional nature of the vectors.

Having written the vector form of Newton's second law for our problem, we next choose a coordinate system and write the components of Newton's law in that system. Here all the forces are vertical, so we choose our y-axis pointing vertically upward (vertically downward would do just as well, and would ultimately result in the same answer). Now we write the components of our vector equation 4–4. In this one-dimensional problem, there are no components of force or acceleration in the x- or z-directions (both horizontal), so that the x- and z-component equations read 0 = 0. Only the y-equation is interesting; formally, it reads

$$T_y + F_{gy} = ma_y. \qquad (4\text{--}5)$$

Now the tension force **T** points upward, or in the +y-direction; its vertical component T_y is positive and is equal to the magnitude T of **T**. The gravitational force **F**$_g$ has magnitude mg and points vertically downward, in the −y direction. Its vertical component F_{gy} is therefore $-mg$. Then Equation 4–5 is

$$T - mg = ma_y,$$

so that

$$T = ma_y + mg = m(a_y + g). \qquad (4\text{--}6)$$

Before putting in specific numbers, let us see if this result makes sense. Suppose the acceleration a_y were zero. Then the net force on the elevator would have to be zero. In this case, Equation 4–6 tells us that $T = mg$, showing that the tension force and gravity have the same magnitude. Since they point in opposite directions, they indeed sum to zero.

If, on the other hand, the elevator is accelerating upward, so that a_y is positive, then Equation 4–6 requires that the magnitude of the tension force exceed that of the gravitational force by an amount ma_y. Why is this? Because in this case the cable not only supports the elevator against gravity, but also provides the upward acceleration. For the numbers of this example, we have

$$T = m(a_y + g) = (740 \text{ kg})(1.1 \text{ m/s}^2 + 9.8 \text{ m/s}^2) = 8100 \text{ N}.$$

What if the elevator were accelerating downward? Then a_y is negative and Equation 4–6 shows that the tension force is less than mg. Does this make sense?

Yes: for a downward acceleration, the net force must be downward so that the magnitude of the downward gravitational force exceeds that of the upward tension force. Were the elevator in free fall, so that $a_y = -g$, the tension force would be exactly zero.

You probably could have reasoned out the answer to this problem in your head. But by applying the steps illustrated here—specifically, writing Newton's second law as a vector equation and then breaking it into components—you will be able to handle more complicated situations without confusion. We will outline the steps in solving a Newton's law problem more formally in the next chapter.

Fig. 4–20
When you push on a book, the book pushes back on you; otherwise you wouldn't feel its presence. The forces F_1 and F_2 have equal magnitudes and constitute an action-reaction pair.

Fig. 4–21
The combustion chamber of a rocket engine exerts a force F_1 on the hot gases, expelling them through the nozzle. In return, the gases exert a force F_2 of equal magnitude on the rocket, accelerating it forward.

action-reaction pair
third law of motion

Fig. 4–22
The horse exerts a force on the cart, and the cart exerts an equal but opposite force on the horse. So how can the two start moving? The answer comes from looking at the *net* force on the horse. This includes not only the backward-pointing force of the cart, but also a forward-pointing force that the road exerts on the horse in reaction to the horse's pushing against the road. As long as that force exceeds the pull of the cart, the pair will accelerate forward.

4.6
NEWTON'S THIRD LAW

Try pushing your book across the table. As you exert a force on the book, you feel the book pushing back on your hand (Fig. 4–20). Kick a ball with bare feet and your toes will hurt. Why? You've exerted a force on the ball, and the ball has also exerted a force back on you. Or imagine a rocket engine, exerting forces that expel hot gases out of its nozzle. Something else happens too: the hot gases exert a force on the rocket, accelerating it forward (Fig. 4–21).

Experimentally, we find that whenever one object exerts a force on the other, the second object also exerts a force on the first. The two forces are in opposite directions, but they have equal magnitudes. The familiar expression that "for every action there is an equal and opposite reaction" is Newton's statement of this fact in seventeenth-century language. By "action" Newton means an applied force. "Reaction" is the second force, equal in magnitude but opposite in direction. Technically, it never makes any difference which force we call the action and which the reaction; they are both always present as an **action-reaction pair.** Newton's statement about action and reaction constitutes his **third law of motion.** In more modern language, we express the third law by stating that

If object *A* exerts a force on object *B*, then object *B* exerts an oppositely directed force of equal magnitude on object *A*.

Notice that Newton's third law deals with *two forces* and also with *two objects*. The two forces of the action-reaction pair act on different objects. Therefore they do not cancel, even though they are of equal magnitude but opposite direction. Misunderstanding this point leads to a contradiction, embodied in the famous horse and cart dilemma: a horse pulls on a cart with a force **F.** But by Newton's third law, the cart pulls back on the horse with an equal but opposite force. So how can the horse-cart combination ever start moving (Fig. 4–22)? The answer lies in looking at *all* the forces on the horse. In addition to the backward-pointing force of the cart, there is also a forward-pointing force that occurs in reaction to the horse's feet pushing against the road. The forces of the road and the cart are *not* an action-reaction pair since one involves the horse-cart pair and the other the horse-road pair. So they need not have the same magnitude; as long as the road force exceeds the cart force, the pair will accelerate forward.

Fig. 4–23
Example 4–10

Example 4–10

Newton's Third Law

On a surface with negligible friction, you push with force **F** on a book of mass m_1 that in turn pushes on a book of mass m_2 (Fig. 4–23). What is the force exerted by the second book on the first?

Solution

Newton's *third* law tells us that the force of the second book on the first is equal in magnitude to that of the first book on the second. But what is that force? We can find it by applying Newton's *second* law to the combination of two books, then individually to the second book.

The total mass m of the two books is $m_1 + m_2$, and the net force applied to this combination is F (actually, this is only the horizontal component; the downward force of gravity and an upward force from the table also act, but they cancel). Then Newton's second law, $F = ma$, gives

$$a = \frac{F}{m} = \frac{F}{m_1 + m_2}.$$

This is the acceleration of the two books as they move together; since they are moving together, it is also the acceleration of each book individually. Now the only (horizontal) force on the second book is the force F_{12} exerted on it by the first book. So we can apply Newton's second law again to find this force:

$$F_{12} = m_2 a = m_2 \frac{F}{m_1 + m_2} = \frac{m_2}{m_1 + m_2} F.$$

Notice how, in applying Newton's second law, we always relate the *net* force on an object to the mass and acceleration *of that object*. Even though the applied force F acts on the first book, the acceleration of the first book is *not* F/m_1, because F is not the *net* force on that book. By Newton's third law, there is also a reaction force F_{21} exerted *by* the second book *on* the first; this force has the same magnitude as the force F_{12} that we just calculated, but it points in the opposite direction:

$$F_{21} = -F_{12} = -\frac{m_2}{m_1 + m_2} F.$$

Does all this make sense? We can see that it does by considering the motion of the first book. It too undergoes an acceleration $a = F/(m_1 + m_2)$. And what is the *net* force on it? For the first book, there are *two* forces acting in the horizontal plane: the applied force F and the reaction force F_{21} exerted by the second book. So the net force on the first book is

$$F_1 = F + F_{21}.$$

Using our expression for F_{21} then gives

$$F_1 = F - \frac{m_2}{m_1 + m_2} F = \frac{F(m_1 + m_2) - m_2 F}{m_1 + m_2} = \frac{m_1}{m_1 + m_2} F = m_1 a.$$

This is consistent with Newton's second law: we know that both books have the same acceleration $a = F/(m_1 + m_2)$, and indeed we find that the force on the first book is the product of that acceleration with the book's mass. Our result shows how Newton's second and third laws are both necessary for a fully consistent description of the motion.

Understanding this example thoroughly will give you confidence in applying Newton's laws of motion correctly.

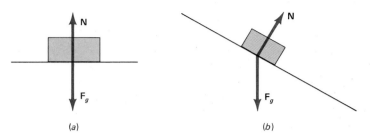

Fig. 4–24 ▲
Normal forces. *(a)* The upward force of a table on a block. *(b)* The normal force of a sloping surface on a block. Also shown in each case is the gravitational force on the block; since both the normal force and the gravitational force act on the same object, they do not constitute an action-reaction pair. In *(a)* the two forces balance, but in *(b)* they add to give a net force that accelerates the block down the slope.

◄ **Fig. 4–25**
Standing on the floor involves two action-reaction pairs: gravitational forces that the earth exerts on me and that I exert on the earth, and contact forces between my feet and the floor. The net force on each object is zero and therefore neither accelerates.

normal force

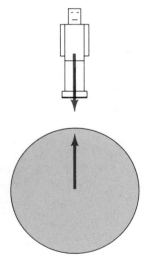

Fig. 4–26
Forces on me and on earth as we fall freely toward one another. The forces constitute an action-reaction pair, but since each acts on a different object and is the only force acting on that object, both objects accelerate. By Newton's third law, the force on each object has the same magnitude, but earth is so much more massive that its acceleration is negligibly small.

A contact force like the force between books in Example 4–10 acts at right angles to the surfaces of the objects that are pushing on each other. Such a force is called a **normal force.** ("Normal" comes from the Latin for "according to the carpenter's square.") Other examples of normal forces include the upward force of a table on an object, or the force normal to a sloping surface supporting an object (Fig. 4–24). (When friction is present, the force between two objects also has a component along the contacting surfaces. In that case, the term normal force refers only to the normal component—the component perpendicular to the surfaces.)

Newton's third law applies even for a force like gravity that doesn't involve direct contact. Since earth exerts a downward force on me, Newton's third law says that I must exert an upward force of equal magnitude on the earth. When I stand on the floor, the force of gravity $\mathbf{F}_{g1}$ on me is balanced by an upward normal force $\mathbf{N}_1$ from the floor. (These two forces don't constitute an action-reaction pair, since they both act on the same object—me.) Similarly, the upward force $\mathbf{F}_{g2}$ that I exert on earth—the reaction to earth's gravitational force on me—is balanced by a downward normal force $\mathbf{N}_2$ from my feet. All these forces are shown in Fig. 4–25. What if I jump off a table? Then the only force acting on me is earth's gravity, and I accelerate downward. But Newton's third law asserts that I exert an upward force on earth; since this force, too, is not cancelled by any other force, earth must accelerate upward as I fall. Does this really happen? Yes—but earth's acceleration is unnoticeably small. Why? Because, according to Newton's third law, the force I exert on earth has the same magnitude mg as the force earth exerts on me (Fig. 4–26). Applying Newton's second law shows that earth's acceleration has magnitude

$$a = \frac{F}{M_e} = \frac{mg}{M_e} = \frac{m}{M_e}\, g,$$

where m is my mass and M_e is the mass of the earth. Because the ratio m/M_e is about 10^{-23}, earth's acceleration toward me is negligibly small.

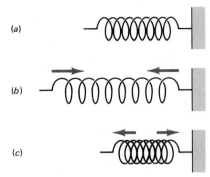

Fig. 4–27
(a) An unstretched spring attached to a wall. *(b)* When stretched, the spring exerts **tension forces** that oppose the stretching. *(c)* When compressed, it exerts **compression forces** that oppose the compression.

When we first listed Newton's laws in Section 4.1, we noted that Newton himself wrote his second law as a relation between force and the rate of change of "quantity of motion," or momentum, defined by $\mathbf{p} = m\mathbf{v}$. In Chapter 9, we will see how Newton's second law in this form combines with the third law to make a powerful statement about the momentum of systems consisting of more than one particle.

4.7
MEASURING FORCE

We have talked a lot about force in this chapter, but have not said much about how to measure this important physical quantity. Newton's second law provides us a direct way of determining force: apply an unknown force to a known mass and measure the resulting acceleration; the force is then the product of mass and acceleration.

Often, though, it is more convenient to use the properties of elastic objects like springs to measure forces. A spring, when stretched or compressed, exerts forces on whatever is deforming it (Fig. 4–27). In the case of a stretched spring, these forces are called **tension forces;** for a compressed spring, they are **compression forces.** In either case, Newton's third law requires that the forces be oppositely directed but of equal magnitude to the external forces acting on the ends of the spring to cause the stretching or compression.

Over a limited range of stretching and compression, the force exerted by a spring is directly proportional to the distance stretched or compressed. When this direct proportionality holds, the spring is said to obey **Hooke's law.** We then write

$$F = -kx, \qquad \text{(Hooke's law; ideal spring)} \qquad (4\text{–}7)$$

where x is the amount by which the spring is stretched or compressed from its normal state, and where the minus sign indicates that the spring force is directed oppositely to the stretching or compression. The constant k is called the **spring constant;** its units are obviously N/m. A spring with $k = 200$ N/m (typical of a spring a few inches long that you might hold in your hand) would exert a force of 2 N when stretched or compressed 1 cm. If it were an **ideal spring**—one that obeyed Hooke's law (Equation 4–7) no matter how much it was deformed—it would exert a force of 200 N when stretched 1 m. A real spring a few inches long would break before reaching 1 m in length, and at any rate would cease to obey Hooke's law well before that point (Fig. 4–28).

We can use a spring to make a **spring scale** by attaching an indicator and a scale calibrated in force units (Fig. 4–29). Common bathroom scales, hanging scales in supermarkets, and laboratory spring scales are all examples of such scales. Even electronic scales widely used at supermarket checkouts are spring scales, with their "spring" a material that produces an electrical signal when it is deformed by an applied force.

We can use a spring scale to weigh objects by attaching one end of the scale to a fixed point and hanging the unknown weight from the other end (Fig. 4–30). When the object hangs at rest on the scale, the scale force is

tension forces
compression forces

Hooke's law

spring constant

ideal spring

spring scale

Fig. 4–28
Force curve for ideal and real springs. The slopes are negative, indicating that the force is opposite to the deformation. Negative values of *x* mean compression; positive values mean stretching.

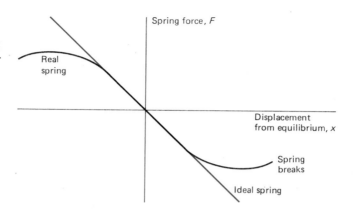

Fig. 4–29
A simple spring scale, made from a spring of known spring constant *k,* an indicating needle, and a scale calibrated in force units.

just enough to keep it from accelerating. By definition, the force of the scale on the object is then equal to the object's weight in the scale's frame of reference. Since mass is proportional to weight in a given frame of reference, the spring scale also provides a measure of the object's mass.

Example 4–11
Weighing a Fish

When a fish is suspended from a spring of spring constant $k = 320$ N/m, the spring stretches 15 cm. What are the weight and mass of the fish?

Solution

From Equation 4–7, a 15-cm stretch corresponds to a spring force of magnitude

$$F = kx = (320 \text{ N/m})(0.15 \text{ m}) = 48 \text{ N}.$$

Since the net force on the fish is zero, the magnitude of the fish's weight is also 48 N. But weight in earth's frame of reference is just mg, so that $m = W/g = (48 \text{ N})/(9.8 \text{ m/s}^2) = 4.9$ kg.

When a spring scale is accelerating, then the weight it reads is that of the object in the accelerating reference frame of the scale. Newton's law shows that this weight must differ from the weight in an inertial (nonaccelerating) frame of reference. Why? Because only in the inertial frame is the net force on the object zero when it is at rest on the scale. In an accelerating frame, there must be a nonzero net force on the object for it to accelerate with the scale; therefore, the scale force and the gravitational force do not balance. When the object and scale are accelerating, the situation is like that of Example 4–9, with the scale playing the role of the elevator cable. The scale reading will be more or less than the actual weight depending on whether the acceleration is upward or downward.

Example 4–12
A Helicopter Ride

A helicopter is rising vertically, carrying a load of concrete to the top of a mountain to make the foundation for a ski lift. A 35-kg bag of concrete is resting on a scale in the helicopter. A construction worker in the copter notes that the scale reads 280 N. What is the acceleration of the copter?

Fig. 4–30
Using a spring scale to determine weight. The scale is a special demonstration model, with the spring mounted outside the scale body.

Fig. 4–31
Forces on the concrete of Example 4–12.

Solution

This problem is similar to Example 4–9. The two forces acting on the bag of concrete are the force of gravity $\mathbf{F}_g$ and the force of the scale $\mathbf{F}_s$ (Fig. 4–31). Newton's second law tells us that the net force is the product of mass and acceleration:

$$\mathbf{F} = \mathbf{F}_g + \mathbf{F}_s = m\mathbf{a}.$$

Since the motion is entirely vertical, we need work only with the vertical component of this equation. With the positive y-direction upward, the vertical component of the downward gravitational force is $-mg$; that of the scale force is positive and is equal to the magnitude F_s of the scale force. Then the y-component of Newton's second law for this case becomes

$$-mg + F_s = ma_y,$$

so that the vertical acceleration is

$$a_y = \frac{-mg + F_s}{m} = -g + \frac{F_s}{m} = -9.8 \text{ m/s}^2 + \frac{280 \text{ N}}{35 \text{ kg}} = -1.8 \text{ m/s}^2.$$

What does this negative result mean? It means that the direction of the helicopter's *acceleration* is downward—even though the copter is *moving* upward. That is, its speed is decreasing at the rate of 1.8 m/s² even as it rises. The result of this example is consistent with that of Example 4–9. There, a downward acceleration would result in a cable tension lower than the weight mg in the earth frame of reference. Here, a downward acceleration results in a scale reading lower than the weight in the earth frame as suggested by the length of the force vectors in Fig. 4–31. The magnitude and direction of the *velocity* are completely irrelevant.

We can also use spring scales to exert known forces on objects, as shown in Fig. 4–32. We attach the scale to the object and pull on the spring scale in such a way that the scale reading remains constant. In the absence of friction or other forces, the scale reading is then the net (horizontal) force on the object. If we measure the resulting acceleration, we can use Newton's law to calculate the object's mass. In a frame of reference at rest on earth, it is much easier to determine mass by hanging an object vertically from a scale. But in a freely falling reference frame like an orbiting spacecraft, this second approach must be used (see Examples 4–6 and 4–13).

Fig. 4–32
Using a spring scale to apply a known force to an unknown mass. In the absence of friction, the force on the mass is equal to the scale reading. (The force applied at the other end of the scale is greater, though, because it also accelerates the scale.)

Example 4–13
Determining Mass in Orbit

A biologist is studying the growth of rats in an orbiting space laboratory. To determine a rat's mass, she puts it in a 320-g cage, attaches a spring scale, and pulls so that the scale reads 0.46 N. If the resulting acceleration of rat and cage is 0.40 m/s², what is the mass of the rat?

Solution

The spring scale reading F_s is the force on the cage and rat, so that Newton's second law gives

$$F_s = (m_r + m_c)a,$$

where m_r and m_c are the rat and cage mass, respectively. Then

$$m_r = \frac{F_s}{a} - m_c = \frac{0.46 \text{ N}}{0.40 \text{ m/s}^2} - 0.32 \text{ kg} = 0.83 \text{ kg}.$$

In pulling on the scale, the biologist must exert a greater force than the 0.46-N scale force. Why? Because in addition to the rat and cage, she is also accelerating the mass of the scale.

accelerometer

Finally, if we attach a known mass to a spring scale and fasten the other end of the scale to a vehicle or other moving object, we then have an **accelerometer** that can be used to measure the acceleration of the object. This application is explored in Problem 28.

SUMMARY

1. Newton's **first law of motion** states that a body continues in uniform motion unless acted on by a force. Philosophically, the first law represents a shift from the Aristotelian notion that the natural state of motion for objects on earth is rest. In Newton's view, uniform motion is a natural state; the study of motion then emphasizes not the cause of motion itself, but the cause of *changes* in motion.

2. Newton's **second law of motion** quantifies the change in motion brought about by a force. The law states that the rate of change of a body's momentum (product of mass and velocity; symbol **p**) is equal to the net force on the body:

$$\mathbf{F} = \frac{d\mathbf{p}}{dt}.$$

As long as the mass of the body does not change, Newton's second law can also be written in the form

$$\mathbf{F} = m\mathbf{a}.$$

Newton's second law is valid only when **F** is the **net force** on a body—that is, the vector sum of all forces acting on the body. The SI unit of force is the **newton**, defined as the force that gives a 1-kg mass an acceleration of 1 m/s².

3. The **weight** of a body is defined as the force that would be required to give the body the acceleration of free fall in a particular frame of reference. In a reference frame fixed with respect to earth or another gravitating object, the magnitude of a body's weight is just the body's mass multiplied by the local acceleration of gravity: $W = mg$. Objects in a freely falling frame of reference have no acceleration relative to their reference frame; therefore they are **weightless.** Weightlessness does not imply the absence of gravitational force; instead, weightlessness arises because all objects at the same place experience the same gravitational acceleration and therefore fall freely without accelerating relative to one another.

4. Newton's **third law of motion** states that forces always come in **action-reaction pairs.** When one object exerts a force on another, the second object exerts an oppositely directed force of equal magnitude back on the first. Newton's second and third laws together permit a consistent description of the motions of interacting objects.

5. Elastic objects like springs provide a practical way of measuring forces. When the force exerted by a spring is directly proportional to the amount of stretch or compression, the spring is said to obey **Hooke's law;** the force is then given by

$$F = -kx, \qquad \text{(Hooke's law)}$$

where k is the **spring constant,** with SI units of N/m.

QUESTIONS

1. Distinguish between the Aristotelian and Galilean/Newtonian view of the natural state of motion.
2. Use Newton's laws of motion to explain the function of a padded dashboard in a car.
3. A ball bounces off a wall with the same speed it had before it hit the wall. Has its momentum changed? Has a force acted on the ball? Has a force acted on the wall? Relate your answers to Newton's laws of motion.
4. Give several examples from the history of physics in which seemingly unrelated forces were found to be related.
5. We often use the term "inertia" to describe human sluggishness. How is this usage related to the meaning of inertia in physics?
6. Why do subway riders lurch?
7. My high school physics teacher defined mass as "inverse pushability aroundness." Comment.
8. Which of the fundamental forces do you deal with in everyday life? Give several examples.
9. Does a body necessarily move in the direction of the net force on it?
10. Given that $\mathbf{F} = m\mathbf{a}$, is it possible to have a net force acting on a body that is at rest? Explain.

11. Can a motorcycle and a truck have the same momentum? Explain.

12. How would you weigh yourself (a) on the moon and (b) in an orbiting spacecraft?

13. Does the length of time that a force is applied to an object affect the change in the object's momentum? Explain.

14. Does the length of time that a force is applied to an object affect the object's acceleration? Explain.

15. An elevator in the physics building at the University of Colorado includes a built-in physics demonstration consisting of a 98-N weight suspended from a spring scale. Is the scale reading more than, less than, or equal to 98 N when the elevator (a) is stationary; (b) first starts moving upward; (c) moves steadily upward; (d) slows down on its way up; (e) starts moving downward; (f) moves steadily downward; (g) slows down on its way down?

16. The surface gravity of Jupiter's moon Io is one-fifth that of earth. What would happen to your weight and to your mass if you were to travel to Io?

17. What does it mean to say that someone "weighs" 50 kilograms?

18. Consider two teams in a tug-of-war (Fig. 4–33). Newton's third law says that the force team A exerts on team B is equal in magnitude to the force team B exerts on team A. How, then, can either team win?

19. Describe the action and reaction forces involved in kicking a football.

20. What is the force that ultimately stops the movement of a braking car?

Fig. 4–33 A tug-of-war (Question 18).

21. If you move from bow to stern of a canoe, the canoe moves in the opposite direction. Why?

22. As you sit in your chair, the chair exerts an upward force on you. Why don't you accelerate upward?

23. As you sit in a car, what direction is the force exerted on you by the car seat (a) when the car moves at constant speed; (b) when the car accelerates in the forward direction; (c) when the car brakes while moving in a straight line; (d) while the car rounds a corner at constant speed?

24. As your plane accelerates down the runway, you take your keys from your pocket and suspend them by a thread. Do they hang vertically? Explain.

25. Since every force has an oppositely directed reaction force of equal magnitude, how can there ever be a net force on an object?

26. A friend thinks that astronauts are weightless because there is no gravity in outer space. Criticize this statement, and supply your friend with a correct explanation for weightlessness.

PROBLEMS

Section 4.3   *Newton's Second Law*

1. A subway train has a mass of 1.5×10^6 kg. What force is required to accelerate the train at 2.5 m/s^2?

2. A railroad locomotive with a mass of 6.1×10^4 kg can exert a force of 1.2×10^5 N. At what rate can it accelerate (a) by itself and (b) when pulling a 1.4×10^6-kg train?

3. The maximum braking force of a 1400-kg car is about 8000 N. Estimate the stopping distance when the car is travelling (a) 40 km/h; (b) 60 km/h; (c) 80 km/h; (d) 55 mi/h.

4. A car leaves the road travelling at 95 km/h and hits a tree, coming to a complete stop in 0.16 s. What force does a seatbelt exert on a 55-kg passenger during this collision?

5. Suppose the passenger in the previous problem were not wearing a seatbelt. What force would the passenger experience in striking a padded dashboard that compresses 8.0 cm on impact? Assume that the car had come to a full stop by the time the passenger struck the dashboard. (Is this a consistent assumption?)

6. As a function of time, the velocity of an object of mass m is given by $\mathbf{v} = bt^2\hat{\mathbf{i}} + (ct + d)\hat{\mathbf{j}}$, where b, c, and d are constants with appropriate units. What is the force acting on the object, as a function of time?

7. In an x-ray tube, electrons are accelerated to speeds on the order of 10^8 m/s, then slammed into a target where they come to a stop in about 10^{-18} s. Estimate the average stopping force on each electron.

8. A 3800-kg jet touches down at 240 km/h on the deck of an aircraft carrier, and immediately deploys a parachute to slow itself down. If the plane comes to a stop in 170 m, what is the average force of air on the parachute? Assume the parachute provides essentially all the stopping force.

Section 4.4   *The Force of Gravity*

9. My spaceship crashes on one of the sun's nine planets. Fortunately, the ship's scales are intact, and show that my weight is 532 N. If I know my mass to be 60 kg, where am I? *Hint:* Consult Appendix F.

10. If I can barely lift a 50-kg concrete block on earth, how massive a block can I lift on the moon?

11. The frictional force between a car's tires and the road has a magnitude that is 75 percent of the car's weight. What is the maximum possible acceleration for this car?

Section 4.5   *Adding Forces*

12. A 65-kg parachute jumper descends at a steady 40 km/h. What is the force of the air on the parachute?

13. A 10-kg mass is suspended at rest by two strings attached to walls, as shown in Fig. 4–34. What are the tension forces in the two strings?

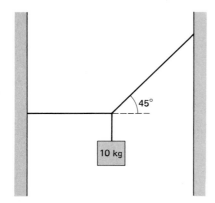

Fig. 4–34   Problem 13

14. A 3700-kg barge is being pulled along a canal by two mules, as shown in Fig. 4–35. The tension in each tow rope is 1100 N, and the ropes make 25° angles with the forward direction. What force does the water exert on the barge (*a*) if it moves with constant velocity and (*b*) if it accelerates forward at 0.16 m/s²?

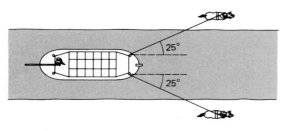

Fig. 4–35   Problem 14

15. At lift-off, a space shuttle with 2.0×10^6 kg total mass undergoes an upward acceleration of 0.60 g. (*a*) What is the total thrust (force) developed by its engines? (*b*) By what factor is the weight of an astronaut increased in the reference frame of the accelerating shuttle?

16. An airplane accelerates down the runway at 3.3 m/s². A passenger suspends a 25-g watch from a thread. (*a*) What angle does the thread make with the vertical? (*b*) What is the tension in the thread?

17. A 15-kg monkey hangs from the middle of a massless rope as shown in Fig. 4–36. What is the tension in the rope? Compare with the monkey's weight.

Fig. 4–36   Problem 17

18. Two forces act on a 3.1-kg mass, which undergoes acceleration $\mathbf{a} = 0.91\hat{\imath} - 0.27\hat{\jmath}$ m/s². If one of the forces is $\mathbf{F}_1 = -1.2\hat{\imath} - 2.5\hat{\jmath}$ N, what is the other force?

19. A block of mass m slides with acceleration a down a frictionless slope that makes an angle θ to the horizontal; the only forces acting on it are the force of gravity $\mathbf{F}_g$ and the normal force $\mathbf{N}$ of the slope, as shown in Fig. 4–37. Show that <u>the magnitude of the normal force is given by $N = m\sqrt{g^2 - a^2}$.</u>

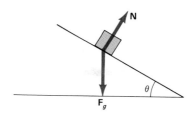

Fig. 4–37   Problem 19

Section 4.6   *Newton's Third Law*

20. In a tractor pulling contest, a 2300-kg tractor pulls a 4900-kg sledge with an acceleration of 0.61 m/s². If the tractor exerts a horizontal force of 7700 N on the ground, determine the magnitudes of (*a*) the force of the tractor on the sledge, (*b*) the force of the sledge on the tractor, and (*c*) the frictional force exerted on the sledge by the ground.

21. A 2200-kg airplane is pulling two gliders, the first of mass 310 kg and the second of mass 260 kg, down the runway with an acceleration of 1.9 m/s² (Fig. 4–38). Neglecting the mass of the two ropes and any frictional forces, determine (*a*) the horizontal thrust of the plane's propeller; (*b*) the tension force in the first rope; (*c*) the tension force in the second rope; and (*d*) the net force on the first glider.

Fig. 4–38 Problem 21

22. A 68-kg astronaut pushes off a 420-kg satellite, exerting a force of 120 N for the 2.9 s they are in contact. How far apart are the two after 1 minute?
23. I have a mass of 65 kg. If I jump off a 120-cm-high table, how far toward me does earth move during the time I fall?

Section 4.7 *Measuring Force*

24. A spring with spring constant $k = 340$ N/m is used to weigh a 6.7-kg fish. How far does the spring stretch?
25. Two springs have the same unstretched length but different spring constants k_1 and k_2. (a) If they are connected side-by-side and stretched a distance x, as shown in Fig. 4–39a, show that the force exerted by the combination is $(k_1 + k_2)x$. (b) If they are now connected end-to-end and the combination is stretched a distance x (Fig. 4–39b), show that they exert a force $k_1 k_2 x/(k_1 + k_2)$.

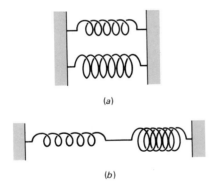

(a)

(b)

Fig. 4–39 Problem 25

26. An elastic tow rope has a spring constant of 1300 N/m. It is connected between a truck and a 1900-kg car. As the truck tows the car, the rope stretches 55 cm. Starting from rest, how far do the truck and car move in 1 min? Assume the car experiences negligible friction.
27. A 7.2-kg mass is hanging from the ceiling of an elevator by a spring of spring constant 150 N/m whose unstretched length is 80 cm. What is the overall length of the spring when the elevator (a) starts moving upward with acceleration 0.95 m/s^2; (b) moves upward at a steady 14 m/s; (c) comes to a stop while moving upward at 14 m/s, taking 9.0 s to do so? (d) If the elevator measures 3.2 m from floor to ceiling,

what is the maximum acceleration it could undergo without the 7.2-kg mass hitting the floor?

28. An accelerometer consists of a spring of spring constant $k = 1.25$ N/m and unstretched length $\ell_0 = 10.0$ cm fastened to a frictionless surface by a pivot that allows it to swivel in any direction in a horizontal plane. A 50.0-g mass is attached to the other end of the spring, as shown in Fig. 4–40. The whole system is mounted securely in an automobile. When the vehicle accelerates, the spring provides a force to keep the 50-g mass accelerating with the vehicle; by measuring the stretch of the spring, the acceleration can then be determined. To calibrate the accelerometer, circles marked with values of acceleration can be drawn on its frictionless surface. (a) How far apart should the circles be if each represents an acceleration of 0.250 m/s^2 larger than the next smaller circle? (b) What should be the radius of the circle marked 2.0 m/s^2? (c) How do you read the direction of the car's acceleration from this device?

Fig. 4–40 Top view of accelerometer for Problem 28.

Supplementary Problems

29. Tarzan (mass 73 kg) slides down a vine that can withstand a maximum tension force of 580 N before breaking. What minimum acceleration must Tarzan have?
30. A 90-kg weightlifter is standing on a scale calibrated in newtons, holding a 140-kg barbell. (a) What does the scale read? (b) The lifter then gives the barbell a constant upward acceleration. If the scale reads 2400 N, what is the acceleration of the barbell? (c) Suppose the lifter were in an orbiting spaceship with his feet contacting an identical scale. If he gave the barbell the same acceleration as in (b), what would the scale read? Assume in (b) and (c) that the lifter keeps his body rigid, bending only his arms, and neglect the mass of the arms and any downward acceleration of the lifter.

31. To escape a dog, a 1.3-kg squirrel runs up a vertical tree trunk, accelerating at 0.82 m/s². What is the average vertical force the tree exerts on the squirrel?

32. The second floor of a house can safely carry a load of 3500 N for each square meter of floor. Can it support a waterbed measuring 1.4 m wide by 1.8 m long by 25 cm thick? (The density of water is 1 g/cm³.)

33. A string is draped over a pulley, and masses m_1 and m_2 are tied to its two ends, as shown in Fig. 4–41. String and pulley have negligible mass, and the pulley is lubricated so that friction is negligible. Show that the magnitude of the two blocks' acceleration is given by

$$a = \frac{m_2 - m_1}{m_2 + m_1}\,g,$$

where a positive result corresponds to an upward acceleration of m_1.

Fig. 4–41 Problem 33

34. A child sends a 2.3-kg stone sliding across a frozen pond at 11 m/s. If the stone slides 67 m before stopping, what is the average frictional force acting on the stone?

35. Three identical massless springs of unstretched length ℓ and spring constant k are connected to three equal masses m as shown in Fig. 4–42. A force is applied at the top of the upper spring to give the whole system the same acceleration a. Determine the length of each spring.

36. A block of mass m_1 on a frictionless table top is connected by a massless string over a massless, frictionless pulley to a mass m_2 (Fig. 4–43). Determine (a) the string tension and (b) the magnitude of the blocks' acceleration.

37. A block of mass M hangs from a rope of length ℓ and mass m. Find an expression for the tension in the rope as a function of the distance y measured vertically downward from the top of the rope.

38. A tow truck exerts a 750-N force on a 54.4-kg tow chain. The other end of the chain is attached to a car, and the whole system accelerates at 0.436 m/s². Find

Fig. 4–42 Problem 35

(a) the force exerted on the truck by the cable, (b) the force exerted on the car by the cable, and (c) the mass of the car. Assume there are no horizontal forces acting on the car except for the cable. Why are your answers to (a) and (b) different?

39. In throwing a 200-g ball, your hand exerts a constant upward force of 9.4 N for 0.32 s. How high does the ball rise after leaving your hand?

40. What downward force is exerted on the air by the blades of a 4300-kg helicopter when it is (a) hovering at constant altitude; (b) dropping at 21 m/s with speed decreasing at 3.2 m/s²; (c) rising at 17 m/s with speed increasing at 3.2 m/s²; (d) rising at a steady 15 m/s; (e) rising at 15 m/s with speed decreasing at 3.2 m/s²?

41. What engine thrust (force) is needed to accelerate a rocket of mass m (a) downward at 1.40g near earth's surface; (b) upward at 1.40g near earth's surface; (c) at 1.40g in interstellar space far from any star or planet?

Fig. 4–43 Problem 36

42. An elevator cable can withstand a maximum tension of 19,500 N before breaking. The elevator has a mass of 490 kg, and a maximum acceleration of 2.24 m/s^2. Engineering safety standards require that the cable tension never exceed two-thirds of the breaking tension. How many 65-kg people can the elevator safely accommodate?

43. You have a mass of 60 kg, and you jump from a 78-cm-high table onto a hard floor. (a) If you keep your legs rigid, you come to a stop in a distance of 2.9 cm, as your body tissues compress slightly. What force does the floor exert on you? (b) If you bend your knees when you land, the bulk of your body comes to a stop over a distance of 0.54 m. Now estimate the force exerted on you by the floor. Neglect the fact that your legs stop in a shorter distance than the rest of you.

44. An electric winch is lifting a 230-kg engine out of a car using a steel cable and pulley, as shown in Fig. 4–44. Find the force of the cable on the pulley if the engine accelerates upward at 0.24 m/s^2. Neglect friction and the mass of the cable.

Fig. 4–44   Problem 44

45. The force of air resistance is roughly proportional to the square of an object's speed, and is directed oppositely to the velocity: $F_{air} = -cv^2$, where c is a constant that depends largely on the shape of the falling body. As a result of air resistance, a falling object eventually reaches a constant **terminal speed**, at which it ceases to accelerate. The constant c for a 70-kg skydiver is approximately 0.30 N·s^2/m^2 (this depends on how the diver's body is oriented). Find (a) the skydiver's acceleration while falling at 25 m/s and (b) find the terminal speed.

46. An F-14 jet fighter has a mass of 1.6×10^4 kg and an engine thrust of 2.7×10^5 N. A 747 jumbo jet has a mass of 3.6×10^5 kg and a total engine thrust of 7.7×10^5 N. Is it possible for either plane to climb vertically, with no lift from its wings? If so, what vertical acceleration could it achieve?

47. A spider of mass m_s drapes a silk thread of negligible mass over a stick with its far end a distance h off the ground as shown in Fig. 4–45. The stick is lubricated by a drop of dew, so that there is essentially no friction between silk and stick. The spider waits on the ground until a fly of mass m_f lands on the other end of the silk and sticks to it. The spider immediately begins to climb her end of the silk. (a) With what acceleration must she climb to keep the fly from falling? (b) If she climbs with acceleration a_s, at what height y above the ground will she encounter the fly?

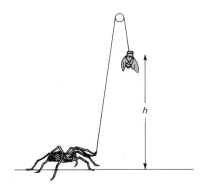

Fig. 4–45   Problem 47

48. Each of the Viking spacecraft that landed on Mars used retrorockets to begin its descent to the Martian surface. At the beginning of the rocket firing, the craft had a mass of 1070 kg, and its rocket engine developed a thrust of 2840 N. If it dropped vertically with its retrorocket firing downward to slow the fall, what was its acceleration? Assume the craft was close enough to the Martian surface to neglect any variation in the local value of g.

5

USING NEWTON'S LAWS

Fig. 5–1
The orbit of Halley's Comet and the trajectory of the European Space Agency's Giotto spacecraft from earth to its encounter with the comet in March, 1986. Careful application of Newton's laws to the motions of both objects made possible Giotto's approach to within 605 km of the comet's nucleus.

With his three laws of motion, Newton gave us the means to understand most aspects of motion throughout the entire universe. The important concepts he codified—such as force and inertia—provide our basic knowledge of how objects move. By quantifying the relation between force and motion, Newton showed how we can solve in detail for the motions of objects in specific cases (Fig. 5–1).

In this chapter, we apply Newton's laws in a variety of physical situations. The basic methods we use are at the heart of all applications of Newton's laws, from the simplest textbook problems to the most complicated computer programs that guide space probes to distant planets. As you read through the examples, don't look on each one as an entirely new thing to learn about. Rather, think about how the examples are related and how they all represent applications of the same basic physical laws.

5.1
USING NEWTON'S SECOND LAW

Newton's second law, $\mathbf{F} = m\mathbf{a}$, is the cornerstone of mechanics. That law relates the *net force* on an object to the acceleration *of that object*. To apply Newton's law, we must identify the object whose motion interests us and all the forces that together provide the net force acting on that object. Only then can we write Newton's law and solve the equations it provides. In working Newton's law problems, you will find the following steps helpful in correctly applying the law and developing from it a mathematical description of each problem:

1. Identify the object of interest.
2. Identify all the forces acting on the object, and draw them on a vector diagram. (This diagram is often called a "free-body diagram.")

3. Write Newton's second law, **F** = m**a**, *in vector form,* using for **F** the vector sum of the forces in your diagram.
4. Choose a convenient coordinate system, and draw the coordinate axes on your force diagram.
5. Write the components of your vector equation in your chosen coordinate system. Be guided in this by the geometry of the force diagram, and by any constraints on the motion (for example, the constraint that an object move along a given surface).
6. Solve the equations symbolically for whatever the problem asks you to find.
7. Ask whether your results make sense. In particular, ask about extreme cases such as purely horizontal or purely vertical motion to see if they lead to results that you have seen before or that are physically obvious.
8. Finally, insert numerical values and work the arithmetic, if numerical answers are called for.

Don't memorize these steps. Rather, you should refer to them as you begin to work problems, and will gradually come to realize that they simply reflect the full meaning of Newton's second law. Later, as you develop confidence in problem solving, you can take short cuts. But whenever you deal with a complicated problem, following these steps will help avoid confusion.

Example 5–1
An Inclined Surface

A block of mass m slides without friction on a surface tilted at an angle θ to the horizontal. Find its acceleration and the magnitude of the force the block exerts on the surface.

Solution

Here we outline the solution in the context of our eight steps:

1. The object of interest is the block.
2. There are two forces on the block: the gravitational force **F**$_g$ and the normal force **N** from the surface. Both are shown in Fig. 5–2.
3. In vector form, Newton's second law becomes

$$\mathbf{F}_g + \mathbf{N} = m\mathbf{a}. \tag{5–1}$$

4. Now we choose a coordinate system. Since gravity points vertically downward, you might pick a system with horizontal and vertical axes. But a better choice has axes parallel and perpendicular to the slope, for then two of the three vectors in Equation 5–1—the acceleration and the normal force—have only one nonzero component. The individual component equations will be simpler in such a coordinate system, which we show superimposed on Fig. 5–2. (In Example 5–1b we repeat this example using a horizontal/vertical coordinate system to show that the choice of coordinate system affects only the ease of computation, not the results.)
5. We now write the components of Equation 5–1. In our tilted coordinated system, the normal force has no x-component, but the gravitational force does. From Fig. 5–3, we see that the x-component of the gravitational force is $F_g \sin\theta$; since the magnitude F_g is mg, we have $F_{gx} = mg \sin\theta$. Are the signs right here? Yes: the gravitational force points vertically downward, and our positive x-direction is downslope, so that the x-component of the gravitational force must be positive.

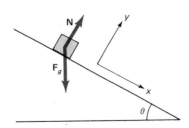

Fig. 5–2
Force diagram for block sliding on incline.

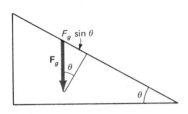

Fig. 5–3
The two triangles shown are similar, so that the angles marked θ are equal. Since the sine of an angle is the ratio of opposite side to hypotenuse, the x-component of the gravitational force **F**$_g$ is $F_g \sin\theta$.

What about the acceleration? The block is constrained to move along the slope, so that there is no y-component of acceleration. Since the x-component of force is positive, so is the x-component of acceleration, which is therefore just the magnitude a. Then the x-component of Newton's law is

$$mg \sin\theta = ma.$$

Similarly, the y-component of the gravitational force is $-mg \cos\theta$; with no acceleration perpendicular to the slope, the y-component of Newton's law reads

$$N - mg \cos\theta = 0.$$

6. Now we solve these equations for the quantities of interest. The x-equation gives immediately

$$a = g \sin\theta,$$

while the y-equation gives

$$N = mg \cos\theta.$$

This is the magnitude of the force that the surface exerts on the block; by Newton's third law, it is also the magnitude of the force that the block exerts on the surface.

7. To check our results, we can consider extreme values for the angle θ. When $\theta = 0$, corresponding to a horizontal surface, we have $\sin\theta = 0$ so that $a = 0$, as we expect. In this case $N = mg$, and the surface supports the entire weight of the block. When $\theta = 90°$, $\sin\theta = 1$ and $a = g$. In this case the block falls freely; the normal force is $mg \cos 90° = 0$, so that the presence of the surface is irrelevant.

8. There are no numerical values in this example.

Our result in this example shows that a frictionless, sloping surface "dilutes" the acceleration of gravity. It was through the use of such "diluted" gravity on inclined planes that Galileo first probed the laws of motion.

Example 5–1a

Leveling an Air Track

An air track used in a physics lab is supported on adjustment screws 88 cm apart (Fig. 5–4). When the track is not quite level, a glider released from rest at one end reaches the other end, 120 cm away, in 6.8 s. By how much should the support near the higher end be dropped in order to level the track?

Solution

From Example 5–1, we know that the acceleration down a sloping track is given by $a = g \sin\theta$. Here we are given the distance the accelerating glider travels in a known time; from this we can use Equation 2–11 to get the acceleration:

$$x - x_0 = \tfrac{1}{2}at^2,$$

so that

$$a = \frac{2(x - x_0)}{t^2},$$

where $x - x_0$ is the 120-cm length of the track. Since $a = g \sin\theta$, the track is tilted at an angle θ given by

$$\sin\theta = \frac{a}{g} = \frac{2(x - x_0)}{gt^2}.$$

In Fig. 5–5, we see an exaggerated view of the sloping track; from the figure, we see that the high end must be dropped by an amount $h = d \tan\theta$, where d is the 88-cm

Fig. 5–4
An air track (Example 5–1a).

Fig. 5–5
Exaggerated view of the sloping track. Angle θ is actually so small that $\sin\theta$ is very nearly equal to $\tan\theta$.

spacing between supports. But for very small angles, sine and tangent are essentially equal (see Appendix A), so that the high end must be dropped by

$$h = d \tan\theta \simeq d \sin\theta = \frac{2d(x - x_0)}{gt^2}$$

$$= \frac{2(0.88 \text{ m})(1.2 \text{ m})}{(9.8 \text{ m/s}^2)(6.8 \text{ s})^2} = 4.7 \times 10^{-3} \text{ m} = 4.7 \text{ mm}.$$

Example 5–1b

Another Coordinate System

Rework Example 5–1, solving for the acceleration using a coordinate system with x- and y-axes horizontal and vertical, respectively.

Solution

Steps 1 to 3 of our solution procedure are independent of the choice of coordinate system, so the forces are still as shown in Fig. 5–2 and Newton's second law is still given by Equation 5–1. The essential physics is summed up in that equation; the rest of the problem is algebra.

In Fig. 5–6 we show the forces on a horizontal/vertical coordinate system. The gravitational force is simpler in this system; it has only a vertical component given by $F_{gy} = -mg$. But now the normal force has two components; from Fig. 5–6, we see that they are $N_x = N \sin\theta$ and $N_y = N \cos\theta$. What about the acceleration? The block is constrained to accelerate down the slope, so from Fig. 5–7 we then have $a_x = a \cos\theta$ and $a_y = -a \sin\theta$, where a is the magnitude of the acceleration. Having resolved the forces and acceleration into components, we rewrite Equation 5–1 and then give its components in our coordinate system:

$$\mathbf{F_g} + \mathbf{N} = m\mathbf{a} \tag{5–1}$$

x-component: $\qquad\qquad\qquad N \sin\theta = ma \cos\theta \tag{5–2}$

y-component: $\qquad\quad -mg + N \cos\theta = -ma \sin\theta. \tag{5–3}$

With our sensible choice of coordinate system in Example 5–1, we needed only one of the component equations to get the acceleration; here, with a less appropriate coordinate system, we must deal with both equations. Solving Equation 5–2 for the unknown normal force N gives

$$N = \frac{ma \cos\theta}{\sin\theta};$$

using this result in Equation 5–3, we have

$$-mg + \frac{ma \cos^2\theta}{\sin\theta} = -ma \sin\theta.$$

Multiplying through by $\sin\theta$ and rearranging the equation gives

$$ma(\cos^2\theta + \sin^2\theta) = mg \sin\theta.$$

But $\cos^2\theta + \sin^2\theta = 1$, so we recover our previous result,

$$a = g \sin\theta.$$

Of course we *had* to get the same result, because we described the same physical situation. But our poor choice of coordinate system resulted in more complicated algebra. Comparison of Examples 5–1 and 5–1b shows that a little thought about coordinate systems can save a good deal of mathematical effort.

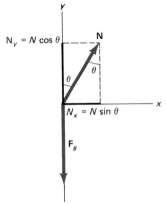

Fig. 5–6
Forces of Example 5–1 on a horizontal/vertical coordinate system. Also shown is the breakdown of the normal force **N** into components $N_x = N \sin\theta$ and $N_y = N \cos\theta$. (The triangle formed by N_x, N_y, and the vector **N** is a right triangle, and the trig functions sine and cosine are defined as ratios of opposite and adjacent sides to the hypotenuse of a right triangle.)

Fig. 5–7
The acceleration vector points downslope, so its components are $a_x = a \cos\theta$ and $a_y = -a \sin\theta$.

Example 5–2

An Equilibrium Situation

A horizontal force of what magnitude is needed to keep the block of Example 5–1 from sliding?

Solution

Now there are three forces acting: gravity, the normal force, and the horizontal restraining force $\mathbf{F}_h$, as shown in Fig. 5–8. Newton's second law then reads

$$\mathbf{F}_g + \mathbf{N} + \mathbf{F}_h = m\mathbf{a} = 0, \qquad (5\text{–}4)$$

where we set the right-hand side to zero because we want $\mathbf{F}_h$ to keep the block from accelerating. Now two of the three nonzero vectors in our equation point in the horizontal or vertical direction, so that we are best off with the horizontal/vertical coordinate system of Example 5–1b. In this system, the gravitational force has only a vertical component $-mg$, and the normal force breaks down as in Example 5–1b into components $N_x = N\sin\theta$ and $N_y = N\cos\theta$. What about $\mathbf{F}_h$? It points in the negative x-direction, so it has only an x-component $-F_h$. Then the components of Newton's second law (Equation 5–4 in this case) become

x-component:
$$N\sin\theta - F_h = 0 \qquad (5\text{–}5)$$

and

y-component:
$$-mg + N\cos\theta = 0. \qquad (5\text{–}6)$$

Solving Equation 5–6 for the normal force gives

$$N = \frac{mg}{\cos\theta}.$$

Using this result in Equation 5–5, we have

$$F_h = \frac{mg}{\cos\theta}\sin\theta = mg\tan\theta.$$

Does this answer make sense? When $\theta = 0$, corresponding to a horizontal surface, then $\tan\theta = 0$ and therefore $F_h = 0$. Of course: it takes no force to prevent acceleration on a horizontal surface. As the slope approaches vertical, however, $\tan\theta \to \infty$, and it becomes impossible for a purely horizontal force $\mathbf{F}_h$ to prevent the acceleration.

Fig. 5–8
Forces on the block of Example 5–2.

5.2
FRICTION

We have seen how the presence of friction prevented scientists before Galileo and Newton from recognizing the true nature of motion. Further, we have generally considered frictionless systems in our examples and problems. But friction does occur in real systems. What is friction, and how can we deal with it?

Friction is a force that acts between two surfaces to oppose their relative motion. Even the smoothest of surfaces is highly irregular on a microscopic scale (Fig. 5–9). When two surfaces are placed in contact, their irregularities adhere because of electrical forces between their molecules (Fig. 5–10). The result is a force that opposes relative motion of the sur-

Fig. 5–9
Electron micrograph of a cracked eggshell shows that the apparently smooth surface is actually rough on a microscopic scale.

Fig. 5–10
(a) When two surfaces are in contact, microscopic irregularities in the two surfaces adhere, giving rise to a force that opposes their relative motion. Only the microscopic irregularities actually touch, so that the actual contact area is much less than the measured area. (b) When the normal force between the surfaces increases, the microscopic contact area increases as the irregularities are crushed together. This increases the frictional force.

(b)

faces; in order to move them, an external force must be applied to break the microscopic electrical bonds.

On earth, friction can rarely be ignored. As much as 20 per cent of the gasoline burned in a car is used to overcome friction in the engine. But frictional forces are also beneficial to the car; without friction between tires and road, the car could not stop, start, or turn corners. And it is friction between your feet and the floor that lets you walk.

We distinguish two types of friction: (1) kinetic, or sliding, friction and (2) static friction.

Kinetic Friction

kinetic friction

Kinetic friction is the friction between surfaces in relative motion. It is kinetic friction that slows down a book you shove across a table, or makes it hard to push a heavy trunk even at constant speed. Experimentally, we find that the force of kinetic friction is independent of the surface areas that seem to be in contact, but is proportional to the normal force acting between the surfaces. Intuitively, you might have expected the frictional force to increase with increasing contact area. On a microscopic scale, your intuition is correct: the greater the area *in actual contact,* the greater the friction. But microscopically, only a small fraction of the area you measure macroscopically is actually in contact with the other surface (Fig. 5–10a). As the normal force between the surfaces increases, the surface irregularities are crushed together and the actual contact area increases, so that the frictional force increases (Fig. 5–10b).

We can characterize the force of kinetic friction mathematically by writing

$$F_k = \mu_k N, \tag{5–7}$$

where F_k is the force of kinetic friction, N the normal force between the two surfaces, and μ_k the **coefficient of kinetic friction,** a quantity that depends on the properties of the two surfaces. Equation 5–7 relates only the magnitudes; the direction of the frictional force is opposite to the relative motion of the surfaces, and is therefore perpendicular to the normal force (Fig. 5–11).

Since both F_k and N have the units of force, the coefficient of kinetic friction is a dimensionless quantity; it has no units. μ_k ranges from about 0.01 for very smooth surfaces to 1.5 for the roughest surfaces. That is, the force of friction on a smooth surface is about 1 per cent of the normal force; if you push an object on a smooth horizontal surface, you must apply a force about 1 per cent of the object's weight. On a rough surface, on the other hand, you may have to push an object with a force greater than its weight just to keep it moving horizontally at constant speed. No wonder Aristotle was confused about the laws of motion!

Fig. 5–11
The force of kinetic friction $\mathbf{F}_k$ acts to oppose relative motion $\mathbf{v}$, and is therefore parallel to the surfaces in contact and perpendicular to the normal force. In the absence of an applied force to the right, the block shown here would be decelerated by the frictional force.

coefficient of kinetic friction

Example 5-3

Pulling a Trunk

A trunk of mass m is being pulled across a heavy floor by means of a massless rope that makes an angle θ with the horizontal. The coefficient of friction between trunk and floor is μ_k. What rope tension is required to move the trunk at constant velocity?

Solution

The trunk is our object of interest; Fig. 5-12 shows that the forces include the rope tension **T**, the force of kinetic friction $\mathbf{F}_k$, the normal force **N**, and the gravitational force $\mathbf{F}_g$. Since the trunk moves with constant velocity, its acceleration is zero and therefore the net force is zero:

$$\mathbf{T} + \mathbf{F}_k + \mathbf{N} + \mathbf{F}_g = 0.$$

The frictional force acts only in the horizontal direction, while the normal and gravitational forces act only in the vertical direction. So we choose a coordinate system with x-axis horizontal and in the direction of the trunk's motion, and with y-axis pointing vertically upward. From Fig. 5-12, we see that the tension force has horizontal and vertical components $T_x = T\cos\theta$ and $T_y = T\sin\theta$, respectively. Equation 5-7 shows that the magnitude of the frictional force is $\mu_k N$; this force points in the negative x-direction to oppose the trunk's motion. Finally, the normal and gravitational forces are entirely vertical, with the vertical component of the gravitational force given by $-mg$ since it points downward. Then the two components of Newton's law are

x-component: $T\cos\theta - \mu_k N = 0$

y-component: $T\sin\theta + N - mg = 0.$

Solving the y-equation for the normal force N gives $N = mg - T\sin\theta$; using this result in the x-equation, we have

$$T\cos\theta - \mu_k(mg - T\sin\theta) = 0,$$

or

$$T(\cos\theta + \mu_k\sin\theta) = \mu_k mg.$$

Then the rope tension T is

$$T = \frac{\mu_k mg}{\cos\theta + \mu_k\sin\theta}.$$

Does this result make sense? As $\mu_k \to 0$, the frictional force vanishes and the force needed to pull the trunk at constant velocity becomes zero, in accordance with Newton's first law. And as the frictional force increases, it becomes more difficult to pull the trunk. We can also look at extreme possibilities for the angle θ: for $\theta = 0$, we have $\cos\theta = 1$ and $\sin\theta = 0$, so that $T = \mu_k mg$. When we pull with a horizontal force on a horizontal surface, the force we must provide is just the coefficient of friction times the object's weight. But in the more general case, the upward component of the tension force helps balance the gravitational force, so that the normal force and therefore the frictional force are lowered. Finally, when $\theta = 90°$, our result gives $T = mg$, independent of μ_k. And this makes sense, too: here we are lifting the trunk vertically; with no acceleration, we provide a force equal to the trunk's weight. Friction plays no role because the trunk is no longer sliding along the surface.

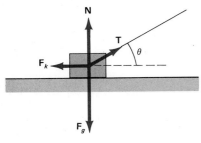

Fig. 5-12
Forces on a trunk being pulled across a level floor include the rope tension **T**, the force of kinetic friction $\mathbf{F}_k$, the normal force **N**, and the gravitational force $\mathbf{F}_g$. Only the tension force has nonzero components in both the horizontal and vertical directions; the figure shows that these are $T_x = T\cos\theta$ and $T_y = T\sin\theta$.

Example 5–4

An Incline with Friction

A child sleds down a 20° snow-covered slope. If the mass of the child and sled together is 38 kg, and the coefficient of kinetic friction is $\mu_k = 0.085$, what is the child's acceleration? At what angle would the child slide with constant speed?

Solution

Here the forces on the child and sled together include only gravity, the normal force, and the frictional force, as shown in Fig. 5–13. Newton's second law then reads

$$\mathbf{F}_g + \mathbf{N} + \mathbf{F}_k = m\mathbf{a}.$$

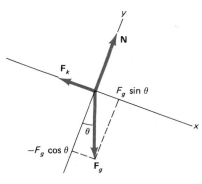

Fig. 5–13
Forces on the child and sled.

As in Example 5–1, the simplest coordinate system is one with axes parallel and perpendicular to the slope. In this system the gravitational force has an x-component $mg \sin\theta$ (see Fig. 5–14), while the frictional force points upslope, or in the negative x-direction; $F_{kx} = -\mu_k N$. So the x-component of Newton's law becomes

x-component: $\qquad mg \sin\theta - \mu_k N = ma.$

There is no acceleration in the y-direction, perpendicular to the slope; forces in the y-direction include the normal force N and the y-component $-mg \cos\theta$ of the gravitational force (see Fig. 5–14), so that the y-component of Newton's law is

y-component: $\qquad N - mg \cos\theta = 0.$

Solving the y-equation gives $N = mg \cos\theta$; using this result in the x-equation, we have

$$a = g \sin\theta - \mu_k g \cos\theta,$$

where the mass m cancels from all terms. Note that if $\mu_k = 0$, we recover the result $a = g \sin\theta$ for acceleration down a frictionless slope.

For the sled to slide with constant velocity, its acceleration must be zero; then

$$g \sin\theta = \mu_k g \cos\theta,$$

so that

$$\mu_k = \frac{\sin\theta}{\cos\theta} = \tan\theta.$$

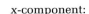

Fig. 5–14
Resolving the forces into components. The magnitude F_g of the gravitational force is mg, so the components become $F_{gx} = mg \sin\theta$ and $F_{gy} = -mg \cos\theta$.

Does this make sense? As the slope becomes very steep, $\tan\theta$ increases without bound and it takes a very large frictional force to counteract gravity. For a horizontal slope, on the other hand, $\tan\theta = 0$ and the sled slides with constant velocity only in the absence of friction: $\mu_k = 0$.

For the numbers of this example, we have

$$a = g(\sin\theta - \mu_k \cos\theta) = (9.8)[\sin 20° - (0.085)(\cos 20°)] = 2.6 \text{ m/s}^2$$

for the acceleration on a 20° slope, and

$$\theta = \tan^{-1}\mu_k = \tan^{-1}(0.085) = 4.9°$$

when the sled undergoes no acceleration.

Note that in working this problem we could not write the frictional force as μ_k times the weight mg. Why not? Because the frictional force depends on the *normal force*, whose magnitude is not equal to the weight when the object is on a sloping surface.

Fig. 5–15
Example 5–5

Example 5–5
Losing a Piano

Workers are pulling a 190-kg piano up a building using a massless rope over a frictionless corner, as shown in Fig. 5–15. When lunchtime arrives, the workers tie the rope to a 210-kg desk, leaving the piano dangling 5.3 m above the ground. Unfortunately, the desk begins to slide; the coefficient of kinetic friction is $\mu_k = 0.71$. What is the acceleration of the piano? At what speed does it hit the ground?

Solution

In this example, we must solve two related Newton's law problems: one for the motion of the piano and one for the desk. Let m_1 be the mass of the piano and m_2 that of the desk. Figure 5–15 shows the forces acting on each. For the piano they are the gravitational force $\mathbf{F}_{g1}$ and the tension force $\mathbf{T}_1$. For the desk they are the gravitational force $\mathbf{F}_{g2}$, the normal force $\mathbf{N}$, the tension force $\mathbf{T}_2$, and the frictional force $\mathbf{F}_k$. So we write Newton's law for each object:

piano: $$\mathbf{F}_{g1} + \mathbf{T}_1 = m\mathbf{a}_1$$

desk: $$\mathbf{F}_{g2} + \mathbf{N} + \mathbf{T}_2 + \mathbf{F}_k = m\mathbf{a}_2,$$

where $\mathbf{a}_1$ and $\mathbf{a}_2$ are the respective accelerations.

Given the geometry of the situation, we can use the same horizontal/vertical coordinate system for each object. (More generally, we might want two different coordinate systems; see Problem 4.) For the piano, the gravitational force points downward and has magnitude $m_1 g$; the tension force points upward and has magnitude T_1. Clearly the acceleration points downward, so that the y-component of Newton's law for the piano becomes

$$-m_1 g + T_1 = -m_1 a_1, \qquad (5\text{–}8)$$

where a_1 is the magnitude of the acceleration. (Had the direction of the acceleration not been obvious, we could have written ma_{y1} on the right-hand side and let the algebra determine the correct sign.)

The desk experiences forces in both horizontal and vertical directions; with its acceleration strictly horizontal, components of Newton's law for the desk are

y-component: $$-m_2 g + N = 0 \qquad (5\text{–}9)$$

x-component: $$T_2 - \mu_k N = m_2 a_2. \qquad (5\text{–}10)$$

Solving Equation 5–9 for the normal force and using the result in Equation 5–10, we have

$$T_2 - \mu_k m_2 g = m_2 a_2. \qquad (5\text{–}11)$$

So far we have not used the fact that the two masses are, in fact, connected by a single rope. Because of this connection, the magnitudes of their accelerations must be the same. Furthermore, the rope is massless and passes over a frictionless corner, so that no force is required to accelerate it; therefore, the tensions at the two ends of the rope are of equal magnitude. So $a_1 = a_2 = a$ and $T_1 = T_2 = T$, so we can drop the subscripts on a and T. Equations 5–8 and 5–11 then become

$$-m_1 g + T = -m_1 a$$

$$T - \mu_k m_2 g = m_2 a.$$

These are two equations in the two unknowns T and a. Solving the first equation for T gives $T = m_1(g - a)$; using this result in the second equation, we have

$$m_1(g - a) - \mu_k m_2 g = m_2 a.$$

Solving for the acceleration a then gives

$$a = \frac{(m_1 - \mu_k m_2)g}{m_1 + m_2}.$$

Does this result make sense? Consider first the frictionless case $\mu_k = 0$. Then $a = m_1 g/(m_1 + m_2)$. This is the acceleration we would expect for an object of mass $m_1 + m_2$ subject to a force $m_1 g$. Next consider the case $m_2 = 0$. Then there is no friction and no force needed on m_2; the rope tension is zero and mass m_1 falls freely with acceleration g. On the other hand, if m_2 or the coefficient of friction become large enough that $m_1 - \mu_k m_2 = 0$, then there is no acceleration and the masses move with constant speed or, if at rest, remain at rest.

For the numbers of this example, we have

$$a = \frac{(m_1 - \mu_k m_2)g}{m_1 + m_2} = \frac{[190 \text{ kg} - (0.71)(210 \text{ kg})](9.8 \text{ m/s}^2)}{190 \text{ kg} + 210 \text{ kg}} = 1.0 \text{ m/s}^2.$$

The piano falls a distance $h = 5.3$ m; Equation 2–14 then shows that it hits the ground with speed

$$v = \sqrt{2ah} = \sqrt{(2)(1.0 \text{ m/s}^2)(5.3 \text{ m})} = 3.3 \text{ m/s}.$$

Smash!

Static Friction

static friction

Kinetic or sliding friction is associated with microscopic bonds that continually form and break as the surfaces slide past each other. In contrast, **static friction** describes the frictional force between two surfaces at rest with respect to each other. When two surfaces are stationary, more bonds have time to form, so that a greater force is needed to initiate relative motion.

coefficient of static friction

The static friction between two surfaces is characterized by the **coefficient of static friction,** μ_s, which relates the frictional force to the normal force. Consider a typical situation involving static friction: a book resting on a table (Fig. 5–16). With no externally applied forces in the horizontal

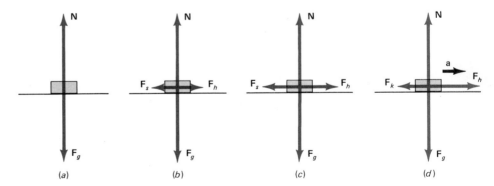

Fig. 5–16
A book on a table. In the vertical direction, the normal force balances the gravitational force. *(a)* With no externally applied horizontal force, the force of static friction is also zero. *(b)* When a horizontal force F_h of magnitude less than $\mu_s N$ is applied, a static frictional force of the same magnitude acts to oppose the applied force. *(c)* An applied force of magnitude $\mu_s N$ is the largest that the static frictional force can balance. *(d)* For applied forces of magnitude greater than $\mu_s N$, the book begins to accelerate; its subsequent motion is determined by the applied force and the force of kinetic friction.

direction, the frictional force must be zero; otherwise there would be an unbalanced frictional force on the book and it would accelerate. If we apply a small force in the horizontal direction, we find that the book still does not move; evidently the force of static friction has the same magnitude as the applied force. As the applied force is increased, there comes a point when the force of static friction can no longer balance the applied force; then the book begins to slide and its subsequent motion is governed by the applied force and the force of kinetic friction. Experimentally, we find that the maximum value for the static frictional force is proportional to the normal force between the surfaces. We are able to describe static friction by writing

$$F_s \leq \mu_s N. \tag{5--12}$$

Because bonds between stationary surfaces are harder to break, the coefficient of static friction μ_s is generally higher than the coefficient of kinetic friction μ_k.

Example 5–6

Static Friction

A 2.5-kg block is placed on a horizontal board, and the board is gradually tilted. The block remains at rest until the board makes an angle of 38° to the horizontal, at which point it begins to slide. What is the coefficient of static friction?

Solution

Figure 5–17 shows the situation, which is identical to that of Example 5–4 except that static friction replaces kinetic friction until the block begins to slide. Following Example 5–4, we can immediately write

$$\mathbf{F}_g + \mathbf{N} + \mathbf{F}_s = 0$$

for Newton's second law before the block starts to slide. Then, using the tilted coordinate system of Example 5–4, and setting the frictional force to its maximum value $\mu_s N$, the components of Newton's law become

x-component: $mg \sin\theta - \mu_s N = 0$

y-component: $-mg \cos\theta + N = 0,$

where θ is the maximum angle at which the block remains at rest. Solving the y-equation for N and using the result in the x-equation gives

$$mg \sin\theta - \mu_s mg \cos\theta = 0,$$

so that

$$\mu_s = \frac{\sin\theta}{\cos\theta} = \tan\theta.$$

Does this make sense? When $\theta = 0$, μ_s must be zero, showing that the block can slide freely without friction. As $\theta \to 90°$, the coefficient of friction must become very large. This is partly because the downslope component of the gravitational force becomes larger, but more importantly it is because the normal force gets smaller, so that a much larger coefficient of friction is needed to counteract the increasing downslope component of gravity. For the numbers of this example, we have

$$\mu_s = \tan 38° = 0.78.$$

Fig. 5–17
Example 5–6

Fig. 5–18
Forces on the hog. The static friction force provides the acceleration of the hog; it points forward to oppose the tendency of the hog to slip backward with respect to the truck.

Example 5–7

Transporting a Hog

A farmer loads a 170-kg hog onto a flatbed truck. If the coefficient of static friction between hog and truck is 0.21, what is the maximum acceleration the truck should undergo if the hog is not to slide out the back?

Solution

Here the object of interest is the hog; as long as the hog is not slipping relative to the truck, the forces on it include static friction, gravity, and a normal force (Fig. 5–18). Are you tempted to draw another force so that the forces on the hog sum to zero? DON'T! If it stays with the truck, the hog is *accelerating*, and there had better be a nonzero net force to provide that acceleration. Static friction ($\mathbf{F}_s$) is that force.

Newton's second law for the hog reads

$$\mathbf{F}_s + \mathbf{F}_g + \mathbf{N} = m\mathbf{a},$$

where **a** is the acceleration of the hog, which is equal to that of the truck as long as the hog does not slip. In a coordinate system with y-axis pointing vertically upward, and x-axis in the direction of the acceleration, the components of Newton's law become

y-component: $-mg + N = 0$

x-component: $\mu_s N = ma.$

Setting the frictional force to its maximum value $\mu_s N$ gives the maximum acceleration; the frictional force enters with a positive sign because it points in the +x-direction, opposing not the motion of the truck but any tendency of the hog to slip backward relative to the truck. Solving the y-equation for the normal force N and using the result in the x-equation, we find that the mass cancels, leaving

$$a = \mu_s g.$$

Does this make sense? Yes: with purely horizontal motion, the normal force is equal to the hog's weight mg, so the maximum frictional force is just the fraction μ_s of the hog's weight. According to Newton's second law, the corresponding maximum acceleration is $a = F/m$, or $\mu_s g$. For this problem, $a = (0.21)(9.8 \text{ m/s}^2) = 2.1 \text{ m/s}^2$ is the maximum acceleration the farmer should give the truck.

Example 5–7 shows that the force of static friction can be useful in accelerating objects. Other cases where static friction plays this accelerating role including walking and driving. When you walk, the foot in contact with the ground is temporarily at rest, pushing back against the ground. The reaction force to this backward push is the forward-pointing force of static friction that accelerates you forward (Fig. 5–19). On a near-frictionless surface, walking becomes very difficult (Fig. 5–20). An accelerating car

Fig. 5–19
Forces involved in walking. The foot in contact with the ground is temporarily at rest. It pushes back against the ground, exerting the static frictional force $\mathbf{F}_1$ on the ground. In reaction, the ground pushes forward on the foot with the equal but opposite frictional force $\mathbf{F}_2$. Transmitted through muscle and bone, this is the force that accelerates your upper body forward.

Fig. 5–20
Walking is difficult on a frictionless surface!

By permission of Johnny Hart and News America Syndicate.

Fig. 5–21
The frictional force between tires and road stops the car. (Here we show only the frictional forces on the tires; each tire exerts an equal but opposite frictional force on the road.)

is in a similar situation. If the tires are not slipping, the bottom of each tire—the part in contact with the road—is instantaneously at rest. The tire pushes back against the road, and in reaction the force of static friction pushes forward to accelerate the car. When the car brakes, the wheel pushes forward against the road, and the reaction force of friction points backward to stop the car (Fig. 5–21). Note that the brakes only stop the wheel's spinning; it is friction that stops the car. You know this if you've ever applied your brakes on ice!

Application

Automotive Safety

Why do we talk about *static* friction in connection with an accelerating car? Because the part of the tire in contact with the road is instantaneously at rest as long as there is no slipping or skidding. That the coefficient of static friction is higher than that of kinetic friction has important implications for automobile safety (Fig. 5–22). When you slam on your brakes so hard that the wheels lock and slide along the road, the force between tires and road is *kinetic* friction. When you pump the brakes so that the wheels keep rolling without slipping, the bottoms of the tires are instantaneously at rest with respect to the road, and the force is that of *static* friction. Since $\mu_s > \mu_k$, the deceleration is greater and therefore the stopping distance is shorter.

To provide the safest possible braking, several manufacturers have developed computer-controlled braking systems. Sensors check the wheel motion many times each second and feed their information to a computer. Just as the car begins to skid, the computer responds by momentarily releasing pressure on the brakes, thereby maintaining a static friction situation and the greatest possible stopping force. Figure 5–23 shows the decrease in stopping distance achieved with such a system.

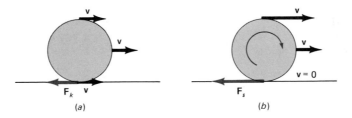

Fig. 5–22
(a) In a wheel that is locked and skidding, all points move with the same velocity. Kinetic friction then acts between the wheel and road. *(b)* When the brakes are pumped so that the wheel keeps rolling, the bottom of the tire is instantaneously at rest so the force acting is that of static friction. Because the coefficient of static friction is greater, the stopping distance is reduced when the wheels are kept rolling.

Asphalt
- 50 km/h: 11.5 m / 13.5 m
- 100 km/h: 45 m / 53 m

Ice
- 30 km/h: 29 m / 32 m
- 50 km/h: 73 m / 103 m

Packed snow
- 30 km/h: 23 m / 34 m
- 50 km/h: 51 m / 85 m

Stopping distance (m): 0   20   40   60   80   100

Fig. 5–23
Stopping distances for computerized braking system (colored bars) and for conventional system (gray bars). Maximum brake pedal pressure is applied in both cases. Computer-controlled system keeps wheels rolling so that the coefficient of static friction remains operative. With the conventional system wheels skid, and the lower coefficient of sliding friction results in a longer stopping distance. (Data from Robert Bosch Automotive Equipment Division.)

Example 5–8
Stopping a Car

The kinetic and static coefficients of friction between a car's tires and a dry road are 0.81 and 0.89, respectively. If the car is travelling at 88 km/h when the brakes are applied, determine (a) the minimum stopping distance and (b) the stopping distance with the wheels fully locked.

Solution

Figure 5–24 shows the forces on the car; they include gravity, the normal force, and a frictional force $\mathbf{F}_f$. We have worked enough examples to see that the normal force in this case of horizontal motion is equal in magnitude to the weight mg. Then the horizontal component of Newton's law reads

$$-\mu mg = ma_x,$$

or

$$a_x = -\mu g,$$

where the negative sign appears because we have taken the positive x-direction in the direction of the car's motion. Equation 2–14 relates distance and acceleration: $v_x^2 = v_{x0}^2 + 2a_x\Delta x$. Putting $v_x^2 = 0$ to get the stopping distance, and using $a_x = -\mu g$, the stopping distance Δx becomes

$$\Delta x = \frac{v_{x0}^2}{-2a_x} = \frac{v_0^2}{\mu g}.$$

The car's initial speed is 88 km/h or 24 m/s; using the appropriate coefficients for μ, the stopping distances are

Fig. 5–24
Forces on a braking car.

$$\Delta x_{\text{no skid}} = \frac{v_0^2}{\mu_s g} = \frac{(24 \text{ m/s})^2}{(0.89)(9.8 \text{ m/s}^2)} = 66 \text{ m}$$

and

$$\Delta x_{\text{skid}} = \frac{v_0^2}{\mu_k g} = \frac{(24 \text{ m/s})^2}{(0.81)(9.8 \text{ m/s}^2)} = 73 \text{ m}.$$

The 7-m difference could well be enough to prevent an accident.

5.3
CIRCULAR MOTION

The giant planet Jupiter, over 300 times more massive than earth, circles the sun at a speed of 13 km/s. A nimble sports car rounds a tight curve at 120 km/h. Protons circle the 2-km Fermilab accelerator at nearly the speed of light.

What keeps these objects in their circular paths? The answer, according to Newton's first law, is a force. For Jupiter, it is a gravitational force; for the sports car, a frictional force between tires and road; and for the proton, a magnetic force. And how big is that force? Newton's second law tells us: the force required to give an object of mass m an acceleration $\mathbf{a}$ is $\mathbf{F} = m\mathbf{a}$. For an object in circular motion at constant speed v, we know from Section 3.4 that the object accelerates—because of its changing direction—at the rate $a = v^2/r$. The direction of the acceleration is toward the center of the circle. So for an object of mass m to be in uniform circular motion, a net force of magnitude

$$F = ma = \frac{mv^2}{r} \qquad \text{(force in uniform circular motion)} \qquad (5\text{–}13)$$

must act on the object; the force vector must be directed toward the center of the circular path. Whenever we see an object in uniform circular motion, we know that a net force of this magnitude must be acting. Something—gravity, tension in a string, an electric or magnetic force, friction, or some other physical mechanism must provide that force.

Newton's second law describes circular motion in exactly the same way that it does any other motion: by relating the net force, the mass, and the acceleration. We can analyze circular motion using exactly the same steps we outlined in Section 5.1, for we are dealing with exactly the same law of motion.

Example 5–9
A Mass on a String

A ball of mass m is whirled around in a horizontal circle at the end of a string of length ℓ. The string makes an angle θ with the horizontal. Determine (a) the speed of the ball and (b) the tension in the string.

Solution

To see that this circular motion problem is like any other Newton's law problem, we apply rigorously the steps outlined in Section 5.1:

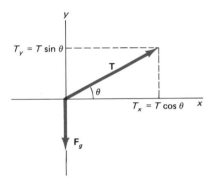

Fig. 5–25
Forces on a ball being whirled about at the end of a string.

1. The object of interest is the ball.
2. There are two forces acting on the ball: the string tension and the gravitational force, as shown in Fig. 5–25. Are you tempted to draw a third force in Fig. 5–25, perhaps pointing outward to balance the other two? DON'T! The tension and gravitational forces *DO NOT BALANCE*. Why not? Because the ball is accelerating, so that there must be a nonzero net force acting on it! Or maybe you're tempted to draw a third force pointing inward, the force mv^2/r. DON'T! mv^2/r is *not* another physical force; it is the magnitude of the mass times the acceleration, and gives the magnitude of the net physical force that must be applied to provide that acceleration. Here, that net force is provided by gravity and the tension force.
3. Newton's law tells us that $\mathbf{F} = m\mathbf{a}$; here we have

$$\mathbf{T} + \mathbf{F}_g = m\mathbf{a}.$$

4. Now we choose a coordinate system. The tension force is at some angle θ to the horizontal. The gravitational force is purely vertical. What about the acceleration? It points toward the center of the circular path—that is, horizontally. So if we choose a horizontal/vertical coordinate system, then two of the three terms in Newton's law will have only one nonzero component. Figure 5–26 shows the forces with appropriate coordinate axes.
5. The downward-pointing gravitational force $\mathbf{F}_g$ has a vertical component $F_{gy} = -mg$; from Fig. 5–26 we see that the tension force $\mathbf{T}$ has a vertical component $T_y = T\sin\theta$, where T is the magnitude of $\mathbf{T}$. The acceleration has no component in the vertical direction, so that the y-component of Newton's law becomes

y-component: $\qquad\qquad T\sin\theta - mg = 0.$

The gravitational force has no horizontal component, while Fig. 5–26 shows that the horizontal component of the tension force is $T_x = T\cos\theta$. At the point where we show the ball in Fig. 5–25, the acceleration points entirely in the x-direction. The constraint that the ball move in a circle tells us that the magnitude of the acceleration is mv^2/r, where r is the radius of the circular path. From Fig. 5–25, we see that this radius is $\ell\cos\theta$. Then the x-component of the acceleration is $mv^2/\ell\cos\theta$, so that the x-component of Newton's law becomes

x-component: $\qquad\qquad T\cos\theta = \dfrac{mv^2}{\ell\cos\theta}.$

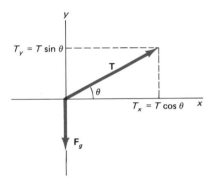

Fig. 5–26
Force components on a horizontal/vertical coordinate system.

6. Now we're ready to solve for the tension and speed. The vertical equation gives the tension:

$$T = \frac{mg}{\sin\theta}.$$

Using this result in the horizontal equation, we have

$$\frac{mg}{\sin\theta}\cos\theta = \frac{mv^2}{\ell\cos\theta},$$

or

$$v = \sqrt{\frac{g\ell\cos^2\theta}{\sin\theta}}.$$

7. Do these results make sense? When $\theta = 90°$, so that the string hangs vertically downward, $\cos\theta = 0$ and therefore $v = 0$. In this case there is no acceleration, and the tension is vertically upward and equal in magnitude to the weight. But as $\theta \to 0°$, $\sin\theta \to 0$ and the speed v becomes very large. This tells us that it is not possible to whirl the ball around with the string exactly horizontal. Why not?

Because there must always be a vertical component of string tension to balance the ball's weight. As the speed increases, so does the string tension, and therefore the vertical component can be a smaller fraction of the total tension. But it can never be zero.

8. There are no numerical values in this example.

Example 5-10
Steering a Car

A level road makes a 90° turn with a 95-m radius of curvature. What is the maximum speed with which a car can negotiate this turn (*a*) when the road is dry and the coefficient of static friction is 0.88 and (*b*) when the road is snow-covered and the coefficient of static friction is 0.21?

Solution

Figure 5-27 shows the forces on the car as it rounds the corner. The only force acting in the horizontal direction is the force of static friction between tires and road. Why *static* friction? Because there is no motion of the tire in the radial direction, perpendicular to the car (Fig. 5-28). This frictional force is what provides the car's acceleration; with the car in a circular path of radius r, we can write

$$\mu_s N = \frac{mv^2}{r}$$

for the horizontal component of Newton's second law. Here we have used the maximum possible value, $\mu_s N$, for the frictional force because we want the maximum possible speed v. In the vertical direction there is no acceleration, so that the normal force balances gravity: $N = mg$. Substituting this result in the horizontal equation, we have

$$\mu_s mg = \frac{mv^2}{r},$$

so that

$$v = \sqrt{\mu_s g r}.$$

Does this make sense? On a frictionless road, $v = 0$: you can't corner without a force to deflect you from a straight-line path. With friction, the maximum safe speed increases as the curve becomes more gradual—that is, with increasing r.

For the numbers of this example, we have

$$v_{\text{dry road}} = [(0.88)(9.8 \text{ m/s}^2)(73 \text{ m})]^{1/2} = 25 \text{ m/s} = 90 \text{ km/h}$$

and

$$v_{\text{snow}} = [(0.21)(9.8 \text{ m/s}^2)(73 \text{ m})]^{1/2} = 12 \text{ m/s} = 44 \text{ km/h}.$$

If you exceed these speeds, your car must inevitably move in a path of greater radius—and that means going off the road!

Example 5-11
Designing a Road

Curves in roads designed for safe, high-speed travel are usually banked so that the normal force of the road has a component toward the center of the curve; this allows vehicles to turn without relying on the force of friction. At what angle should the road of the previous example be banked, if it is designed for travel at 55 km/h (15 m/s) without relying on friction?

Fig. 5-27
Forces on a car rounding a corner include gravity, the normal force, and the force of static friction between tires and road.

Fig. 5-28
Cornering at high speed. The force of static friction acts on the bottom of the tire and is directed toward the center of the turn. Tension in the tire, evident in this picture through the distortion of the tire, exerts a force on the rest of the car.

Fig. 5–29
Forces on a car rounding a banked turn. The horizontal component of the normal force provides the acceleration.

Solution

Figure 5–29 shows the forces acting on a car as it rounds the banked turn. They include only gravity and the normal force; we do not show a frictional force because we want to calculate the angle at which the frictional force can be zero. Newton's second law then reads

$$\mathbf{F}_g + \mathbf{N} = m\mathbf{a}.$$

The gravitational force points vertically downward, and the vertical component of the normal force is $N \cos\theta$. There is no acceleration in the vertical direction, so the vertical component of Newton's second law is

$$N \cos\theta - mg = 0.$$

The only force component in the horizontal direction is $N \sin\theta$; since the car describes a circular path, the horizontal component of Newton's law becomes

$$N \sin\theta = \frac{mv^2}{r}.$$

Substituting $N = mg/\cos\theta$ from the vertical equation gives

$$\frac{mg}{\cos\theta} \sin\theta = \frac{mv^2}{r},$$

so that

$$\tan\theta = \frac{v^2}{gr}.$$

Does this make sense? At very low speeds, banking is hardly needed. But at high speeds, the force needed to maintain circular motion increases, and so does the banking angle.

For the numbers of this example,

$$\theta = \tan^{-1}\left(\frac{v^2}{gr}\right) = \tan^{-1}\left[\frac{(15 \text{ m/s})^2}{(9.8 \text{ m/s}^2)(73 \text{ m})}\right] = 17°.$$

Example 5–12

Weight at the Equator and Poles

A 60.00-kg person stands on a spring scale. What does the scale read (*a*) at the north pole and (*b*) at the equator? Assume (unrealistically!) that g has the value 9.810 m/s² everywhere on earth's surface.

Solution

Why should the scale give a different reading at the equator than at the pole? Because earth rotates, and therefore a person standing at the equator is accelerating, while a person standing at the pole is not. Figure 5–30 shows the forces on the person at both locations. They include the upward force $\mathbf{F}_s$ of the spring scale and the downward force $\mathbf{F}_g$ of gravity. According to Newton's second law, the vector sum of the two forces is equal to the product of the mass and acceleration:

$$\mathbf{F}_s + \mathbf{F}_g = m\mathbf{a}.$$

In a coordinate system with the positive direction upward, we have at the pole

$$F_s - mg = 0,$$

so that the spring force is equal to the gravitational force mg, or

pole: $\qquad F_s = mg = (60.00 \text{ kg})(9.810 \text{ m/s}^2) = 588.6 \text{ N}.$

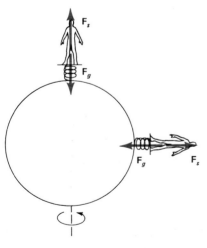

Fig. 5–30
Forces on a person standing on a spring scale at the pole and the equator. In both cases, the only forces acting are the spring force and gravity. At the pole they sum to zero because the person is not accelerating. At the equator they sum to *m***a,** where **a** is the acceleration associated with the circular motion of the rotating earth.

Fig. 5–31
A loop-the-loop roller coaster. At the top of the loop, net force on the train and its passengers is downward; that force provides the acceleration that keeps them in their circular path.

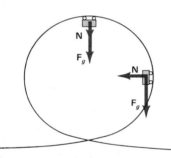

Fig. 5–32
Forces on the train include gravity and the normal force. At the top of the loop, both point downward.

Fig. 5–33
If the train's speed is too low, it leaves the track on a parabolic trajectory, subject only to the gravitational force.

At the equator, however, the person moves in a circular path as earth rotates, and therefore experiences an acceleration directed toward the center of the earth—that is, downward. So at the equator the two forces don't balance; in a coordinate system with the upward direction positive, we have

equator: $$F_s - mg = -\frac{mv^2}{r},$$

where the minus signs show that the gravitational force and the acceleration are both toward the center of the earth. Now earth takes a time $T = 1$ day to rotate about its axis; in this time a point on the equator moves one earth circumference, or $2\pi R_e$, where R_e is earth's radius. So $v = 2\pi R_e/T$, and Newton's law becomes

$$F_s - mg = -\frac{m(2\pi R_e/T)^2}{R_e} = -\frac{4\pi^2 mR_e}{T^2}.$$

Then the spring force—that is, the scale reading—is

$$F_s = mg - \frac{4\pi^2 mR_e}{T^2}$$

$$= (60.00 \text{ kg})(9.810 \text{ m/s}^2) - \frac{(4\pi^2)(60.00 \text{ kg})(6.37 \times 10^6 \text{ m})}{[(24 \text{ h})(3600 \text{ s/h})]^2}$$

$$= 586.6 \text{ N},$$

or about 0.34 per cent below the weight at the pole. For points between the equator and pole, the difference is correspondingly smaller (see Problem 65). Actually, the difference is about 50 per cent greater because g varies due to the nonspherical shape of the earth.

Example 5–13
Loop-the-Loop

The "Great American Revolution" roller coaster at Valencia, California, includes a loop-the-loop section whose radius is 6.3 m (Fig. 5–31). What is the minimum speed of a train at the top of the loop if it is not to leave the track?

Solution

What does it mean for the train to stay on the track? It means that there must be a nonzero normal force between train and track; if that force goes to zero, then the train and track are no longer in contact. The only forces acting on the train are gravity and the normal force of the track; Fig. 5–32 shows these forces at two points on the loop. Newton's second law relates the net force to the acceleration:

$$\mathbf{F}_g + \mathbf{N} = m\mathbf{a}.$$

At the top of the loop, both forces point downward. In a coordinate system with the positive direction downward, the vertical component of Newton's law then becomes

$$mg + N = ma = \frac{mv^2}{r},$$

so that

$$v^2 = gr + \frac{N}{m}.$$

At the minimum speed, the normal force barely reaches zero as the train passes the top of the loop; at that instant the gravitational force alone provides the acceleration keeping the train in its circular path. The minimum speed is then given by setting $N = 0$ at the top of the loop:

$$v_{min} = \sqrt{gr}.$$

For speeds lower than v_{min}, the normal force goes to zero before the train reaches the top of the loop, and the train leaves the track travelling in the parabolic trajectory of a projectile (Fig. 5–33). For speeds greater than v_{min}, the normal force is everywhere nonzero, and the train remains in contact with the track. For the "Great American Revolution," $r = 6.3$ m so that $v_{min} = \sqrt{gr} = [(9.8 \text{ m/s}^2)(6.3 \text{ m})]^{1/2} = 7.9$ m/s. The actual speed of the train at the top of the loop is 9.7 m/s to maintain a margin of safety.

SUMMARY

1. Newton's second law provides a universal description of motion in the realm of classical physics. The following steps will help you apply Newton's law correctly in a variety of situations:
   1. Identify the object of interest.
   2. Identify all forces acting on the object, and draw the force vectors on a single diagram.
   3. Write Newton's law in vector form: $\mathbf{F} = m\mathbf{a}$, where $\mathbf{F}$, the net force, is the vector sum of the forces you have identified.
   4. Choose a suitable coordinate system.
   5. Write the components of Newton's law in your coordinate system.
   6. Solve algebraically for the quantities of interest.
   7. Check some special cases to see if your answers make sense.
   8. Insert numerical values into the equations to obtain numerical answers.
2. **Friction** is a force associated with microscopic bonds between two contacting surfaces. The frictional force always acts to oppose motion. Its magnitude depends on the normal force between the two surfaces. When the surfaces are moving relative to one another, the frictional force is the force of **kinetic friction, $\mathbf{F}_k$** (also called **sliding friction**); in that case the relation between friction and normal forces is quantified by the **coefficient of kinetic friction, μ_k**:

$$F_k = \mu_k N.$$

When the surfaces are at rest, the force of **static friction** opposes an applied force:

$$F_s \le \mu_s N,$$

where μ_s is the **coefficient of static friction**. In general, $\mu_s > \mu_k$. Once an applied force exceeds the maximum static frictional force $\mu_s N$, the surfaces start moving relative to one another and the subsequent motion is governed by the applied force and the force of kinetic friction.

3. When an object undergoes circular motion at speed v in a circle of radius r, it accelerates at the rate v^2/r in the direction toward the center of the circle. Newton's second law shows that a force of magnitude mv^2/r must then be acting in the same direction.

QUESTIONS

1. Compare the net force on a heavy trunk when it is (a) at rest on the floor; (b) being slid across the floor at constant speed; (c) being pulled upward in an elevator whose cable tension equals the combined weight of the elevator and trunk; (d) sliding down a frictionless ramp.
2. Can an object move if there is no net force on it? Can it start moving if there is no net force?
3. If you take your foot off the gas pedal while driving on a horizontal road, your car soon coasts to a stop. Is there a net force on the car during this time? If not, why not? If so, what forces might contribute to it?
4. The force of static friction acts only between surfaces at rest. Yet that force is essential in walking and in accelerating or braking a car. Explain.

5. A jet plane flies at constant speed in a vertical circular loop (Fig. 5–34). At what point in the loop does

Fig. 5–34 Question 5

the seat exert the greatest force on the pilot? The least force?

6. In cross-country skiing, skis should easily glide forward but should remain at rest when the skier pushes back against the snow. What frictional properties should the ski wax have to achieve this goal?

7. Why is it easier for a child to stand nearer the inside of a rotating merry-go-round?

8. Can a coefficient of friction exceed 1?

9. By pushing horizontally with your hand, you can hold a book at rest on a perfectly vertical wall (Fig. 5–35). How is this possible?

Fig. 5–35   Question 9

10. In general, a mass suspended from a string will not point exactly toward the center of the earth. Explain in terms of earth's rotation. Are there places on earth where the string will point toward the center of the earth?

11. Earth's gravity pulls a satellite toward the center of the earth. So why doesn't the satellite actually fall to earth?

12. Why can front-wheel-drive cars corner better on slippery roads than do rear-wheel-drive cars? Explain in terms of the forces acting on the wheels.

13. Explain why stepping as hard as you can on the brake pedal does not necessarily result in the shortest stopping distance for your car.

14. A fishing line has a breaking strength of 20 lb. Is it possible to break the line while reeling in a 15-lb fish? Explain.

15. Two blocks rest on slopes of unequal angle, connected by a rope passing over a pulley (Fig. 5–36). If the blocks have equal masses, will they remain at rest? Why? Neglect friction.

Fig. 5–36   Question 15

16. Why do a car's front brakes usually wear out before the rear brakes?

17. The dominant aerodynamic force on an airplane is the force of air approximately perpendicular to the wings. Why do airplanes bank when turning?

18. Someone once tried to describe the orbital motion of a satellite by saying that "the gravitational force balances the force mv^2/r." Criticize this statement.

19. In what sense is the force of friction between two surfaces independent of their contacting surface areas? In what sense does the force depend on surface area?

20. On landing, jet aircraft brake by reversing their engine thrust. Is the stopping distance affected by the coefficient of friction between the plane's tires and the runway?

21. If surfaces are very highly polished, friction actually increases. Why might this be?

22. A car rounds a banked turn at a speed lower than the design speed. Which way does the frictional force point?

23. For safety, automobile racetracks are banked as shown in Fig. 5–37. Explain why this improves the safety of the track.

Fig. 5–37   Banking of an automobile racetrack. Inside edge of turn is to left (Question 23).

24. In contrast to the automobile racetrack of the previous question, well-designed running tracks are sometimes banked as shown in Fig. 5–38. Explain why, neglecting safety considerations, this is a more appropriate banking scheme.

Fig. 5–38   Banking of a running track. Inside edge of turn is to left (Question 24).

25. Would the difference between apparent weights at the equator and pole be measurable with a pan balance? Why or why not?

PROBLEMS

Section 5.1 *Using Newton's Second Law*

1. A 20-kg fish at the end of a fishing line is being lifted vertically into a boat. When its acceleration reaches 1.2 m/s², the line breaks and the fish goes free. What is the maximum allowable tension in the line?
2. At what angle should you tilt an air table to simulate motion on the moon's surface, where g = 1.6 m/s²?
3. A tow truck is connected to a 1400-kg car by a cable that makes a 25° angle to the horizontal, as shown in Fig. 5–39. If the truck accelerates at 0.57 m/s², what is the magnitude of the cable tension? Neglect friction and the mass of the cable.

Fig. 5–39 Problem 3

4. A 2.0-kg mass and an unknown mass are on frictionless surfaces and are connected by a massless string over a frictionless pivot, as shown in Fig. 5–40. If the 2.0-kg mass accelerates downslope at 1.8 m/s², what is the unknown mass?

Fig. 5–40 Problem 4

5. Your 12-kg baby sister is pulling on the bottom of the tablecloth with all her weight. In the middle of the table, 60 cm from each edge, is a 6.8-kg roast turkey. (*a*) What is the acceleration of the turkey? (*b*) From the time she starts pulling, how long do you have to intervene before the turkey goes over the edge of the table?
6. Find expressions for the acceleration of the blocks in Fig. 5–41, where the string is fastened securely to the ceiling. Neglect friction and assume that the masses of pulley and string are negligible.
7. A block is launched up a frictionless ramp that makes an angle of 35° to the horizontal. If the block's initial speed is 2.2 m/s, how far up the ramp does it slide?
8. A 1300-kg car is being pulled up a 20° incline using a tow rope that makes a 30° angle with the incline, as shown in Fig. 5–42. If the car moves with constant speed, what is the tension in the rope? Neglect friction.

Fig. 5–41 Problem 6

Fig. 5–42 Problem 8

9. A skier starts from rest at the top of a 24° slope 1.3 km long. Neglecting friction, how long does it take to reach the bottom?
10. A 73,200-kg space shuttle is in circular orbit at an altitude of 250 km above earth, where the acceleration of gravity is 0.93 times its surface value. With what magnitude and direction should rocket thrust be applied so that it begins moving in a straight line tangent to its orbit?
11. At the start of a race, a 70-kg swimmer pushes off the starting block with a force of 950 N directed at 15° below the horizontal. (*a*) What is the swimmer's horizontal acceleration? (*b*) If the swimmer is in contact with the starting block for 0.29 s, what is the horizontal component of his velocity when he hits the water?

Section 5.2 *Friction*

12. Eight rugby players push on a scrum machine—a device with vertically mounted pads for pushing and a horizontal surface where additional players stand to increase the total weight. The scrum machine has a mass of 70 kg, and holds eight more 80-kg players. The coefficient of friction between the scrum machine and ground is 0.78. If the pushing players push the scrum machine at constant speed, what total force do they exert?
13. The handle of a 22-kg lawnmower makes a 35° angle with the horizontal. If the coefficient of friction between lawnmower and ground is 0.68, what magnitude of force is required to push the mower at constant speed? Assume the force is applied in the

direction of the handle. Compare with the mower's weight.

14. The coefficient of friction between a suction cup and window glass is 1.3. If the suction cup is mounted on a vertical window, and if the net force of air on the cup is 85 N, how much mass can the cup support?

15. During an ice storm, the coefficients of friction between car tires and road are reduced to $\mu_k = 0.088$ and $\mu_s = 0.14$. (a) What is the maximum slope on which a car can be parked without sliding? (b) On a slope just steeper than this maximum, with what acceleration will a car slide down the slope?

16. A bat crashes into the vertical front of an accelerating subway train. If the coefficient of friction between bat and train is 0.86, what is the minimum acceleration of the train that will allow the bat to remain in place?

17. In a factory, boxes drop vertically onto a conveyor belt moving horizontally at 1.7 m/s. If the coefficient of kinetic friction is 0.46, how long does it take each box to come to rest with respect to the belt?

18. The coefficient of static friction between steel train wheels and steel rails is 0.58. The engineer of a train moving at 140 km/h spots a stalled car on the tracks 150 m ahead. If he applies the brakes so that the wheels do not slip, will the train stop in time?

19. If you neglect to fasten your seatbelt, and if the coefficient of friction between you and your car seat is 0.42, what is the maximum deceleration for which you can remain in your seat? Compare with the deceleration in an accident that brings a 60-km/h car to rest in a distance of 1.6 m.

20. A 310-g paperback book rests on a 1.2-kg textbook. A force is applied to the textbook, and the two books accelerate together from rest to 96 cm/s in 0.42 s. The textbook is then brought to a stop in 0.33 s, during which time the paperback slides off. Within what range does the coefficient of static friction between the two books lie?

21. A 2.5-kg block and a 3.1-kg block slide down a 30° incline as shown in Fig. 5–43. The coefficient of kinetic friction between the 2.5-kg block and the slope is 0.23; between the 3.1-kg block and the slope it is 0.51. Determine the (a) acceleration of the pair and (b) force the lighter block exerts on the heavier one.

Fig. 5–43   Problem 21

22. Children sled down a 41-m-long hill inclined at 25°. At the bottom the slope levels out. If the coefficient of friction is 0.12, how far do the children slide on the level?

23. In a typical front-wheel-drive car, 70 per cent of the car's weight rides on the front wheels. If the coefficient of friction between tires and road is 0.61, what is the maximum acceleration of the car?

24. Repeat the previous problem for a rear-wheel-drive car with the same portion of its weight over the front wheels.

25. A police officer investigating an accident estimates from the damage done that a moving car hit a stationary car at 25 km/h. If the moving car left skid marks 47 m long, and if the coefficient of kinetic friction is 0.71, what was the initial speed of the moving car?

26. A skier finds she must give herself a push to get started on slopes of less than 8°. What is the coefficient of static friction?

27. Starting from rest, the skier of the previous problem traverses a 1.8-km-long trail in 65 s. If the trail is inclined at 12°, what is the coefficient of kinetic friction?

28. A slide inclined at 35° takes bathers into a swimming pool. With water sprayed onto the slide to make it essentially frictionless, a bather spends only one-third as much time on the slide as when it is dry. What is the coefficient of friction on the dry slide?

29. Planes operated by USAir have tables at their forward-most seats. (a) Sitting in the rear-facing seat at the forward side of the table, I place a book on the table during take-off. If the coefficient of static friction is 0.33, and if the plane accelerates at 2.4 m/s² during its take-off roll, will my book stay in place? (b) Once the plane is airborne, it heads upward at an 18° angle but with constant speed. Now will the book stay in place?

30. You try to push a heavy trunk, exerting a force at an angle of 50° below the horizontal (Fig. 5–44). Show that, no matter how hard you try to push, it is impossible to budge the trunk if the coefficient of static friction exceeds 0.84.

Fig. 5–44   Problem 30

31. A block of mass m is being pulled at constant speed v down a slope that makes an angle θ with the horizontal. The pulling force is applied through a horizontal rope, as shown in Fig. 5–45. If the coefficient of kinetic friction is μ_k, what is the rope tension?

32. A block is shoved down a 22° slope with an initial speed of 1.4 m/s. If it slides 34 cm before stopping, what is the coefficient of friction?

33. If the block in the previous problem were shoved up the slope with the same initial speed, (a) how far

Fig. 5–45   Problem 31

would it go? (b) Once it stopped, would it slide back down?

Section 5.3   *Circular Motion*

34. Suppose the moon were held in its orbit not by gravity but by the tension in a massless cable. Estimate the magnitude of the cable tension. (See Appendix F for relevant data.)

35. Show that the force needed to keep a mass m in a circular path of radius r with period T is $4\pi^2 mr/T^2$.

36. A mass m_1 undergoes circular motion of radius R on a horizontal frictionless table, connected by a massless string through a hole in the table to a second mass m_2 (Fig. 5–46). If m_2 is stationary, find (a) the tension in the string and (b) the period of the circular motion.

Fig. 5–46   Problem 36

37. A bug starts walking outward from the center of a $33\frac{1}{3}$-rpm record. If the coefficient of friction between bug and record is 0.15, how far does the bug get before it starts to slip?

38. A 340-g rock is whirled in a horizontal circle at the end of a 1.3-m-long string. If the breaking strength of the string is 250 N, what is the maximum speed of the rock? Assume that the string is very nearly horizontal at this speed. (How do you know that this assumption is reasonable?)

39. If the rock of the previous problem is whirled in a vertical circle, what is the minimum speed necessary at the top of the circle in order that the string remain taut?

40. A subway train rounds an unbanked curve at 67 km/h. A passenger hanging onto a strap notices that an adjacent unused strap makes an angle of 15° to the vertical. What is the radius of the turn?

41. An Olympic hammer thrower whirls a 7.3-kg hammer on the end of a 120-cm chain. If the chain makes a 10° angle with the horizontal, what is the speed of the hammer?

42. A Volvo model 240 sedan has a minimum turning radius of 9.8 m. If the coefficient of static friction between tires and road is 0.81, what is the maximum speed the car can have without skidding if the steering wheel is turned fully to the right?

43. A drum major whirls a ball of mass m in a vertical circle at the end of a massless rope of length ℓ. The ball's speed is constant, and is just fast enough to keep the rope always taut. If the drum major releases the rope when the ball is headed vertically upward, to what height h does it rise above its release point?

44. The world's largest Ferris wheel, at the Tsukuba Exposition in Japan, is 100 m in diameter and rotates once every 15 min. By what percentage would your weight in the frame of reference of the rotating wheel differ from your weight in earth's frame of reference when you are (a) at the top and (b) at the bottom of the wheel?

45. A space station is in the shape of a hollow ring with an outer diameter of 150 m. How fast should it rotate to simulate earth's surface gravity—that is, so that the force exerted on an object by the outside wall is equal to the object's weight on earth's surface?

46. A 45-kg skater rounds a 5.0-m-radius turn at 6.3 m/s. (a) What are the horizontal and vertical components of the force the ice exerts on her skate blades? (b) At what angle can she lean without falling over?

47. An indoor running track is square-shaped with rounded corners; each corner has a radius of 6.5 m on its inside edge. The track includes six 1.0-m-wide lanes. What should be the banking angles on (a) the innermost and (b) the outermost lanes if the design speed of the track is 24 km/h?

48. A jetliner flying horizontally at 850 km/h banks at 32° to make a turn. What is the radius of the turn? Note: the main aerodynamic force on an airplane is normal to the wing surfaces.

49. A 550-g rock is whirled in a horizontal circle at the end of a string 80 cm long. If the period of the circular motion is 1.6 s, what angle does the string make with the vertical?

50. A bucket of water is whirled in a vertical circle of radius 85 cm. What is the minimum speed that will keep the water from falling out?

51. A child is sitting on the edge of a merry-go-round 2.8 m in diameter. When the speed of the merry-go-round reaches one revolution in 3.2 s, the child slides off. What is the coefficient of static friction?

52. Riders on the "Great American Revolution" loop-the-loop roller coaster of Example 5–13 wear seatbelts as the roller coaster negotiates its 6.3-m-radius loop with a speed of 9.7 m/s. At the top of the loop, what are the magnitude and direction of the force exerted on a 60-kg rider (a) by the roller-coaster seat and (b) by the seatbelt? (c) What would happen if the rider unbuckled at this point?

53. A 1200-kg car drives on the country road shown in Fig. 5–47. The radius of curvature of the crests and dips is 31 m. (a) What is the maximum speed at which the car will always maintain contact with the road? (b) If the maximum rated load for the car is 450 kg, and if it carries four 65-kg people, what is the maximum speed for which it will not exceed its rated load?

Fig. 5–47   Problem 53

54. The Tethered Satellite System (TSS) is a proposed NASA experiment consisting of a 500-kg satellite connected to the space shuttle by a 20-km long cable whose mass is negligible compared with the satellite's mass. Suppose the shuttle is placed in a 250-km high circular orbit, where the acceleration of gravity is 0.926 times its value at earth's surface. The TSS hangs vertically on its tether (Fig. 5–48), and at its 230-km altitude the acceleration of gravity is 0.932 times its surface value. What is the tension in the cable? Assume that the shuttle's orbit is not significantly affected by the TSS, but that the TSS is forced by the cable to have the same orbital period as the shuttle. (Why is this assumption reasonable?)

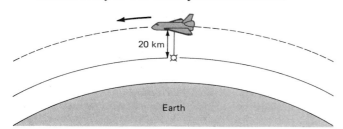

Fig. 5–48   NASA's Tethered Satellite System (Problem 54).

55. A block of mass m slides in a circle around the inside of a frictionless cone, as shown in Fig. 5–49. Find an expression for the speed of the block, if it is a vertical distance h above the apex of the cone.

Supplementary Problems

56. An astronaut is training in a centrifuge that consists of a small chamber whirled around horizontally at the end of a 5.1-m-long shaft. The astronaut places a notebook on the vertical wall of the chamber and it stays in place. If the coefficient of static friction is 0.62, what is the minimum rate at which the centrifuge must be revolving?

57. A block of mass m is given an initial speed v_0 on a horizontal table of height h. It slides a distance x_1

Fig. 5–49   Problem 55

across the table and lands on the floor a horizontal distance x_2 from the edge of the table. Find an expression for the coefficient of friction between block and table.

58. Driving in thick fog on a horizontal road, a driver spots a tractor-trailer truck jackknifed across the road, as in Fig. 5–50. To avert a collision, the driver could brake to a stop or swerve in a circular arc, as suggested in Fig. 5–50. Which offers the greater margin of safety? Assume that the same coefficient of static friction is operative in both cases, and that the car maintains constant speed if it swerves.

Fig. 5–50   Problem 58

59. A highway turn of radius R is banked for a design speed v_d. If a car enters the turn at speed $v = v_d + \Delta v$, where Δv can be positive or negative, show that the minimum coefficient of static friction needed to prevent slipping is

$$\mu_s = \frac{|\Delta v|}{gR} (2v_d + \Delta v).$$

Show that your result is consistent with Example 5–6 for $\Delta v = -v_d$—that is, for a car at rest on the banked highway.

60. Suppose the coefficient of friction between a block and a horizontal surface is proportional to the block's speed: $\mu = \mu_1 v/v_1$, where μ_1 and v_1 are constants. If the block is given an initial speed v_0, show that it comes to rest in a distance $x = v_0 v_1 / \mu g$.

61. A block is projected up an incline making an angle θ with the horizontal. It returns to its initial position with half its initial speed. Show that the coefficient of friction is $\mu = \frac{3}{5} \tan\theta$.

62. A conical pendulum consists of a mass m whirled in a horizontal circle at the end of a massless string of length ℓ. Show that in the limit when the string is nearly vertical, the period of the circular motion is $2\pi\sqrt{\ell/g}$.

63. A 2.1-kg mass is connected to a spring of spring constant $k = 150$ N/m and unstretched length 18 cm. The pair are mounted on a frictionless air table, with the free end of the spring attached to a frictionless pivot. The mass is set into circular motion at 1.4 m/s. Find the radius of its path.

64. The victim of a political kidnapping is forced into a north-facing car and then blindfolded. The car pulls into traffic and, from the sound of the surrounding traffic, the victim knows that the car is moving at about the legal speed limit of 85 km/h. The car then turns to the right; the victim estimates that the force the seat exerts on him is one-fifth of his weight. The victim experiences this force for 28 s. At the end of that time, in what direction can the victim conclude that he is heading?

65. A mass m is suspended from a spring scale at latitude θ on earth's surface. (a) Show that the spring and mass make an angle ϕ with the radial direction to earth's center, where ϕ in radians is given by

$$\phi = \frac{\pi}{2} - \theta - \tan^{-1}\left[\cot\theta\left(1 - \frac{4\pi^2 R_e}{gT^2}\right)\right],$$

with R_e the earth's radius and T its rotation period. (b) Show that the weight read by the spring scale is

$$F_s = \frac{mg\,\sin\theta}{\cos\left(\dfrac{\pi}{2} - \theta - \phi\right)}.$$

(c) Show that the equations you write in deriving these results are consistent with $\phi = 0$ at poles and equator, and that in these cases the spring scale force is as given in Example 5–12. (d) Evaluate ϕ and F_s for the case when you weigh yourself at your present latitude. Assume throughout that g is constant.

6

WORK, ENERGY, AND POWER

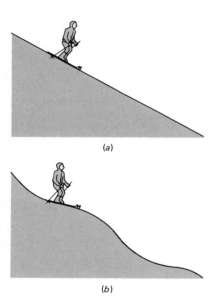

Fig. 6–1
Skier on (a) a uniform slope and (b) a nonuniform slope.

In Fig. 6–1a, a skier starts from rest at the top of a uniform slope. What is the skier's speed at the bottom? You could easily solve this problem by applying Newton's second law to find the acceleration, then using the appropriate constant acceleration equation to find the speed. But what about the skier in Fig. 6–1b? Here the slope is continuously changing, and so is the acceleration. Constant acceleration equations do not apply, so that solving for the details of the skier's motion would prove very difficult. Nevertheless, by introducing two important new concepts—work and energy—we will see how to "shortcut" the detailed application of Newton's law to arrive very easily at the answers to this and many other practical problems.

6.1
WORK

work

We all have an intuitive sense of the term "work." Carrying a piece of furniture upstairs involves work. The heavier the furniture, or the higher the stairs, the greater the work we must do. Pushing a stalled car involves work. Again, the heavier the car or the farther we push it, the more work we must do. Our precise definition of work reflects this intuition. For an object moving in one dimension—say, along the x-axis—the **work** W done on the object by an applied force $\mathbf{F}$ is

$$W = F_x \Delta x, \tag{6–1}$$

where F_x is the component of the force in the direction of the object's motion and where Δx is the distance moved. The force $\mathbf{F}$ need not be the net force; if we are interested, for example, in how much work *we* must do to drag a heavy box across the floor, then $\mathbf{F}$ is the force *we apply* and W is the work *we do*.

joule

Equation 6–1 shows that the SI unit of work is the newton-meter (N·m). One newton-meter is given the name **joule,** in honor of the nineteenth-century British physicist and brewer James Joule (Fig. 6–2). Since a newton is a kilogram-meter/second^2, the units of work can also be expressed as kg·m^2/s^2. In the English system, where the unit of force is the pound and the unit of distance is the foot, work is measured in **foot-pounds** (ft·lb).

foot-pound

Equation 6–1 shows that the person pushing the car in Fig. 6–3 does work equal to the force he applies times the distance the car moves. But the person pulling the suitcase in Fig. 6–4 does work equal only to the horizontal component of the force she applies times the distance the suitcase moves.

Furthermore, by our definition, the waiter of Fig. 6–5 does no work on the tray. Why not? Because the direction of the force he applies is perpendicular to the horizontal motion of the tray; there is no component of force along the direction of motion. Similarly, the weightlifter of Fig. 6–6 does no work while he holds the barbell steady over his head. Now you know both the waiter and weightlifter get tired. What is going on is that their muscles are undergoing minuscule contractions and lengthenings, so that on a small scale the muscles are doing work. But according to our definition, no work is being done on the tray or barbell. Similarly, a normal force from the road acts to support a moving car against gravity. But because that force is always perpendicular to the motion, it does no work on the car. Only the component of force in the direction of motion contributes to the work.

Fig. 6–2
James Joule.

Fig. 6–3
When pushing in the direction of the car's motion, the person does work equal to the force he applies times the distance the car moves.

Example 6–1
Pushing a Trunk

You push a 75-kg trunk 6.4 m across a floor, exerting a horizontal force of 540 N. How much work do you do?

Solution

Since the force is in the direction of motion, Equation 6–1 gives simply

$$W = F\Delta x = (540 \text{ N})(6.4 \text{ m}) = 3500 \text{ N·m} = 3500 \text{ J}.$$

If the trunk is pushed at constant speed, then this work is expended to overcome the frictional force.

Example 6–2
A Garage Lift

A garage lift raises a 1300-kg car a vertical distance of 2.3 m at constant speed. How much work does it do?

Solution

To find the work, we need the force the lift exerts on the car. Since the car is raised at constant speed, it is not accelerating and therefore the *net* force on it is zero. The two forces acting are the upward lift force and the downward force of gravity; with no acceleration, they have the same magnitude, *mg*. The lift force is in the same direction as the motion, so that the work done by the lift is

$$W = F\Delta x = mg\Delta x = (1300 \text{ kg})(9.8 \text{ m/s}^2)(2.3 \text{ m})$$

$$= 2.9 \times 10^4 \text{ kg·m}^2/\text{s}^2 = 2.9 \times 10^4 \text{ J}.$$

Fig. 6–4
Here only the component of force in the direction of motion contributes to the work.

Fig. 6–5
The waiter applies a vertical force to the tray; since this is perpendicular to the tray's horizontal motion, the waiter does no work on the tray.

Fig. 6–6
This weightlifter, strain though he may, is not doing work in the sense the word is used in physics.

Fig. 6–7
Example 6–3

In the previous two examples, the force we were interested in was in the same direction as the motion. When that is not the case, we must first determine the component of force along the direction of motion, as the next example shows.

Example 6–3
Pulling a Suitcase

An airline passenger pulls a wheeled suitcase, exerting a 60-N force at a 35° angle to the horizontal. How much work does she do in pulling the suitcase 45 m from a taxi to the check-in counter?

Solution

Figure 6–7 shows that the horizontal component of the force is $F_x = F \cos\theta$, so that the work is

$$W = F_x \Delta x = F \cos\theta \, \Delta x = (60 \text{ N})(\cos 35°)(45 \text{ m}) = 2200 \text{ J}.$$

Work can be positive or negative. When a force acts in the same general direction as the motion, the work it does is positive. Acting at 90° to the direction of motion, a force does no work. And when a force acts to oppose motion, it does negative work (Fig. 6–8).

Example 6–4
Stopping a Car

The coefficient of kinetic friction between a wet, horizontal road and the wheels of a skidding car is 0.21. The mass of the car is 1500 kg. How much work is done on the car by the frictional force if the car comes to a stop in 54 m?

Solution

To find the work, we need to know the frictional force. On a horizontal road, the normal force balances gravity, so that $N = mg$. Then the magnitude of the frictional force is $\mu_k N = \mu_k mg$. The direction of this force is opposite the car's motion. If we take the positive x-direction in the direction of the car's motion, then the component of force along this direction is negative: $F_x = -\mu mg$. So the work done by friction is

$$W = F_x \Delta x = (-\mu_k mg)(\Delta x) = -(0.21)(1500 \text{ kg})(9.8 \text{ m/s}^2)(54 \text{ m})$$

$$= -1.7 \times 10^5 \text{ kg·m}^2/\text{s}^2 = -1.7 \times 10^5 \text{ J}.$$

6.2
WORK AND THE SCALAR PRODUCT

Work is a *scalar* quantity: it is specified completely by a single number, and has no direction associated with it. But Fig. 6–8 shows clearly that work involves a relation between two *vectors*—the force vector **F** and the displacement vector **Δr**. If θ is the angle between those two vectors, then the component of the force along the direction of motion is $F \cos\theta$. If the length of the displacement vector is Δr, then the work is simply

$$W = (F \cos\theta)(\Delta r) = F\,\Delta r \cos\theta. \tag{6-2}$$

(Equation 6–2 is really the same as our definition 6–1, written in slightly more general terms. If we choose the x-axis along the displacement vector $\Delta \mathbf{r}$, then $F_x = F \cos\theta$ and $\Delta r = \Delta x$, and we recover Equation 6–1.)

Equation 6–2 shows that the work is the product of the magnitudes of the vectors $\mathbf{F}$ and $\Delta \mathbf{r}$ and the cosine of the angle between them. This combination—the product of vector magnitudes with the cosine of the angle between the vectors—occurs so often in physics and mathematics that it is given a special name: the **scalar product** of two vectors. If $\mathbf{A}$ and $\mathbf{B}$ are any two vectors, their scalar product is defined as

scalar product

$$\mathbf{A}\cdot\mathbf{B} = AB \cos\theta, \tag{6-3}$$

where A and B are the magnitudes of the vectors and θ the angle between them. Note that we use a centered dot to designate the scalar product; for this reason the scalar product is often called the **dot product**. Although the scalar product $\mathbf{A}\cdot\mathbf{B}$ is formed from two vectors, the product itself is a scalar.

dot product

Since scalar multiplication is commutative, we can rearrange terms on the right-hand side of Equation 6–3 to get $\mathbf{A}\cdot\mathbf{B} = BA\cos\theta$. But $BA\cos\theta$ is, by definition, the scalar product $\mathbf{B}\cdot\mathbf{A}$, so that the scalar product is itself commutative: $\mathbf{A}\cdot\mathbf{B} = \mathbf{B}\cdot\mathbf{A}$. Problems 11 and 12 ask you to confirm that the scalar product is also distributive:

$$\mathbf{A}\cdot(\mathbf{B} + \mathbf{C}) = \mathbf{A}\cdot\mathbf{B} + \mathbf{A}\cdot\mathbf{C}$$

and that it has the property

$$(c\mathbf{A})\cdot\mathbf{B} = \mathbf{A}\cdot(c\mathbf{B}),$$

where c is a scalar. (In Chapter 11 we will define a way of multiplying vectors to form another vector; we will find that that operation is not commutative.)

Comparing Equation 6–2 with the definition 6–3 of the scalar product, we see immediately that work is given by

$$W = \mathbf{F}\cdot\Delta\mathbf{r}. \tag{6-4}$$

This vector notation expresses the work in a compact way that accounts for both direction and magnitude of the vectors involved.

The forms 6–3 and 6–4 are convenient when we are given the magnitudes and directions of both vectors. But often vectors are expressed in unit vector notation. In that case, we can apply the distributive law to derive a simple form for the scalar product. Let $\mathbf{A} = A_x\hat{\mathbf{i}} + A_y\hat{\mathbf{j}} + A_z\hat{\mathbf{k}}$ and $\mathbf{B} = B_x\hat{\mathbf{i}} + B_y\hat{\mathbf{j}} + B_z\hat{\mathbf{k}}$. Then the scalar product $\mathbf{A}\cdot\mathbf{B}$ is

$$\mathbf{A}\cdot\mathbf{B} = (A_x\hat{\mathbf{i}} + A_y\hat{\mathbf{j}} + A_z\hat{\mathbf{k}})\cdot(B_x\hat{\mathbf{i}} + B_y\hat{\mathbf{j}} + B_z\hat{\mathbf{k}}).$$

Multiplying this out would give a sum of nine terms. The first term, for example, is $A_x\hat{\mathbf{i}}\cdot B_x\hat{\mathbf{i}}$. This can be written $A_x B_x\hat{\mathbf{i}}\cdot\hat{\mathbf{i}}$. But what is the scalar product $\hat{\mathbf{i}}\cdot\hat{\mathbf{i}}$? The vector $\hat{\mathbf{i}}$ is a *unit* vector—it has length 1—and the angle between any vector and itself is zero, so that

Fig. 6–8
(a) A force applied in the same general direction as the motion does positive work. (b) A force acting at right angles to the motion—like the normal force of the floor—does no work. (c) A force acting to oppose the motion—like the frictional force—does negative work.

$$\hat{\imath} \cdot \hat{\imath} = (1)(1)(\cos 0°) = 1.$$

Thus the term $A_x\hat{\imath} \cdot B_x\hat{\imath}$ becomes A_xB_x. Clearly there are two similar terms, A_yB_y and A_zB_z. What about the other six terms? They involve expressions like $A_x\hat{\imath} \cdot B_y\hat{\jmath} = A_xB_y\hat{\imath} \cdot \hat{\jmath}$. But the different unit vectors are perpendicular, so $\hat{\imath} \cdot \hat{\jmath} = 0$ and the six "cross terms" vanish. Then the scalar product becomes simply

$$\mathbf{A} \cdot \mathbf{B} = A_xB_x + A_yB_y + A_zB_z. \qquad (6–5)$$

Since Equation 6–5 follows directly from the definition 6–3, either form may be used in computing the scalar product of two vectors.

Example 6–5
Work and Unit Vectors

A force $\mathbf{F} = 33\hat{\imath} + 14\hat{\jmath}$ N acts to move an object on a straight path from the origin to the point $x = 4.0$ m, $y = 2.0$ m. How much work is done by the force?

Solution

The work is given by Equation 6–4: $W = \mathbf{F} \cdot \Delta\mathbf{r}$. Here the displacement vector from the origin to the point (4.0 m, 2.0 m) is $\Delta\mathbf{r} = 4.0\hat{\imath} + 2.0\hat{\jmath}$ m, so that Equation 6–5 gives immediately

$$W = \mathbf{F} \cdot \Delta\mathbf{r} = F_x\Delta x + F_y\Delta y = (33\text{ N})(4.0\text{ m}) + (14\text{ N})(2.0\text{ m}) = 160\text{ J},$$

where Δx and Δy are the components of the displacement vector.

Equation 6–5 provides the best approach here since the vectors are given in unit vector notation. If you insist on using Equation 6–3, you must first compute the magnitudes of both vectors and the angle between them. Problem 15 explores this approach.

6.3
A VARYING FORCE

Often the force applied to an object varies with position. Especially important examples include the fundamental forces of nature; the electrical and gravitational forces, for example, vary as the inverse square of the distance between interacting objects. The force of a spring that we encountered in Chapter 4 provides another example; as the spring stretches, the force increases.

How are we to calculate the work done by a varying force? We consider first the case of one-dimensional motion, with the force in the same direction as the motion. Figure 6–9 is a plot of a force F that varies with position x. We would like to find the work done by the force as an object moves from x_1 to x_2. We can't simply write $F(x_2 - x_1)$, since the force varies so that there is no single value for F. What we can do, though, is to divide the region into a series of small rectangles of width Δx, as shown in Fig. 6–10. If we make the width Δx small enough, the force will be nearly constant over the width of each rectangle. Then the work ΔW done in moving the width Δx of one such rectangle is approximately $F(x)\Delta x$, where $F(x)$ is the

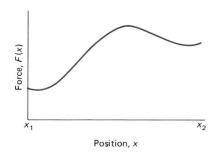

Fig. 6–9
A force $F(x)$ that varies with position x.

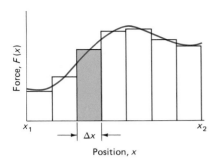

Fig. 6–10
The work done by the varying force is the area under the force versus position curve, and is approximated as the sum of the areas of many narrow rectangles.

magnitude of the force at the midpoint x of that rectangle; we write $F(x)$ to show explicitly that the force is a function of position. Note that the quantity $F(x)\Delta x$ is simply the area of the rectangle, expressed in the appropriate units (N·m, or J). Suppose there are N rectangles. Let x_i be the midpoint of the ith rectangle. Then the total work done in moving from x_1 to x_2 is given approximately by the sum of the individual amounts of work ΔW_i associated with each rectangle, or

$$W \simeq \sum_{i=1}^{N} W_i = \sum_{i=1}^{N} F(x_i)\Delta x. \qquad (6\text{–}6)$$

How good is this approximation? That depends on how small we make the rectangles. Suppose we let them get arbitrarily small. Then the number of rectangles must grow arbitrarily large. In the limit of infinitely many infinitesimally small rectangles, the approximation in Equation 6–6 becomes exact. Then we have

$$W = \lim_{\Delta x \to 0} \sum_{i} F(x_i)\Delta x, \qquad (6\text{–}7)$$

definite integral

where the sum is over all the infinitesimal rectangles between x_1 and x_2. The sum of infinitely many infinitesimal quantities occurs frequently in physics and mathematics, and is called a **definite integral.** The quantity on the right-hand side of Equation 6–7 is the definite integral of the function $F(x)$ over the interval from x_1 to x_2. We introduce a special symbolism for the limiting process of Equation 6–7, writing

$$W = \int_{x_1}^{x_2} F(x)\ dx. \qquad \left(\begin{array}{l}\text{work done by a varying} \\ \text{force in one dimension}\end{array}\right) \qquad (6\text{–}8)$$

What does expression 6–8 mean? It means, by definition, exactly the same thing as Equation 6–7: it tells us to break the interval from x_1 to x_2 into many small rectangles of width Δx, to multiply the value of the function $F(x)$ at each rectangle by the width Δx, and to sum those products. As we take arbitrarily many arbitrarily small rectangles, the result of this process gives us the value of the definite integral. You can think of the symbol $\int$ in Equation 6–8 as standing for "sum," and of the symbol dx as a limiting case of arbitrarily small Δx. The definite integral has a simple geometrical interpretation: as the sum of the areas of the many rectangles, it is the area under the curve $F(x)$ between the limits x_1 and x_2.

How are we ever to evaluate the infinite sum that is implied in Equation 6–8? One way is to back off and take a sum over a large but finite number of small but not infinitesimally small rectangles. This method gives an approximation that can be very accurate if the rectangle width Δx is small enough. It is widely used in computer calculations and for integrals that cannot be handled in any other way.

Calculus provides us with a powerfully simple way to evaluate many integrals. In the box below, we show how and why this is so. If you are familiar with integrals from your calculus course, you can skip the box and move on to more physics. But even if you are comfortable with integrals, you may find the box useful in refreshing your sense of just what an integral means.

Box 6–1
Integrals and Derivatives

The limiting process defining the integral, and even the symbol dx in the expression 6–8, should remind you of our definition of the derivative in Chapter 2. Integration and differentiation are related processes—in fact, they are inverses. You either have proved or will soon prove this rigorously in your calculus course; here we give a graphical illustration of the relation between differentiation and integration.

Figure 6–11a again shows our force function $F(x)$, with the area under it divided into small rectangles. We define a new function, called $A(x)$, which gives the area under the $F(x)$ curve between x_1 and some arbitrary point x. That is,

$$A(x) = \int_{x_1}^{x} F(x)\, dx. \tag{6–9}$$

(Setting $x = x_2$ in the upper limit of the integral gives the area from x_1 to x_2.) In Fig. 6–11b, we plot the function $A(x)$. At the end of the first interval in Fig. 6–11a, the total area under the curve is the area marked A_1; we plot the value of this area at the appropriate point in Fig. 6–11b. At the end of the second interval in Fig. 6–11a, the total area under the curve is the sum of the areas A_1 and A_2; we plot this area on Fig. 6–11b as well. We continue this process for the intervals of Fig. 6–11a, obtaining the points shown on Fig. 6–11b. We could fill in intermediate points by considering smaller intervals in Fig. 6–11a; the result is the smooth curve shown in Fig. 6–11b.

What is the *rate* at which the function $A(x)$ increases with increasing x? That depends on the *value* of the function $F(x)$ at the point x. If $F(x)$ were everywhere constant, $A(x)$ would increase at a steady rate (Fig. 6–12). What does all this mean? Simply this: the rate of change of the area $A(x)$ under a curve $F(x)$ is given by the value of $F(x)$. But, as we found in Chapter 2, the rate of change of a function is the *derivative* of that function. So we have

$$\frac{dA(x)}{dx} = F(x). \tag{6–10}$$

Equations 6–9 and 6–10 are both relations between $A(x)$ and $F(x)$. Equation 6–9 tells us that $A(x)$ is the integral of $F(x)$; conversely, Equation 6–10 tells us that $F(x)$ is the derivative of $A(x)$. Differentiation and integration are therefore inverse operations.

In particular, the integral of $F(x)$ must be a function that, when differentiated, gives the function $F(x)$. Now there are many

such functions; if $A(x)$ is one of them, so that $dA(x)/dx = F(x)$, then so is $A(x) + $ constant, since the derivative of any constant is zero. So how are we to choose? In calculus, we distinguish between the **indefinite integral** of $F(x)$, defined as any function $A(x)$ whose derivative is $F(x)$, and the **definite integral,** which we defined earlier as the area under the curve $F(x)$ between two specific limits. If we want the area between some point x_1 and another point x_2, then our result should reduce to zero when $x_2 = x_1$. We can ensure this by adding to $A(x)$ a constant equal to $-A(x_1)$. Then our definite integral is

$$\int_{x_1}^{x_2} F(x)\, dx = A(x_2) - A(x_1) \equiv A(x)\Big|_{x_1}^{x_2}, \tag{6–11}$$

where the term $A(x)\Big|_{x_1}^{x_2}$ is a shorthand for $A(x_2) - A(x_1)$. The expression 6–11 has all the features we want: its derivative (with respect to x_2) is the function F, and it correctly gives zero when $x_2 = x_1$.

We learned in Chapter 2 that the derivative of the function x^n is nx^{n-1}. Since we have just shown that integration and differentiation are inverse relations, this means that x^n (plus any constant) is the indefinite integral of nx^{n-1}. That is, to integrate a power of x, we increase the exponent by one and divide by the new exponent. If we start with x^n, we end up, after integrating, with

$$\int x^n\, dx = \frac{x^{n+1}}{n+1} + \text{constant.} \tag{6–12}$$

You can verify this equation by differentiating the right-hand side; the result is just x^n. Equation 6–12 gives the indefinite integral of x^n; the definite integral is given by applying Equation 6–11:

$$\int_{x_1}^{x_2} x^n\, dx = \frac{x^{n+1}}{n+1}\Big|_{x_1}^{x_2} = \frac{x_2^{n+1}}{n+1} - \frac{x_1^{n+1}}{n+1}, \tag{6–13}$$

and is equal to the area under the curve x^n between x_1 and x_2. In your calculus course, you either have learned or will learn how to integrate other functions. Appendix B lists integrals of some common functions.

Example 6–6
Stretching a Spring

A spring of constant k is stretched a distance x_1 from its equilibrium position. How much work does this take?

Solution

We learned in Section 4.7 that an ideal spring exerts a force $-kx$, where x is the distance it has been stretched or compressed and where the minus sign indicates that the spring opposes the stretching or compression. To stretch a spring, we must exert a force $+kx$ to overcome the spring force. The work we do is then given

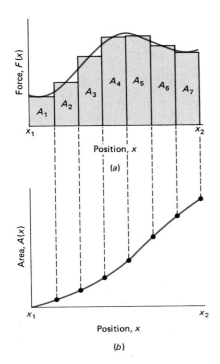

Fig. 6–11
(a) The force function $F(x)$, showing the area under the curve divided into small rectangles. (b) The function $A(x)$ is the area under the curve $F(x)$ from the point x_1 to an arbitrary point x.

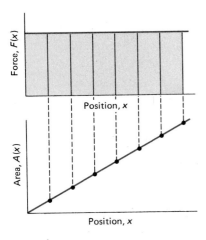

Fig. 6–12
With constant $F(x)$, the area $A(x)$ under the $F(x)$ curve increases at a constant rate; that rate depends on the *value* of the function F. The $F(x)$ curve is therefore the slope, or derivative, of the $A(x)$ curve.

by the definite integral in Equation 6–8:

$$W = \int_0^{x_1} kx\, dx = \left.\frac{kx^2}{2}\right|_0^{x_1} = \tfrac{1}{2}kx_1^2 - \tfrac{1}{2}k(0)^2 = \tfrac{1}{2}kx_1^2.$$

Since x_1 is quite arbitrary, we can drop the subscript and say that the work needed to stretch a spring of constant k a distance x from its equilibrium position is

$$W = \tfrac{1}{2}kx^2. \qquad \text{(work to stretch spring)} \qquad \text{(6–14)}$$

In this simple case, we can also solve the problem graphically. Figure 6–13 graphs the force kx we apply to stretch the spring. The work required is the area under the line $F = kx$ between $x = 0$ and $x = x_1$. Here the area is that of a triangle: one-half of the base times the height, or $(\tfrac{1}{2})(x_1)(kx_1) = \tfrac{1}{2}kx_1^2$, as before.

Notice that in this example we could not simply multiply the force kx_1 by the stretch x_1 to get kx_1^2 for the work. Why not? Because the force does not always have the value kx_1; rather, it increases steadily from zero. To evaluate the work, we must go through the procedure of adding up the small amounts of work done as we stretch the spring over small intervals, each of which has a *different* value of the force. The definite integral we used provides us the exact results of carrying out this procedure in the limit of arbitrarily small intervals. You will find integrals appearing in physics any time you are involved with quantities that vary continuously over an interval.

Example 6–7
Rough Sliding

Workers pushing a 180-kg crate across a level floor encounter a 9.5-m-long region where the floor becomes increasingly rough; the coefficient of friction increases from 0.17 to 0.87, according to the expression

$$\mu_k = ax^2 - bx^3 + \mu_0,$$

where $a = 0.022$ m^{-2}, $b = 1.5 \times 10^{-3}$ m^{-3}, $\mu_0 = 0.17$, and where x is the distance in meters from the beginning of the rough region. How much work does it take to push the crate at constant speed across this region?

Solution

Pushing at constant speed on a level floor, the workers must supply just enough force to balance the frictional force $\mu_k N$; here the normal force balances gravity, so that $N = mg$. Then the frictional force is $\mu_k mg = (ax^2 - bx^3 + \mu_0)mg$. As in the previous example, the force varies with position, so that we must effectively add the contributions from many small intervals over which we can consider the force roughly constant. Equation 6–8 expresses this procedure and Equation 6–13 lets us evaluate the result:

$$W = \int_{x_1}^{x_2} F(x)\, dx = \int_{x_1}^{x_2} mg\,(ax^2 - bx^3 + \mu_0)\, dx = \left. mg\left(\frac{ax^3}{3} - \frac{bx^4}{4} + \mu_0 x\right)\right|_{x_1}^{x_2}.$$

Here $x_1 = 0$, the start of the rough interval, and $x_2 = 9.5$ m. Putting in the values for a and b, we then have

$$W = mg\left(\frac{ax_2^3}{3} - \frac{bx_2^4}{4} + \mu_0 x_2\right) - mg\left(\frac{ax_1^3}{3} - \frac{bx_1^4}{4} + \mu_0 x_1\right)$$

$$= (180 \text{ kg})(9.8 \text{ m/s}^2)\left[\frac{(0.022 \text{ m}^{-2})(9.5 \text{ m})^3}{3} - \frac{(1.5 \times 10^{-3} \text{ m}^{-3})(9.5 \text{ m})^4}{4}\right.$$

$$\left. + (0.17)(9.5 \text{ m})\right] - 0 = 8.6 \times 10^3 \text{ J}.$$

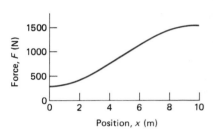

Fig. 6–13
The force required to stretch a spring increases linearly with distance x. The work done in stretching the spring an amount x_1 is the area under the force-distance curve, or $\frac{1}{2}kx_1^2$.

Fig. 6–14
Force versus position for Example 6–7.

Does this result make sense? It is well above the 2.8×10^3 J we get by calculating $\mu_k mg\Delta x$ with μ_k taking its value 0.17 at the beginning of the rough region. On the other hand, it's well below the 1.5×10^4 J we get using the value $\mu_k = 0.87$ appropriate to the end of the interval. Since the actual coefficient varies between these limits, we expect the work to lie between those extremes.

Figure 6–14 shows the force $\mu_k mg$ as a function of position. Unlike the previous example, we cannot calculate the work from the graph using a simple geometrical formula; to get the exact area under the curve we must do the integral. However, we can approximate the work by estimating the area graphically; Problem 24 explores this approach.

6.4
FORCE AND WORK IN THREE DIMENSIONS

What if a force varies not only in magnitude but also in direction? Or what if an object's path is not straight but curved? Then how do we calculate work? Our basic definition $W = \mathbf{F} \cdot \Delta\mathbf{r}$ provides the answer. Figure 6–15a shows the curved path of an object and several vectors of an applied force for which we would like to know the work. In this most general case, both the direction of the path and the direction and magnitude of the force vary. But if we magnify a small section $\Delta\mathbf{r}$ of the path (Fig. 6–15b), it will appear essentially straight and the force will not vary significantly over the segment. What if the path is sharply bent, or the force is changing rapidly? Then just make the segment smaller. Eventually it will be small enough to look approximately straight. Over this short segment, with the force a nearly constant quantity $\mathbf{F}$, the work ΔW is approximately

$$\Delta W = \mathbf{F} \cdot \Delta\mathbf{r}.$$

If we determine the work ΔW associated with each small segment of the path from some point $\mathbf{r}_1$ to another point $\mathbf{r}_2$, then the total work is given by

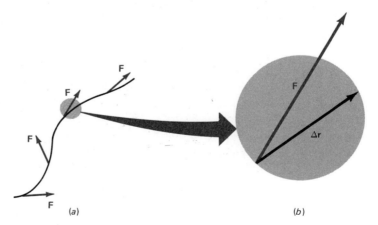

Fig. 6–15
(a) An object moves on a curved path. We want to know the work done by a force that may vary in direction and/or magnitude along the path. (b) A very small segment $\Delta\mathbf{r}$ of the path appears straight and the force does not vary significantly over that segment. The work involved in traversing the short segment is $\Delta W = \mathbf{F} \cdot \Delta\mathbf{r}$.

summing all the ΔW's:

$$W \approx \sum \Delta W = \sum \mathbf{F} \cdot \Delta \mathbf{r}.$$

If we let the size of the segments grow arbitrarily small and their number increase without bound, this approximation becomes increasingly accurate. In the limit $\Delta \mathbf{r} \rightarrow 0$, the sum becomes an integral and we write

$$W = \int_{\mathbf{r}_1}^{\mathbf{r}_2} \mathbf{F} \cdot d\mathbf{r}, \tag{6-15}$$

where the limits $\mathbf{r}_1$ and $\mathbf{r}_2$ imply that the integral is taken over the specified path from point $\mathbf{r}_1$ to $\mathbf{r}_2$. An integral like that in Equation 6–15, involving the dot product of a vector with a particular path, is called a **line integral.** You will encounter line integrals again when you study electromagnetism.

line integral

What does the line integral 6–15 mean? Its meaning comes from the procedure through which we arrived at it: form the many scalar quantities $\mathbf{F} \cdot \Delta \mathbf{r}$ over the path of interest and sum them, taking the limit as $\Delta \mathbf{r}$ becomes arbitrarily small. Example 6–8 illustrates the use of a line integral.

Example 6–8
A Line Integral and the Gravitational Force

A car drives down the hill shown in Fig. 6–16a. How much work does the force of gravity do on the car as it drives from the top of the hill $(y=h)$ to the bottom $(y=0)$?

Solution

Figure 6–16b shows a small segment $\Delta \mathbf{r}$ of the path, which can be written $\Delta \mathbf{r} = \Delta x \hat{\imath} + \Delta y \hat{\jmath}$ in a coordinate system with x-axis horizontal and y-axis vertically upward. The force of gravity is always downward: $\mathbf{F}_g = -mg\hat{\jmath}$. Then the amount of work ΔW done by gravity as the car undergoes the displacement $\Delta \mathbf{r}$ is

$$\Delta W = \mathbf{F} \cdot \Delta \mathbf{r} = -mg\hat{\jmath} \cdot (\Delta x \hat{\imath} + \Delta y \hat{\jmath}) = -mg\Delta y.$$

Summing over the entire path and taking the limit as $\Delta y \rightarrow 0$ gives

$$W = \int_{y=h}^{y=0} (-mg\ dy) = -mgy \Big|_{h}^{0} = -mg(0) - (-mgh) = mgh.$$

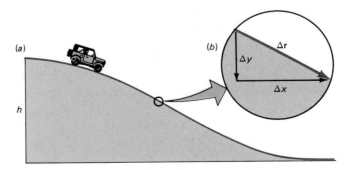

Fig. 6–16
(a) Hill of Example 6–8; (b) shows a small portion of the hill where the car undergoes displacement $\Delta \mathbf{r} = \Delta x \hat{\imath} + \Delta y \hat{\jmath}.$

In this case the details of the path don't matter at all; the work depends only on the vertical distance h. This illustrates a property of the gravitational force that we will explore further in the next chapter.

An interesting case involving work as a line integral is provided by uniform circular motion. Here the force **F** is always perpendicular to the displacement vector $\Delta\mathbf{r}$; the product $\mathbf{F}\cdot\Delta\mathbf{r}$ is therefore always zero and no work is done, no matter how far the object moves in its circular path. Thus it takes no work to whirl a ball around on the end of a horizontal string; similarly, earth's gravity does no work on a satellite in a circular orbit.

6.5
KINETIC ENERGY

So far we have discussed only the work done by a particular force acting on an object. We didn't distinguish between the case when that was the only force acting—in which case the object must be accelerating—and the case where other forces act as well, perhaps giving zero net force. We did not need to make a distinction because the work done by the one force of interest is $\int\mathbf{F}\cdot d\mathbf{r}$ regardless of what other forces may be acting.

We now turn our attention to the *net* force on an object. The *total* work done *on* an object is given by summing the work associated with each individual force. Since the sum of the forces is the net force, this amounts to using the net force in our expression for work:

$$W_{\text{total}} = \int \mathbf{F}_{\text{net}}\cdot d\mathbf{r}. \qquad (6\text{--}16)$$

For example, if you push a heavy crate across the floor at constant speed, you do work on the crate. But the frictional force does negative work of equal magnitude; the net force is zero and so is the total mechanical work done on the crate.

energy   Considering the total work in relation to the net force leads to the important concept of **energy**—a concept that will become increasingly vital as your understanding of physics develops. Here we consider the case of one-dimensional motion; the general case is readily treated by retaining all three terms that form the dot product in Equation 6–16. In one dimension, Equation 6–16 becomes

$$W = \int F\,dx,$$

where we have dropped the subscripts "total" and "net" because it is understood we are talking about total work and net force. But the net force can be written in terms of Newton's second law: $F = ma$, or $F = m\,dv/dt$, so that

$$W = \int m\,\frac{dv}{dt}dx. \qquad (6\text{--}17)$$

The quantities dv, dt, and dx arose as the limits of small numbers Δv, Δt, and Δx. In your calculus class, you have by now shown that the limit of a product or quotient is just the product or quotient of the individual terms involved. For these reasons, we can rearrange the symbols dv, dt, and dx

to rewrite Equation 6–17 in the form

$$W = \int m \, dv \, \frac{dx}{dt}.$$

But $dx/dt = v$, so we have

$$W = \int mv \, dv.$$

The integral is simple; it is just like the form $\int x \, dx$, which we integrate by raising the exponent and dividing by the new exponent. What about the limits? Suppose our object starts out at some speed v_1 and ends up at v_2. Then we have

$$W = \int_{v_1}^{v_2} mv \, dv = \tfrac{1}{2}mv^2 \Big|_{v_1}^{v_2} = \tfrac{1}{2}mv_2^2 - \tfrac{1}{2}mv_1^2. \qquad (6\text{–}18)$$

kinetic energy

What is the significance of Equation 6–18? It shows that an object has associated with it a quantity $\tfrac{1}{2}mv^2$ that changes when, and only when, work is done on the object. The quantity $\tfrac{1}{2}mv^2$ is called the **kinetic energy,** K. Equation 6–18 shows that the change in an object's kinetic energy is equal to the total work done on the object; we often rewrite Equation 6–18 in the form

$$\Delta K = W, \qquad (6\text{–}19)$$

work-energy theorem

where ΔK is the change in kinetic energy. Equations 6–18 and 6–19 are equivalent forms of the **work-energy theorem.**

In particular, an object accelerated from rest to speed v experiences a change $\tfrac{1}{2}mv^2$ in kinetic energy; we then say that an object moving at speed v has kinetic energy $\tfrac{1}{2}mv^2$ by virtue of its motion. Like velocity, kinetic energy is a relative term; its value depends on the reference frame in which it is measured. Unlike velocity, though, kinetic energy is a scalar. Since it depends on the square of the speed, it is always positive.

What if we stop a moving object? Then the kinetic energy changes from $\tfrac{1}{2}mv^2$ to zero—a change of $-\tfrac{1}{2}mv^2$. So we must do negative work on the object to stop it—that is, we must apply a force directed oppositely to the motion. By Newton's third law, the object exerts an equal but oppositely directed force on us, therefore doing positive work $\tfrac{1}{2}mv^2$ on us. So an object of mass m moving at speed v can do work equal to its initial kinetic energy if it is brought to rest.

Example 6–9
Work-Energy Theorem

A biologist uses a spring-loaded gun to shoot tranquilizer darts into an elephant. The gun's spring has spring constant $k = 940$ N/m, and is compressed 25 cm from its equilibrium position before firing a 38-g tranquilizer dart. At what speed does the dart leave the gun?

Solution

From Example 6–6, we know that the work required to compress the spring is $\tfrac{1}{2}kx^2$. When the spring is released, it exhibits the same force-distance relation as when it was compressed, so it now does positive work $\tfrac{1}{2}kx^2$ on the dart. The work-energy theorem tells us that this is also the change in the dart's kinetic energy; since the dart starts from rest, we then have

$$\tfrac{1}{2}kx^2 = \tfrac{1}{2}mv^2,$$

so that

$$v = \sqrt{\frac{k}{m}}\,x = \left(\sqrt{\frac{940\text{ N/m}}{0.038\text{ kg}}}\right)(0.25\text{ m}) = 39\text{ m/s}.$$

Does this result make sense? Yes: in algebraic form, our answer $v = \sqrt{k/m}\,x$ shows that the stiffer the spring, the higher the speed; the greater the mass, the lower the speed, as we expect from Newton's second law. And the further we compress the spring, the greater the speed as well.

Notice how easy the work-energy theorem made this problem. Had we tried to calculate the speed using Newton's second law, we would have had a hard time because the force, and therefore the acceleration, is not constant.

As Example 6–9 shows, the work-energy theorem gives us a quick way to solve problems that might be difficult using Newton's second law. Of course, the work-energy theorem is itself an application of Newton's second law; we used Newton's law to replace the net force with ma in deriving that theorem. But in our calculus derivation of the work-energy theorem, we developed a shortcut way of applying Newton's law that bypasses the details we would have to work out if we applied the law directly.

6.6
ENERGY UNITS

Since work is equal to the change in kinetic energy, the units of kinetic energy are the same as those of work. In SI, the unit of kinetic energy is the joule, equal to one newton-meter.

erg

In the centimeter-gram-second (cgs) system of units still commonly used in several branches of physics, the unit of energy (and work) is the **erg,** equal to one dyne-centimeter (the dyne is the cgs force unit, and is equal to 10^{-5} N). One erg is equal to 10^{-7} J.

foot-pound

We have already seen that the unit of work in the English system is the **foot-pound.** This is therefore also the English unit of energy, and is equal to 1.356 J.

kilowatt-hour

When you pay your electric bill, you are charged for your energy usage in **kilowatt-hours** (kW·h or kWh). One kWh is the amount of energy consumed by a 100-watt light bulb burning for 10 hours and is equal to 3.6×10^6 J.

electron-volt

All these energy units are most useful on the macroscopic scale. In atomic physics and molecular chemistry, scientists often use the **electron-volt** (eV), an energy unit equal to 1.60×10^{-19} J. The electron-volt is based on the energy gained by an electron under specified circumstances that we will discuss in Chapter 23. Chemical reactions between individual atoms and molecules typically involve energies on the order of 1 eV. Nuclear reactions involve energies on the order of 10 MeV (1 MeV $= 10^6$ eV; see Table 1–1). The factor of 10 million between chemical and nuclear reactions shows why the invention of nuclear weapons so radically changed our world. Our largest particle accelerators, probing the fundamental structure of matter, accelerate elementary particles to energies measured in TeV (1 TeV $= 10^{12}$ eV). And physicists seeking a single unified force law governing all of physics consider elementary particle energies of 10^{24} eV—about the kinetic energy of a car moving at 50 km/h.

Appendix D contains an extensive table of energy conversion factors.

Example 6–10
Kinetic Energy

Evaluate and compare the kinetic energies of a 1200-kg car moving at 50 km/h, 100 km/h, and 150 km/h.

Solution

To work in SI units, we convert km/h to m/s; the conversion factor is 1 km/h $=(1000$ m$)/(3600$ s$)=0.278$ m/s, so that the speeds become 14 m/s, 28 m/s, and 42 m/s. Then our energies are

$$K_{50 \text{ km/h}} = \tfrac{1}{2}(1200 \text{ kg})(14 \text{ m/s})^2 = 1.2 \times 10^5 \text{ J},$$

$$K_{100 \text{ km/h}} = \tfrac{1}{2}(1200 \text{ kg})(28 \text{ m/s})^2 = 4.7 \times 10^5 \text{ J},$$

$$K_{150 \text{ km/h}} = \tfrac{1}{2}(1200 \text{ kg})(42 \text{ m/s})^2 = 1.1 \times 10^6 \text{ J}.$$

Since the speed is squared, the kinetic energy is four times as high when the speed is doubled, and more than double when the speed is increased by 50 per cent. Since all the kinetic energy must be removed to stop the vehicle, this example suggests the hazard of high-speed driving.

Example 6–11
A Falling Coconut

What is the kinetic energy of a 1.5-lb coconut landing on your head after falling 30 ft starting from rest? Express in foot-pounds and joules. Determine also the final speed of the coconut.

Solution

The only force acting on the falling coconut is the constant downward force of gravity, which is the weight of the coconut. Acting over a distance $\Delta y = 30$ ft, this force does work

$$W = F_g \Delta y = (1.5 \text{ lb})(30 \text{ ft}) = 45 \text{ ft·lb}.$$

Since the gravitational force is the net force, the work-energy theorem tells that this is the kinetic energy gained by the coconut. With 1 ft·lb $=1.356$ J, the kinetic energy of the coconut is (45 ft·lb)(1.356 J/ft·lb)$=61$ J.

The speed is given by solving $K=\tfrac{1}{2}mv^2$ for v. Here the *weight* of the coconut is 1.5 lb, or 6.7 N (see Appendix D for conversion tables); the mass is then $(6.7 \text{ N})/(9.8 \text{ m/s}^2) = 0.68$ kg. So

$$v = \sqrt{\frac{2K}{m}} = \sqrt{\frac{(2)(61 \text{ J})}{0.68 \text{ kg}}} = 13 \text{ m/s}.$$

Example 6–12
A Falling Snowflake

What is the kinetic energy of a 10-mg snowflake settling on your hand at 90 cm/s? Express in joules, ergs, and eV.

Solution

In SI, we have

$$K = \tfrac{1}{2}mv^2 = \tfrac{1}{2}(10 \times 10^{-6}\ \text{kg})(0.90\ \text{m/s})^2 = 4.1 \times 10^{-6}\ \text{J}.$$

With 10^7 erg/J, this is $(4.1 \times 10^{-6}\ \text{J})(10^7\ \text{erg/J}) = 41$ erg. Or, dividing by the conversion factor 1.6×10^{-19} J/eV, it is also equivalent to $(4.1 \times 10^{-6}\ \text{J})/(1.6 \times 10^{-19}\ \text{J/eV})$ $= 2.6 \times 10^{13}$ eV. This is only slightly higher than the energy given to individual protons in the largest particle accelerators.

6.7
POWER

Climbing stairs at constant speed requires the same amount of work no matter how fast you go. Why? Because at constant speed, you exert an average force exactly equal to your weight, and do so over a fixed distance; work is the product of force and distance. But of course it's much harder to run up the stairs than to walk. In a case like this, we are concerned not so much with the total work done as with the *rate* at which we do work.

power
average power

Power is defined as the rate of doing work. If an amount of work ΔW is done in a time Δt, then the **average power** $\overline{P}$ is

$$\overline{P} = \frac{\Delta W}{\Delta t}. \tag{6-20}$$

instantaneous power

Often the rate of doing work varies with time. Then we define the **instantaneous power** as the average power taken in the limit of arbitrarily small time interval Δt:

$$P = \lim_{\Delta t \to 0} \frac{\Delta W}{\Delta t} = \frac{dW}{dt}. \tag{6-21}$$

Equations 6–20 and 6–21 both show that the units of power are joules/second. One J/s is given the name watt (W) in honor of James Watt, a Scottish engineer and inventor who was instrumental in developing the steam engine as a practical power source. It is ironic that the SI unit, the watt, supersedes the English unit of power suggested by Watt himself, the horsepower. Watt defined one horsepower as 550 ft·lb/s; he chose this figure—somewhat greater than the experimentally measured output of a horse—so that buyers of his steam engines would not feel short-changed. Since a ft·lb is 1.356 J, one horsepower is about 746 J/s or 746 W.

Example 6–13
Climbing Mt. Washington

A 55-kg hiker ascends New Hampshire's Mount Washington, a vertical rise of 1300 m from the base elevation. The hike takes 2 hours. A 1500-kg car drives up the Mount Washington Auto Road, the same vertical rise, in half an hour. What is the average power output in each case? Assume the hiker and car maintain constant speed and neglect friction, so that each does work only against the gravitational force.

Solution

In Example 6–8, we found that the work done by gravity depends only on the overall change in vertical position. Here the hiker and car do positive work $\Delta W = mgh$ to overcome the negative work $-mgh$ done by gravity. So the average power outputs are

$$\overline{P}_{\text{hiker}} = \frac{\Delta W}{\Delta T} = \frac{(55 \text{ kg})(9.8 \text{ m/s}^2)(1300 \text{ m})}{(2.0 \text{ h})(3600 \text{ s/h})} = 97 \text{ W}$$

and

$$\overline{P}_{\text{car}} = \frac{\Delta W}{\Delta t} = \frac{(1500 \text{ kg})(9.8 \text{ m/s}^2)(1300 \text{ m})}{(0.50 \text{ h})(3600 \text{ s/h})} = 1.1 \times 10^4 \text{ W}.$$

These values correspond to 0.13 hp and 15 hp, respectively. The figure of 97 W is typical of the sustained long-term power output of the human body. Remember that next time you leave a 100-W light bulb burning! The power plant supplying the electricity is doing work at about the rate your body can (actually, it's doing work about three times this rate, for reasons we will examine in Chapter 19). You may be surprised at the low output of the car, given that it probably has an engine rated at several hundred horsepower. Actually, only a small fraction of a car engine's rated horsepower is available in mechanical power to the wheels. The rest is lost in friction and heating.

When the power is constant, so that the average and instantaneous power are the same, then Equation 6–20 shows that the amount of work W done in a time Δt is just

$$W = P\Delta t. \tag{6–22}$$

When the power is not constant, we can consider small amounts of work ΔW, each taken over so small a time interval Δt that the power is nearly constant. Adding all these small amounts of work, and taking the limit as Δt becomes arbitrarily small, we have

$$W = \lim_{\Delta t \to 0} \sum P\Delta t = \int_{t_1}^{t_2} P \, dt, \tag{6–23}$$

where t_1 and t_2 are the beginning and end of the time interval over which we calculate the power.

Example 6–14

An Electric Bill: Yankee Stadium

Each of the 500 floodlights at Yankee Stadium uses electrical energy at the rate of 1.0 kW. How much does it cost to run these lights during a 4-hour night game, if electricity costs 9.5 cents per kilowatt-hour?

Solution

The total power consumption of the 500 lights is 500 kW. Since the power is constant, the total work done to run the lamps is given by Equation 6–22:

$$W = P\Delta t = (500 \text{ kW})(4.0 \text{ h}) = 2000 \text{ kWh}.$$

The cost is then (2000 kWh)(9.5 cents/kWh) = $190.

Example 6–15

Variable Power

Figure 6–17 shows the rate of electrical energy use in a typical home between the hours of 3 PM and 9 PM. The curve shown is given by

$$P = at^2 + bt + c,$$

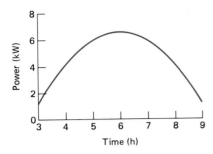

Fig. 6–17
Electrical power consumption in a home
(Example 6–15).

where t is the time in hours and where $a = -0.60$ kW/h², $b = 7.2$ kW/h, and $c = -15$ kW. Find the total energy consumption during this interval.

Solution

Now the power varies with time, so we must evaluate the integral in Equation 6–23:

$$W = \int_{t_1}^{t_2} P \, dt = \int_{t_1}^{t_2} (at^2 + bt + c) \, dt$$

$$= \left(\frac{at^3}{3} + \frac{bt^2}{2} + ct \right) \Bigg|_{t_1}^{t_2} = \frac{a(t_2^3 - t_1^3)}{3} + \frac{b(t_2^2 - t_1^2)}{2} + c(t_2 - t_1),$$

where we have used the usual rule for integrating a power of a variable: raise the exponent by 1 and divide by the new exponent. Putting in numbers including the limits $t_1 = 3$ h and $t_2 = 9$ h, we have

$$W = \frac{(-0.60)(9^3 - 3^3)}{3} + \frac{(7.2)(9^2 - 3^2)}{2} + (-15)(9 - 3) = 29 \text{ kWh},$$

where we have left off the units in doing the calculation. Note that with power in kW and time in hours, our answer must come out in kWh.

Does our result make sense? Figure 6–17 shows a maximum power of about 6.5 kW; at this rate we would use about 40 kWh in the 6-hour period. The minimum power in Fig. 6–17 is a little over 1 kW; at this rate we would use 6 kWh in the period. Our answer, 29 kWh, lies in between and is toward the high end because the curve rises rapidly. The average power consumption during the interval is just 29 kWh/6 h or 4.8 kW.

We can derive an expression relating power, applied force, and velocity by noting that the work ΔW done by a force **F** acting on an object that undergoes a small displacement $\Delta \mathbf{r}$ is given by Equation 6–4:

$$\Delta W = \mathbf{F} \cdot \Delta \mathbf{r}.$$

Dividing both sides by the time interval Δt in which the displacement $\Delta \mathbf{r}$ occurs, and taking the limit as $\Delta t \to 0$, we have

$$\lim_{\Delta t \to 0} \frac{\Delta W}{\Delta t} = \lim_{\Delta t \to 0} \mathbf{F} \cdot \frac{\Delta \mathbf{r}}{\Delta t} = \mathbf{F} \cdot \frac{d\mathbf{r}}{dt}.$$

But the limit of $\Delta W / \Delta t$ is just the instantaneous power, P, and $d\mathbf{r}/dt$ is the velocity, **v,** so that

$$P = \mathbf{F} \cdot \mathbf{v}. \tag{6–24}$$

Example 6–16
Bicycling

As you ride your 14-kg bicycle on level ground, you must overcome a frictional force of 30 N. If your mass is 65 kg, what is the power you must supply to maintain a steady 25 km/h (*a*) on level ground and (*b*) going up a 5° incline?

Solution

The force of friction opposes your motion; to overcome friction, you must apply a force of equal magnitude in the direction of motion. The 25-km/h speed is equivalent to $(25 \times 10^3 \text{ m})/(3600 \text{ s}) = 6.9 \text{ m/s}$, so the power you supply is

$$P = \mathbf{F} \cdot \mathbf{v} = Fv = (30 \text{ N})(6.9 \text{ m/s}) = 210 \text{ W},$$

or a little over one-fourth horsepower. (In writing $\mathbf{F} \cdot \mathbf{v} = Fv$, we used the fact that the force is in the same direction as the velocity, so the cosine in the dot product is 1.)

In climbing the hill, you must overcome not only friction but also the down-slope component of the gravitational force. From Example 5–1, this downslope component is $mg \sin\theta$, here equal to $(14 \text{ kg} + 65 \text{ kg})(9.8 \text{ m/s}^2)(\sin 5°) = 67 \text{ N}$. Also from Example 5–1, we know that the normal force is $mg \cos\theta$, so that the frictional force is reduced from its level-ground value by a factor $\cos\theta$. But here $\cos\theta = \cos 5° = 0.996$, so that the frictional force is still essentially 30 N. Then the power you must supply is

$$P = Fv = (30 \text{ N} + 67 \text{ N})(6.9 \text{ m/s}) = 670 \text{ W},$$

or nearly one horsepower. Here again we wrote $P = Fv$ since the applied force is in the direction of the velocity.

SUMMARY

This chapter introduces the important concepts of work and energy, whose meanings in physics are similar but not identical to their meanings in everyday language.

1. **Work** is defined as the product of the component of force in the direction an object moves and the distance through which the object moves. Taking the x-direction as the direction of motion, work is

$$W = F_x \Delta x.$$

The SI unit of work is the newton-meter, given the special name **joule** (J).

2. The **scalar product** or **dot product** of two vectors provides a convenient shorthand for writing work in terms of the force and displacement vectors. The scalar product of any two vectors $\mathbf{A}$ and $\mathbf{B}$ is defined as the product of their magnitudes with the cosine of the angle between them:

$$\mathbf{A} \cdot \mathbf{B} = AB\cos\theta.$$

In terms of the dot product, the work done by a force $\mathbf{F}$ acting on an object undergoing displacement $\Delta\mathbf{r}$ is

$$W = \mathbf{F} \cdot \Delta\mathbf{r}.$$

3. When force varies with distance, work must be calculated by summing the terms $\mathbf{F} \cdot \Delta\mathbf{r}$ in the limit of arbitrarily small $\Delta\mathbf{r}$:

$$W = \lim_{\Delta r \to 0} \sum \mathbf{F} \cdot \Delta\mathbf{r}.$$

This limiting process defines the **definite integral:**

$$W = \int_{r_1}^{r_2} \mathbf{F} \cdot d\mathbf{r}.$$

Written in terms of a dot product of force with the infinitesimal displacement $d\mathbf{r}$, this form of the definite integral is called a **line integral.** In the case of one-dimensional motion along the x-axis, the line integral reduces to

$$W = \int_{x_1}^{x_2} F \, dx.$$

Integration is the inverse of differentiation; the methods of calculus show how to evaluate integrals. In particular, the integral of a power of a variable is obtained by raising the exponent and dividing by the new exponent:

$$\int_{x_1}^{x_2} x^n \, dx = \left. \frac{x^{n+1}}{n+1} \right|_{x_1}^{x_2},$$

where the $\left. \vphantom{x} \right|_{x_1}^{x_2}$ means to evaluate the expression at x_2 and subtract from it the same expression evaluated at x_1.

4. Work done by a nonzero net force results in a change in an object's **kinetic energy,** a scalar quantity given by $K = \frac{1}{2}mv^2$. The **work-energy theorem** shows that the change in kinetic energy is exactly equal to the work done by the net force:

$$W = \Delta K = \tfrac{1}{2}mv_2^2 - \tfrac{1}{2}mv_1^2,$$

where v_1 and v_2 are the speeds before and after the work is done, respectively. The units of energy are the same as those of work. In addition to the SI unit, the joule, other common units include the English foot-pound; the kilowatt-hour; the cgs unit erg; and the electron-volt, widely used in atomic, nuclear, and high-energy physics.

5. **Power** is the rate at which work is done. In SI units, power is measured in joules/second, or **watts;**

1 W = 1 J/s. The average power $\overline{P}$ is given by

$$\overline{P} = \frac{\Delta W}{\Delta t},$$

while the instantaneous power is

$$P = \frac{dW}{dt}.$$

Inverting this last expression allows us to calculate work as the integral of the power:

$$W = \int_{t_1}^{t_2} P \, dt.$$

When a force **F** acts on an object moving with velocity **v**, the instantaneous power supplied by that force is

$$P = \mathbf{F} \cdot \mathbf{v}.$$

QUESTIONS

1. Give two examples of situations in which you might think you are doing work but in which, in the technical sense, you do no work.
2. If the scalar product of two nonzero vectors is zero, what can you conclude about their relative directions?
3. Must you do work to whirl a ball around on the end of a string? Explain.
4. If you pick up a suitcase and put it down, how much total work have you done on the suitcase? Does your answer change if you pick up the suitcase and drop it?
5. You lift a book from your desk to a bookshelf. It is initially at rest and ends up at rest, so that its kinetic energy has not changed. Yet you have certainly done work on the book. Explain why this is not a violation of the work-energy theorem.
6. Would Equation 6–5 hold in a coordinate system whose axes were not perpendicular?
7. A given force F is applied to move a crate a fixed distance across the floor. Does the amount of work done by the force depend on the coefficient of friction? Does the total work done on the crate depend on the coefficient of friction?
8. Discuss the relation between a sum and an integral.
9. Two cross-country skiers race up opposite sides of the mountain shown in Fig. 6–18. If the skier coming up the steeper side wins, compare the work and the average power associated with each skier. Assume that no work is done by friction (although static friction, which does no work, is what makes the climb possible).

Fig. 6–18   Question 9

10. With a given nonzero coefficient of friction, compare the force required to slide a piano up a steep ramp versus a gradual ramp. Compare also the work done in raising the piano the same height on each ramp.
11. Does the gravitational force of the sun do work on a planet in a circular orbit? On a comet in an elliptical orbit? Explain.
12. How does the dependence of a car's kinetic energy on speed affect its stopping distance, assuming a constant braking force?
13. Give an example showing that kinetic energy depends on frame of reference.
14. Can kinetic energy ever be negative? Explain.
15. A pendulum bob swings back and forth on the end of a string, describing a circular arc. Does the tension force in the string do any work?
16. In the preceding question, does the kinetic energy of the bob change as it swings back and forth? Why?
17. Does your car's kinetic energy change if you drive at constant speed for 1 hour?
18. List in order of increasing size: erg, kWh, eV, ft·lb, J. Which units are most appropriate in discussing the energetics of macroscopic systems? Which is most appropriate in atomic physics?
19. A watt-second is a unit of what quantity? Relate it to a more standard SI unit.
20. A body collides with a spring and compresses it an amount Δx. How will Δx change if you double the impact velocity? Half the mass of the body? Triple the spring constant?
21. In the absence of air resistance, it would take the same time for a fly ball to rise as to fall. In the presence of air resistance, however, the ball will take longer to fall. Use the work-energy theorem to explain this difference.
22. Two particles of different mass have the same momentum. Compare their kinetic energies.
23. A truck is moving northward at 55 mph. Later, it is moving eastward at the same speed. Has its kinetic energy changed? Has its momentum changed? Has work been done on the truck? Has a force acted on the truck? Explain.

_____ **PROBLEMS** _____

Section 6.1   *Work*

1. How much work do you do as you exert a 95-N force to push a 30-kg shopping cart through a 14-m-long supermarket aisle?

2. If the coefficient of kinetic friction is 0.21, how much work do you do when you slide a 50-kg box at constant speed across a 4.8-m-wide room?

3. A crane lifts a 500-kg beam vertically upward 12 m, then swings it eastward 6.0 m. How much work does the crane do? Neglect friction, and assume the beam moves with constant speed.

4. You lift a 45-kg barbell from the ground to a height of 2.5 m. (*a*) How much work do you do on the barbell? (*b*) You hold the barbell aloft for 2.0 min. How much work do you do on the barbell during this time? (*c*) You lower the barbell to the ground. Now how much work do you do on it?

5. You slide a box of books at constant speed up a 30° ramp, applying a force of 200 N directed up the slope. The coefficient of sliding friction is 0.18. (*a*) How much work have you done when the box has risen 1 m vertically? (*b*) What is the mass of the box?

6. Two people push a stalled car at its front doors, each applying a 330-N force at 25° to the forward direction, as shown in Fig. 6–19. How much work does each do in pushing the car 6.2 m?

W = F Δr cos θ
W = 330 N 6.2 25°

Fig. 6–19   Problem 6

7. A locomotive does 8.8×10^{11} J of work in pulling a 2×10^6-kg train 150 km. What is the average force in the coupling between the locomotive and the rest of the train?

8. An elevator of mass m rises a distance h up a vertical shaft with upward acceleration equal to one-tenth g. How much work does the elevator cable do on the elevator?

9. A 20-kg child lies on her back and scoots 7.4 m across the floor at constant speed by applying a 50-N force with the soles of her feet (Fig. 6–20). (*a*) How much work does she do? (*b*) What is the coefficient of friction between the child's back and the floor?

10. The mass of a hydrogen atom is 1.67×10^{-27} kg. How many eV of work does gravity do on the atom when it falls a distance of 10 cm? (See Section 6.6 for the definition of the eV.)

Fig. 6–20   Problem 9

Section 6.2   *Work and the Scalar Product*

11. Show that the scalar product is distributive: $\mathbf{A} \cdot (\mathbf{B} + \mathbf{C}) = \mathbf{A} \cdot \mathbf{B} + \mathbf{A} \cdot \mathbf{C}$.

12. Show that the scalar product has the property that $(c\mathbf{A}) \cdot \mathbf{B} = \mathbf{A} \cdot (c\mathbf{B})$, where c is a scalar.

13. Given the following vectors:

   A has length 10 and points 30° above the x-axis

   B has length 4.0 and points 10° to the left of the y-axis

   $\mathbf{C} = 5.6\hat{\imath} - 3.1\hat{\jmath}$

   $\mathbf{D} = 1.9\hat{\imath} + 7.2\hat{\jmath},$

   compute the scalar products (*a*) $\mathbf{A} \cdot \mathbf{B}$; (*b*) $\mathbf{C} \cdot \mathbf{D}$; (*c*) $\mathbf{B} \cdot \mathbf{C}$.

14. (*a*) Find the scalar product of the vectors $a\hat{\imath} + b\hat{\jmath}$ and $b\hat{\imath} - a\hat{\jmath}$, and (*b*) determine the angle between them. (*a* and *b* are arbitrary constants.)

15. Rework Example 6–5 using Equation 6–3 instead of Equation 6–5.

16. Use Equations 6–3 and 6–5 to show that the angle between the vectors $\mathbf{A} = a_x\hat{\imath} + a_y\hat{\jmath}$ and $\mathbf{B} = b_x\hat{\imath} + b_y\hat{\jmath}$ is

$$\theta = \cos^{-1}\left\{ \frac{a_x b_x + a_y b_y}{[(a_x^2 + a_y^2)(b_x^2 + b_y^2)]^{1/2}} \right\}$$

17. Given that $\mathbf{A} = 2\hat{\imath} + 2\hat{\jmath}$, $\mathbf{B} = 5\hat{\imath}$, and $\mathbf{C} = \sqrt{2}\hat{\imath} - \pi\hat{\jmath}$, find the angles between (*a*) **A** and **B**; (*b*) **A** and **C**; (*c*) **B** and **C**. *Hint:* See previous problem.

18. A force $\mathbf{F} = 67\hat{\imath} + 23\hat{\jmath} + 55\hat{k}$ N is applied to a body as it moves in a straight line from $\mathbf{r}_1 = 16\hat{\imath} + 31\hat{\jmath}$ to $\mathbf{r}_2 = 21\hat{\imath} + 10\hat{\jmath} + 14\hat{k}$ m. How much work is done by the force?

19. A rope pulls a box a horizontal distance of 23 m, as shown in Fig. 6–21. If the rope tension is 120 N, and if the rope does 2500 J of work on the box, what angle does it make with the horizontal?

Fig. 6–21   Problem 19

Section 6.3   A Varying Force

20. Find the total work done by the force shown in Fig. 6–22, as the object on which it acts moves from $x = 0$ to $x = 5.0$ m.

Fig. 6–22   Problem 20

21. A force F acts in the x-direction, its magnitude given by $F = ax^2$, where x is in meters and a is exactly 5 N/m². (a) Find an exact value for the work done by this force as it acts on a particle moving from $x = 0$ to $x = 6$ m. Now find approximate values for the work by dividing the area under the force curve into rectangles of width (b) $\Delta x = 2$ m; (c) $\Delta x = 1$ m; (d) $\Delta x = \frac{1}{2}$ m with height equal to the magnitude of the force in the center of the interval. Calculate the per cent error in each case.

22. A spring has spring constant $k = 200$ N/m. How much work does it take to stretch the spring (a) 10 cm from equilibrium and (b) from 10 cm to 20 cm from equilibrium?

23. A certain amount of work is required to stretch spring A a certain distance. Twice as much work is required to stretch spring B half that distance. Compare the spring constants of the two springs.

24. On graph paper, draw an accurate force-distance curve for the force of Example 6–7, and obtain a solution to that example by determining graphically the area under the curve.

25. A force $\mathbf{F}$ acts in the x-direction, its magnitude given by $F = F_0 \cos(x/x_0)$, where $F_0 = 51$ N and $x_0 = 13$ m. Calculate the work done by this force acting on an object as it moves from $x = 0$ to $x = 37$ m. *Hint:* Consult Appendix B for the integral of the cosine function, and treat the argument of the cosine as a quantity in radians.

26. Work the preceding problem graphically, by making an accurate plot of the force versus distance curve on graph paper, and determining the area (in units of work) under the curve.

27. A force given by $F = a\sqrt{x}$ acts in the x-direction, where $a = 14$ N/m$^{1/2}$. Calculate the work done by this force acting on an object as it moves (a) from $x = 0$ to

$x = 2.2$ m; (b) from $x = 2.2$ m to $x = 4.4$ m; (c) from 4.4 m to 6.6 m.

28. A force given by $F = b/\sqrt{x}$ acts in the x-direction, where b is a constant with the units N·m$^{1/2}$. Show that even though the force becomes arbitrarily large as x approaches 0, the work done in moving from x_1 to x_2 remains finite even as x_1 approaches zero. Find an expression for that work in the limit $x_1 \to 0$.

29. The force exerted by a rubber band is given approximately by

$$F = F_0\left[\frac{\ell_0 + x}{\ell_0} - \frac{\ell_0^2}{(\ell_0 + x)^2}\right],$$

where ℓ_0 is the unstretched length, x the stretch, and F_0 is a constant (although F_0 varies with temperature). Find the work needed to stretch the rubber band a distance x.

Section 6.4   Force and Work in Three Dimensions

30. You put your little sister (mass m) on a swing whose chains have length ℓ, and pull slowly back until the swing makes an angle ϕ with the vertical. Show that the work you do is $mg\ell(1 - \cos\phi)$.

31. A cylindrical log of radius R lies half buried in the ground, as shown in Fig. 6–23. An ant climbs the log at constant speed, supplying just enough force to balance gravity. Show by evaluating $\int \mathbf{F} \cdot d\mathbf{r}$ that the work required to reach the top is mgR.

Fig. 6–23   Problem 31

32. A particle of mass m moves from the origin to the point $x = 3$, $y = 6$ along the curve $y = ax^2 - bx$, where $a = 2$ m^{-1} and $b = 4$. It is subject to a force $\mathbf{F} = cxy\hat{\mathbf{i}} + d\hat{\mathbf{j}}$, where $c = 10$ N/m² and $d = 15$ N. Calculate the work done by the force.

33. Repeat the preceding problem for the case when the particle moves first along the x-axis from the origin to the point (3,0), then parallel to the y-axis until it reaches (3,6).

34. A playground structure is in the form of a spherical cap of radius R; an arc from the top of the cap to the ground subtends an angle θ, as shown in Fig. 6–24. A child of mass m slides from the top of the structure to the ground. If the coefficient of friction is μ, show that the work done on the child by the frictional force is $-\mu mgR \sin\theta$.

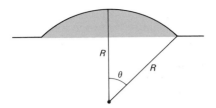

Fig. 6–24 Problem 34

Sections 6.5–6.6 *Kinetic Energy and Energy Units*

35. A 3.5×10^5-kg jumbo jet is cruising at 1000 km/h. (*a*) What is its kinetic energy relative to the ground? A 85-kg passenger strolls down the aisle at 2.9 km/h. What is the passenger's kinetic energy (*b*) relative to the ground and (*c*) relative to the plane?

36. Electrons in a color TV tube are accelerated to 25% of the speed of light. How much work does the TV tube do on each electron? (At this speed, relativity theory introduces small but measurable corrections; here you neglect these effects.) See inside front cover for the electron mass.

37. In a cyclotron used to produce radioactive isotopes for medical research at the Massachusetts General Hospital, deuterium nuclei (mass 3.3×10^{-27} kg) are given kinetic energies of 5.5 MeV. What is their speed? Compare with the speed of light.

38. At what speed must a 950-kg subcompact car be moving to have the same kinetic energy as a 3.2×10^4-kg truck going 20 km/h?

39. A 60-kg skateboarder comes over the top of a hill at 5.0 m/s, and reaches 10 m/s at the bottom of the hill. Find the total work done on the skateboarder between the top and bottom of the hill.

40. Two unknown elementary particles pass through a detection chamber. If they have the same kinetic energy and their mass ratio is 4:1, what is the ratio of their speeds?

41. A 300-kg boulder rolls after an intrepid explorer at a speed of 10 m/s (Fig. 6–25). The explorer is running away at 3.0 m/s. What is the kinetic energy of the boulder as it hits the explorer, measured in the explorer's frame of reference? (Photo from *Raiders of the Lost Ark* © MCMLXXXI by Lucasfilm, Ltd. All rights reserved.)

42. After a tornado, a 0.50-g drinking straw was found embedded 4.5 cm in a tree. Subsequent measurements showed that the tree would exert a stopping force of 70 N on the straw. What was the straw's speed when it hit the tree?

43. You drop a 150-g baseball from a sixth-story window 16 m above the ground. What are (*a*) its kinetic energy and (*b*) its speed when it hits the ground? Neglect air resistance.

44. A hospital patient was being wheeled in for x-ray when his leg slipped off the stretcher and his heel hit the concrete floor. As a physicist, you are called to testify about the forces involved in this accident. You estimate that the foot and leg had an effective mass of 8 kg, that they dropped freely a distance of 70 cm, and that the stopping distance was 2 cm. What force can you claim was exerted on the foot by the floor? Give your answer in pounds so the jury will have a feel for the size of the force.

45. From what height would you have to drop a car for its impact to be equivalent to a collision at 20 mph?

46. A 2.3-kg particle's position as a function of time is given by $x = bt^3 - ct$, where $b = 0.41$ m/s^3 and $c = 1.9$ m/s. Find the work done on the particle between the time $t = 0$ and $t = 2.0$ s.

47. In a switchyard, freight cars start from rest and roll down a 2.8-m incline and come to rest against a spring bumper at the end of the track (Fig. 6–26). If the spring constant is 4.3×10^6 N/m, how much is the spring compressed when hit by a 57,000-kg freight car?

2.8 m

Fig. 6–26 Problem 47

48. Catapults run by high-pressure steam from the ship's nuclear reactor are used on the aircraft carrier Enterprise to launch jet aircraft to takeoff speed in only 76 m of deck space. A catapult exerts a 1.1×10^6 N force on a 3.3×10^4 kg aircraft. What are (*a*) the kinetic energy and (*b*) the speed of the aircraft as it leaves the catapult? (*c*) How long does the catapulting operation take? (*d*) What is the acceleration of the aircraft?

49. A block of mass *m* slides from rest without friction down the slope shown in Fig. 6–27. (*a*) How much work is done on the block by the normal force of the slope? (*b*) Show that the final speed is $\sqrt{2gh}$ regardless of the details of the slope.

Fig. 6–25 Problem 41

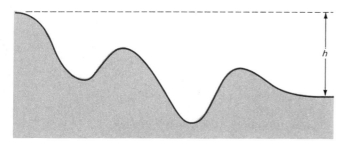

Fig. 6–27   Problem 49

Section 6.7   *Power*

50. A horse plows a 200-m-long furrow in 5.0 min, exerting a force of 750 N. What is its power output, measured in watts and in horsepower?
51. A typical car battery stores about 1 kWh of energy. What is its power output if it is drained completely in (*a*) 1 minute; (*b*) 1 hour; (*c*) 1 day?
52. Herschel Walker's mass is 90 kg. (*a*) When he is running at 7.0 m/s, what is his kinetic energy? (*b*) If a tackler grabs him, and slows him to 3.0 m/s over a 1.0-s interval, what power does Herschel supply?
53. A "mass driver" is designed to launch raw materials mined on the moon to a factory in lunar orbit. The driver can accelerate a 1000-kg package to 2.0 km/s (just under lunar escape speed) in 55 s. (*a*) What is its power output during a launch? (*b*) If the driver makes one launch every 30 minutes, what is its average power consumption?
54. An 85-kg long-jumper takes 3.0 s to reach a prejump speed of 10 m/s. What is his power output?
55. Estimate your power output as you do deep knee bends at the rate of one per second.
56. At what rate can a one-half horsepower well pump deliver water to a tank 60 m above the water level in the well? Give your answer in kg/s and gal/min.
57. A young boy, fortified by a hearty lunch, straps himself into his human-powered go-cart and begins to expend his bodily energy in such a way that his vehicle's speed increases quadratically with time. Show that his power output must increase in proportion to t^3.
58. With your car initially at rest, you depress the accelerator pedal in such a way that the power delivered by the car's engine is proportional to the time since you started. Neglecting losses to air and road friction, show that the car's speed also increases linearly with time.

Supplementary Problems

59. If the ant of Problem 31 climbs with constant speed v along the log surface, (*a*) what is its power output as a function of time? (*b*) Integrate your expression for power to show that the total work to climb the log is the same as that obtained in Problem 31.
60. You need to purchase a refrigerator, and are looking at an energy-efficient, 250-W model for $950 and a

standard, 450-W model for $800. If each refrigerator is actually running 20% of the time, and if electricity costs 9 cents/kWh, how long would you have to own the refrigerator for the energy-efficient model to be more economical? Work your answer (*a*) neglecting interest on your money and (*b*) assuming you can earn 7.4% interest on your savings, compounded continuously. *Note:* Part (*b*) calls for an iterative calculation.

61. A machine delivers power at a decreasing rate $P = W_0/(t+1)^2$, where W_0 is a constant with the units of work, and t is the time in seconds. The machine starts at time $t=0$ and continues forever. Show that it nevertheless does only a finite amount of work, equal to W_0.

62. An unusual spring has the force-distance curve in Fig. 6–28. This curve is described analytically by $F=100x^2$ for $0 \leq x \leq 1$ and $F=100(4x-x^2-2)$ for $1 \leq x \leq 2$, where x is the displacement in meters from the equilibrium position and F is in newtons. Find the work done in stretching this spring (*a*) from equilibrium to 1 m and (*b*) from 1 m to 2 m. (*c*) Show that the work done in stretching the spring from equilibrium to 2 m is the same as for an ideal spring with $k=100$ N/m. (*d*) Explain, in terms of the shape of the graph, why this is true. Is it true for any other distance stretched?

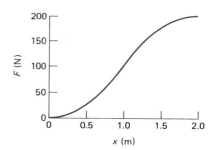

Fig. 6–28   Problem 62

63. The force of earth's gravity on an object of mass m is given by mgR_e^2/r^2, where g is the acceleration of gravity at earth's surface, R_e is earth's radius, and r is the distance in meters from the center of the earth. (*a*) Show that the work required to move an object from earth's surface to a distance r from the center of the earth is given by

$$W = mgR_e \left(1 - \frac{R_e}{r} \right).$$

Calculate and compare the work needed to boost an 850-kg satellite (*b*) to low earth orbit, 250 km above earth's surface; (*c*) to geosynchronous orbit, 36,000 km above earth's surface; (*d*) to the moon's orbit, 390,000 km from earth. (Your answers do not include additional work needed to achieve orbital speed.)

64. A spring scale hangs vertically. A mass is attached to the unstretched scale and released from rest. It bounces up and down awhile until friction eventually brings it again to rest, with the final scale reading equal to the weight. Show that the maximum scale reading is twice the object's weight.

65. A locomotive accelerates a freight train of total mass M, applying constant power P from rest. Determine the velocity and position of the train as functions of time.

66. A possible reaction for a nuclear fusion reactor involves the fusing of two deuterium nuclei (each consisting of one proton and one neutron) to form helium, a process that releases 24 MeV of energy. In the fusion process, the two nuclei are bound tightly by the strong nuclear force. But the nuclear force is effective only when the nuclei are closer than about 10^{-15} m; beyond this their interaction is dominated by a repulsive electrical force given in newtons by $F = 2.3 \times 10^{-28}/r^2$, where r is the distance in meters between the two nuclei. Consider one deuterium nucleus held at rest and another a long way from it. (a) Calculate the work needed to overcome the electrical force and bring the second nucleus to within 10^{-15} m of the first. (b) If the electric force alone acts between the nuclei, what initial speed should the second nucleus have if it is to fuse with the first? (c) A typical large nuclear fission power plant has an electrical power output of 1000 MW. If a fusion plant with the same power output converts fusion energy to electricity with 40% efficiency, at what rate must deuterium-deuterium fusion reactions occur in its reactor?

7

CONSERVATION OF ENERGY

(a)

(b)

Fig. 7–1
Both the rock climber (a) and the mover (b) do work, but only the climber can recover that work as kinetic energy.

conservative force

nonconservative force

The rock climber of Fig. 7–1a does work as she ascends the vertical cliff. So does the mover of Fig. 7–1b, as he pushes a heavy chest across the floor. But there is a difference. If the rock climber lets go, down she goes; the work she put into the climb comes back as kinetic energy of her fall. If the mover lets go of the trunk, though, it just sits there; it has no tendency to return to its starting place.

The contrast between the two situations of Fig. 7–1 illustrates an important distinction between two types of forces. In this chapter, we explore that distinction and from it develop one of the most important principles in all of physics: conservation of energy. In later chapters, we will expand the conservation of energy principle to include new forms of energy we encounter. Ultimately, in Chapter 33, we will see how Einstein's theory of relativity subsumes two great principles—conservation of energy and conservation of matter—into a single statement.

7.1
CONSERVATIVE AND NONCONSERVATIVE FORCES

Both the climber and the mover of Fig. 7–1 are working against external forces—gravity for the climber and friction for the mover. The difference between the two situations is this: if the climber lets go, the gravitational force "gives back" the work that she did; that work manifests itself as a gain in her kinetic energy. But the frictional force does not "give back" the work that the mover did; that work has disappeared, and cannot be recovered as kinetic energy.

We use the term **conservative force** to describe a force that, like gravity, "gives back" work that has been done against it. A force like friction is **nonconservative.** We can give a more precise mathematical sense of this distinction by considering the work involved in moving an object over a closed path—that is, **a** path that ends up at the same point where it started. Suppose, for example, that our rock climber ascends a cliff of height h and then returns to her starting point. How much work has the gravitational force done on her? That force has magnitude mg, and points downward. Going up, the force is directed opposite to her motion, so that the work done by gravity is $-mgh$. Coming down, the force is in the same direction as the motion, so that the work done by gravity is $+mgh$. The total work that gravity does on the climber as she traverses the closed path from the bottom to the top of the cliff and back again is therefore zero.

(We're concerned here only with the work done by gravity, so other forces don't affect this result. For example, if the climber falls from the top of the cliff, then the only work done during her descent is that of gravity, so that she gains kinetic energy on the way down. But if she climbs carefully down, she exerts upward forces so that there is no net work done on the way down, and she arrives safely at the bottom. But in either case, the work done on her *by gravity* is mgh.)

Now suppose the mover of Fig. 7–1b pushes the chest a distance ℓ across a room, discovers it's the wrong room, and pushes it back to the door. Like the climber, the chest describes a closed path. How much work is done by the frictional force acting over this path? That force has magnitude μN, where the normal force in this case of horizontal motion is just mg. But the frictional force *always* acts to oppose the motion, so that it *always* does negative work. With frictional force μmg opposing the motion, the work done in crossing the width ℓ of the room is $-\mu mg\ell$. Coming back, it is also $-\mu mg\ell$, so that the total work done by the frictional force is $-2\mu mg\ell$.

The difference between our answers for the total work done by the gravitational and frictional forces acting over closed paths provides one precise definition of the distinction between conservative and nonconservative forces:

When the total work done by a force acting as an object moves over any closed path is zero, then the force is conservative. Mathematically,

$$\oint \mathbf{F}\cdot d\mathbf{r} = 0. \qquad \text{(conservative force)} \qquad (7\text{–}1)$$

The circle on the integral sign indicates that the integral is taken over a *closed* path. A force for which the integral is nonzero, like the frictional force, is nonconservative.

You can see why the mathematical definition Equation 7–1 is equivalent to our more physical statement that a conservative force "gives back" work that was done against it. When we do work against a conservative force, it simultaneously does negative work on us. But for the total work done by the force to be zero, it must subsequently do positive work on us; during this time it "gives back" the work we did earlier.

Equation 7–1 suggests a related property of conservative forces. Suppose we move an object along the straight path between points A and B shown in Fig. 7–2, along which a conservative force acts; let the work done by the conservative force be W_{AB}. Since the work done by a conservative force over any closed path is zero, the work W_{BA} done in moving back from

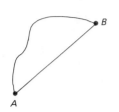

Fig. 7–2
Since the work done by a conservative force over a closed path is zero, the work done in moving from point A to point B must be independent of the path.

Fig. 7–3
Movers raise identical boxes a vertical distance *h*. The work done by gravity is the same for the box lifted vertically and for the box pushed up the ramp. (The horizontal location of the starting point doesn't matter here, since gravity does no work on an object moved horizontally.)

Fig. 7–4
Top view of boxes being pushed along a horizontal floor. The work done by friction is least for the straight-line path.

B to *A* must be $-W_{AB}$ whether we return along the straight path or take the curved path shown or any other path. That is, the work done by a conservative force as we move between two points is *independent of the path taken*: $\int_A^B \mathbf{F} \cdot d\mathbf{r}$ is path-independent. We saw this in Example 6–8, where we found that the work done by gravity does not depend on the details of the path taken (Fig. 7–3). In contrast, the work done by a nonconservative force is *not* path-independent. On a frictional surface, for example, the least work is done over a straight-line path; any other path involves more work (Fig. 7–4).

Important examples of conservative forces include gravity and the static electric force. The force of an ideal spring—fundamentally an electric force—is also conservative. Nonconservative forces include friction and the electric force in the presence of time-varying magnetic effects.

Example 7–1
Conservative and Nonconservative Forces

Two forces point in the y-direction; the first is given by $\mathbf{F}_1 = ay\hat{\jmath}$ and the second by $\mathbf{F}_2 = bx\hat{\jmath}$, where *a* and *b* are constants. For each force, determine the work done in moving from the origin to the point (ℓ, ℓ) by first moving up the y-axis to $(0, \ell)$, then moving straight over to (ℓ, ℓ). Compare with the work done in moving first along the x-axis to $(\ell, 0)$, then straight up to (ℓ, ℓ). Comment on the conservative or nonconservative nature of the forces.

Solution

Figure 7–5a shows some force vectors for $\mathbf{F}_1$ on the two paths *ABC* and *ADC*. If we start at the origin and go upward, we have

$$W_{AB} = \int_A^B \mathbf{F} \cdot d\mathbf{r} = \int_{(0,0)}^{(0,\ell)} ay\hat{\jmath} \cdot d\mathbf{r}$$

for the work done by $\mathbf{F}_1$ along the vertical segment *AB*. But along this segment, *d***r** is vertical; $d\mathbf{r} = \hat{\jmath} \, dy$. Then we have

$$W_{AB} = \int_{y=0}^{y=\ell} a \, y \, dy = \left. \frac{ay^2}{2} \right|_0^\ell = \tfrac{1}{2}a\ell^2.$$

Going across the top of the square, from *B* to *C*, the force and displacement are perpendicular, so that no work is done; therefore, $W_{ABC} = \tfrac{1}{2}a\ell^2$ for force $\mathbf{F}_1$. Going

Fig. 7–5
Force vectors and paths for the forces $\mathbf{F}_1$ and $\mathbf{F}_2$ of Example 7–1.

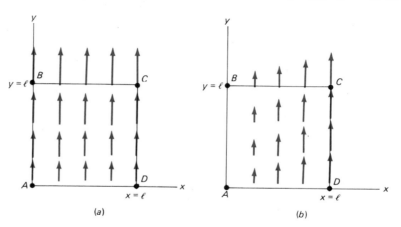

along the x-axis from A to D, the force and displacement are again perpendicular and no work is done. Going up from D to C, we again have $d\mathbf{r} = \hat{\jmath}\,dy$; then

$$W_{DC} = \int_{y=0}^{y=\ell} a\,y\,dy = \tfrac{1}{2}a\ell^2,$$

so that the work W_{ADC} is equal to the work W_{ABC}, and the force could be conservative. (Problem 2 asks you to verify that the work is the same along the diagonal path AC.)

For the force $\mathbf{F}_2$, on the other hand, $x = 0$ and therefore $\mathbf{F}_2 = 0$ along the segment AB. With $\mathbf{F}_2$ perpendicular to displacement along BC, the work $W_{ABC} = 0$ for this force. Along AD, the work is again zero, but going up from D to C we have $d\mathbf{r} = \hat{\jmath}\,dy$, so that with $x = \ell$ along this segment, the work becomes

$$W_{DC} = \int_{y=0}^{y=\ell} b\,\ell\,dy = b\ell y \Big|_0^\ell = b\ell^2.$$

Then the total work W_{ADC} is $b\ell^2$ for the force $\mathbf{F}_2$; since this differs from the work over the path W_{ABC}, the work is not path-independent and therefore the force is not conservative.

Although we calculated the work integrals in detail here, you should be able to see directly from Fig. 7–5 that $\mathbf{F}_1$ is conservative and $\mathbf{F}_2$ is not. Question 1 explores other examples like this one.

7.2
POTENTIAL ENERGY

Work done against a conservative force is somehow "stored," in the sense that we can get it back again in the form of kinetic energy. The climber of Fig. 7–1a is acutely aware of that "stored work"; it gives her the potential for a dangerous fall. So is the archer of Fig. 7–6; the work he did against the springiness of his bow has the potential to propel the arrow at high speed. "Potential" is an appropriate word here: we can consider the "stored work" as **potential energy**, potential in the sense that it can become actualized as kinetic energy.

potential energy

We define potential energy formally in terms of the the work done by a conservative force. Specifically, the change ΔU_{AB} in potential energy associated with moving an object from point A to point B is the negative of the work done by the conservative force acting on that object:

$$\Delta U_{AB} = -\int_A^B \mathbf{F}\cdot d\mathbf{r}. \qquad \text{(potential energy)} \qquad (7\text{–}2)$$

Why the minus sign? Because we want the potential energy to represent stored work. When you lift a book from the floor to your desk, for example, *you* do positive work on the book. But gravity—the conservative force of interest—does negative work; putting the minus sign in our definition of potential energy then gives a positive value for the "stored work."

Our definition speaks only of *changes* in potential energy. In fact, only changes in potential energy ever matter physically. The actual value of potential energy is physically meaningless. Often, though, it is convenient to

Fig. 7–6
The archer's taut bow stores potential energy that can become kinetic energy of the arrow.

establish a reference point at which the potential energy is defined to be zero. When we then speak of "the potential energy U," we really mean the potential energy difference ΔU between that reference point and some other point. The rock climber of Fig. 7–1a, for example, would find it convenient to take the zero of potential energy at the base of the cliff. When dealing with the gravity of the earth in relation to the sun and other planets, we will find the mathematics simplified if we take the zero of potential energy at an infinite distance from the earth. But the choice is purely for convenience; only potential energy *differences* ever matter, and no physically significant result ever depends on the choice for the zero of potential energy.

Fig. 7–7
The work done by gravity as the book moves from floor to shelf is the same for both paths shown, but is more easily calculated for the path composed of horizontal and vertical sections.

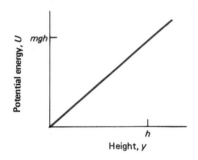

Fig. 7–8
Since the gravitational force is constant, the potential energy increases linearly with height.

Example 7–2
Gravitational Potential Energy

A book of mass m is moved from the floor to a shelf of height h. (a) What is the change in its potential energy? (b) Taking the zero of potential energy at the floor, what is the potential energy when the book is on the floor and when it is on the shelf? (c) Taking the zero of potential energy at the shelf, what is the potential energy when the book is on the floor and when it is on the shelf?

Solution

The potential energy difference is given by Equation 7–2. Here **F** is the gravitational force, $-mg\hat{\jmath}$. Over what path are we to evaluate the integral in Equation 7–2? It doesn't matter: gravity is a conservative force, so the work is path-independent. The simplest path involves only horizontal and vertical motion (Fig. 7–7); the work done by gravity on the horizontal sections is zero, and on the vertical section is just $-mgh$. So the potential energy change—the negative of the work done by gravity—is mgh. If we take the zero of potential energy at the floor, then the potential energy at the shelf is mgh. If we take the zero of potential energy at the shelf, then the potential energy at the floor must be such that its value plus the change $\Delta U = mgh$ gives zero. So the potential energy at the floor must be $-mgh$. We can get these results formally by applying Equation 7–2. With $U = 0$ at the shelf height $y = h$, for example, we have

$$U_{\text{floor}} = -\int_{y=h}^{y=0} (-mg\hat{\jmath})\cdot\hat{\jmath}\,dy = -(-mgy)\Big|_{h}^{0} = -[0 - (-mgh)] = -mgh.$$

Figure 7–8 shows potential energy as a function of vertical position for this example, with the zero of potential energy taken at the floor. The *linear* increase in potential energy with height is a reflection of the *constant* gravitational force.

Just where is the "stored work" represented by the potential energy actually stored? We often speak loosely of the potential energy of a particular object, like the book of Example 7–2. But the book itself hasn't changed as we raise it to the shelf. What has changed is the configuration of a system consisting of the book and the earth. The potential energy change is associated with that change in configuration; potential energy resides not in the book but in the altered gravitational situation between earth and book. We will explore this notion further when we study gravity in the next chapter, and again when we examine the electric force. A spring provides a clearer example that potential energy is associated with a

Fig. 7–9
A mass attached to a spring. When the spring is stretched, the increased potential energy is associated not with the mass but with the altered configuration of the spring.

Potential energy, U

$x = 0$

Compression   Equilibrium   Stretch

Fig. 7–10
The potential energy curve for a spring is a parabola.

change in configuration. In Fig. 7–9, the increase in potential energy is clearly associated not with the mass but with the altered configuration of the spring.

Example 7–3
The Potential Energy of a Spring

Find the potential energy of a spring of spring constant k when it is stretched or compressed a distance x from equilibrium. Take $U = 0$ in the spring's equilibrium configuration.

Solution

The spring exerts a force $-kx$, so that Equation 7–2 becomes

$$U = -\int_0^x (-kx)\, dx = \int_0^x kx\, dx = \tfrac{1}{2}kx^2 \Big|_0^x$$
$$= \tfrac{1}{2}kx^2. \quad \text{(potential energy of a spring)} \tag{7–3}$$

This result is the same as the expression we found in Example 6–6 for the work done by an applied force in stretching the spring. Of course: we defined potential energy so it would represent the "stored work" done by an applied force acting to oppose a given conservative force.

Figure 7–10 shows the potential energy as a function of position for the spring. The *parabolic* shape of the potential energy curve—U varying in proportion to x^2—reflects the *linear* relation between force and position.

Example 7–4
Electric Potential Energy

In the vicinity of an electrically charged wire of radius R, a proton experiences a force given by

$$\mathbf{F} = F_0 \frac{R}{r}\hat{\mathbf{r}},$$

where $\hat{\mathbf{r}}$ is a unit vector directed radially outward from the center of the wire, r is the distance from the center of the wire, and F_0 is the force that would act on the proton at $r = R$ (F_0 is related to the electric charge on the wire and on the proton). Taking the zero of potential energy at the surface of the wire, calculate the potential energy at an arbitrary point outside the wire.

Solution

Moving radially outward from the wire, we can write our infinitesimal displacement $d\mathbf{r}$ as $\hat{\mathbf{r}}dr$, where dr is a scalar (in the same way, we wrote $d\mathbf{r} = \hat{\jmath}dy$ when we moved along the y-axis in Example 7–1). Then Equation 7–2 gives

$$U = -\int_R^r \mathbf{F}\cdot d\mathbf{r} = -\int_R^r F_0 \frac{R}{r}\hat{\mathbf{r}}\cdot\hat{\mathbf{r}}\, dr = -F_0 R \int_R^r \frac{dr}{r},$$

where the dot product of $\hat{\mathbf{r}}$ with itself is simply 1 and where we have taken constants outside the integral sign (we can always do this using the distributive law, remembering that an integral is just the limit of a sum). The integral of $1/r$, or r^{-1}, is the one exception to our rule for integrating powers. This integral, in fact, defines the natural logarithm: $\int r^{-1}dr \equiv \ln(r)$. So we have

$$U = -F_0 R \ln(r) \Big|_R^r = -F_0 R\,[\ln(r) - \ln(R)] = -F_0 R \ln\!\left(\frac{r}{R}\right).$$

Fig. 7–11
Potential energy curve for Example 7–4. (Curve does not extend to $r < R$ since force was only given for $r \geq R$.)

Fig. 7–12
Since potential energy is independent of the path taken, it can be calculated using any path. The potential energy change is zero over the two segments *AB* and *BC* of the path shown, and is given by the result of Example 7–4 for the segment *CD*.

Does this result make sense? For positive F_0, the force is directed away from the wire. We must then do work to move the proton toward the wire, thereby increasing the stored potential energy. So the potential energy must get lower as we move away from the wire. Since we chose $U = 0$ at $r = R$, the potential energy must be negative for $r > R$, as our expression indeed shows. Note again that only potential energy differences matter. There is nothing impossible or unusual about our negative answer for the potential energy itself; it is significant only in telling us that potential energy decreases as we move away from the wire.

Figure 7–11 shows the potential energy curve for this example, and is analogous to Fig. 7–8 and Fig. 7–10 for the gravitational and spring forces. The potential energy decreases rapidly near the wire, reflecting the strong force there, but soon decreases more gradually as the force and therefore the work done in moving a given distance also decrease.

We worked this example as though we were considering a path radially outward from the wire. But what if we had moved between the points *A* and *D* shown in Fig. 7–12? Since potential energy is path-independent (we are dealing with a conservative force whenever we talk about potential energy), we can use *any* path to evaluate the integral for potential energy. In Fig. 7–12, we show a path that extends first in a straight line *AB* along the wire surface, then in a circular arc *BC* around the wire, and finally radially outward along a line *CD*. Along the first two segments, the radially outward force is at right angles to the displacement, and the potential energy change $-\int \mathbf{F} \cdot d\mathbf{r}$ over these segments is zero. Over the segment *CD*, the potential energy change has the value we calculated in this example; since the changes over the other segments are zero, segment *CD* gives the overall change in potential energy from *A* to *D*. So the potential energy in this case depends only on the radial distance from the center of the wire, and not on how far we move along or around the wire.

7.3
CONSERVATION OF MECHANICAL ENERGY

In the preceding chapter, we introduced the work-energy theorem, which shows that the change ΔK in a body's kinetic energy is equal to the total work done on it:

$$\Delta K = W.$$

Consider separately the work W_c done by conservative forces and the work W_{nc} done by nonconservative forces, so that

$$\Delta K = W_c + W_{nc}.$$

But we have defined the change in potential energy, ΔU, as the negative of the work done by conservative forces. So we can write

$$\Delta K = -\Delta U + W_{nc},$$

or

$$\Delta K + \Delta U = W_{nc}. \qquad (7\text{--}4)$$

mechanical energy   We define the sum of the kinetic and potential energy as the **mechanical energy.** Then Equation 7–4 can be written

$$\Delta(K + U) = W_{nc}, \qquad (7\text{--}5)$$

showing that the change in mechanical energy is equal to the work done by nonconservative forces.

In the absence of nonconservative forces (or when those forces are perpendicular to displacement, so they do no work), then Equations 7–4 to 7–6 show that the mechanical energy is unchanged:

$$\Delta K + \Delta U = 0 \qquad (7\text{--}6)$$

and, equivalently,

$$K + U = \text{constant}. \qquad (7\text{--}7)$$

law of conservation of mechanical energy   Equations 7–6 and 7–7 express the **law of conservation of mechanical energy.** They show that, in the absence of nonconservative forces, there is a quantity $K+U$ that remains always the same. The kinetic energy K may change, but that change is always compensated by an equal but opposite change in potential energy.

Conservation of mechanical energy is a powerful principle, one that is grounded in Newton's laws and in the nature of conservative forces. Throughout physics, from the subatomic realm through practical problems in engineering and on to astrophysics, the principle of energy conservation is widely used in solving problems that would be intractable without it.

Applying the conservation of energy principle is as simple as writing $K+U=$ constant, with the form of U appropriate to the situation at hand and the constant arrived at from the statement of the problem. In classical physics, the kinetic energy K is given by $\frac{1}{2}mv^2$. But the form of the potential energy depends on the details of the conservative force; in Examples 7–2, 7–3, and 7–4 we worked out some specific cases. Usually we are given the speed at some position; then we can find the kinetic energy K_0 and potential energy U_0 at that position. Since mechanical energy is constant, the quantity K_0+U_0 is the constant in Equation 7–7. In the examples below, we show how the conservation of energy principle is applied.

Example 7–5
Accelerating a Proton

The proton of Example 7–4 is released from rest at the surface of the wire. How fast is it moving when it is a distance r from the wire?

Solution

Since only the conservative electric force acts, the mechanical energy $K+U$ is conserved. So we can write

$$K + U = K_0 + U_0,$$

where K_0 and U_0 are the kinetic and potential energy at the surface of the wire. The proton is released from rest, so $K_0 = 0$. In Example 7–4, we choose $U=0$ at the surface of the wire, so that $U_0 = 0$ as well [we can also get this by setting $r=R$ in our expression for U in Example 7–4, noting that $\ln(R/R) = \ln(1) = 0$]. So the mechanical energy with the proton at the wire surface is 0; since mechanical energy is conserved, this must be its value anywhere else. (Again, remember that only differences in potential energy matter; the actual value of the potential energy and therefore of the total mechanical energy has no significance, so you should not be bothered by zero total energy.) The kinetic energy anywhere is given by $K=\frac{1}{2}mv^2$. From Example 7–4, we know that the potential energy in this case is $U= -F_0R \ln(r/R)$. So we can write

$$K + U = \tfrac{1}{2}mv^2 - F_0R \ln(r/R) = 0.$$

This is the statement of mechanical energy conservation—Equation 7–7—specialized to this particular example. Solving for the speed v gives

$$v = \sqrt{\frac{2F_0R \ln(r/R)}{m}}.$$

Does this result make sense? Yes: Fig. 7–13 shows a plot of speed versus distance r from the center of the wire. At first the speed increases rapidly, as the proton experiences a strong repulsive force. But the force decreases with distance, and while the proton continues to accelerate, it does so at an ever-decreasing rate.

This example illustrates the power of the conservation of energy principle. Applying Newton's second law in this case of a force and therefore acceleration that varies as $1/r$ would prove quite difficult. But conservation of energy bypasses the details of the acceleration and gets us directly to an expression for speed as a function of position. What conservation of energy cannot do, though, is give us all the details; in particular, it can never give us position and speed as functions of *time*. Only the full application of Newton's second law—often requiring computer calculations—can do that.

Fig. 7–13
Speed as a function of position for the proton in Example 7–5.

Fig. 7–14
Example 7–6

Example 7–6
Conservation of Energy: A Spring and Gravity

The spring in Fig. 7–14 has spring constant $k = 140$ N/m. A 50-g block is placed against the spring, which is then compressed 11 cm. When the block is released, how high up the slope does it rise? Both the horizontal surface and the slope are frictionless.

Solution

To solve this problem, we equate the total energy $K_0 + U_0$ in the initial position with the total energy $K_1 + U_1$ at the maximum height:

$$K_1 + U_1 = K_0 + U_0.$$

Initially, the block is at rest, so $K_0 = 0$. At maximum height on the slope, it is also at rest, so $K_1 = 0$. The initial potential energy is that of a compressed spring, or $\frac{1}{2}kx^2$ from Example 7–3. The final potential energy is the gravitational potential energy mgh, as we found in Example 7–2. So our statement of energy conservation reads simply

$$\tfrac{1}{2}kx^2 = mgh.$$

Solving for the height h and using the values given, we have

$$h = \frac{kx^2}{2mg} = \frac{(140\ \text{N/m})(0.11\ \text{m})^2}{(2)(0.050\ \text{kg})(9.8\ \text{m/s}^2)} = 1.7\ \text{m}.$$

You might have been tempted in working this example to solve for the speed after the block left the spring, and then equate $\frac{1}{2}mv^2$ to mgh to find the height. And you certainly could have done that. But you don't have to! Conservation of energy short-cuts all details of the motion, and allows you to equate directly the total energy at two points of interest. Here the speed is zero at both these points, so you need not be concerned with kinetic energy.

Example 7–7
A Pendulum

The pendulum of Fig. 7–15 is pulled back until its string makes an angle θ_0 with the vertical, then released from rest. (a) How fast is it going when it reaches its lowest point? (b) At its lowest point, the string catches on a nail located a distance a above the bottom of the string. Assuming the string remains taut, what is the maximum angle θ_1 that the string makes with the vertical?

Solution

Here two forces are acting: the conservative force of gravity and the string tension. But the string tension is perpendicular to the motion, and so does no work. So the total energy remains constant, and the potential energy is associated with the gravitational force alone:

$$K + U = K_0 + U_0.$$

Fig. 7–15
Example 7–7

To write out the potential energy terms, we need an expression for the potential energy as a function of angle. Figure 7–16 shows that an angle θ corresponds to a height $h = \ell(1 - \cos\theta)$. Setting the zero of potential energy at the lowest point, we can then write $U_0 = mgh = mg\ell(1 - \cos\theta_0)$, where m is the mass of the pendulum bob (we assume the string has negligible mass). Since the pendulum is released from rest, $K_0 = 0$, so that $K_0 + U_0 = mg\ell(1 - \cos\theta_0)$.

(a) To find the speed at the bottom, we equate the energy at the bottom to our total energy $K_0 + U_0$. At the bottom, we have defined $U = 0$, so that $K + U = \frac{1}{2}mv^2$ at the bottom. Then

$$\tfrac{1}{2}mv^2 = mg\ell(1 - \cos\theta_0),$$

so that

$$v = \sqrt{2g\ell(1 - \cos\theta_0)}.$$

(b) To find the maximum angle as the pendulum swings to the right, we equate the energy in the rightmost position to the total energy $K_0 + U_0$. On the right, the geometry is the same as in Fig. 7–16 but with the length a replacing ℓ. So the potential energy in the rightmost position is $mga(1 - \cos\theta_1)$. Since the pendulum is instantaneously at rest in this position, $K = 0$, and conservation of energy becomes

$$mga(1 - \cos\theta_1) = mg\ell(1 - \cos\theta_0).$$

Solving for θ_1 gives

$$\theta_1 = \cos^{-1}\left(\frac{\ell}{a}\cos\theta_0 + \frac{a - \ell}{a}\right).$$

Does this result make sense? When $a = \ell$, so that the nail is the pivot for the pendulum, then $\theta_1 = \theta_0$, and the pendulum swings symmetrically about its lowest position. And no matter where the nail, our conservation of energy statement shows that $a(1 - \cos\theta_1) = \ell(1 - \cos\theta_0)$; from Fig. 7–16, we see that this means the pendulum rises to the same height on either side, regardless of the presence of the nail. Of course it must! At its extreme positions, it has only gravitational potential energy. Since gravitational potential energy is mgh regardless of the details of the path taken to rise a distance h, the heights must be the same on both sides of the pendulum's arc.

Will the string really remain taut, as we have assumed? Not always! This question is explored in Problems 27 and 60.

How long does it take the pendulum to complete its swing? That is a much harder question, one that energy conservation cannot answer. We will solve Newton's second law for the pendulum in Chapter 14; only then can we determine the time-dependence of the motion.

Fig. 7–16
When the pendulum makes an angle θ with the vertical, it is a distance $h = \ell(1 - \cos\theta)$ above its lowest position.

Example 7–8
Stopping an Electron

An electron with kinetic energy of 25 keV is moving in the $+x$-direction. At $x = 0$, it enters a region where it experiences a conservative force pointing in the $-x$-direction; the force is given by $F = -ax^2$, where $a = 18$ eV/cm³. (You should verify that these are reasonable units for a.) How far into the region does the electron penetrate?

Solution

Again, mechanical energy is conserved, so that

$$K + U = K_0 + U_0.$$

If we take $U = 0$ at $x = 0$, then the right-hand side of the equation is known: $U_0 = 0$ by definition, and K_0 is given as 25 keV. We don't have an expression for U, but can get this by integrating the force as described by Equation 7–2:

$$U(x) = -\int_0^x F\,dx = -\int_0^x(-ax^2)dx = \int_0^x ax^2\,dx = \tfrac{1}{3}ax^3.$$

(Since a has units eV/cm^3, the units of U are eV when x is measured in cm.) With $K=0$ at maximum x, our conservation of energy statement becomes

$$\tfrac{1}{3}ax^3 = K_0,$$

or

$$x = \left(\frac{3K_0}{a}\right)^{1/3} = \left[\frac{(3)(25 \times 10^3 \text{ eV})}{18 \text{ eV/cm}^3}\right]^{1/3} = 16 \text{ cm.}$$

Note how the units work out without our ever needing to convert eV to joules. Atomic and high-energy physicists often work in the "mixed units" of this example.

7.4
POTENTIAL ENERGY CURVES

Figure 7–17 shows a frictionless roller-coaster track. How fast must a car be coasting at point A if it is to reach point D? What happens if it is going more slowly than this?

The answers to our questions are provided by the conservation of energy principle. If we take the zero of potential energy at the lowest point on the track, then the energy at point A is $\tfrac{1}{2}mv_A{}^2 + mgh_A$; since mechanical energy is conserved, this is the energy anywhere. To reach point D, the car must clear the highest peak C, where its potential energy is mgh_C. If it just barely clears the peak, its kinetic energy is arbitrarily close to zero on the peak; then the statement of energy conservation becomes $U_C = K_A + U_A$, or

$$mgh_C = \tfrac{1}{2}mv_A{}^2 + mgh_A,$$

so that

$$mg(h_C - h_A) = \tfrac{1}{2}mv_A{}^2.$$

In other words, the initial kinetic energy must be at least equal to the potential energy difference between the highest point and the initial point. Solving for v_A would give our answer for the minimum speed required.

What if the car is moving only a little more slowly? Then it won't ever get to the top of the second peak, but will reverse direction before then. Where? At the height h where the kinetic energy becomes zero: $mgh = \tfrac{1}{2}mv_A{}^2 + mgh_A$. It will head back, clearing peak B, then down and up past point A until its kinetic energy is again zero. Where is this? Again, at a point where $mgh = \tfrac{1}{2}mv_A{}^2 + mgh_A$—that is, at the same height where it turned earlier. So the car will run back and forth between two **turning points** set by the value of its total energy. With still lower speed, the car won't clear peak B; then its motion will be confined to the first valley alone.

turning points

Fig. 7–17
A roller-coaster track.

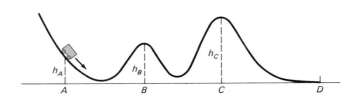

potential energy curve

Figure 7–17 is a drawing of the actual roller-coaster track. But, because gravitational potential energy near earth's surface is directly proportional to height, we can also regard it as a plot of potential energy versus position: a **potential energy curve.** We can understand the car's motion graphically by plotting the car's total energy on the same graph as the potential energy curve. Since total energy is constant, the total energy curve is a straight, horizontal line. Figure 7–18 shows the potential energy curve and the total energy curve for several values of the total energy. These graphs tell us immediately about the motion of the car. In Fig. 7–18a, the total energy exceeds the potential energy at peak C; therefore, the car will reach C with kinetic energy to spare, and will make it all the way to D. In Fig. 7–18b, the total energy is less than the potential energy at C; the car must stop when its total energy is entirely potential. This happens when the total energy curve intersects the potential energy curve; the points of intersection are the turning points that bound the car's motion. In Fig. 7–18c, the energy is still lower, and the turning points closer together. We say that the car is **trapped** in the **potential well** between its turning points.

trapped
potential well

In both Fig. 7–18b and Fig. 7–18c, the car's total energy exceeds the potential energy in the rightmost region, so that motion in this region is energetically possible. But starting at point A, the car is blocked from this region by the **potential barrier** of peak C. In the case of Fig. 7–18c, peak B poses an additional potential barrier that keeps the car out of the valley between B and C where motion is also energetically possible. The terminology of this example—potential wells and barriers—is widely used in many fields of physics.

potential barrier

Although we phrased our discussion in terms of a potential energy curve corresponding directly to physical hills and valleys of a roller-coaster track, potential energy curves remain useful even when such a correspondence is absent. For example, Fig. 7–19 shows the potential energy versus separation distance for a pair of deuterium (heavy hydrogen) nuclei. The potential barrier is associated with the repulsive electric force, while the deep potential well arises from the strongly attractive but short-range nuclear force. Even though the forces here are not gravitational, you can picture the potential barrier as a "hill" with a deep hole on the other side. If you can get a nucleus over the hill, it will "fall" into the hole. The result is a fusion reaction in which two deuterium nuclei fuse to form a helium nucleus, releasing a great deal of energy in the process. (This classical description of fusion is only partially correct; quantum-mechanical effects actually permit "barrier penetration" by nuclei whose energies are below the barrier height.) If nuclear fusion could be harnessed to produce electricity, each gallon of seawater would be energetically equivalent to 400 gallons of gasoline. Since the 1950's, scientists have made slow progress toward the

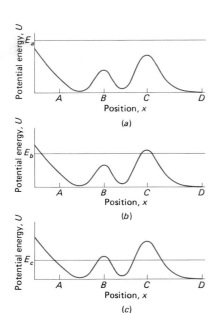

Fig. 7–18
Potential and total energy for a car on a roller coaster. (a) The total energy E_a exceeds the potential energy at peak C, and the car can move over the entire track. (b) The total energy E_b is lower than the potential energy at C, and the car's motion is confined between the turning points where the total and potential energy curves intersect. (c) The total energy E_c is lower than the potential energy at B, limiting the car's motion still further. Although motion between B and C is energetically possible, a car starting at A with this total energy cannot overcome the potential energy barrier of peak B to reach the region between B and C.

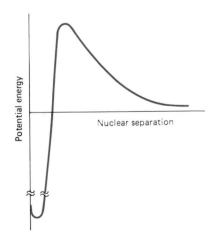

Fig. 7–19
Potential energy curve for a pair of deuterium nuclei. Break in curve indicates that nuclear potential energy well is really much deeper than shown.

goal of developing a controlled fusion reactor—a device in which nuclei are given the high energies needed for fusion, in an environment where there are enough nuclei to ensure frequent collisions that result in fusion reactions. Unfortunately, we've long known how to make fusion work in an uncontrolled fashion, by using fissioning plutonium to "ignite" the fusion reaction in thermonuclear weapons (hydrogen bombs).

Example 7–9
A Diatomic Molecule

The force between the atoms of a diatomic molecule arises from the electrical interactions of the electrons and nuclei in each atom. For simple diatomic molecules, the associated potential energy is given, to a good approximation, by the so-called Lennard-Jones potential:

$$U = U_0\left[\left(\frac{a}{x}\right)^{12} - \left(\frac{a}{x}\right)^{6}\right], \qquad (7\text{–}8)$$

where x is the distance between the two atoms and where U_0 and a are constants. For oxygen (O_2), $U_0 = 5.6 \times 10^{-21}$ J and $a = 3.5 \times 10^{-10}$ m. (a) Plot the potential energy curve for oxygen, and from it determine the spacing between atoms at the minimum possible energy for the molecule. (b) If the molecule has more than this minimum energy, it may vibrate between two extreme sizes. Find these extrema for the case when the molecule's total energy is 1.0×10^{-21} J over the minimum. (c) What will happen if the molecule is given an energy 2.0×10^{-21} J over the minimum?

Solution

Figure 7–20 shows a plot of Equation 7–8. The minimum possible energy is at the lowest point on the curve, or -1.4×10^{-21} J; if the molecule has this minimum value, its energy is all potential and the two atoms cannot move. At this point, Fig. 7–20 shows that the atomic separation is 3.9×10^{-10} m. Figure 7–20 also shows horizontal lines representing total energies of 1.0×10^{-21} J and 2.0×10^{-21} J above the minimum. From the graph, we see in the case of 1.0×10^{-21} J that the turning points—here the points of maximum and minimum atomic separation—occur at about 3.6×10^{-10} m and 5.4×10^{-10} m. But what happens when the total energy is 2.0×10^{-21} J over the minimum? Then there is a minimum atomic separation of about 3.5×10^{-10} m, but no maximum: the total energy exceeds the potential energy no matter how far apart the atoms get. What does this mean? As would be the case

Fig. 7–20
Potential energy curve for diatomic oxygen, showing three possible values for total energy.

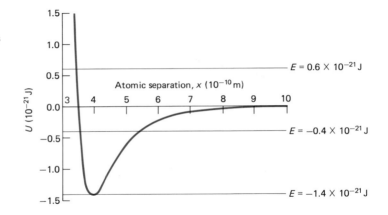

with a roller-coaster track shaped like Fig. 7–20, it means that the atoms get arbitrarily far apart. In other words, they do not stay together to form a molecule. High-speed collisions in a high-temperature gas, for example, might give a molecule enough energy to dissociate in this way.

Note that the zero of potential energy implicit in Equation 7–9 occurs when the atoms are a great distance apart. This is often a convenient choice when dealing with isolated but interacting particles. With this choice, total energies below zero result in two turning points and therefore correspond to the two atoms being bound together; total energies greater than zero correspond to unbound atoms.

7.5
FORCE AND POTENTIAL ENERGY

Figure 7–20 describes the potential energy of an oxygen molecule as a function of atomic separation. But it also tells us about the force acting between the atoms. As they get very close—specifically, to the left of the low point in Fig. 7–20—they experience a repulsive force. This is evident in Fig. 7–20 because the potential energy increases as the molecules move closer, indicating that the interatomic force does negative work on the atoms. Equivalently, if you tried to push the atoms together, you would have to do positive work to overcome the interatomic force. How strong is the repulsive force? That depends on *how rapidly* the potential energy increases with decreasing atomic separation—that is, on the *slope* of the potential energy curve. This makes sense mathematically, too. We wrote the potential energy as the integral of the force; now we find that the force is related to the slope, or derivative, of the potential energy curve. Again, we see the inverse relation between differentiation and integration.

What, exactly, is the relation between potential energy and force? In Fig. 7–20, the repulsive force to the left of the energy minimum points in the +x-direction; the slope of the curve in this region is negative. So our relationship must be

$$F_x = -\frac{dU}{dx}.$$

(7–9)

You can confirm that dU/dx has the units of force, so that no dimensional proportionality constant is needed in Equation 7–9. To the right of the energy minimum, the force is attractive and therefore points in the −x-direction; the slope dU/dx is positive, and therefore Equation 7–9 again correctly gives the force. What about the minimum point? Here the slope dU/dx is zero, so there must be no force. That is the one place where the atoms can remain at rest. We will explore such **equilibrium points** in more detail in Chapter 11.

equilibrium points

Example 7–10
Force and Potential Energy

Find an expression for the force between atoms in an oxygen molecule. Use your result to find the force when the atoms are separated by 5.0×10^{-10} m and to determine the equilibrium separation.

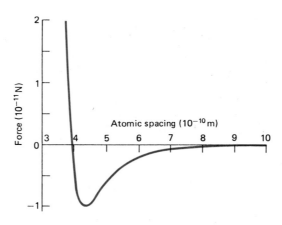

Fig. 7–21
Interatomic force in diatomic oxygen, as
a function of atomic separation.

Solution

Equation 7–9 gives the potential energy as a function of separation:

$$U = U_0 \left[\left(\frac{a}{x} \right)^{12} - \left(\frac{a}{x} \right)^{6} \right].$$

Differentiating this expression with respect to x gives the force:

$$F = -\frac{dU}{dx} = -U_0 \left[-12 \left(\frac{a^{12}}{x^{13}} \right) + 6 \left(\frac{a^{6}}{x^{7}} \right) \right] = \frac{6U_0}{a} \left[2 \left(\frac{a}{x} \right)^{13} - \left(\frac{a}{x} \right)^{7} \right]. \quad (7\text{–}10)$$

Evaluating this expression at $x = 5.0 \times 10^{-10}$ m, using values of U_0 and a from Example 7–9, gives $F = -6.0 \times 10^{-12}$ N. The minus sign indicates that at this separation the force is attractive.

Setting $F = 0$ in Equation 7–10 allows us to find the equilibrium separation:

$$2 \left(\frac{a}{x} \right)^{13} - \left(\frac{a}{x} \right)^{7} = 0,$$

so that, on dividing by $(a/x)^7$, we have

$$\left(\frac{a}{x} \right)^{6} = \frac{1}{2},$$

or

$$x = 2^{1/6} a = (2^{1/6})(3.5 \times 10^{-10} \text{ m}) = 3.9 \times 10^{-10} \text{ m},$$

in agreement with our graphical result from Example 7–9. Figure 7–21 shows a plot of the interatomic force as a function of separation. The graph shows clearly that the force on either side of the equilibrium point tends to restore the molecule to equilibrium. We will explore the significance of such a restoring force further in Chapters 11 and 13.

We developed Equation 7–9, $F = -dU/dx$, for the case when the potential energy depends on only one position variable. In such a case, we may regard Equation 7–9 as the inverse of the potential energy equation $U = -\int F_x dx$. But what about the more general case when U may vary in more than one direction? Imagine you're standing on the side of a mountain. Your gravitational potential energy mgh is directly proportional to

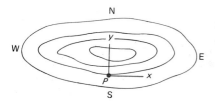

Fig. 7–22
Contour map of a mountain. Contours are lines of equal height and therefore of equal potential energy. At the point P, eastward (x) component of the gravitational force is zero. Gravitational force is a maximum in the southward (−y) direction.

your altitude h. Figure 7–22 shows a contour map of the mountain. The contour lines—lines of constant altitude—are also lines of constant potential energy. If you walk eastward from the point P—that is, along a contour line—your potential energy does not change. And the component of the gravitational force in the direction of your motion is also zero. Mathematically, we can write $F_x = -dU/dx = 0$. But if you walk southward—at right angles to the contour lines—your potential energy changes rapidly and the component of gravitational force in your direction of motion is large. Mathematically, we now write $F_y = -dU/dy$; the minus sign arises because the potential energy increases up the slope, while the force is downslope. More generally, if you walk in some direction along the mountainside, the component of gravitational force in that direction is the negative of the rate of change of your potential energy as you walk; we write

$$F_\ell = -\frac{dU}{d\ell},\tag{7–11}$$

where ℓ designates an arbitrary direction and F_ℓ the component of force in that direction.

Can we write an expression for the actual force vector itself? Yes: we already wrote $F_x = -dU/dx$ and $F_y = -dU/dy$. Just what do the derivatives mean here? dU/dx means the rate of change of U as we move *in the x-direction only*; that is, the derivative of U with respect to x *while y is held constant*. Similarly, dU/dy means the derivative of U with respect to y *while x is held constant*. To avoid confusion in cases like this where a quantity (here U) depends on more than one variable (here x and y), we

partial derivative   define a **partial derivative** as a derivative taken with respect to only one variable while all other variables are held constant. Partial differentiation is indicated by the special symbol ∂ instead of the usual d; we then write $F_x = -\partial U/\partial x$ and $F_y = -\partial U/\partial y$. So, using unit vector notation, we can write the vector force itself:

$$\mathbf{F} = -\left(\frac{\partial U}{\partial x}\hat{\mathbf{i}} + \frac{\partial U}{\partial y}\hat{\mathbf{j}}\right).\tag{7–12}$$

The combination $\hat{\mathbf{i}}\partial/\partial x + \hat{\mathbf{j}}\partial/\partial y$ acting on a scalar function occurs often in physics and mathematics, and is given the special symbol $\boldsymbol{\nabla}$:

$$\boldsymbol{\nabla} \equiv \hat{\mathbf{i}}\frac{\partial}{\partial x} + \hat{\mathbf{j}}\frac{\partial}{\partial y}.\tag{7–13}$$

[The extension to a three-dimensional dependence is obvious; we just add a term $(\partial U/\partial z)\hat{\mathbf{k}}$ to Equation 7–12 and a term $\hat{\mathbf{k}}\partial/\partial z$ to the definition 7–13.] Using the definition 7–13, we can write the force in terms of the potential energy in compact vector notation:

$$\mathbf{F} = -\boldsymbol{\nabla}U.\tag{7–14}$$

gradient   The vector quantity $\boldsymbol{\nabla}U$ is called the **gradient** of U; it is a vector whose magnitude is the maximum rate of change of U with position, and whose direction is that in which U increases most rapidly. Equation 7–12 shows how to interpret the compact notation of Equation 7–14.

Example 7–11

The Gradient

The potential energy of a particle moving through a region is given by $U = ax^2y + bx$, where a and b are constants. Obtain an expression for the force as a function of position, and show that there is no point where the force is zero.

Solution

The force is given by Equation 7–14, whose interpretation is Equation 7–12:

$$\mathbf{F} = -\nabla U = -\left(\hat{\mathbf{i}}\frac{\partial U}{\partial x} + \hat{\mathbf{j}}\frac{\partial U}{\partial y}\right) = -[(2axy + b)\hat{\mathbf{i}} + ax^2\hat{\mathbf{j}}].$$

Note that, in taking derivatives, we treated y as a constant in the x-differentiation and vice versa. For a vector to be zero, all its components must be zero. So we must have $x = 0$ for the y-component, $F_y = -ax^2$, to be zero. But then the x-component is the nonzero constant $-b$, so that the force cannot be zero anywhere.

7.6
NONCONSERVATIVE FORCES

We developed the conservation of energy principle and the notion of potential energy on the assumption that only conservative forces were acting. But with nonconservative forces like friction, mechanical energy is not conserved and we must go back to Equation 7–5:

$$\Delta(K + U) = W_{nc}, \tag{7–5}$$

where K is the kinetic energy, U the potential energy associated with any conservative forces acting, and W_{nc} the work done by nonconservative forces. It makes no sense to define a potential energy associated with nonconservative forces, since these forces do not "give back" work done against them. When you do work to push a trunk along a floor, there is no tendency for the trunk to slide back when you let go; the trunk gains no potential for doing work.

If we have an expression for W_{nc} in Equation 7–5, we can use that equation as we did the conservation of energy principle to provide a shortcut to the solution of many practical problems.

Example 7–12

A Nonconservative Force

A cross-country skier moving at 4.8 m/s on level ground encounters a nearly frictionless downward slope 6.1 m high. On the level ground below, the snow has been worn thin and consequently the coefficient of friction is 0.27. After coasting down the hill, how far will the skier glide across the level stretch?

Solution

The skier starts with mechanical energy $K + U = \frac{1}{2}mv_0^2 + mgh$, where v_0 is the speed at the top of the slope and h the height of the hill, and where we have taken the zero of potential energy at the bottom of the slope. When the skier has stopped on the level stretch, both the kinetic and potential energy are zero; the total change in mechanical energy is therefore $\Delta(K+U) = -(\tfrac{1}{2}mv_0^2 + mgh)$. The work done by friction is $\mathbf{F}_f \cdot \Delta\mathbf{r}$ where $\mathbf{F}_f$ is the frictional force and $\Delta\mathbf{r}$ the displacement. On level ground, the frictional force has magnitude μmg; if we take the x-direction as the direction of motion, the work is then $-\mu mg\Delta x$, where the minus sign arises because the force is opposite the direction of motion. Then Equation 7–5, $\Delta(K+U) = W_{mc}$, becomes

$$-(\tfrac{1}{2}mv_0^2 + mgh) = -\mu mg\Delta x.$$

so that

$$\Delta x = \frac{\tfrac{1}{2}v_0^2}{\mu g} + \frac{h}{\mu} = \frac{(\tfrac{1}{2})(4.8 \text{ m/s})^2}{(0.27)(9.8 \text{ m/s}^2)} + \frac{6.1 \text{ m}}{0.27} = 27 \text{ m}.$$

7.7
CONSERVATION OF ENERGY AND MASS-ENERGY

When a conservative force acts, work done against that force is "stored" as potential energy. Potential energy comes in many forms. Gravity provides one example of a conservative force and its associated potential energy. So does the force of a spring—ultimately electrical—and the force—also electrical—associated with the interactions of atoms and molecules. The energy contained in a fuel like gasoline is, in fact, electrical potential energy associated with the particular configuration of atoms in the gasoline molecules. When you burn gasoline, those molecules are reconfigured into substances—mostly carbon dioxide and water—whose potential energy is lower. The excess energy becomes kinetic energy of the individual molecules, which in turn may do work as they collide with pistons in an automobile engine. The forces binding atomic nuclei together provide yet another example of stored potential energy. Liberation of this nuclear potential energy powers the sun as well as our nuclear power plants and nuclear weapons.

But what about nonconservative forces? Is energy really lost when they act? No: but it is converted to forms that we don't normally associate with mechanical energy. Friction, for example, converts the kinetic energy of a moving object like a car into randomly directed kinetic energies of individual molecules in the frictional surfaces. The energy is still there; it's just in a form where it's not as obvious or, for reasons we detail in Chapter 19, as useful. (The term "heat" is sometimes used to describe this random molecular kinetic energy, although in Chapter 16 we will find that the term "internal energy" is more accurate.) And what about the electrical energy we supply to a light bulb? It, too, turns into random kinetic energy of atoms in the bulb's filament. Those atoms, in turn, convert their energy into electromagnetic radiation, a form of energy that travels through space at 3×10^8 m/s. We'll see just how that comes about in Chapter 32; leading up to our study of electromagnetic radiation, we will see also how energy can be stored in both electrical and magnetic forms.

Energy can take a variety of forms. Much of physics and engineering involves identifying, following, or controlling the interchanges of energy among its different forms. In classical physics, one overriding principle

conservation of energy

governs those interchanges: the principle of **conservation of energy.** If we keep track of all forms of energy involved, we find that energy is never lost in any interchange; it is just converted to another form. The interchange of potential and kinetic energy is just one example that we examined in detail in this chapter. If we account for the random kinetic energy of molecular motion, we find that even a "nonconservative" force like friction conserves energy; we examine this situation further in Chapters 16 to 19. If we account for electromagnetic radiation, we find that processes like the operation of a radio transmitter, the cooling of a hot stove burner, or the death of a star also conserve energy; Chapters 20 to 32 amount to a detailed study of electromagnetic energy.

The conservation of energy principle stands at the heart of classical physics. Alongside it is the principle of conservation of mass. But if we look closely, we find that neither principle really stands by itself. If, for example, we determine the mass of two deuterium nuclei before they fuse to form helium, we find their total mass to be slightly greater than the mass of the helium. Some mass seems to have disappeared; at the same time, energy has been released. Albert Einstein explained this phenomenon as a consequence of his special theory of relativity. Mass and energy, said Einstein, are interchangeable. His equation $E = mc^2$ describes that interchangeability; it says that a quantity of matter m is equivalent to a quantity of energy mc^2 (check the units: they work out!). In deuterium fusion, the energy released is exactly Δmc^2, where Δm is the mass difference between the deuterium nuclei before they react and the helium nucleus after the reaction. We can describe the reaction by saying that a small fraction of the original mass ends up after the reaction as kinetic energy. In more extreme cases, all the mass of a pair of reacting particles may change form. When an electron encounters its antimatter opposite, a positron, the pair annihilate completely; all the mass disappears in a burst of electromagnetic radiation. So much energy is produced in this total annihilation that the mc^2 energy of a single raisin could supply the energy needs of a major city for a day! And the opposite process occurs, too: under suitable conditions, a pair of particles can form out of pure energy (Fig. 7–23). Such total interchange of matter and energy is rare on earth; it occurs only in our large particle accelerators and in some reactions involving cosmic rays. But in some astrophysical situations, and especially in the very early universe, these events play a major role.

Fig. 7–23
Pair creation. This photograph, taken in the bubble chamber of the Stanford Linear Accelerator, shows the spiral tracks of an electron and positron that materialized out of pure electromagnetic energy. They are curving oppositely in the strong magnetic field that is present.

Conversion of matter to energy is popularly associated with nuclear energy only. That misconception does an injustice to Einstein's universal statement of mass-energy equivalence. Any time there is a net energy loss from a system, its mass goes down by an amount E/c^2. This occurs in burning gasoline just as it does in fissioning uranium; it's just that nuclear reactions convert a much greater portion of their mass to energy than do chemical reactions. Even a stretched spring is more massive than the same spring at equilibrium. The extra mass is given by $\frac{1}{2}kx^2/c^2$, since $\frac{1}{2}kx^2$ is the potential energy stored in the spring. It is only because the speed of light is so large that we do not notice the general equivalence of mass and energy.

conservation of mass-energy

Einstein's mass-energy equivalence replaces the two conservation statements for mass and energy separately with a single statement: the **conservation of mass-energy.** Whatever interchanges occur among different forms of energy, or among energy and matter, we find that the total mass-energy of a closed system remains the same. In this sense, matter and energy are essentially the same basic "stuff," just manifesting itself in different forms. We will see how mass-energy equivalence arises when we examine the theory of relativity in Chapter 33; in Chapter 36 we will see how, at the atomic level, the theory of quantum mechanics further erodes the distinction between matter and energy.

═══════ SUMMARY ═══════

1. A **conservative force** is one that "stores" work done against it. Mathematically, a conservative force is one that does zero work on an object moved around any closed path:

$$\oint \mathbf{F} \cdot d\mathbf{r} = 0. \quad \text{(conservative force)}$$

A corollary is that the work done by a conservative force as an object is moved between two points is independent of the path taken. Gravity is a familiar example of a conservative force.

2. With a **nonconservative force,** like friction, the work done by the force is not path-independent, and the total work done on an object describing a closed path need not be zero.

3. **Potential energy** describes the "stored work" associated with a conservative force. Mathematically, the potential energy difference as an object moves from point A to point B is defined as the negative of the work done on the object by the conservative force:

$$\Delta U_{AB} = \int_A^B \mathbf{F} \cdot d\mathbf{r}. \quad \text{(potential energy)}$$

Only potential energy differences have physical significance. We are free to assign zero potential energy to any point we choose; when we then speak of the potential energy U at some other point, we really mean the potential energy difference between that point and the point where $U = 0$.

   The form of the potential energy function depends on the specific conservative force involved. Two com-monly encountered cases include gravitational potential energy near earth's surface:

$$U = mgh, \quad \text{(gravitational potential energy)}$$

and the potential energy of an ideal spring:

$$U = \frac{1}{2}kx^2. \quad \text{(ideal spring)}$$

4. When only conservative forces act, the **mechanical energy**—the sum $K + U$ of the kinetic and potential energies—remains constant. This statement is the principle of **conservation of mechanical energy.** The conservation of energy principle allows us to solve easily problems that would be difficult to solve using Newton's second law.

5. Graphs of potential energy as a function of position—**potential energy curves**—reveal features of an object's motion. In particular, from such curves we can identify **turning points** where an object's kinetic energy goes to zero; when there are two such points, the object is confined to a **potential well** by **potential barriers** on either side.

6. Potential energy is related to the integral of force over distance; inversely, force can be expressed as the derivative of potential energy. Specifically, the component of force in some direction designated by ℓ is

$$F_\ell = -\frac{dU}{d\ell},$$

where the derivative indicates the rate of change of the potential energy U as one moves in the ℓ-direction.

The force vector may be written in terms of the **gradient** of the potential energy:

$$\mathbf{F} = -\boldsymbol{\nabla}U,$$

where

$$\boldsymbol{\nabla}U = \hat{\mathbf{i}}\frac{\partial U}{\partial x} + \hat{\mathbf{j}}\frac{\partial U}{\partial y} + \hat{\mathbf{k}}\frac{\partial U}{\partial z}.$$

The **partial derivatives** in this expression mean differentiation with respect to one variable while the others are held constant.

7. Energy exists in many forms besides kinetic and potential. These include the internal energy associated with random molecular motions, electrical energy, magnetic energy, and the energy of electromagnetic radiation. The **conservation of energy** principle states that, when all forms are taken into account, energy is neither created nor destroyed; it only changes form.

8. Einstein showed that energy and matter are interchangeable according to the equation $E = mc^2$. His theory of relativity therefore replaces the classical principles of conservation of energy and conservation of matter with the single **conservation of mass-energy** principle.

QUESTIONS

1. Figure 7–24 shows force vectors associated with four different forces. Which are conservative?

(a)   (b)

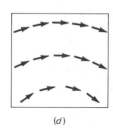

(c)   (d)

Fig. 7–24   Question 1

2. Is the conservation of energy principle related to Newton's laws, or is it an entirely separate physical principle? Discuss.
3. Why can't we define a potential energy associated with friction?
4. Why are you free to choose the zero of potential energy?
5. Can potential energy be negative? Can kinetic energy? Can total mechanical energy? Explain.
6. If the potential energy is zero at a point, must the force also be zero at that point? Give an example.
7. If the force is zero at a point, must the potential energy also be zero at that point? Give an example.
8. Explain how path-independence of the work done by a conservative force follows from the fact that the work done over a closed path is zero.
9. If the difference in potential energy between two points is zero, does that necessarily mean that an object moving between those points experiences no force?
10. A tightrope walker follows an essentially horizontal rope between two mountain peaks of equal altitude. A climber descends from one peak and climbs the other. Compare the work done by the gravitational force on the tightrope walker and on the climber.
11. A bowling ball is tied to the end of a long rope and suspended from the ceiling. A student climbs a stool at one side of the room and holds the ball to her nose, then releases it from rest (Fig. 7–25 left). Should she duck as it swings back (Fig. 7–25 right)? Argue from conservation of energy.
12. An avalanche thunders down a mountainside. Discuss the various energy transfers that resulted in water from the ocean eventually ending up as snow in the avalanche.

Fig. 7–25   Question 11

13. Could you define a potential energy function for a velocity-dependent force?

14. A block of mass m is held against a spring of constant k while the spring is compressed a distance x. Discuss how the speed of the block when released scales with k, x, and m.

15. Figure 7–26 shows a potential energy curve along with total energies for three particles. If the particles are all initially at x_0 and moving to the right, discuss qualitatively their subsequent motions.

16. A block *slides* down a frictionless incline. (a) Is its mechanical energy conserved? (b) If the incline is not frictionless, is mechanical energy conserved? (c) Now consider a cylinder that *rolls* without slipping down the incline. Note that friction is necessary to make the cylinder roll instead of sliding. Nevertheless, energy is conserved in this case. Why?

17. If potential energy is an even function, meaning that $U(x) = U(-x)$, what can you conclude about the force acting at the origin?

18. Why is it a misconception to apply $E = mc^2$ only to nuclear reactions?

19. High-energy physicists often give the mass of elementary particles in eV; for example, the "mass" of an electron is 511 keV. Explain.

20. You use a microwave oven to boil a cup of coffee.

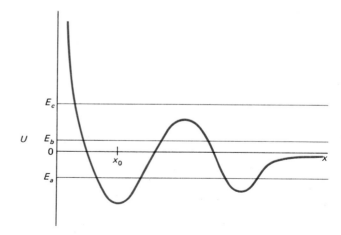

Fig. 7–26   Question 15

Assuming that your electricity comes from a hydro-electric power plant, trace the energy of your hot coffee as far back as you can.

21. In terms of potential energy, how do a new and a run-down battery differ?

PROBLEMS

Section 7.1   *Conservative and Nonconservative Forces*

1. Determine the work done by the frictional force in moving a block of mass m from point 1 to point 2 over the two paths shown in Fig. 7–27. The coefficient of friction has the constant value μ over the surface.

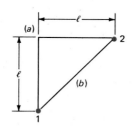

Fig. 7–27   Problem 1

2. Calculate the work done by each of the forces in Example 7–1 as the object is moved along a diagonal straight line from A to C in Fig. 7–5, and compare with the results of Example 7–1.

3. Force $\mathbf{F}_1$ points only in the x-direction, and its magnitude varies with x only. Force $\mathbf{F}_2$ points only in the x-direction, and its magnitude varies with y only. Draw diagrams showing some force vectors for forces with these general properties, and by drawing appropriate closed paths show that one force is conservative and the other nonconservative.

4. A force is given by $\mathbf{F} = F_0 \, (-\hat{\mathbf{i}} \sin\theta + \hat{\mathbf{j}} \cos\theta)$, where θ is the angle from the x-axis to the point where the force is being evaluated, and F_0 is a constant. Find the work done by the force as an object moves around a circle of radius R centered on the origin. Is the force conservative?

Section 7.2   *Potential Energy*

5. Show using Equation 7–2 that the potential energy difference between the ground and a distance h above the ground is mgh regardless of whether you choose the y-axis upward or downward.

6. An incline makes an angle θ with the horizontal. Find the gravitational potential energy associated with a mass m located a distance x measured along the incline. Take the zero of potential energy at the bottom of the incline.

7. The force exerted by a rubber band is given approximately by

$$F = F_0 \left[\frac{\ell + x}{\ell} - \frac{\ell^2}{(\ell + x)^2} \right],$$

where ℓ is the unstretched length and F_0 a constant. Find the potential energy of the rubber band as a function of the distance x it is stretched. Take the zero of potential energy in the unstretched position.

8. The force on a particle is given by $\mathbf{F} = A\hat{\mathbf{i}}/x^2$, where A is a positive constant. (a) Find the potential energy difference between two points x_1 and x_2, where $x_1 > x_2$. (b) Show that the potential energy difference remains finite even when $x_1 \to \infty$.

9. A 1.50-kg brick measures 20.0 cm $\times$ 8.00 cm $\times$ 5.50 cm. Taking the zero of potential energy when the brick lies on its broadest face, what is the potential energy (a) when the brick is standing on end and (b) when it is balanced on its 8-cm edge, with its center directly above that edge? *Note:* You can treat the brick as though all its mass is concentrated at its center.

10. Can you define a potential energy associated with a force $\mathbf{F} = -bx^4\hat{\mathbf{i}}$, where b is a positive constant? If so, give the potential energy as a function of position. If not, why not?

11. Can you define a potential energy associated with a force $\mathbf{F} = -bx^4\hat{\mathbf{j}}$, where b is a positive constant? If so, give the potential energy as a function of position. If not, why not?

12. The top of the volcano Haleakala on Maui, Hawaii, is 3050 m above sea level and 18 km inland from the sea. By how much does your gravitational potential energy change as you come down from the mountaintop observatory to swim in the ocean? Assume your mass is 75 kg.

13. A particle moves along the x-axis under the influence of a force $F = ax^2 + b$, where a and b are constants. Find its potential energy as a function of position, taking $U = 0$ at $x = 0$.

14. A 60-kg hiker ascending 1250-m-high Camel's Hump mountain in Vermont has potential energy -2.4×10^5 J; the zero of potential energy is taken at the mountain top. What is her altitude?

15. A 3.0-kg fish is hanging from a spring scale whose spring constant is 240 N/m. (a) What is the potential energy of the spring? (b) If the fish were moved slowly upward to the equilibrium position of the spring, by how much would its gravitational potential energy change? (c) In case (b), by how much would the spring's potential energy change? Explain any apparent discrepancies.

Section 7.3   *Conservation of Mechanical Energy*

16. A skier starts down a frictionless 30° slope. After a vertical drop of 22 m, the slope temporarily levels out, then drops at 20° an additional 31 m vertically before levelling out again. What is the skier's speed on the two level stretches?

17. A Navy jet of mass 10,000 kg lands on an aircraft carrier and snags a cable to slow it down. The cable is attached to a spring with spring constant 40,000 N/m. If the spring stretches 25 m to stop the plane, what was the landing speed of the plane?

18. A child is on a swing whose 3.2-m-long chains make a maximum angle of 50° with the vertical. What is the child's maximum speed?

19. Derive Equation 2–18 using the conservation of energy principle.

20. A 200-g block slides back and forth on a frictionless surface between two springs, as shown in Fig. 7–28. The left-hand spring has $k = 130$ N/m and its maximum compression is 16 cm. The right-hand spring has $k = 280$ N/m. Find (a) the maximum compression of the right-hand spring and (b) the speed of the block as it moves between the springs.

Fig. 7–28   Problem 20

21. A ball of mass m is being whirled around on a string of length R in a vertical circle; the string does no work on the ball. (a) Show from force considerations that the speed at the top of the circle must be at least $\sqrt{Rg}$ if the string is to remain taut. (b) Show that, as long as the string remains taut, the speed at the bottom of the circle can be no more than $\sqrt{5}$ times the speed at the top.

22. An 840-kg roller-coaster car is launched from a giant spring of constant $k = 31,000$ N/m into a frictionless loop-the-loop track of radius 6.2 m, as shown in Fig. 7–29. What is the minimum amount that the spring must be compressed if the car is to stay on the track? *Hint:* See preceding problem.

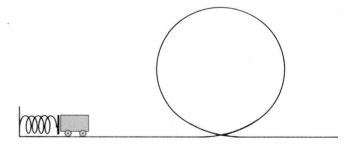

Fig. 7–29   Problem 22

23. An initial speed of 2.4 km/s (the "escape speed") is required for an object launched from the moon to get arbitrarily far from the moon. At a mining operation on the moon, 1000-kg packets of ore are to be launched to a smelting plant in orbit around the earth. If they are launched with a large spring whose maximum compression is 15 m, what should be the spring constant of the spring?

24. A runaway truck lane heads uphill at 30° to the horizontal. If a 16,000-kg truck goes out of control and enters the lane going 110 km/h, how far along the ramp does it go? Neglect friction.

25. A low-damage bumper on a 1500-kg car is mounted on springs whose total effective spring constant is 8.0×10^5 N/m. The springs can undergo a maximum compression of 18 cm without damage to the bumper,

springs, or car. What is the maximum speed at which the car can collide with a stationary object without sustaining damage?

26. A block slides on the frictionless loop-the-loop track shown in Fig. 7–30. What is the minimum height h at which it can start from rest and still make it around the loop?

Fig. 7–30   Problem 26

27. Show that the pendulum string in Example 7–7 can remain taut all the way to the top of its smaller loop only if $a \leq \frac{2}{5}\ell$. (Note that the maximum release angle is $90°$ for the string to be taut on the way down.)
28. The maximum speed of the pendulum bob in a grandfather clock is 0.55 m/s. If the pendulum makes a maximum angle of $8.0°$ with the vertical, what is the length of the pendulum?
29. A 2.0-kg mass rests on a frictionless table and is connected over a frictionless pulley to a 4.0-kg mass, as shown in Fig. 7–31. Use conservation of energy to calculate the speed of the masses after they have moved 50 cm.

Fig. 7–31   Problem 29

30. Your shot in a pinball game falls short; you would have wanted the 100-g ball to move 15.0 cm farther along the game. You had drawn a spring of constant $k = 140$ N/m back 6.6 cm. If the game and spring are inclined at $20°$, how much farther should the next player pull back the spring?
31. Boyoma Falls in Zaire has the largest flow of any waterfall on earth, with 2×10^7 kg of water plunging over the 60-m-high falls each second. If all the energy gained in this fall could be converted to electricity in a hydroelectric generating plant, what would be the power output of the plant? Compare with the 1000-MW output of a typical large nuclear plant.

32. A mass m is dropped from a height h above the top of a spring of constant k that is mounted vertically on the floor (Fig. 7–32). Show that the maximum compression of the spring is given by $(mg/k)(1 + \sqrt{1 + 2kh/mg})$. What is the significance of the other root of the quadratic equation?

Fig. 7–32   Problem 32

33. A uranium nucleus has a radius of 1.43×10^{-10} m. An alpha particle (mass 6.7×10^{-27} kg) leaves the surface of the nucleus with negligible speed, subject to a repulsive force whose magnitude is $F = A/x^2$, where $A = 4.1 \times 10^{-26}$ N·m^2, and where x is the distance from the alpha particle to the center of the nucleus. What is the speed of the alpha particle when it is (a) 4 nuclear radii from the nucleus; (b) 100 nuclear radii from the nucleus; (c) very far from the nucleus $(x \to \infty)$?

Section 7.4   Potential Energy Curves

34. Derive an expression for the potential energy of an object subject to a force $\mathbf{F} = (ax - bx^3)\hat{\mathbf{i}}$, where $a = 5$ N/m and $b = 2$ N/m^3. Graph the potential energy curve, and use your graph to determine the turning points and the points of maximum speed.
35. The potential energy associated with a conservative force is shown in Fig. 7–33. Consider particles with

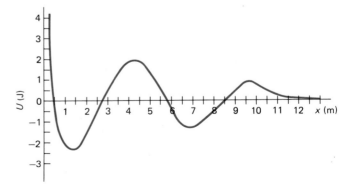

Fig. 7–33   Problem 35

total energies $E_1 = -1.5$ J, $E_2 = -0.5$ J, $E_3 = 0.5$ J, $E_4 = 1.5$ J, and $E_5 = 3.0$ J. Discuss the subsequent motion, including the approximate location of any turning points, if the particles are initially at point $x = 1$ m and moving in the $-x$-direction.

36. Make an accurate potential energy curve, covering the region -8 m $< x < 8$ m, for potential energy $U = (ax^2 - b)e^{-x^2/c^2}$, where $a = 1.5$ J/m^2, $b = 5.0$ J, and $c = 3.0$ m. Discuss the subsequent motion of 1-kg particles starting from the origin and moving initially in the $+x$-direction with total energies -3 J, 1 J, and 4 J. Include the location of any turning points. Determine also the speed of the highest-energy particle when it is a great distance from the origin.

Section 7.5   *Force and Potential Energy*

37. (a) Find an expression for the force in the preceding problem as a function of position. (b) Plot your result and compare with the graph of the preceding problem.

38. (a) Find the force as a function of position for potential energy given by $U = Axy + Bx^2$, where $A = 2$ J/m^2 and $B = 3$ J/m^2. (b) Find all points where the force is directed at 45° counterclockwise from the positive x-axis.

39. The potential energy associated with a conservative force is given by $U = bx^2$, where b is a constant. Show that the force always tends to accelerate a particle toward the origin if b is positive, and away from the origin if b is negative.

40. The potential energy of a spring is given by $U = ax^2 - bx + c$, where $a = 5.20$ N/m, $b = 3.12$ N, and $c = 0.468$ J, and where x is the *overall* length of the spring (not the stretch!). (a) What is the equilibrium length of the spring? (b) What is the spring constant?

Section 7.6   *Nonconservative Forces*

41. Repeat Problem 16 for the case when the coefficient of friction is 0.11.

42. A spring of constant $k = 280$ N/m is used to launch a 2.5-kg block along a horizontal surface whose coefficient of sliding friction is 0.24. If the spring is compressed 15 cm, how far does the block slide?

43. A 2.5-kg block strikes a horizontal spring at a speed of 1.8 m/s, as shown in Fig. 7–34. The spring constant is 100 N/m. If the maximum compression of the spring is 21 cm, what is the coefficient of friction between the block and the surface on which it is sliding?

3.1 m/s

Fig. 7–34   Problem 43

44. A meteorite strikes earth and embeds itself 1.7 m into the ground. Scientists dig up the meteorite and find that its mass is 400 g; they estimate that the ground exerted a retarding force of 10^6 N on the meteorite. Estimate the impact speed of the meteorite.

45. In the presence of time-varying magnetic effects, an electron experiences a nonconservative force. In a particular situation, the force vectors lie tangent to concentric circles (Fig. 7–35), and have magnitude given by $F = \frac{1}{2}e\dot{B}r$, where e and $\dot{B}$ are constants (they are the electron charge and the rate of change of the magnetic field), and r the distance from the origin. If an electron starts from rest a distance R from the origin and is constrained by some force to move on a circle of this radius, find its speed after it has made one complete circle.

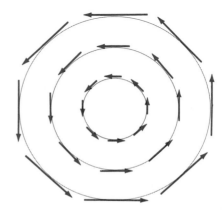

Fig. 7–35   Problem 45

46. A biologist uses a spring-loaded dart gun to shoot a 50-g tranquilizing dart into an elephant 21 m away. The gun's spring has spring constant $k = 690$ N/m, and is pulled back 14 cm to launch the dart. The dart embeds itself 2.2 cm in the elephant. (a) What is the average stopping force exerted on the dart by the elephant's flesh? (b) How long does it take the dart to reach the elephant? Assume the dart's trajectory is nearly horizontal.

47. A surface is frictionless except for a region between $x = 1$ m and $x = 2$ m, where the coefficient of friction is given by $\mu = ax^2 + bx + c$, with $a = -2$ m^{-2}, $b = 6$ m^{-1}, and $c = -4$. A block is sliding in the $+x$-direction when it encounters this region. What is the minimum speed it must have to get all the way across the region?

48. An object starts at rest from point A as shown in Fig. 7–36 and slides down the straight incline (path 1), reaching point B with speed v. The coefficient of friction on the incline is μ. If the coefficient of friction has the same value on the other paths shown, (a) show that the object will reach point B with the same speed v on either path 2 or path 3. (Assume there is a gradual bend at the bottom, but neglect the

Fig. 7–36   Problem 48

Fig. 7–38   Problem 51

details of this turn.) (*b*) Make a general argument, based on your result in part (*a*), to show that the speed will be the same for an arbitrary path that lies in the plane of the page, like path 4. (*c*) Explain why, in this problem, the work done by friction seems to be path-independent, even though friction is a non-conservative force. Give an example of a path for which your result (*b*) does not hold.

49. Two mountain peaks are a horizontal distance of 3400 m apart. One peak rises 1100 m above the valley between them, the other 900 m. Find the maximum coefficient of friction that will allow a skier starting from rest at the higher peak to reach the lower peak.

50. A bug slides back and forth in a hemispherical bowl of 11 cm radius, starting from rest at the top, as shown in Fig. 7–37. The bowl is frictionless except for a 1.5-cm-wide sticky patch at the bottom, where the coefficient of friction is 0.87. How many times does the bug cross the sticky region?

Fig. 7–37   Problem 50

51. A 190-g block is launched by compressing a spring of constant $k = 200$ N/m a distance of 15 cm. The spring is mounted horizontally and the surface directly under it is frictionless. But beyond the equilibrium position of the spring end, the surface has coefficient of friction $\mu = 0.27$. This frictional surface extends 85 cm, followed by a frictionless curved rise, as shown

in Fig. 7–38. After launch, where does the block finally come to rest? Measure from the left end of the frictional zone.

Section 7.7   *Conservation of Energy and Mass-Energy*

52. Particle physicists often describe the "mass" of the proton as 938 MeV. To what mass in kg does this correspond?

53. A hypothetical power plant converts matter entirely into electrical energy. Each year, a worker at the plant buys a box of 1-g raisins at the grocery store; each day, he drops one raisin into the plant's energy conversion unit. Estimate the average power output of the plant. Compare with that of a 500-mW coal-burning power plant, which consumes a 100-car trainload of coal every 3 days.

54. The sun's total power output is 4×10^{26} W. What is the associated rate at which the sun loses mass?

Supplementary Problems

55. Show that, for small displacements from the origin, the potential energy associated with the mass-spring system of Fig. 7–39 is given approximately by $U = \frac{1}{2}kr^2$, where $r^2 = x^2 + y^2$. Take the origin and the zero of potential energy when the mass is centered between the springs. All four springs have the same spring constant k. Why is your result only approximately correct?

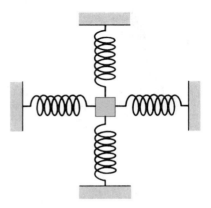

Fig. 7–39   Problem 55

56. A mass m is attached to a spring of constant k that is hanging from the ceiling. (a) Taking the zero of potential energy when the spring is in its normal unstretched position, derive an expression for the total potential energy (gravitational plus spring) as a function of distance y taken positive downward. (b) Find the point where the potential energy is a minimum, and explain its significance. (c) Find a second point where the total potential energy is zero. Discuss its significance in terms of an experiment where you attach the mass to the unstretched spring and let go.

57. With the brick of Problem 9 standing on end, what is the minimum kinetic energy that can be given the brick to make it fall over?

58. A bug lands on top of the frictionless, spherical head of a bald man. It begins to slide down the head (Fig. 7–40). Show that the bug leaves the head when it has dropped a vertical distance one-third the radius of the head.

Fig. 7–40 Problem 58

59. Together, the springs in a 1200-kg car have an effective spring constant of 110,000 N/m, and can compress a maximum distance of 40 cm. What is the maximum abrupt drop in road level (Fig. 7–41) that the car can tolerate without "bottoming out"—that is, without its springs reaching maximum compression? Assume the car is driving fast enough that it becomes temporarily airborne.

Fig. 7–41 Problem 59

60. Show that the pendulum string in Example 7–7 will cease to be taut when the string has caught on the nail and makes an angle

$$\theta = \cos^{-1}\left[\frac{2\ell}{3a}\left(\cos\theta_0 + \frac{a}{\ell} - 1 \right) \right]$$

with the vertical. Show that your answer is consistent with that of Problem 27, in that when $\theta_0 = 90°$ and $a = \frac{2}{5}\ell$, the string remains taut all the way to the top of the small circle.

61. An electron with kinetic energy of 10 keV enters a region where its potential energy is $U = ax^2 - bx$, where $a = 1.7$ keV/cm^2, $b = 2.6$ keV/cm, and x is the distance in cm from the start of the region. (a) How far into the region does the electron penetrate? (b) What is the maximum speed of the electron? (c) At what point does this maximum speed occur?

62. A particle of mass m is subject to a force $\mathbf{F} = (a\sqrt{x})\hat{\mathbf{i}}$, where a is a constant. The particle is initially at rest at the origin, and is given a slight nudge in the positive x-direction. Find an expression for the particle's speed as a function of position x.

63. (a) Repeat the previous problem for a force $\mathbf{F} = (ax - bx^3)\hat{\mathbf{i}}$, where a and b are positive constants. (b) What is the significance of the negative square root that can occur for some values of x? (c) Find an expression for the particle's maximum speed.

64. A 17-m-long vine hangs vertically from a tree on one side of a 10-m-wide gorge, as shown in Fig. 7–42. Tarzan runs up, hoping to grab the vine, swing over the gorge, and drop vertically off the vine to land on the other side. At what minimum speed must he be running?

Fig. 7–42 Problem 64

65. A force points in the $-x$-direction with magnitude given by $F = ax^b$, where a and b are constants. Evaluate the potential energy as a function of position, taking $U = 0$ at some point $x_0 > 0$. Use your result to show that an object of mass m released infinitely far from x_0 will reach x_0 with finite velocity provided $b < -1$. Find the velocity for this case.

66. A block slides on a horizontal surface with coefficient of sliding friction $\mu_k = 0.37$. It collides with a spring and stops at the point of maximum compression. If the block hit the spring at 1.79 m/s, and if the spring compressed 22 cm, and if these are the maximum speed and compression for which the block stops, show that the coefficient of static friction is twice the coefficient of sliding friction.

8

GRAVITATION

In 1684, Isaac Newton was a professor at Cambridge University when he received a visit from the young astronomer Edmond Halley. Halley had been discussing orbits with colleagues at London's Royal Society, a scientific organization. The London scientists had reasoned from Johannes Kepler's description of planetary orbits that the force acting on the planets must decrease with the square of their distance from the sun.

Halley asked Newton whether he knew what shape orbit such a force would imply. Though Kepler had shown empirically that planetary orbits were ellipses, Halley and his colleagues had been unable to prove this from their conjecture about the inverse-square dependence of the force. "Sr Isaac replied immediately that it would be an Ellipsis [an ellipse]," as was later reported by a person to whom Newton told the story. "The Doctor struck with joy & amazement asked him how he knew it, why saith he I have calculated it."*

After some months, Newton sent Halley a 9-page piece called *De Moto Corporum in Gyrum* (On the Motion of Bodies in an Orbit). In it, he proved all three of Kepler's three empirical rules of planetary motion. Newton became consumed with his work, and by 1686 he submitted to the Royal Society his masterwork *Philosophiae Naturalis Principia Mathematica* (The Mathematical Principles of Natural Philosophy). Halley saw the book through the press, and it was published in 1687 (Fig. 8–1). It was soon recognized as a monumental work that changed the course of science.

In addition to the three laws of motion that we introduced in Chapter 4, Newton advanced a law describing a force that tended to pull masses together. In his successive works in the 1680's he called it "gravity," from the Latin word *gravitas*, meaning "heaviness." We now know gravity as one of the fundamental forces of the universe (Section 4.2). In this chapter, we explore Newton's law of gravity and its application in the context of Newton's laws of motion and the concepts of work and energy.

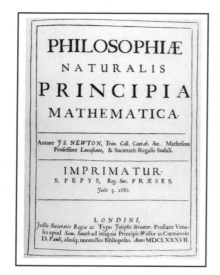

Fig. 8–1
Title page of Newton's *Principia*.

*See R. Westfall, *Never at Rest* (Cambridge University Press, 1980) for an authoritative account of Newton's life and work.

8.1
TOWARD THE CONCEPT OF UNIVERSAL GRAVITATION

Newton's theory of gravity was the culmination of two centuries of scientific revolution that began in 1543 when the Polish astronomer Nicolaus Copernicus made his radical suggestion that the planets orbit not the earth but the sun. Before that time, theories of motion and astronomy had been dominated by the views of the Greek philosopher-scientists Aristotle (ca. 350 B.C.) and Ptolemy (ca. A.D. 140). The Greeks held that the earth was the center of the universe, and the realm of imperfection. The natural tendency of terrestrial objects was to move toward the earth. The heavens, in contrast, were the realm of perfection, the home of the gods and of perfect celestial spheres like stars and planets. In the celestial realm, objects moved in the most perfect way possible—in perfect circles (Fig. 8–2). Even Copernicus maintained the sharp distinction between terrestrial and celestial motion; although he correctly placed the sun at the center of the solar system, he still insisted that planetary motion be described entirely in terms of circles (Fig. 8–3).

Fifty years after Copernicus' work was published, the Danish noble Tycho Brahe began a program of accurate observations of planetary motion (Fig. 8–4). After Tycho's death in 1601, his assistant Johannes Kepler worked for years to make sense of these observations. Success came when Kepler took a radical step: he gave up the requirement that planetary motion involve only perfect circles. In 1609 Kepler published his first two laws:

Fig. 8–2
In the Aristotelian scheme, planets moved about the earth in perfect circles. To match the observed planetary behavior, though, additional circular motions about the main circular path had to be postulated. Ptolemy made this addition.

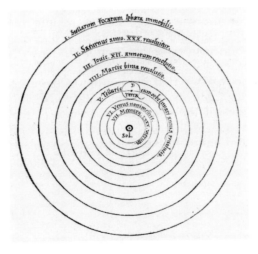

Fig. 8–3
The Copernican theory shifted the center from earth to sun, but maintained that celestial motion involved only circles. We see here the original diagram from Copernicus' book *De Revolutionibus,* published in 1543. Note *sol* (sun) at the center with *telluris* (earth) moving around it.

Fig. 8–4
Before the invention of the telescope, Tycho Brahe developed instruments for accurate measurements of planetary motion. Here Tycho demonstrates a mural quadrant used to measure the altitudes of stars and planets as they crossed the meridian.

Kepler's first law: The planets orbit the sun in ellipses, with the sun at one focus.

Kepler's second law: The line joining the sun and a planet sweeps out equal areas in equal times.

The first law sets the shape of the orbit (Fig. 8–5), while the second law describes the speed at which the planet moves along its orbit (Fig 8–6). In 1618 Kepler added his third law, relating the period (the time to complete one orbit) and the semimajor axis of the orbit (half the length of the major axis shown in Fig. 8–5):

Kepler's third law: The square of a planet's orbital period is proportional to the cube of the semimajor axis of its orbit.

These laws were all empirical—worked out to describe the data—and had no theoretical basis. So Kepler knew *how* the planets moved in their orbits, but not *why* they did so.

Shortly after Kepler published his first two laws, Galileo became the first to use a telescope to observe the heavens. With his first telescopes, no more powerful than today's binoculars, he discovered that Jupiter had moons orbiting it, that earth's moon was not perfect but pocked with craters, that the sun was blemished by sunspots, that the Milky Way was made of uncountable stars, and a host of other facts that are now common astronomical knowledge. His observations of Venus (Fig. 8–7) provided strong support for the Copernican theory. For favoring Copernican theory, the church condemned Galileo to life imprisonment, later commuted to house arrest.

By Newton's time the intellectual climate was ripe for the culmination of the revolution that had begun with Copernicus. The popular story is that Newton was sitting under an apple tree when a falling apple struck him on the head and caused him to discover gravity. That story is a myth, but if it were true the other half would be that Newton was staring at the moon when the apple hit him (Fig. 8–8). And Newton's stroke of genius was this: he realized that **the motion of the apple and the motion of the moon were the *same* motion; that both were "falling" toward earth under the influence of the same force.** In one of the most sweeping syntheses in all of human thought, Newton eliminated forever the distinction between terrestrial and celestial realms, suggesting that the behavior of everything in the universe follows a single set of physical laws.

Fig. 8–5
Kepler's first law asserts that planetary orbits are ellipses with the sun at one focus. The ellipse shown here is highly exaggerated; the orbits of all the planets but Pluto are nearly but not exactly circular. (A circle is an ellipse with both foci at the center.) Straight line is the major axis of the ellipse; the points are the foci.

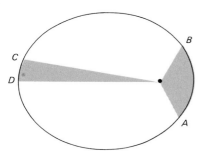

Fig. 8–6
Kepler's equal-area law. If the planet takes the same time to go from A to B and from C to D, then the shaded areas are the same. Note that this means the planet must be moving faster when it is closer to the sun.

8.2

THE LAW OF UNIVERSAL GRAVITATION

law of universal gravitation

In his *Principia*, Newton quantified his three laws of motion, and proposed further his **law of universal gravitation.** Newton suggested that any two particles in the universe exert an attractive force on each other, with the magnitude of the force given by

$$F = \frac{Gm_1m_2}{r^2}, \quad \text{(universal gravitation)} \qquad (8–1)$$

where m_1 and m_2 are the masses of the particles, r the distance between them, and G a constant. The value of G—called the **constant of universal gravitation**—is 6.67×10^{-11} N·m²/kg², although this value was not determined until after Newton's time. G is truly universal; both observation and theory suggest that it has the same value throughout the universe.

The force of gravity acts *between* the two particles m_1 and m_2. That is, m_1 exerts an attractive force on m_2, and m_2 exerts an equal but oppositely directed force on m_1. The two gravitational forces therefore obey Newton's third law, and constitute an action-reaction pair.

Newton's law of universal gravitation applies strictly only to pointlike particles that have no extent. But, as Newton showed and as we will prove in Section 8.5, it also holds for spherically symmetric objects of any size, provided that the distance r is measured from the centers of the objects. Thus the law 8–1 applies to planets and stars. It also applies approximately to arbitrarily shaped objects provided that the distance between them is large compared with their sizes (see Problem 29). For example, the gravitational force of earth on a space shuttle is given accurately by Equation 8–1 because (1) the earth is spherical and (2) the space shuttle, although irregular in shape, is much smaller than its distance from the center of the earth. To apply Equation 8–1 accurately to closely spaced irregular objects, we add vectorially the gravitational forces between all the individual particles making up the objects. We discuss this process further in Section 8.5.

Example 8–1
The Acceleration of Gravity

(*a*) Use Newton's law of universal gravitation to find an expression for the force of earth's gravity on a mass m, and apply Newton's second law of motion to calculate the corresponding acceleration. (*b*) Evaluate this acceleration at earth's surface and the 250-km altitude of a space shuttle. (*c*) Adapt your calculations to find the acceleration due to the moon's gravity at the lunar surface.

Solution

Since earth is spherical, Equation 8–1 gives the gravitational force of earth on a mass m:

constant of universal gravitation

Fig. 8–7
The phases of Venus. In an earth-centered universe, Venus would not show the full range of phases from crescent to full, and its apparent size would remain constant because of its constant distance from earth. Galileo's observations of the phases of Venus and the associated variation in its apparent size were strong evidence for Copernicus' heliocentric theory.

Fig. 8–8
Newton's stroke of genius was the realization that terrestrial and celestial objects move under the influence of the same force: gravity.

$$F = \frac{GM_e m}{R_e^2},$$

where M_e and R_e are the mass and radius of the earth. We use R_e because the mass m is at earth's surface, and the distance r in Equation 8–1 is measured from the *center* of the gravitating object.

Newton's second law, $F = ma$, shows that the acceleration is F/m. So

$$a = \frac{F}{m} = \frac{GM_e}{R_e^2}. \tag{8–2}$$

Taking values of M_e and R_e from Appendix F gives

$$a = \frac{(6.67 \times 10^{-11} \text{ N·m}^2/\text{kg}^2)(5.97 \times 10^{24} \text{ kg})}{(6.37 \times 10^6 \text{ m})^2} = 9.8 \text{ m/s}^2.$$

This, of course, is just the value of g—the acceleration of gravity at earth's surface. Our calculation shows clearly the difference between the two numbers G and g commonly associated with gravity. G is a truly universal constant, and is not a measure of acceleration; g is the acceleration of gravity at a particular place in the universe—the surface of the earth—and happens to have the value it does because of the size and mass of the earth.

At the altitude of the space shuttle, $r = R_e + 250$ km, so

$$a = \frac{F}{m} = \frac{GM_e}{r^2} = \frac{(6.67 \times 10^{-11} \text{ N·m}^2/\text{kg}^2)(5.97 \times 10^{24} \text{ kg})}{(6.37 \times 10^6 \text{ m} + 250 \times 10^3 \text{ m})^2} = 9.1 \text{ m/s}^2,$$

or about 93 per cent of its surface value. This calculation supports our contention in Chapter 4 that weightlessness does not mean the absence of gravitational force. The gravitational force on the orbiting astronauts is about 93 per cent of its value at earth's surface. But, as Equation 8–2 shows, the acceleration of an object arising from the gravitational force is independent of the object's mass. So the astronauts experience the same acceleration as their spacecraft, and are therefore weightless in the spacecraft's frame of reference.

Finally, we can find lunar surface gravity by replacing M_e and R_e with the appropriate values for the moon, also listed in Appendix F:

$$g_{\text{moon}} = \frac{GM_m}{R_m^2} = \frac{(6.67 \times 10^{-11} \text{ N·m}^2/\text{kg}^2)(7.35 \times 10^{22} \text{ kg})}{(1.74 \times 10^6 \text{ m})^2} = 1.6 \text{ m/s}^2,$$

or about one-sixth the value at earth's surface. How can this be, when the moon has only about one one-hundredth of earth's mass? Surface gravity depends on both the mass and the radius of the gravitating object; although the moon is less massive than earth, it is also smaller. An object on the lunar surface is therefore closer to the center, and this effect increases the gravitational acceleration even as the effect of lower mass decreases it.

Although we treated earth and moon as perfectly spherical in Example 8–1, they are actually not. Deviations of earth from spherical symmetry are associated with the overall shape of the planet as well as with geological features like mountains and subsurface rock formations. Using sensitive instruments called gravimeters, geologists map minute variations in g, and interpret their results to help locate mineral and oil deposits (Fig. 8–9). Tracking spacecraft in lunar orbit has led similarly to the discovery of "mascons"—concentrations of mass beneath the lunar surface.

Fig. 8–9
(Above) Student using a gravimeter to determine the local value of *g*. (Below) Contour map produced from gravimeter data shows variation of *g* in the vicinity of Middlebury, Vermont. The area shown measures 10 by 15 km; the value of *g* on adjacent contour lines differs by one milligal or 0.001 cm/s^2. Structure at the left is a trough of decreased gravitational acceleration associated with the Champlain Thrust, where low-density layers overlie the deeper bedrock.

Example 8–2 _____
The Gravitational Force between Small Objects

(a) Estimate the gravitational force between a 55-kg woman and a 75-kg man when they are 1.6 m apart. (b) Find the gravitational force between two electrons 1.0 cm apart, and compare with the 2.3×10^{-24} N repulsive electrical force that the two electrons also experience.

Solution

The people are hardly spherical, and their separation is not large compared with their sizes, so that Equation 8–1 can provide at best an order-of-magnitude estimate of the force:

$$F \sim \frac{Gm_1m_2}{r^2} = \frac{(6.67 \times 10^{-11} \text{ N·m}^2/\text{kg}^2)\,(55 \text{ kg})\,(75 \text{ kg})}{(1.6 \text{ m})^2} = 10^{-7} \text{ N}.$$

This force is far smaller than typical forces we usually discuss in connection with people-sized objects.

Electrons are essentially point particles, so Equation 8–1 applies exactly. Taking the electron mass from the list of fundamental constants inside the front cover, we have for two electrons

$$F = \frac{Gm_e^2}{r^2} = \frac{(6.67 \times 10^{-11} \text{ N·m}^2/\text{kg}^2)(9.1 \times 10^{-31} \text{ kg})^2}{(0.010 \text{ m})^2} = 5.5 \times 10^{-67} \text{ N},$$

or about 10^{42} times smaller than the electrical force.

Example 8–2 suggests that the gravitational force between subatomic particles and even ordinary-sized objects like people is very small compared with other forces that usually act. Why, then, is gravity the dominant force on the large scale? Because, unlike the electrical force, gravity is always attractive. No antigravity, or negative mass, has ever been found.* So the gravitational force is always cumulative, and large concentrations of matter like stars and planets give rise to substantial gravitational forces. Electrical forces, in contrast, can be attractive or repulsive because there are two kinds of electric charge. A large object like the earth contains nearly equal amounts of positive and negative charge, and therefore exerts no significant electrical force. We will discuss this fundamental difference between the gravitational and electrical forces further in Chapter 20.

The Cavendish Experiment: Weighing the Earth

We showed in Example 8–1 that the acceleration of gravity at earth's surface is given by $g = GM_e/R_e^2$. Given the radius and mass of the earth, and the measured value of *g*, we could determine *G*, the constant of universal gravitation. Or we might determine *G* using the parameters of earth's orbit in conjunction with the mass of the sun. Unfortunately, though, there is no way to determine accurately the masses of planets and stars except by ob-

_____
*Even antimatter should be attracted by the gravitational force of ordinary matter.

serving their gravitational effects and then using Newton's law of gravity to calculate the mass. For this we need to know G.

The only way to determine G is to measure the gravitational force arising from a *known* mass. Given the very weak gravitational force of ordinary-sized objects, though, this is a difficult task. That task was accomplished in 1798 through an ingenious experiment by the British physicist Henry Cavendish. Cavendish mounted two 5-cm-diameter lead spheres on the ends of a rod that was suspended from a thin fiber. He then brought two 30-cm lead spheres near the smaller spheres (Fig. 8–10). The gravitational attraction caused a slight twisting of the fiber. Knowing the properties of the fiber, Cavendish could determine the force involved. From the known masses and separation of the lead spheres, he then used Equation 8–1 to determine G. His result was within 1 per cent of the currently accepted value. Cavendish used his value of G to compute the mass of the earth; indeed, his published paper was titled "On Weighing the Earth."

Improved versions of the Cavendish apparatus are used today both in introductory physics laboratories and in experiments aimed at providing more accurate values of G. Modern experiments often use a laser beam reflected from a mirror mounted on the twisting fiber.

After his death, Cavendish left his considerable fortune to relatives, who later endowed the Cavendish Laboratory at Cambridge University. In "the Cavendish," many of the key discoveries about the nature of matter were made, including the discovery of the electron in 1897, of alpha and beta particles from radioactive decay in 1898, and of the neutron in 1932. Research on the nature of DNA by James Watson and Francis Crick in 1953 was done in the Cavendish as well.

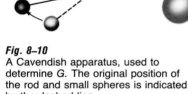

Fig. 8–10
A Cavendish apparatus, used to determine G. The original position of the rod and small spheres is indicated by the dashed line.

8.3
ORBITAL MOTION

orbital motion

Orbital motion refers not just to spacecraft and planets, but quite generally to objects moving under the influence of gravity alone. Minor constituents of the solar system—comets, asteroids, meteors—are, like the planets, in orbital motion about the sun. An individual astronaut, floating outside a spacecraft, is in earth orbit. And the sun itself orbits the center of the galaxy, taking about 250 million years to complete one revolution. Neglecting air resistance, even a baseball is temporarily in orbit. Here we discuss quantitatively the special case of circular orbits, then describe qualitatively the general case.

Circular Orbits

Newton's genius was to recognize that the moon is held in its circular orbit by the same force that pulls an apple to the ground. From there, it was a short step for Newton to grasp the possibility that human-made objects could be put into orbit. Nearly 300 years before the first artificial satellites were launched, he imagined a projectile launched horizontally from a high mountain (Fig. 8–11). If the projectile is simply dropped, it falls vertically like an apple from a tree. But given an initial horizontal velocity, the projectile describes a curve as the gravitational force pulls it from a

Fig. 8–11
Newton's thought experiment, showing the relation between projectile motion and orbital motion. This is from his *System of the World*, published in 1728.

straight-line path. As the initial horizontal speed is increased, the projectile travels farther before striking earth. But always gravity pulls it out of a straight-line path. Finally, there comes a speed for which the rate at which the projectile is pulled out of its straight-line path is exactly equal to the rate at which earth's surface curves away beneath it. It is then in **circular orbit,** returning eventually to its starting point and continuing forever unless a nongravitational force acts.

circular orbit

Why doesn't the orbiting object fall toward earth? It does! It falls toward earth in the sense that its motion deviates from a straight line, and the direction of that deviation is toward earth. Under the influence of earth's gravity, it is always getting closer to earth than it would be on a straight-line path (Fig. 8–12). It is behaving exactly as Newton's second law suggests it should. Remember that Newton's laws are not so much about *motion* as they are about *changes in motion.* That emphasis on change is what distinguishes Newton's view from the earlier and misleading Aristotelian view. If you ask why a satellite doesn't fall down, you are adopting the archaic Aristotelian view. The Newtonian question is: why doesn't the satellite move in a straight line? And the answer is simple: because a force is acting. That gravitational force is exactly analogous to the tension force that keeps a ball on a string whirling in a circular path (Fig. 8–13).

We can analyze circular orbits quantitatively because we know that any object in uniform circular motion is undergoing an acceleration v^2/r, where v is its speed and r the radius of the circular path. Newton's first law of motion tells us that a force is necessary to provide this acceleration. Newton's second law tells us the magnitude of that force:

$$F = ma = \frac{mv^2}{r}.$$

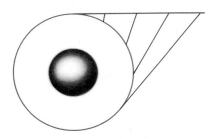

Fig. 8–12
An object in circular orbit is falling away from the straight-line path it would follow in the absence of gravity.

Some physical force of this magnitude must act to maintain the circular motion. In the case of an orbit, that force is gravity. Newton's law of gravity tells the strength of the gravitational force:

$$F = \frac{GMm}{r^2},$$

where M is the mass of the gravitating object and m the mass of the orbiting object. (We assume here that $M \gg m$, so we can consider the gravitating object to be at rest, essentially unaffected by the gravitational force.) Why do we have two equations for the same force F? The first, $F = mv^2/r$, is Newton's second law. It tells us nothing about the *physical nature* of the force, but only what its magnitude must be to keep the object in its circular path. The second, $F = GMm/r^2$, is a description of the particular physical force acting, in this case the gravitational force. The two describe the same force; equating them gives a relation between v and r that is necessary for a circular orbit:

$$\frac{GMm}{r^2} = \frac{mv^2}{r},$$

Fig. 8–13
A ball whirling on a string is like a satellite in circular orbit. The tension force pulls the ball toward the center of the circle, but the ball never gets closer to the center. Similarly, the gravitational force pulls the satellite toward earth's center, but the satellite never gets closer to the earth.

or

$$v^2 = \frac{GM}{r}. \qquad (8\text{–}3)$$

orbital period

Fig. 8–14
Astronaut Robert L. Stewart floats motionless with respect to the Space Shuttle from which this picture was taken. Because orbital parameters are independent of the orbiting mass, Stewart remains in the same orbit as the Shuttle, both circling earth at nearly 8 km/s.

Often we're interested in the **orbital period,** or time to complete one orbit. In one period T, the orbiting object moves the orbital circumference $2\pi r$, so that its speed is $2\pi r/T$. Using this expression for v in Equation 8–3 gives

$$\frac{4\pi^2 r^2}{T^2} = \frac{GM}{r},$$

or

$$T^2 = \frac{4\pi^2 r^3}{GM}. \qquad \text{(orbital period, circular orbit)} \qquad (8\text{–}4)$$

In deriving Equation 8–4, we have proved Kepler's third law—that the square of the orbital period is proportional to the cube of the semimajor axis—for the special case of a circular orbit, whose semimajor axis is just its radius.

Note that neither the orbital speed nor the orbital period depends on the mass m of the orbiting object. This is another indication that all objects experience the same gravitational acceleration, and is what allows an astronaut to remain motionless with respect to an orbiting spacecraft (Fig. 8–14).

Example 8–3 ——————————————————————————————
A Space Shuttle Orbit

A space shuttle is in circular orbit 250 km above earth's surface. What are its orbital speed and period?

Solution

Remember that the r appearing in Equations 8–3 and 8–4 is the distance from the *center* of the gravitating object. So here r is the earth's radius plus the 250-km altitude, or $r = 6.37 \times 10^6$ m $+ 0.25 \times 10^6$ m $= 6.62 \times 10^6$ m. Then, taking the mass of the earth from Appendix F, Equation 8–3 gives

$$v^2 = \frac{GM_e}{r} = \frac{(6.67 \times 10^{-11}\ \text{N·m}^2/\text{kg}^2)(5.97 \times 10^{24}\ \text{kg})}{6.62 \times 10^6\ \text{m}} = 6.0 \times 10^7\ \text{m}^2/\text{s}^2,$$

so that $v = 7.8$ km/s, or about 17,500 mph. Astronauts have no choice; if they want a circular orbit 250 km up, they must achieve this speed.

We can get the orbital period either from the speed and radius, or directly from Equation 8–4:

$$T^2 = \frac{4\pi^2 r^3}{GM_e} = \frac{(4\pi^2)\,(6.62 \times 10^6\ \text{m})^3}{(6.67 \times 10^{-11}\ \text{N·m}^2/\text{kg}^2)(5.97 \times 10^{24}\ \text{kg})} = 2.88 \times 10^7\ \text{s}^2,$$

so that $T = 5363$ s, or about 90 minutes. Again, there is no choice: as long as gravity is the only force acting, an orbit at 250 km altitude must take this much time.

Since 250 km is small compared with earth's radius, the orbital speed and 90-minute period found in this example are approximately correct for any near-earth orbit.

———————————————————————————————————————

Example 8–3 showed that the orbital period in near-earth orbit is about 90 minutes. The moon, on the other hand, takes 27.3 days to complete its nearly circular orbit. (Comparison of the moon's acceleration with that of an object falling at earth's surface helped Newton verify the inverse-square

Fig. 8–15
Weather over Africa and the South Atlantic as photographed by the European Space Agency's METEOSAT satellite from its geosynchronous orbit.

Fig. 8–16
This TV satellite dish antenna is trained on a communications satellite 36,000 km above the equator.

perihelion
aphelion
perigee
apogee

Fig. 8–17
(a) Two masses interacting by gravity alone describe elliptical orbits with one focus at the center of mass of the system (small dot). (b) When one object is much more massive, and it remains essentially fixed and the other orbits in an ellipse with one focus very near the center of the massive object.

dependence of the gravitational force; see Problem 8.) So there must be a distance where the orbital period is 24 h—the same as the rotation period of the earth. A satellite at this altitude whose orbital motion is parallel to earth's equator will remain at rest with respect to the earth. For this reason, weather and communications satellites are placed in geosynchronous orbit (Fig. 8–15). The increasingly popular home TV dish antennas are trained on geosynchronous satellites (Fig. 8–16).

Example 8–4

Geosynchronous Orbit

At what altitude may a satellite be placed in geosynchronous orbit?

Solution

We want the period T to be 24 h or 8.64×10^4 s. Solving Equation 8–4 for r gives

$$r = \left(\frac{GM_eT^2}{4\pi^2} \right)^{1/3}$$

$$= \left(\frac{(6.67 \times 10^{-11} \text{ N·m}^2/\text{kg}^2)(5.97 \times 10^{24} \text{ kg})(8.64 \times 10^4 \text{ s})^2}{4\pi^2} \right)^{1/3}$$

$$= 4.22 \times 10^7 \text{ m},$$

or 42,000 km. This is the distance from earth's center; the altitude above earth's surface is then 36,000 km or about 22,000 miles.

Elliptical Orbits

Using his laws of gravity and motion, Newton was able to prove Kepler's first law: that the planets move in elliptical paths with the sun at one focus. Since Newton's law of gravity is truly universal, Kepler's law applies to objects orbiting any spherical, gravitating body (here we assume the gravitating body is much more massive than its satellite; if this is not true, both bodies describe ellipses with one focus at the so-called center of mass of the system; see Fig. 8–17).

The circular orbits we discussed in the preceding section represent the special case when the two foci of the ellipse coincide, and the distance from the gravitating body remains constant. In the more general case, the orbit is distinctly noncircular. For bodies orbiting the sun, the point of closest approach is the **perihelion;** the most distant point is the **aphelion.** For bodies orbiting earth, the corresponding points are **perigee** and **apogee.** The orbits of the planets are nearly circular; earth's distance from the sun, for example, varies by only 3 per cent throughout the year. But the orbits of

(a)   (b)

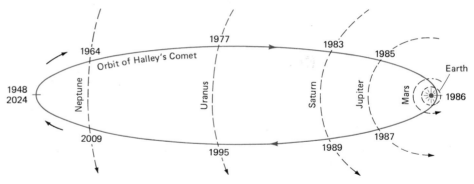

Fig. 8–18
Orbits of Halley's Comet and the planets, showing the years when the comet crosses each planetary orbit.

Fig. 8–19
Halley's Comet as imaged by the European Space Agency's Giotto spacecraft from a distance of 18,000 km. The comet's nucleus, the dark potato-shaped object at upper left, is 15 km long. From cracks in its crust, bright jets of dust erupt in the direction of the sun.

comets are typically quite elongated. Figure 8–18 is an accurately scaled diagram showing the orbit of Halley's Comet in relation to the planetary orbits. From the dates of each orbit crossing, you can see the comet falling toward the sun, picking up speed on its inward journey, then whipping around the sun under the influence of the strong gravitational force well inside earth's orbit, and finally slowing as it climbs away from the sun. Halley's most recent dash through the inner solar system occurred in the winter of 1986, with perihelion on February 9. The comet is now outbound, and will spend most of its 76-year period moving slowly through the outer solar system. Although Halley's 1986 journey did not take it as close to earth as in 1910, the comet was visited by an international armada of spacecraft that returned spectacular pictures along with much scientific data (Fig. 8–19).

When we discussed projectile motion in Chapter 3, we concluded that the trajectory of a projectile is a parabola. But in our derivation, we neglected the curvature of the earth and the associated decrease in the acceleration of gravity with altitude. In fact, a projectile launched from earth is just like any other orbiting body. Neglecting air resistance, it too obeys Kepler's first law, describing an elliptical orbit with earth's center at one focus. For trajectories small compared with earth's radius, the true elliptical path and the parabolic path of Chapter 3 are indistinguishable (Fig. 8–20). Un-

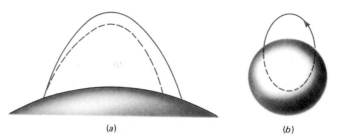

Fig. 8–20
(a) For projectiles of limited range, the true elliptical trajectory (solid line) differs only slightly from the parabolic trajectory calculated on the assumption of a flat earth. (b) Long-range trajectories, like those of intercontinental ballistic missiles, are clearly elliptical. Were earth's mass concentrated at the center, such a projectile would continue forever in its elliptical orbit.

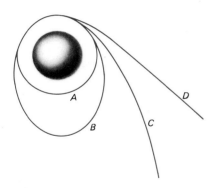

Fig. 8–21
As the projectile speed is increased above that required for circular orbit (A), the trajectory becomes first an elongated ellipse (B), then a parabola (C), and finally a hyperbola (D).

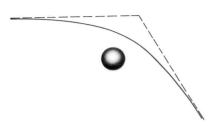

Fig. 8–22
Hyperbolic orbit of an object starting far from the sun with nonzero velocity. Only near the sun does the orbit deviate significantly from a straight line; at great distances the orbit approaches the asymptotes of the hyperbola (dashed lines).

Fig. 8–23
The change in gravitational potential energy between points r_1 and r_2 is found by integrating the gravitational force; along the path of integration the force **F** and path element dr are oppositely directed.

like a spacecraft orbit, the orbit of a projectile intersects the earth; at that point, nongravitational forces quickly put an end to the orbital motion. Even a baseball is in an elliptical orbit, and would continue forever in this orbit if earth were suddenly shrunk to the size of a grapefruit. Newton's ingenious insight was correct: barring air resistance, there is truly no difference between the motion of everyday objects near earth and the motion of celestial objects. A continuous range of orbits—from the straight-line path of a falling apple to the circular orbit of the moon—includes all such motions.

Open Orbits

The elliptical and circular orbits we have just discussed are all closed—that is, the same motion is repeated over and over because the orbital path closes back on itself. But closed orbits are not the only ones possible. Imagine again Newton's thought experiment (Fig. 8–21). Firing the projectile at the appropriate speed gives a circular orbit. Firing it faster causes it to rise higher above the earth, giving an elongated ellipse. But for great enough speeds—which we will derive quantitatively in the next section—the projectile travels in a path that takes it ever farther from earth. Eventually it gets so far that the influence of the gravitating mass becomes negligible, and the trajectory approaches a straight line. Mathematically, the shape of the trajectory is a hyperbola (Fig. 8–22). At the dividing line between closed elliptical and open hyperbolic orbits is the parabolic orbit C of Fig. 8–21, in which the initial velocity is just barely enough to prevent the orbit from closing. In the next section, we show how orbital energy determines these possibilities.

8.4
GRAVITATIONAL POTENTIAL ENERGY

How much work does it take to boost a satellite from earth's surface to geosynchronous orbit? Equivalently, what is the satellite's gravitational potential energy as a function of height? Our simple answer mgh won't do here, since the acceleration of gravity varies with height over the substantial distances involved. The expression mgh for potential energy, like the parabolic projectile trajectories of Chapter 3, is an approximation based on the assumption that g is constant—an approximation that is valid only for heights much smaller than the radius of the earth or other gravitating body.

Figure 8–23 shows two points at distances r_1 and r_2 from the center of a gravitating mass M. To find the change in potential energy associated with moving a mass m from r_1 to r_2, we use Equation 7–2:

$$U_{12} = -\int_{r_1}^{r_2} \mathbf{F} \cdot d\mathbf{r}.$$

Here the force points radially inward, and has magnitude GMm/r^2, while the path element $d\mathbf{r}$ points radially outward. Then $\mathbf{F} \cdot d\mathbf{r} = -(GMm/r^2)\,dr$, and the potential energy becomes

$$\Delta U_{12} = \int_{r_1}^{r_2} \frac{GMm}{r^2}\, dr = GMm \int_{r_1}^{r_2} r^{-2}\, dr$$

$$= GMm \left. \frac{r^{-1}}{-1} \right|_{r_1}^{r_2} = GMm\left(\frac{1}{r_1} - \frac{1}{r_2}\right).$$

(8–5)

Does this result make sense? Yes: for $r_1 < r_2$, the potential energy change is positive, showing that potential energy increases with increasing height. The result 8–5 is thus consistent with our result $\Delta U = mg\,\Delta y$ for the potential energy change associated with a change Δy in vertical position near earth's surface. Problem 34 shows that $\Delta U = mg\,\Delta y$ is a special case of the form 8–5 when $r_1 \approx r_2$. Although we derived Equation 8–5 for two points along a radial line, it holds for any two points at distances r_1 and r_2 from the gravitating center, as suggested by Fig. 8–24.

The potential energy difference 8–5 has an interesting feature: it remains finite even when the points are infinitely far apart. As a result, it takes only a finite amount of work to propel a spacecraft arbitrarily far from earth. Even though the gravitational force is always doing work on the spacecraft as it moves away, that force drops off so rapidly that its cumulative effect remains finite.

This property of the gravitational potential energy makes it convenient to set the zero of potential energy an infinite distance from the gravitating mass. Setting $r_1 = \infty$, and dropping the subscript on r_2, we then have an expression for the potential energy at an arbitrary distance r from the gravitating center:

$$U(r) = -\frac{GMm}{r}. \qquad \text{(gravitational potential energy)} \qquad (8\text{–}6)$$

The potential energy is negative because we chose $U = 0$ at $r = \infty$; any point $r < \infty$ is closer to the gravitating center and therefore has lower potential energy.

Knowing the form 8–6 for the gravitational potential energy allows us to apply the powerful conservation of energy principle. Figure 8–25 shows the potential energy curve for a gravitating mass. Superimposing several total energy curves shows immediately that an object with $E_{\text{total}} < 0$ is in a bound orbit, for there is a maximum distance beyond which it cannot move. In general, the orbit for $E_{\text{total}} < 0$ is an ellipse. But for $E_{\text{total}} > 0$, the object is not bound and can move infinitely far from the gravitating center. This corresponds to the case of a hyperbolic orbit. The case $E_{\text{total}} = 0$ is the intermediate case of a parabolic orbit; here the object has just barely enough energy to move infinitely far from the gravitating center.

Fig. 8–24
The path between two arbitrary points can be broken into an arc at fixed radius and a radial line. Since the gravitational force is perpendicular to the arc, there is no potential energy change along the arc. Potential energy change along the line is given by Equation 8–5.

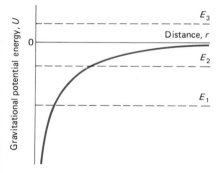

Fig. 8–25
Potential energy curve—a graph of Equation 8–6—for a mass m moving under the gravitational influence of a fixed mass M. Total energies E_1 and E_2, both less than zero, represent bound orbits; positive total energy E_3 represents an unbound orbit.

Example 8–5

Steps to the Moon

Materials to construct a 11,000-kg lunar base module are boosted from earth to geosynchronous orbit. There they are assembled, then launched to the moon, 390,000 km from earth. Compare the work that must be done against earth's gravity on the two steps of the trip.

Solution

As we saw in the preceding chapter, the work that must be done against a conservative force is equal to the associated potential energy difference. That difference is given by Equation 8–5. For the first step we have $r_1 = R_e$ and, from Example 8–4, $r_2 = 42,000$ km. So

$$W = \Delta U_{12} = GM_e m\left(\frac{1}{r_1} - \frac{1}{r_2}\right)$$

$$= (4.38 \times 10^{18} \text{ N·m}^2)\left(\frac{1}{6.37 \times 10^6 \text{ m}} - \frac{1}{4.2 \times 10^7 \text{ m}}\right)$$

$$= 5.8 \times 10^{11} \text{ J},$$

where the quantity 4.38×10^{18} N·m^2 is the value of $GM_e m$ calculated from G, M_e, and $m = 11,000$ kg. From geosynchronous orbit to the moon,

$$W = (4.38 \times 10^{18} \text{ N·m}^2)\left(\frac{1}{4.2 \times 10^7 \text{ m}} - \frac{1}{3.9 \times 10^8 \text{ m}}\right)$$

$$= 9.3 \times 10^{10} \text{ J}.$$

Even though the trip from geosynchronous orbit to the moon is much longer, the rapid drop-off of the gravitational force means that more work is required for the boost from earth to geosynchronous orbit.

The work calculated in this problem is solely the work done against earth's gravity. It does not include the work done to accelerate the lunar module material to orbital speed, and does not take into account work done by the moon. In Section 8.5 we show how to handle the moon's effect as well, while Problem 24 addresses the work associated with orbital speed.

Example 8–6
Halley's Comet

At perihelion on February 9, 1986, Halley's Comet was 8.79×10^7 km from the sun and was moving at 54.6 km/s relative to the sun. Find its speed at its March 13 encounter with the Giotto spacecraft, when the comet was 1.16×10^8 km from the sun, and its speed at its next aphelion in the year 2024, when the comet will be 5.28×10^9 km from the sun.

Solution

The comet's total energy is conserved, so we can write

$$K + U = K_p + U_p,$$

where the subscript p denotes perihelion. The kinetic energy is $\frac{1}{2}mv^2$, while the potential energy is given by Equation 8–6, so that

$$\tfrac{1}{2}mv^2 - \frac{GM_\odot m}{r} = \tfrac{1}{2}mv_p^2 - \frac{GM_\odot m}{r_p},$$

where $M_\odot$ is the sun's mass ($\odot$ is used by astronomers to designate the sun) and m the comet's mass. The comet mass cancels, and we can solve for the speed v:

$$v = \left[v_p^2 + 2GM_\odot\left(\frac{1}{r} - \frac{1}{r_p}\right)\right]^{1/2}.$$

Evaluating this expression at the Giotto encounter gives

$$
\begin{aligned}
v_{\text{encounter}} = \Bigg[(5.46 \times 10^4 \text{ m/s})^2 &+ (2)(6.67 \times 10^{-11} \text{ N} \cdot \text{m}^2/\text{kg}^2)(1.99 \times 10^{30} \text{ kg}) \\
&\left(\frac{1}{1.16 \times 10^{11} \text{ m}} - \frac{1}{8.79 \times 10^{10} \text{ m}} \right) \Bigg]^{1/2} \\
&= 4.74 \times 10^4 \text{ m/s} = 47.4 \text{ km/s}.
\end{aligned}
$$

A similar calculation gives $v_{\text{aphelion}} = 2.92$ km/s. The substantial difference between speeds at perihelion and aphelion results from Halley's highly elliptical orbit (see Fig. 8–18). As the comet climbs to aphelion well beyond Neptune's orbit, its gravitational potential energy increases greatly, leaving very little kinetic energy.

Escape Speed

Throw a ball straight up and eventually it comes down. Is this always true? No! Since there is a finite difference in gravitational potential energy between earth's surface and infinity, an object with enough total energy can escape all the way to infinity, and will never come back.

How much energy is needed for escape? At infinity, the potential energy is zero. If an object has barely enough energy, it will reach infinity with no kinetic energy remaining. So zero total energy is required (we saw this graphically in our analysis of Fig. 8–25):

$$K + U = 0.$$

If v is the speed of a mass m at some distance r from a gravitating mass M, then $K = \frac{1}{2}mv^2$ and $U = -GMm/r$, and we have

$$\frac{1}{2}mv^2 - \frac{GMm}{r} = 0,$$

so that

$$v = \sqrt{\frac{2GM}{r}}. \qquad \text{(escape speed)} \qquad (8\text{–}7)$$

escape speed

The speed v in Equation 8–7 is known as the **escape speed.** It is the speed that must be given an object at the distance r in order for it to escape all the way to infinity. At earth's surface, $v_{\text{esc}} = 11.2$ km/s. Earth-orbiting spacecraft are given somewhat lower speeds, depending on the desired orbital parameters. Moon-bound spacecraft are given speeds just under escape speed, so that if anything goes wrong (as happened with Apollo 13) they will return to earth. Spacecraft headed for other planets have speeds greater than v_{esc}; Pioneer and Voyager missions to the outer solar system left earth's vicinity at 14 km/s. In their encounters with Jupiter these spacecraft gained additional energy, giving them escape speed relative to the sun as well. Leaving the solar system altogether, these craft will coast through the galaxy for the foreseeable future (Fig. 8–26).

On a much grander scale, the concept of escape speed applies to the universe itself. Our universe is known to be expanding; cosmologists ask whether that expansion will continue forever or whether the universe will eventually collapse on itself. Although detailed analysis requires the general theory of relativity (Section 8.8), the question is basically whether or not the expansion speed exceeds the escape speed associated with the gravitational attraction of all the matter in the universe.

Energy and Circular Orbits

In the special case of a circular orbit, the potential and kinetic energies are related in a very simple way. In Section 8.3, we found that the speed in a circular orbit is given by

$$v^2 = \frac{GM}{r},$$

where r is the distance from a gravitating center of mass M. So the kinetic energy of the object is

$$K = \tfrac{1}{2}mv^2 = \frac{GMm}{2r}.$$

The potential energy is given by Equation 8–6:

$$U = -\frac{GMm}{r}.$$

Comparison of these two expressions shows that

$$U = -2K. \quad \text{(circular orbit)}$$

The total energy $U + K$ is therefore given by

$$E_{\text{total}} = U + K = -2K + K = -K, \quad \text{(circular orbit)} \tag{8–8}$$

or, equivalently,

$$E_{\text{total}} = \tfrac{1}{2}U. \quad \text{(circular orbit)} \tag{8–9}$$

Equation 8–8 shows that for circular orbits, higher kinetic energy corresponds to lower total energy. This surprising result arises because *higher* orbital speeds correspond to *lower* orbits. The implications for space flight

Fig. 8–27
(a) Thrusting toward the target only takes the spacecraft into a higher-energy—and therefore higher but slower—orbit. (b) The correct maneuver is counterintuitive. The spacecraft thrusts *away from* its target, decreasing its total energy and dropping into an elliptical orbit. A second thrust circularizes the orbit; the lower circular orbit is faster than the target's orbit. After coming ahead of the target, the spacecraft reverses this series of maneuvers.

are counterintuitive. To get to a faster orbit, a spacecraft must *lose* energy—as if a car, to speed up, had to apply its brakes. Astronauts Ed White and Jim McDivitt, attempting the first orbital rendezvous in 1965, experienced this firsthand. As they fired their thruster rockets in a direction they thought would take them toward their target, they found that they only moved farther away (Fig. 8–27a). Figure 8–27b shows the correct maneuvers, which involve thrusting opposite the desired direction to achieve a lower but faster orbit.

Example 8–7

Maneuvering a Spacecraft

A shuttle crew is sent to service the Hubble Space Telescope in its 600-km-altitude circular orbit. They maneuver into the same orbit, but find themselves 1.8 km behind the telescope. With two quick thrusts, they drop into an elliptical and then a circular orbit 250 m below the telescope. How long should they stay in this orbit before reversing the procedure to rendezvous with the telescope? Neglect the thrusting time and the time spent in the elliptical transfer orbits. How many orbits does the spacecraft complete during this maneuver?

Solution

Equation 8–3 shows that the speed in circular earth orbit is $v = \sqrt{GM_e/r}$. The telescope's speed v_t is therefore

$$v_t = \left(\frac{GM_e}{r_t}\right)^{1/2} = \left[\frac{(6.67 \times 10^{-11} \text{ N·m}^2/\text{kg}^2)(5.97 \times 10^{24} \text{ kg})}{6.97 \times 10^6 \text{ m}}\right]^{1/2} = 7560 \text{ m/s},$$

where $r_t = R_e + 600 \text{ km} = 6.97 \times 10^6$ m is the telescope's orbital radius. Speed in the lower orbit is given by the same expression, with r lower by an amount $\Delta r = 250$ m. Although we could solve directly for the speed in the lower orbit, it is more convenient with such a small Δr to use the binomial approximation, $(1 + x)^n \simeq 1 + nx$, which holds for $|nx| \ll 1$, and is described in Appendix A. We can write the shuttle speed v_s as

$$v_s = \left(\frac{GM_e}{r_t - \Delta r}\right)^{1/2} = \left(\frac{GM_e}{r_t}\right)^{1/2}\left(\frac{1}{1 - \Delta r/r_t}\right)^{1/2}.$$

The term $(GM_e/r_t)^{1/2}$ is just the telescope speed v_t; rewriting the second term as a quantity to the $-\frac{1}{2}$ power, we have

$$v_s = v_t \left(1 - \frac{\Delta r}{r_t}\right)^{-1/2}.$$

The term in parentheses has the form $(1+x)^n$, with $x = -\Delta r/r_t$ and $n = -\frac{1}{2}$. Since $\Delta r \ll r_t$, we can apply the binomial approximation and write

$$v_s \simeq v_t \left(1 + \frac{\Delta r}{2r_t}\right).$$

The difference between the two speeds—that is, the shuttle speed *relative* to the telescope—is therefore

$$v_{\text{rel}} = v_s - v_t = \frac{v_t \Delta r}{2r_t} = \frac{(7.56 \times 10^3 \text{ m/s})(250 \text{ m})}{(2)(6.97 \times 10^6 \text{ m})} = 0.136 \text{ m/s}.$$

Since the upper and lower orbits have nearly the same radius, the shuttle must travel very nearly the entire 1.8 km relative to the telescope in order to catch up. With relative speed v_{rel}, this takes a time Δt given by

$$\Delta t = \frac{\Delta x}{v_{\text{rel}}} = \frac{1800 \text{ m}}{0.136 \text{ m/s}} = 1.32 \times 10^4 \text{ s} = 221 \text{ min}.$$

Since the period in near-earth orbit is about 90 min, the spacecraft completes more than two orbits during the maneuver.

8.5
THE SUPERPOSITION PRINCIPLE

So far we have considered only the effect of a single gravitating mass. But things are more complicated than that! The moon, for example, experiences substantial gravitational forces from both earth and sun, as well as smaller forces from the other planets. How are we to handle such cases? Experimentally, we find that gravitational forces given by Equation 8–1 simply add vectorially (Fig. 8–28). This experimental fact is an instance of the **superposition principle.**

superposition principle

To determine the motion of several gravitating masses, we must first add vectorially the gravitational forces acting on each, and then solve Newton's second law for the motion. So complicated is this process that, in general, it is impossible to solve exactly for the motions of even three objects. In practice, computer calculations are used to provide highly accurate approximation in these cases. Before the age of computers, orbital calculations often involved years of tedious work (Fig. 8–29).

Fig. 8–28
The net force on the moon is the sum of the gravitational forces of earth and sun.

Fig. 8–29
Halley's original observations of his comet in 1682. The left-hand page shows observations of September 4, 1682, followed by calculations of the orbit. The right-hand page shows a sketch of the inner orbit.

Much of the difficulty in treating complicated gravitational situations involves the vector addition of forces that vary in both direction and magnitude. But because forces add, so do the potential energies associated with these forces. Then the gravitational potential energy of a mass m a distance r_1 from a gravitating mass M_1 and a distance r_2 from a second gravitating mass M_2 is just the *scalar* sum

$$U = -\frac{GM_1 m}{r_1} - \frac{GM_2 m}{r_2} = -Gm\left(\frac{M_1}{r_1} + \frac{M_2}{r_2}\right), \qquad (8\text{--}10)$$

regardless of the directions of the *vectors* **r₁** and **r₂**. In the preceding chapter, we found that the force is given by the gradient of the potential energy, so that we can in principle calculate the gravitational force from the associated potential energy function.

Example 8–8
Potential Energy and Superposition

(a) Find an expression for the gravitational potential energy of a mass m located a distance r from earth's center along a line joining earth and moon. (b) Revise accordingly the calculation in Example 8–5 for the work done in boosting the 11,000-kg lunar base module from geosynchronous orbit to the moon's surface. (c) Use your potential energy function to find an expression for the net gravitational force, and find a point where the force vanishes.

Solution

(a) Letting R be the 390,000-km distance from earth to moon, Equation 8–10 becomes

$$U = -Gm\left(\frac{M_e}{r} + \frac{M_m}{R-r}\right).$$

(b) At geosynchronous orbit, $r = 42{,}000$ km and $R - r = 350{,}000$ km, so that for the 11,000-kg lunar base module

$$U_{geo} = (-6.67 \times 10^{-11}\ \text{N·m}^2/\text{kg}^2)(11 \times 10^3\ \text{kg})\left(\frac{5.97 \times 10^{24}\ \text{kg}}{42 \times 10^6\ \text{m}} + \frac{7.35 \times 10^{22}\ \text{kg}}{350 \times 10^6\ \text{m}}\right)$$

$$= -1.0 \times 10^{11}\ \text{J}.$$

At the moon's surface, r is nearly the full 390,000 km and $R - r$ is one lunar radius, or 1740 km, so that

$$U_{moon} = -(6.67 \times 10^{-11} \text{ N} \cdot \text{m}^2/\text{kg}^2)(11 \times 10^3 \text{ kg})\left(\frac{5.97 \times 10^{24} \text{ kg}}{390 \times 10^6 \text{ m}} + \frac{7.35 \times 10^{22} \text{ kg}}{1.74 \times 10^6 \text{ m}}\right)$$

$$= -4.2 \times 10^{10} \text{ J}.$$

Then the work needed to lift the module from geosynchronous orbit to the moon is

$$W = U_{moon} - U_{geo} = (-4.2 \times 10^{10} \text{ J}) - (-1.0 \times 10^{11} \text{ J}) = 6 \times 10^{10} \text{ J},$$

about 35 per cent lower than the 9.3×10^{10} J we found in Example 8–5 when we neglected the moon's gravity. (c) In this one-dimensional situation, the gravitational force lies along the earth-moon line; Equation 7–11 then shows that $F = -dU/dr$, or

$$F = Gm\frac{d}{dr}\left(\frac{M_e}{r} + \frac{M_m}{R-r}\right) = -\frac{GmM_e}{r^2} + \frac{GmM_m}{(R-r)^2}.$$

Here $R - r$ is the distance from the moon, so that the second term is the force of the moon's gravity, while the first is that of earth's gravity. The positive term indicates a force in the direction of increasing r—that is, toward the moon—while the negative term indicates an earthward force. The force is zero when

$$\frac{M_m}{(R-r)^2} = \frac{M_e}{r^2},$$

or

$$r\sqrt{M_m} = (R-r)\sqrt{M_e},$$

so that

$$r = R\frac{\sqrt{M_e}}{\sqrt{M_e} + \sqrt{M_m}}.$$

Using the appropriate values shows that the gravitational force vanishes at a point 350,000 km from earth's center. (Because earth and moon are in orbit about each other, this zero-gravity point does not stay fixed, so a particle would not remain at rest there.)

The Gravitational Effect of a Spherical Mass

Newton was delayed 20 years in the publication of his ideas about gravity, until he could prove that a spherical body's gravity acted as though all the mass of the body were concentrated at its center. Here we determine the gravitational effect of a spherical mass by calculating the gravitational potential energy.

We begin by considering a thin spherical shell of mass M and radius R, with a small mass m located some distance r from the center of the shell (Fig. 8–30). We seek an expression for the gravitational potential energy of this configuration, as a function of the distance r. Spherical symmetry ensures that the potential energy depends only on r, and not on angular position, so that the position of our "test mass" m is quite general.

Now imagine dividing the shell into many mass elements ΔM_i. If the mass elements are small enough, they behave essentially like point particles, and each gives rise to a gravitational potential energy given by Equation 8–6:

Fig. 8–30
A small mass m located a distance r from the center of a spherical shell of mass M. Also shown is a hoop-shaped mass element, all of which is a distance s from the test mass m.

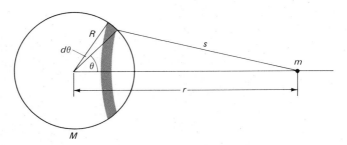

$$\Delta U = -\frac{Gm\,\Delta M_i}{s_i},$$

where s_i is the distance from the mass element ΔM_i to the test mass m. Generalizing Equation 8–10, we can write the total potential energy of the mass m as the sum of the potential energies associated with each of the mass elements:

$$U = -\sum\frac{Gm\,\Delta M_i}{s_i}.$$

In the limit $\Delta M_i\to0$, our approximation of the mass elements as point particles becomes exact, and the sum becomes an integral:

$$U = -\int\frac{Gm\,dM}{s}, \tag{8–11}$$

where the integration is taken over all mass elements making up the shell.

What constitutes a suitable mass element? Applying Equation 8–6 to write the potential energy of a mass element as $\Delta U = -Gm\Delta M/s$ did not really require that each mass element resemble a point particle, but only that it be small enough so the distance s is the same for all parts of the mass element. Suitable mass elements with this property are narrow hoops like the one shown in Fig. 8–30. In the limit that led to the integral 8–11, such a hoop has infinitesimal mass dM; since the shell is uniform, the ratio dM/M is the same as the ratio of the hoop area to the total area of the shell. Figure 8–30 shows that the hoop subtends an angle $d\theta$, so that its width is $R\,d\theta$. The radius of the hoop is $R\sin\theta$, where θ is shown in Fig. 8–30. Now imagine "unrolling" the hoop; the result is a thin, nearly rectangular strip of area $2\pi R^2\sin\theta\,d\theta$ (Fig. 8–31). Since the area of the entire shell is $4\pi R^2$, we have

Fig. 8–31
Unrolling a hoop-shaped mass element gives a rectangular strip of length $2\pi R\sin\theta$ and width $R\,d\theta$; the area of the strip is $2\pi R^2\sin\theta\,d\theta$.

$$\frac{dM}{M} = \frac{\text{hoop area}}{\text{shell area}} = \frac{2\pi R^2\sin\theta\,d\theta}{4\pi R^2} = \tfrac12\sin\theta\,d\theta.$$

Solving for dM and using the result in Equation 8–11 gives

$$U = -\int\frac{GMm}{2s}\sin\theta\,d\theta.$$

To evaluate this integral, we must relate the variables s and θ. Such a relationship is provided by the law of cosines (see Appendix A); applying that law to the triangle shown in Fig. 8–30 gives

$$s^2 = R^2 + r^2 - 2rR\cos\theta.$$

Both the shell radius R and the distance r to the test mass are independent of θ, so that differentiating this expression with respect to θ gives

$$2s\,\frac{ds}{d\theta} = 2rR\sin\theta,$$

since $d(\cos\theta)/d\theta = -\sin\theta$. We can rearrange this expression to get

$$\frac{\sin\theta\,d\theta}{s} = \frac{ds}{rR};$$

using this result in our integral then gives

$$U = -\frac{GMm}{2rR}\int ds.$$

The limits of this integral must be chosen to cover the entire shell; that is, they must include all values of the distance s corresponding to all the hoops making up the shell. Calling s_1 the smallest such value and s_2 the largest, our integral becomes

$$U = -\frac{GMm}{2rR}\int_{s_1}^{s_2} ds = -\frac{GMm}{2rR}(s_2 - s_1). \tag{8-12}$$

We now consider the two distinct cases of (1) the test mass m outside the shell and (2) the test mass m inside the shell.

Test mass outside shell: In this case, Fig. 8–30 shows that the smallest value of s is $s_1 = r - R$, while the largest is $s_2 = r + R$. Then Equation 8–12 becomes

$$U = -\frac{GMm}{2rR}\,[(r+R) - (r-R)] = -\frac{GMm}{r}.$$

This result is identical to Equation 8–6 for the potential energy of a mass m a distance r from a point mass M. Thus for a test mass outside the shell, the shell's gravitational effect is the same as if all the shell's mass were concentrated at its center.

Since a solid sphere can be considered to be composed of a nested set of shells (Fig. 8–32), with each shell acting as if its mass were concentrated at the center, the total gravitational effect of the sphere is still that of a mass point at the sphere's center. Note that the density does not even have to be constant from shell to shell. As long as there is only a radial variation in density, so that the sphere remains spherically symmetric, then the gravitational effect remains that of a mass point concentrated at the center.

Fig. 8–32
A solid sphere can be considered to be composed of a nested set of shells.

Test mass inside shell: Figure 8–33 shows that in this case $s_1 = R - r$ while $s_2 = R + r$. Then Equation 8–12 gives

$$U = -\frac{GMm}{2rR}\,[(R+r) - (R-r)] = -\frac{GMm}{R}.$$

Since all the quantities in this expression are constants, the potential energy has the same value everywhere inside the shell. That means no work is involved in moving the test mass around inside the shell, and therefore the force must be zero everywhere inside the shell! How can this be? The answer lies in the inverse-square dependence of the force associated with

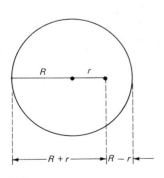

Fig. 8–33
With the test mass inside the shell, values of s range from $R - r$ to $R + r$.

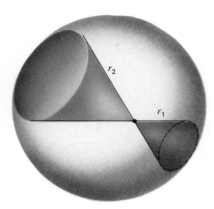

Fig. 8–34
Within any cone of arbitrary angle, the amount of mass on the more distant part of the shell is larger than that on the nearer part by a factor r_2^2/r_1^2. But the force from each mass point on the more distant part is weaker by r_1^2/r_2^2. The result is equal forces in two opposite directions, so that there is no net force anywhere inside the shell.

a point mass. At any point inside the shell, the force from nearby portions of the shell is exactly compensated by the greater mass associated with more distant parts of the shell (Fig. 8–34).

Our results for the gravitational force within and without a shell can be combined to give the force inside a solid sphere like the earth. Since a shell exerts no force on a test mass inside it, the overlying layers have no effect on a test mass inside the sphere (Fig. 8–35). The underlying layers, meanwhile, act as though their mass were concentrated at the center, and provide the total force on the test mass. So we can write

$$F = \frac{GM(r)m}{r^2}, \qquad (8\text{–}13)$$

where $M(r)$ signifies the total mass interior to the radius r. The direction of this force is, of course, toward the center. In the case of a *uniform* solid sphere (a poor approximation to the earth, whose density is much greater at the center), the mass within a given radius is proportional to the volume within that radius, so that

$$M(r) = \frac{r^3}{R^3} M,$$

with M the total mass and R the radius of the sphere. Using this expression in Equation 8–13 gives

$$F = G\left(\frac{Mr^3}{R^3}\right)\left(\frac{m}{r^2}\right) = \frac{GMmr}{R^3},$$

so that the gravitational force increases linearly from the center to the surface, after which it decreases with the $1/r^2$ dependence characteristic of a point mass (Fig. 8–36).

8.6
THE GRAVITATIONAL FIELD

Our description of gravity so far has been one in which a massive object like the earth somehow "reaches out" across empty space and tugs on external objects like the moon or a baseball. Such a description is termed **action at a distance** because of its obvious assumption that earth can somehow exert its influence on distant objects.

action at a distance

There is an alternative way of looking at gravity that avoids explicit reference to a force acting between distant objects. A 1-kilogram object placed at some point in earth's vicinity experiences a force of 9.8 newtons, directed downward. A 2-kilogram object placed at the same point experiences twice the force. We ascribe this force not to a direct interaction between earth and each object but rather to a **gravitational field** that exists in the vicinity of earth. Near earth, the field produces a force of 9.8 newtons on every kilogram, directed downward. Since we need to specify both magnitude and direction, the gravitational field is a vector. At every point in space there is a gravitational field vector, giving the magnitude and direction of the gravitational force on a 1-kilogram mass placed at that point. Mathematically, we can write the gravitational field **g** as

gravitational field

Fig. 8–35
A test mass inside a solid sphere. Matter outside the radius r where the test mass is located exerts no force on the test mass, since that matter is composed of spherical shells of which the test mass is on the inside. The gravitational force arises entirely from the mass interior to the radius r, and that mass behaves as though it were concentrated at the center.

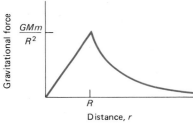

Fig. 8–36
Gravitational force on a test mass m inside and outside a uniform sphere of mass M and radius R. Inside the sphere, force increases with radius because the r^3 increase in enclosed mass overcomes the $1/r^2$ drop-off in strength. Once outside, the enclosed mass remains constant and the force drops as $1/r^2$.

$$\mathbf{g} = \frac{\mathbf{F}_g}{m}. \quad \text{(gravitational field)} \qquad (8\text{--}14)$$

where $\mathbf{F}_g$ is the gravitational force on a mass m (we assume the mass m is small enough that its own gravitational effects do not alter the arrangement of matter giving rise to the field). Since the force on a mass m in the field of a point particle or spherical mass M has magnitude GMm/r^2 and is directed toward the mass M, we have

$$\mathbf{g} = -\frac{GM}{r^2}\hat{\mathbf{r}}. \quad \left(\begin{array}{c}\text{gravitational field}\\\text{of a spherical mass}\end{array}\right) \qquad (8\text{--}15)$$

for the associated gravitational field, where $\hat{\mathbf{r}}$ is a unit vector pointing radially outward and where the minus sign shows that the field points toward the gravitating center. Both the definition 8–14 and Equation 8–15 show that the magnitude of the gravitational field $\mathbf{g}$ is just the local acceleration of gravity, g. The units of $\mathbf{g}$—N/kg—are equivalent to those of acceleration—m/s^2. The difference is one of interpretation; g reminds us of the acceleration of a mass falling freely under the influence of gravity, while $\mathbf{g}$ tells us the gravitational force per unit mass that arises whether or not the object is allowed to accelerate.

Near earth's surface, g is approximately constant and Equation 8–14 gives $\mathbf{g} = -g\hat{\mathbf{j}}$, where the unit vector $\hat{\mathbf{j}}$ points upward. The gravitational field is uniform, with field vectors of the same magnitude and direction everywhere (Fig. 8–37a). On a larger scale, the field is given by Equation 8–15, and the field vectors differ in magnitude and direction from point to point (Fig. 8–37b).

What is this field? Is it really "something," or just a mathematical construct we use to describe the gravitational interaction? At present you are perfectly justified in arguing the latter point of view. As you progress in

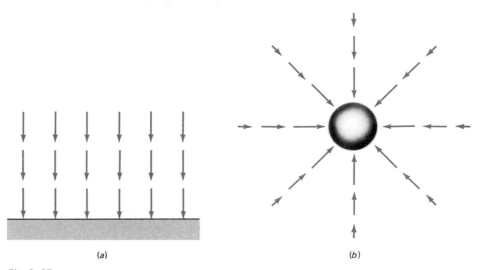

Fig. 8–37
(a) Gravitational field vectors in a small region near earth's surface have the same magnitude and direction. (b) On a larger scale, the field vectors vary in both direction and magnitude.

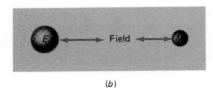

Fig. 8–38
(a) In the action-at-a-distance view, the earth interacts directly with a distant object, for example, the moon. (b) In the field view, earth gives rise to a field everywhere in space. The moon, in turn, responds to the field in its immediate vicinity.

your study of physics, though, you will encounter other forces—particularly those of electricity and magnetism—that are most easily described using the field concept. Gradually that concept will become almost indispensable, and the fields will become increasingly real to you. To a physicist, fields are every bit as real as matter.

Using the field concept, our description of the force on the moon becomes slightly more involved. We now say that the moon interacts only with the field in its immediate vicinity. The field, in turn, is produced by the earth. The field becomes an intermediary between earth and moon (Fig. 8–38).

What do we gain with this more complicated description? If we know the field at a point, we can readily calculate the force on *any* object placed in that field. We gain a more general description that applies to any object. But there is a far more important reason for speaking of fields rather than of action at a distance. It might bother you to think that the moon can somehow "know" that the earth is there to pull on it. It should bother you even more to imagine what would happen if the earth suddenly disappeared. Would the moon know immediately to stop feeling a force? Would it immediately fly off in the straight-line path required by Newton's first law? How could something that happens elsewhere—namely, at earth—instantaneously affect what goes on where the moon is? With the field concept these problems are avoided. The moon responds only to the field in its immediate vicinity. There is no question of its needing to know instantaneously what is going on in some distant place. The field concept makes the interaction a local one, in which what happens at some point depends only on conditions (that is, the field vector) right at that point.

As long as we deal with situations in which nothing changes, the field concept and the action-at-a-distance explanation give the same results. The choice of which to use is a matter of convenience or philosophical inclination. But as soon as we allow objects to move, only the field description can be correct. The reason lies in Einstein's special theory of relativity, which asserts that information cannot be transmitted instantaneously. If the earth disappears or simply jumps sideways so that "down" becomes a new direction, the field in the moon's vicinity cannot change instantaneously. Instead, a change in the field propagates outward from earth at a high, but finite, speed (in fact, it is the speed of light). The moon experiences the changed field only after a small but nonzero time has elapsed. Only when the field has changed will the direction or magnitude of the force on the moon also change. This field description is consistent with the requirement that information not be transmitted instantaneously. The action-at-a-distance view is not.

8.7
TIDAL FORCES AND THE ROCHE LIMIT

When the gravitational field is uniform, all parts of a freely falling object experience exactly the same gravitational acceleration (Fig. 8–39a). But when the field is nonuniform, the acceleration of gravity varies in magnitude and/or direction from place to place (Fig. 8–39b). The result is a

Fig. 8–39
(a) In a uniform gravitational field, all parts of an object experience the same gravitational acceleration. (b) When the field is not uniform, gravity acts differently on the different parts of the object. The result is a differential force that tends to stretch an object along the field and compress it at right angles to the field.

differential force

tidal forces

differential force—depending not on the strength of gravity but on how gravity varies from place to place—that tends to stretch or compress the object.

Ocean tides are an important manifestation of this differential force (Fig. 8–40). Because of the association with ocean tides, the differential forces of gravity are usually called **tidal forces.** In reality, the effects of continents and sea floor topography greatly alter the simplified tidal picture of Fig. 8–40. And the differential force of the sun, although weaker than that of the moon, still has a significant effect. As a result, tides are highest when the sun, moon, and earth are in a line and weakest when they make a right angle.

The force of the sun's gravity on earth is far greater than that of the moon (see Problem 37). Why, then, should the moon's gravity be the dominant influence on the tides? The answer lies in the very rapid drop-off of tidal forces with distance. Consider an object consisting of two small masses m separated by a distance $2a$, and located some distance r from a gravitating mass M (Fig. 8–41). The tidal force arises from the *difference* in gravitational field across the object. With the object oriented as in Fig. 8–41, the gravitational force points in the same direction at both ends of the object; its magnitude at either end is given by Equation 8–1, using $r \pm a$ for the distance. So the tidal force on the object—the difference between

Earth

Moon

Fig. 8–40
Ocean tides result primarily from the differential force of the moon's gravity. The gravitational force is strongest on the moonward ocean, weaker on the solid earth, and weakest on the distant ocean. Thus the water on the moonward side is pulled away from the solid earth, while earth itself is pulled away from the distant water. Two tidal bulges result, so that a given location experiences two high tides each day as earth rotates. (Not shown is the differential force associated with the sun's gravity, which is weaker but also important.)

Fig. 8–41
The tidal force on an object arises from the difference in gravitational field strength across the object.

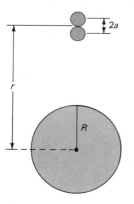

Fig. 8–42
Two volcanic eruptions on Jupiter's moon Io are visible in this image from Voyager I. The volcanic plume at right extends for 250 km. The bright spot on the terminator—the line between night and day—is another erupting volcano. Io's volcanism is thought to arise from heat generated internally by tidal stresses.

the gravitational forces on either end—is

$$F_T = \frac{GMm}{(r-a)^2} - \frac{GMm}{(r+a)^2} = GMm\frac{(r+a)^2 - (r-a)^2}{(r-a)^2(r+a)^2}.$$

Expanding both terms in the numerator, and noting that $(r-a)(r+a) = r^2 - a^2$, we have

$$F_T = GMm\frac{(r^2 + 2ra + a^2) - (r^2 - 2ra + a^2)}{(r^2 - a^2)^2} = \frac{4GMmra}{(r^2 - a^2)^2}.$$

If the object's size $2a$ is small compared with the distance r from the gravitating object—as is the case with earth's diameter in relation to the earth-moon distance—then we can neglect a^2 compared with r^2 in the denominator, so that the tidal force becomes very nearly

$$F_T = \frac{4GMma}{r^3}. \qquad \text{(tidal force)} \qquad (8\text{--}16)$$

This equation shows that the tidal force drops off as the inverse cube of the distance—much more rapidly than the gravitational force itself. For this reason the tidal force of the moon is greater than that of the more massive but more distant sun.

Tidal forces exert stresses on any extended object in a nonuniform gravitational field, and the astronomical consequences of tidal forces are therefore numerous. The extensive volcanic activity of Jupiter's moon Io (Fig. 8–42) is thought to arise from heat generated by tidal stresses. Tidal forces can even become strong enough to break an object apart. This happened to the Comet Biela in 1846, when it was split into two pieces by the strong tidal forces at perihelion.

Since astronomical objects are generally held together by their own gravity, we can ask when tidal forces might become strong enough to overcome the internal gravitational force. Figure 8–43 shows an object consisting of two small spheres of mass m and radius a in free fall a distance r from a planet of mass M. Since the small masses are spherical, they attract each other gravitationally as though they were point masses located at their centers, a distance $2a$ apart. So the magnitude of the attractive force between them is

$$F_g = \frac{Gm^2}{(2a)^2} = \frac{Gm^2}{4a^2}.$$

In the configuration of Fig. 8–43, the tidal force associated with differences in the planet's gravity tends to pull the spheres apart; since the spheres are small compared with their distance to the planet's center, and their own centers are a distance $2a$ apart, the magnitude F_T of the tidal force is given by Equation 8–16:

$$F_T = \frac{4GMma}{r^3}.$$

The object will be pulled apart if $F_T > F_g$, so that

$$\frac{4GMma}{r^3} > \frac{Gm^2}{4a^2}$$

Fig. 8–43
Two small spheres attracted by their own gravity, but pulled apart by the tidal force of the planet they orbit. Which dominates depends on how close they are to the planet.

Fig. 8–44
The rings of a planet lie within the planet's Roche limit, where tidal forces overcome the gravitational forces that would hold a moon together. Here, left to right, are the rings of Jupiter, Saturn, and Uranus.

or when

$$r^3 < \frac{16 M a^3}{m}.$$

If we let ρ_p be the density of the planet, R its radius, and ρ_s the density of its satellite—the composite object we are considering—then $M = \frac{4}{3}\pi R^3 \rho_p$ and $m = \frac{4}{3}\pi a^3 \rho_s$. Then our condition for tidal break-up becomes

$$r < \left(\frac{16 \rho_p}{\rho_s} \right)^{1/3} R. \qquad (8\text{–}17)$$

Roche limit

The critical radius r for tidal break-up is called the **Roche limit,** after the French scientist Edouard Roche, who suggested in 1848 that a moon would break up within this distance of a planet's center. Equation 8–17 shows that the Roche limit occurs at about 2.5 times the planet's radius when planet and satellite densities are comparable. A less simplified analysis would show the Roche limit depends also on the composition of the planet and satellite and whether the satellite material is liquid or solid.

Within the Roche limits of the planets Jupiter, Saturn, Uranus, and Neptune we find rings rather than moons (Fig. 8–44), showing that the tidal force prevents material within that limit from collapsing gravitationally to form moons. Beyond their Roche limits, all these planets have moons. We regularly place artificial satellites in orbit within earth's Roche limit, but these are held together by bolts, welds, and the strengths of materials rather than by gravitational forces, so that our force analysis does not apply.

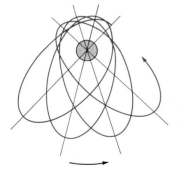

Fig. 8–45
The shift in Mercury's perihelion results in an orbit that does not quite close on itself. Both the shift and ellipticity of the orbit are greatly exaggerated; the actual orbit is nearly circular, and the perihelion shift amounts to only 43 seconds of arc per century.

8.8
GRAVITY AND THE GENERAL THEORY OF RELATIVITY

Although Newton's theory of gravity provided a brilliantly successful explanation of planetary motion, and today guides space probes like Voyager on billion-mile journeys to the outer planets, that theory is not perfectly correct. In very strong gravitational fields deviations from Newtonian predictions become evident. For decades the only evidence for this was a very slight shift in the position of the perihelion of Mercury's orbit (Fig. 8–45),

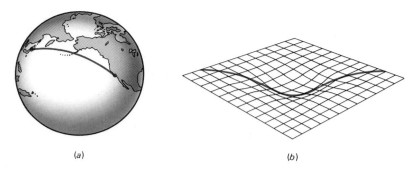

(a)   (b)

Fig. 8–46
(a) The "straightest" path between San Francisco and Tokyo is a great circle skirting the Aleutian Islands. (b) Similarly, the "straightest" path in the curved space and time near a massive object is not a straight line in the Newtonian sense. Depression in the surface shown represents the effect of a massive object on space and time.

Fig. 8–47
This supercomputer simulation shows the results of a calculation of the motion of gas as it spirals into a black hole. The black hole itself is invisible at the center, but we see the disk of gas that forms around it. X-rays emitted by the hot gas allow astronomers to study such systems.

amounting to only 43 seconds of arc per century (one second is 1/3600 of a degree).

That shift is consistent with the general theory of relativity, a radically different description of gravity completed by Albert Einstein in 1916. Unlike his special theory of relativity, which we discuss in detail in Chapter 33, Einstein's general theory is largely beyond the scope of this book. Here we note only that Einstein describes gravity as a geometrical effect resulting from the curvature of space and time caused by the presence of matter. In Einstein's theory, the natural state of motion is not uniform motion but free fall. An object moving under the influence of gravity alone follows the "straightest" path in curved space and time. But that straightest path need not be a true straight line, just as the straightest path on the surface of the round earth is not a straight line (Fig. 8–46).

The general theory predicts deviations from the Newtonian description of space, time, and gravity that become more significant as the gravitational field increases. Within our solar system, careful measurements of Mercury's orbit along with more recent precision spacecraft experiments have confirmed Einstein's remarkable theory. So have earth-based experiments that measure the minute effect of earth's gravity on time itself. And sensitive measurements of star positions during solar eclipses have confirmed Einstein's prediction of the influence of gravity on light.

Only with the past two decades' advances in astrophysics, though, have the effects of general relativity provided more than minor corrections to Newtonian theory. Today we observe extraordinarily dense collapsed stars, some in such close orbits about each other that relativistic effects on their

Fig. 8–48
This massive aluminum bar was built at Bell Laboratories to detect gravitational waves. Sensitive instruments on the bar could detect vibrations whose amplitude is no larger than an atomic nucleus. Such vibrations might be caused by gravitational waves from an exploding star elsewhere in our galaxy.

black holes

gravitational waves

orbits are quite obvious. Other collapsed stars, we speculate, may involve **black holes**—objects so dense that they warp space and time until not even light can escape (Fig. 8–47). Finally, scientists are testing general relativity's prediction that **gravitational waves** can exist. Literally ripples in the fabric of space and time, these waves could be generated in violent stellar explosions, and might be detected by the minute vibrations they set up in massive objects (Fig. 8–48).

SUMMARY

1. The concept of **universal gravitation** represents a major philosophical shift in human understanding of the universe. In contrast to the ancients' view that the celestial and terrestrial realms were entirely distinct and governed by different laws, Newton's universal gravitation provides, in conjunction with his laws of motion, a coherent description of motion throughout the entire universe. In particular, Kepler's laws of planetary motion follow as a natural consequence of universal gravitation.

2. Newton's **law of universal gravitation** states that any two particles in the universe exert a mutually attractive force, whose magnitude is given by

$$F = \frac{Gm_1m_2}{r^2},$$

where m_1 and m_2 are the particle masses and r the distance between them. Although the law applies strictly only to point particles, Newton showed that it is also exactly true for spherically symmetric masses of any size. Furthermore, it remains approximately true for arbitrarily shaped objects whose separation is much greater than their size.

3. The **constant of universal gravitation,** G, was first determined by Cavendish, who measured the gravitational attraction of lead spheres in the laboratory. The value of G is approximately 6.67×10^{-11} N·m²/kg².

4. An **orbit** is the path of an object moving under the influence of gravity. Orbital motion is generally very complicated, but the case of two isolated objects interacting gravitationally is more simple.
   a. Objects whose total energy is negative travel in closed, **elliptical orbits.**
   b. A special case of an ellipse is the **circular orbit,** for which gravity provides the mv^2/r force needed for circular motion. For an object in orbit about a much more massive object M, the orbital period and radius are related by

$$T^2 = \frac{4\pi^2r^3}{GM}. \quad \text{(circular orbit)}$$

This expression is a special case of Kepler's third law, which states that the square of the period of an elliptical orbit is proportional to the cube of the semimajor axis. An especially important earth orbit

is the equatorial **geosynchronous orbit,** where a satellite's orbital period equals one day so that the satellite remains fixed over a point on earth's equator. Geosynchronous orbit occurs at about 36,000 km above earth's surface.
   c. Objects whose total energy is greater than zero travel in open, **hyperbolic orbits** that take them infinitely far from the gravitating center. The intermediate case of zero total energy corresponds to a parabolic orbit.

5. The gravitational potential energy of two masses M and m is given by

$$U = -\frac{GMm}{r}, \quad \text{(gravitational potential energy)}$$

where r is the distance between their centers and where the zero of potential energy is taken at infinity.
   a. Because the potential energy difference remains finite even over infinite distances, it is possible to launch an object with sufficient speed that it will never return to its starting point. The required speed is the **escape speed,** given by

$$v_{\text{esc}} = \sqrt{\frac{2GM}{r}}. \quad \text{(escape speed)}$$

   b. For an object in circular orbit, the potential and kinetic energies are related in a simple way:

$$U = -2K, \quad \text{(circular orbit)}$$

so that the total energy is

$$E_{\text{total}} = \tfrac{1}{2}U = -K. \quad \text{(circular orbit)}$$

6. The **superposition principle** states that gravitational forces add vectorially. Consequently, the scalar potential energies also add. Integrating the potential energy associated with a spherical mass proves Newton's assertion that the gravitational force outside a spherically symmetric body is the same as if the body's mass were concentrated at its center.

7. The **gravitational field** describes the force per unit mass at each point in space. The field concept avoids the action-at-a-distance view that the earth or other massive object somehow "reaches out" across empty space to pull on distant objects. Instead, earth gives

rise to a gravitational field that pervades space, and a distant object responds to the field in its vicinity.

8. **Tidal forces** result from the difference in gravitational force over an extended body. Tidal forces give rise to stresses within astronomical objects; within the so-called **Roche limit,** tidal forces are strong enough to break apart objects held together by their own gravitation.

9. The **general theory of relativity** is Einstein's description of gravity in terms of the geometry of space and time. The predictions of general relativity differ only very slightly from those of Newtonian theory in the weak gravitational fields of the solar system, but in more exotic astrophysical situations the general relativistic description of gravity must be used.

QUESTIONS

1. What is the difference between Kepler's and Newton's assertions that planetary orbits are elliptical?
2. Explain the difference between G and g.
3. Earth's orbital motion is fastest in January and slowest in June. When is earth closest to the sun? Explain.
4. Newton was unable to determine the value of G, yet he managed to show that Kepler's laws followed from his law of universal gravitation. Why was this possible?
5. When you stand on the earth, the distance between you and earth is zero. So why isn't the gravitational force infinite?
6. The force of gravity on an object is proportional to the object's mass, and yet all objects fall with the same acceleration. Why?
7. A friend who knows nothing about physics asks what keeps an orbiting space shuttle from falling to earth. Give an answer that will satisfy your friend.
8. Could you put a satellite in an orbit that kept it stationary over the south pole? Explain.
9. It takes more energy to launch a satellite into the polar orbit shown in Fig. 8–49 than into the equatorial orbit shown. Why?

Fig. 8–49   Polar and equatorial orbits (Question 9).

10. Why are satellites generally launched to the east?
11. Can you launch a projectile that will travel three-fourths of the way around the earth, as suggested in Fig. 8–50? Why or why not?
12. Why was the United States' first satellite launching facility (at Cape Canaveral, Florida) in the southern part of the country?
13. Given the mass of the earth, the distance to the moon, and the period of the moon's orbit, could you calculate the mass of the moon? How or why not?

Fig. 8–50   Question 11

14. How should a satellite be launched so that its orbit takes it over every point on earth?
15. Does escape speed depend on the angle at which an object is launched? See Fig. 8–51.

Fig. 8–51   Question 15

16. Name some advantages and disadvantages of choosing the zero of gravitational potential energy at earth's surface rather than at infinity.
17. Is it possible for a spacecraft to reach Jupiter if launched from earth with less than escape speed relative to earth? Explain.
18. Is it possible to launch a projectile to the moon using a high-speed slingshot mounted on the earth?
19. Is it possible to launch a projectile into circular earth orbit using a high-speed slingshot mounted on the earth?
20. Describe the maneuvers necessary for a spacecraft to catch up with another that is ahead of it in the same circular orbit.

21. Are there any points not on a line between two masses where a third mass would experience zero gravitational force?
22. If the sun suddenly shrank to a white dwarf star the size of the earth, but with no loss of mass, what would happen to earth's orbit?
23. Newton asserted that a spherical object of radius R behaves gravitationally as though all its mass were concentrated at the center. Is this an approximation valid only at distances r large compared with the object's radius ($r \gg R$), or is it exactly true for any distance $r > R$?

24. Why is it significant whether the total energy of a comet is greater or less than zero?
25. Satellites in orbits lower than a few hundred km experience significant frictional drag due to residual air at these altitudes. Is the ultimate effect of this frictional drag to slow down or speed up a satellite? Explain.
26. Inside a spherical shell of matter, the gravitational force of the shell is zero. Does this mean that you can shield yourself from all gravitational forces by going inside such a shell?

PROBLEMS

Section 8.2   *The Law of Universal Gravitation*

1. Space explorers land on a planet with the same mass as the earth, but find that they weigh twice what they would on earth. What is the radius of the planet?
2. Jupiter's satellites Himalia and Io have masses of 9×10^{18} kg and 8.9×10^{22} kg, respectively. Their radii are 93 km and 1820 km, respectively. Determine the acceleration of gravity on the surface of each.
3. If you are standing on the ground 15 m directly below the center of a spherical water tank containing 4×10^6 kg of water, by what fraction is your weight reduced?
4. Compare the gravitational attraction of the earth for an astronaut on the surface of the moon with the gravitational attraction of the moon for the astronaut.
5. A sensitive gravimeter is carried to the top of Chicago's Sears Tower, where its reading of the acceleration of gravity is 0.00136 m/s² lower than at street level. What is the height of the building?
6. The density of lead is 11 g/cm³. What was the gravitational attraction between the 5.0-cm- and 30-cm-diameter lead spheres in Cavendish's experiment when they were nearly touching?

Section 8.3   *Orbital Motion*

7. Mars' orbit has a diameter 1.52 times that of earth's orbit. How long does it take Mars to orbit the sun?
8. Calculate the acceleration of the moon in its circular orbit (radius 390,000 km, period 27.3 days), and compare with the acceleration of gravity at earth's surface. Show that the acceleration of the moon is smaller by a factor (radius of moon's orbit)²/(radius of earth)², thereby confirming the inverse-square nature of the gravitational force.
9. Comets are thought to originate in a cloud of ice chunks orbiting in roughly circular orbits at a distance of almost one light-year (the distance light travels in one year) from the sun. Effects of collisions or gravitational interactions with other stars occasionally send a chunk out of its circular orbit and into the elliptical orbit of the comets we observe. What is the orbital period of the cometary ice chunks in their distant circular orbits?
10. The asteroid Icarus has an orbital period of 410 days. What is the semimajor axis of its orbit? Compare with earth's orbital radius.
11. During the Apollo moon landings, one astronaut remained with the command module in lunar orbit, about 130 km above the surface. For half of each orbit, this astronaut was the "loneliest man in the universe," as his spacecraft rounded the back side of the moon and he was cut off from visual or radio contact with earth and with his fellow astronauts. How long did this period last?
12. Derive an expression for the period of a circular orbit in terms of the orbital speed.
13. We derived Equation 8–4 for the period of a circular orbit on the assumption that the massive gravitating center remained fixed. Now consider the case of two objects of equal mass M orbiting about each other as shown in Fig. 8–52. Show that the orbital period is given by

$$T^2 = \frac{16\pi^2 r^3}{GM},$$

where r is the orbital radius, or half the distance between the objects.

Fig. 8–52   Problem 13

14. Use the result of the preceding problem to determine the mass of two equal-mass stars in a binary star system, if the stellar separation is 2.4 AU (one AU, or

astronomical unit, is the distance from earth to sun) and the orbital period is 180 days.

15. A white dwarf is a collapsed star with roughly the mass of the sun but the radius of the earth. What would be the orbital period of a spaceship in low orbit around such a white dwarf?

16. Our Milky Way galaxy belongs to a large group of galaxies known as the Virgo Cluster, which contains about 1000 times the mass of our galaxy, which in turn contains about 10^{11} times the mass of the sun. We are roughly 50 million light-years (1 light-year is the distance light travels in 1 year) from the center of this approximately spherical distribution of galaxies. Could our galaxy have completed a full orbit of the cluster in the time since the universe began, some 15 billion years ago?

Section 8.4   *Gravitational Potential Energy*

17. Show that an object released from rest very far from earth ($r \gg R_e$) reaches earth's surface at nearly escape speed.

18. What is the total mechanical energy associated with earth's orbital motion?

19. By what factor must the speed of an object in circular orbit be increased to reach escape speed from its orbital altitude?

20. Two meteoroids are 250,000 km from earth and are moving at 2.1 km/s. One is headed straight for earth, while the other is on a path that will miss earth by a distance of 8500 km from earth's center (Fig. 8–53). (a) What is the speed of the first meteoroid when it strikes earth? (Neglect air resistance.) (b) What is the speed of the second meteoroid at its closest approach to earth? (c) Will the second meteoroid return to earth's vicinity again?

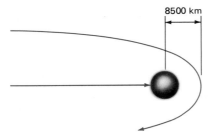

Fig. 8–53 Partial trajectories of two meteoroids (Problem 20).

21. Neglecting air resistance, to what height would you have to fire a rocket for the constant acceleration equations of Chapter 3 to give a height that is in error by 1%? Would those methods provide an overestimate or an underestimate?

22. Recent estimates suggest that efficient rockets of the twenty-first century may be able to place payloads in low earth orbit (altitude 300 km) for as little as

$700/kg. (This compares with 1985 space shuttle costs of about $18,000/kg.) If most of this cost is for fuel, and if fuel efficiency is independent of altitude, what would be the twenty-first century cost of getting 1 kg into geosynchronous orbit?

23. One component of the proposed Strategic Defense Initiative ballistic missile defense calls for powerful ground-based lasers aimed at their targets by space-based mirrors. Tentative plans call for 30-m-diameter mirrors in geosynchronous orbit to reflect the laser beam to low-orbit "battle mirrors." One simple means of foiling this delicate technology is to put a load of rocks in the same orbit as the mirrors, but going in the opposite direction. At what relative speed would the rocks hit a mirror in geosynchronous orbit?

24. Neglecting earth's rotation, show that the energy needed to launch a satellite of mass m into a circular orbit of altitude h is

$$\frac{GM_e m}{R_e} \frac{R_e + 2h}{2(R_e + h)}.$$

25. Satellites are usually launched eastward to take advantage of earth's rotation. Show that 0.30% more energy is needed to launch a satellite into a 1000-km-high equatorial orbit than into a polar orbit at the same altitude.

26. Late twentieth-century humanity consumes energy at the rate of about 10^{13} W. Suppose a method were invented to extract usable energy from the moon's orbital motion. If all our energy were supplied from this source, and our energy use remained constant, by how much would (a) the moon's orbital radius and (b) its orbital period change in a century?

27. A projectile is launched vertically upward from a planet of mass M and radius R; its initial speed is twice the escape speed. Derive an expression for its speed as a function of distance r from the center of the planet.

28. A spacecraft is in circular earth orbit at an altitude of 5500 km. By how much will its altitude decrease if it moves to a new circular orbit where (a) its orbital speed is 10% higher or (b) its orbital period is 10% shorter?

Section 8.5   *The Superposition Principle*

29. Two particles of equal mass M are located a distance ℓ apart. (a) Determine the gravitational potential energy of a third mass m at an arbitrary point on the perpendicular bisector shown in Fig. 8–54. (Take the bisector to be the x-axis, and give your answer as a function of x.) (b) Show that your result approaches the potential energy associated with the gravity of a point particle of mass 2M when $x \gg \ell$. (c) Show with a simple sketch that the gravitational force on the mass m must point in the x-direction, and differentiate your expression for potential energy to get an expression for the force. (d) Show that the gravita-

tional force is zero midway between the two masses, and that it drops off as $1/x^2$ for $x \gg \ell$.

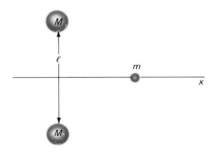

Fig. 8–54   Problem 29

30. An advanced galactic civilization constructs a solid shell of mass M_s and radius R_s around a planet of mass M_p and radius R_p. The shell has negligible thickness. Find expressions for the acceleration of gravity (a) for $R_p < r < R_s$ and (b) for $r > R_s$, where r is the radial distance from the center of the planet. Make a sketch of the gravitational acceleration as a function of r.

31. Show, by integrating the gravitational force, that the work needed to move a mass m from the center to the surface of a uniform sphere of mass M and radius R is $GMm/2R$.

32. Suppose earth's density were uniform, and that a small hole was drilled to the center of the earth. If an object were dropped from rest at the top of the hole, with what speed would it reach the center of the earth? Compare with the speed in a circular orbit just above earth's surface. *Hint:* See result of preceding problem.

33. (a) Use the result of Problem 31 to show that the potential energy of a mass m inside a uniform sphere of mass M and radius R is

$$U = -\frac{GMm}{2R}\left[3 - \left(\frac{r}{R}\right)^2\right],$$

where r is the distance from the center and where $U = 0$ at $r = \infty$. (b) Sketch the potential energy as a function of position both inside and outside the sphere.

Supplementary Problems

34. Show that the form $\Delta U = mg\Delta r$ follows from Equation 8–5 for the case $r_2 - r_1 \ll r_1$.

35. Although the study of black holes necessarily involves general relativity, one way to think about a black hole is to consider it an object so dense that the escape speed is the speed of light. (a) Using this criterion, show that the radius R_s of a black hole of mass M is given by $R_s = 2GM/c^2$, where c is the speed of light. What are the radii of black holes with (b) the mass of the earth and (c) the mass of the sun?

36. When a star with a mass twice that of the sun exhausts its nuclear fuel, it collapses into a neutron star with a radius of about 10 km. (a) What would be the acceleration of gravity on the surface of such a neutron star? Neutron stars are usually in rapid rotation, for reasons we will examine in Chapter 12. (b) If your mass is 70 kg, what would be your weight at the pole of the neutron star? (c) If the star is rotating once per second, by what fraction would your weight at the equator differ from your weight at the pole?

37. Show that the force of the sun's gravity on earth is nearly 200 times that of the moon's gravity, but that the tidal force associated with the sun's gravity is about half that associated with the moon's gravity.

38. The innermost satellites of Mars, Jupiter, and Saturn lie at distances of 9400 km, 128,000 km, and 138,000 km, respectively, from their respective planets' centers. Use data from Appendix F to compare these orbital radii with the appropriate Roche limits.

39. A uniform solid sphere of radius R and initial mass M is hollowed out to make a cavity of radius $R/2$ that just touches the center of the sphere, as shown in Fig. 8–55. Use the superposition principle to show that the gravitational field a distance $r > R$ to the right of the center of the sphere is

$$\frac{GM}{r^2}\left(1 - \frac{1}{8(1 - R/2r)^2}\right),$$

where r is the distance from the large sphere.

Fig. 8–55   Problem 39

40. A straight tunnel is drilled from New York to San Francisco, a surface distance of 4900 km, as shown in Fig. 8–56. If a vehicle is released from rest at New York and if friction is negligible, what is the maximum speed it achieves? *Hint:* See Problem 33.

Fig. 8–56   Problem 40

41. Two satellites are in geosynchronous orbit, but in diametrically opposite positions (Fig. 8–57). Into how much lower a circular orbit should one spacecraft descend if it is to catch up with the other after 10 complete orbits? Neglect rocket firing time and time spent in transfer orbits.

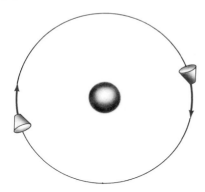

Fig. 8–57   Problem 41

42. A black hole (see Problem 35) has the same mass as the sun. Estimate how close you could get to the black hole before the tidal force stretching you apart had a magnitude of 1 ton.

9

SYSTEMS OF PARTICLES

In the previous chapters, we treated most objects as point particles. That is, we neglected any effects associated with the nonzero size of objects. But in reality, the sizes of objects may greatly affect their physical interactions. We have seen, for example, how the fact that earth is essentially a large sphere rather than a point delayed Newton for many years when he was considering his law of universal gravitation.

rigid bodies

In this chapter, we deal with systems composed of many particles. These include **rigid bodies**—objects like baseballs, cars, and planets composed of many particles linked together at fixed distances and with fixed orientations, as well as systems whose constituent parts move with respect to one another, like a gymnast, an exploding star, or a cup of coffee being stirred. In Chapter 12, we will concentrate specifically on the rotational motion of rigid bodies, and in Chapter 15 will deal with fluid systems. Our work in the present chapter is an important stage on the route to understanding these more complex and realistic systems. Some systems, like the air masses that determine earth's weather, are still too complicated for us to predict their motion. The advance of supercomputers, though, is enhancing our ability to apply the laws of physics in such situations.

Fig. 9–1
Most parts of the hammer move in complicated paths. But one point—the center of mass—follows the simple parabolic trajectory of a projectile.

center of mass

9.1
CENTER OF MASS

Figure 9–1 shows a hammer tossed into the air. The motion of most parts of the hammer is quite complex. But the curve superimposed on the photograph shows that one point seems to follow the parabola that we expect of a point projectile (Section 3.3). This point is known as the **center of mass,** since the force of gravity acts as though all the mass were concentrated there.*

---

*Actually, the point where gravity seems to act is called the **center of gravity.** For objects small enough that the acceleration of gravity doesn't vary over their size, the center of mass and center of gravity coincide. We discuss this point further in Section 11.3.

How do we find out where the center of mass is? Figure 9–1 shows that the center of mass obeys Newton's second law just as would a point particle. If we can find a point whose acceleration **A** obeys Newton's second law **F** = M**A,** where **F** is now the net force on an entire system and M the mass of that system, then we will have found the center of mass. (Note that we use capital letters for quantities associated with the center of mass.)

Consider a system consisting of many particles. Our system could be a rigid body, or its constituent particles could be moving relative to one another; we only require that the total mass remain constant. To find the center of mass, we want an equation that looks like Newton's second law but involves the total mass of the system and the net force on the entire system. If we apply Newton's second law to the ith particle in the system, we have

$$\mathbf{F}_i = m_i\mathbf{a}_i = m_i\frac{d^2\mathbf{r}_i}{dt^2} = \frac{d^2m_i\mathbf{r}_i}{dt^2},$$

where $\mathbf{F}_i$ is the net force on the particle, m_i its mass, and where we have written the acceleration $\mathbf{a}_i$ as the second derivative of the position $\mathbf{r}_i$. Now consider the entire object. The net force is $\mathbf{F} = \Sigma\mathbf{F}_i$, where we sum the forces acting on all the particles making up the object. Thus

$$\mathbf{F} = \sum \frac{d^2m_i\mathbf{r}_i}{dt^2},$$

where the sum is taken over all values of i that label the individual particles. But the sum of derivatives is the same as the derivative of the sum, so that

$$\mathbf{F} = \frac{d^2(\sum m_i\mathbf{r}_i)}{dt^2}.$$

We can now put this equation in the form of Newton's second law. Multiplying and dividing the right-hand side by the total mass $M = \Sigma m_i$, and distributing this constant M through the differentiation, we have

$$\mathbf{F} = M\frac{d^2}{dt^2}\left(\frac{\sum m_i\mathbf{r}_i}{M}\right). \tag{9–1}$$

Equation 9–1 has the desired form $\mathbf{F} = M\mathbf{A} = M(d^2\mathbf{R}/dt^2)$ if we define

$$\mathbf{R} = \frac{\sum m_i\mathbf{r}_i}{M}. \qquad \text{(center of mass)} \tag{9–2}$$

We have almost reached our goal of showing that the point **R** moves according to Newton's law $\mathbf{F} = Md^2\mathbf{R}/dt^2$. Why aren't we there now? Because the force **F** in Equation 9–1 is the sum of *all* the forces acting on all the particles of the system, including the **internal forces** that act between the particles. We would like the force **F** in Newton's law to be the net **external force**—the net force applied from outside the system. We can write the force **F** in Equation 9–1—the total force on all the particles of the system—as

internal forces

external force

$$\mathbf{F} = \sum\mathbf{F}_{\text{ext}} + \sum\mathbf{F}_{\text{int}},$$

where $\Sigma\mathbf{F}_{ext}$ is the sum of all the external forces and $\Sigma\mathbf{F}_{int}$ the sum of the internal forces. According to Newton's third law of motion, each of the internal forces has an equal but oppositely directed reaction force that itself acts on a particle of the system and is therefore included in the sum $\Sigma\mathbf{F}_{int}$. (Each external force also has a reaction force, but these reaction forces act *outside* the system and are therefore not included in the sum.) Added vectorially, the reaction forces therefore cancel in pairs, so that $\Sigma\mathbf{F}_{int}=0$, and the force $\mathbf{F}$ in Equation 9–1 is just the net *external* force applied to the system. So the point $\mathbf{R}$ defined in Equation 9–2 does obey Newton's law, written in the form

$$\mathbf{F} = M\frac{d^2\mathbf{R}}{dt^2}, \tag{9–3}$$

where $\mathbf{F}$ is the net external force applied to the system and M the total mass.

We have defined the center of mass $\mathbf{R}$ so that we can apply Newton's second law to the entire system rather than to each individual particle. As far as its overall motion is concerned, a complex system acts as though all its mass were concentrated at the center of mass. Physically, the center of mass represents a kind of "average position," determined from the positions of all the individual particles weighted according to their masses.

Finding the Center of Mass

Equation 9–2 expresses the center of mass in vector form; taking components gives three separate scalar equations for the xyz-coordinates of the center of mass. If we consider only a one-dimensional situation, in which the constituent particles lie along a single line, then the center of mass must lie along that line. Similarly, for a two-dimensional object, the center of mass lies in the plane of the object. For the simple case of two point masses, we can take the x-axis along the line joining the masses, and write Equation 9–2 in the form

$$X = \frac{m_1x_1 + m_2x_2}{m_1 + m_2}. \tag{9–4}$$

Example 9–1
Weightlifter

You want to lift a barbell at its center of mass. (*a*) Suppose there are equal 60-kg masses at either end of the 1.5-m-long bar. (*b*) Suppose someone put unequal masses of 50 kg and 80 kg on the ends. Where is the center of mass in each case? Assume that the size of each of the masses is negligible compared with the distance between them.

Solution

In (*a*) it's obvious that the center of mass must lie at the center of the barbell. If we choose the origin to lie at one of the masses, then $x_1=0$ m and $x_2=1.5$ m; applying Equation 9–4 then gives

$$X = \frac{m_1x_1 + m_2x_2}{m_1 + m_2} = \frac{(60\ kg)(0\ m)\ +\ (60\ kg)(1.5\ m)}{60\ kg\ +\ 60\ kg} = 0.75\ m,$$

CM

60 kg   60 kg

(a)

CM

50 kg   80 kg

(b)

Fig. 9–2
Center of mass of a barbell. (*a*) Two
equal masses. (*b*) 50-kg and 80-kg
masses.

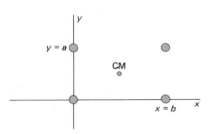

Fig. 9–3
Example 9–2

as expected. In case (*b*), with the origin at the 50-kg mass, we have

$$X = \frac{m_1 x_1 + m_2 x_2}{m_1 + m_2} = \frac{(50 \text{ kg})(0 \text{ m}) + (80 \text{ kg})(1.5 \text{ m})}{50 \text{ kg} + 80 \text{ kg}} = 0.92 \text{ m}.$$

Again, the result makes sense: the center of mass is closer to the more massive constituent of the system (Fig. 9–2). Our choice of origin at one of the masses was convenient because it made one of the terms in the sum $\Sigma m_i x_i$ zero. But that choice is purely for convenience; it cannot influence the actual physical location of the center of mass (see Problem 2).

Example 9–2
Center of Mass in a Plane

Four equal masses m lie at the corners of a rectangle of width a and length b. Where is the center of mass?

Solution

A convenient coordinate system has two sides of the rectangle along the x- and y-axes, with one corner at the origin (Fig. 9–3). Then the x- and y-components of Equation 9–2 are

$$X = \frac{\sum m_i x_i}{M} = \frac{m(0 + b + b + 0)}{4m} = \frac{b}{2}$$

and

$$Y = \frac{\sum m_i y_i}{M} = \frac{m(0 + 0 + a + a)}{4m} = \frac{a}{2},$$

where in both cases we summed going counterclockwise around the rectangle, starting at the origin. Our result is hardly surprising: the center of mass lies at the center of the rectangle.

It is no accident that the center of mass in Example 9–2 lies in the center of the rectangle. For any object with an axis of symmetry, the center of mass must lie along that axis. This is because particles on opposite sides of the symmetry axis cancel each other's effect on the component of the center-of-mass position in a direction perpendicular to the axis. The rectangle of Example 9–2 has *two* symmetry axes; they are vertical and horizontal lines through its center. The center of mass must lie on *both* symmetry axes, and is therefore at their one point of intersection, the center. Attention to symmetry here and in many other areas of physics can save a great deal of calculation.

We have expressed the center of mass in terms of sums over individual particles. Ultimately, matter is composed of individual particles. But it is often a convenient approximation to consider that matter is continuously distributed; after all, we don't want to deal with 10^{23} or so atoms to find the center of mass of a book or other macroscopic object. We can consider a chunk of continuous matter to be composed of individual pieces of mass Δm_i, with position vectors $\mathbf{r}_i$; we call these pieces **mass elements** (Fig. 9–4). The center of mass of the entire chunk is then given by Equation 9–2:

$$\mathbf{R} = \frac{\sum \Delta m_i \mathbf{r}_i}{M},$$

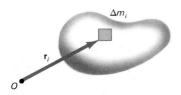

Fig. 9–4
A chunk of continuous matter, showing one mass element Δm_i and its position vector $\mathbf{r}_i$ from an arbitrary origin.

where $M = \Sigma \Delta m_i$ is the total mass. This expression is slightly vague, for we don't know exactly where within a mass element its position vector should terminate. But in the limit as the mass elements become arbitrarily small, like point particles, the expression becomes exact. As in Chapter 6, that limiting process defines an integral, giving

$$\mathbf{R} = \lim_{\Delta m_i \to 0} \frac{\sum \Delta m_i \mathbf{r}_i}{M} = \frac{1}{M}\int \mathbf{r}\, dm, \quad \left(\begin{array}{c}\text{center of mass,}\\ \text{continuous matter}\end{array}\right) \quad (9\text{--}5)$$

where the integration is over the entire volume of the object. Like the sum 9–2, the vector form 9–5 stands for three separate integrals for the three components of the center-of-mass position. Example 9–3 shows how to evaluate these integrals.

Example 9–3

An Aircraft Wing

The wing of a supersonic aircraft is in the form of an isosceles triangle of length ℓ, width w, and negligible thickness (Fig. 9–5). It has total mass M, distributed uniformly over the wing. Where is its center of mass?

Solution

Figure 9–5 shows the wing with a suitable coordinate system. Since the wing is flat and of negligible thickness, its center of mass must lie in the x-y plane. The wing is symmetric about the x-axis, so that the center of mass must lie on the x-axis; that is, $Y = 0$. So we need to integrate only to find the x-coordinate. Figure 9–5 shows an appropriate mass element, here in the form of a strip of width dx located a distance x along the axis. To find the mass dm of the strip, we first find its area. Figure 9–5 shows that the equations describing the sloping sides of the wing are $y = \pm wx/2\ell$, so that our strip extends from $x = -wx/2\ell$ to $+wx/2\ell$; its length is therefore wx/ℓ. Since its width is dx, its area is then $dA = (wx\,dx)/\ell$. [Here we've treated the strip as a rectangle, which is not quite right because of its sloping sides. But in the limit of arbitrarily small dx, the area of the strip and the rectangle area $(wx\,dx)/\ell$ become the same (Fig. 9–6).] Since mass is distributed uniformly over the wing, the mass dm of the strip is the same fraction of the total mass as its area is of the total area:

$$\frac{dm}{M} = \frac{dA}{A} = \frac{(wx\,dx)/\ell}{\frac{1}{2}w\ell} = \frac{2x\,dx}{\ell^2},$$

so that $dm = (2Mx\,dx)/\ell^2$. The x-component of the center-of-mass position is given by the x-component of Equation 9–5:

$$X = \frac{1}{M}\int x\, dm.$$

Using our expression for dm, and integrating over the entire triangle—that is, from $x = 0$ to $x = \ell$—we have

$$X = \frac{1}{M}\int_0^\ell \frac{2M}{\ell^2}x^2\, dx = \frac{2}{\ell^2}\frac{x^3}{3}\bigg|_0^\ell = \tfrac{2}{3}\ell.$$

Does this make sense? Yes: more of the wing's mass is concentrated near the wide end at $x = \ell$, so the center of mass should be located closer to that end.

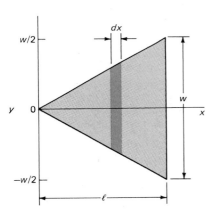

Fig. 9–5
A supersonic aircraft wing (Example 9–3). Shaded area is a mass element of width dx.

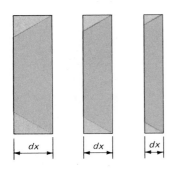

Fig. 9–6
As the width dx of the strip becomes arbitrarily small, its area approaches that of the rectangle.

Fig. 9–7
The center of mass of the airplane is found by treating the wing and fuselage as point particles located at their respective centers of mass. Given the center-of-mass location, is the wing or the fuselage more massive?

Fig. 9–8
An irregular object, showing centers of mass of the constituent rectangles and of the object itself. Note that the center of mass lies outside the object.

Fig. 9–9
The high jumper's center of mass does not clear the bar, even though his entire body does. This is possible because the entire body is not above the bar at the same time.

With still more complex objects, it is convenient to find the centers of mass of major subpieces, then treat those subpieces as point particles to find the center of mass of the entire object. If the wing of Example 9–3 is placed on a cylindrical airplane fuselage, for example, then we can find the center of mass of the entire plane by treating the wing and fuselage as point particles located at their respective centers of mass (Fig. 9–7). And an irregular object like that of Fig. 9–8 is treated by locating the centers of mass of its three constituent rectangles (see Problem 5).

Figure 9–8 shows that the center of mass need not lie within the object. A high jumper (Fig. 9–9) takes advantage of this fact by arching his body into a shape qualitatively like that of Fig. 9–8. The jumper's center of mass never has to get as high as the bar, thereby reducing the amount of work he must do against gravity. Similarly, a ballet dancer can appear to float through the air, her head and torso following a horizontal trajectory, by raising her legs and therefore the position of the center of mass relative to her torso. The center of mass, of course, follows a parabolic trajectory, but that's not what the audience notices (Fig. 9–10).

Motion of the Center of Mass

We defined the center of mass (Equation 9–2) so that its motion would obey Newton's law $\mathbf{F} = M\mathbf{A}$, where $\mathbf{F}$ is the net external force applied to a system and M the total mass. When, for example, gravity is the only external force acting on a system, then its center of mass follows the trajectory appropriate to a point particle. We saw this in Fig. 9–1 and Fig. 9–10, and see it again with the exploding fireworks rocket of Fig. 9–11. An example similar to Fig. 9–11 is provided on a grander scale by the breakup of comet Biela by tidal forces as it passed the sun in the mid-1800's. Today, the Andromedid swarm of meteors orbits the sun in similar but not identical orbits. But the center of mass of the swarm remains in the orbit of the original comet, despite the fact that there is no longer any matter there!

When there is no net external force on a system, then the center of mass acceleration $\mathbf{A}$ is zero, and the center of mass moves with constant velocity. In the special case of a system at rest and subject to no net external force, the center of mass remains at rest despite any internal motions of the system's constituents.

Example 9–4 _____
Leaping to Shore

You are standing 1.8 m from the shoreward end of a 4.2-m-long boat; from the end to shore is another 1.1 m (Fig. 9–12). Your mass is 70 kg and the boat's mass is 150 kg. The center of mass of the boat lies at its center. You walk to the shoreward end of the boat, preparing to leap to shore. How far do you have to leap? Where is the boat at the instant you reach shore? Neglect any frictional effects.

Solution

The net external force on the system consisting of you and the boat is zero, so that the center of mass of the system remains fixed. Letting m_1 and x_1 be your mass and position, and m_2 and x_2 the mass and position of the boat (that is, of the boat's

Fig. 9–10
Performing a grand jeté, Jennifer Davis of the Pittsburgh Ballet Theatre keeps her head and torso moving nearly horizontally while her center of mass describes a parabolic trajectory.

Fig. 9–11
An exploding fireworks rocket. The center of mass of the system follows a parabolic trajectory despite the strong internal forces of the explosion.

center of mass), and designating the initial and final values by the subscripts i and f, respectively, we equate the initial and final positions of the center of mass:

$$\frac{m_1 x_{1i} + m_2 x_{2i}}{m_1 + m_2} = \frac{m_1 x_{1f} + m_2 x_{2f}}{m_1 + m_2}.$$

The total mass $m_1 + m_2$ cancels, so that

$$m_1 x_{1i} + m_2 x_{2i} = m_1 x_{1f} + m_2 x_{2f}. \tag{9–6}$$

Since we're interested in the final position with respect to the shore, an appropriate choice of coordinate system has the origin at the shore. Then Fig. 9–12 shows that $x_{1i} = 1.1 \text{ m} + 1.8 \text{ m} = 2.9 \text{ m}$ and $x_{2i} = 1.1 \text{ m} + 2.1 \text{ m} = 3.2 \text{ m}$. x_{1f} and x_{2f} are still unknown. But they are related: when you reach the end of the boat, you are half a boat length closer to shore than the center of the boat. Therefore, $x_{2f} = x_{1f} + \frac{1}{2}L$, where L is the 4.2-m length of the boat. Using this result in Equation 9–6 gives

$$m_1 x_{1i} + m_2 x_{2i} = m_1 x_{1f} + m_2 (x_{1f} + \tfrac{1}{2}L).$$

Solving for x_{1f}, we then have

$$x_{1f} = \frac{m_1 x_{1i} + m_2 x_{2i} - \frac{1}{2} m_2 L}{m_1 + m_2}$$

$$= \frac{(70 \text{ kg})(2.9 \text{ m}) + (150 \text{ kg})(3.2 \text{ m}) - \frac{1}{2}(150 \text{ kg})(4.2 \text{ m})}{70 \text{ kg} + 150 \text{ kg}} = 1.7 \text{ m}.$$

This is the distance you have to leap from the end of the boat to shore. When you reach shore, you are at the origin: $x_{1f} = 0$. Solving Equation 9–6 for the boat's position then gives

Fig. 9–12
Example 9–4

$$x_{2f} = \frac{m_1 x_{1i} + m_2 x_{2i}}{m_2} = \frac{(70 \text{ kg})(2.9 \text{ m}) + (150 \text{ kg})(3.2 \text{ m})}{150 \text{ kg}} = 4.6 \text{ m}.$$

After the instant you reach shore, we can no longer argue that the center of mass remains fixed. Why not? Because an external force—the stopping force of the ground—has acted on part of the system, so that the center of mass is no longer fixed. Indeed, the boat continues to drift away from shore. Question 10 explores this situation further.

9.2
MOMENTUM

When we introduced Newton's second law of motion in Chapter 4, we defined the linear momentum $\mathbf{p} = m\mathbf{v}$ of a particle, and first wrote Newton's law in the form $\mathbf{F} = d\mathbf{p}/dt$. We subsequently applied the law to single particles, using the form $\mathbf{F} = m\mathbf{a}$, but suggested that the momentum concept would play an important role in many-particle systems.

Consider the total momentum of a system of particles:

$$\mathbf{P} = \sum \mathbf{p}_i = \sum m_i \mathbf{v}_i,$$

where m_i and $\mathbf{v}_i$ are the masses and velocities of the individual particles, and $\mathbf{p}_i$ their corresponding momenta. But $\mathbf{v} = d\mathbf{r}/dt$, so that

$$\mathbf{P} = \sum m_i \frac{d\mathbf{r}_i}{dt} = \frac{d}{dt} \sum m_i \mathbf{r}_i,$$

where the last step follows because the individual particle masses are constant and because the sum of derivatives is the derivative of the sum. In Section 9.1 we defined the center-of-mass position $\mathbf{R}$ as $\sum m_i \mathbf{r}_i / M$, where M is the total mass. So the total momentum can be written

$$\mathbf{P} = \frac{d}{dt} M\mathbf{R},$$

or, assuming the system mass M remains constant,

$$\mathbf{P} = M\frac{d\mathbf{R}}{dt} = M\mathbf{V}, \qquad (9\text{--}7)$$

where $\mathbf{V} = d\mathbf{R}/dt$ is the center-of-mass velocity. So the momentum of a system is given by an expression similar to that of a single particle; it is the product of the system mass with the system velocity—that is, with the velocity of the center of mass. If this seems so obvious as not to need deriving, watch out! We'll see in Section 9.3 that the same is *not* true for the system's total energy.

If we differentiate Equation 9–7 with respect to time, we have

$$\frac{d\mathbf{P}}{dt} = M\frac{d\mathbf{V}}{dt} = M\mathbf{A},$$

where $\mathbf{A}$ is the center-of-mass acceleration. But we defined the center of mass so that its motion obeyed Newton's second law, $\mathbf{F} = M\mathbf{A}$, with $\mathbf{F}$ the net external force on the system. So we can write simply

$$\mathbf{F} = \frac{d\mathbf{P}}{dt}, \tag{9-8}$$

showing that the momentum of a system of particles changes only if there is a net external force on the system. Remember the hidden role of Newton's third law in all this: only because the forces *internal* to the system cancel in pairs can we ignore them and consider just the *external* force.

Conservation of Momentum

In the special case when the net external force is zero, Equation 9–8 gives

$$\frac{d\mathbf{P}}{dt} = 0, \qquad \text{(no net external force)}$$

so that

$$\mathbf{P} = \text{constant.} \qquad \text{(conservation of momentum)} \tag{9-9}$$

law of conservation of momentum

Equation 9–9 expresses the **law of conservation of momentum.** It says that, in the absence of a net external force, the total momentum **P** of a system—the vector sum $\Sigma m_i\mathbf{v}_i$ of the momenta of the individual particles—remains constant. (More explicitly, we have written the "law of conservation of linear momentum." We will deal with "angular momentum" in Chapter 12.)

Equation 9–9 holds no matter how many particles are involved, and no matter how they may be moving. It is valid for a set of pool balls both before and after they are struck by the cue ball (Fig. 9–13). It is also valid for a globular cluster containing 1,000,000 stars interacting by their mutual gravity (Fig. 9–14), to the extent that we can ignore the external force from the rest of the galaxy (since the cluster takes hundreds of millions of years to orbit the galaxy, that is a reasonable approximation for an astrophysicist studying the much more rapid internal dynamics of the cluster). And it is valid for a system consisting of 10^{23} air molecules and a closed vessel containing them. We will, in fact, use momentum conservation in Chapter 17 to show how the behavior of gases follows from Newton's laws.

We derived the conservation of momentum principle from Newton's laws. But in a fundamental sense, momentum conservation is more basic than Newton's laws. Momentum is conserved even in subatomic and nuclear systems where the laws and even language of Newtonian physics are hopelessly inadequate. The examples below show the wide range and power of the momentum conservation principle.

Example 9–5
Momentum Conservation in a Canoe

Amy (mass 55 kg) and George (mass 70 kg) are sitting at opposite ends of a canoe (mass 22 kg) at rest on frictionless water. She tosses him a 14-kg pack, giving it a speed of 3.1 m/s relative to the water. What is the speed of the canoe (*a*) while the pack is in the air and (*b*) after George catches it?

Solution

We're interested here in the horizontal motion of the canoe. With no external forces acting in the horizontal direction, the horizontal component of the momentum is conserved. Originally, everything is at rest and the total momentum is zero.

Fig. 9–13
(Above) The momentum **P** of the system of pool balls is that of the cue ball alone. (Below) After the cue ball has struck the others, the total momentum $\Sigma m_i\mathbf{v}_i$ is still equal to the original **P.**

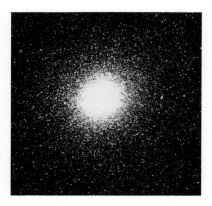

Fig. 9–14
A globular cluster, containing about 10^6 stars interacting via gravitational forces. In the absence of external forces, the total momentum of the system remains constant.

While the pack is in the air, it has horizontal momentum $m_p v_p$. The canoe and its passengers are all moving together; they have momentum $(m_a + m_g + m_c)v_c$, where m_a, m_g, and m_c are the masses of Amy, George, and the canoe, respectively, and where v_c is the canoe's horizontal velocity. Since horizontal momentum is conserved, it must still be zero when the pack is in the air, so that

$$m_p v_p + (m_a + m_g + m_c)v_c = 0,$$

or

$$v_c = -\frac{m_p v_p}{m_a + m_g + m_c} = -\frac{(14 \text{ kg})(3.1 \text{ m/s})}{55 \text{ kg} + 70 \text{ kg} + 22 \text{ kg}} = -0.30 \text{ m/s.}$$

The minus sign tells us that the canoe moves in the opposite direction from the pack.

There is no need to calculate the speed after George catches the pack: canoe, passengers, and pack all have the same velocity then. For the total momentum to remain zero, that velocity must be zero.

Example 9–6
The Speed of a Hockey Puck

A hockey coach enlists a physics student on his team to measure the speed of a hockey puck. The student loads a small styrofoam chest with sand, giving it a total mass of 6.4 kg. He places the chest, at rest on frictionless ice, in the path of the hockey puck, whose mass is 160 g. The puck embeds itself in the styrofoam, and the chest moves off at 1.2 m/s. What was the speed of the puck?

Solution

Since there is no net external force, momentum is conserved. Originally, all the momentum of the puck+chest system is in the puck: $P = m_p v_p$, where we do not need vector notation because the motion is in one dimension. After the puck hits the chest, the two move off together at the same speed: $P = (m_p + m_c)v_c$. So the statement that momentum is conserved becomes

$$m_p v_p = (m_p + m_c)v_c,$$

so that

$$v_p = \frac{(m_p + m_c)v_c}{m_p} = \frac{(0.16 \text{ kg} + 6.4 \text{ kg})(1.2 \text{ m/s})}{0.16 \text{ kg}} = 49 \text{ m/s.}$$

Variations of this technique are routinely used to measure the speeds of rapidly moving objects like bullets.

Example 9–7
Radioactive Decay

A lithium-5 nucleus (^{5}Li) is moving at 1.6×10^6 m/s when it decays into a proton (^{1}H) and an alpha particle (^{4}He). [The superscripted numbers are the total number of nucleons (neutrons and protons) in a nucleus, and give the approximate nuclear mass in atomic mass units.] The alpha particle is detected moving at 1.4×10^6 m/s, at 33° to the original velocity of the ^{5}Li nucleus. What are the magnitude and direction of the proton's velocity?

Solution

Again, momentum is conserved. Before the decay, we have only the lithium nucleus. After the decay, there are two particles whose individual momenta contribute to the total. So the statement that momentum is conserved becomes

$$m_{Li}\mathbf{v}_{Li} = m_H\mathbf{v}_H + m_{He}\mathbf{v}_{He},$$

where we keep the full vector notation because the motion involves two dimensions. If we choose the x-axis along the direction of $\mathbf{v}_{Li}$, then we can write separately the two components of the momentum conservation equation:

x-component: $$m_{Li}v_{Li} = m_H v_H \cos\theta + m_{He} v_{He} \cos\phi$$

y-component: $$0 = m_H v_H \sin\theta + m_{He} v_{He} \sin\phi,$$

where θ and ϕ are the angles that the velocities $\mathbf{v}_H$ and $\mathbf{v}_{He}$ make with the positive x-axis (Fig. 9–15). Writing these two equations completes the physics of the problem; the rest is the mathematics of solving them. Moving the terms involving the unknown proton speed v_H to one side of each equation, we can write

$$m_H v_H \cos\theta = m_{Li} v_{Li} - m_{He} v_{He} \cos\phi$$
$$m_H v_H \sin\theta = -m_{He} v_{He} \sin\phi.$$

Squaring both sides of each equation and adding the resulting equations gives

$$(m_H v_H)^2 = (m_{Li} v_{Li} - m_{He} v_{He} \cos\phi)^2 + (m_{He} v_{He} \sin\phi)^2$$

where we used the fact that $\cos^2\theta + \sin^2\theta = 1$. Then

$$v_H = \left[\left(\frac{m_{Li}}{m_H} v_{Li} - \frac{m_{He}}{m_H} v_{He} \cos\phi \right)^2 + \left(\frac{m_{He}}{m_H} v_{He} \sin\phi \right)^2 \right]^{1/2}.$$

Since the proton mass is 1 u, the mass ratios m_{Li}/m_H and m_{He}/m_H are equal to the nucleon numbers of ^5Li and ^4He, respectively. So

$$v_H = [(5v_{Li} - 4v_{He}\cos\phi)^2 + (4v_{He}\sin\phi)^2]^{1/2}$$
$$= \{[(5)(1.6 \times 10^6 \text{ m/s}) - (4)(1.4 \times 10^6 \text{ m/s})(\cos 33°)]^2$$
$$+ [(4)(1.4 \times 10^6 \text{ m/s})(\sin 33°)]^2\}^{1/2}$$
$$= 4.5 \times 10^6 \text{ m/s}.$$

Knowing the speed of the proton, we can solve the y-component of the momentum conservation equation for the angle θ:

$$\theta = \sin^{-1}\left(\frac{-m_{He} v_{He} \sin\phi}{m_H v_H} \right) = \sin^{-1}\left[\frac{-(4\text{ u})(1.4 \times 10^6 \text{ m/s})(\sin 33°)}{(1\text{ u})(4.5 \times 10^6 \text{ m/s})} \right] = -43°,$$

where the minus sign indicates that the proton's velocity vector points below the x-axis. We can see graphically that our results make sense by redrawing Fig. 9–15 as a momentum vector diagram—that is, by multiplying each velocity vector by the appropriate mass. The result, Fig. 9–16, shows that the y-components of the He and H momenta cancel, and that their x-components sum to the momentum of the original nucleus.

With no external forces acting, momentum had to be conserved in this decay. But kinetic energy is not conserved, as you will find if you evaluate the kinetic energies before and after decay (see Problem 39). Internal potential energy of the ^5Li nucleus is converted to kinetic energy in the decay process.

How do we decide whether or not the forces acting on a system are external? That depends on our choice of what to include in the system. In Example 9–6, for example, we chose to include both the hockey puck and the styrofoam chest in our system; the force exerted on the chest by the puck was then an internal force and we did not consider it explicitly. On the other hand, we could have chosen our system to include just the chest;

Fig. 9–15
Decay of a ^5Li nucleus (Example 9–7).

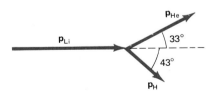

Fig. 9–16
Momentum diagram for Example 9–7.

then the force of the puck would be an external force, and the momentum of the system—the chest alone—would change. Of course, our definition of the system cannot affect what actually happens. Either description of the puck-chest interaction is equally valid; our choice was made so we could apply the conservation of momentum principle.

Sometimes we're interested in the force exerted on a particular object. Then it is convenient to redefine our system to include only that object, so that the force of interest is an external force. The example below illustrates this situation.

Example 9–8

Fighting a Fire

A firefighter directs a stream of water against the window of a burning building, hoping to break it so the water can get to the fire. The hose delivers water at the rate of 45 kg/s; the water hits the window moving horizontally at 32 m/s. After hitting the window, the water drops vertically downward. What is the horizontal force exerted on the window?

Solution

The horizontal motion of the water stops abruptly at the window; since the water is moving initially at 32 m/s, each kg of water loses 32 kg·m/s of momentum. But water strikes the window at the rate of 45 kg/s, so that the rate of momentum loss is

$$\frac{dP}{dt} = (45 \text{ kg/s})(32 \text{ kg·m/s/kg}) = 1400 \text{ kg·m/s}^2.$$

If we regard the water alone as our system, then this change in the system's momentum means that an external force of magnitude 1400 N is acting. That force is provided by the window. By Newton's third law, the water must therefore exert an oppositely directed force of equal magnitude on the window. Because the window is attached to the building, and the building to the earth, the force does not give rise to any significant acceleration. Once the window breaks, though, the glass fragments will be accelerated violently.

Rockets

Almost everyone knows that a rocket moves forward by ejecting gas backward. Its motion is a consequence of Newton's third law. Yet in the 1920's, *The New York Times* criticized the American rocket pioneer Robert Goddard, claiming that his rockets would never work in space because they had nothing to push against (Fig. 9–17). The *Times* was wrong; today we routinely use rocket engines in space to deploy satellites from space shuttles, to point space-based telescopes at their targets, to make midcourse corrections to planetary probes, and to return manned spacecraft from orbit.

Consider a rocket in deep space, where we can neglect gravity. The rocket has a total mass M including fuel, and is moving with velocity $\mathbf{v}$ relative to some nonaccelerating frame of reference. Its engine is then fired for a time Δt, during which time its mass changes by an amount ΔM, where ΔM is a *negative* quantity. The mass lost by the rocket appears as exhaust gas, moving with velocity $\mathbf{v}_{ex}$ relative to the rocket. At the end of the interval, the rocket is moving with velocity $\mathbf{v} + \Delta\mathbf{v}$ (Fig. 9–18). Before

His Plan Is Not Original. That Professor Goddard, with his "chair" in Clark College and the countenancing of the Smithsonian Institution, does not know the relation of action to reaction, and of the need to have something better than a vacuum against which to react—to say that would be absurd. Of course he only seems to lack the knowledge ladled out daily in high schools.

But there are such things as intentional mistakes or oversights, and, as it happens, Jules Verne, who also knew a thing or two in assorted sciences—and had, besides, a surprising amount of prophetic power—deliberately seemed to make the same mistake that Professor Goddard seems to make. For the Frenchman, having got his travelers to or toward the moon into the desperate fix of riding a tiny satellite of the satellite, saved them from circling it forever by means of an explosion, rocket fashion, where an explosion would not have had in the slightest degree the effect of releasing them from their dreadful slavery. That was one of Verne's few scientific slips, or else it was a deliberate step aside from scientific accuracy, pardonable enough in him as a romancer, but its like is not so easily explained when made by a savant who isn't writing a novel of adventure.

All the same, if Professor Goddard's rocket attains sufficient speed before it passes out of our atmosphere—which is a thinkable possibility—and if its aiming takes into account all of the many deflective forces that will affect its flight, it may reach the moon. That the rocket could carry enough explosive to make on impact a flash large and bright enough to be seen from the earth by the biggest of our telescopes—that will be believed when it is done.

Fig. 9–17
New York Times editorial of January 13, 1920, criticizing Robert Goddard's suggestion that rockets might be used for space travel.

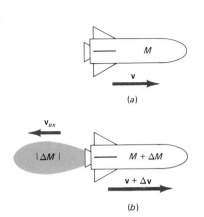

Fig. 9–18
A rocket (a) before and (b) after a short firing of its engine. The change ΔM in the rocket's mass is negative, so that $M+\Delta M < M$. Rocket speed is relative to a nonaccelerating frame of reference; exhaust speed v_{ex} is relative to the rocket.

engine firing, the total momentum is

$$P_{\text{initial}} = Mv,$$

where we drop the vector notation for the case of one-dimensional motion. What is the momentum after firing? The rocket's mass has changed by ΔM, and its speed by Δv, so its new momentum is $(M+\Delta M)(v+\Delta v)$. (Remember that ΔM is a negative quantity, so that the mass has actually decreased.) The gas is exhausted backward at speed v_{ex} relative to the rocket, so that the exhaust velocity in our reference frame is $v - v_{ex}$. (Actually, this is only approximately true, since the rocket speed changes during the firing. But when we take the limit $\Delta t \to 0$, this approximation will become exact.) The mass of the ejected gas is the positive quantity $-\Delta M$, where ΔM—a negative quantity—is the change in the rocket's mass as a result of its ejecting the gas. So the momentum of the gas is given by $p_{\text{gas}} = -\Delta M(v - v_{ex})$, and therefore the total momentum after firing is

$$P_{\text{final}} = p_{\text{rocket}} + p_{\text{gas}} = (M+\Delta M)(v+\Delta v) - \Delta M(v-v_{ex}).$$

There are no external forces acting on the rocket-gas system, so the initial and final momenta are the same. Expanding the products in the expression for the final momentum, and equating to the initial momentum, we have

$$Mv = Mv + v\Delta M + M\Delta v + \Delta M\Delta v - v\Delta M + v_{ex}\Delta M,$$

or

$$0 = M\Delta v + \Delta M\Delta v + v_{ex}\Delta M.$$

Rearranging and dividing by the time interval Δt gives

$$M\frac{\Delta v}{\Delta t} = -(v_{ex} + \Delta v)\frac{\Delta M}{\Delta t}.$$

In the limit $\Delta t \to 0$, the ratios $\Delta v/\Delta t$ and $\Delta M/\Delta t$ become derivatives, while $\Delta v \to 0$, so that

$$M\frac{dv}{dt} = -v_{ex}\frac{dM}{dt}. \qquad \text{(rocket equation)} \qquad (9\text{–}10)$$

The quantity $-v_{ex}dM/dt$ is defined by rocket engineers to be the **thrust** of the rocket. Thrust has the dimensions of force; physically, it is the force exerted on the interior of the rocket engine by the exhaust gases. We see from Equation 9–10 that the thrust can be increased by ejecting the gases at a higher exhaust speed, by ejecting gas at a greater rate, or both. The minus sign in Equation 9–10 shows that an *increase* in speed—positive dv/dt—corresponds to a *decrease* in rocket mass—negative dM/dt. In practice, the exhaust gas plume does not point straight backward, but fans out somewhat, thereby reducing the forward thrust (Fig. 9–19).

thrust

Example 9–9 ————————————————————————————
    On to Neptune!
    Several weeks after its rendezvous with Uranus in January 1986, the 815-kg Voyager 2 spacecraft was moving at 19.698 km/s relative to the sun. To set its course for an August 1989 rendezvous with Neptune, Voyager's rocket thrusters

were fired for a period of 2 h 33 min, to give the craft an acceleration in the same direction as its velocity. During the rocket firing 9.59 kg of fuel was ejected at 1448 m/s relative to the spacecraft. By how much did Voyager's speed increase?

Solution

For this firing $|\Delta M| \ll M$, so that we can "back off" just slightly from the limit $\Delta t \to 0$ that led to Equation 9–10, and write approximately

$$M \frac{\Delta v}{\Delta t} = -v_{ex} \frac{\Delta M}{\Delta t},$$

so that

$$\Delta v = -v_{ex} \frac{\Delta M}{M} = -(1448 \text{ m/s})\left(\frac{-9.59 \text{ kg}}{815 \text{ kg}}\right) = 17 \text{ m/s}$$

is the increase in Voyager's speed. That $\Delta v \ll v_{ex}$ is another indication that our approximation is reasonable.

Fig. 9–19
The exhaust plume of a rocket fans out slightly, reducing thrust from the theoretical value given by Equation 9–10. The photo shows the launch of the Solar Maximum Mission, a satellite that has carried out extensive studies of the sun.

What if the rocket engine is fired for so long a time that the mass changes substantially? Then we cannot use the approximation in Example 9–9. But if we multiply both sides of Equation 9–10 by dt/M, we obtain

$$dv = -v_{ex} \frac{dM}{M}.$$

Integrating this expression from some initial speed v_0 to some final speed v, during which the mass goes from M_0 to M, gives

$$\int_{v_0}^{v} dv = -v_{ex} \int_{M_0}^{M} \frac{dM}{M}.$$

The integral on the left is just $v - v_0$, while the integral on the right is the one we encountered in Example 7–4; it defines the natural logarithm. So we have

$$v - v_0 = -v_{ex}[\ln(M) - \ln(M_0)] = v_{ex}[\ln(M_0) - \ln(M)].$$

But $\ln(a) - \ln(b) = \ln(a/b)$, so that

$$v = v_0 + v_{ex} \ln\left(\frac{M_0}{M}\right). \tag{9–11}$$

Since $M_0 > M$, this equation gives the expected result that speed increases as the rocket ejects fuel.

A rocket carries only a finite amount of fuel, so that the mass ratio from fully loaded to fully empty fuel tanks sets the maximum achievable speed—the **terminal speed** of the rocket. For a given mass ratio, the terminal speed can be increased by increasing the velocity of the exhaust gases.

terminal speed

Example 9–10
Terminal Speed

A spacecraft is being designed to probe the interstellar medium beyond the solar system. The craft is to be boosted from earth and sent on an outbound trajectory by conventional rockets. At the orbit of Pluto, it is to be moving away from the sun at 34 km/s; at that point an advanced rocket engine will fire to accelerate the craft to its terminal speed of 150 km/s. If the mass of the spacecraft alone is 750 kg, and if the advanced rocket exhausts fuel at 47 km/s, how much fuel must be carried to Pluto's orbit? Plot the speed of the craft as a function of time during the rocket firing, assuming that fuel is exhausted at the rate of 19 kg/s. At Pluto, the sun's gravity has a negligible effect on the spacecraft.

Solution

Let M be the spacecraft mass and M_0 the mass of the spacecraft plus fuel. To solve Equation 9–11 for the fuel mass, we first write

$$\ln\left(\frac{M_0}{M}\right) = \frac{v - v_0}{v_{ex}} = \frac{150 \text{ km/s} - 35 \text{ km/s}}{47 \text{ km/s}} = 2.45,$$

so that

$$\frac{M_0}{M} = e^{2.45} = 11.6,$$

where we used the fact that natural logarithm and exponential are inverse functions: $e^{\ln x} = x$. So the total mass before the rocket firing is $11.6M$, or 8700 kg. Subtracting the 750-kg spacecraft mass leaves 7950 kg of fuel. This example shows why the achievement of very high exhaust speeds is crucial to long-distance space travel; even in this case the useful payload is dwarfed by the fuel mass, and the situation would be far worse with present-day rockets whose exhaust speeds are typically several km/s.

If fuel is burned at a steady rate dM/dt, the mass at time t is given by $M_0 - t(dM/dt)$, so that the speed is

$$v = v_0 + v_{ex} \ln\left[\frac{M_0}{M_0 - t(dM/dt)}\right].$$

Fig. 9–20
Speed versus time for the spacecraft of Example 9–10. The craft coasts at its terminal speed once all its fuel is exhausted. Note that the acceleration increases as the craft loses mass.

The general principle of rocket propulsion applies as well to jet aircraft engines. In analyzing a jet engine, however, we must account also for the momentum of the air that is drawn into the intake of the jet (see Problem 47).

9.3

KINETIC ENERGY IN MANY-PARTICLE SYSTEMS

We have seen in this chapter how the center-of-mass concept allows us to treat the overall motion of many-particle systems using the laws we introduced earlier for individual point particles. In particular, we've seen that the total momentum of a system is determined completely by the motion of its center of mass; motions and interactions of the constituent particles don't matter. For example, a firecracker sliding on ice has the same total momentum before and after it explodes.

The same, however, is not true of a system's kinetic energy. Energetically, our firecracker is very different after it explodes; internal potential energy has been converted to kinetic energy of the fragments. Nevertheless, the center-of-mass concept remains useful in categorizing the kinetic energy associated with a system of particles.

The total kinetic energy of a system is simply the sum of the kinetic energies of the constituent particles:

$$K = \sum \tfrac{1}{2} m_i v_i{}^2.$$

But the velocity $\mathbf{v}_i$ of a particle can be written as the vector sum of the center-of-mass velocity $\mathbf{V}$ and a velocity $\tilde{\mathbf{v}}_i$ of that particle relative to the center of mass:

$$\mathbf{v}_i = \mathbf{V} + \tilde{\mathbf{v}}_i.$$

Then the total kinetic energy of the system is

$$\begin{aligned} K &= \sum \tfrac{1}{2} m_i (\mathbf{V} + \tilde{\mathbf{v}}_i) \cdot (\mathbf{V} + \tilde{\mathbf{v}}_i) \\ &= \sum \tfrac{1}{2} m_i V^2 + \sum m_i \mathbf{V} \cdot \tilde{\mathbf{v}}_i + \sum \tfrac{1}{2} m_i \tilde{v}_i{}^2, \end{aligned} \tag{9–12}$$

where in the middle term the $\tfrac{1}{2}$ cancelled the 2 from the cross terms in multiplying out the dot product.

Let us examine the three sums making up the total kinetic energy. Since the center-of-mass speed V is common to all particles, it can be factored out of the first sum, so that

$$\sum \tfrac{1}{2} m_i V^2 = \tfrac{1}{2} V^2 \sum m_i = \tfrac{1}{2} M V^2,$$

kinetic energy of the center of mass

where M is the total mass. So what is this term? It is just the kinetic energy associated with a particle of mass M moving with speed V; we call this term K_{cm}, the **kinetic energy of the center of mass.**

The center-of-mass velocity can also be factored out of the second term in Equation 9–12, giving

$$\sum m_i \mathbf{V} \cdot \tilde{\mathbf{v}}_i = \mathbf{V} \cdot \sum m_i \tilde{\mathbf{v}}_i.$$

But what is $\sum m_i \tilde{\mathbf{v}}_i$? Because the $\tilde{\mathbf{v}}_i$'s are the particle velocities relative to the center of mass, that sum is just the total momentum measured in a frame of reference moving with the center of mass. But we found earlier that the total momentum is $\mathbf{P} = m\mathbf{V}$, with $\mathbf{V}$ the center of mass velocity. In a frame of reference where $\mathbf{V} = 0$—that is, a frame of reference moving with the center of mass—the total momentum must be zero. So the entire second term in Equation 9–12 is zero.

internal kinetic energy

The third term in Equation 9–12, $\sum \tfrac{1}{2} m_i \tilde{v}_i{}^2$, is just the sum of the individual kinetic energies measured in a frame of reference moving with the center of mass. We call this term K_{int}, the **internal kinetic energy.**

With the middle term gone, Equation 9–12 shows that the kinetic energy of a system breaks down into two terms:

$$K = K_{cm} + K_{int}. \tag{9–13}$$

The first term, the kinetic energy of the center of mass, depends only on the motion of the center of mass. In our firecracker example, K_{cm} cannot change when the firecracker explodes. The second term, the internal kinetic energy, depends only on the motions of the constituent particles relative to the center of mass. It is therefore unchanged by external forces acting on the system, but it can be changed by internal forces. The internal kinetic energy of our firecracker increases dramatically when it explodes.

SUMMARY
---

1. A system of particles of total mass M has associated with it a point called the **center of mass** to which Newton's laws of motion apply as they do to a point particle:

$$\mathbf{F} = M \frac{d^2\mathbf{R}}{dt^2} = M\mathbf{A},$$

where $\mathbf{F}$ is the net external force on the system and $\mathbf{A}$ the acceleration of the center of mass. The position $\mathbf{R}$ of the center of mass is given by

$$\mathbf{R} = \frac{\sum m_i \mathbf{r}_i}{M}, \qquad \text{(center of mass)}$$

where m_i and $\mathbf{r}_i$ represent the masses and positions of the individual particles in the system. For continuously distributed matter, the center-of-mass position is given by an integral:

$$\mathbf{R} = \frac{1}{M} \int \mathbf{r}\, dm,$$

where the integration is taken over the entire system. That the center-of-mass concept is useful is a consequence of Newton's third law, which requires that internal forces cancel in pairs, leaving the overall system motion determined only by external forces.

2. In the absence of a net external force, the center-of-mass velocity $\mathbf{V} = \sum m_i \mathbf{v}_i$ remains constant. In particular, if the center of mass is at rest, then it remains at rest regardless of the motions of the constituent particles.

3. The total momentum $\mathbf{P}$ of a system is the vector sum of the momenta $\mathbf{p}_i = m_i \mathbf{v}_i$ of the constituent particles:

$$\mathbf{P} = \sum m_i \mathbf{v}_i.$$

Application of Newton's third law, as embodied in the center-of-mass concept, shows that the system obeys Newton's second law in the form

$$\mathbf{F} = \frac{d\mathbf{P}}{dt},$$

where $\mathbf{F}$ is the net external force applied to the system.

4. In the absence of a net external force, the momentum of a system remains constant. This statement is known as the **law of conservation of momentum.** It is a fundamental principle of physics, extending even into realms where Newtonian mechanics is not applicable.

5. The motion of a rocket is a manifestation of the momentum principle. The rate of change of a rocket's speed v is given by

$$M \frac{dv}{dt} = -v_{\text{ex}} \frac{dM}{dt},$$

where M is the rocket's mass, v_{ex} the speed of the exhaust gas relative to the rocket, and dM/dt the rate of change of the rocket's mass due to the ejection of gas.

6. The total kinetic energy of a system of particles includes the kinetic energy of the center of mass, given by

$$K_{\text{cm}} = \tfrac{1}{2}MV^2,$$

where M is the total mass and V the speed of the center of mass, and the **internal kinetic energy,** given by

$$K_{\text{int}} = \sum \tfrac{1}{2}m_i \tilde{v}_i^2,$$

where m_i is the mass of an individual particle and $\tilde{v}_i$ its speed relative to the center of mass. The total kinetic energy is the sum of these two:

$$K_{\text{total}} = K_{\text{cm}} + K_{\text{int}}.$$

QUESTIONS
---

1. Roughly where is your center of mass when you are standing?
2. Can you form your body into a shape so that your center of mass is not within your body? If not, why not? If so, describe.
3. Where is the center of mass of a solid wooden wheel? Of a wagon wheel, with spokes?
4. Earth and moon are both in nearly circular orbits about a point 4600 km from the center of the earth. Explain in terms of the center-of-mass concept as applied to the earth-moon system.
5. Hunters drive a herd of bison over the edge of a cliff. As they fall, what happens to the center of mass of the earth + bison system? What happens to the centers of mass of the herd and the earth separately? Explain.
6. Explain why a high jumper's center of mass need not clear the bar.

7. Where would our derivation of the center-of-mass position $\mathbf{R}$ fail if the number of particles in the system were not constant?
8. The center of mass of a solid sphere is clearly at its center. If the sphere is cut in half, and the two halves are stacked as in Fig. 9–21, is the center of mass at the point where they touch? If not, roughly where is it? Explain.

Fig. 9–21 Question 8

9. How can a jet engine work when it takes air in the front as well as exhausting it out the back?

10. When you reach shore in Example 9–4, the center of mass of the boat + you system suddenly begins moving. What force accelerates it?

11. In Example 9–4, does the motion of the boat change when you reach shore?

12. Does the momentum of a basketball change as it rebounds off a backboard? What happens to the momentum of the backboard?

13. The momentum of a system of pool balls is the same before and after they are hit by the cue ball. Is it still the same after one of the balls strikes the edge of the table? Explain.

14. If all the cars in the world started driving eastward, what would happen to the length of the day?

15. When the chest of Example 9–6 hits the wall of the hockey rink, its momentum is no longer conserved. How would you redefine the system so that momentum is still conserved?

16. Two unequal masses are attached to the ends of an ideal spring. The spring is then compressed and the system placed at rest on a frictionless horizontal surface. When the masses are released, they oscillate back and forth, alternately stretching and compressing the spring. (a) Does the center of mass move during this process? (b) Now suppose the spring is not ideal, so that energy is dissipated in the spring and the motion eventually stops. Has the center of mass moved from its original position? (c) Now suppose the surface is not frictionless, so that again the motion eventually stops. Has the center of mass moved from its original position? Explain your answers.

17. Consider the system consisting of a shot putter and his shot; the mass of the shot is about 10% that of the shot putter. Describe the motion of the system's center of mass (a) if the shot putter is standing on a concrete pad with high coefficient of friction and (b) if he is standing on a frictionless surface.

18. An asteroid 100 km in diameter is discovered to be on collision course with earth. In a show of international cooperation and mutual disarmament, the superpowers launch all their nuclear missiles at the asteroid and succeed in blowing it to smithereens. Will the center of mass of the asteroid still hit earth?

19. Soon after the event of the previous question, a smaller asteroid is discovered heading for earth. Having used all their nuclear missiles on the first asteroid, the superpowers now cooperate in the manufacture of a huge rocket engine, which they transport to the asteroid. The rocket is strapped to the asteroid and fired long enough to move the asteroid off its collision course. Now does the center of mass of the asteroid hit earth?

20. Can you make a sailboat go by blowing air onto the sails with a fan mounted on the boat? With air from a compressed-air cylinder mounted on the boat? [See *The Physics Teacher*, vol. 24, pp. 38–39, 392–393 (1986).]

21. Criticize the editorial shown in Fig. 9–17.

22. An hourglass is inverted and placed on a scale. Compare scale readings (a) before sand begins to hit the bottom; (b) while sand is hitting the bottom; (c) when all the sand is on the bottom.

23. The momentum of the center of mass of a system is the sum of the momenta of the individual particles, but the same is not true for kinetic energy. Why not?

============================ **PROBLEMS** ============================

Section 9.1   *Center of Mass*

1. Four masses lie at the corners of a square 1.0 m on a side, as shown in Fig. 9–22. Where is the center of mass?

6.6 kg   5.5 kg
●   ●

2.2 kg   3.3 kg
●   ●

Fig. 9–22   Problem 1

2. Rework Example 9–1 with the origin at the center of the barbell, showing that the physical location of the center of mass is independent of the choice of coordinate system.

3. Three equal masses lie at the corners of an equilateral triangle of side ℓ. Where is the center of mass?

4. How far from the center of the earth is the center of mass of the earth-moon system? *Hint:* Consult Appendix F.

5. Find the center of mass of the plane object shown in Fig. 9–8, assuming uniform density.

6. Find the center of mass of the solar system at a time when all the planets are lined up on the same side of the sun. *Hint:* Consult Appendix F.

7. Find the center of mass of a pentagon of side a with one triangle missing, as shown in Fig. 9–23. *Hint:* See Example 9–3.

8. Find the center of mass of a uniformly solid cone of height h and base radius a.

9. A water molecule (H_2O) consists of two hydrogen atoms, each of mass 1.0 u, and one oxygen atom of mass 16 u. The hydrogen atoms are 0.96 Å (1 Å = 10^{-10} m) from the oxygen and are separated by an angle of 105° (Fig. 9–24). Where is the center of mass of the molecule?

Fig. 9–23 Problem 7

Fig. 9–24 A water molecule (Problem 9).

10. A flat, T-shaped structure is made from two identical rectangles of length ℓ and width w (Fig. 9–25). Find its center of mass.

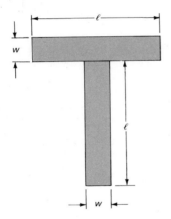

Fig. 9–25 Problem 10

11. Consider a system of three equal mass particles moving in a plane; their positions are given by $a_i\hat{\imath} + b_i\hat{\jmath}$, where a_i and b_i are functions of time with the units of position. Particle 1 has $a_1 = 3t^2 + 5$ and $b_1 = 0$; particle 2 has $a_2 = 7t + 2$ and $b_2 = 2$; particle 3 has $a_3 = 3t$ and $b_3 = 2t + 6$. Find the position, velocity, and acceleration of the center of mass as functions of time.

12. A 50-kg woman on a 650-kg boat hooks a 150-kg blue marlin fish on the end of a nearly horizontal line 35 m long. If fish and boat are originally at rest on a frictionless sea, how far does the boat move as she reels in the fish?

13. Estimate how much the earth would move if its entire human population of 4.5 billion jumped simultaneously into the 1-mile-deep Grand Canyon.

14. You are with 19 other people on a boat at rest in frictionless water. Your total mass is 1500 kg, and the mass of the boat itself is 12,000 kg. The entire party walks the 6.5-m distance from bow to stern. How far does the boat move?

15. A hemispherical bowl is at rest on a frictionless kitchen counter. A mouse drops onto the rim of the bowl from a cabinet directly overhead. The mouse climbs down the inside of the bowl to eat the crumbs at the bottom. If the bowl moves along the counter a distance equal to one-tenth of its diameter, how does the mouse's mass compare with the bowl's mass?

16. An 850-kg elevator is balanced perfectly by a counterweight connected to the elevator by a cable running over a pulley (Fig. 9–26). When the elevator is at the first floor, the counterweight is at the seventeenth floor. (a) Where is the center of mass of the elevator and counterweight system? (b) If a 60-kg passenger boards the elevator when it is at rest on the fifth floor, what is the subsequent motion of the center of mass of the system consisting of elevator, counterweight, and person?

Fig. 9–26 Problem 16

Section 9.2 *Momentum*

17. The Olympic-champion ice dancers Torville and Dean start from rest and push off each other. Torville's mass is 70 kg and Dean's mass is 50 kg, and the ice is essentially frictionless. If Torville's speed is 6.2 m/s, how far apart are they after 2.0 s?

18. A plutonium-239 nucleus at rest decays into a uranium-235 nucleus by emitting an alpha particle (^{4}He) with kinetic energy of 5.15 MeV. What is the speed of the uranium nucleus?

19. A runaway toboggan of mass 8.6 kg is moving horizontally at 23 km/h. As it passes under a tree, 15 kg of snow drop onto it. What is its subsequent speed?

20. A 950-kg airplane touches down on an icy runway, heading northward at 150 km/h. It collides with a 1200-kg plane taxiing eastward at 85 km/h. Find the speed and direction of the combined wreckage.

21. During a heavy storm, rain falls at the rate of 2.0 cm/hour; the speed of the individual raindrops is 25 m/s. (a) If the rain strikes a flat roof and then flows off the roof with negligible speed, what is the force exerted per square meter of roof area? (b) How much water would have to stand on the roof to exert the same force? The density of water is 1.0 g/cm^3.

22. A circle of Ice Capades clowns contains six individuals with masses of 50, 55, 60, 65, 70, and 75 kg. If they are at rest and evenly spaced around a circle, then start skating radially outward each with the same momentum $p = 200$ kg·m/s, describe the subsequent motion of their center of mass.

23. An 11,000-kg freight car is resting against a spring bumper at the end of a railroad track. The spring has constant $k = 3.2 \times 10^5$ N/m. The car is hit by a second car of 9400 kg mass moving at 8.5 m/s, and the two cars couple together. (a) What is the maximum compression of the spring? (b) What is the speed of the two cars together when they rebound from the spring?

24. On an icy road, a 1200-kg car moving at 50 km/h strikes a 4400-kg truck moving in the same direction at 35 km/h. The combination is soon hit from behind by a 1500-kg car speeding at 65 km/h. If all three vehicles stick together, what is the speed of the wreckage?

25. A 1600-kg automobile is resting at one end of a 4500-kg railroad flatcar that is also at rest. The automobile then drives along the flatcar at 15 km/h relative to the flatcar. Unfortunately, the flatcar brakes are not set. How fast does it move?

26. One plan for a space-based anti-ballistic-missile weapon involves shooting a beam of 100-MeV hydrogen atoms at an approaching missile. The power delivered by the beam is 100 MW. To destroy a missile, the beam should be turned on for 2 s, and should cover an area of 1 m^2. Determine (a) the momentum in the beam and (b) the average force exerted on the missile. Assume the beam is absorbed by the missile. (c) If the beam hits a 100-kg warhead moving at 8 km/s, will the warhead's trajectory be affected significantly?

27. An alternative to the anti-missile weapon of the previous problem is to hit the missile with objects of about 1-kg mass travelling at 20 km/s. Assuming that such a "kinetic kill weapon" embeds itself in the missile, (a) how much momentum does it impart to the missile; (b) how much kinetic energy does it carry; (c) does it significantly affect the trajectory of a 100-kg warhead moving at 8 km/s? (d) Compare the energy and momentum in this problem with that of the preceding problem. Explain any similarities and differences.

28. A ^{238}U nucleus is moving in the x-direction at 5.0×10^5 m/s, when it decays into an alpha particle (^{4}He) and a ^{234}Th nucleus. If the alpha particle moves off at 22° above the x-axis with a speed of 1.4×10^7 m/s, what is the recoil velocity of the thorium nucleus?

29. An ideal spring of spring constant k rests on a frictionless surface. Blocks of mass m_1 and m_2 are pushed against the two ends of the spring until it is compressed a distance x from its equilibrium length. The blocks are then released. What are their speeds when they leave the spring?

30. A car of mass M is initially at rest on a frictionless surface. A jet of water carrying mass at the rate dm/dt and moving horizontally at speed v_0 strikes the rear window of the car, which makes a 45° angle with the horizontal; the water bounces off at the same relative speed with which it hit the window, as shown in Fig. 9–27. (a) Find an expression for the initial acceleration of the car. (b) What is the maximum speed reached by the car?

Fig. 9–27   Problem 30

31. A 950-kg compact car is moving with velocity $\mathbf{v}_1 = 32\hat{\imath} + 17\hat{\jmath}$ m/s. It skids on a frictionless icy patch, and collides with a 450-kg hay wagon moving with velocity $\mathbf{v}_2 = 12\hat{\imath} + 14\hat{\jmath}$ m/s. If the two stay together, what is their velocity?

32. The 975-kg Giotto spacecraft, when it was close to Halley's Comet in 1986, passed through cometary dust of density 0.10 g/m^3 at a speed of 200 m/s. Its frontal surface area was 10 m^2. Assuming that the dust stuck to the front of the spacecraft, at what rate was the spacecraft decelerated?

33. A biologist fires 20-g rubber bullets at a rhinoceros that is charging at 1.9 m/s. If the gun fires 5 bullets per second, with a speed of 1600 m/s, and if the biologist fires for 13 s to stop the rhino in its tracks, what is the mass of the rhino? Assume the bullets drop vertically after striking the rhino.

34. A wedge-shaped block of mass M, length ℓ, and angle θ is at rest on a frictionless surface. A small block of mass m is released from rest at the top of the wedge, and slides without friction to the bottom and onto the horizontal surface (Fig. 9–28). Show that the speed of the wedge after the block leaves it is

$$v = m\sqrt{\frac{2g\ell\,\sin\theta\,\cos\theta}{(M+m)(M+m\,\sin^2\theta)}}.$$

Fig. 9–28 Problem 34

35. An Ariane rocket ejects 1.0×10^5 kg of fuel in the 90 s after launch. (a) How much thrust is developed if the fuel is ejected at 3.0 km/s with respect to the rocket? (b) What is the maximum total mass of the rocket if it is to get off the ground?

36. 90% of a rocket's initial mass is fuel. If the fuel is exhausted at 3500 m/s, what is the terminal speed of the rocket?

37. If a rocket's exhaust speed is 200 m/s, what fraction of its initial mass must be ejected to increase the rocket's speed by 50 m/s?

38. A space shuttle's main engines develop a thrust of 35×10^6 N as they eject gas at 2500 m/s. (a) How much fuel must the shuttle carry to permit a 5-minute engine firing? (b) At 200 kg/m^3, how large a cubical fuel tank would be required?

Section 9.3   *Kinetic Energy in Many-Particle Systems*

39. Determine the center of mass and internal kinetic energies before and after decay of the lithium nucleus of Example 9–7. Treat the individual nuclei as point particles.

40. A 150-g trick baseball is thrown at 60 km/h. It explodes in flight into two pieces, with a 38-g piece continuing straight ahead at 85 km/h. How much energy is released in the explosion?

41. The solar corona is a gas containing predominantly electrons and protons. The electrons are moving in random directions at speeds on the order of 10^7 m/s; this speed corresponds to a temperature of about 2 million K. The average coronal density near the sun is about 10^9 electrons/cm^3, with an equal density of protons. Large volumes of coronal material are sometimes ejected into space at speeds on the order of 300 km/s. Assuming that the protons partake only in this overall motion, while the electrons have superimposed their random 10^7 m/s motions, determine the center of mass and internal kinetic energies in a 1000 km^3 volume of such ejected coronal matter. Which particles make the dominant contribution to the center of mass and internal energies?

Supplementary Problems

42. The triangle of Fig. 9–29 has a density that varies in proportion to y^α, where α is a constant. Show that its center of mass is located at $y = (\alpha + 2)h/(\alpha + 3)$.

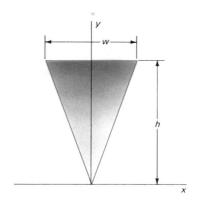

Fig. 9–29 Problem 42

43. While standing on frictionless ice, you (mass 65.0 kg) toss a 4.50-kg rock with initial speed of 12.0 m/s. If the rock is 15.2 m from you when it lands, (a) at what angle did you toss it? (b) How fast are you moving?

44. A drunk driver in a 1600-kg car plows into a 1300-kg parked car with its brake set. Police measurements show that the two cars skid together a distance of 25 m before stopping. If the effective coefficient of friction is 0.77, how fast was the drunk going just before the collision?

45. A fireworks rocket is launched vertically upward at 40 m/s. At the peak of its trajectory, it explodes into two equal-mass fragments. One reaches the ground 2.87 s after the explosion. When does the second reach the ground?

46. A fire hose delivers 50 kg/s of water at 30 m/s. How many 75-kg firefighters are needed to hold the hose on muddy ground for which the coefficient of static friction is 0.35?

47. (a) Derive an expression for the thrust of a jet aircraft engine. Moving through the air with speed v, the engine takes in air at the rate dM_{in}/dt. It uses the air to burn fuel with a fuel/air ratio f (that is, f kg of fuel burned for each kg of air), and ejects the exhaust gases at speed v_{ex} with respect to the engine. (b) Use your result to find the thrust of a JT-8D engine on a Boeing 727 jetliner, for which $v_{ex} = 1034$ ft/s and $dM_{in}/dt = 323$ lb/s, and which consumes 3760 lb of fuel per hour while cruising at 605 mi/h.

48. Two blocks are sliding along a one-dimensional frictionless surface with speeds v_1 and v_2, when they collide. Use the conservation of momentum principle to show that the most kinetic energy is lost if they stick together.

10

COLLISIONS

On the highway, we try to avoid colliding with other cars. On the pool table, we tailor collisions to suit our purposes. In particle accelerators, we interpret collisions to reveal the innermost structure of matter. On a cosmic scale, we wonder if a collision with an asteroid led to the extinction of the dinosaurs, and whether such occasional collisions will have drastic effects in the future. Collisions are important features of our physical universe (Fig. 10–1).

collision

A **collision** is a relatively violent interaction of objects that lasts for a short time. By "violent interaction" we mean that forces associated with the collision are much greater than any other forces that may be acting on the objects. By "short time" we mean short compared with time scales appropriate in describing the overall motion of the objects. A collision between two airplanes, for example, involves forces much greater than the gravitational and aerodynamic forces; the time interval over which the collision occurs is short compared with the overall flight times. Similarly, a collision between two galaxies (Fig. 10–2) may take millions of years, but that period is still short compared with the ages of the galaxies.

Fig. 10–1
Artist's conception of an asteroid colliding with the earth. Statistics show that an asteroid larger than 1 km probably hits our planet every few hundred million years. Some scientists have suggested that such a collision 65 million years ago created a cloud of dust and soot that led to the extinction of the dinosaurs.

impulsive force

10.1
IMPULSE AND COLLISIONS

In a collision of two objects—like the foot and football in Fig. 10–3—the velocity of one or both objects is abruptly changed. We know, from Newton's laws of motion, that such a change means a force has been applied. The strong but short-duration force associated with a collision is called an **impulsive force.** Figure 10–4 shows force as a function of time for the football of Fig. 10–3. Although the gravitational force also acts on the ball, during the collision the impulsive force is overwhelmingly dominant. We can relate the impulsive force to the change in an object's momen-

Fig. 10–2
Colliding galaxies.

Fig. 10–3
High-speed photo of a collision between a foot and a football. The strong impulsive force is evident in the deformation of the football. This force causes a rapid change in the ball's velocity.

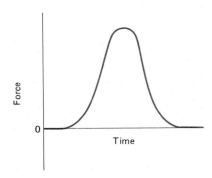

Fig. 10–4
Force as a function of time for the football of Fig. 10–3. The impulse is given by the area under the force versus time curve, and is equal to the change in the football's momentum.

tum through Newton's second law:

$$\mathbf{F} = \frac{d\mathbf{p}}{dt}.$$

Multiplying this equation by dt and integrating from some time t_1 before the collision to a time t_2 after the collision, we have

$$\int_{t_1}^{t_2} \mathbf{F}\,dt = \int_{t_1}^{t_2} d\mathbf{p}.$$

The right-hand integral is just the change $\Delta\mathbf{p}$ that occurs during the collision. The integral on the left is known as the **impulse, I,** associated with the collision. Our result then shows that the change in an object's momentum is equal to the impulse:

$$\mathbf{I} \equiv \int_{t_1}^{t_2} \mathbf{F}\,dt = \Delta\mathbf{p}. \qquad (10\text{--}1)$$

The units of impulse are the same as those of momentum: kg·m/s, or, equivalently, N·s. Since the definite integral corresponds to the area under a curve, Equation 10–1 shows that the impulse is given geometrically by the area under the force versus time curve. It doesn't much matter whether the force curve includes any non-impulsive forces that may be present, for our definition of a collision ensures that the change in momentum associated with non-impulsive forces is small during the time of the collision.

Although the impulsive force in a collision may be a very complicated function of time (Fig. 10–5), the overall effect of a collision on the motion of an object is summed up by the change in the object's momentum. We can work backward from that change to determine the **average impulsive force $\overline{\mathbf{F}}$**—the force that, if applied constantly during the collision time Δt, would give the same change in momentum. That is,

$$\overline{\mathbf{F}} = \frac{\mathbf{I}}{\Delta t} = \frac{\Delta\mathbf{p}}{\Delta t}. \qquad (10\text{--}2)$$

impulse

average impulsive force

Fig. 10–5
Impulsive force in the crash of a 1986 Suzuki Samurai into a rigid barrier. Horizontal line is the average force; area under the rectangle is the same as under the jagged curve.

Graphically, the average force is represented by the height of a rectangle whose area is the same as the actual impulse area $\int Fdt$ (see Fig. 10–5).

Example 10–1
Impulse

A 150-g baseball is moving horizontally at 30 m/s just before reaching the bat. Bat and ball are then in contact for 2.0 ms (Fig. 10–6). Find the impulse and the average impulsive force (a) if the hit is a line drive to center field at 45 m/s and (b) if the hit is a pop foul that starts straight up at 22 m/s.

Solution

In a coordinate system with x-axis along the line from home plate to center field, the incoming momentum is

$$\mathbf{p}_1 = m\mathbf{v}_1 = (0.15 \text{ kg})(-30\mathbf{\hat{\imath}} \text{ m/s}) = -4.5\mathbf{\hat{\imath}} \text{ kg·m/s}.$$

For the line drive, the outgoing momentum is

$$\mathbf{p}_2 = m\mathbf{v}_2 = (0.15 \text{ kg})(45\mathbf{\hat{\imath}} \text{ m/s}) = 6.8\mathbf{\hat{\imath}} \text{ kg·m/s},$$

giving an impulse

$$\mathbf{I} = \Delta\mathbf{p} = (6.8\mathbf{\hat{\imath}} \text{ kg·m/s}) - (-4.5\mathbf{\hat{\imath}} \text{ kg·m/s}) = 11\mathbf{\hat{\imath}} \text{ kg·m/s}$$

and an average force

$$\overline{\mathbf{F}} = \frac{\Delta\mathbf{p}}{\Delta t} = \frac{11\mathbf{\hat{\imath}} \text{ kg·m/s}}{2.0\times10^{-3} \text{ s}} = 5.5\times10^{3}\mathbf{\hat{\imath}} \text{ N}.$$

This is a large force, nearly 4000 times the gravitational force on the ball.

For the pop foul, the outgoing momentum is in the y-direction:

$$\mathbf{p}_2 = m\mathbf{v}_2 = (0.15 \text{ kg})(22\mathbf{\hat{\jmath}} \text{ m/s}) = 3.3\mathbf{\hat{\jmath}} \text{ kg·m/s},$$

so that

$$\mathbf{I} = \Delta\mathbf{p} = (3.3\mathbf{\hat{\jmath}} \text{ kg·m/s}) - (-4.5\mathbf{\hat{\imath}} \text{ kg·m/s}) = 4.5\mathbf{\hat{\imath}} + 3.3\mathbf{\hat{\jmath}} \text{ kg·m/s}$$

and

$$\overline{\mathbf{F}} = \frac{\Delta\mathbf{p}}{\Delta t} = \frac{4.5\mathbf{\hat{\imath}} + 3.3\mathbf{\hat{\jmath}} \text{ kg·m/s}}{2.0\times10^{-3} \text{ s}} = 2.3\times10^{3}\mathbf{\hat{\imath}} + 1.7\times10^{3}\mathbf{\hat{\jmath}} \text{ N},$$

or an average impulse force of magnitude 2800 N. Large forces like this are typical of collisions, and explain why collisions often involve so much damage.

Fig. 10–6
High-speed photo of ball and bat. The two are in contact for only about 2 ms.

10.2
COLLISIONS AND THE CONSERVATION LAWS

Often we know no more about the impulsive force of a collision than that it acts for a short time and produces abrupt changes in motion. Nevertheless, we can use the conservation laws developed in earlier chapters to relate the interacting objects' motions before and after collision. As always, conservation laws provide a "shortcut," giving us an overall picture lacking in some details. In the case of a collision involving an unknown impulsive force, those missing details are confined to the very short time of the collision.

Momentum

One thing we do know about impulsive forces between colliding objects is that they are *internal* to a system comprising those objects. We found in the preceding chapter that the momentum of a system can be changed only by external forces. Therefore, the impulsive forces of a collision leave the total momentum of the colliding objects unchanged. What about any external forces that may also act during a collision, like the gravitational force on a tennis ball as it collides with the racket? Our definition of a collision requires that the collision take place in a very short time, so that external forces do not have time to alter the system momentum significantly during the collision. To a very good approximation, therefore, the total momentum of a colliding system is conserved during a collision. This conclusion is valid regardless of the details of the impulsive force.

Energy

elastic collision

What about mechanical energy? It may or may not be conserved during a collision. If mechanical energy is conserved, the collision is termed elastic. Like a completely frictionless surface, an **elastic collision** is an impossible idealization in the macroscopic world. In a macroscopic collision, some mechanical energy is inevitably transformed to other forms like sound, random molecular motions, or the energy associated with permanently deforming materials (Fig. 10–7). But some interactions in the atomic, nuclear, and elementary particle realms are completely elastic. And macroscopic objects like billiard balls, trampolines, and hockey pucks undergo nearly elastic collisions. The important criterion is that in an elastic collision, the internal forces must be conservative. Then kinetic energy is stored temporarily as potential energy, all of which is again released as kinetic energy before the collision is over.

inelastic collision
totally inelastic collision

When mechanical energy is lost during a collision, the collision is **inelastic.** In a **totally inelastic collision,** the colliding objects stick together to form one composite object. Even then, mechanical energy is usually not

Fig. 10–7
(Left) The superball on the left undergoes a nearly elastic collision with the ground, rebounding with much greater speed than the squash ball on the right. (Above) An automobile collision is invariably inelastic, with much of the kinetic energy lost to permanent deformation of the colliding vehicles.

all lost; complete loss of mechanical energy in most cases would violate conservation of momentum. But a totally inelastic collision involves the maximum loss of mechanical energy that is consistent with momentum conservation. In general, we can determine the motion after collision only for the case of completely elastic or totally inelastic collisions; in intermediate cases we must know just how much energy is lost before we can solve for the post-collision motion (see Problem 47).

10.3
INELASTIC COLLISIONS

The motion after a totally inelastic collision is determined entirely by the conservation of momentum principle. We analyzed some totally inelastic collisions in the previous chapter; for instance, measuring the speed of the hockey puck in Example 9–6 involved a totally inelastic collision.

Consider two objects with masses m_1 and m_2 and initial velocities $\mathbf{v}_{1i}$ and $\mathbf{v}_{2i}$ that undergo a totally inelastic collision. That is, after collision they stick together to form a single composite body of mass $m_1 + m_2$ and final velocity $\mathbf{v}_f$. Conservation of momentum states that the initial and final momenta of this two-particle system must be the same:

$$m_1\mathbf{v}_{1i} + m_2\mathbf{v}_{2i} = (m_1 + m_2)\mathbf{v}_f. \qquad \text{(inelastic collision)} \qquad (10\text{–}3)$$

Given four of the five quantities m_1, $\mathbf{v}_{1i}$, m_2, $\mathbf{v}_{2i}$, and $\mathbf{v}_f$, we can solve for the fifth. Often but not always, the unknown is the final velocity:

$$\mathbf{v}_f = \frac{m_1\mathbf{v}_{1i} + m_2\mathbf{v}_{2i}}{m_1 + m_2}. \qquad (10\text{–}4)$$

Calculating the total kinetic energy before and after the collision will convince you that this collision is indeed inelastic (see Problem 13).

Example 10–2
The Ballistic Pendulum

The ballistic pendulum is a device used to measure the speeds of fast-moving objects like bullets. It consists of a wooden block of mass M suspended from vertical strings (Fig. 10–8). When a bullet strikes the block, it undergoes an inelastic collision and embeds itself in the block. If the bullet has mass m, and if the block rises a maximum height h after the collision, show that the speed of the bullet is $(m + M)\sqrt{2gh}/m$.

Solution

To solve this problem, we deal separately first with the collision and then with the subsequent rise of the block. Understanding the difference in the way we handle these two steps will strengthen your confidence in applying the conservation laws.

1. The incoming bullet undergoes an inelastic collision with the block. Mechanical energy is not conserved. But because the collision takes such a short time, external forces—here gravity and the string tension—have little effect and the momentum of the bullet + block system is essentially conserved. So we can write:

$$mv = (m + M)V,$$

Fig. 10–8
A ballistic pendulum (Example 10–2).

where v is the initial speed of the bullet and V the speed of the bullet/block combination after the collision. Solving for V gives $V = mv/(m+M)$.

2. As the block swings upward, the external forces of gravity and string tension act to alter the momentum of the bullet + block system. Momentum is not conserved. But gravity is a conservative force, and the string tension acts at right angles to the motion and therefore does no work. So mechanical energy is conserved in the upward swing of the block. Taking the zero of potential energy in the block's initial position, we can then equate the kinetic energy just after the collision to the potential energy when the block is at its maximum height:

$$\tfrac{1}{2}(m+M)V^2 \; = \; (m+M)gh.$$

Now we relate the two parts of the problem. Using our expression for V in the statement of energy conservation, we have

$$\frac{1}{2}\left(\frac{mv}{m+M}\right)^2 \; = \; gh,$$

so that

$$v \; = \; \frac{(m+M)\sqrt{2gh}}{m}.$$

Example 10–3

A Fusion Reaction

In a fusion reaction, two deuterium nuclei (^{2}H) combine to form a helium nucleus (^{4}He). One of the incident nuclei is originally moving in the +x-direction at 3.50×10^6 m/s, and the helium nucleus is subsequently detected moving at 1.62×10^6 m/s at an angle of $\theta = 36°$ to the x-axis (Fig. 10–9). Find the initial velocity of the second deuterium nucleus.

Solution

Momentum conservation entirely determines the outcome of this totally inelastic collision. The statement of momentum conservation is given by Equation 10–3; solving for the initial velocity $\mathbf{v}_2$ of the second deuterium nucleus, we have

$$\mathbf{v}_2 \; = \; \frac{(m_1+m_2)\mathbf{v} \; - \; m_1\mathbf{v}_1}{m_2}.$$

Fig. 10–9
Velocity vectors for Example 10–3.

Breaking this vector equation into its two components gives

x-component: $$v_2\cos\phi \; = \; \frac{(m_1+m_2)v\,\cos\theta \; - \; m_1v_1}{m_2}$$

y-component: $$v_2\sin\phi \; = \; \frac{(m_1+m_2)v\,\sin\theta}{m_2},$$

where we have made use of the fact that $\mathbf{v}_1$ is entirely in the x-direction. Squaring and adding these two equations, and using $\cos^2\phi + \sin^2\phi = 1$, we get

$$v_2^2 \; = \; \frac{(Mv\,\cos\theta - m_1v_1)^2 \; + \; M^2v^2\,\sin^2\theta}{m_2^2},$$

where $M = m_1 + m_2$ is the total mass. Using the given values of m_1, m_2, v_1, v_2, and θ, we find that $v_2 = 2.1 \times 10^6$ m/s. Solving the y-component equation for ϕ then gives

$$\phi \; = \; \sin^{-1}\left(\frac{Mv\,\sin\theta}{m_2v_2}\right) \; = \; \sin^{-1}\left[\frac{(4\text{ u})(1.62 \times 10^6 \text{ m/s})(\sin 36°)}{(2\text{ u})(2.1 \times 10^6 \text{ m/s})}\right] \; = \; 65°.$$

Figure 10–9 shows the velocity vectors for the deuterium and helium nuclei.

Does this problem remind you of the radioactive decay of Example 9–7? It should: fusion and radioactive decay are essentially inverse processes. The same momentum conservation principle governs both, and even the same mathematical techniques apply.

10.4
ELASTIC COLLISIONS

We have seen that momentum is essentially conserved in any collision. In an elastic collision, kinetic energy is conserved as well. In the most general case of a two-body collision, we consider two objects of masses m_1 and m_2, moving initially with velocities $\mathbf{v}_{1i}$ and $\mathbf{v}_{2i}$, respectively. Their final velocities after collision are $\mathbf{v}_{1f}$ and $\mathbf{v}_{2f}$. Then the conservation statements for momentum and kinetic energy become

$$m_1\mathbf{v}_{1i} + m_2\mathbf{v}_{2i} = m_1\mathbf{v}_{1f} + m_2\mathbf{v}_{2f} \qquad (10–5)$$

and

$$\tfrac{1}{2}m_1 v_{1i}^2 + \tfrac{1}{2}m_2 v_{2i}^2 = \tfrac{1}{2}m_1 v_{1f}^2 + \tfrac{1}{2}m_2 v_{2f}^2. \qquad (10–6)$$

Given the initial velocities, we would like to be able to predict the outcome of a collision. In the preceding section, we did just that for an arbitrary inelastic collision. In a two-dimensional inelastic collision, we had two equations (the two components of the vector momentum conservation equation) and two unknowns (the magnitude and direction of the one final velocity). Mathematically, we had enough information to solve the system. Here, in the elastic case, we have the two components of the momentum conservation equation 10–5 and the single scalar equation for energy conservation 10–6. But we have four unknowns—the magnitudes and directions of both final velocities. With three equations and four unknowns, we do not have enough information to solve the general two-dimensional elastic collision. Later in this section we will see how other information can help us solve such problems. First, though, we look at the special case of a one-dimensional elastic collision.

Elastic Collisions in One Dimension

When two objects collide head-on, the internal forces act along the same line as the incident motion, and the objects' subsequent motion must therefore be along that same line (Fig. 10–10). Although such one-dimensional collisions are clearly a very special case, they do occur and they provide much insight into the more general case.

In the one-dimensional case, the momentum conservation equation 10–5 has only one nontrivial component:

$$m_1 v_{1i} + m_2 v_{2i} = m_1 v_{1f} + m_2 v_{2f}, \qquad (10–5a)$$

where the v's stand for velocity components, rather than magnitudes, and can therefore be positive or negative. If we collect together the terms in Equations 10–5a and 10–6 that are associated with each mass, we have

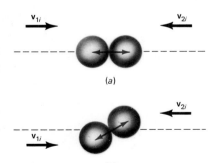

Fig. 10–10
(a) When two objects collide head-on, internal forces act along the same line as the incident motion, and the subsequent motion is also along this line. The collision is one-dimensional. (b) If the collision is not head-on, internal forces act in new directions, and the motion is necessarily two-dimensional.

$$m_1(v_{1i} - v_{1f}) = m_2(v_{2f} - v_{2i}) \tag{10-5b}$$

and

$$m_1(v_{1i}^2 - v_{1f}^2) = m_2(v_{2f}^2 - v_{2i}^2). \tag{10-6a}$$

But $a^2 - b^2 = (a+b)(a-b)$, so that Equation 10–6a can be written

$$m_1(v_{1i} - v_{1f})(v_{1i} + v_{1f}) = m_2(v_{2f} - v_{2i})(v_{2f} + v_{2i}). \tag{10-6b}$$

Dividing the left and right sides of Equation 10–6b by the corresponding sides of Equation 10–5a then gives

$$v_{1i} + v_{1f} = v_{2f} + v_{2i}. \tag{10-7}$$

(In performing this division, we assumed that we were not dividing by zero; that is, we assumed that the velocities were indeed changed by the collision.) Rearranging Equation 10–7 shows that

$$v_{1i} - v_{2i} = v_{2f} - v_{1f}. \tag{10-8}$$

What does this equation tell us? Both sides describe the relative velocity between the two particles; the equation therefore shows that the relative speed remains unchanged after the collision, although the direction reverses. If one object is approaching another at a relative speed of 5 m/s, then after collision it will be receding at 5 m/s.

Continuing our search for the final velocities, we solve Equation 10–8 for v_{2f}:

$$v_{2f} = v_{1i} - v_{2i} + v_{1f},$$

and use this result in Equation 10–5a:

$$m_1 v_{1i} + m_2 v_{2i} = m_1 v_{1f} + m_2(v_{1i} - v_{2i} + v_{1f}).$$

Solving for v_{1f} then gives

$$v_{1f} = \frac{m_1 - m_2}{m_1 + m_2} v_{1i} + \frac{2m_2}{m_1 + m_2} v_{2i}. \tag{10-9a}$$

Problem 32 asks you to show similarly that

$$v_{2f} = \frac{2m_1}{m_1 + m_2} v_{1i} + \frac{m_2 - m_1}{m_1 + m_2} v_{2i}. \tag{10-9b}$$

Equations 10–9a and 10–9b are our desired result, expressing the final velocities in terms of the initial velocities alone. To see that these results make sense, we suppose that $v_{2i} = 0$. (This is really not a special case, since we can always work in a frame of reference in which m_2 is initially at rest.) Now consider several special cases.

Case 1: $m_1 \ll m_2$

For this case, picture a Ping-Pong ball colliding with a bowling ball, or any object colliding elastically with a perfectly rigid wall. Setting $v_{2i} = 0$ in Equations 10–9, and dropping m_1 as being negligible compared with m_2, Equations 10–9 become simply

$$v_{1f} = -v_{1i}$$

and

$$v_{2f} = 0.$$

That is, the lighter object rebounds with no change in speed, while the heavier object remains at rest. Does this make sense in light of the conservation laws that Equations 10–9 are supposed to reflect? Clearly energy is conserved: the kinetic energy of m_2 remains zero and the kinetic energy $\frac{1}{2}m_1 v_1^2$ is unchanged. But what about momentum? The momentum of the lighter object has changed, from $m_1 v_{1i}$ to $-m_1 v_{1i}$. But momentum is conserved; the momentum given up by the lighter object is absorbed by the heavier object. In the limit of an arbitrarily large m_2, though, the heavier object can absorb huge amounts of momentum without acquiring significant speed. If we "back off" from the extreme case that m_1 can be neglected altogether compared with m_2, we would find that the lighter object rebounds with slightly reduced speed and that the heavier object begins moving very slowly in the opposite direction (see Problem 41).

An important example of a case (1) collision is that of an electron and a proton, nearly 2000 times more massive than the electron. We have just seen that such collisions result in very little energy transfer from the lighter to the heavier object. For this reason, energy imparted to the electrons in a gas of electrons and protons—a plasma—is not readily transferred to the protons. Particle energy is associated with temperature, as we will see in Chapter 17, so that an electron-proton gas can actually have two quite different temperatures.

Case 2: $m_1 = m_2$

Again setting $v_{2i} = 0$, Equations 10–9 now give

$$v_{1f} = 0$$

and

$$v_{2f} = v_{1i}.$$

So the first object stops abruptly, transferring all its energy and momentum to the second object (Fig. 10–11). Case (2) collisions have important implications for the design of nuclear reactors. The fission reactions that power a reactor are most easily initiated by slowly moving neutrons, while each uranium atom that fissions releases fast-moving neutrons. The reactor's fuel rods are therefore surrounded by a moderator—a substance that slows down the neutrons. Our case (2) analysis shows that the most effective slowing-down is achieved in collisions of nearly equal masses. Most nuclear reactors use water as a moderator; the protons comprising the nuclei of the hydrogen atoms have almost the same mass as a neutron and are therefore efficient absorbers of neutron energy. Case (2) also shows why ordinary air does not have the dual-temperature complexity of the plasma described under case (1). In air, all the molecules have similar masses, and therefore energy is readily transferred in intermolecular collisions.

For purposes of energy transfer, two equal-mass particles are perfectly "matched." We will encounter analogous instances of energy transfer "matching" when we discuss wave motion and again in connection with electric circuits.

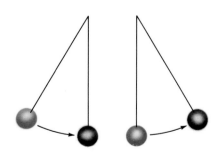

Fig. 10–11
During a collision between two pendulums of equal mass, the initially moving pendulum transfers all of its energy to the initially stationary one.

Case 3: $m_1 \gg m_2$

Now, with v_{2i} again set to zero, Equations 10–9 give

$$v_{1f} = v_{1i}$$

and

$$v_{2f} = 2v_{1i},$$

where we have neglected m_2 compared with m_1. So here the more massive object barrels right on with no change in motion, while the lighter one heads off in the same direction with twice the speed. How are momentum and energy conserved in this case? In the extreme limit where we neglect the mass m_2, the energy and momentum associated with m_2 are negligible. Essentially all the energy and momentum remain with the more massive object, and both these quantities are unchanged in the collision. If we "back off" from the extreme case where we neglect m_2 altogether, we find that the more massive object's speed is reduced slightly, while the lighter object heads off with a speed just under twice the initial speed of the heavier object (see Problem 42). The collision of a baseball bat and ball is a case (3) collision; in a reference frame moving with the ball's initial velocity, the massive bat hits the ball, which then heads out at a higher speed than that of the bat. The bat's motion is hardly altered.

Example 10–4 _____

Car-Truck Collisions

A truck of mass $9M$ is moving at speed $v = 15$ km/h when it collides head-on with a parked car of mass M. Spring-mounted bumpers ensure that the collision is essentially elastic. Describe the subsequent motion of each vehicle. Repeat for the case of the car moving at speed $v = 15$ km/h and colliding with the stationary truck. What fraction of the incident vehicle's kinetic energy is transferred in each case?

Solution

For the first case, we can set $m_1 = 9M$, $v_{1i} = v = 15$ km/h, $m_2 = M$, and $v_{2i} = 0$. Then Equations 10–9 give

$$v_{1f} = \frac{9M - M}{9M + M}v = \tfrac{4}{5}v = 12 \text{ km/h}$$

and

$$v_{2f} = \frac{(2)(9M)}{9M + M}v = \tfrac{9}{5}v = 27 \text{ km/h}.$$

So both vehicles move off in the same direction, with the truck's speed reduced by 20 per cent and the car "kicked up" to 27 km/h. The initial energy of the truck is $\tfrac{9}{2}Mv^2$ or $4.5Mv^2$; the final energy of the car is $\tfrac{1}{2}M(\tfrac{9}{5}v)^2$ or $1.6Mv^2$. So 1.6/4.5, or 36 per cent of the truck's energy is transferred in this case.

For the second collision, we set $m_1 = M$ and $m_2 = 9M$, giving

$$v_{1f} = \frac{M - 9M}{M + 9M}v = -\tfrac{4}{5}v = -12 \text{ km/h}$$

and

$$v_{2f} = \frac{2M}{M + 9M}v = \tfrac{1}{5}v = 3.0 \text{ km/h},$$

so that the car rebounds with 80 per cent of its initial speed and the truck picks up a relatively small speed. Now the initial energy of the car is $\frac{1}{2}Mv^2$, while the final energy of the truck is $\frac{9}{2}M(\frac{1}{5}v)^2 = 0.18Mv^2$, so that again 36 per cent of the energy is transferred. Even though the mass ratio is quite large, neither collision approaches closely the case (1) or case (3) limit. Problem 26 explores the approach to those limits.

Example 10–5
"Weighing" an Elementary Particle

In a nuclear experiment, a particle of unknown mass moving at 460 km/s undergoes a head-on elastic collision with a carbon nucleus (^{12}C; mass approximately 12 u) moving at 220 km/s. After collision, the carbon continues in the same direction at 340 km/s. Find the mass and final velocity of the unknown particle.

Solution

If we designate the carbon as particle 2, we then know all quantities in Equation 10–9b except the unknown mass m_2. Multiplying that equation through by $(m_1 + m_2)$, we have

$$(m_1 + m_2)v_{2f} = 2m_1 v_{1i} + (m_2 - m_1)v_{2i}.$$

Solving for m_1 then gives

$$m_1 = \frac{m_2(v_{2i} - v_{2f})}{v_{2f} - 2v_{1i} + v_{2i}} = \frac{(12 \text{ u})(220 \text{ km/s} - 340 \text{ km/s})}{340 \text{ km/s} - (2)(460 \text{ km/s}) + 220 \text{ km/s}} = 4 \text{ u}.$$

The unknown particle is therefore probably an alpha particle (^{4}He, or helium nucleus). Knowing m_1, we use Equation 10–9a to find v_{1f}:

$$v_{1f} = \frac{4 \text{ u} - 12 \text{ u}}{16 \text{ u}}(460 \text{ km/s}) + \frac{(2)(12 \text{ u})}{16 \text{ u}}(220 \text{ km/s}) = 100 \text{ km/s}.$$

Are these results consistent with our earlier finding that a less massive particle should rebound off a more massive one? After all, both particles now seem to continue in the same direction. But there is no inconsistency; our earlier conclusion was based on one particle's being initially at rest, while here both have nonzero initial velocities. If we look at the situation in a reference frame where the carbon is initially at rest, we have $v_{1i} = 460$ km/s $- 220$ km/s $= 240$ km/s, while $v_{1f} = 100$ km/s $- 220$ km/s $= -120$ km/s. The less massive nucleus does rebound, as expected. Figure 10–12 summarizes the collision in both reference frames; the change of reference frames is explored further in Problem 27.

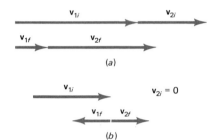

Fig. 10–12
The collision of Example 10–5 (a) in the original reference frame and (b) in a reference frame moving with the initial 220 km/s velocity of the carbon nucleus.

Fig. 10–13
The impact parameter is the perpendicular distance b between centers of the colliding spheres. In this simple case of equal-sized spheres, knowing the impact parameter allows us to find the line along which the internal forces act, and therefore to solve for the subsequent motion.

Elastic Collisions in Two Dimensions

To analyze an elastic collision in two dimensions, we must use the full vector statement of momentum conservation (Equation 10–5), along with the energy conservation equation 10–6. But we found earlier that these equations alone do not provide enough information to solve the problem. In a collision between reasonably simple macroscopic objects, that information may be provided by the so-called **impact parameter,** a measure of how much the collision differs from being head-on (Fig. 10–13). More typically, though, and especially with atomic and nuclear interactions, the needed information must be supplied by measurements done after the collision. Knowing the direction of motion of one particle after collision, for example, provides enough information to analyze the collision if the masses and initial velocities are also known.

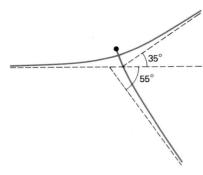

Fig. 10–14
A close encounter between two stars, in a frame of reference in which one star is initially at rest.

Example 10–6
Stars in a Close Encounter

A star of mass 1.4 $M_\odot$ ($M_\odot$ is the sun's mass, a convenient mass unit in astronomy) is a great distance from another star of equal mass, and is approaching the second star at 680 km/s. The two stars undergo close encounter, and much later the first star is moving at a 35° angle to its initial direction, as shown in Fig. 10–14. In the frame of reference in which the second star is initially at rest, find the final speeds of both stars and the direction of motion of the second star.

Solution

Since the force acting between the stars is the conservative gravitational force, the encounter is elastic.* Designating the initially moving star by the subscript 1, and taking the x-axis along the direction of its initial motion, the two components of the momentum conservation equation 10–5 become

x-component:
$$m_1 v_{1i} = m_1 v_{1f}\cos\theta_1 + m_2 v_{2f}\cos\theta_2 \qquad (10\text{–}10)$$

y-component:
$$0 = m_1 v_{1f}\sin\theta_1 + m_2 v_{2f}\sin\theta_2, \qquad (10\text{–}11)$$

where $\theta_{1,2}$ are the angles the final velocities make with the x-axis. A third equation is provided by energy conservation:

$$\tfrac{1}{2}m_1 v_{1i}^2 = \tfrac{1}{2}m_1 v_{1f}^2 + \tfrac{1}{2}m_2 v_{2f}^2, \qquad (10\text{–}12)$$

so we have three equations in the three unknowns v_{1f}, v_{2f}, and θ_2. Since the masses are equal, they cancel from all three equations. Isolating the unknown θ_2 on one side of Equations 10–10 and 10–11 gives

$$v_{2f}\cos\theta_2 = v_{1i} - v_{1f}\cos\theta_1$$

$$v_{2f}\sin\theta_2 = -v_{1f}\sin\theta_1.$$

Squaring and adding these two equations, and using $\cos^2\theta + \sin^2\theta = 1$ on both sides of the equation, we have

$$v_{2f}^2 = (v_{1i} - v_{1f}\cos\theta_1)^2 + v_{1f}^2\sin^2\theta_1 = v_{1i}^2 - 2v_{1i}v_{1f}\cos\theta_1 + v_{1f}^2.$$

Using this result in the energy conservation equation 10–12 gives

$$v_{1i}^2 = v_{1f}^2 + v_{2f}^2 = v_{1f}^2 + v_{1i}^2 - 2v_{1i}v_{1f}\cos\theta_1 + v_{1f}^2,$$

or

$$v_{1f}^2 = v_{1i}v_{1f}\cos\theta_1,$$

so that

$$v_{1f} = v_{1i}\cos\theta_1 = (680 \text{ km/s})(\cos 35°) = 557 \text{ km/s}.$$

From Equation 10–12, we can then write

$$v_{2f} = [v_{1i}^2 - v_{1f}^2]^{1/2} = [(680 \text{ km/s})^2 - (557 \text{ km/s})^2]^{1/2} = 390 \text{ km/s}.$$

Finally, the y-momentum equation 10–11 gives

$$\theta_2 = \sin^{-1}\left(\frac{-v_{1f}\sin\theta_1}{v_{2f}}\right) = \sin^{-1}\left[\frac{-(557 \text{ km/s})(\sin 35°)}{390 \text{ km/s}}\right] = -55°.$$

This angle is shown on Fig. 10–14. Note that the angle between the outgoing velocity vectors is 90°. Problem 29 asks you to prove that this is always true in an elastic collision of equal masses, one of which is initially at rest.

---

*This neglects tidal effects that might transform kinetic energy of stellar motion into internal energy.

Is this event really a collision? After all, the two stars interact only through the gravitational force which acts all the time. We certainly wouldn't consider a satellite in earth orbit—again interacting only via gravity—to be "colliding" with the earth. But our stellar encounter really is a collision. The two stars are in hyperbolic orbits; their energy exceeds escape energy, and they interact strongly only when they are very close. Far from each other, the stars travel in nearly straight lines, approaching the asymptotes of their hyperbolic orbits. So their interaction really does involve a strong force acting for only a short time, and therefore meets our definition of a collision. On the astronomical and subatomic scale, most collisions actually involve such "close encounters" in which particles interact without touching.

SUMMARY

1. A **collision** is a relatively violent interaction between two objects that takes place in a short time. An **impulsive force** acts between the colliding objects; this force is much stronger than the net external force acting on either object.
2. The **impulse** imparted to an object is given by integrating the impulsive force over time; Newton's second law shows that the impulse is equal to the change in the object's momentum:

$$\mathbf{I} = \int_{t_1}^{t_2} \mathbf{F} \, dt = \Delta \mathbf{p}.$$

The average value $\overline{\mathbf{F}}$ of the impulsive force is given by the impulse divided by the time interval Δt over which the force acts:

$$\overline{\mathbf{F}} = \frac{\mathbf{I}}{\Delta t} = \frac{\Delta \mathbf{p}}{\Delta t}.$$

3. Because impulsive forces acting during a collision are internal to the system of colliding objects, they cancel in pairs and therefore cannot change the momentum of the system. Since a collision takes place in a short time, any external forces have little effect on the system momentum, so that to a good approximation **momentum is conserved during a collision.**
4. If kinetic energy is not conserved during a collision, the collision is **inelastic.** The maximum loss of kinetic energy occurs when the colliding objects stick to-

gether; then the collision is **totally inelastic.** In a totally inelastic collision, the final velocity $\mathbf{v}_f$ is determined entirely by the initial velocities through the momentum conservation equation:

$$m_1\mathbf{v}_{1i} + m_2\mathbf{v}_{2i} = (m_1 + m_2)\mathbf{v}_f,$$

where m_1 and m_2 are the masses of the colliding objects.
5. In an **elastic collision,** kinetic energy is conserved. The relation between the initial and final velocities is governed by conservation of momentum and conservation of energy:

$$m_1\mathbf{v}_{1i} + m_2\mathbf{v}_{2i} = m_1\mathbf{v}_{1f} + m_2\mathbf{v}_{2f}$$

$$\tfrac{1}{2}m_1v_{1i}^2 + \tfrac{1}{2}m_2v_{2i}^2 = \tfrac{1}{2}m_1v_{1f}^2 + \tfrac{1}{2}m_2v_{2f}^2.$$

In the general case, these equations are not sufficient to solve for the final velocities. Additional information, such as the direction of one of the final velocities or the details of the collision, must also be used. In the special case of a one-dimensional collision, the momentum and energy conservation equations combine to determine completely the final velocities:

$$v_{1f} = \frac{m_1 - m_2}{m_1 + m_2}v_{1i} + \frac{2m_2}{m_1 + m_2}v_{2i}$$

$$v_{2f} = \frac{2m_1}{m_1 + m_2}v_{1i} + \frac{m_2 - m_1}{m_1 + m_2}v_{2i}.$$

QUESTIONS

1. Halley's Comet spends most of its 76-year orbital period moving slowly a long way from the sun. Does it make sense to treat its roughly 6-month close encounter with the sun as a collision? Discuss.
2. Why do we require a short time interval and strong impulsive forces for an interaction to qualify as a collision? What is meant by "short" and "strong" in this context?
3. Can the impulse associated with an impulsive force be zero even if the force is not always zero?
4. When a ball bounces off a wall, its momentum is reversed. How can this be, in view of the law of conservation of momentum?
5. A high jumper runs to the takeoff point with horizontal but no vertical momentum. When he jumps, where does his vertical momentum come from?

6. As you jump off a table, you bend your knees on landing. How does this lessen the shock to your body?

7. To what height does a bouncing ball return if the collision is elastic? Explain.

8. Must the analysis of a collision between two objects ever require consideration of all three dimensions? Explain.

9. Why are cars designed so that their front ends crush during an accident?

10. Discuss the relative advantages and disadvantages of air bags and seat belts for automotive safety during collisions.

11. Give three everyday examples of inelastic collisions.

12. Is it possible to have an inelastic collision in which *all* the kinetic energy of the colliding objects is lost? If not, why not? If so, give an example.

13. In our discussion of equal-mass elastic collisions, we argued that hydrogen-containing substances should make good moderators for nuclear reactors. Yet some reactors use graphite (a form of carbon) moderators. What can you say about the amount of graphite needed versus the amount of water in a water-moderated reactor? (The reactor that exploded at Chernobyl in the Soviet Union in 1986 used graphite as its moderator; the large amounts of burning graphite made the accident especially serious.)

14. If you want to stop the neutrons in a reactor, why not use massive nuclei like lead?

15. Photons—particles of light—carry momentum and energy but have no intrinsic mass. When an electron and a positron (the electron's antiparticle) collide, they annihilate to form a pair of photons. If the electron and positron were initially moving straight toward each other at the same speed, what can you conclude about the directions of the two photons? Would it be possible for just one photon to be created in this annihilation? Why or why not? Is mass conserved in the annihilation? Could energy be conserved?

16. Discuss the conservation principles used in the analysis of the ballistic pendulum. When is each valid?

17. A truck collides with an identical-looking truck initially at rest. The two move off together with more than half the original speed of the moving truck. What can you conclude about their relative loads?

18. Is it possible to have a collision during which the kinetic energy of the colliding particles increases? Explain.

19. How could you generalize the concept of energy to reinstitute the conservation of energy principle for inelastic collisions?

20. Ty Cobb slides into second base. His kinetic energy has been dissipated as heat, but where did his momentum go?

21. Does a batted ball go farther if the pitch is thrown faster, all other factors being equal? Explain.

22. Why is it relatively safe (though not recommended, of course!) to drop a lead weight on your foot if your foot is not in direct contact with the ground?

23. A downward-moving gas molecule collides with a downward-moving piston in an automobile engine. Comment on the speeds of each after the collision, and on any transfer of energy that might take place. How are such collisions important to the operation of the engine?

24. Two identical satellites are going in opposite directions in the same circular orbit, when they collide head-on. Describe their subsequent motion if the collision is (a) elastic or (b) inelastic.

___ **PROBLEMS** ___

Section 10.1 *Impulse and Collisions*

1. While doing aerobic dancing, you jump up 32 cm (that is, your center of mass rises that far). On the way down, you bend your knees as your feet hit the ground, lowering your center of mass an additional 12.0 cm in the 0.050 s it takes for your body to stop. If your mass is 60 kg, what are (a) the impulse and (b) the average impulsive force? Compare with the force of gravity on you.

2. A 59-g tennis ball is thrown straight up, and at the peak of its trajectory is hit by a racket that exerts a horizontal force given by $F = at - bt^2$, where t is the time in milliseconds from the instant the racket first contacts the ball, and where $a = 1200$ N/ms and $b = 400$ N/ms^2. The ball separates from the racket after 3.0 ms. Find (a) the impulse, (b) the average impulsive force, and (c) the ball's speed just after it leaves the racket.

3. What is the impulse imparted by the force shown in Fig. 10–15?

Fig. 10–15 Problem 3

4. Explosive bolts separate a 950-kg communications satellite from its 640-kg booster rocket. If the impulse of the explosion is 350 N·s, at what relative speed do the satellite and booster separate?

5. A 727 jetliner in level flight with a total mass of 8.6×10^4 kg encounters a downdraft lasting 1.3 s. During this time, the plane acquires a downward velocity component of 85 m/s. Find (a) the impulse and (b) the average impulsive force on the plane.

6. Find the magnitude of the impulse imparted to the stars in Example 10-6.

Section 10.2   *Collisions and the Conservation Laws*

7. At the peak of its trajectory, a 1.0-kg projectile moving horizontally at 15 m/s collides with a 2.0-kg projectile at the peak of a vertical trajectory. If the collision takes 0.10 s, how good is the assumption that momentum is conserved during the collision? To find out, compare the change in momentum of the colliding system with the system's total momentum.

8. An object like a ball used in a sporting event can be characterized by its **coefficient of restitution,** defined as the ratio of outgoing to incident speed when the ball collides with a rigid surface. The coefficient of restitution of a typical tennis ball is about 0.7. What fraction of the ball's kinetic energy is lost at each bounce?

Section 10.3   *Inelastic Collisions*

9. In a railroad switchyard, a 45-ton freight car is sent at 8.0 mi/h toward a 28-ton car that is moving in the same direction at 3.4 mi/h. (a) What is the speed of the pair after they couple together? (b) What fraction of the initial kinetic energy was lost in the collision?

10. In a totally inelastic collision between two equal masses, one of which is initially at rest, show that half the initial kinetic energy is lost.

11. A sled and child with a total mass of 33 kg are moving horizontally at 10 m/s when a second child leaps on with negligible speed. If the sled's speed drops to 6.4 m/s, what is the mass of the second child?

12. In an ice-show stunt, a 70-kg skater dressed as a baseball player catches a 150-g baseball moving at 23 m/s. (a) If the skater was initially at rest, what is his final speed? (b) If the catch takes 36 ms, what is the average impulsive force exerted by the ball?

13. A mass m collides totally inelastically with a mass M initially at rest. Show that a fraction $M/(m+M)$ of the initial kinetic energy is lost in the collision.

14. A 1200-kg Toyota and a 2200-kg Buick collide at right angles in an intersection. They lock together and skid 22 m; the coefficient of friction is 0.91. Show that at least one car must have exceeded the 25 km/h speed limit in effect at the intersection.

15. Astronomers warn that there is a nonzero chance of earth colliding inelastically with a substantial asteroid (Fig. 10-1). Impact speed of the asteroid might be 10 km/s. Estimate the mass of an asteroid needed (a) to alter earth's orbital speed by 0.01%; (b) to release energy equivalent to all the world's nuclear arsenal, about 16,000 megatons. (See Appendix D.)

16. Two identical trucks have mass 5500 kg when empty. One truck carries a 9500-kg load and is moving at 65 km/h. It collides inelastically with the second truck, which is initially at rest, and the pair moves off at 40 km/h. What is the load of the second truck?

17. Two pendulum bobs of equal length are suspended from the same point, and one is released from a distance h as shown in Fig. 10-16. When the first bob hits the second, the two stick together. Show that the maximum height to which the combination rises is $\frac{1}{4}h$.

Fig. 10-16   Problem 17

18. A 5.4-kg hawk is diving at 18 m/s on a northward path at 65° to the horizontal when it grabs a 1.2-kg pigeon in its talons. If the pigeon was flying horizontally at 14 m/s in the same direction as the hawk's horizontal motion, what is the velocity of the pair just after the catch?

19. A 400-mg popcorn kernel is skittering across a nonstick frying pan at 8.2 cm/s when it pops and breaks into two equal-mass pieces. If one piece ends up at rest, how much energy was released in the popping?

20. A 1300-kg car moving at 10 km/h collides with a 1600-kg car moving in the same direction at 6.6 km/h. The first car is equipped with spring-loaded bumpers to prevent damage. If the spring constant is 28,000 N/m, find the maximum compression of the spring.

21. Two identical objects with the same initial speed collide and stick together. If the composite object moves with half the initial speed of either object, what was the angle between the initial velocities?

Section 10.4   *Elastic Collisions*

22. An alpha particle (^{4}He) strikes a stationary gold nucleus (^{197}Au) head-on. What fraction of the alpha particle's kinetic energy is transferred to the gold nucleus? Assume the collision is totally elastic.

23. While playing ball in the street, a child accidentally tosses a ball at 18 m/s toward the front of a car moving toward him at 14 m/s. What is the speed of the ball after it rebounds elastically from the car?

24. A block of mass m undergoes a one-dimensional elas-

tic collision with a block of mass M initially at rest. If both blocks have the same speed after the collision, how are their masses related?

25. Blocks B and C have masses $2m$ and m, respectively, and are at rest on a frictionless surface. Block A, also of mass m, is heading at speed v toward block B, as shown in Fig. 10–17. If all subsequent collisions are elastic, determine the final velocity of each block.

Fig. 10–17 Problem 25

26. A block of mass m_1 undergoes a one-dimensional elastic collision with an initially stationary block of mass m_2. Find an expression for the fraction of the initial kinetic energy transferred to the second block, and plot your result for mass ratios m_1/m_2 from 0 to 20. Show also that, for a given mass ratio, the energy transfer is the same no matter which mass is initially at rest.

27. Rework Example 10–5 using a frame of reference in which the carbon nucleus is initially at rest.

28. Two buses are approaching each other at 60 km/h relative to the road. The driver of one bus tosses a tennis ball straight ahead at 20 km/h relative to his bus. The ball bounces elastically off the vertical windshield of the second bus, and back to the driver who threw it. At what speed relative to the driver is it going when caught? Neglect gravity.

29. An object collides elastically with an equal-mass object initially at rest. If the collision is not head-on, show that the final velocity vectors are perpendicular.

30. On ice, a 3.2-kg rock moving at 1.0 m/s collides elastically with a 0.35-kg rock initially at rest. The smaller rock goes off at an angle of 45° to the larger rock's initial motion. What are the final speeds of the two rocks? What is the direction of the larger rock?

31. Two pendulums of equal length $\ell = 50$ cm are suspended from the same point. The pendulum bobs are steel spheres with masses of 140 and 390 g. The more massive bob is drawn back to make a 15° angle with the vertical (Fig. 10–18). When it is released the bobs

Fig. 10–18 Problem 31

collide elastically. What is the maximum angle made by the less massive pendulum?

32. Derive Equation 10–9b.

33. A particle of mass m collides elastically with a particle of mass $3m$. The more massive particle moves off at 1.2 m/s at 17° to the original direction of the less massive particle. The less massive particle moves off at 0.92 m/s at 48° to its original direction. Find the initial speeds of both particles.

34. A proton of mass 1.007 u is travelling through the bubble chamber of a particle accelerator at 2.4×10^5 m/s when it strikes a stationary deuteron (mass 2.014 u). The proton is deflected through an angle of 37°. Assuming the collision is elastic, what are the final velocities of the two particles?

35. A tennis ball moving at 18 m/s strikes the 45° hatchback of a car moving away at 12 m/s, as shown in Fig. 10–19. Both speeds are given with respect to the ground. What is the velocity of the ball with respect to the ground after it rebounds elastically from the car? *Hint:* Work in the frame of reference of the car; then transform to the ground frame.

Fig. 10–19 Problem 35

36. Rework Example 10–6 for the case when the star initially at rest is three times as massive as the other star.

37. Two identical billiard balls are initially at rest when they are struck symmetrically by a third identical ball moving with velocity $\mathbf{v}_0 = v_0\hat{\mathbf{i}}$, as shown in Fig. 10–20. Find the velocities of all three balls after they undergo an elastic collision.

Fig. 10–20 Problem 37

Supplementary Problems

38. You set a small ball of mass m atop a large ball of mass $M \gg m$ and drop the pair from a height h. Assuming the balls are perfectly elastic, show that the smaller ball rebounds to a height $9h$.

39. A 1400-kg car moving at 75 km/h runs into a 1200-kg car moving in the same direction at 50 km/h. The two cars lock together and both drivers immediately slam on their brakes. If the cars come to rest in a distance of 18 m, what is the coefficient of friction?

40. To show that elastic collisions among electrons and

protons are not very effective at transferring energy, estimate the number of head-on collisions an electron must make with stationary protons ($m_p = 1800m_e$) before it has lost half its *initial* energy. *Hint:* Determine the fractional energy *remaining* with the electron. With each collision, the energy is further reduced by that factor. See Problem 26.

41. Consider a one-dimensional elastic collision with $m_1 \ll m_2$ and m_2 initially at rest. In discussing this extreme case, we neglected m_1 altogether and showed that m_1 then rebounds with its initial speed. Now use the binomial theorem (see Appendix A) to show that a better approximation gives a rebound speed that is less than the incident speed by an amount $2m_1v_1/m_2$ for the case $m_1 \ll m_2$. In applying the binomial theorem, keep terms of order m_1/m_2, but neglect terms of order m_1^2/m_2^2.

42. Repeat the preceding problem for the case $m_1 \gg m_2$, and show that the less massive object moves off with speed given approximately by $2v_1(1 - m_2/m_1)$, where v_1 is the initial speed of the more massive object.

43. How many head-on collisions must a neutron (mass 1.0087 u) make with stationary ^{12}C nuclei (mass 11.9934 u) in a graphite-moderated nuclear reactor in order to lose as much energy as it would in a water-moderated reactor where it collides with a single proton (mass 1.0073 u)? *Hint:* See hint in Problem 40.

44. A 200-g block is released from rest 25 cm high on a frictionless 30° incline. It slides down the incline, then along a frictionless surface until it collides elastically with an 800-g block at rest 1.4 m from the bottom of the incline (Fig. 10–21). How much later do the two blocks collide again?

Fig. 10–21 Problem 44

45. A block of mass M is moving at speed v_0 on a frictionless surface that ends in a rigid wall. Farther from the wall is a more massive block of mass αM, initially at rest (Fig. 10–22). The less massive block undergoes elastic collisions with the other block and with the wall, and the motion of both blocks is confined to one dimension. (a) Show that the two blocks will undergo only one collision if $\alpha \leq 3$. (b) Show that the two blocks will undergo two collisions if $\alpha = 4$, and determine their final speeds. (c) Find out how many collisions the two blocks will undergo if $\alpha = 10$, and determine their final speeds.

Fig. 10–22 Problem 45

46. Use a computer to investigate the number of collisions in the previous problem as a function of the mass ratio α, and plot the collision number versus α for values of α from 1 to 500.

47. A 1200-kg car moving at 25 km/h undergoes a one-dimensional collision with an 1800-kg car initially at rest. The collision is neither elastic nor totally inelastic; the kinetic energy lost is 5800 J. Find the speeds of both cars after the collision.

11

TORQUE AND STATIC EQUILIBRIUM

What keeps the steelworker of Fig. 11–1 alive? Two things: First, the cable is strong enough to provide the tension force necessary to counteract the weight of the beam and the steelworker. Second, the forces on the beam are applied in such a way that there is no tendency for the beam to rotate. The steelworker remains in static equilibrium, neither accelerating nor rotating. Both conditions—force balance and no tendency to rotate—are necessary to maintain static equilibrium. In this chapter, we explore these conditions and their application in practical situations.

Fig. 11–1
A steelworker in static equilibrium.

11.1
TORQUE

The first condition for static equilibrium—zero net force on a body—is familiar from our study of Newton's laws. If there is no net force on a body, then its center of mass cannot accelerate. If at rest, the center of mass will remain at rest. But the body could still rotate, as in Fig. 11–2. To prevent such rotation, it is not enough that the forces on a body sum to zero; those forces must also be applied in such a way that they cancel each other's tendency to rotate the body.

Figure 11–3 shows a beam supported by a cable. The beam, in turn, supports two equal weights hung from its ends. The tension in the cable is equal to the total weight, so that there is no net force on the beam. The right-hand weight tends to rotate the beam clockwise, but this tendency is counteracted by an equal counterclockwise effect from the left-hand weight, so that the system is in static equilibrium. If we move one of the weights, the system will begin to rotate (Fig. 11–4).

This simple example suggests that the tendency of a system to rotate is determined not only by the magnitude and direction of applied forces, but also by *where* those forces are applied. The concept of **torque** quantifies the

Fig. 11–2
Even though there is no net force on the beam, it may still rotate!

torque

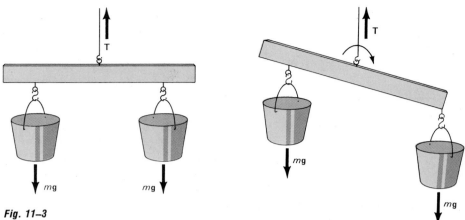

Fig. 11–3
A system in static equilibrium.

Fig. 11–4
If one of the weights in Fig. 11–3 is moved, the system goes out of equilibrium.

relation between applied force and the tendency of a body to rotate. As Fig. 11–5 suggests, the torque—the tendency to rotate—is greater for greater distances from the pivot point to the point where the force is applied. Figure 11–6 suggests further that for a given force, the important quantity is the perpendicular distance from the pivot point to the line along which the force acts. We call this distance the **lever arm,** $r_\perp$, and write

lever arm

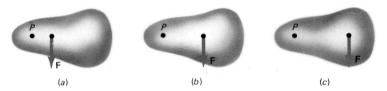

(a)   (b)   (c)

Fig. 11–5
Torque increases with distance from pivot P to the force application point. The same force **F** produces the greatest torque in (c).

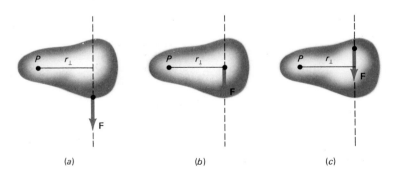

(a)   (b)   (c)

Fig. 11–6
Torque depends on the perpendicular distance $r_\perp$—called the lever arm—from the pivot P to the line along which the force acts. Because $r_\perp$ and **F** are the same in cases (a) through (c), the torque in each case is the same.

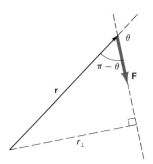

Fig. 11–7
The lever arm is given by
$r \sin(\pi - \theta) = r \sin\theta$.

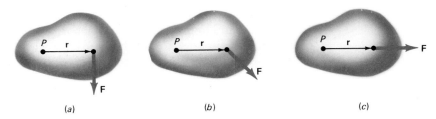

Fig. 11–8
The torque is greatest with **F** and **r** at right angles, and is zero when they are collinear.

$$\tau = r_{\perp}F \qquad (11-1)$$

for the magnitude τ of the torque about a pivot point arising from a force **F** with lever arm $r_{\perp}$. Equation 11–1 shows that the units of torque are newton-meters (N·m), the same as those of energy. However, torque and energy are two different things, so that we call one newton-meter a joule only when it refers to energy.

Figure 11–7 shows that the lever arm $r_{\perp}$ is given by $r_{\perp} = r \sin\theta$, where r is the length of the vector **r** from the pivot point to the force application point, and θ the angle between **r** and the force vector **F**. Then Equation 11–1 for the magnitude of the torque may be written.

$$\tau = rF \sin\theta. \qquad (11-2)$$

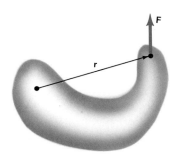

Fig. 11–9
The vector **r** always extends from the pivot point to the force application point, even for a concave body.

For a given force F and distance r, the torque is greatest when the vectors **F** and **r** are at right angles, and goes to zero as the two vectors become collinear (Fig. 11–8). Physically, you can see that no matter how hard you pull to the right in Fig. 11–8c, you can't cause the body to rotate about P because you are pulling in line with the pivot point. We emphasize that the vector **r** always points straight from the pivot point to the force application point. Although this vector often lies entirely within the body, this need not be the case (Fig. 11–9).

Example 11–1
Torque

A square slab of wood 20 cm on a side is free to pivot about a horizontal axis through its center. A 200-g mass is suspended from the lower right corner of the body, as shown in Fig. 11–10. Find the torque exerted by the weight of the 200-g mass about the axis of the slab.

Solution

To find the torque we must evaluate the right-hand side of Equation 11–1 or 11–2. For Equation 11–2 the distance r from the pivot point to the force application point is half a diagonal, or $10\sqrt{2}$ cm, while the angle θ is $\pi/4$ radians, or 45°, whose sine is $\sqrt{2}/2$. The mass exerts a force mg, so that the torque is

$$\tau = r F \sin\theta = (0.10\sqrt{2} \text{ m})(0.20 \text{ kg})(9.8 \text{ N/kg})(\sqrt{2}/2) = 0.20 \text{ N·m}.$$

We could solve this problem more easily by noting from Fig. 11–10 that the lever arm $r_{\perp}$ is just 10 cm, so that the torque is

$$\tau = r_{\perp}F = (0.10 \text{ m})(0.20 \text{ kg})(9.8 \text{ N/kg}) = 0.20 \text{ N·m}.$$

Fig. 11–10
Example 11–1

Rotation

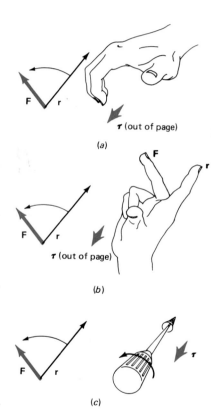

Fig. 11–11
The right-hand rule. Curl the fingers of your right hand in the direction that a torque would tend to rotate a system. Then your right thumb points in the direction of the torque.

τ (out of page)

(a)

τ (out of page)

(b)

τ (out of page)

(c)

Fig. 11–12
Right-hand rules for the direction of torque and, more generally, for the cross product of two vectors. Rules (a), (b), and (c) are equivalent.

Does torque have direction? The torque in Example 11–1 tends to rotate the slab clockwise. The torques due to the weights in Fig. 11–3 are in opposite directions, and therefore cancel. We could specify the direction of a torque by its tendency to rotate a system either clockwise or counterclockwise (we call this the "sense" of the rotation), and it is often simplest to visualize torques in this way. But it is mathematically more convenient to treat torque like any other quantity with magnitude and direction—like a vector. We define the direction of the torque vector to be at right angles to the plane in which the torque tends to rotate a body, and in a sense given by the right-hand rule (Fig. 11–11). This definition may seem a little strange, since all the action is in the plane perpendicular to the torque. But there is no unique vector direction within the plane of rotation; in fact, only the direction perpendicular to that plane specifies the orientation of the plane. Torque is only the first of several vector quantities that we will define in this way; we do so because we obtain a unique vector representation that allows us to state physical laws in compact, powerful mathematical form.

Our right-hand rule definition for the direction of the torque is based on a physical consideration—the sense in which the torque would tend to rotate a body. We can form an equivalent but more mathematical right-hand rule for the torque vector by placing the vectors **r** and **F** tail-to-tail and curling the fingers of the right hand in a direction that would rotate **r** until it is aligned with **F**. The right thumb then points in the direction of the torque (Fig. 11–12a). Figure 11–12b and c show equivalent right-hand rules for the direction of the torque vector. Using our right-hand rule and Equation 11–2, we can say that the torque vector has magnitude $\tau = rF\sin\theta$, where θ is the angle between the vectors **r** and **F,** and that its direction is given by applying the right-hand rule to the vectors **r** and **F**. This definition makes it explicit that torque is always specified *with respect to some point*, for the vector **r** is drawn from that point.

Example 11–2

Torque as a Vector

Figure 11–13 shows a 1.8-N force applied 2.5 m from a point O and 1.3 m from a point P. What are the torques about O and P due to **F?**

Solution

Equation 11–2 gives the magnitudes of the torques:

$$\tau_O = r\,F\sin\theta = (2.5\text{ m})(1.8\text{ N})(\sin30°) = 2.3\text{ N·m}$$

and

$$\tau_P = r\,F\sin\theta = (1.3\text{ m})(1.8\text{ N})(\sin45°) = 1.7\text{ N·m}.$$

To determine the direction of the torque about O, we place the two vectors **r** and **F** tail-to-tail (Fig. 11–14) and apply the right-hand rule of Fig. 11–12, showing that the torque is into the page. Equivalently, we could imagine the force **F** rotating a physical object about the point O. Curling our fingers in the clockwise direction of such a rotation, we find again that the torque vector is into the page. A similar analysis shows that the torque about P is out of the page.

The Vector Cross Product

Torque is a vector that is determined entirely by the two other vectors **r** and **F** as described by Equation 11–2 and the right-hand rule. This operation—forming from two vectors **A** and **B** a third vector **C** of magnitude $C = AB\sin\theta$ and direction given by the right-hand rule—occurs frequently in physics. We will encounter it in discussing rotational motion in the next chapter, and later in connection with magnetism. We therefore give this operation a name: the **vector cross product**, often called simply the **cross product**. The vector cross product **C** of two vectors **A** and **B** is written

$$\mathbf{C} = \mathbf{A} \times \mathbf{B}.$$

This expression means to form the vector **C** with magnitude $AB\sin\theta$, where θ is the angle between **A** and **B**, and with **C** perpendicular to both **A** and **B**, as described by the right-hand rule of Fig. 11–12.

Torque is a particular example of a vector cross product, and we can write the torque vector simply as

$$\boldsymbol{\tau} = \mathbf{r} \times \mathbf{F}. \tag{11–3}$$

Having once defined the cross product, we need not give separate and wordy descriptions of the magnitude and direction of torque; both aspects of the torque vector are contained succinctly in Equation 11–3.

The vector cross product **A** × **B** bears some similarity to the dot product $\mathbf{A} \cdot \mathbf{B} = AB\cos\theta$ that we encountered in Chapter 7. Both depend on the product of the magnitudes of the vectors **A** and **B**, and on the angle between them. But where the dot product depends on the cosine of the angle, and is therefore maximum when $\theta = 0$, the cross product depends on the sine, and is maximum for two vectors at right angles. And most significantly, the dot product is a *scalar*—a single number, without direction—while the cross product is a *vector*. Because of this distinction, the two products are often called the scalar product of two vectors and the vector product of two vectors, respectively.

The vector cross product obeys some of the common rules for ordinary multiplication. For example, it is distributive over addition:

$$\mathbf{A} \times (\mathbf{B} + \mathbf{C}) = \mathbf{A} \times \mathbf{B} + \mathbf{A} \times \mathbf{C}.$$

But it is *not* commutative: the order of multiplication *does* matter. In fact

$$\mathbf{B} \times \mathbf{A} = -\mathbf{A} \times \mathbf{B}.$$

You can see this result from the right-hand rule, where rotating **B** into **A** points your thumb in the opposite direction from rotating **A** into **B**.

Fig. 11–13
Example 11–2

Fig. 11–14
Right-hand rule for the vectors of Example 11–2.

Example 11–3
The Vector Cross Product

Find the cross product of the vectors $\mathbf{A} = 3\hat{\imath}$ and $\mathbf{B} = \sqrt{3}\hat{\imath} + \hat{\jmath}$. Do so in two ways: (a) by first finding the directions and magnitudes of the two vectors, and (b) by working in unit vector notation and using the distributive law for cross products.

Solution

To calculate the vector cross product, we need the magnitudes of two vectors and the angle between them. Applying the Pythagorean theorem, we find that

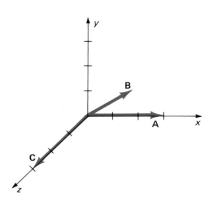

Fig. 11–15
The cross product **C** = **A** × **B** points out
of the page, or in the +z direction.

$$B = \sqrt{B_x^2 + B_y^2} = \sqrt{3 + 1} = 2.$$

The angle **B** makes with the x-axis is

$$\theta = \tan^{-1}\left(\frac{1}{\sqrt{3}}\right) = 30°.$$

The vector **A** lies along the x-axis, so that 30° is the angle between the two vectors. **A** has magnitude 3, so that the magnitude of the cross product is

$$|\mathbf{A} \times \mathbf{B}| = AB\sin\theta = (3)(2)\sin 30° = 3.$$

Rotating **A** into **B** shows that the direction of **A** × **B** is out of the page, or in the +z direction (Fig. 11–15). Then in compact vector notation, we can write

$$\mathbf{A} \times \mathbf{B} = 3\hat{\mathbf{k}}.$$

We could also obtain this result using unit vectors:

$$\mathbf{A} \times \mathbf{B} = (3\hat{\mathbf{i}}) \times (\sqrt{3}\hat{\mathbf{i}} + \hat{\mathbf{j}}) = 3\sqrt{3}(\hat{\mathbf{i}} \times \hat{\mathbf{i}}) + 3(\hat{\mathbf{i}} \times \hat{\mathbf{j}}).$$

What about the cross products of the unit vectors? The angle between $\hat{\mathbf{i}}$ and itself is zero, so that the first cross product is simply zero. The angle between $\hat{\mathbf{i}}$ and $\hat{\mathbf{j}}$ is 90°, and each unit vector has length 1. Therefore, the magnitude of $\hat{\mathbf{i}} \times \hat{\mathbf{j}}$ is 1 and from the right-hand rule we see that $\hat{\mathbf{i}} \times \hat{\mathbf{j}}$ points in the +z direction (Fig. 11–16). Therefore, $\hat{\mathbf{i}} \times \hat{\mathbf{j}}$ is simply the unit vector $\hat{\mathbf{k}}$. In general, the cross product of any two different unit vectors is ± the third unit vector, with the + sign taken when the vectors are in cyclic order $\hat{\mathbf{i}}\hat{\mathbf{j}}\hat{\mathbf{k}}\hat{\mathbf{i}} \ldots$.* Our product **A** × **B** is therefore simply $3\hat{\mathbf{k}}$, as we found before.

11.2
STATIC EQUILIBRIUM

Having defined torque, we are now ready to make a rigorous statement of the conditions for a body to be in static equilibrium:

static equilibrium   A body is in static equilibrium when the net force and the net torque on the body are both zero.

Zero net force ensures that the center of mass does not accelerate; zero net torque ensures that the body has no tendency to rotate.

To determine whether a body is in static equilibrium, we draw a diagram showing all forces acting on the body. The first condition for equilibrium is met by requiring that there be no net force:

$$\sum \mathbf{F}_i = 0. \tag{11–4}$$

The second condition requires zero net torque:

$$\sum \boldsymbol{\tau}_i = \sum (\mathbf{r}_i \times \mathbf{F}_i) = 0. \tag{11–5}$$

The subscripts i in Equations 11–4 and 11–5 label the different forces that act on a body, the radius vectors from a pivot point to the different force application points, and the associated torques.

---

right-handed coordinate
system *If you ever wonder which way to put the axes in an xyz coordinate system, just choose their directions so that these unit vector cross products work out. Then you have a **right-handed coordinate system,** consistent with all the right-hand rules used in physics.

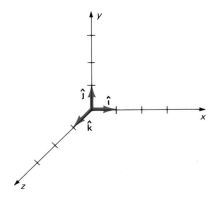

Fig. 11–16
Cross product of any two unit vectors is the third unit vector when the two are taken in cyclic order $\hat{\imath}\hat{\jmath}\hat{k}\hat{\imath}$ . . . and is the opposite of the third unit vector when taken in the reverse order.

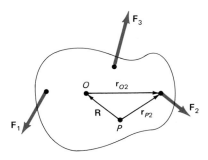

Fig. 11–17
The forces sum to zero, and the torques about O sum to zero. Is the net torque about P also zero?

There seems to be an ambiguity in Equation 11–5, for we have not specified the point to be used in evaluating the radius vectors $\mathbf{r}_i$. But a body in equilibrium must not rotate about *any* point, so that Equation 11–5 must hold no matter what point we choose to evaluate the torques. Must we then apply Equation 11–5 to every possible point? No! If the first equilibrium condition ($\Sigma\mathbf{F}_i = 0$) is satisfied, then it suffices to show that the sum of the torques about any arbitrary point is zero. We can prove this fact using Fig. 11–17, which shows an object subject to several forces whose vector sum is zero. Suppose also that the net torque about point O is zero. What about the torque about point P? This torque is given by

$$\boldsymbol{\tau}_P = \sum(\mathbf{r}_{Pi} \times \mathbf{F}_i), \qquad (11\text{–}6)$$

where $\mathbf{r}_{Pi}$ is the vector from P to the application point of $\mathbf{F}_i$. Let $\mathbf{R}$ be the vector from P to O. Then, as suggested in Fig. 11–17 for the case $i = 2$, we can write

$$\mathbf{r}_{Pi} = \mathbf{R} + \mathbf{r}_{Oi},$$

where $\mathbf{r}_{Oi}$ is the vector from O to the application point of $\mathbf{F}_i$. Using this expression in Equation 11–6, we have

$$\begin{aligned}\boldsymbol{\tau}_P &= \sum(\mathbf{r}_{Oi} + \mathbf{R})\times\mathbf{F}_i = \sum(\mathbf{r}_{Oi}\times\mathbf{F}_i + \mathbf{R}\times\mathbf{F}_i)\\ &= \sum(\mathbf{r}_{Oi}\times\mathbf{F}_i) + \sum(\mathbf{R}\times\mathbf{F}_i) = \sum(\mathbf{r}_{Oi}\times\mathbf{F}_i) + \mathbf{R}\times\sum\mathbf{F}_i,\end{aligned} \qquad (11\text{–}7)$$

where, in the last step, we have taken $\mathbf{R}$ outside the summation since it is the same vector for each term in the sum. The first term on the rightmost side of Equation 11–7 is just the net torque about O, which we have assumed to be zero. The second term is the cross product of the vector $\mathbf{R}$ with the net force on the body. But we have assumed the net force to be zero. Thus the net torque about P is also zero. Since the location of P is quite arbitrary, our result shows that if the net force on an object is zero, and the net torque about *some* point is zero, then the net torque about *any* point is also zero.

This result is useful in solving equilibrium problems, for it allows us to choose any convenient point about which to evaluate the torques. An appropriate point is usually the point of application of one of the forces, for then the torque due to that force is zero. The problem is thus simplified, since the torque sum in Equation 11–5 has one fewer term than it would otherwise.

Example 11–4
Equilibrium and the Choice of Pivot Point

A 5.0-m-long canoe is tied at bow and stern to a pair of trees so that it rides parallel to the shore, as shown in Fig. 11–18. The tie ropes are perpendicular to the shore. A paddler boards the canoe 1.0 m from the stern, in the process exerting an outward force of 200 N at right angles to the shore. Find the tensions in the two ropes, if the canoe remains in static equilibrium. Assume that buoyancy of the water balances the gravitational force and that the torques resulting from these two forces exactly cancel, so that you need only consider equilibrium in the horizontal plane.

Fig. 11–18
Top view of canoe in Example 11–4.

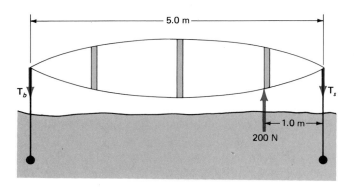

Solution

All three horizontal forces are perpendicular to the shore, so that the first equilibrium condition, Equation 11–4, becomes the single scalar equation

$$T_b + T_s - 200 \text{ N} = 0. \tag{11–8}$$

We can choose any point for our pivot; if we choose one of the force application points, then that force will not appear in the torque equation. Since the tensions are the unknowns, choosing either end of the canoe as our pivot will eliminate one unknown from the torque equation. Choosing the stern, the torque equation 11–5 becomes

$$(5.0 \text{ m})(T_b) - (200 \text{ N})(1.0 \text{ m}) = 0,$$

where the first term is the torque due to the force of the paddler and the second is the torque due to the bow-rope tension T_b. Here we take as positive a torque tending to produce counterclockwise rotation, so that the bow-rope torque has a negative sign. Solving for T_b gives

$$T_b = \frac{(200 \text{ N})(1.0 \text{ m})}{5.0 \text{ m}} = 40 \text{ N}.$$

Using this result in Equation 11–8 gives

$$T_s = 200 \text{ N} - T_b = 200 \text{ N} - 40 \text{ N} = 160 \text{ N}.$$

Suppose we had chosen the center of the canoe as our pivot point. The force-balance equation 11–8 would be unchanged, but the torque equation would now contain three terms:

$$(2.5 \text{ m})(T_b) + (1.5 \text{ m})(200 \text{ N}) - (2.5 \text{ m})(T_s) = 0,$$

where again we adopt the convention that a torque tending to produce counterclockwise rotation is positive. The three terms are due to the bow rope, the paddler, and the stern rope, respectively, and the distances are measured from the canoe center. Note that now the bow-rope and paddler torques have the same sign, since both tend to produce counterclockwise rotation about the canoe center. We can solve Equation 11–8 for T_s to get

$$T_s = 200 \text{ N} - T_b.$$

Using this result in the torque equation gives

$$(2.5 \text{ m})(T_b) + (1.5 \text{ m})(200 \text{ N}) - (2.5 \text{ m})(200 \text{ N} - T_b) = 0,$$

so that

$$T_b = \frac{(2.5 \text{ m})(200 \text{ N}) - (1.5 \text{ m})(200 \text{ N})}{5.0 \text{ m}} = 40 \text{ N},$$

as before. Although we get the same answer, the algebra is considerably more complicated with this choice of pivot point.

In Example 11–4, all the forces are perpendicular to the shore, and, as the right-hand rule shows, all the torque vectors point either vertically upward or downward. As a result, the two vector equations 11–4 and 11–5 reduce to two scalar equations in two unknowns. More generally, though, the forces can have components along any of three mutually perpendicular directions. With all three force components present, there will also be three components of torque that must sum to zero. In this most general case, then, Equations 11–4 and 11–5 become six scalar equations in six unknowns.

Often we have a situation in which all the forces lie in a single plane, so that Equation 11–4 has only two components. If we choose our pivot point to lie in the plane defined by the force vectors, then all torques will be perpendicular to that plane, so that the torque equation has only one component, making a total of three equations in three unknowns.

11.3
CENTER OF GRAVITY

One force often present is gravity, which acts on all parts of a body (Fig. 11–19). We already know how to calculate the vector sum of these gravitational forces—it is just $M\mathbf{g}$. But what about the torques due to all the gravitational forces acting on different parts of the body? Summing these torques, we have

$$\boldsymbol{\tau} = \sum \mathbf{r}_i \times \mathbf{F}_i = \sum \mathbf{r}_i \times m_i \mathbf{g} = \left(\sum m_i \mathbf{r}_i \right) \times \mathbf{g}, \qquad (11\text{–}9)$$

where $\mathbf{F}_i$ is the gravitational force on the ith mass element, and $\mathbf{r}_i$ is the vector from some pivot point to that mass element (Fig. 11–20). We can rewrite Equation 11–9 by multiplying the right-hand side by M/M, where M is the total mass of the body:

$$\boldsymbol{\tau} = \left(\frac{\sum m_i \mathbf{r}_i}{M} \right) \times M\mathbf{g}.$$

The term in parentheses is just the location of the center of mass (see Section 9.1), while the right-hand term is the total weight of the body. Therefore, the net torque on the body due to gravity is just that of the gravitational force $M\mathbf{g}$ acting at the center of mass. In general, the point at which the gravitational force seems to act is called the **center of gravity**. We have just proven that the center of gravity coincides with the center of mass when the gravitational field is uniform—that is, when $\mathbf{g}$ is the same for all mass elements in the body. If a body is large enough that the variation in magnitude or direction of $\mathbf{g}$ is significant over the object, then the two

Fig. 11–19
The gravitational force acts everywhere on an extended body.

Fig. 11–20
Calculating the torque produced by an individual mass element about the pivot point O.

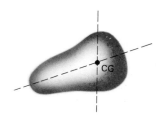

(a)   (b)

Fig. 11–21
The object is in equilibrium only when its center of gravity lies directly below the suspension point.

Fig. 11–22
The intersection of vertical lines from each suspension point is at the center of gravity.

points may not coincide (see Problem 35), although this is not a situation we usually encounter.

We can easily locate the center of gravity by suspending an object from a string or rope attached to its edge. The torque about the suspension point is due entirely to gravity, and is zero only if the center of gravity lies directly beneath that point (Fig. 11–21). In equilibrium, a vertical line from the suspension point must therefore pass through the center of gravity. If we now change the suspension point, we can determine another line that passes through the center of gravity. These two lines intersect in a single point, which must be the center of gravity (Fig. 11–22).

Example 11–5
Static Equilibrium

A 25-kg traffic signal is suspended over the center of a road by the structure shown in Fig. 11–23. The structure is secured to a concrete foundation with two bolts, as shown. What is the tension in the left-hand bolt?

Solution

Figure 11–24 shows a force diagram for the structure. There are four downward forces, which are the weights of each of the components of the structure. These forces are applied at the centers of gravity of the various components. There is also a downward force **T**, exerted by the tension in the left-hand bolt, and an upward contact force F_c, exerted by the foundation at the point where the right-hand bolt attaches. The condition of force balance (Equation 11–4) becomes

$$m_1g + m_2g + m_3g + m_4g + T - F_c = 0, \qquad (11\text{–}10)$$

where we have adopted the convention that a downward force is positive. We are free to evaluate torques about any point. A convenient choice is the point O, where the axis of the vertical member intersects the concrete base. Then the lever arm, $r\sin\theta$, for each force is the horizontal distance x_i from the vertical axis to the force application point, so the torque-balance condition (Equation 11–5) becomes

$$m_1gx_1 + m_2gx_2 + m_3gx_3 + m_4gx_4 - Tx_5 - F_cx_6 = 0. \qquad (11\text{–}11)$$

Here we adopt the convention that a torque tending to produce clockwise rotation is positive, and that all distances x_i are positive numbers, so that the last two terms are negative. The fourth term, m_4gx_4, is actually zero since $x_4 = 0$, but we retain this term in symbolic form for mathematical convenience.

We can solve Equation 11–10 for the contact force F_c to get

$$F_c = g\sum m_i + T,$$

where we have factored out g and used the summation symbol, $\sum$, to indicate the sum of the four masses. Using this expression in Equation 11–11 gives

$$g\sum m_ix_i - Tx_5 - (g\sum m_i + T)x_6 = 0,$$

where again we have factored out g and used the summation symbol. We can now solve for T:

$$g\sum m_ix_i - gx_6\sum m_i - T(x_5 + x_6) = 0,$$

so that

$$T = \frac{g\left(\sum m_ix_i - x_6\sum m_i\right)}{x_5 + x_6}.$$

Fig. 11–23
Example 11–5

Fig. 11–24
Force diagram for structure of Fig.
11–23. Force vectors are not drawn to
scale.

The second sum is just the total mass, 495 kg, while the first is

$$\sum m_i x_i = (25\ \text{kg})(8.0\ \text{m}) + (150\ \text{kg})(4.0\ \text{m}) + (20\ \text{kg})(1.5\ \text{m}) + 0 = 830\ \text{kg·m},$$

where we have neglected the relatively small radius of the vertical member in figuring the distances to the centers of mass of the horizontal and diagonal members. The fourth term in this sum is zero because the vertical member stands directly above the point about which the torques are evaluated (that is, $x_4 = 0$), and thus contributes nothing to the net torque. Then the bolt tension is

$$T = \frac{(9.8\ \text{m/s}^2)[830\ \text{kg·m} - (0.38\ \text{m})(495\ \text{kg})]}{0.38\ \text{m} + 0.38\ \text{m}} = 8.3 \times 10^3\ \text{N},$$

or nearly one ton! Engineers are responsible for ensuring that bolts and fittings on structures like this are sufficiently strong.

Example 11–6

Static Equilibrium

A board of mass m and length L is resting against a wall, as shown in Fig. 11–25. The wall is frictionless, while the coefficient of static friction between board and floor is μ. What is the minimum angle θ at which the board can be placed without slipping? Evaluate for the case $\mu = 0.27$, $L = 2.4$ m, $m = 5.0$ kg.

Solution

Figure 11–26 shows a force diagram for the board. In addition to the board's weight, there are normal forces F_1 and F_2 at the floor and wall, and a frictional force at the floor. We have expressed the frictional force in terms of the normal force of the floor, F_1, and the coefficient of static friction, μ (see Section 5.2), because the

Fig. 11–25
Example 11–6

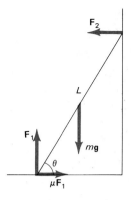

Fig. 11–26
In addition to its weight, two normal forces and a frictional force act on the board.

minimum angle occurs when the force of static friction takes its maximum value μF_1. This frictional force acts to oppose slipping of the board, and so points toward the wall. The equation of force balance now has both horizontal and vertical components:

$$F_1 - mg = 0; \quad \text{(vertical)} \tag{11–12}$$

$$\mu F_1 - F_2 = 0. \quad \text{(horizontal)} \tag{11–13}$$

Two forces are applied at the bottom of the board, so that if we choose this point to calculate the torques, we eliminate two of the forces from the torque equation. The remaining torques arise from the normal force $\mathbf{F}_2$ acting through the lever arm $L\sin\theta$ and from the gravitational force mg acting through the lever arm $\frac{1}{2}L\cos\theta$, as suggested in Fig. 11–26. Taking counterclockwise rotation as positive, the torque balance equation may then be written

$$LF_2\sin\theta - \tfrac{1}{2}Lmg\cos\theta = 0.$$

Having written the equations of force and torque balance, we have completed the essential physics of the problem. The rest is just algebra. We rewrite the torque equation in the form

$$\tan\theta = \frac{\sin\theta}{\cos\theta} = \frac{mg}{2F_2}. \tag{11–14}$$

We can find F_2 by solving Equations 11–12 and 11–13 for both normal forces F_1 and F_2. Equation 11–12 gives

$$F_1 = mg,$$

so that Equation 11–13 can be written

$$\mu mg = F_2.$$

Using this result in Equation 11–14 gives

$$\tan\theta = \frac{mg}{2\mu mg} = \frac{1}{2\mu},$$

so that

$$\theta = \tan^{-1}\left(\frac{1}{2\mu}\right).$$

This is a remarkably simple result—it doesn't depend on the length or mass of the board, or on g. Does it make sense? As the coefficient of friction goes to zero, the tangent of θ grows without bound, and θ approaches 90°. With no friction, we can lean the board against the wall only if it is vertical. Increasing the coefficient of friction allows us to lean the board at ever lower angles. When $\mu = 0.27$, we have

$$\theta = \tan^{-1}\left[\frac{1}{(2)(0.27)}\right] = 62°.$$

What if the wall had not been frictionless? Then we would have had an additional frictional force at the top. Although the physics of the situation would have been nearly the same, the algebra would be more complicated. Problem 20 explores this more realistic case.

Example 11–7

Equilibrium in the Human Body

Figure 11–27 depicts a section of a human arm. The forearm measures 32 cm from elbow joint to center of palm and has a mass $m = 2.7$ kg, with center of mass located 14 cm from the elbow joint. The biceps muscle attaches to the radius (fore-

Fig. 11–27
A human arm.

Biceps

Humerus

80°

Elbow pivot

CM

3.6 cm

14 cm

32 cm

arm bone) 3.6 cm from the elbow joint. With the humerus (upper arm bone) vertical and the forearm horizontal, the biceps muscle makes an 80° angle with the horizontal. If a pumpkin of mass $M = 4.5$ kg rests on the palm, what are the tensions in the biceps and the forces exerted on the elbow joint?

Solution

To solve this problem, we redraw the arm in schematic form, showing all the forces acting on it (Fig. 11–28). In addition to the weights **m**g and **M**g of the arm and pumpkin, the tension force **T** in the biceps and the contact force **F**$_c$ at the elbow joint also act on the arm. Denoting the horizontal and vertical components of the contact force by F_1 and F_2, the equations of force balance become

$$T \cos\theta - F_1 = 0, \quad \text{(horizontal)} \tag{11–15}$$

and

$$T \sin\theta - F_2 - mg - Mg = 0. \quad \text{(vertical)} \tag{11–16}$$

We now have two equations in the three unknowns T, F_1, and F_2. A third equation is provided by the condition that there be no net torque on the arm. Choosing the elbow joint as our pivot to eliminate the contact force from the torque equation gives

$$\ell_1 T \sin\theta - \ell_2 mg - \ell_3 Mg = 0$$

for the condition of torque balance. Here the ℓ's are the distances from the elbow to the biceps, the center of mass of the arm, and the pumpkin, respectively. We have taken a counterclockwise rotation as positive. Solving the torque equation for the biceps tension T gives

$$T = \frac{(\ell_2 m + \ell_3 M)g}{\ell_1 \sin\theta}$$

$$= \frac{[(0.14 \text{ m})(2.7 \text{ kg}) + (0.32 \text{ m})(4.5 \text{ kg})](9.8 \text{ N/kg})}{(0.036 \text{ m})(\sin 80°)}$$

$$= 500 \text{ N}.$$

Equations 11–15 and 11–16 then give the components of the elbow contact force:

$$F_1 = T \cos\theta = (500 \text{ N})(\cos 80°) = 87 \text{ N},$$

and

$$F_2 = T \sin\theta - (m + M)g$$

$$= (500 \text{ N})(\sin 80°) - (2.7 \text{ kg} + 4.5 \text{ kg})(9.8 \text{ N/kg}) = 420 \text{ N}.$$

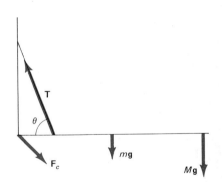

T

θ

F_c

m**g**

M**g**

Fig. 11–28
A simplified picture of the arm, showing the forces acting.

This example shows that the human body often sustains forces far larger than the weights of objects it may be lifting.

Application

Restoring the Statue of Liberty

In 1986, workers completed major renovation of the Statue of Liberty, France's famous gift to the United States that was first dedicated in 1886. Although its designer, French sculptor Frédéric-Auguste Bartholdi, suggested that his creation should last as long as Egypt's pyramids, many factors conspired to make major renovation necessary after only one century. These include corrosion from air pollution and from a chemical reaction between the iron framework and the copper skin, as well as an assembly change that resulted in excess torques on the statue's structural members.

Sculptor Bartholdi was no engineer, and without the work of the French engineer Eiffel (of tower fame) the statue could not have maintained itself in static equilibrium. Eiffel designed an inner skeleton of iron to provide the forces necessary to counteract the weights and torques associated with components of the statue, as well as with the force exerted by wind (Fig. 11–29). The statue was constructed in France in 300 separate pieces, then shipped to New York. During assembly, probably as a conscious aesthetic decision, Liberty's head and upraised arm were mounted 2 feet from their locations on Eiffel's plan, with the arm making a

Fig. 11–29
The interior skeleton of the Statue of Liberty counteracts forces and torques associated with the statue itself as well as with the wind. This computer drawn image of Liberty's skeleton aided architects planning the restoration. (See color plate 1.)

Fig. 11–30
The Statue of Liberty's head and arm are offset from their originally planned positions, resulting in greater than expected forces and torques on structural members.

As built

Eiffel's plan

greater angle to the vertical than planned (Fig. 11–30). As a result, the statue's head had a nonzero lever arm about the central support, resulting in a significant torque. More importantly, the arm exerted a much greater torque about the shoulder than planned, resulting in forces greater than anticipated on structural components. For historical integrity, renovators did not return to Eiffel's original design; instead, they reinforced the support structure to withstand better the excess forces and torques.

11.4
STABILITY OF STATIC EQUILIBRIA

Fig. 11–31
Stable (left) and unstable (right) equilibria.

What if a body is disturbed from static equilibrium? Then, in general, it will experience nonzero net forces or torques, and it will accelerate or begin to rotate. Figure 11–31 shows two very different possibilities for the subsequent behavior of a body displaced slightly from equilibrium. On the left, a slight displacement results in a torque that moves the body back toward its equilibrium position. Although the body may rock back and forth for a while, any friction or other dissipation will soon sap the body's energy and it will settle back into its original equilibrium. On the right in Fig. 11–31, the torque arising from a slight displacement swings the body away from its original equilibrium. The former situation is an example of **stable equilibrium,** the latter of **unstable equilibrium.** Nearly all the equilibria we encounter in nature are stable, for a body in unstable equilibrium will not remain that way for any significant time. The slightest disturbance will set it in motion, and if it eventually stops, it will be in a very different equilibrium state from its original one.

stable equilibrium

unstable equilibrium

neutral stability

metastability

The distinction between stable and unstable equilibria is often subtler than Fig. 11–31 would imply. Figure 11–32 shows a ball in four different equilibrium situations. Clearly situation (a) is stable, while (b) is unstable. Situation (c) is neither stable nor unstable; it is termed **neutrally stable.** But what about situation (d)? For very small disturbances, the ball will return to its original state, so that the equilibrium is stable. But for larger disturbances—large enough to push the ball just over the highest points on the hill—it is unstable. Such an equilibrium is called **conditionally stable** or **metastable.** Most equilibria are conditionally stable. Figure 11–33 shows a rectangular block in two equilibrium situations. Although both are stable against small disturbances, the vertical orientation is less stable in the sense that it is easier to dislodge it from its stable situation and send it crashing down on its side.

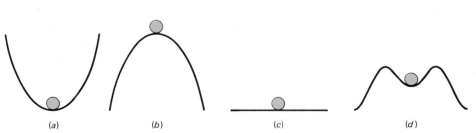

(a)   (b)   (c)   (d)

Fig. 11–32
Stable, unstable, neutrally stable, and conditionally stable equilibria.

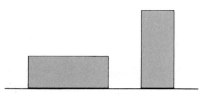

Fig. 11–33
Both equilibria are stable against very small disturbances, but even a modest disturbance will bring the vertical block into an unstable situation.

The stability of an equilibrium is closely associated with the potential energy of the system in equilibrium. In Fig. 11–32, for example, the shapes of the hills and valleys reflect the gravitational potential energy of the ball as a function of position. In all cases of equilibrium, the ball is at a minimum or maximum of the potential energy curve—at a place where the derivative of potential energy with respect to position is zero. For the stable and metastable equilibria, the potential energy at equilibrium is a minimum, at least with respect to positions immediately adjacent to equilibrium. A deviation from equilibrium requires that work be done against a net force that tends to restore the ball to its equilibrium position. The unstable equilibrium, in contrast, occurs at a maximum in the potential energy. Here, a deviation from equilibrium results in lower potential energy and in a net force that tends to accelerate the ball farther from equilibrium. For the neutrally stable equilibrium, there is no change whatever in potential energy as we move away from equilibrium; consequently the ball experiences no force.

The potential energy curve for the rectangular block of Fig. 11–33 is less obvious. But we can develop that curve by considering the height of the center of mass as the block is tipped. In both cases, tipping the block requires that the center of mass be raised, thereby raising the potential energy. Figure 11–34 shows the location of the center of mass as we tilt the block through various orientations. The path traced out by the center of mass is the potential energy curve for the block. From this curve we see immediately that there are two stable equilibria of lowest potential energy corresponding to the block lying on either side. Similarly, there are two metastable states corresponding to the block standing vertically on either end. In between are unstable equilibria that occur when the block is balanced on a corner so that its center of mass is just over the balance point. Disturbed from these unstable states, the block experiences a net torque that rotates it toward one of the stable or metastable states.

We can sum up our understanding of equilibrium and potential energy in two simple mathematical statements. First, equilibrium requires a local maximum or minimum in the potential energy, so that

$$\frac{dU}{dx} = 0, \qquad \text{(equilibrium condition)} \qquad (11\text{–}17)$$

where U is the potential energy of a system and x is a variable describing the configuration of that system. For the simple systems we have been considering, x measures the position or orientation of an object, but with more complicated systems it may represent other quantities such as the system's volume or even its composition. For a stable equilibrium, we require a local

Fig. 11–34
As the block is tilted, its center of mass traces out a potential energy curve. Shown are two stable equilibria (ends), a metastable equilibrium (center), and two unstable equilibria (tilted blocks).

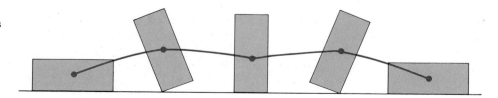

minimum, so that the potential energy curve is concave upward. Mathematically,

$$\frac{d^2U}{dx^2} > 0. \quad \text{(stable equilibrium)} \quad (11\text{--}18)$$

This condition applies to metastable equilibria as well, for they are *locally* stable. In contrast, unstable equilibrium occurs where the potential energy has a local maximum, so that

$$\frac{d^2U}{dx^2} < 0. \quad \text{(unstable equilibrium)} \quad (11\text{--}19)$$

The intermediate case $d^2U/dx^2 = 0$ corresponds to neutral stability.

Example 11–8

Stability of Equilibria

Solid-state physicists developing a new semiconductor device theorize that the potential energy of an electron in a region of the device should be given by

$$U(x) = ax^2 - bx^4,$$

where x is the electron's position measured in angstrom units (1 Å $= 10^{-10}$ m), U is its energy in electron volts (1 eV $= 1.6 \times 10^{-19}$ J), and constants a and b are given by $a = 8$ eV/Å^2 and $b = 1$ eV/Å^4. Locate the equilibrium positions for the electron, and describe their stability.

Solution

Equilibrium occurs where the potential energy has a minimum or maximum, so that $dU/dx = 0$. Taking the derivative of the potential energy and setting it to zero gives

$$0 = \frac{dU}{dx} = 2ax - 4bx^3 = 2x(a - 2bx^2) = 2x(8 - 2x^2) = 4x(4 - x^2) \text{ eV/Å},$$

where for mathematical clarity we have not bothered to write the units except in the final answer. This equation is satisfied if $x = 0$ or if $4 - x^2 = 0$, so that $x = \pm 2$. Therefore, the electron is in equilibrium at $x = -2$ Å, at $x = 0$ Å, or at $x = 2$ Å. To determine the stability of these equilibria, we evaluate the second derivative at each equilibrium position:

$$\frac{d^2U}{dx^2} = 2a - 12bx^2 = 16 - 12x^2 \text{ eV/Å}^2,$$

so that

$$\left(\frac{d^2U}{dx^2}\right)_{x = \pm 2} = 16 - (12)(4) = -32 \text{ eV/Å}^2$$

and

$$\left(\frac{d^2U}{dx^2}\right)_{x = 0} = 16 - 0 = 16 \text{ eV/Å}^2.$$

From conditions 11–18 and 11–19, we see that the equilibria at $x = \pm 2$ Å are unstable, while the equilibrium at $x = 0$ Å is locally stable. Figure 11–35 shows a plot of the potential energy curve, which makes clear the location and stability of the equilibria.

Fig. 11–35
Potential energy curve for Example 11–8.

Questions of stability apply not only to the physical locations of individual particles but also to the overall arrangements of the basic constituent particles that comprise matter. A mixture of hydrogen and oxygen, for example, is in metastable equilibrium at room temperature—the individual atoms are at local minima in their potential energy curves, as in Fig. 11–32d or Fig. 11–35. Applying a lighted match to the mixture adds enough energy to bring some of the atoms over the maxima in their potential energy curves, at which point the atoms can rearrange into a state of much lower potential energy—the state we call water (H_2O). Energy released in the process maintains the reaction, until virtually all the atoms have rearranged themselves into the lower-energy state. Since no state of lower potential energy is available to its constituent particles, the water molecule is quite stable, as opposed to the explosively metastable mixture of hydrogen and oxygen. Similarly, a uranium nucleus is at a local minimum in its potential energy curve—a minimum determined by the interplay of nuclear and electrical forces. But if it gains a small amount of excess energy, the nucleus may fission—split—into two smaller nuclei whose total potential energy is much lower. This transition from a less stable to a more stable equilibrium describes the basic physics of nuclear fission.

Potential energy curves for complex structures like molecules or skyscrapers cannot be described fully by simple one-dimensional graphs, for the configurations of these structures can be altered in many different ways. If potential energy varies with position in several different directions, for example, then we must consider all possible changes in potential energy in order to determine stability. A snowbank sitting on a saddle-shaped pass between two mountain peaks, or any other system with a saddle-shaped potential energy curve (Fig. 11–36), is stable with respect to displacements in one direction but not in another. Stability analysis of complex physical systems, ranging from nuclei and molecules to bridges and fusion reactors and on to stars and galaxies, is an important part of contemporary work in engineering and science.

Fig. 11–36
A saddle-shaped potential energy curve. Saddle point P is an equilibrium position that is stable in one direction but not in another.

SUMMARY

1. **Torque** describes the tendency of a force to produce a rotation of an object about a point. The torque about a given pivot point depends on the magnitude of the force and on the perpendicular distance, or **lever arm,** from the pivot point to the line along which the force vector lies. Mathematically, the torque about a point O is a vector given by

   $$\boldsymbol{\tau} = \mathbf{r} \times \mathbf{F},$$

   where $\mathbf{r}$ is a vector from point O to the point where the force $\mathbf{F}$ is applied. The product in this expression is the **vector cross product,** defined as a vector whose magnitude is given by

   $$\tau = rF \sin\theta$$

   and whose direction is determined by the right-hand rule: curl the fingers of your right hand in a way that rotates the vector $\mathbf{r}$ onto the vector $\mathbf{F}$, and your right thumb points in the direction of the cross product $\boldsymbol{\tau} = \mathbf{r} \times \mathbf{F}$.

2. A body at rest is in **static equilibrium** only when there is no net force on the body and no net torque about any point:

   $$\sum \mathbf{F} = 0$$

   and

   $$\sum \boldsymbol{\tau} = 0.$$

   If the first condition is met, and the second holds for some point, then it holds for all points.

3. When the gravitational force acts on an extended body, its effect in producing a torque is that of a single force acting at a point that is called the **center of gravity.** If the gravitational field is the same throughout the body, the center of gravity coincides with the center of mass.

4. An equilibrium state is **stable** if a small displacement from equilibrium results in forces and/or torques that tend to restore the equilibrium. It is **unstable** if small displacements result in forces and/or torques that move the system farther from its original equilibrium. A **metastable** equilibrium is stable against very small displacements but becomes unstable if larger displacements occur. Stability properties of a system are closely related to its potential energy curve. Stable and metastable equilibria occur at minima of the potential energy curve, unstable equilibria at maxima. Mathematically,

$$\frac{dU}{dx} = 0, \quad \text{(equilibrium condition)}$$

$$\frac{d^2U}{dx^2} > 0, \quad \text{(stable or metastable equilibrium)}$$

and

$$\frac{d^2U}{dx^2} < 0. \quad \text{(unstable equilibrium)}$$

The intermediate case $d^2U/dx^2 = 0$ is termed **neutral stability.**

QUESTIONS

1. Why is the direction of the torque vector taken to be perpendicular to the plane in which the torque tends to rotate a body?
2. Figure 11–37 shows four forces acting on a body. What are the directions of each of the associated torques about the point O? About the point P?

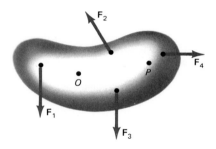

Fig. 11–37   Question 2

3. The best way to lift a heavy weight is to squat with your back vertical, rather than to lean over (Fig. 11–38). Why?

Right   Wrong

Fig. 11–38   Right and wrong ways to lift a heavy weight (Question 3).

4. Give an example of an object on which the net force is zero but which is not in static equilibrium.

5. As the beam of Fig. 11–4 rotates, does the torque on it remain constant? Explain.
6. Give an example of an object on which the net torque about the center of gravity is zero but which is not in static equilibrium. Is the net torque about all points zero in this case? Explain.
7. Estimate the torque you apply when tightening the wheel nuts of a car after changing a flat tire.
8. Some screwdrivers have flat shanks to which a wrench can be attached. How does this help increase the torque applied to a screw?
9. Pregnant women often assume a posture in which the shoulders are held well back of their normal position. Explain in terms of torque and center of gravity.
10. A large, irregularly shaped asteroid of uniform density is falling toward earth in the orientation shown in Fig. 11–39. Which is closer to earth, the asteroid's center of gravity or its center of mass?

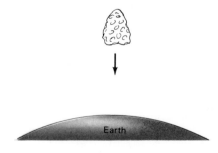

Fig. 11–39   Question 10

11. When you carry a bucket full of water with one hand, you often find it easier if you extend your opposite arm. Why?
12. Is a ladder more likely to slip when you stand near the top or the bottom? Explain.
13. How does a heavy keel on a boat help prevent the boat from tipping over?
14. In addition to wings, most airplanes have a smaller set of horizontal surfaces near the tail. Why? What

does this configuration suggest about the location of the wings relative to the center of gravity of the plane?

15. Why is a beer bottle less stable if stood on its top rather than on its base?

16. Stars end their lives containing a greater proportion of helium and other heavier elements than they had originally. What does this change say about the relative stability of matter arranged as helium and heavier elements versus the same matter arranged as hydrogen?

17. Why is a "balancing rock" (Fig. 11–40) such an unusual phenomenon?

Fig. 11–40   A balancing rock (Question 17).

PROBLEMS

Section 11.1   *Torque*

1. A rod is free to pivot about one end, and a force is applied at the other end, as shown in Fig. 11–41. What is the torque about the pivot point?

Fig. 11–41   Problem 1

Fig. 11–42   Problem 2

2. A pulley 12 cm in diameter is free to rotate about a horizontal axle. A 220-g mass and a 470-g mass are tied to either end of a massless string, and the string is hung over the pulley, as shown in Fig. 11–42. If the string does not slip, what torque must be applied to keep the pulley from rotating?

3. A car tune-up manual calls for tightening the spark plugs to a torque of 25 ft·lb. If the plugs are tightened by pulling at right angles to the end of a wrench 10 in long, how much force must be applied to the wrench?

4. Two arm wrestlers are deadlocked in the position shown in Fig. 11–43. Each arm is 34 cm long and makes a 60° angle with the horizontal; the contact force at the hands is 180 N. What is the torque each exerts about the other's elbow? Neglect the weights of the wrestlers' arms.

Fig. 11–43   Problem 4

5. Figure 11–44 shows the forces acting on a sailboat. These include the weight of the boat, 2200 N, acting at the center of gravity C; the upward buoyancy force of the water, acting at point B; and the force of the wind, acting horizontally at point A. Along an axis through the mast of the boat, point C lies 1.4 m below point B, and point A lies 4.2 m above B. The boat is heeled with its mast 30° to the vertical. What is the force of the wind?

6. What are the net force and the net torque about the origin due to the following forces?

$\mathbf{F}_1 = 2.0\hat{\imath} - 0.80\hat{\jmath}$ N,
applied at $\mathbf{r}_1 = -1.3\hat{\imath}$ m

$\mathbf{F}_2 = 1.0\hat{\imath} + 2.6\hat{\jmath} - 1.4\hat{k}$ N,
applied at $\mathbf{r}_2 = -0.70\hat{\imath} + 1.1\mathbf{j}$ m

$\mathbf{F}_3 = 1.7\hat{\jmath}$ N,
applied at $\mathbf{r}_3 = -2.6\hat{k}$ m

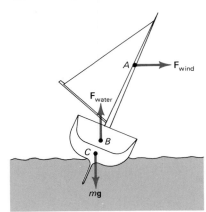

Fig. 11–44   Problem 5

7. What is the cross product of the vectors $\mathbf{A} = \hat{\imath} - 2\hat{\jmath} + 3\hat{k}$ and $\mathbf{B} = 2\hat{\imath} + 4\hat{\jmath} + 2\hat{k}$?

8. Vector **A** has length 1 and points along the positive x-axis. Vector **B** extends from the origin to the point (2,2). Evaluate the vector cross product $\mathbf{A} \times \mathbf{B}$.

9. Given the vectors $\mathbf{A} = 2\hat{\imath} + 3\hat{\jmath}$, $\mathbf{B} = \hat{\imath} - 2\hat{\jmath}$, and $\mathbf{C} = 4\hat{\imath} + 2\hat{\jmath}$, find the following: (a) $\mathbf{A} \times \mathbf{B}$; (b) $\mathbf{A} \times \mathbf{C}$; (c) $\mathbf{B} \times \mathbf{C}$; (d) $\mathbf{A} \times (\mathbf{B} \times \mathbf{C})$; (e) $(\mathbf{A} \times \mathbf{B}) \times \mathbf{C}$; (f) $\mathbf{C} \cdot (\mathbf{A} \times \mathbf{B})$.

10. A rod of length ℓ has forces acting everywhere perpendicular to its length, as shown in Fig. 11–45. The rod lies along the x-axis, and the force per unit length is given by

$$\frac{dF}{dx} = \frac{F_0}{\ell}\left[1 - \left(\frac{x}{\ell}\right)^2\right].$$

Determine the magnitude of (a) the total force on the rod; (b) the torque about the end $x = 0$; (c) the torque about the end $x = \ell$.

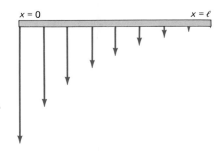

Fig. 11–45   Problem 10

Sections 11.2 and 11.3   *Static Equilibrium and Center of Gravity*

11. A 4.2-m-long beam is supported by a cable at its center. A 65-kg steelworker stands at one end of the beam. Where should a 190-kg bucket of concrete be suspended if the beam is to be in static equilibrium?

12. Two pulleys are mounted on a horizontal axle, as shown in Fig. 11–46. The inner pulley has a diameter of 6.0 cm, the outer a diameter of 20 cm. Cords are wrapped around both pulleys so that they do not slip. In the configuration shown, with what force must a person pull on the outer rope in order to support the 40-kg mass?

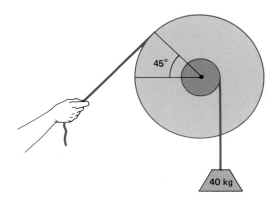

Fig. 11–46   Problem 12

13. A 23-m-long log of irregular cross section is lying horizontally, supported by a wall at one end and a cable attached 4.0 m from the other end, as shown in Fig. 11–47. The log weighs 7.5×10^3 N, and the tension in the cable is 6.2×10^3 N. Where is the log's center of gravity?

Fig. 11–47   Problem 13

14. Figure 11–48 shows an outstretched arm with a mass of 4.2 kg. The arm is 56 cm long, and its center of gravity is 21 cm from the shoulder. The hand at the end of the arm holds a 6.0-kg mass. (a) What is the torque about the shoulder due to the weights of the arm and the 6.0-kg mass? (b) If the arm is held in

equilibrium by the deltoid muscle, whose force on the arm acts 5.0° below the horizontal at a point 18 cm from the shoulder joint (Fig. 11–49), what is the force exerted by the muscle?

Fig. 11–48   Problem 14

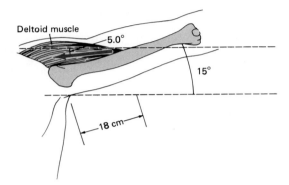

Fig. 11–49   Deltoid muscle (Problem 14).

15. Figure 11–50 shows how a scale with a capacity of only 250 N can be used to weigh a much heavier person. The board is 3.0 m long, has a mass of 3.4 kg, and is of uniform density. It is free to pivot about the end farthest from the scale. What is the weight of a person standing 1.2 m from the pivot end, if the scale reads 210 N? Assume that the beam remains nearly horizontal.

Fig. 11–50   Problem 15

16. Figure 11–51 shows a portable infant seat that is supported by the edge of a table. The mass of the seat is 1.5 kg, and its center of mass is located 16 cm from the table edge. A 12-kg baby is sitting in the seat with her center of mass over the seat's center of mass. Find the forces F_A and F_B that the seat exerts on the table.

Fig. 11–51   Problem 16

17. A 15.0-kg door measures 2.00 m high by 75.0 cm wide. It hangs from hinges mounted 18.0 cm from top and bottom. Assuming that each hinge carries half the door's weight, determine the horizontal and vertical forces that the door exerts on each hinge.

18. Figure 11–52 shows a popular system for mounting bookshelves. An aluminum bracket is mounted on a vertical aluminum support by small tabs inserted into vertical slots. If each bracket in a shelf system supports 32 kg of books, with center of gravity 12 cm out from the vertical support, what is the horizontal component of the force exerted on the upper of the two bracket tabs? Assume contact between the bracket and support occurs only at the upper tab and at the bottom of the bracket, 4.5 cm below the upper tab.

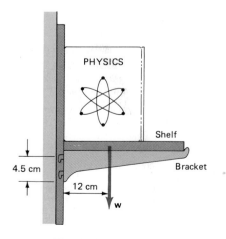

Fig. 11–52   Problem 18

19. Figure 11–53 shows a house designed to have high "cathedral" ceilings. Following a heavy snow, the total mass supported by each diagonal roof rafter is 170 kg, including building materials as well as snow. Under these conditions, what is the force in the horizontal tie beam near the roof peak? Is this force a compression or a tension? Neglect any horizontal component of force due to the vertical walls below the roof. Ignore the widths of the various structural components, treating contact forces as though they were concentrated at the roof peak and at the outside edge of the rafter/wall junction.

Fig. 11–53   Problem 19

20. Repeat Example 11–6, now assuming that the coefficient of friction at the floor is μ_1 and that at the wall μ_2. Show that the minimum angle at which the ladder will not slip is now given by

$$\theta = \tan^{-1}\left(\frac{1-\mu_1\mu_2}{2\mu_1}\right).$$

21. A uniform sphere of radius R is supported by a rope attached to a vertical wall, as shown in Fig. 11–54. The point where the rope is attached to the sphere is

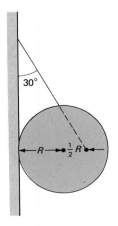

Fig. 11–54   Problem 21

located so that a continuation of the rope would intersect a horizontal line through the sphere's center a distance $R/2$ beyond the center, as shown. What is the smallest possible value for the coefficient of friction between wall and sphere?

22. Show that if the wall in the previous problem is frictionless, then a continuation of the rope line must pass through the center of the sphere.

23. A garden cart loaded with firewood is being pushed horizontally when it encounters a step 8.0 cm high, as shown in Fig. 11–55. The mass of the cart and its load is 55 kg, and the cart is balanced so that its center of mass is directly over the axle. The wheel diameter is 60 cm. What is the minimum horizontal force that will get the cart up the step?

Fig. 11–55   Problem 23

24. A 3.0-m-long ladder is leaning against a frictionless vertical wall, with which it makes a 15° angle. The mass of the ladder is 5.0 kg, uniformly distributed over its length. The coefficient of friction between ladder and ground is 0.42. Can a 65-kg person climb to the top of the ladder without its slipping? If not, how high can the person climb? If so, how massive a person would make the ladder slip?

25. The boom in the crane of Fig. 11–56 is free to pivot about point P and is supported by the cable that joins halfway along its 18-m total length. The cable passes over a pulley and is anchored at the back of the crane. The boom has a mass of 1700 kg, distributed uniformly along its length, and the mass hanging from

Fig. 11–56   Problem 25

the end of the boom is 2200 kg. The boom makes a 50° angle with the horizontal. What is the tension in the cable that supports the boom?

26. A uniform board of length ℓ and weight W is suspended between two vertical walls by ropes of length $\ell/2$ each. When a weight w is placed on the left end of the board, it assumes the configuration shown in Fig. 11–57. Find weight w in terms of the board weight W.

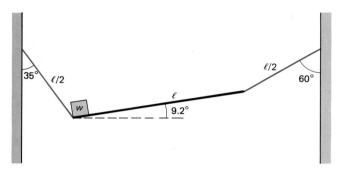

Fig. 11–57   Problem 26

Section 11.4   *Stability of Static Equilibria*

27. A roly-poly toy clown is made from part of a sphere topped by a cone. The sphere is truncated at just the right point so that there is no discontinuity in angle as the surface changes from sphere to cone (Fig. 11–58a). If the clown always returns to an upright position, what is the maximum possible height for its center of mass? Would your answer change if the continuity-of-angle condition were not met, as in Fig. 11–58b?

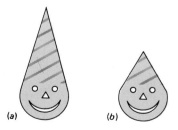

Fig. 11–58   Problem 27

28. The potential energy as a function of position for a certain electron is given by

$$U = U_0[1 - e^{(x-x_1)^2/x_2^2}],$$

where x is the electron's position and x_1 and x_2 are constants. Find any equilibria of this electron, and determine their stability.

29. A uniform rectangular block is twice as long as it is wide. Letting θ be the angle that the long dimension makes with the horizontal (Fig. 11–59), determine the angular positions of any static equilibria, and comment on their stability.

Fig. 11–59   Problem 29

30. The potential energy as a function of position for a certain particle is given by

$$U(x) = U_0\left(\frac{x^3}{x_0^3} + a\frac{x^2}{x_0^2} + 4\frac{x}{x_0}\right),$$

where U_0, x_0, and a are constants. For what values of a will there be two static equilibria? Comment on the stability of these equilibria.

Supplementary Problems

31. Suppose that the forces of Problem 6 are applied to a body. Show that it is not possible using a single additional force to put the body into static equilibrium. Find two additional forces, and their application points, that will result in static equilibrium. *Hint:* Think about the geometrical relationship of vectors in the cross product. You may also find the vector dot product useful.

32. Show that the cross product $\mathbf{A} \times \mathbf{B}$ of vectors $\mathbf{A} = a_x\hat{\mathbf{i}} + a_y\hat{\mathbf{j}} + a_z\hat{\mathbf{k}}$ and $\mathbf{B} = b_x\hat{\mathbf{i}} + b_y\hat{\mathbf{j}} + b_z\hat{\mathbf{k}}$ is given by

$$\mathbf{A} \times \mathbf{B} = (a_yb_z - a_zb_y)\hat{\mathbf{i}} + (a_zb_x - a_xb_z)\hat{\mathbf{j}} + (a_xb_y - a_yb_x)\hat{\mathbf{k}}.$$

33. Show that $\mathbf{A} \cdot (\mathbf{A} \times \mathbf{B})$ is zero for any two vectors $\mathbf{A}$ and $\mathbf{B}$.

34. A uniform solid cone of height h and base diameter $\frac{1}{3}h$ is placed on an incline, as shown in Fig. 11–60. The coefficient of static friction between cone and in-

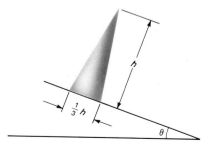

Fig. 11–60   Problem 34

cline is 0.63. As the slope of the incline is increased, will the cone first begin to slip or to tip over? At what angle would each occur? *Hint:* Begin with an integration to locate the center of mass of the cone.

35. A huge interstellar spacecraft from an advanced civilization is hovering above earth, as shown in Fig. 11–61. The ship consists of two small pods, each of mass m, separated by a rigid shaft of negligible mass that is one earth radius (R_e) long. The ship is hovering with one pod a distance R_e directly above earth's north pole and with the main axis of the ship parallel to the equatorial plane. (a) Find the net gravitational force on the ship (magnitude and direction), expressed in terms of the pod mass m and earth's surface gravity g. (b) Find the net torque on the ship about its center of mass. (c) Locate the center of gravity of the ship, and compare with the location of the center of mass.

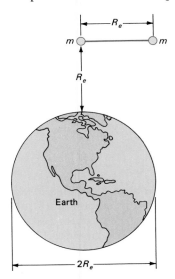

Fig. 11–61 Problem 35

12

ROTATIONAL MOTION

When a nonzero net force acts on an object, Newton's law tells us that the object accelerates. What happens when a nonzero net torque acts? Then the rotational motion of the object changes. We could describe this rotation without reference to torque, if we chose to consider the forces, accelerations, and velocities associated with each particle making up an object. That would be a difficult task, and would not give us much insight into the behavior of the object as a whole. Instead, we will develop a description of rotational motion that closely parallels what we know about motion as described by Newton's laws. We already established part of that description when we defined torque, which we can think of as the rotational analog of force.

12.1
ANGULAR VELOCITY AND ACCELERATION

Angular Speed

angular speed

Consider a record rotating on a turntable. If we described this motion in terms of linear velocity and acceleration, we would have to say that each point on the record has a different speed—depending on its distance from the center of the record—and a different acceleration to hold it in its circular path. But the record is a rigid body—all its parts maintain fixed positions relative to one another—so it is simpler to say that the entire record rotates at $33\frac{1}{3}$ revolutions per minute (rpm). When we say this, we are talking about **angular speed**—the rate at which the angular position of any point on the record changes. In this case, our unit of angle is one full revolution (360° or 2π radians), and our unit of time is the minute. We could equally well have expressed angular speed in revolutions per second (rev/s), degrees per second (°/s), or radians per second (rad/s). Because of the mathematically simple status of radian measure, we often use radians in calculations involving rotational motion.

We use the Greek symbol ω (omega) for angular speed, and define

average angular speed $\overline{\omega}$ as:

$$\overline{\omega} = \frac{\Delta\theta}{\Delta t}, \tag{12–1}$$

where $\Delta\theta$ is the change in angle occurring in the time Δt (Fig. 12–1). When the angular speed is constant, its value at any instant is the same as its average value. When angular speed is changing, we define **instantaneous angular speed** as the limit of the average angular speed taken over arbitrarily short time intervals:

$$\omega = \lim_{\Delta t \to 0} \frac{\Delta\theta}{\Delta t} = \frac{d\theta}{dt}. \tag{12–2}$$

These definitions are analogous to our definitions of average and instantaneous linear speed introduced in Chapter 2. The only difference is the use of angular displacement $\Delta\theta$, rather than linear displacement Δx.

Knowing the angular speed of a rotating object, we can easily find the linear speed of any point on the object. Recall that an angle in radian measure is defined as the ratio of subtended arc length to radius (Fig. 12–2):

$$\theta = \frac{s}{r}. \tag{12–3}$$

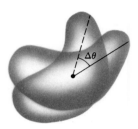

Fig. 12–1
A rigid body rotates through the angle $\Delta\theta$ in time Δt. Its average angular speed is $\Delta\theta/\Delta t$.

Differentiating this expression with respect to time gives

$$\frac{d\theta}{dt} = \frac{1}{r}\frac{ds}{dt},$$

since the radius r is constant. But $d\theta/dt$ is the angular speed, and ds/dt is the linear speed, v, so that $\omega = v/r$, or

$$v = \omega r. \tag{12–4}$$

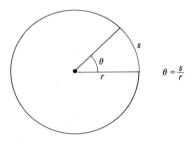

Fig. 12–2
The angle θ in radians is the ratio of the arc length s to the radius r.

Thus the linear speed of any point on a rotating object is proportional both to the angular speed of the object and to the distance from that point to the axis of rotation (Fig. 12–3). A word of caution: Equation 12–4 was derived from the definition of angle in radians, and holds only for angular speed measured in radians per unit time. For other measures of angle, a proportionality constant must be included in the relation among v, ω, and r (see Problem 3). Furthermore, Equation 12–4 is valid only for rotation about a fixed rotation axis. In Section 12.3 we will consider the more general case of an object—like a rolling wheel—whose rotation axis is itself in motion.

Example 12–1
Angular Speed

A record 30.5 cm in diameter is rotating at $33\frac{1}{3}$ rpm. Find its angular speed in rad/s, and determine the linear speed of a point on its outer edge.

Solution

One revolution is 2π radians, and one minute is 60 seconds, so that

$$\omega = 33\tfrac{1}{3} \text{ rpm} = \frac{(33\tfrac{1}{3} \text{ rev/min})(2\pi \text{ rad/rev})}{60 \text{ s/min}} = 3.49 \text{ rad/s}.$$

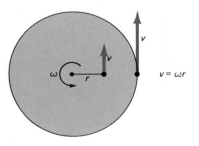

Fig. 12–3
The linear speed of a point in a rotating object is proportional to the angular speed of rotation and the distance from the rotation axis.

This result makes sense, for at $33\frac{1}{3}$ rpm, the record turns a little more than half a revolution—π radians—in one second. From Equation 12–4, we then have

$$v = \omega r = (3.49 \text{ rad/s})\left(\frac{30.5 \text{ cm}}{2}\right) = 53.2 \text{ cm/s.}$$

Angular Acceleration

angular acceleration

If the angular speed of a rotating object changes, then the object undergoes an **angular acceleration,** α, defined analogously to linear acceleration:

$$\alpha = \lim_{\Delta t \to 0} \frac{\Delta\omega}{\Delta t} = \frac{d\omega}{dt}. \tag{12–5}$$

Taking the limit in Equation 12–5 gives the instantaneous angular acceleration; if we do not take the limit, then we have an average value over the time interval Δt. The SI units for angular acceleration are rad/s^2, although we will sometimes use other units such as rpm/s or rev/s^2. Having defined angular acceleration, we can differentiate Equation 12–4 to get a relation between angular acceleration and tangential acceleration a_t of a point a distance r from the axis of rotation:

$$a_t = \frac{dv}{dt} = r\frac{d\omega}{dt} = r\alpha. \tag{12–6}$$

This equation gives only the tangential acceleration—the component tangent to the circular path of a rotating point. There is also a radial acceleration a_r given by

$$a_r = \frac{v^2}{r} = \omega^2 r, \tag{12–7}$$

where we have used Equation 12–4 to express v in terms of ω.

Because angular speed and acceleration are defined in a way that is mathematically analogous to linear speed and acceleration, all the relations among linear position, speed, and acceleration automatically apply among angular position, angular speed, and angular acceleration. For example, angular acceleration is the second time derivative of angular position; angular speed is the integral of angular acceleration. And if angular acceleration is constant, then all our constant-acceleration formulas of Chapter 2 apply when we make the substitutions θ for x, ω for v, and α for a. Table 12–1 summarizes this direct analogy between linear and rotational quantities. With the analogies of Table 12–1, problems involving rotational motion are just like the one-dimensional linear problems you solved in Chapter 2.

Example 12–2
Constant Angular Acceleration

When the record of Example 12–1 finishes, the turntable shuts off and coasts to a halt in 17 s. If the angular acceleration is constant, how many revolutions does the turntable make during this time?

TABLE 12–1 ▬▬▬▬▬▬▬▬▬▬▬▬▬▬▬▬▬▬▬▬▬▬▬▬▬
Angular and Linear Position, Speed, and Acceleration

Linear Quantity or Equation	Angular Quantity or Equation
Position x	Angular position θ
Speed $v = \dfrac{dx}{dt}$	Angular speed $\omega = \dfrac{d\theta}{dt}$
Acceleration $a = \dfrac{dv}{dt} = \dfrac{d^2x}{dt^2}$	Angular acceleration $\alpha = \dfrac{d\omega}{dt} = \dfrac{d^2\theta}{dt^2}$

Equations for Constant Acceleration

$\bar{v} = \frac{1}{2}(v_0 + v)$	(2–12)	$\bar{\omega} = \frac{1}{2}(\omega_0 + \omega)$	(12–8)
$v = v_0 + at$	(2–10)	$\omega = \omega_0 + \alpha t$	(12–9)
$x = x_0 + v_0 t + \frac{1}{2}at^2$	(2–11)	$\theta = \theta_0 + \omega_0 t + \frac{1}{2}\alpha t^2$	(12–10)
$v^2 = v_0^2 + 2a(x - x_0)$	(2–14)	$\omega^2 = \omega_0^2 + 2\alpha(\theta - \theta_0)$	(12–11)

Solution

With constant angular acceleration, the average angular speed during the 17-s stopping time is just the average of the initial $33\frac{1}{3}$ rpm and the final speed of 0 rpm. Then the number of revolutions travelled in this time is

$$\theta = \bar{\omega}t = \tfrac{1}{2}(\omega_0 + \omega)t = \tfrac{1}{2}(33\tfrac{1}{3}\ \text{rev/min} + 0)\left(\frac{17\ \text{s}}{60\ \text{s/min}}\right) = 4.7\ \text{revolutions.}$$

Alternatively, we could have solved for the angular acceleration using $\alpha = \Delta\omega/\Delta t$. Then Equation 12–10 would give the angular displacement $\theta - \theta_0$ during the stopping time. Or we could have used Equation 12–11, setting the final angular speed ω to zero and solving for $\theta - \theta_0$.

Example 12–3 _____

Constant Angular Acceleration

A rotating wheel 80 cm in diameter is decelerating at 0.21 rad/s². What should be the initial angular speed if the wheel is to stop after exactly one revolution? What is the tangential linear deceleration of a point on the wheel's rim?

Solution

Can you see that this problem is exactly like one in which you are asked to find the initial vertical speed needed to throw a ball to a given height? We apply Equation 12–11, setting the final angular speed ω to zero and taking $\theta_0 = 0$ for convenience:

$$0 = \omega_0^2 + 2\alpha\theta.$$

Setting θ to 2π because we want exactly one revolution, and noting that α is negative because it is a deceleration, we solve for ω_0 to get

$$\omega_0 = \sqrt{-2\alpha\theta} = [(-2)(-0.21\ \text{rad/s}^2)(2\pi)]^{1/2} = 1.6\ \text{rad/s.}$$

The tangential acceleration of a point on the rim is then given by Equation 12–6:

$$a = r\alpha = (80\ \text{cm})(-0.21\ \text{rad/s}^2) = -17\ \text{cm/s}^2,$$

where the minus sign tells us that the tangential acceleration is directed oppositely to the linear velocity of the rim.

Fig. 12–4
The direction of the angular velocity vector is given by the right-hand rule.

Angular Velocity and Acceleration Vectors

angular velocity

So far, we have treated angular quantities as scalars, with magnitude but not direction. But rotation of a wheel about a horizontal axis, for example, is not quite the same motion as rotation about a vertical axis. To distinguish these cases from each other and from all other possible orientations of the rotation axis, we define **angular velocity, ω,** as a vector whose magnitude is the angular speed ω and whose direction is parallel to the rotation axis. Specifically, the direction of the angular velocity is given by the right-hand rule: curl the fingers of your right hand so as to follow the rotation, and your right thumb points in the direction of the angular velocity (Fig. 12–4). Note that this definition of angular velocity is like our definition of torque, in that the vector direction is perpendicular to the plane of rotation.

By analogy with the linear acceleration vector, we define angular acceleration as the rate of change of the angular velocity vector:

$$\boldsymbol{\alpha} = \frac{d\boldsymbol{\omega}}{dt}.$$

(12–12)

This definition says that the angular acceleration vector points in the direction of the *change* in the angular velocity. If the angular velocity changes only in magnitude but not in direction, then **ω** simply grows or shrinks, so that **α** lies parallel or antiparallel to the rotation axis (Fig. 12–5). In this case, the magnitude of the angular acceleration is just the rate of change of

Fig. 12–5
(a) An increase in angular speed alone corresponds to a change Δω in the angular velocity that is parallel to the angular velocity vector. Therefore, the angular acceleration vector **α** is also parallel to angular velocity. *(b)* With a decrease in ω, Δω and **α** are antiparallel to **ω**.

(a)   (b)

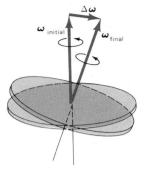

Fig. 12–6
When the angular velocity ω changes only in direction, the change Δω and therefore the angular acceleration vector α are perpendicular to the angular velocity.

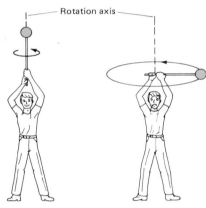

Fig. 12–7
A body's resistance to changes in rotational motion depends on the body itself and on the axis about which rotational motion is changed.

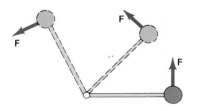

Fig. 12–8
A force applied perpendicular to the rod results in angular acceleration. (Here we assume no other external forces, such as gravity, are acting.)

angular speed, as in our scalar definition 12–5. But as with linear velocity, a change in the *direction* of angular velocity is also associated with acceleration. When **ω** changes only in direction, the angular acceleration vector is perpendicular to **ω** (Fig. 12–6). In the most general case, both the direction and magnitude of the angular velocity may change, and then **α** is neither parallel nor perpendicular to **ω.** These situations are exactly analogous to the linear case, where an acceleration that is parallel or antiparallel to velocity produces only a change in speed, while an acceleration that is perpendicular to velocity produces only a change in direction.

12.2
ROTATIONAL INERTIA AND THE ANALOG OF NEWTON'S LAW

Newton's second law, **F** = m**a,** proved very powerful in our study of linear motion. Ultimately, of course, Newton's law itself governs all motion, including rotation, but its application to every particle in a rotating object would be terribly cumbersome. Can we instead formulate an analogous law that deals directly with rotational quantities?

To develop such a law, we need rotational analogs of the three quantities **F, a,** and m. In torque and angular acceleration, we already have the analogs of force and linear acceleration. But what rotational quantity might be analogous to mass?

The mass m in Newton's law is a measure of a body's inertia—its resistance to changes in motion. We want a quantity that, analogously, describes a body's resistance to changes in rotational motion. Consider an object consisting of a small ball of mass m at the end of a rigid, massless rod of length R. This composite object is easy to start rotating about an axis that coincides with the rod, but much harder to start rotating about a perpendicular axis through the end of the rod (Fig. 12–7). Why is this? In the first case, no point is very far from the rotation axis, so that the linear speeds of all parts of the object remain small. But in the second case, the mass is far from the rotation axis, and to achieve a given change in angular speed requires a large change in linear speed. The rotational analog of mass must therefore depend both on the mass of the rotating object and on how far that mass is from the axis of rotation.

Suppose that we start our mass-rod object rotating by attaching one end to a frictionless pivot and applying a force **F** that is always at right angles to the rod (Fig. 12–8). That force results in an angular acceleration of the object about an axis perpendicular to the page. Starting from rest, it begins to rotate counterclockwise at an ever-increasing rate. Applying the right-hand rule, we see that the angular velocity vector **ω** is out of the page. Since **ω** is increasing in length, the angular acceleration vector **α** is also out of the page. We now develop a simple description of this situation in terms of angular quantities alone. Writing Newton's second law*, and using

---
*Actually, we are writing only the tangential component of Newton's law. There must also be a radial force acting at right angles to the applied force **F**. This force is provided automatically by the tension in the rod, and will not concern us further. Because it lies along a line from the mass to the rotation axis, the radial force contributes nothing to the torque.

Equation 12–6 to express the tangential acceleration a_t in terms of α and the distance R from the axis of rotation, we have

$$F = ma_t = mR\alpha. \qquad (12\text{–}13)$$

Here we have assumed the ball small enough that all parts of it are essentially the same distance R from the pivot point. The force **F** produces a torque about the pivot point. From Equation 11–2, this torque has magnitude

$$\tau = RF,$$

and, by the right-hand rule, it points out of the page. Solving for F and using the result in Equation 12–13, we have

$$\frac{\tau}{R} = mR\alpha,$$

or

$$\tau = (mR^2)\alpha.$$

Here we have Newton's second law, $F = ma$, written in terms of rotational quantities. The torque—analogous to force—is the product of the angular acceleration with the quantity mR^2, which must therefore be the rotational analog of mass. We call this quantity mR^2 the **rotational inertia** or **moment of inertia,** and represent it by the symbol I. Rotational inertia has the units kg·m², and accounts both for mass and for the location of mass relative to the axis of rotation. We can therefore write, in analogy with Newton's second law,

rotational inertia
moment of inertia

$$\boldsymbol{\tau = I\alpha,} \qquad (12\text{–}14)$$

where the fact that torque and angular acceleration are in the same direction allows us to write this as a vector equation.

Although we derived Equation 12–14 for a single mass point, we can apply it to extended objects if we interpret $\boldsymbol{\tau}$ as the net torque on the object and I as the sum of the rotational inertias of all masses making up the object. The first subsection below shows how to calculate the rotational inertia for extended objects. The second subsection then explores the meaning of the net torque on such an object, and illustrates the practical application of Equation 12–14 to the dynamics of rotating objects.

Calculating the Rotational Inertia

When an object consists of a number of discrete mass points, its rotational inertia about an axis is just the sum of the rotational inertias of the individual mass points about that axis:

$$I = \sum m_i r_i^2. \qquad (12\text{–}15)$$

Here m_i is the mass of the ith mass point, and r_i its distance from the rotation axis.

Example 12–4
Rotational Inertia

A dumbbell-shaped object consists of two equal masses $m = 0.64$ kg on the end of a massless rod of length $\ell = 85$ cm. Calculate the rotational inertia of this object about an axis one-fourth of the way from one end of the rod and perpendicular to it. If the object is accelerated from rest by a torque of 1.2 N·m pointing along the same axis, how many revolutions will it turn in 2.5 s?

Solution

The situation is shown in Fig. 12–9. Summing the individual rotational inertias, we have

$$I = \sum m_i r_i^2 = m\left(\frac{1}{4}\ell\right)^2 + m\left(\frac{3}{4}\ell\right)^2 = \tfrac{5}{8}m\ell^2$$

$$= \tfrac{5}{8}(0.64 \text{ kg})(0.85 \text{ m})^2 = 0.29 \text{ kg·m}^2.$$

From Equation 12–14, the angular acceleration is

$$\alpha = \frac{\tau}{I}.$$

Using this result in Equation 12–10 then gives the angular displacement:

$$\theta = \frac{1}{2}\alpha t^2 = \frac{1}{2}\left(\frac{\tau}{I}\right)t^2 = \frac{1}{2}\left(\frac{1.2 \text{ N·m}}{0.29 \text{ kg·m}^2}\right)(2.5 \text{ s})^2 = 13 \text{ rad} = 2.1 \text{ rev.}$$

Fig. 12–9
Example 12–4

When an object consists of a continuous distribution of matter rather than a number of point masses, then we consider a large number of very small mass elements dm throughout the object, and sum the individual rotational inertias $r^2 dm$ over the entire object (Fig. 12–10). In the limit of an arbitrarily large number of very small mass elements, the sum becomes an integral, and we have

$$I = \int r^2 dm, \tag{12–16}$$

where the limits of integration are chosen to include the entire object.

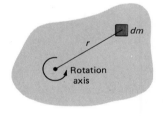

Fig. 12–10
To find the rotational inertia of a solid object, we imagine it divided into small elements dm, then integrate over the rotational inertias $r^2 dm$ of the individual mass elements.

Example 12–5
Rotational Inertia of a Rod

Find the rotational inertia of a uniform, narrow rod of mass M and length ℓ about an axis through its center and perpendicular to the rod.

Solution

Let the rod coincide with the x-axis, with origin at the center of the rod, and consider mass elements of mass dm and length dx, as shown in Fig. 12–11. The distance x from the center of the rod to the mass element dm plays the role of r in Equation 12–16, so that

$$I = \int_{x=-\ell/2}^{x=\ell/2} x^2 \, dm, \tag{12–17}$$

Fig. 12–11
A uniform rod, showing mass element of mass dm and length dx.

where we have chosen the limits to include the entire rod. To do the integration, we must relate x and dm so that we have a single variable under the integral sign. The length dx of the mass element is some tiny fraction of the total length ℓ. Since the rod is uniform, the mass dm is the *same* fraction of the total mass M. Therefore

$$\frac{dm}{M} = \frac{dx}{\ell}.$$

Solving for dm and using the result in Equation 12–17, we have

$$I = \int_{-\ell/2}^{\ell/2} \frac{M}{\ell} x^2 \, dx = \frac{M}{\ell} \int_{-\ell/2}^{\ell/2} x^2 \, dx$$

$$= \frac{M}{\ell} \left. \frac{x^3}{3} \right|_{-\ell/2}^{\ell/2} = \frac{1}{12} M\ell^2. \quad \text{(rod about bisector)}$$

(12–18)

Does this make sense? Yes: much of the rod's mass is near the axis of rotation, and therefore contributes little to the rotational inertia. The result is a much lower rotational inertia than if all the mass were at the ends of the rod.

Example 12–6
Rotational Inertia of a Ring

Find the rotational inertia of a thin ring of radius R and mass M about the ring's axis (Fig. 12–12).

Solution

We divide the ring into mass elements dm, one of which is shown in Fig. 12–12. All the mass elements in the ring are the same distance R from the rotational axis, so that r in Equation 12–16 is the constant R, and the equation becomes

$$I = \int R^2 \, dm = R^2 \int dm,$$

where the integration is over the ring. But the sum of mass elements over the ring is just the total mass, M, so that

$$I = MR^2. \quad \text{(thin ring)} \tag{12–19}$$

The rotational inertia of the ring is the same as if all the mass were concentrated in one place a distance R from the rotation axis; the angular distribution of the mass about the axis does not matter. Notice, too, that it does not matter whether the ring is narrow like a loop of wire or long like a section of hollow pipe, as long as it is thin enough that all of it is essentially equidistant from the rotation axis (Fig. 12–13).

Example 12–7
Rotational Inertia of a Disk

A disk of radius R and mass M has uniform density. Find the rotational inertia of the disk about an axis through its center and perpendicular to the disk.

Solution

Not all parts of the disk are the same distance from the axis, so that r is not constant in Equation 12–16. Since we already know the rotational inertia of a ring, we can divide the disk into mass elements that are themselves rings, as shown in Fig. 12–14. A given mass element is a ring of radius r, width dr, and mass dm. Its rotational inertia is $r^2 dm$, so that the total rotational inertia of the disk is

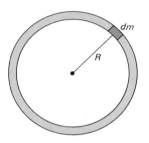

Fig. 12–12
A thin ring, showing one mass element dm.

Fig. 12–13
The rotational inertia is MR^2 for any thin ring, whether it is narrow like a wire loop (left) or long like a section of pipe (right).

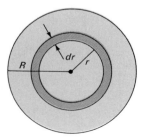

Fig. 12–14
A disk may be divided into ring-shaped mass elements of mass dm, radius r, and width dr.

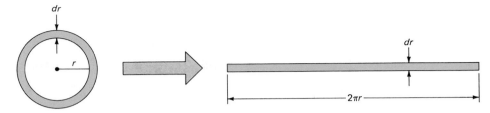

Fig. 12–15
The mass element *dm* may be "unwound" into a thin rectangle of length $2\pi r$ and width *dr*.

$$I = \int_{r=0}^{r=R} r^2 \, dm, \qquad (12\text{–}20)$$

where the limits are chosen to include all the ring-shaped mass elements in the entire disk. To evaluate this integral, we must relate the variables m and r. The mass element dm is a tiny fraction of the total mass M—but it is the *same* fraction of the total mass as its area is of the total disk area, πR^2. Since the ring dm is very thin, we can imagine "unwinding" it to get a thin rectangle of length $2\pi r$ and width dr (Fig. 12–15). Then the area of the ring is $2\pi r \, dr$, and we have

$$\frac{dm}{M} = \frac{2\pi r \, dr}{\pi R^2}.$$

Solving for dm and using the result in Equation 12–20 leaves only the variable r under the integral, allowing us to do the integration:

$$I = \int_{r=0}^{r=R} r^2 \, dm = \int_0^R r^2 \frac{2M}{R^2} r \, dr = \frac{2M}{R^2} \int_0^R r^3 \, dr \qquad (12\text{–}21)$$

$$= \frac{2M}{R^2} \frac{r^4}{4} \Big|_0^R = \tfrac{1}{2} M R^2. \quad \text{(disk)}$$

Does this make sense? In the disk, mass is distributed from the axis out to the edge. Mass nearer the axis contributes less to the rotational inertia, so that we expect a lower rotational inertia for the disk than for a ring of the same mass and radius.

The rotational inertias of other shapes about various axes may be found by integration as in these three examples. Table 12–2 lists results for some common shapes. Note that more than one rotational inertia is listed for some shapes, since the rotational inertia depends on the rotation axis.

If we know the rotational inertia, I_{cm}, about an axis through the center of mass of a body, a useful relation called the **parallel axis theorem** allows us to calculate the rotational inertia, I, through any parallel axis. The parallel axis theorem states that

parallel axis theorem

$$I = I_{cm} + Mh^2, \qquad (12\text{–}22)$$

where h is the distance from the center of mass axis to the parallel axis and M the total mass of the object. Problem 14 explores the proof of this theorem.

TABLE 12–2
Rotational Inertias

Thin rod about center
$I = \frac{1}{12}M\ell^2$

Thin rod about end
$I = \frac{1}{3}M\ell^2$

Thin ring or hollow cylinder
about its axis
$I = MR^2$

Disk or solid cylinder
about its axis
$I = \frac{1}{2}MR^2$

Solid cylinder about
perpendicular bisector
$I = \frac{1}{4}MR^2 + \frac{1}{12}M\ell^2$

Solid sphere about diameter
$I = \frac{2}{5}MR^2$

Hollow spherical shell about
diameter
$I = \frac{2}{3}MR^2$

Sphere about tangent line
$I = \frac{7}{5}MR^2$

Flat plate about perpendicular
axis
$I = \frac{1}{12}M(a^2 + b^2)$

Flat plate about central axis
$I = \frac{1}{12}Ma^2$

Example 12–8 _____

The Parallel Axis Theorem

Find the rotational inertia of a uniform, narrow rod of length ℓ and mass M about an axis through one end and perpendicular to the rod.

Solution

In Example 12–5, we found the rotational inertia through the center of mass of the rod to be $I_{cm} = M\ell^2/12$. Our new rotation axis is a distance $\ell/2$ from the axis through the center of mass, so that the parallel axis theorem becomes

$$I = I_{cm} + Mh^2 = \tfrac{1}{12}M\ell^2 + M\left(\frac{\ell}{2}\right)^2 = \tfrac{1}{3}M\ell^2.$$

Use of the parallel axis theorem can eliminate a great deal of integration!

Rotational Dynamics

Knowing the rotational inertia of a body, we can use the rotational analog of Newton's second law (Equation 12–14) to determine the behavior of the body just as we used $\mathbf{F} = m\mathbf{a}$ itself to determine the dynamics of linear motion. The torque in Equation 12–14 is the *net* torque on the object in question. As with forces in the linear case, we must be careful to isolate the object and determine *all* torques that act on it, then take their vector sum to get the net torque.

When we studied the linear motion of a composite system, we found that only external forces matter; internal forces cancel in pairs according to Newton's third law. Can we similarly disregard torques due to internal forces among the various parts of an object? The answer is yes, if we make one further assumption about those internal forces—that they act along a line joining the two mass elements in question (Fig. 12–16). Then the lever arm $r \sin\theta$ for each torque is the same, as shown in Fig. 12–16. By Newton's third law, the forces are equal but opposite; since the lever arms $r \sin\theta$ are the same, the torques are also equal and opposite. Therefore, internal torques cancel in pairs, and the torque in Equation 12–14 is the net *external* torque.

We now apply Equation 12–14 in two examples. These examples are analogous to one-dimensional linear motion, in that torque and angular

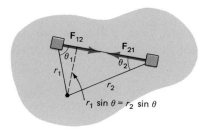

Fig. 12–16
When internal forces act along the line joining two mass elements, then the associated torques cancel in pairs.

velocity are in the same direction. Later, in Section 12.4, we consider the case in which a torque acts to change the direction of angular velocity.

Example 12–9
De-spinning a Satellite

A cylindrical satellite is 1.4 m in diameter, with its mass of 940 kg distributed approximately uniformly throughout its volume. The satellite is spinning at 10 rpm about its axis, but must be stopped so that a space shuttle crew can make repairs. Two small gas jets, each with a thrust of 20 N, are mounted on opposite sides of the satellite and are aimed tangent to the satellite's surface (Fig. 12–17). How long must the jets be fired in order to stop the satellite's rotation?

Solution

The satellite's angular speed must change by $\Delta\omega = 10$ rpm. At constant angular acceleration α, this takes time

$$\Delta t = \frac{\Delta\omega}{\alpha} = \frac{\Delta\omega I}{\tau}, \tag{12–23}$$

where we have used Equation 12–14 to write $\alpha = \tau/I$. From Table 12–2 the rotational inertia of the cylindrical satellite is $I = \frac{1}{2}MR^2$. The torque exerted by the two jets, each a distance R from the rotational axis and directed perpendicular to the radius, is $\tau = 2RF$, with F the thrust of one jet. Then Equation 12–23 becomes

$$\Delta t = \frac{(\Delta\omega)(\frac{1}{2}MR^2)}{2RF} = \frac{\Delta\omega MR}{4F} = \frac{(10 \text{ rpm})(2\pi \text{ rad/rev})}{60 \text{ s/min}} \frac{(940 \text{ kg})(0.70 \text{ m})}{(4)(20 \text{ N})} = 8.6 \text{ s},$$

where we have converted the change in angular speed from rpm to rad/s.

Fig. 12–17
Satellite with gas jets.

Often, rotational and linear motion are coupled in a single problem, as in Example 12–10.

Example 12–10
Rotational and Linear Dynamics

A solid cylinder of mass M and radius R is mounted on a frictionless horizontal axle over a well, as shown in Fig. 12–18. A rope of negligible mass is wrapped around the cylinder, and a bucket of mass m is suspended from the rope. Find an expression for the acceleration of the bucket as it falls down the empty well shaft.

Solution

Were it not connected to the cylinder, the bucket would, of course, accelerate downward with linear acceleration g. But now the rope exerts an upward tension force T on the bucket, reducing the net downward force and at the same time exerting a torque on the cylinder. The downward force on the bucket is $F = mg - T$ (Fig. 12–19), so that Newton's second law gives

$$ma = mg - T, \tag{12–24}$$

where a is the linear acceleration of the bucket. Looking at the cylinder end-on (Fig. 12–20), we see that the rope exerts a torque $\tau = RT$ on the cylinder, giving it an angular acceleration

$$\alpha = \frac{\tau}{I} = \frac{RT}{I}, \tag{12–25}$$

where I is the rotational inertia.

Fig. 12–18
Example 12–10

Fig. 12–19
Force diagram for the bucket. The net downward force is $mg - T$.

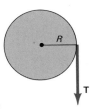

Fig. 12–20
End view of cylinder, showing that the rope tension T exerts a torque RT on the cylinder.

The linear acceleration of the bucket and angular acceleration of the cylinder are related, for as the rope unwinds without slipping, the tangential acceleration of a point on the cylinder edge is equal to the linear acceleration of rope and bucket. Therefore $a = \alpha R$, or, using Equation 12–25,

$$a = \alpha R = \frac{R^2 T}{I}. \tag{12–26}$$

The tension T is the same throughout the massless rope. Solving Equation 12–26 for this tension and using the result in Equation 12–24 gives

$$ma = mg - \frac{I}{R^2}a,$$

so that

$$\left(m + \frac{I}{R^2}\right)a = mg.$$

Solving for the acceleration a, and noting that the rotational inertia of a solid cylinder about its axis is $I = \frac{1}{2}MR^2$, we have

$$a = \frac{mg}{m + \frac{1}{2}M}.$$

Is this result reasonable? If the cylinder mass M is small compared with the bucket mass m, the rotation of the cylinder is unimportant and the acceleration is simply g. But more generally, the gravitational force on the bucket provides not only the bucket's linear acceleration, but also the angular acceleration of the cylinder. As a result, the linear acceleration is decreased. This example is similar to Example 5–5, in which a falling mass also accelerates a horizontally moving mass rather than a rotating mass. Problem 15 explores a combination of these two examples.

12.3
ENERGY AND ROTATIONAL MOTION

A rotating object clearly has kinetic energy. Even if the whole object is not going anywhere, its individual mass elements are moving, and the sum of their kinetic energies is the object's **rotational kinetic energy.** Invoking the analogy with linear motion, we can speculate that the kinetic energy of a rotating body should be the rotational analog of $K = \frac{1}{2}mv^2$:

rotational kinetic energy

$$\boxed{K_{\text{rot}} = \tfrac{1}{2}I\omega^2.} \tag{12–27}$$

We can prove that this is a valid expression by summing the kinetic energies of the individual mass elements. Figure 12–21 shows that the kinetic energy of a mass element dm a distance r from the rotation axis is

$$dK = \tfrac{1}{2}(dm)(v^2) = \tfrac{1}{2}(dm)(\omega r)^2.$$

The total kinetic energy of the rotating object is given by summing—that is, integrating—over the entire object:

$$K_{\text{rot}} = \int \tfrac{1}{2}(dm)(\omega r)^2 = \tfrac{1}{2}\omega^2 \int r^2\, dm,$$

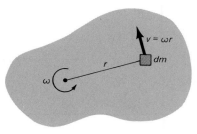

Fig. 12–21
A mass element dm a distance r from the rotation axis has linear velocity $v = \omega r$, giving it a kinetic energy $dK = \frac{1}{2}(dm)(\omega r)^2$.

where we have taken ω^2 outside the integral because it is a constant characterizing the rotation of the whole object. But the remaining integral is simply the rotational inertia, I (Equation 12–16), so that $K_{rot} = \frac{1}{2}I\omega^2$, just as we expected from our rotational/linear motion analogy.

Example 12–11
Rotational Kinetic Energy

Estimate the rotational kinetic energy of the earth, assuming it to be a solid sphere of uniform density.

Solution

To use Equation 12–27 for rotational kinetic energy, we need the rotational inertia and angular velocity of the earth. From Table 12–1, we find that $I = \frac{2}{5}MR^2$ for a uniform solid sphere, so that

$$K_{rot} = \tfrac{1}{2}I\omega^2 = \tfrac{1}{5}MR^2\omega^2.$$

Obtaining M and R from Appendix F, and converting earth's angular speed of 1 rev/day to rad/s, we have

$$K_{rot} = \frac{(6.0 \times 10^{24}\text{ kg})(6.4 \times 10^6\text{ m})^2}{5}\left(\frac{(1.0\text{ rev/day})(2\pi\text{ rad/rev})}{(3600\text{ s/h})(24\text{ h/day})}\right)^2 = 2.6 \times 10^{29}\text{ J}.$$

Actually, more of earth's mass is concentrated toward the center, reducing the rotational inertia and making this value an overestimate.

The work-energy theorem developed in Chapter 6 states that the work done on a system is equal to the change in its kinetic energy. In general, the work is given by Equation 6–15:

$$W = \int \mathbf{F}\cdot d\boldsymbol{\ell},$$

where we now write $d\boldsymbol{\ell}$ instead of $d\mathbf{r}$ for the path element to avoid confusion with the radius $\mathbf{r}$. When a torque τ acts on an object, we can consider it caused by a tangentially directed force $F = \tau/r$ applied some arbitrary distance r from the rotation axis (Fig. 12–22). As the object rotates through a small angle $d\theta$, the point of application of the force moves tangentially a distance $r\,d\theta$. With force and displacement both in the tangential direction, the work becomes

$$W = \int \mathbf{F}\cdot d\boldsymbol{\ell} = \int F\,d\ell = \int \frac{\tau}{r}r\,d\theta = \int \tau\,d\theta. \tag{12–28}$$

In the case of a constant torque, this equation reduces to

$$W = \tau\,\Delta\theta, \tag{12–29}$$

in analogy with $W = F\Delta x$ for a constant force.

Fig. 12–22
A torque τ may be considered to be caused by a force $F = \tau/r$.

Example 12–12
Work and Rotational Energy

A toy gyroscope consists of a ring of mass $M = 85$ g and radius $R = 2.6$ cm, connected by essentially massless spokes to an axle of negligible mass. The ring and axle are mounted in a frame in which they are free to rotate (Fig. 12–23). A massless string of length $\ell = 45$ cm is wrapped around the axle and pulled with a

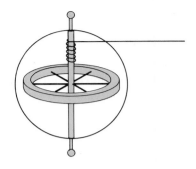

Fig. 12–23
A toy gyroscope (Example 12–12).

steady force $F = 3.7$ N. If the string unwinds without slipping, what is the final rotational speed of the gyroscope? If the torque due to the string is 7.4×10^{-3} N·m, how many revolutions does the gyroscope make while the string is being pulled?

Solution

With constant force, the work integral reduces to the simple product $W = F\ell$; since mechanical energy is conserved, all this work ends up as rotational kinetic energy of the gyroscope, so that

$$\tfrac{1}{2}I\omega^2 = F\ell.$$

Solving for ω^2 and using $I = MR^2$ for the ring gives

$$\omega^2 = \frac{2F\ell}{I} = \frac{2F\ell}{MR^2} = \frac{(2)(3.7 \text{ N})(0.45 \text{ m})}{(0.085 \text{ kg})(0.026 \text{ m})^2} = 5.8 \times 10^4 \text{ (rad/s)}^2,$$

so that $\omega = 240$ rad/s, or about 38 rev/s. As with a linear problem, conservation of energy provides a quick route to the final velocity that is independent of the details of the acceleration.

Since the string is massless and therefore has no kinetic energy, the work $F\ell$ is the same as the work $\tau \, \Delta\theta$ done on the gyroscope by the torque associated with the string, so that

$$F\ell = \tau\Delta\theta,$$

or

$$\Delta\theta = \frac{F\ell}{\tau} = \frac{(3.7 \text{ N})(0.45 \text{ m})}{7.4 \times 10^{-3} \text{ N·m}} = 225 \text{ rad} = 36 \text{ rev}.$$

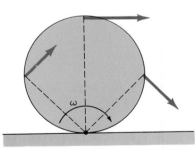

Fig. 12–24
A rolling object exhibits both translational and rotational motion.

Fig. 12–25
The point of contact with the ground is instantaneously at rest. The motion may be thought of as a pure rotation about that point. Arrows represent the linear velocities of several points on the wheel's rim.

Rolling Objects

A rolling object exhibits both rotational and translational motion—motion of the whole object from one place to another. As the object moves forward, it rotates about a point that is itself moving in a straight line (Fig. 12–24). The total kinetic energy of the object must reflect both its translation and its rotation. How are we to determine separately the translational and rotational kinetic energies? The obvious thing would be to consider the translational motion of the whole object—that is, of its center of mass—along with rotation about the center of mass. In fact, this is possible, as we now show for the special case of a round object whose center of mass and geometrical center coincide.

When an object rolls without slipping, the point in contact with the ground is instantaneously at rest with respect to the ground (Fig. 12–25). The entire motion may be thought of instantaneously as a pure rotation about this contact point. We may write the entire kinetic energy as energy of rotation about the contact point:

$$K_{\text{total}} = \tfrac{1}{2}I_c\omega_c^{\,2}, \tag{12–30}$$

where I_c and ω_c are the rotational inertia and angular speed *about the contact point.*

We would like to rewrite this energy in terms of the translational energy of the center of mass and the rotation about the center of mass. The parallel axis theorem (Equation 12–22) provides the link we need. Using this theorem, we may write the rotational inertia I_c about the contact point in terms of the rotational inertia I_{cm} about the center of mass:

$$I_c = I_{cm} + MR^2, \qquad (12\text{–}31)$$

where M and R are the mass and radius of the rolling object. We must also compare the angular speed about the contact point with the angular speed about the center of mass. From Fig. 12–25, we see that the horizontal speed of the center of mass is given by $v = \omega_c R$. In the center-of-mass frame of reference, however, the ground and contact point are moving backward at the same speed v, so that $v = \omega_{cm} R$, where ω_{cm} is the angular speed about the center of mass. Comparing our two expressions for v, we see immediately that the rotational speed ω_c and ω_{cm} must be the same. Then we can use Equation 12–31 in Equation 12–30, giving

$$K_{total} = \tfrac{1}{2}(I_{cm} + MR^2)\omega^2 = \tfrac{1}{2}I_{cm}\omega^2 + \tfrac{1}{2}MR^2\omega^2,$$

where we have dropped the subscript on ω since the angular speeds about the contact point and center of mass are the same. But $\omega R = v$, the translational speed of the center of mass, so that the second term in our expression for the total energy becomes $\tfrac{1}{2}Mv^2$, and we have

$$K_{total} = \tfrac{1}{2}I_{cm}\omega^2 + \tfrac{1}{2}Mv^2 = K_{rot} + K_{trans}. \qquad (12\text{–}32)$$

The total energy can indeed be written as the sum of the translational energy of the center of mass and the rotational energy about the center of mass. Although we derived Equation 12–32 for the special case of a rolling object whose center of mass and geometrical center coincide, it is in fact possible to write the kinetic energy of any object in this way, as long as v is taken to be the speed of the center of mass.

Example 12–13 _____

Rolling Down an Incline

A solid sphere and a solid cylinder, each of the same mass M and radius R, start from rest and roll without slipping down an incline. If they drop a total vertical distance h, what is the linear speed of each at the bottom?

Solution

Were the objects sliding instead of rolling, we would apply conservation of energy by equating the initial potential energy, Mgh, to the final kinetic energy, $\tfrac{1}{2}Mv^2$, and solve for v. But now some of the energy goes into rotation, so that we must equate the potential energy to the total kinetic energy given by Equation 12–32:

$$Mgh = \tfrac{1}{2}I_{cm}\omega^2 + \tfrac{1}{2}Mv^2.$$

But for a rolling object, the linear speed v and angular speed ω are related by $v = \omega R$, so we can write

$$Mgh = \frac{1}{2}I_{cm}\left(\frac{v}{R}\right)^2 + \tfrac{1}{2}Mv^2 = \frac{1}{2}\left(\frac{I_{cm}}{R^2} + M\right)v^2.$$

Solving for v gives

$$v = \sqrt{\frac{2Mgh}{I_{cm}/R^2 + M}}.$$

Using $I_{cm} = \tfrac{2}{5}MR^2$ for the sphere and $I_{cm} = \tfrac{1}{2}MR^2$ for the cylinder, we have

$$V_{\text{sphere}} = \sqrt{\frac{2Mgh}{\frac{2}{5}M + M}} = \sqrt{\frac{10}{7}gh}$$

and

$$V_{\text{cylinder}} = \sqrt{\frac{2Mgh}{\frac{1}{2}M + M}} = \sqrt{\frac{4}{3}gh}.$$

Neither object acquires as much linear velocity as the $\sqrt{2gh}$ it would have if it simply slipped down the incline without rolling. And the cylinder, with its larger rotational inertia, has a slightly lower final speed than the sphere. The energy is the same in all cases, but as the rotational inertia increases, more of that energy is in rotation and less in translational motion.

Example 12–14
A 747 on the Runway

With its fuel tanks nearly empty, a 747 jetliner has a mass of 1.6×10^5 kg. Its landing gear consists of 18 wheels, each of rotational inertia 30 kg·m² and radius 62 cm. As it taxis toward the terminal gate with its wheels rolling, what per cent of its total kinetic energy is in the rotational motion of the wheels?

Solution

The translational kinetic energy is given by $K_{\text{trans}} = \frac{1}{2}Mv^2$, while the rotational energy is $K_{\text{rot}} = \frac{1}{2}NI\omega^2$, where N is the number of wheels and I the rotational inertia of each. Since the wheels roll without slipping, $\omega = v/R$, where R is the wheel radius. Then the fraction of the energy that is rotational is

$$\frac{K_{\text{rot}}}{K_{\text{trans}} + K_{\text{rot}}} = \frac{\frac{1}{2}NI(v/R)^2}{\frac{1}{2}Mv^2 + \frac{1}{2}NI(v/R)^2} = \frac{NI}{MR^2 + NI}$$

$$= \frac{(18)(30 \text{ kg·m}^2)}{(1.6 \times 10^5 \text{ kg})(0.62 \text{ m})^2 + (18)(30 \text{ kg·m}^2)} = 0.0087 = 0.87\%.$$

Note that this result is independent of the plane's speed; as long as the wheels roll without slipping, the rotational and translational energies are in a fixed ratio. On landing, the wheels' rotational energy comes at the expense of the plane's translational energy (although frictional losses are involved too); the rapid spin-up of the wheels contributes slightly to the jolt you experience when the plane lands.

12.4
ANGULAR MOMENTUM

angular momentum

Angular momentum (symbol **L**) is the rotational analog of linear momentum. Like torque and other rotational quantities, angular momentum is meaningful only in relation to a specified point. If a particle of linear momentum **p** is at position **r** with respect to some point, then its angular momentum about that point is defined to be

$$\mathbf{L} = \mathbf{r} \times \mathbf{p}. \tag{12–33}$$

You might also suspect that the analogy between linear and rotational quantities should allow us to write

$$\mathbf{L} = I\boldsymbol{\omega},\tag{12–34}$$

in analogy with the definition $\mathbf{p}=m\mathbf{v}$ for linear momentum. Equations 12–33 and 12–34 are indeed equivalent, as Example 12–15 suggests.

Example 12–15
Angular Momentum

A small particle of mass m moves counterclockwise at speed v around a circle of radius r. Use the definition 12–33 to find its angular momentum about the center of the circle, and show that the result is equivalent to Equation 12–34.

Solution

From Fig. 12–26, we see that the particle's linear momentum $m\mathbf{v}$ and the radius $\mathbf{r}$ are always at right angles, so that $\sin\theta$ in the cross product $\mathbf{r}\times\mathbf{p}$ is just 1. Applying the right-hand rule, we find that the angular momentum $\mathbf{r}\times\mathbf{p}$ points out of the page. Denoting this direction by $\hat{\mathbf{k}}$, we have

$$\mathbf{L} = \mathbf{r}\times\mathbf{p} = \mathbf{r}\times m\mathbf{v} = mvr\,\hat{\mathbf{k}}.$$

The angular velocity of the particle also points out of the page, and may be written

$$\boldsymbol{\omega} = \frac{v}{r}\,\hat{\mathbf{k}},$$

so that our expression for angular momentum becomes

$$\mathbf{L} = mvr\,\hat{\mathbf{k}} = m\frac{v}{r}r^2\,\hat{\mathbf{k}} = mr^2\boldsymbol{\omega}.$$

Since mr^2 is the rotational inertia of a single particle, we have

$$\mathbf{L} = I\boldsymbol{\omega}.$$

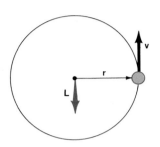

Fig. 12–26
The angular momentum **L** of a particle moving at speed v around a circle of radius r has magnitude mvr and points out of the page.

Example 12–15 shows that Equations 12–33 and 12–34 are equivalent for a single particle moving in a circular path. A rigid, rotating object consists of many such particles in circular motion with a common angular speed. At any given instant, each mass element dm has linear momentum $m\mathbf{v}$, with $\mathbf{v}$ at right angles to the radius vector $\mathbf{r}$ from the rotation axis to the point in question. Then the magnitude of the angular momentum, dL, due to one mass element is just

$$dL = rv\,dm = \omega r^2\,dm.$$

By the right-hand rule, the angular momenta of all the mass elements in the rigid object point in the same direction (Fig. 12–27), parallel to the angular velocity vector. Then the magnitude of the total angular momentum is just the sum, or integral, of the individual dL's:

$$L = \int \omega r^2\,dm = \omega\int r^2\,dm,$$

where the integration is over all the mass elements in the object, and where we have taken ω outside the integral because it is the same for all points in a rigid, rotating object. We recognize the integral on the rightmost side of this equation as the rotational inertia, I (Equation 12–16), so that

$$L = \omega I.$$

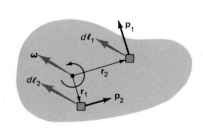

Fig. 12–27
When a rigid object rotates, the angular momentum vectors associated with each of the individual mass elements all point in the same direction, parallel to the angular velocity vector.

Since **L** and **ω** are in the same direction* we can write this equation vectorially:

$$\mathbf{L} = I\boldsymbol{\omega},$$

showing that Equations 12–33 and 12–34 are indeed equivalent for a rigid object.

For a rotating object, it is usually easier to use Equation 12–34 to calculate angular momentum. But the concept of angular momentum applies, more generally, even to systems of particles that do not share a common circular motion. Equation 12–33 remains the fundamental definition, and may be used to calculate angular momentum in all cases.

Example 12–16

Angular Momentum of a Particle in Uniform Motion

An electron of mass m moves in a straight line at constant speed v past a neutron, with b its distance of closest approach (Fig. 12–28). Determine the angular momentum of the electron about the neutron, and show that it remains constant.

Solution

From Equation 12–33, the magnitude of **L** is

$$L = rp \sin\theta = mvr \sin\theta.$$

But from Fig. 12–28, we see that $r \sin\theta = b$, so that

$$L = mvb,$$

which is independent of the electron's position on its straight-line trajectory. What about the direction of the angular momentum vector? From the right-hand rule, we see that $\mathbf{r} \times \mathbf{v}$ is everywhere into the page, so that the angular momentum is constant in magnitude and direction.

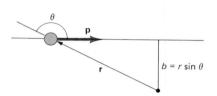

Fig. 12–28
The angular momentum of an object moving uniformly in a straight line is constant.

$b = r \sin\theta$

Torque and Angular Momentum

In Section 12.2, we considered the rotational analog of Newton's law $\mathbf{F} = m\mathbf{a}$. Newton's law in this form holds when the mass m of a system is constant; analogously, our equation $\boldsymbol{\tau} = I\boldsymbol{\alpha}$ holds when the rotational inertia I is constant. More generally, we saw in Chapter 9 that Newton's law applied to a system of particles has the form

$$\mathbf{F} = \frac{d\mathbf{P}}{dt},$$

where **F** is the sum of the external forces acting on the system, and **P** is the total momentum of the system. Can we write, by analogy,

$$\boldsymbol{\tau} = \frac{d\mathbf{L}}{dt}?$$

To see that we can, we write the angular momentum of a system as the sum of the angular momenta of its constituent particles:

---

*Actually, this is true only when the rotation axis is stationary. In more complicated situations involving asymmetric objects, the angular momentum and angular velocity may be in different directions. In that case the rotational inertia cannot be described by a single number but instead is described by a more complicated mathematical entity called a tensor.

$$\mathbf{L} = \sum \mathbf{L}_i = \sum \mathbf{r}_i \times \mathbf{p}_i,$$

where the subscript i refers to the ith particle of the system. Differentiating this equation with respect to time gives

$$\frac{d\mathbf{L}}{dt} = \sum \left(\mathbf{r}_i \times \frac{d\mathbf{p}_i}{dt} + \frac{d\mathbf{r}_i}{dt} \times \mathbf{p}_i \right),$$

where we have applied the product rule for differentiation, being careful to preserve the order of the cross product since it is not commutative. But $d\mathbf{r}_i/dt$ is the velocity of the ith particle, so that the second term in the sum is the cross product of velocity $\mathbf{v}$ and momentum $\mathbf{p} = m\mathbf{v}$. Since these two vectors are parallel, their cross product is zero, and we are left with only the first term in the sum:

$$\frac{d\mathbf{L}}{dt} = \sum \mathbf{r}_i \times \frac{d\mathbf{p}_i}{dt} = \sum \mathbf{r}_i \times \mathbf{F}_i,$$

where we have used Newton's law to write $d\mathbf{p}_i/dt = \mathbf{F}_i$. But $\mathbf{r}_i \times \mathbf{F}_i$ is the torque, $\boldsymbol{\tau}_i$, on the ith particle, so that

$$\frac{d\mathbf{L}}{dt} = \sum \boldsymbol{\tau}_i.$$

As we discussed in Section 12.2, the internal torques cancel in pairs as long as the internal forces in a system of particles act along the lines between the particles. Under these conditions, the sum of all the torques on all the particles reduces to the net *external* torque on the system, and we have

$$\frac{d\mathbf{L}}{dt} = \boldsymbol{\tau}, \qquad (12\text{--}35)$$

where $\boldsymbol{\tau}$ is the net external torque. Thus our analogy between linear and rotational motion holds for momentum as well as for the other quantities we have discussed.

Conservation of Angular Momentum

When there is no external torque on a system, Equation 12–35 tells us that angular momentum is constant. This statement—that the angular momentum of an isolated system cannot change—is of fundamental importance in physics, and applies to systems ranging from subatomic particles to galaxies (Fig. 12–29). In deriving Equation 12–35, we did not require that the system in question be a rigid object, so that conservation of angular momentum applies even to systems that undergo changes in configuration and therefore in rotational inertia. The classic example of such a change is a figure skater, who starts spinning relatively slowly with arms extended, then pulls her arms in to spin much more rapidly (Fig. 12–30). Why does this happen? As the skater's arms move in, her mass is concentrated more toward the rotation axis, lowering her rotational inertia, I. But her angular momentum $I\omega$ is conserved, so that her angular speed ω must increase. A much more dramatic example is illustrated in Example 12–17: the collapse

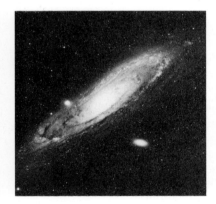

Fig. 12–29
The Andromeda galaxy, nearest large galaxy to our own Milky Way. The galaxy is a complex system of 100 billion stars and clouds of gas and dust, undergoing slow rotation. But the galaxy is essentially isolated, so that no matter how complex the interactions among its constituent parts, its total angular momentum remains constant.

Fig. 12–30
As the skater pulls in her arms, her rotational inertia *I* decreases. To conserve her angular momentum *I*ω, her angular speed ω must increase.

of a star at the end of its lifetime. Again, the rotational inertia decreases, requiring an increase in the star's rotational speed.

Example 12–17

Pulsars and the Conservation of Angular Momentum

A certain star rotates about its axis once every 45 days. At the end of its life, when the star has exhausted its nuclear fuel, it undergoes a colossal outburst called a supernova explosion. During this event, much of the star's mass is flung outward into the interstellar medium, where it will eventually condense into new stars and planets and perhaps find its way into living creatures (Fig. 12–31). But the inner core of the star, whose initial radius was 2×10^7 m, collapses into an object only 6 km in radius. This **neutron star** is so dense that one teaspoonful of its material has a mass of a billion tons! Calculate the rotation rate of the neutron star, assuming that no torque acts on the stellar core during the collapse. Consider the core to be a uniform sphere both before and after collapse.

Solution

This situation is exactly like that of the figure skater, in that a decrease in rotational inertia requires an increase in angular speed. Conservation of angular momentum states that

$$I_1\omega_1 = I_2\omega_2,$$

where the subscripts 1 and 2 refer to conditions before and after the collapse, respectively. For a uniform sphere, $I = \tfrac{2}{5}MR^2$, so that

$$\tfrac{2}{5}MR_1^2\omega_1 = \tfrac{2}{5}MR_2^2\omega_2.$$

Solving for ω_2 and using the known values of ω_1, R_1, and R_2 gives

$$\omega_2 = \omega_1\left(\frac{R_1}{R_2}\right)^2 = \left(\frac{1\text{ rev}}{45\text{ day}}\right)\left(\frac{2\times 10^7\text{ m}}{6\times 10^3\text{ m}}\right)^2 = 2.5\times 10^5\text{ rev/day} = 3\text{ rev/s}.$$

This neutron star is a fantastic thing—an object with more mass than the entire sun, rotating three times a second. Often intense radio waves, light, or x-rays radiate in a narrow beam from the magnetic axis of the neutron star. As the neutron star

neutron star

Fig. 12–31
The Crab Nebula is the remains of a supernova explosion as it looks 1000 years after the explosion.

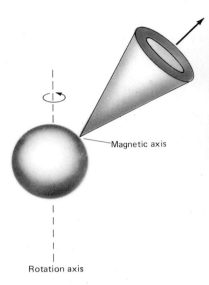

Magnetic axis

Rotation axis

Fig. 12–32
A rotating neutron star emits a beam of radiation, much like a searchlight.

Fig. 12–33
This series of optical images shows the pulsar in the Crab Nebula at different times in its 33-ms cycle. The object on the left is a normal star and remains at constant brightness. The object on the right is the pulsar; its intensity is lowest in the first frame.

rotates, this beam of radiation sweeps through space like a searchlight beacon (Fig. 12–32). As this beam repeatedly sweeps past earth, we detect a series of regular pulses of radiation that give the rotating neutron star the name "pulsar" (Fig. 12–33). Over 300 pulsars have been identified, with rotation periods ranging from 1.6 ms to 4 s. Pulsar rotation rates actually decrease slowly, as magnetic forces exert slight torques on the neutron stars.

Example 12–18
Conservation of Angular Momentum

A merry-go-round of radius $R = 1.3$ m has a rotational inertia $I = 240$ kg·m², and is rotating freely at $\omega_1 = 11$ rpm. A child of mass $m_1 = 28$ kg leaps onto the edge of the merry-go-round, heading directly toward the center (Fig. 12–34). What is the new angular speed of the merry-go-round? Later a second child, of mass $m_2 = 32$ kg, leaps onto the merry-go-round by running tangentially at speed $v = 3.7$ m/s. If the direction of the child's motion is the same as that of the merry-go-round (see Fig. 12–34), what is the new angular speed?

Solution

Moving directly toward the rotation axis, the first child carries no angular momentum relative to the axis, so that the total angular momentum is $I\omega_1$. But sitting at the edge of the merry-go-round, the child adds rotational inertia m_1R^2 to the system. Then conservation of angular momentum may be written

$$I\omega_1 = (I + m_1R^2)\omega_2,$$

where ω_2 is the angular speed after the child is on the merry-go-round. Solving for ω_2 gives

$$\omega_2 = \frac{I\omega_1}{I + m_1R^2} = \frac{(240 \text{ kg·m}^2)(11 \text{ rpm})}{240 \text{ kg·m}^2 + (28 \text{ kg})(1.3 \text{ m})^2} = 9.2 \text{ rpm.}$$

Notice that in this calculation, where we dealt with a ratio of angular speeds, we did not need to convert from rpm to rad/s.

The second child, running tangentially to the merry-go-round, carries angular momentum m_2vR, in the same direction as the merry-go-round's angular momen-

Fig. 12–34
Running toward the axis, child A brings no angular momentum relative to the axis of the merry-go-round. Running tangentially, child B brings angular momentum mvR.

tum (see Example 12–16), so that the total angular momentum of the system is now $I\omega_1 + m_2vR$. After the second child leaps on, the total rotational inertia includes that of the merry-go-round along with a contribution mR^2 from each child. Calling the final angular speed ω_3, conservation of angular momentum may then be written

$$I\omega_1 + m_2vR = (I + m_1R^2 + m_2R^2)\omega_3,$$

so that

$$\omega_3 = \frac{I\omega_1 + m_2vR}{I + (m_1 + m_2)R^2}.$$

With m_2 in kg, v in m/s, and R in m, the angular momentum m_2vR of the second child has the units of kg·m²·rad/s, while all our other angular momenta have been expressed implicitly in kg·m²·rpm. To solve for ω_3 in rpm, we convert the second child's angular momentum into the latter unit:

$$\omega_3 = \frac{(240 \text{ kg·m}^2)(11 \text{ rpm}) + (32 \text{ kg})(3.7 \text{ m/s})(1.3 \text{ m})(1 \text{ rev}/2\pi \text{ rad})(60 \text{ s/min})}{240 \text{ kg·m}^2 + (28 \text{ kg} + 32 \text{ kg})(1.3 \text{ m})^2} = 12 \text{ rpm}.$$

Is mechanical energy conserved as the children leap onto the merry-go-round? No! In each case frictional forces are involved in bringing children and merry-go-round to rest with respect to each other, so that the situation is like an inelastic collision.

Rotational Dynamics in Three Dimensions

Although we developed rotational analogs of Newton's law (Equations 12–14 and 12–35) in vector form, so far we have explored rotational dynamics only in cases where the angular momentum vector and torque are in the same direction. When these two vectors are not collinear, new and often startling behavior results. However strange this behavior may seem, you can always understand it if you really accept the rotational analog of Newton's law—that the rate of change of the angular momentum *vector* is equal to the applied torque *vector*.

A toy gyroscope provides a common example of rotational dynamics in three dimensions. This device seems to defy gravity, balanced on a single point with most of its mass clearly unsupported (Fig. 12–35). What is going on here? The downward force of gravity produces a torque whose direction is into the page for the orientation shown in Fig. 12–35. Were the gyroscope not spinning, this torque would cause it to fall over, gaining angular momentum about its pivot point (Fig. 12–36). The change in angular momentum—here an increase—is in the same direction as the torque, in agreement with the rotational analog of Newton's law. When the gyroscope is spinning, the gravitational torque is still into the page. But now the gyroscope already has angular momentum that points along its rotation axis. The rotational analog of Newton's law states that this angular momentum *vector* must change at a rate given by the torque, and that this change must be in the same direction as the torque—at right angles to the angular momentum vector. As a result the gyroscope moves around so that its rotation axis sweeps out a circle—a phenomenon called **precession**. The torque and angular momentum vectors remain always at right angles (Fig. 12–37), so that the torque changes only the direction but not the magnitude of the angular momentum vector.

Fig. 12–35
A gyroscope.

τ, L, ΔL
into
page

Fig. 12–36
Were it not spinning, the gyroscope would fall over, gaining angular momentum about its pivot point. The change in angular momentum points in the same direction as the torque, satisfying the rotational analog of Newton's law.

precession

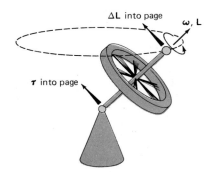

Fig. 12–37
With **L** and τ at right angles, the gyroscope precesses, its rotation axis describing a circle. The *change* in angular momentum is still in the same direction as the torque.

So why doesn't the gyroscope fall over? The reason is analogous to why a satellite doesn't fall to earth. There is a gravitational force on the satellite, but it is providing just the right force to hold the satellite in orbit. Analogously, there is a torque on the gyroscope, but it has all it can do to change the angular momentum at a rate required to maintain precession.

We can analyze the gyroscope's behavior quantitatively through Fig. 12–38, which shows a gyroscope spinning with its axis in a horizontal plane. The downward force of gravity on the unbalanced gyroscope produces a torque that is into the page in Fig. 12–38a—that is, at right angles to the angular momentum vector. In a short time dt, the angular momentum vector changes by an amount $d\mathbf{L}$ given by Equation 12–35:

$$d\mathbf{L} = \tau dt. \tag{12–36}$$

This change is shown in Fig. 12–38b, and represents a rotation of the angular momentum vector through a small angle $d\phi$. For an arbitrarily small time interval dt, and correspondingly small angle $d\phi$, the magnitude dL of the change in angular momentum is essentially equal to the arc length through which the tip of the angular momentum vector swings in Fig. 12–38b. From the definition of angle (Equation 12–3), this arc length is just $Ld\phi$, so that

$$dL = Ld\phi.$$

Combining this result with Equation 12–36 gives

$$\tau dt = Ld\phi. \tag{12–37}$$

The angular speed of precession, called Ω, is the rate at which the angular momentum vector rotates, or $d\phi/dt$. Solving Equation 12–37 for this quantity gives

$$\Omega = \frac{d\phi}{dt} = \frac{\tau}{L}. \tag{12–38}$$

Although we derived Equation 12–38 for the case of a gyroscope whose angular momentum is horizontal,* it holds true for any angle the gyroscope

*Actually, **L** in this example is not quite horizontal. The gyroscope also has a small vertical component of angular momentum associated with its precession. But if the angular momentum associated with spin about the axis is large, the precession rate and vertical component of **L** are small.

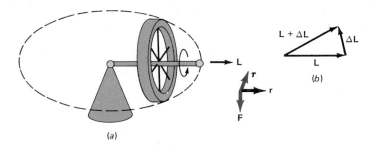

Fig. 12–38
(a) A gyroscope spinning with its axis in the horizontal plane. (b) Top view showing change in the angular momentum vector.

might make with the horizontal (see Problem 39). To use Equation 12–38 it is, of course, necessary to know both the angular momentum L and the torque τ. Problems 40 and 41 explore practical applications of this equation.

The motion of a gyroscope can be more complicated than we have described. The gyroscope's precession represents a component of angular momentum about a vertical axis. But unless it is given an initial impulse in the direction of precession, the gyroscope has initially no vertical component of angular momentum. Since the gravitational torque acts only in the horizontal direction, the vertical component of the gyroscope's angular momentum must remain zero. As a result, a gyroscope released with its angular momentum vector strictly horizontal will drop slightly as it begins to precess, gaining a downward component of angular momentum that compensates for the upward component associated with precession. In the absence of friction, it overshoots the position at which the two would balance, resulting in a slight oscillation that is called **nutation** (Fig. 12–39). If the angular momentum associated with the spin of the gyroscope is large, this nutation is very small. In any event, torques that are associated with friction at the gyroscope support usually damp out the nutation in a short time.

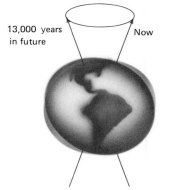

An important example of precession is provided by the earth itself. The earth is slightly bulged at its equator, and the gravitational force of the sun and moon on this bulge results in a slight torque on the tilted, spinning earth. In response, the rotation axis of the earth precesses, taking about 26,000 years to complete a full circle (Fig. 12–40). Although earth's axis points now toward the star Polaris, which we call the North Star, it will not always do so! When astronomers measure star positions in earth-based coordinates, they must take account of precession and, for extreme accuracy, of nutation as well.

Fig. 12–39
Nutation.

nutation

13,000 years in future

Now

Fig. 12–40
Torque due to the sun's gravity on earth's equatorial bulge (shown highly exaggerated) results in precession of the planet's rotation axis with a period of about 26,000 years.

Conservation of Angular Momentum in Three Dimensions

When no external torques act on a system, both the direction and magnitude of its angular momentum remain constant. For example, a spinning gyroscope that is supported at both ends maintains its rotation axis in the same direction even as it is moved about the earth (Fig. 12–41). Gyroscopes of this sort are used extensively in navigation systems. Changes in the orientation of the rotation axis relative to a submarine, ship, or aircraft are "remembered" by a computer that can consequently calculate where the craft is relative to its starting point.

Fig. 12–41
A gyrocompass. When no external torques act, the rotation axis of the shipboard gyroscope always points in the same direction.

Application

Pointing a Satellite

One way to steer a satellite (for example, to point at an astronomical object under study) is to apply torques using small gas jets. But eventually these jets run out of gas and the satellite can no longer be controlled. Another approach involves angular momentum conservation. The satellite is equipped with three internal

Fig. 12–42
The Solar Maximum Mission satellite is aimed at the sun by a reaction wheel system. An electrical failure crippled the reaction wheels about six months after launch in 1980. In 1984 Solar Max became the first satellite to be repaired in space. Here an astronaut attempts to link with the slowly spinning satellite prior to the actual repair.

Fig. 12–43
Close-up of the Solar Maximum Mission satellite reaction wheel system. Arrows at rear point to three reaction wheels with mutually perpendicular axes. At front is a fourth wheel mounted at an angle to provide redundancy should one of the others fail.

wheels whose axes are mutually perpendicular (Figs. 12–42 and 12–43). Each wheel has a motor and brakes to start and stop its rotation. When a wheel starts rotating, the satellite rotates in the opposite direction to conserve angular momentum. After the satellite has rotated through the desired angle, the wheel is stopped and the satellite also stops. The use of three wheels allows the satellite to be pointed in any direction. Electricity generated by solar panels powers the motors and brakes, so there is no fuel to run out.

SUMMARY

Rotational motion is described using quantities analogous to those of linear motion. These rotational quantities satisfy the same relations as their linear counterparts, making problems involving rotational motion similar to the linear motion problems of previous chapters.

1. The rotational analog of displacement is **angular displacement,** defined as the angle through which an object has rotated. The SI unit of angular displacement is the radian. The first and second time derivatives of angular displacement are **angular speed,** ω, and **angular acceleration,** α. **Angular velocity** ω is a vector whose magnitude is the angular speed and whose direction is along the rotation axis, as given by the right-hand rule. The **angular acceleration vector** α is the time derivative of the angular velocity vector, and points in the direction of the change in the angular velocity.

2. The rotational analog of mass is **rotational inertia,** a quantity that measures the resistance of a body to changes in rotational motion. Rotational inertia depends on the mass of a body and on the distribution of mass about the rotation axis, and is given by

$$I = \sum m_i r_i^2$$

for a body consisting of discrete masses, and by

$$I = \int r^2 dm$$

for a continuous distribution of matter.

3. **Torque** is the rotational analog of force; torque, rotational inertia, and angular acceleration are related by the rotational analog of Newton's second law:

$$\tau = I\alpha.$$

4. **Rotational kinetic energy** is calculated from rotational inertia and angular speed in the same way that translational kinetic energy is calculated from mass and linear speed:

$$K_{\text{rot}} = \tfrac{1}{2}I\omega^2.$$

The total kinetic energy of a rigid, rotating object may be written as the sum of the translational kinetic energy of its center of mass and the rotational kinetic energy about its center of mass.

5. The **angular momentum L** of a particle about some point is defined in terms of the particle's linear momentum **p** and its displacement **r** from that point:

$$\mathbf{L} = \mathbf{r} \times \mathbf{p}.$$

The angular momentum of a system of particles is the sum or integral of the angular momenta of the constituent particles. For a rigid, rotating object, the angular momentum may also be written in terms of strictly rotational quantities:

$$\mathbf{L} = I\boldsymbol{\omega},$$

in analogy with linear momentum $\mathbf{p} = m\mathbf{v}$.

The rotational analog of Newton's law may be written in terms of angular momentum as

$$\boldsymbol{\tau} = \frac{d\mathbf{L}}{dt}.$$

In the absence of external torques, the angular momentum of a system is conserved. The application of external torques to a rotating system results in a change in angular momentum. When the external torque is at right angles to the angular momentum, the angular momentum vector **precesses,** describing a circular path as its direction changes.

Table 12–3 summarizes the analogy between linear and rotational quantities.

TABLE 12–3
Linear and Angular Quantities

Linear Quantity or Equation	Angular Quantity or Equation	Relation Between Linear and Angular Quantities
Position x	Angular position θ	
Speed $v = dx/dt$	Angular speed $\omega = d\theta/dt$	$v_t = \omega r$
Velocity $\mathbf{v}$	Angular velocity $\boldsymbol{\omega}$	
Acceleration $\mathbf{a}$	Angular acceleration $\boldsymbol{\alpha}$	$a_t = \alpha r$
Mass m	Rotational inertia I	$I = \int r^2 \, dm$
Force $\mathbf{F}$	Torque $\boldsymbol{\tau}$	$\boldsymbol{\tau} = \mathbf{r} \times \mathbf{F}$

Newton's second law (constant mass or rotational inertia):

$\mathbf{F} = m\mathbf{a}$ $\boldsymbol{\tau} = I\boldsymbol{\alpha}$

Kinetic energy:

$K_{\text{trans}} = \frac{1}{2}mv^2$ $K_{\text{rot}} = \frac{1}{2}I\omega^2$

Momentum:

$\mathbf{p} = m\mathbf{v}$ (linear) $\mathbf{L} = I\boldsymbol{\omega}$ (angular) $\mathbf{L} = \mathbf{r} \times \mathbf{p}$

Newton's second law in terms of momentum:

$\mathbf{F} = d\mathbf{p}/dt$ $\boldsymbol{\tau} = d\mathbf{L}/dt$

QUESTIONS

1. Do all points on a rigid, rotating object have the same angular speed? linear speed? radial acceleration?
2. Suppose you mount tires on your car that are slightly larger in diameter than factory-supplied tires. If you are in a 55-mi/h zone and your speedometer says 55 mi/h, are you speeding? Explain.
3. A wheel undergoes a constant angular acceleration. How do each of the following depend on time: (a) tangential acceleration of a point on the rim? (b) radial acceleration of a point on the rim? (c) angular speed of the wheel?
4. Part of a train wheel extends below the point of contact with the rails, as shown in Fig. 12–44. It is often said that this part of the train moves backward. Explain.

Fig. 12–44 Question 4

5. An electric circular saw takes a long time to stop rotating after the power is turned off. Without the saw blade mounted, the motor stops much more quickly when turned off. Why?
6. A solid sphere and a solid cube have the same mass, and the side of the cube is equal to the diameter of the sphere. Which has the greatest rotational inertia about an axis through the center of mass? The rotational axis for the cube is perpendicular to two of the cube faces.
7. A badly unbalanced wheel has its center of mass located closer to its rim than to its geometrical center. The wheel is released from rest on a slope where it is free to roll without slipping. Describe its initial motion when released from each of the orientations shown in Fig. 12–45.
8. The lower leg of a horse contains essentially no muscle. How does this help the horse to run fast? Explain in terms of rotational inertia.
9. You wish to store energy in a rotating flywheel. Given a fixed amount of material, what shape should you make the flywheel so that it will store the most energy at a given angular speed?

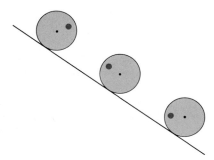

Fig. 12–45 The darker circle indicates the center of mass of the wheel (Question 7).

10. A ball starts from rest and rolls without slipping down an incline, then across a horizontal surface. It then starts up a *frictionless* incline (Fig. 12–46). Compare its maximum height on the frictionless incline with its starting height on the first incline.

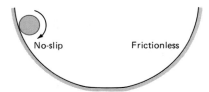

No-slip   Frictionless

Fig. 12–46 Question 10

11. Two solid cylinders of the same mass but different radii are rolling with the same linear speed. How do their translational and rotational kinetic energies compare?
12. A raw egg and a hard-boiled egg, otherwise identical, are rolled down an incline. Which hits the bottom first? Explain.
13. A cloud of interstellar matter collapses to form a star. Under what conditions will the star *not* be rotating?
14. What happens to the rotational inertia of a washing machine tub and its contents when the spin portion of the cycle starts?
15. A bug, initially at rest on a stationary record turntable, begins walking around the turntable. After a while the bug stops. Must the turntable stop immediately? Or must it first return to its initial angular position? Or must it keep rotating?
16. Tornadoes in the northern hemisphere rotate counterclockwise, as viewed from above. A farfetched suggestion was once made that tornadoes occur more frequently in the northern hemisphere because most vehicles drive on the right-hand side of the road. Could there by any physical basis for this suggestion? Explain in terms of the angular momentum imparted to the air by vehicles passing in opposite directions.
17. As they are launched, rockets are often set rotating about a vertical axis. Why does this help stabilize the rockets?

18. A physics student is standing on a nonrotating platform that is free to rotate, and is holding a wheel that is rotating about a vertical axis (Fig. 12–47). Describe what happens if she turns the wheel upside down.

Fig. 12–47 Question 18

19. How does angular momentum conservation help explain why there are seasons on earth?
20. A gyroscope is spinning with its rotation axis horizontal, and is precessing about a vertical axis. If a weight is hung from the end of the gyroscope (Fig. 12–48), its precession rate increases. Why does this happen?

w

Fig. 12–48 The gyroscope precesses faster when a weight is hung from its end (Question 20).

21. A balanced gyroscope is spinning without precessing, its rotation axis horizontal. If you push with your finger in a horizontal direction at right angles to the rotation axis (Fig. 12–49), what happens?

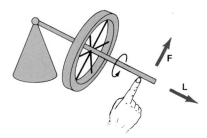

F

L

Fig. 12–49 Question 21

PROBLEMS

Section 12.1 *Angular Velocity and Acceleration*

1. Determine the angular speed, in rad/s, of (a) earth about its axis; (b) the minute hand of a clock; (c) the hour hand of a clock; (d) an egg beater turning at 300 rpm.

2. What is the linear speed of a point on earth's equator? At your latitude?

3. Express Equation 12–4 with constants appropriate to angular speed in (a) rpm, (b) rev/s, (c) °/s.

4. A 25-cm-diameter circular saw blade spins at 3500 rpm. How fast would you have to push a straight hand saw to have the teeth move through the wood at the same rate as the circular saw teeth?

5. A wheel is turned through 2.0 revolutions while being accelerated at 18 rpm/s. (a) What is the final angular speed? (b) How long does it take to turn the 2.0 revolutions?

6. You switch a record turntable from 45 rpm to $33\frac{1}{3}$ rpm. The turntable takes 2.2 s to reach the new speed. Assuming that the deceleration is constant, how many revolutions does the turntable make during this time?

7. The angular acceleration of a wheel in rad/s² is given by $24t^2 - 16t^3$, where t is the time in seconds. The wheel starts from rest at $t = 0$. (a) When is it again at rest? (b) How many revolutions has it turned between $t = 0$ and when it is again at rest?

8. A circular saw blade completes 1200 revolutions in 40 s while coasting to a stop after being turned off. Assuming constant deceleration, what are (a) the angular deceleration and (b) the initial angular speed?

Section 12–2 *Rotational Inertia and the Analog of Newton's Law*

9. Each propeller on a King Air twin engine airplane consists of three blades, each of mass 10 kg and length 125 cm. The blades may be treated approximately as uniform, thin rods. (a) What is the rotational inertia of the propeller? (b) If the propeller is driven by an engine that develops a torque of 2700 N·m, how long will it take to change the propeller's angular speed from 1400 rpm to 1900 rpm? Neglect the rotational inertia of the engine and any aerodynamic forces on the propeller.

10. A neutron star is an extremely dense, rapidly spinning object that results from the collapse of a star at the end of its life (see Example 12–17). A neutron star of 1.8 times the sun's mass has an approximately uniform density of 1×10^{18} kg/m³. (a) What is its rotational inertia? (b) The neutron star's spin rate slowly decreases as a result of torque associated with magnetic forces. If the spin-down rate is 5×10^{-5} rad/s², what is the magnetic torque?

11. Verify by direct integration the formula given in Table 12–2 for the rotational inertia of a flat plate about a central axis.

12. Use the parallel axis theorem to derive the rotational inertia of a sphere about a tangent line from that of a sphere about a diameter (see Table 12–2).

13. A square frame is made from four thin rods, each of length ℓ and mass m. Calculate its rotational inertia about the three axes shown in Fig. 12–50.

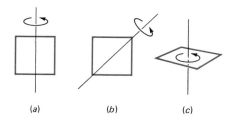

(a)   (b)   (c)

Fig. 12–50 Problem 13

14. Proof of the parallel axis theorem: Fig. 12–51 shows an object of mass M with axes through the center of mass and through an arbitrary point A. Both axes are perpendicular to the page. Let **h** be a vector from the axis through the center of mass to the axis through point A, $\mathbf{r}_{cm}$ a vector from the axis through the CM to an arbitrary mass element dm, and **r** a vector from the axis through point A to the mass element dm, as shown. (a) Use the law of cosines to show that

$$r^2 = r_{cm}^2 + h^2 - 2\mathbf{h} \cdot \mathbf{r}_{cm}.$$

(b) Use this result in the expression $I = \int r^2 dm$ to calculate the rotational inertia of the object about the axis through A. Each of the three terms in your expression for r^2 leads to a separate integral. Identify one as the rotational inertia about the CM, another as the quantity Mh^2, and show that the third is zero because it involves the position of the center of mass relative to the center of mass. Your result is then a statement of the parallel axis theorem.

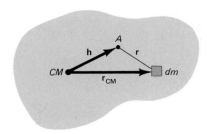

Fig. 12–51 Problem 14

15. Two blocks of mass m_1 and m_2 are connected by a massless string that passes over a solid cylindrical pulley, as shown in Fig. 12–52. The surface under the block m_2 is frictionless, and the pulley rides on frictionless bearings. The string passes over the pulley

without slipping. When released, the masses accelerate at $\frac{1}{3}g$. The tension in the lower half of the string is 2.7 N and that in the upper half, 1.9 N. What are the masses of the pulley and of the two blocks?

Fig. 12–52   Problem 15

16. A disk of radius R and thickness w has a mass density that increases from the center outward, being given by $\rho = \rho_0 r/R$, where r is the distance from the axis of the disk. (a) Calculate the total mass M of the disk. (b) Calculate the rotational inertia about the disk axis, in terms of M and R. Compare with the results for a solid disk of uniform density and for a ring.

17. A space station is constructed in the shape of a wheel 22 m in diameter, with essentially all of its 5.0×10^5-kg mass at the rim (Fig. 12–53). Once the station is completed, it is set rotating at a rate that requires an object at the rim to have radial acceleration g, thereby simulating earth's surface gravity. This is accomplished using two small rockets, each with 100 N thrust, that are mounted on the rim of the station as shown. (a) How long will it take to reach the desired spin rate? (b) How many revolutions will the station make in this time?

Fig. 12–53   Problem 17

18. A standard 108-g Frisbee is 24 cm in diameter and has about half its mass spread uniformly in a disk, and the other half concentrated in the rim. With a quarter-turn flick of the wrist, a student sets the Frisbee rotating at 550 rpm. (a) What is the rotational inertia of the Frisbee? (b) What is the magnitude of the torque, assumed constant, that the student applies?

19. The crane shown in Fig. 12–54 contains a hollow drum of mass 150 kg and radius 0.80 m that is driven by an engine to wind up a cable. The cable passes over a solid cylindrical 30-kg pulley 0.30 m in radius to lift a 2000-N weight. How much torque must the engine apply to the drum to lift the weight with an acceleration of 1.0 m/s²? Neglect the rotational inertia of the engine and the mass of the cable.

Fig. 12–54   Problem 19

20. A 2.4-kg block rests on a 30° slope, and is attached by a string of negligible mass to a solid drum of mass 0.85 kg and radius 5.0 cm, as shown in Fig. 12–55. When released, the block accelerates down the slope at 1.6 m/s². What is the coefficient of friction between block and slope?

Fig. 12–55   Problem 20

21. A bicycle is under repair, and is upside-down with its 66-cm-diameter wheel spinning freely at 230 rpm. The mass of the wheel is 1.9 kg, and is concentrated mostly at the rim. The cyclist holds a wrench against the tire for 3.1 s, with a normal force of 2.7 N. If the coefficient of friction between the wrench and the tire is 0.46, what is the final angular speed of the wheel?

22. At the National Magnet Laboratory at MIT, energy is stored in huge solid flywheels of mass 7.7×10^4 kg and radius 2.4 m. If the flywheels ride on shafts 41 cm in diameter, and if the coefficient of friction between shafts and bearings is 0.018, how long would it take a flywheel to coast to a stop from its normal rotation rate of 360 rpm?

Section 12.3   *Energy and Rotational Motion*

23. The flywheel of the previous problem is used to generate a large amount of electric power for a short time. If the wheel's rotation rate is dropped from 390 to 300 rpm in 5.0 s, (a) what is the average power output and (b) what fraction of the rotational kinetic energy has been removed?

24. A 25-cm-diameter circular saw blade has a mass of 0.85 kg, distributed uniformly as in a disk. (a) What is its rotational kinetic energy at 3500 rpm? (b) What average power must be applied to bring the blade from rest to 3500 rpm in 3.2 s?

25. In the stellar collapse of Example 12–17, by what factor does the rotational kinetic energy of the star change?

26. An object of rotational inertia I is initially at rest. A torque is then applied to the object, causing it to begin rotating. The torque is applied for only one-quarter of a revolution, during which time its magnitude is given by $\tau = A\cos\theta$, where A is a constant and θ is the angle through which the object has rotated. What is the final angular speed of the object?

27. The rotational kinetic energy of a rolling automobile wheel is 40% of its translational kinetic energy. The wheel is then redesigned to have 10% lower rotational inertia and 20% less mass, while keeping its radius the same. By what percentage does its total kinetic energy at a given speed decrease?

28. Two solid cylinders of the same mass roll without slipping down an incline. If they start from the same height h, show that they reach the bottom with the same linear speed, even if their radii are not the same. What is the linear speed at the bottom?

29. A ball rolls without slipping down a slope of vertical height 35 cm, and reaches the bottom moving at 2.0 m/s. Is the ball hollow or solid?

30. A solid ball of mass M and radius R starts at rest at height h above the bottom of the path shown in Fig. 12–56. It rolls without slipping down the left side of the path. The right side of the path, starting at the bottom, is frictionless. To what height does the ball rise on the right?

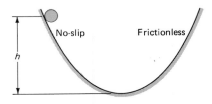

Fig. 12–56   Problem 30

31. A solid marble of radius r starts from rest and rolls without slipping on the loop-the-loop track shown in Fig. 12–57. Find the minimum starting height of the marble from which it will remain on the track through the loop.

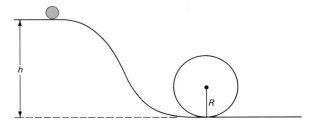

Fig. 12–57   Problem 31

32. A 100-g yo-yo consists of two disks joined by a narrower shaft. The rotational inertia of the yo-yo is 600 g·cm². A string 80 cm long is wound around the narrow shaft of the yo-yo. With the yo-yo initially 50 cm off the ground, the string is pulled vertically upward with a force of 0.98 N until the string comes entirely free of the yo-yo. The yo-yo then falls freely. What are its rotational and translational kinetic energies just before it hits the ground?

Section 12.4   *Angular Momentum*

33. What is the angular momentum of the earth about its own axis? About an axis through the center of the sun and perpendicular to earth's orbital plane? See Appendix F, and consider earth to be a uniform sphere.

34. A 150-g baseball has an angular momentum of 7.7 kg·m²/s about a vertical axis through the batter. If it is moving at 43 m/s without spinning, by how much does it miss the axis of the batter?

35. About 99.9% of the mass of the solar system lies in the sun. Referring to Appendix F, estimate what fraction of the angular momentum of the solar system about the sun's axis is associated with the sun. Where is most of the rest of the angular momentum?

36. Two ants, each of mass 0.012 g, are standing at rest on a motionless record turntable with rotational inertia 0.010 kg·m², one 5.0 cm from the center and the other 11 cm from the center. The ants start walking in the same direction around the turntable, at 0.90 cm/s relative to the turntable. How long will it take the turntable to complete one revolution?

37. A physics student is standing on an initially motionless, frictionless turntable with rotational inertia 0.31 kg·m². She is holding a wheel of rotational inertia 0.22 kg·m² spinning at 130 rpm about a vertical axis, as shown in Fig. 12–58. When she turns the wheel upside down, the student and turntable begin rotating at 70 rpm. (a) What is the student's mass, considering her to be a cylinder 30 cm in diameter? (b) How much work did it take to turn the wheel upside down?

38. A 3.0-m-diameter merry-go-round with a rotational inertia of 120 kg·m² is spinning freely at 0.50 rev/s. Four 25-kg children sit suddenly on the edge of the merry-go-round. Find the new angular speed and de-

Fig. 12–58   Problem 37

termine the total energy lost to friction between the children and the merry-go-round.

39. Derive Equation 12–38 for the case of a gyroscope whose angular momentum vector is not necessarily in a horizontal plane.

40. After being "spun up," the gyroscope of Example 12–12 is placed with one end on a frictionless stand, with its axis horizontal. The rotating ring of the gyroscope is 3.0 cm from the end, and the mass of the rest of the gyroscope is negligible compared with that of the ring. What is the precession rate of the gyroscope?

41. A gyroscope consists of a disk and shaft mounted on frictionless bearings in a circular frame of diameter d. Initially the gyroscope is spinning with angular speed ω, and is perfectly balanced so it is not precessing (Fig. 12–59). When a mass m is hung from the frame at one of the shaft bearings, the gyroscope precesses with angular speed Ω. Find the rotational inertia of the disk in terms of the quantities given.

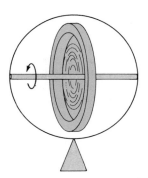

Fig. 12–59   Problem 41

Supplementary Problems

42. A 55-kg diver is spinning forward in a tuck position at 2.1 rev/s, as shown in Fig. 12–60a. In this position, the diver's rotational inertia is 3.9 kg·m². At the peak of her trajectory, the diver suddenly straightens out in a horizontal position as shown in Fig. 12–60b. In this new position, the diver has an overall length of 2.2 m with center of mass midway along this length, and a rotational inertia of 21 kg·m² about the rotation axis. What is the minimum height of the diver above the water if she is to enter the water hands first? Neglect the diver's horizontal translational motion.

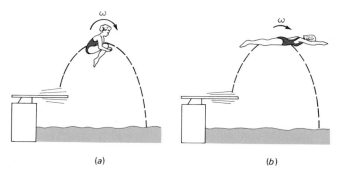

(a)   (b)

Fig. 12–60   Problem 42

43. A rod of length ℓ and mass M is suspended from a pivot, as shown in Fig. 12–61. The rod is struck midway along its length by a wad of putty of mass m moving horizontally at speed v. The putty sticks to the rod. What is the minimum speed v that will result in the rod's making a complete circle rather than swinging like a pendulum?

Fig. 12–61   Problem 43

44. A 30-cm-diameter phonograph record is dropped onto a turntable being driven at $33\frac{1}{3}$ rpm. If the coefficient of friction between record and turntable is 0.19, how far will the turntable rotate between the time when the record first contacts it and when the record is rotating at the full $33\frac{1}{3}$ rpm? Assume that the record is a homogeneous disk. *Hint:* You will need to do an integral to calculate the torque.

45. The contraption shown in Fig. 12–62 consists of two solid rubber wheels each of mass M and radius R that are mounted on an axle of negligible mass in a rigid square frame made of thin rods of mass m and length

ℓ. The axle bearings are frictionless, and the wheels are mounted symmetrically about the center line of the frame, just far enough apart that they don't touch. The whole contraption is floating freely in space, and the frame is not rotating. The wheels are rotating with angular speed ω in the same direction, as shown. A mechanism built into the frame moves the axles very slightly so that the wheels touch and frictional forces act between them. Describe quantitatively the motion of the system after the wheels have stopped slipping against each other.

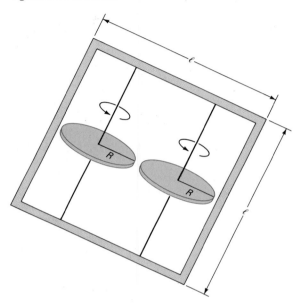

Fig. 12–62   Problem 45

46. A small mass m slides on the inside of a frictionless, cone-shaped surface as shown in Fig. 12–63. At its highest point, it is a distance h_0 above the vertex of the cone, and has speed v_0. What is the minimum height above the vertex that the mass reaches as it moves around the surface? *Hint:* What quantities are conserved?

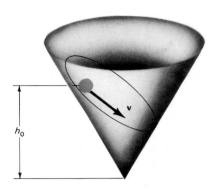

Fig. 12–63   Problem 46

47. In 1609, Johannes Kepler presented his famous equal-area law, stating that the planets move in such a way that a line from a planet to the sun sweeps out equal areas in equal times (Fig. 12–64). Later, Newton showed that the equal-area law is a consequence of his law of universal gravitation. In fact, the equal-area law holds for any *central* force—any force, like the gravitational force of the sun, that is always directed toward the same point. Show that a central force cannot exert any torque about the center of force, and that the angular momentum of an object moving under the influence of such a force cannot change. Use this result to prove the equal-area law. *Hint:* Consider the small area dA swept out in a small time dt, and show that the "areal velocity," dA/dt, is constant.

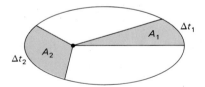

Fig. 12–64   (Problem 47) Kepler's equal-area law. If the time intervals Δt_1 and Δt_2 are equal, then so are the areas A_1 and A_2.

13

OSCILLATORY MOTION

oscillatory motion

When we disturb a system in stable equilibrium, forces within the system tend to restore its equilibrium. For example, if the ball of Fig. 13–1 is disturbed, it experiences a net force toward its equilibrium position at the bottom of the valley. This force accelerates the ball toward equilibrium, and if frictional energy losses are not too great it reaches the bottom with some kinetic energy. As a result, it overshoots its equilibrium, now moving up the opposite side of the valley. Again, a force develops that points back toward equilibrium. This force decelerates the ball, which eventually stops and then heads back toward the bottom. Again it may overshoot. The result is **oscillatory motion**—the movement of the ball back and forth about its equilibrium position. Were there no friction, this oscillation would continue forever. In a real system, of course, friction eventually dissipates the energy, and the system settles into equilibrium.

A wide variety of physical systems are in stable equilibrium, but subject to occasional disturbances. As a result, these systems frequently undergo oscillatory motion. Examples of oscillatory motion can therefore be found throughout the vast realm of physical phenomena. A uranium nu-

Fig. 13–1
(a) A ball in stable equilibrium at the bottom of a valley. *(b)* If the ball is disturbed from equilibrium, it oscillates about its equilibrium position.

(a)   (b)

Fig. 13-2
The collapse of the Tacoma Narrows Bridge in Washington occurred because the bridge design did not anticipate large-scale oscillatory motion of the structure; see also Fig. 13–37.

cleus undergoes oscillations before it fissions. The oscillatory motion of the atoms in water molecules is responsible for cooking in a microwave oven. When your professor squeaks chalk on the blackboard, contact between chalk and board disturbs the equilibrium state of the chalk, setting up an oscillation that produces the horrible sound you hear. The timekeeping mechanism of a watch—whether an old-fashioned spring and balance wheel or a modern quartz crystal—is a carefully engineered system whose disturbance from equilibrium results in a very precise oscillatory motion. Musical instruments work because of oscillatory motion. Even large-scale structures like buildings and bridges undergo oscillatory motions about their equilibria; if these oscillations are not accounted for in the design of the structure, the result can be disaster (Fig. 13–2). Finally, many stars undergo oscillations about their equilibrium sizes (Fig. 13–3). Oscillatory motion is a universal phenomenon. In this chapter, we develop a detailed description of oscillatory motion and apply that description to a variety of physical systems.

13.1
PROPERTIES OF OSCILLATORY MOTION

amplitude
period
frequency

Oscillatory motion is characterized by the maximum size of the displacement from equilibrium—called the **amplitude** of oscillation—and by the time it takes for the motion to repeat itself—the **period** of oscillation. Closely related to the period is the **frequency** of oscillation, defined as the number of oscillation cycles per unit time. The frequency and period are simply inverses:

$$f = \frac{1}{T}, \tag{13–1}$$

hertz

where f is the frequency and T the period. The unit of frequency is the cycle/second, which is given the name **hertz** (Hz), after the German physicist, engineer, and mathematician Heinrich Hertz (1857–1894), who was the first to produce and detect radio waves.

Fig. 13-3
The star δ Cephei exhibits periodic variations in brightness, corresponding to oscillatory motion of the star about its equilibrium configuration. Magnitude (vertical axis) is an astronomical measure of brightness, with lower magnitude representing higher brightness.

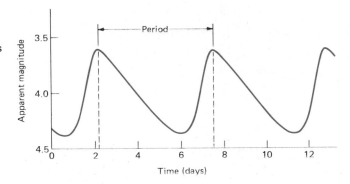

Example 13–1
Amplitude, Period, and Frequency

Bored by a physics lecture, a student holds one end of a flexible plastic ruler against a book and idly strikes the other end, setting it into oscillation (Fig. 13–4). The student notes that 28 complete cycles occur in 10 s, and that the end of the ruler moves a total distance of 8.0 cm, as shown in Fig. 13–4. What are the amplitude, period, and frequency of this oscillatory motion?

Solution

We have defined amplitude as the maximum displacement from equilibrium. Since the end of the ruler moves both left and right of equilibrium, the amplitude of the motion is 4.0 cm. (The full 8.0-cm motion is called the **peak-to-peak** amplitude.) With 28 cycles in 10 s, the time per cycle, or period, is

$$T = \frac{10 \text{ s}}{28} = 0.36 \text{ s}.$$

The frequency in Hz is the inverse of the period:

$$f = \frac{1}{T} = \frac{1}{0.36 \text{ s}} = 2.8 \text{ Hz}.$$

peak-to-peak

Fig. 13–4
Top view of a ruler undergoing oscillatory motion (Example 13–1).

8.0 cm

Amplitude and period or frequency do not completely characterize an arbitrary oscillatory motion, for they do not describe in detail how a system behaves over one cycle. The behavior of a ball bouncing between two rigid walls (Fig. 13–5a) is quite different from that of a ball rolling in a U-shaped valley (Fig. 13–5b). The difference lies in the force as a function of position. For the ball bouncing between rigid walls, the force acts only when the ball is in contact with the walls; between bounces, the ball moves with constant speed. For the ball in the valley, a force acts as soon as the ball moves from its equilibrium position, and the force increases as the ball moves up the ever-steepening sides of the valley. In the rest of this chapter, we examine the important case of oscillatory motion that results from a force that is proportional to displacement from equilibrium.

13.2
SIMPLE HARMONIC MOTION

For a wide variety of physical systems, the force that develops when a body is displaced from a stable equilibrium is directly proportional to the displacement. For many other systems, this proportionality is an approximation that becomes increasingly accurate for small displacements. The kind of motion that results from such a force is therefore common in physical systems, and is called **simple harmonic motion:**

simple harmonic motion

> Simple harmonic motion is the motion that results when an object is subject to a restoring force proportional to its displacement from equilibrium.

Mathematically, we can describe such a force by writing

$$F = -kx,$$

(13–2)

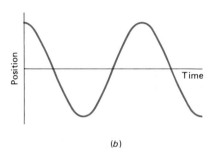

Fig. 13–5
Displacement as a function of time
(a) for a ball bouncing between rigid
walls and *(b)* for a ball rolling in a U-
shaped valley like that of Fig. 13–1.

SIMPLE HARMONIC MOTION IS
THE MOTION THAT RESULTS FROM
A RESTORING FORCE THAT IS
PROPORTIONAL TO ITS DISPLACEMENT
FROM EQUILIBRIUM.

Fig. 13–6
Simple harmonic motion results from a
restoring force that is *proportional* to
the displacement from equilibrium.

differential equation
dependent variable
independent variable

Fig. 13–7
A mass attached to an ideal spring
undergoes simple harmonic motion.
The mass is on a frictionless surface,
and the spring exerts a force if it is
either stretched or compressed from its
equilibrium position.

where F is the force, x the displacement, and k a constant giving the proportionality between force and displacement. The minus sign in Equation 13–2 indicates a *restoring* force: if the object is displaced in some direction, the force is in the *opposite* direction, so that it tends to *restore* the equilibrium (Fig. 13–6).

Although we have phrased our definition of simple harmonic motion and Equation 13–2 in terms of force F and linear displacement x, simple harmonic motion also results if a body is subject to a restoring torque proportional to its angular displacement from equilibrium. More generally, any system whose tendency to return to equilibrium is proportional to how far it is displaced from equilibrium will exhibit simple harmonic motion.

Comparison with Equation 4–7 shows that Equation 13–2 is the equation for the force in an ideal spring, where k is the spring constant. For this reason, a system consisting of a mass on a spring (Fig. 13–7) undergoes a simple harmonic motion. Many other systems—even atoms and molecules—can often be understood by modelling them as miniature mass-spring systems (see Example 13–7 and Problem 5).

We have defined simple harmonic motion, but we have not described it. How does a body in simple harmonic motion actually move? We can find out by applying Newton's second law, $\mathbf{F} = m\mathbf{a}$, to the mass-spring system of Fig. 13–7. For this system, the force on the mass m is $-kx$ from Equation 13–2, so that Newton's law becomes

$$ma = -kx, \qquad (13–3)$$

where we take the x-axis to be along the direction of the motion with origin at the equilibrium position. To describe the motion in detail, we need to know how the position x depends on time. Although time does not appear explicitly in Equation 13–3, it is implicitly present because the acceleration a is the second time derivative of position. Thus Equation 13–3 may be written

$$m \frac{d^2x}{dt^2} = -kx. \qquad (13–4)$$

The unknown in Equation 13–4 is the displacement, x. But the solution to this equation is not a simple number like $x = 5.0$ m, but is rather a function of time. Equation 13–4 is a **differential equation**: the unknown (or **dependent**) variable—in this case x—appears in a derivative with respect to the known (or **independent**) variable—in this case t. Differential equations occur throughout physics and engineering, and finding their solutions often presents fascinating challenges to the theoretical physicist, applied mathematician, or computer scientist.

What does it mean to solve an equation? To solve the equation $2x = 6$ means to find a value for x that, when substituted into the equation, yields an identity—in this case $6 = 6$. Similarly, to solve Equation 13–4 means to find a function of time which, when substituted for x in the equation, results in an identity. What function might it be? We expect the system to undergo oscillatory motion. This *physical* insight suggests a *mathematical* solution that is periodic. Equation 13–4 tells us further that our solution x must be proportional to its own second derivative. You know two periodic functions with this property: sine and cosine. (Differentiate sine and you get cosine; differentiate cosine and you get −sine. Similarly, start with cosine and after two differentiations you have −cosine.) So we might expect our solution to Equation 13–4 to involve sine or cosine functions whose arguments depend on the time t. We know physically that we can have oscillatory motions with different amplitudes and frequencies; our solution should therefore be flexible enough to accommodate these differences. Just as we need an origin—the equilibrium position—from which to measure distances, so we also need to define an initial time $t=0$ from which our times are measured. A mathematical form that accommodates different amplitudes, frequencies, and initial times is

$$x = x_0 \cos(\omega t + \phi), \tag{13–5}$$

where x_0, ω, and ϕ are constants.

What is the physical significance of the constants in Equation 13–5? Since the cosine function itself varies between $+1$ and -1, the quantity x_0 multiplying the cosine is just the amplitude, or greatest displacement from equilibrium (Fig. 13–8).

The cosine—and thus the oscillatory motion that is described by Equation 13–5—undergoes a full cycle as its argument increases by 2π. In Equation 13–5, the argument of the cosine is $(\omega t + \phi)$. Since the time for one full cycle of the oscillatory motion is the period T, the argument of the cosine must increase by 2π as time increases by T:

$$\omega(t + T) + \phi = \omega t + \phi + 2\pi,$$

so that $\omega T = 2\pi$, or

$$T = \frac{2\pi}{\omega}. \tag{13–6}$$

The frequency of the motion is then

$$f = \frac{1}{T} = \frac{\omega}{2\pi}. \tag{13–7}$$

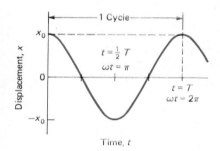

Fig. 13–8
The function $x_0 \cos\omega t$. This function varies between $\pm x_0$, and undergoes one full cycle as ωt increases by 2π.

Equation 13–7 shows that ω is a measure of the frequency, although it differs from the frequency in Hz by a factor of 2π. ω is called the **angular frequency**, and is measured in rad/s or, since radians are dimensionless, simply in s^{-1}. The relation between angular frequency and frequency in Hz is the same as that between angular speed in rad/s and in rev/s that we encountered in the previous chapter. Here, as there, we introduce the quantity ω because it affords the simplest mathematical description of the motion we are studying—in this case simple harmonic motion. This similarity between the descriptions of simple harmonic motion and of rotational motion is no coincidence, as we will explore further in Section 13.4.

Finally, as Fig. 13–9 shows, the constant ϕ—called the **phase constant**—is related to our choice for $t=0$, or, equivalently, to the initial displacement of the oscillating mass. You might wonder why we chose a cosine instead of a sine in writing Equation 13–5. It really doesn't matter which we use; our freedom to choose the phase constant ϕ means that the special cases $\cos\omega t$ and $\sin\omega t$ are included in Equation 13–5. In the former case $\phi = 0$, while in the latter $\phi = -\pi/2$, as you can see from the trigometric identity $\cos(\alpha - \pi/2) = \sin\alpha$.

angular frequency

phase constant

Fig. 13–9
The phase constant φ determines the displacement x at time t=0. *(a)* φ=0 corresponds to oscillation with maximum displacement at t=0, while *(b)* φ = −π/4 shifts the cosine curve to the right by π/4. *(c)* φ = −π/2 corresponds to oscillation passing through equilibrium at time t=0.

Merely writing the displacement x in the form 13–5 does not guarantee that we have a solution; we must now find out if the assumed solution 13–5 makes Equation 13–4 into an identity. Equation 13–4 contains both x and its second derivative. If x is given by Equation 13–5, then its first derivative is

$$\frac{dx}{dt} = \frac{d}{dt}[x_0 \cos(\omega t + \phi)] = -x_0\omega \sin(\omega t + \phi), \qquad (13\text{–}8)$$

where we have used the chain rule for differentiation (see Appendix B). Then the second time derivative is

$$\frac{d^2x}{dt^2} = \frac{d}{dt}\left(\frac{dx}{dt}\right) = \frac{d}{dt}[-x_0\omega \sin(\omega t + \phi)] = -x_0\omega^2 \cos(\omega t + \phi). \qquad (13\text{–}9)$$

We can now try out the assumed solution for x (Equation 13–5), and its second time-derivative (Equation 13–9), in the differential equation 13–4. Substituting x and d^2x/dt^2 in the appropriate places gives

$$m[-x_0\omega^2 \cos(\omega t + \phi)] \overset{?}{=} -k[x_0 \cos(\omega t + \phi)], \qquad (13\text{–}10)$$

where the ? indicates that we are still trying to find out if this is indeed an equality. Now Equation 13–10 must be true *for all values of time t*. Why? Because Newton's law holds at all times, and Equation 13–10 is derived from Newton's law for the mass-spring system. Fortunately, the time-dependent term $\cos(\omega t + \phi)$ appears on both sides of the equation, so that we can cancel it. Had this not been possible, there would have been no way to make Equation 13–10 an identity for all times. We notice, too, that the constant x_0 and the minus sign cancel from the equation, leaving only

$$m\omega^2 = k. \qquad (13\text{–}11)$$

What is Equation 13–11 telling us? This equation follows directly from Newton's law, if we assume a solution of the form 13–5. If that solution is to be correct, then Equation 13–11 must be an identity. This is possible, but only if the angular frequency ω is given by

$$\omega = \sqrt{\frac{k}{m}}. \qquad (13\text{–}12)$$

So what does all this mean physically? Equation 13–5 *is* a possible description of the motion of a mass m on a spring of spring constant k, provided the angular frequency ω is given by Equation 13–12. Equivalently, using Equation 13–7, we can write the frequency in Hz as

$$f = \frac{\omega}{2\pi} = \frac{1}{2\pi}\sqrt{\frac{k}{m}}, \qquad (13\text{–}13)$$

so that the period of the motion is

$$T = \frac{1}{f} = \frac{2\pi}{\omega} = 2\pi\sqrt{\frac{m}{k}}. \qquad (13\text{–}14)$$

Does the relation of frequency to mass m and spring constant k make physical sense? If we increase the mass m, it becomes harder to accelerate, so that we expect slower oscillation. Indeed, this is reflected in Equations 13–12 and 13–13, where m appears in the denominator. Similarly, if we increase the spring constant k, the spring becomes stiffer, and able to provide larger accelerations. As a result, the frequency should increase—and it does, as shown by the presence of k in the numerator of Equations 13–12 and 13–13. Physical systems display a large range of m and k values and a correspondingly large range of oscillation frequencies. An atom, with its small mass and its "springiness" provided by electrical forces, may oscillate at 10^{13} Hz or more (see Problem 5 and Example 13–7). A massive skyscraper, whose "springiness" is in the inherent flexibility of its construction materials, may oscillate at frequencies around 0.1 Hz (see Example 13–2). You can verify that Equations 13–12 and 13–13 give the right units for frequency (see Problem 1).

What about the amplitude x_0? It cancelled from our equations, showing that Equation 13–5 is a solution of Equation 13–4 for *any* value of x_0. Physically, this means that we can have simple harmonic motion of any amplitude we choose, and that the frequency of that motion does not depend on amplitude. Independence of frequency and amplitude is one of the particularly simple features of simple harmonic motion, and arises because the restoring force is *directly proportional* to the displacement. When the restoring force does not take the mathematically simple form $F = -kx$, then the frequency does depend on amplitude and the analysis of oscillatory motion becomes much more complicated (see Problem 55). In particular, if a real spring is stretched too far, the force it develops is no longer directly proportional to displacement. For this reason, simple harmonic motion occurs in real springs and other systems usually only for relatively small-amplitude oscillations.

Just as the amplitude x_0 dropped out of our equations, so did the phase constant ϕ. Again, this shows that a solution of the form 13–5 satisfies Newton's law—Equation 13–4 for the mass-spring system—for any choice of phase constant. Thus of the three constants x_0, ω, and ϕ that appear in our solution, one—the angular frequency ω—is determined by the physical properties m and k of the system, while the other two can take on arbitrary values. What determines those values? They are determined by initial conditions—x_0 by how far the spring is stretched initially, and ϕ by the exact time when the motion starts.

You might wonder whether Equation 13–4 admits solutions other than Equation 13–5. The answer is no. In the study of differential equations, it is shown that an equation like 13–5 that contains a second derivative as its highest derivative has as its most general solution a function that, like Equation 13–5, contains two arbitrary constants. Specification of those constants in accordance with initial conditions then gives the particular solution valid in specific circumstances. So *all* oscillating mass-spring systems are described by Equation 13–5; specification of amplitude x_0 and phase constant ϕ then gives a description applicable in a specific situation.

Since Equation 13–5 is indeed a solution for the position of the oscillating mass as a function of time, the first and second derivatives of that

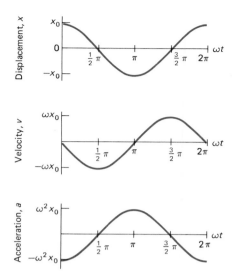

Fig. 13–10
Graphs of displacement, velocity, and acceleration in simple harmonic motion. The phase constant ϕ has been taken to be zero.

equation—Equations 13–8 and 13–9—must be the velocity and acceleration, respectively. From Equation 13–8, we see that the velocity is a sine function when the displacement is a cosine function. The velocity is therefore a maximum when the displacement is zero, and vice versa. As the mass moves through its equilibrium position, it has its maximum speed; at the extremes of its displacement, it is instantaneously stopped. Equation 13–8 also shows that the maximum velocity is given by $x_0\omega$. This makes sense because, for a fixed amplitude x_0, a higher-frequency oscillation requires a larger velocity in order to traverse the same distance in a shorter time. Similar analysis of Equation 13–9 shows that the displacement and acceleration reach their extremes at the same time, but with opposite signs. When the displacement has its greatest positive value, the acceleration has its greatest negative value, showing that the spring force tends to restore the system to equilibrium. This relation between acceleration and displacement makes good physical sense, for at maximum displacement the spring exerts its greatest force, and therefore provides the greatest acceleration. Figure 13–10 summarizes the relations among displacement, velocity, and acceleration over one cycle.

Example 13–2

A Skyscraper in Simple Harmonic Motion

The huge mass-spring system shown in Fig. 13–11 is mounted on the top floor of New York's 300-m (900-ft) high Citicorp Tower. It is engineered to oscillate at the same frequency as the building itself, but out of phase, thereby reducing the overall oscillation amplitude of the building. The 3.73×10^5-kg concrete block completes one oscillation in 6.80 s, and the oscillation amplitude in a high wind is 110 cm. Determine the spring constant and the maximum speed and acceleration experienced by the concrete block. Write an equation describing the position x of the block as a function of time, assuming it is in equilibrium and moving toward positive x at time $t = 0$.

Fig. 13–11
(Left) New York's 59-floor Citicorp Tower. Like other skyscrapers, this building can be set into simple harmonic motion by the force of the wind. (Center) To reduce the building's tendency to oscillate, this huge mass-spring system was constructed on the top floor. The 410-ton mass and springs are engineered to have the same oscillation frequency as the building. The mass rides on a film of oil, and is set oscillating 180° out of phase with the building, thereby reducing the amplitude of the building's oscillation. (Right) A similar "tuned mass damper" in action on Boston's John Hancock Building. (See also color plate 2.)

Solution

Since we know the frequency and period, we can solve Equation 13–12 for the spring constant k:

$$k = \frac{4\pi^2 m}{T^2} = \frac{(4\pi^2)(3.73 \times 10^5 \text{ kg})}{(6.80 \text{ s})^2} = 3.18 \times 10^5 \text{ N/m}.$$

Equations 13–8 and 13–9 show that the maximum speed and acceleration are $v_{max} = \omega x_0$ and $a_{max} = \omega x_0^2$. In terms of the period, the angular frequency may be obtained from Equation 13–6:

$$\omega = \frac{2\pi}{T} = \frac{2\pi}{6.80 \text{ s}} = 0.924 \text{ s}^{-1},$$

so that

$$v_{max} = \omega x_0 = (0.924 \text{ s}^{-1})(1.10 \text{ m}) = 1.02 \text{ m/s}$$

and

$$a_{max} = \omega^2 x_0 = (0.924 \text{ s}^{-1})^2(1.10 \text{ m}) = 0.939 \text{ m/s}^2.$$

Finally, the position as a function of time is given by Equation 13–5, with our values $x_0 = 1.10$ m and $\omega = 0.924$ s^{-1}. What about the phase constant ϕ? We want a sinusoidal curve that has $x = 0$ at $t = 0$, with x increasing at that point. The appropriate form is $\cos(\omega t - \pi/2)$ or simply $\sin \omega t$. So we have

$$x = 1.10 \sin(0.924t),$$

with x in m and t in s.

13.3
APPLICATIONS OF SIMPLE HARMONIC MOTION

Simple harmonic motion occurs in many physical situations analogous to the mass-spring system. The basic criterion for simple harmonic motion is that the force or other physical quantity driving the system back toward equilibrium must be directly proportional to displacement from equilibrium. We now explore a number of instances in which this occurs. As you study each, consider how it meets the basic criterion for simple harmonic motion and yet differs from the mass-spring system we studied previously.

The Vertical Mass-Spring System

Shown in Fig. 13–12, this system is like the horizontal mass-spring system except that the force of gravity acts in addition to the spring force. What effect does gravity have? First, it changes the equilibrium position, since the spring must now exert an upward force to counteract the weight. If we take the origin at the end of the unstretched spring, and let the positive x-axis point downward, then in the new equilibrium the force-balance condition reads

$$mg - kx_1 = 0,$$

where x_1 is the new equilibrium position with the weight attached. Solving

Fig. 13–12
A vertical mass-spring system.

for x_1 gives

$$x_1 = \frac{mg}{k}.$$

The motion of the system is described by Newton's second law, which, with the gravitational force included, becomes

$$m\frac{d^2x}{dt^2} = -kx + mg, \qquad (13\text{--}15)$$

where x is measured from the original, horizontal equilibrium. This equation resembles Equation 13–4 for the horizontal mass-spring system, except for the additional constant term mg. To solve the equation, we introduce a new position variable x', defined as the displacement from the new equilibrium position x_1:

$$x' = x - x_1 = x - \frac{mg}{k}.$$

Solving for x and substituting into Equation 13–15, we have

$$m\frac{d^2}{dt^2}\left(x' + \frac{mg}{k}\right) = -k\left(x' + \frac{mg}{k}\right) + mg.$$

The derivative of the constant mg/k is zero, so the left-hand side of this equation is just d^2x'/dt^2. Then, distributing the $-k$ on the right-hand side, we have

$$m\frac{d^2x'}{dt^2} = -kx' - k\left(\frac{mg}{k}\right) + mg,$$

or

$$m\frac{d^2x'}{dt^2} = -kx'. \qquad (13\text{--}16)$$

Equation 13–16 is identical to Equation 13–4 except for the substitution of x' for x. The analysis of Equation 13–4 therefore applies here, and we conclude that the vertical mass-spring system oscillates about its equilibrium position in the same sinusoidal way and at the same frequency as its horizontal counterpart oscillates about its equilibrium. The effect of gravity is *only* to displace the equilibrium; it has no effect on the frequency or time dependence of the motion.

The Torsional Oscillator

A torsional oscillator is a system that is subject to a restoring torque when it is displaced from equilibrium. Common examples include the balance wheel in a mechanical watch (Fig. 13–13) and a child who twists up the ropes on a swing (Fig. 13–14). In these and all other torsional oscillators, the restoring torque sets up a back-and-forth rotational motion about the torque-free equilibrium state. When the restoring torque is directly proportional to the angular displacement from equilibrium, then the result is simple harmonic motion.

Fig. 13–13
The balance wheel in a watch is a torsional oscillator whose period is the basic time interval of the watch. The coiled hairspring provides the restoring torque.

Fig. 13–14
Twisting the swing ropes gives rise to a torque that tends to untwist them. The result is torsional oscillation about the untwisted equilibrium position.

A simple example of a torsional oscillator consists of an object of rotational inertia I suspended from a string, rope, or wire that develops a torque when it is twisted (Fig. 13–15). When the restoring torque is directly proportional to the angular displacement, we can write

$$\tau = -\kappa\theta, \tag{13-17}$$

where τ is the torque and θ the angular displacement. The constant κ is called the **torsional constant,** and is the rotational analog of the spring constant; it gives the torque developed per radian of twist.

The behavior of the torsional oscillator is described by the rotational analog of Newton's law (Equation 12–14):

$$\tau = I\alpha,$$

where α is the angular acceleration. Using Equation 13–17 for τ, and writing α as the second time derivative of angular displacement, the analog of Newton's law becomes

$$I\frac{d^2\theta}{dt^2} = -\kappa\theta. \tag{13-18}$$

This equation is identical to Equation 13–4 for the linear oscillator, except that I replaces m, θ replaces x, and κ replaces k. We need not repeat the mathematical analysis that led to the solution of Equation 13–4; rather, in direct analogy with the solution 13–15, we can write

$$\theta = \theta_0 \cos(\omega t + \phi), \tag{13-19}$$

where θ_0 and ϕ are the amplitude and phase constant as determined by the initial conditions, and where ω is given by analogy with Equation 13–12:

$$\omega = \sqrt{\frac{\kappa}{I}}. \tag{13-20}$$

Expressions for the period and frequency in Hz follow directly from Equations 13–6 and 13–7.

In addition to its timekeeping functions, the torsional oscillator provides an accurate way of measuring rotational inertia, as the example below illustrates.

torsional constant

Fig. 13–15
A simple torsional oscillator, consisting of a disk suspended by a wire.

Example 13–3
A Torsional Oscillator

An irregular object is suspended from a fiber of torsional constant $\kappa = 3.1$ N·m/rad. When the system is set into torsional oscillation, 68 complete oscillations occur in 2.0 minutes. What is the rotational inertia of the object about an axis lying along the fiber?

Solution

Solving Equation 13–20 for I, we have

$$I = \frac{\kappa}{\omega^2} = \frac{\kappa}{(2\pi f)^2} = \frac{3.1 \text{ N·m/rad}}{[(2\pi)(68 \text{ cycles}/120 \text{ s})]^2} = 0.24 \text{ kg·m}^2.$$

The Pendulum

simple pendulum

Fig. 13–16
A simple pendulum, showing the forces acting.

A **simple pendulum** consists of a point mass suspended from a massless cord that cannot stretch. This idealization is approximated by many physical systems in which a mass of small extent is suspended by a long structure of much lower mass.

Figure 13–16 shows a pendulum of mass m and length ℓ displaced slightly from its equilibrium. We could analyze this situation either in terms of the forces on the mass m or, because the motion is a rotation about the suspension point, in terms of torque. We choose the latter because it is readily generalized to other types of pendulum. (Problem 20 analyzes the simple pendulum in terms of forces alone.) From Fig. 13–16, we see that tension force in the cord, acting along the line between the suspension point and the mass, exerts no torque. When the pendulum is displaced from equilibrium, however, the gravitational force does exert a torque whose magnitude is given by Equation 11–2:

$$\tau = mg\ell \sin\theta$$

(see Fig. 13–16). The direction of this torque is such that it tends to rotate the pendulum back toward equilibrium. Writing the rotational analog of Newton's law, $\tau = I\alpha$, we then have

$$I\frac{d^2\theta}{dt^2} = -mg\ell \sin\theta, \qquad (13\text{–}21)$$

where the minus sign shows that the torque is opposite to the angular displacement, and where we have written the angular acceleration α as the second time derivative of angular displacement. Equation 13–21 looks somewhat analogous to Equation 13–4, with θ replacing x, I replacing m, and $mg\ell$ replacing k. But not quite—the right-hand side contains not θ but $\sin\theta$, so that the restoring torque is not *directly proportional* to the angular displacement. Because of this, Equation 13–21 does not, in general, describe simple harmonic motion. Although the motion of the system is usually oscillatory,* it does not have the simple sinusoidal time dependence of Equation 13–5, and the frequency is not truly independent of amplitude. The exact solution of Equation 13–21 is very difficult, and is usually done only in advanced mechanics courses. Problem 55 explores some aspects of the full pendulum problem.

If, however, the amplitude of the pendulum motion is small, then it *approximates* simple harmonic motion. For small angles (much less than 1 radian), the sine of the angle is approximately equal to the radian measure of the angle itself (Fig. 13–17). For example, an angle of 0.11 rad has a sine equal to 0.1097—a difference of only 0.3 per cent—while even a 30° angle (0.52 rad) has a sine of 0.50, within 4 per cent of its radian measure. Thus if we restrict ourselves to small-amplitude oscillations, we can obtain an approximate equation by replacing $\sin\theta$ with θ itself:

$$I\frac{d^2\theta}{dt^2} = -mg\ell\theta.$$

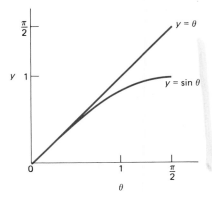

Fig. 13–17
For small values of θ measured in radians, $\sin\theta$ and θ itself are nearly equal.

*It may not even be oscillatory. If given enough energy, the mass may go "over the top," exhibiting circular motion with nonuniform speed.

Comparing this approximate equation with Equation 13–4, we see immediately that the pendulum will exhibit simple harmonic motion. Since I plays the role of m, and $mg\ell$ plays the role of k, we can find the frequency by replacing m with I and k with $mg\ell$ in Equation 13–12:

$$\omega = \sqrt{\frac{mg\ell}{I}}.\tag{13–22}$$

For a *simple* pendulum, the rotational inertia I is that of a point mass m a distance ℓ from the rotational axis, or $I = m\ell^2$ (see Equation 12–15). Then we have

$$\omega = \sqrt{\frac{mg\ell}{m\ell^2}} = \sqrt{\frac{g}{\ell}}, \quad \text{(simple pendulum)}\tag{13–23}$$

or, from Equation 13–6,

$$T = \frac{2\pi}{\omega} = 2\pi\sqrt{\frac{\ell}{g}}. \quad \text{(simple pendulum)}\tag{13–24}$$

These equations show that the frequency and period of a simple pendulum are independent of its mass, depending only on length and gravitational acceleration. You can confirm this prediction experimentally by sitting on a swing next to another swing with a small child on it. Even though your mass is greater, both of you have nearly the same swing period.

Example 13–4
Tarzan and the Simple Pendulum

Tarzan stands on a branch, petrified with fear as a leopard approaches. Fortunately, Jane is on a branch of the same height in a nearby tree, 8.0 m away, and she is holding a 25-m-long vine of negligible mass attached directly above the point midway between her and Tarzan (Fig. 13–18). Seeing Tarzan in trouble, Jane grasps the vine and steps off her branch with negligible initial velocity. How soon does she reach Tarzan? When she does reach him, she grabs him and lets the vine take the two of them back to safety. How long does the return journey take, if Tarzan's mass is 50 per cent greater than Jane's? Use the approximation $\sin\theta \approx \theta$ throughout. How good is this approximation?

Solution

Jane and the vine constitute a pendulum that takes half a period to reach Tarzan. The period is given by Equation 13–24:

$$T = 2\pi\sqrt{\frac{\ell}{g}} = 2\pi\sqrt{\frac{25 \text{ m}}{9.8 \text{ m/s}^2}} = 10 \text{ s},$$

so that Jane reaches Tarzan in 5.0 s. Since the period of a simple pendulum is independent of its mass, the return trip with Tarzan takes the same time.

How good is the approximation $\sin\theta \approx \theta$? From Fig. 13–18, we see that

$$\sin\theta_0 = \frac{4.0 \text{ m}}{25 \text{ m}} = 0.16.$$

Then $\theta_0 = \sin^{-1}(0.16) = 0.1607$ rad, for a difference of only 0.43 per cent at the greatest angular displacement. Remember to set your calculator to radians for this comparison of $\sin\theta$ with θ.

Fig. 13–18
Tarzan in trouble (Example 13–4).
Lengths are not to scale.

physical pendulum

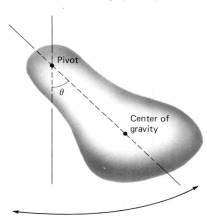

Fig. 13–19
A physical pendulum.

A **physical pendulum** is an object of arbitrary shape that is free to swing in a plane (Fig. 13–19). The physical pendulum differs from the simple pendulum in that its mass is distributed over the whole length of the object, rather than being concentrated at the end. In our analysis of the simple pendulum, we used this distinction only at the very end, when we wrote $m\ell^2$ for the rotational inertia. Therefore, our analysis before that point applies to the physical pendulum as well. In particular, Equation 13–22 gives correctly the frequency of a physical pendulum executing small-amplitude oscillations, provided we interpret ℓ as the distance from the pivot to the center of gravity, rather than the overall length.

Example 13–5
A Physical Pendulum

A thin rod of mass m and length ℓ is suspended from a pivot at one end. Find the period of small-amplitude oscillations. What would be the length of a simple pendulum of the same period?

Solution

The center of gravity lies halfway along the rod, so we use $\ell/2$ in place of ℓ in Equation 13–22. Combining Equation 13–22 with Equation 13–6 then gives the period:

$$T = \frac{2\pi}{\omega} = 2\pi\sqrt{\frac{I}{mg\ell/2}}.$$

Table 12–2 shows that the rotational inertia of a rod about one end is $I = \frac{1}{3}m\ell^2$. Then we have

$$T = 2\pi\sqrt{\frac{m\ell^2}{3mg\ell/2}} = 2\pi\sqrt{\frac{2\ell}{3g}}.$$

Comparing this result with Equation 13–24, we see that this is the same period as that of a simple pendulum with length $\frac{2}{3}\ell$. Does this make sense? Yes: in the physical pendulum, much of the mass is concentrated more closely to the pivot, making the effective length shorter than the overall length.

13.4

SIMPLE HARMONIC MOTION IN TWO DIMENSIONS

So far, we have discussed systems in which motion is confined to a single one-dimensional path—either the straight line of a mass-spring system or the arc of a pendulum. But for many systems, oscillatory motion in several directions is possible at once. One example is a pendulum that is free to swing in any direction (Fig. 13–20). We could set this pendulum into one-dimensional simple harmonic motion by displacing it in some direction and then releasing it. But suppose we displace it in the x-direction, and as we release it give it an impulse in the y-direction. The result is a composite motion whose maximum x-displacement (and therefore zero x-velocity) occurs when the y-displacement is zero and the y-velocity a maximum. As the pendulum swings in toward $x = 0$, it moves rapidly away from $y = 0$. Since the periods of the x- and y-motions are the same (we are making the assumption of small amplitude oscillations), the pendulum reaches its maximum y-displacement as it passes through $x = 0$. The result is a curved path—in fact, an ellipse (Fig. 13–21).

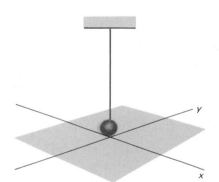

Fig. 13–20
The pendulum is free to swing in any direction. We can analyze its motion in terms of components along the x- and y-axes.

If the amplitudes of the x- and y-motions are equal, then the motion is circular. We can prove this by describing the motion vectorially. With maximum x-displacement at $t = 0$, the x-motion is described by $x = r_0\cos\omega t$, where r_0 is the amplitude of both x- and y-components. With maximum velocity at $t = 0$, the y-motion is described by $y = r_0\cos(\omega t - \pi/2) = r_0\sin\omega t$. A vector description of the motion is then given by

$$\mathbf{r} = x\hat{\mathbf{i}} + y\hat{\mathbf{j}} = r_0(\cos\omega t\ \hat{\mathbf{i}} + \sin\omega t\ \hat{\mathbf{j}}), \qquad (13\text{–}25)$$

where $\mathbf{r}$ is the displacement from equilibrium. The magnitude of $\mathbf{r}$ is then given by the Pythagorean theorem:

$$r^2 = x^2 + y^2 = r_0^2(\cos^2\omega t + \sin^2\omega t) = r_0^2,$$

since $\cos^2\omega t + \sin^2\omega t = 1$ for any value of ωt.

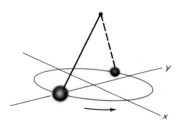

Fig. 13–21
When the motions are out of phase, the pendulum traces out an ellipse.

We could have analyzed this circular pendulum motion without any reference to simple harmonic motion. In fact, we did so in Example 5–9, to illustrate uniform circular motion. In these two different approaches to the same physical situation, we can see the link between simple harmonic motion and uniform circular motion, and can understand why we speak of angular frequency in simple harmonic motion even when there are no physical angles involved. Our analysis of the circular pendulum in this chapter shows that its motion may be resolved into two simple harmonic motions, at right angles in space and $\pi/2$ rad out of phase. If we look at the pendulum from above, we see it trace out the circle—the composite motion. But if we peer in a horizontal plane at the pendulum bob (Fig. 13–22), we see only the projection of that circular motion onto one of the coordinate axes; it appears to us that the bob is executing simple harmonic motion. The period of the circular motion is the same as that of each simple harmonic motion component, and therefore the angular frequencies of the circular and harmonic motions are equal as well. The angular frequency of the circular motion has obvious physical meaning—it is the number of radians swept out in a unit time. We can think of the angular frequency of simple harmonic motion as the angular frequency of a circular motion of which that simple harmonic motion might be a component. The "angle" ωt then corresponds directly to a physical angle in the circular motion. Similarly, the phase constant ϕ corresponds to the initial angular displacement in the circular motion (Fig. 13–23).

We have considered the cases of two harmonic motions either in phase or $\pi/2$ rad out of phase. In the most general case, we can have two motions of different amplitudes with arbitrary phase difference. In that case, the motion is elliptical, but the axes of the ellipse do not generally correspond with the x- and y-axes. Problem 53 explores this situation further.

With the pendulum we have been discussing, the frequencies of the x and y harmonic motions are necessarily the same. But other two-dimensional oscillators may have different frequencies for the two perpendicular components of motion (Fig. 13–24). In this case the motion becomes interestingly complex. If, for example, the frequencies form a 2:1 ratio, the

Fig. 13–22
If we observe an object in the plane of its circular motion, we see only one component of that motion. This component is simple harmonic motion.

Fig. 13–23
Simple harmonic motion as a projection of uniform circular motion. The quantities ωt and ϕ in simple harmonic motion correspond to physical angles in the associated uniform circular motion.

lissajous figures

Fig. 13–24
A two-dimensional mass-spring system.
If the spring constants differ in the x-
and y-directions, the frequencies of the
associated simple harmonic motions
also differ.

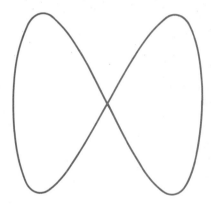

Fig. 13–25
A 2:1 frequency ratio gives rise to a
figure-eight-shaped path.

oscillating object traverses a figure-eight-shaped path (Fig. 13–25). In general, such paths are called **lissajous figures.** They can be quite complex, striking,
and even beautiful (Fig. 13–26). If the frequencies are not related as the
ratio of a pair of integers, then the path is not closed but actually fills an
entire region bounded by the amplitudes in both directions (Fig. 13–27).

13.5
ENERGY IN SIMPLE HARMONIC MOTION

Displacing an object from stable equilibrium requires energy, as we do
work against the restoring force. In a mass-spring system, that work goes
into increasing the potential energy of the spring. If we then release the
mass, it accelerates toward its equilibrium position, gaining kinetic energy.
Where does it get the kinetic energy? From the potential energy of the
spring, which consequently decreases. When the mass moves through its
equilibrium position, its potential energy is zero, and all its energy is now
kinetic. As it moves away from equilibrium, the mass slows down as the
spring stretches. Its kinetic energy decreases and potential energy again increases. If there is no energy loss or gain, this process repeats indefinitely.
Oscillatory motion is therefore a process whereby energy is transferred
back and forth between its kinetic and potential forms (Fig. 13–28).

In the case of a mass-spring system, the potential energy is given by
Equation 7–3:

$$U = \tfrac{1}{2}kx^2,$$

where x is the displacement from equilibrium. Meanwhile, the kinetic energy is $K = \tfrac{1}{2}mv^2$. We can illustrate explicitly the interchange of kinetic and
potential energy in simple harmonic motion by using x from Equation 13–
5 and v (that is, dx/dt) from Equation 13–8 in the expressions for potential
and kinetic energy. Then we have

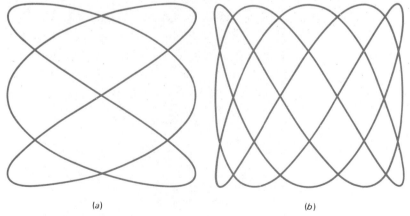

(a)   (b)

Fig. 13–26
Lissajous figure produced by perpendicular oscillations with (a) 2:3 and (b) 5:3 frequency ratios.

Fig. 13–27
In this case the frequency ratio is π, and the curve shown results after 7 cycles of the lower-frequency oscillator. Eventually the entire rectangular area would be traversed.

$$U = \tfrac{1}{2}kx^2 = \tfrac{1}{2}k(x_0\cos\omega t)^2 = \tfrac{1}{2}kx_0^2\cos^2\omega t \qquad (13\text{–}26a)$$

and

$$K = \tfrac{1}{2}mv^2 = \tfrac{1}{2}m(-x_0\omega\sin\omega t)^2 = \tfrac{1}{2}m\omega^2 x_0^2\sin^2\omega t = \tfrac{1}{2}kx_0^2\sin^2\omega t, \qquad (13\text{–}26b)$$

where we have used the fact that $\omega^2 = k/m$ in writing the final form of Equation 13–26. We set the phase constant to zero in Equation 13–26 to describe motion starting from maximum displacement. Comparing our expressions for potential and kinetic energy, we see that both have the same maximum value—$\tfrac{1}{2}kx_0^2$—equal to the initial potential energy of the stretched spring. Since $\sin\omega t = \cos(\omega t - \pi/2)$, the only difference between the two lies in their relative phase—the potential energy is a maximum when the kinetic energy is zero, and vice versa. What about the total energy? It is

$$E = U + K = \tfrac{1}{2}kx^2 + \tfrac{1}{2}mv^2 \qquad (13\text{–}27)$$

or

$$E = \tfrac{1}{2}kx_0^2\cos^2\omega t + \tfrac{1}{2}kx_0^2\sin^2\omega t = \tfrac{1}{2}kx_0^2,$$

where we have used the fact that $\sin^2\omega t + \cos^2\omega t = 1$. Although both kinetic and potential energy vary with time, their sum remains constant (Fig. 13–29).

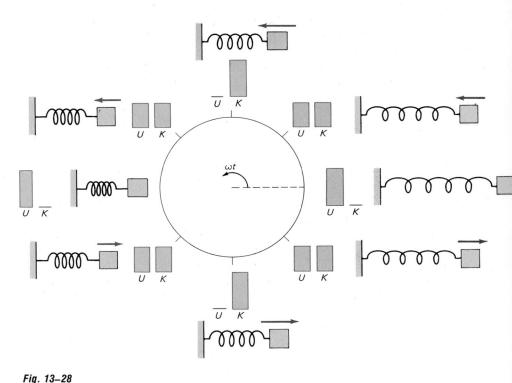

Fig. 13–28
Kinetic and potential energy in a simple harmonic oscillator. Figure shows the spring compression and velocity of oscillating mass, along with relative amounts of potential and kinetic energy, at eight points in the cycle.

Fig. 13–29
The potential and kinetic energy of a simple harmonic oscillator vary with time, but their sum is constant.

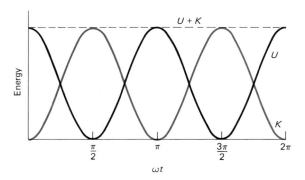

Example 13–6
Energy in Simple Harmonic Motion

A mass m is mounted on a spring of constant k, and the system is displaced a distance x_0 from equilibrium. Use energy conservation to find the maximum velocity attained by the mass once it is released, and show that the result is consistent with Equation 13–8. Find also the velocity when the potential and kinetic energies are equal.

Solution

The initial potential energy, which is the total energy, is $\frac{1}{2}kx_0^2$. At maximum velocity, all of this energy has been converted to kinetic energy, so that

$$\tfrac{1}{2}mv_{\max}^2 = \tfrac{1}{2}kx_0^2,$$

or

$$v_{\max} = \sqrt{\frac{k}{m}}\, x_0 = \omega x_0,$$

in agreement with the maximum velocity from Equation 13–8. A third way to obtain this maximum velocity would be to integrate the acceleration over time (see Problem 13).

When the kinetic and potential energies are equal, each must be equal to half the total energy. Therefore, for the kinetic energy,

$$\frac{1}{2}mv^2 = \frac{1}{2}\left(\frac{1}{2}mv_{\max}^2\right),$$

so that

$$v = \frac{1}{\sqrt{2}}v_{\max} = \frac{\sqrt{2}}{2}\omega x_0.$$

Recall that Equation 7–3 for the potential energy of a spring was derived by integrating the spring force, $-kx$, over distance. Since every simple harmonic oscillator has a restoring force or torque that is directly proportional to displacement, integration of that force or torque always results in a potential energy function that depends on the square of the displacement. Conversely, any system whose potential energy function is quadratic in the displacement exhibits simple harmonic motion. For many systems, it is easier to evaluate the potential energy than the force, so that this criterion is often a more useful one. Also, complicated potential energy func-

Fig. 13–30
Near its minima, which are points of stable equilibrium, the potential energy curve approximates a parabola.

tions are often approximately quadratic near their stable equilibrium points (Fig. 13–30), so that small-amplitude oscillations about these points represent simple harmonic motion. As the example below illustrates, we can determine the properties of the motion by comparing the potential energy function with that of a linear or torsional oscillator, as appropriate.

Example 13–7

The Potential Energy Function for a Molecule

When a molecule of hydrochloric acid (HCl) is stretched or compressed from its equilibrium, its potential energy increases. For small displacements from equilibrium, the potential energy of the molecule is given by

$$U = \alpha x^2,$$

where $\alpha = 247$ J/m^2, and where we take the zero of potential energy at equilibrium. Determine the oscillation frequency of this molecule, under the approximation that the more massive chlorine remains essentially at rest while the hydrogen undergoes oscillatory motion.

Solution

The expression for the potential energy of HCl resembles that of a spring, $\frac{1}{2}kx^2$, with the quantity α playing the role of $\frac{1}{2}k$. So the effective "spring constant" of the molecule is 2α or 594 N/m. The mass of the hydrogen is essentially that of its single proton (see table inside the front cover), so that the oscillation frequency as given by Equation 13–13 is

$$f = \frac{1}{2\pi} \sqrt{\frac{k}{m}} = \frac{1}{2\pi} \sqrt{\frac{594 \text{ N/m}}{1.67 \times 10^{-27} \text{ kg}}} = 9.49 \times 10^{13} \text{ Hz}.$$

Like most molecular oscillations, this one occurs at a frequency associated with infrared radiation; for this reason the structure of molecules can be studied by measuring precisely the amounts of infrared radiation absorbed by a substance at different infrared frequencies, a process known as infrared spectroscopy.

13.6
DAMPED HARMONIC MOTION

In real oscillating systems, forces like friction are always present that dissipate the oscillation energy. Unless energy is somehow added, dissipation eventually brings the system to rest at equilibrium. The motion in this case

damped harmonic motion

is said to be **damped.** If the dissipation is sufficiently weak that only a small fraction of the system's energy is removed in each oscillation cycle,

Fig. 13–31
Damped oscillatory motion.

then we expect that the system should behave essentially as in the un-damped case, except for a gradual decrease in the oscillation amplitude (Fig. 13–31).

Can we describe damped motion more quantitatively? Yes, but only if we have a mathematical expression for the damping force. In many systems—especially those involving friction associated with slow motion through a viscous fluid—the damping force is approximately proportional to the velocity, and in the opposite direction:

$$F_d = -bv = -b\frac{dx}{dt},$$

where b is a constant giving the strength of the damping. We can write Newton's law as before, now including the damping force along with the restoring force. For a mass-spring system, we have

$$m\frac{d^2x}{dt^2} = -kx - b\frac{dx}{dt},$$

or

$$m\frac{d^2x}{dt^2} + b\frac{dx}{dt} + kx = 0. \qquad (13\text{–}28)$$

We will not solve this equation, but simply state that its solution, provided the damping is not too large, is

$$x = x_0 e^{-bt/2m} \cos(\omega t + \phi). \qquad (13\text{–}29)$$

The solution 13–29 describes sinusoidal motion whose amplitude decreases exponentially with time. How fast the amplitude drops depends on the damping constant b and mass m: when $t = 2m/b$, the amplitude has dropped to $1/e$ of its original value (Fig. 13–32a). When the damping is so weak that only a small fraction of the total energy is lost in each cycle, then the frequency ω in Equation 13–29 is essentially equal to the undamped frequency $\sqrt{k/m}$. But with stronger damping, the damping force slows the motion, and the frequency becomes lower. At the same time, the oscillation amplitude decreases more rapidly with time (Fig. 13–32b). As long as any underdamped oscillation occurs, the motion is said to be **underdamped.** For sufficiently strong damping, though, the effect of the damping force is as great as that critical damping of the spring force. Under this condition, called **critical damping,** the system returns to its equilibrium state without undergoing any oscillations (Fig. 13–32c). If the damping is made still stronger, the system becomes

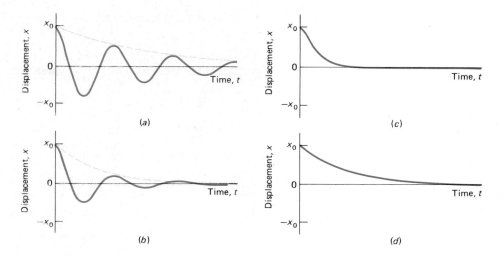

Fig. 13–32
(a) Weak damping, showing sinusoidal oscillations confined within the "envelope" of a decreasing exponential. The time in which the amplitude decreases to 1/e—about one-third—of its original value is considerably longer than the oscillation period, T. (b) Stronger damping, but still underdamped. (c) Critical damping. (d) Overdamping.

overdamped

Fig. 13–33
Dampers resting on piano strings cause the sound-producing oscillations to die out quickly.

overdamped. The damping force now dominates the motion, and as a result the system returns to equilibrium more slowly than with critical damping (Fig. 13–32d).

Many physical systems, ranging from atoms to the human leg, can be modelled as damped oscillators. Engineering systems are often designed with very specific amounts of damping. For example, automobile shock absorbers—the damping element in the automobile suspension—are designed along with the springs to give critical damping. This results in the most rapid return to equilibrium while successfully absorbing the energy imparted to the car by road bumps. When the shock absorbers wear out, the car's suspension becomes underdamped, and the whole car bounces up and down after hitting a bump. Similarly, the strings of a piano are damped—although not critically—immediately after a key is struck so that the note will die out quickly. Depressing the right foot pedal on the piano lifts the dampers from the strings, allowing them to vibrate much longer (Fig. 13–33).

Example 13–8
Damped Harmonic Motion

A damped mass-spring system has $m = 85$ g, $k = 22$ N/m, and $b = 0.016$ kg/s. How many oscillations will it make while its amplitude falls to half its original value?

Solution

The amplitude will be half its original value when the factor $e^{-bt/2m}$ in Equation 13–29 has the value one-half:

$$e^{-bt/2m} = \tfrac{1}{2}.$$

Taking the natural logarithm of both sides gives

$$\frac{-bt}{2m} = -\ln 2,$$

where we have used the facts that $\ln(x)$ and e^x are inverse functions and that $\ln(1/x) = -\ln(x)$. Then

$$t = \frac{2m}{b}\ln 2 = \frac{(2)(0.085 \text{ kg})}{0.016 \text{ kg/s}}\ln 2 = 7.4 \text{ s}$$

is the time for the amplitude to drop to half its original value. For small damping, the period is very close to the undamped period, which is

$$T = 2\pi\sqrt{\frac{m}{k}} = 2\pi\sqrt{\frac{0.085 \text{ kg}}{22 \text{ N/m}}} = 0.39 \text{ s}.$$

Then the number of cycles during the 7.4 s it takes the amplitude to drop in half is

$$\frac{7.4 \text{ s}}{0.39 \text{ s}} = 19.$$

That the number of oscillations is much greater than 1 tells us that the damping is fairly small, justifying our use of the undamped period.

13.7
DRIVEN OSCILLATIONS AND RESONANCE

The left photograph in Figure 13–34 shows a child pushing steadily on a tree with very little effect. Yet on the right we see the same child producing large-amplitude motion of the treetop—an experiment you may have performed in your own childhood. How is this possible? In the vibrating tree, we have a system analogous to a mass-spring system, one that has a natural frequency of oscillation. By pushing the tree at its own natural frequency,

Fig. 13–34
(Left) A child pushing steadily near the bottom of a tree produces very little displacement of the treetop. (Right) By applying small pushes at the tree's natural oscillation frequency, the same child produces large-amplitude motion of the treetop.

the child supplies a small amount of energy each cycle, and that energy accumulates to produce large-amplitude motion.

What would happen if the child pushed the tree very slowly—at a frequency much lower than the natural frequency? This would be very much like the steady push of Fig. 13–34 on the left, and amplitude of the motion would be very small. How about a very high frequency, much higher than the natural frequency? Try it! Vibrate a tree very fast near the bottom, and not much happens at the top. Only when you push at a frequency near the natural frequency can you build up energy in the oscillation.

driven harmonic motion

driving frequency

When an oscillating system is pushed by an external force, we say that the system is **driven,** and the resulting motion is **driven harmonic motion.** We can understand this motion quantitatively by writing Newton's law for a driven system. Consider a mass-spring system, and suppose that the driving force is given by $F = F_0 \cos\omega_d t$, where ω_d is the **driving frequency,** not necessarily the natural frequency of the system. Then Newton's law is

$$m\frac{d^2x}{dt^2} = -kx - b\frac{dx}{dt} + F_0 \cos\omega_d t, \qquad (13\text{–}30)$$

where the first term on the right-hand side is the restoring force, the second the damping force, and the third the driving force. Since the system is being pushed at the driving frequency ω_d, we expect that it will undergo oscillatory motion at this frequency. (It might also oscillate at its natural frequency. But this undriven **transient solution** soon damps out, leaving only **steady-state** motion at the driving frequency.) So we guess that the solution to Equation 13–30 might have the form

transient solution

steady state

$$x = x_0 \cos(\omega_d t + \phi). \qquad (13\text{–}31)$$

By substituting this expression and its derivatives into Equation 13–30 and using trig identities (see Problem 48), it is possible to satisfy Equation 13–30, provided that

$$x_0 = \frac{F_0}{m\sqrt{(\omega_d^2 - \omega_0^2)^2 + b^2\omega_d^2/m^2}} \qquad (13\text{–}32)$$

and

$$\phi = \tan^{-1}\left(\frac{\omega_d b}{m(\omega_0^2 - \omega_d^2)}\right), \qquad (13\text{–}33)$$

where ω_0 is the undamped natural frequency $\sqrt{k/m}$, as distinguished from the driving frequency ω_d.

resonance curve

Equations 13–32 and 13–33 show that the amplitude and phase of the motion vary with driving frequency for a fixed amplitude F_0 of the driving force. Figure 13–35 shows a **resonance curve,** which is just a plot of the amplitude 13–32 as a function of driving frequency, for several values of the damping. As long as the system is underdamped, the curve has a maximum at some nonzero frequency (see Problem 49), and for weak damping that maximum occurs at very nearly the natural frequency. The weaker the damping, the more sharply peaked is the resonance curve. Thus in a weakly damped system, it is possible to build up large-amplitude oscillations with relatively small driving forces. Such **resonance** can cause serious problems in physical systems. For example, we would not want a vary-

resonance

Fig. 13–35
Resonance curves for several damping strengths. ω_0 is the undamped natural frequency $\sqrt{k/m}$.

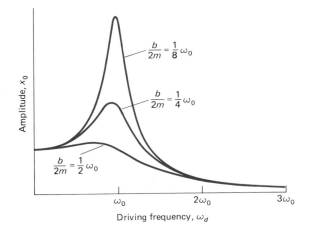

$\frac{b}{2m} = \frac{1}{8}\omega_0$

$\frac{b}{2m} = \frac{1}{4}\omega_0$

$\frac{b}{2m} = \frac{1}{2}\omega_0$

Amplitude, x_0

Driving frequency, ω_d

ω_0 $2\omega_0$ $3\omega_0$

Fig. 13–36
Resonant vibrations in the structure housing a large telescope would cause unacceptable blurring of astronomical images. This housing for the Multiple-Mirror Telescope on Mt. Hopkins in Arizona was intentionally made as small as possible, in part to limit such vibrations.

ing wind to set up vibrations in a skyscraper analogous to those of the tree in Fig. 13–34! (In fact, the device described in Example 13–2 is designed to minimize just such oscillations.) The building housing a large telescope (Fig. 13–36) must be free of resonant vibrations if the telescope is to produce clear images. A famous disaster involving resonance is the 1940 collapse of the Tacoma Narrows Bridge in Washington state (Fig. 13–37). Resonance is also important at the microscopic level. Microwave ovens work by pumping energy into food at a resonant frequency of the water molecule; the resulting oscillation energy is eventually dissipated as heat by damping forces. At the nuclear level, the process called nuclear magnetic resonance (NMR) uses resonant behavior of protons to probe the structure of matter and to produce images useful in medical diagnosis.

Fig. 13–37
(Left and center) Wind-driven resonant oscillations of the Tacoma Narrows Bridge caused its collapse in 1940 only 4 months after it was opened. (Right) The bridge has since been rebuilt, with additional bracing.

SUMMARY
---

1. **Oscillatory motion** occurs when a system is displaced from stable equilibrium. Restoring forces bring the system back toward equilibrium, and if friction is not great enough to prevent overshoot, the system oscillates back and forth about equilibrium.

2. **Simple harmonic motion** is a special case of oscillatory motion that occurs when the restoring force is directly proportional to displacement, a situation that holds approximately for many systems subject to small displacements from equilibrium. Simple harmonic motion is described by the equation

$$x = x_0 \cos(\omega t + \phi),$$

where x_0 is the maximum displacement, or **amplitude,** and ϕ the **phase constant,** which tells when the maximum amplitude occurs in relation to the time $t = 0$. ω is the **angular frequency** of oscillation, and is given by $\omega = \sqrt{k/m}$ for a mass m oscillating on a spring of constant k. Analogous expressions hold for other systems, including torsional oscillators and pendulums:

$$\omega = \sqrt{\frac{\kappa}{I}}, \quad \text{(torsional oscillator)}$$

$$\omega = \sqrt{\frac{g}{\ell}}, \quad \text{(simple pendulum)}$$

and

$$\omega = \sqrt{\frac{mg\ell}{I}}. \quad \text{(physical pendulum)}$$

The frequency in Hz (or cycles/second) and the period can be found from the angular frequency by using the equations

$$f = \frac{\omega}{2\pi}$$

and

$$T = \frac{1}{f} = \frac{2\pi}{\omega}.$$

3. When an object undergoes simple harmonic motion in two perpendicular directions, the resulting composite motion is, most generally, elliptical. For the special case when the two component motions have the same amplitude but differ in phase by $\pi/2$, the composite motion is circular. Conversely, simple harmonic motion may be considered a component of circular motion, with the quantities ωt and ϕ corresponding to real angles in the related circular motion.

4. In oscillatory motion, energy is transferred back and forth between potential and kinetic forms. In the absence of energy input or loss mechanisms, the total energy remains constant even as the relative amounts of potential and kinetic energy change. The special case of simple harmonic motion results when the potential energy is a quadratic function of displacement—a condition that is met approximately for many systems near stable equilibrium.

5. When energy loss occurs—for example, through friction—then the motion is **damped.** In an **underdamped** system, the damping force is relatively small, and the resulting damped motion is described by

$$x = x_0 \, e^{-bt/2m} \cos(\omega t + \phi),$$

where b is a proportionality constant between damping force and velocity. When the damping is very small, the frequency ω is essentially the same as the undamped frequency $\sqrt{k/m}$; for larger damping, the frequency drops because of the slowing effect of friction. As the damping force is increased, the system eventually undergoes **critical damping,** in which the system reaches equilibrium without oscillation. For even greater damping, the system is **overdamped,** reaching equilibrium without oscillation, but more slowly than with critical damping.

6. When an oscillatory system is driven by an external force, it responds with motion at the driving frequency. The amplitude of motion is greatest for driving frequencies near the natural frequency of the system. Called **resonance,** this phenomenon is most prominent in weakly damped systems. The amplitude of resonant oscillations is given by

$$x_0 = \frac{F_0}{m\sqrt{(\omega_d^2 - \omega_0^2)^2 + b^2\omega_d^2/m^2}},$$

where F_0 is the amplitude of the driving force, ω_d its frequency, m the mass, b the damping constant, and $\omega_0 = \sqrt{k/m}$ the undamped natural frequency of the system.

QUESTIONS
---

1. Is a vertically bouncing ball an example of oscillatory motion? Of simple harmonic motion? Explain.
2. The vibration frequencies of atomic-sized systems are much higher than those of macroscopic mechanical systems. Why should this be?
3. What happens to the frequency of a simple harmonic oscillator when the spring constant is doubled? When the mass is doubled?
4. If the spring of a simple harmonic oscillator is cut in half, what happens to the frequency?

5. How does the frequency of a simple harmonic oscillator depend on its amplitude?
6. How would the frequency of a horizontal mass-spring system change if it were taken to the moon? Of a vertical mass-spring system? Of a simple pendulum?
7. In what ways is the motion of a damped pendulum not exactly periodic?
8. When is the acceleration of an undamped simple harmonic oscillator zero? When is the velocity zero?
9. Is the acceleration of a damped harmonic oscillator ever zero? Explain.
10. If the spring in a mass-spring system is not massless, how will this affect the frequency?
11. What will happen to the period of a mass-spring system if it is placed in a jetliner accelerating down the runway? What will happen to the period of a pendulum in the same situation?
12. Even if the springs in the two-dimensional oscillator of Fig. 13–24 are ideal, the system exhibits simple harmonic motion only for small-amplitude oscillations. Why?
13. Explain how simple harmonic motion might be used to determine the mass of objects in an orbiting spacecraft.
14. What is the phase constant of each of the simple harmonic motions shown in Fig. 13–38?

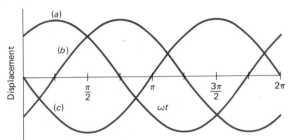

Fig. 13–38   Question 14

15. How does the solution of a differential equation differ from that of an algebraic equation?
16. One pendulum consists of a solid rod of mass m and length ℓ, another of a compact ball of the same mass m on the end of a massless string of the same length ℓ. Which has the greater period? Why?

17. Give an example of a system that can simultaneously undergo mass-spring simple harmonic motion, torsional simple harmonic motion, and pendulum motion.
18. Why doesn't the period of a simple pendulum depend on its mass?
19. When the amplitude of a pendulum's motion becomes large enough that the approximation $\sin\theta \approx \theta$ is no longer valid, the period lengthens with increasing amplitude. Why should this be?
20. Could a mass suspended from a string ever undergo non-oscillatory motion?
21. The needle of a sewing machine moves up and down, yet its driving force comes from an electric motor executing rotary motion. What sort of mechanism might convert rotary to up-and-down motion? *Hint:* What relevance would this conversion mechanism have for the present chapter?
22. The x- and y-components of motion of a body are both simple harmonic with the same frequency and amplitude. What shape is the path of the body if the component motions are (a) in phase; (b) $\pi/2$ out of phase; (c) $\pi/4$ out of phase?
23. List five oscillatory systems and identify the damping forces that act on each.
24. Why is critical damping desirable in many mechanical systems?
25. Explain why the frequency of a damped system is lower than that of the equivalent undamped system.
26. The quantity $2m/b$ in Equation 13–29 has the units of time. How should this time compare with the period of the motion if damping is to be considered small?
27. Opera singers have been known to break glasses with their voices. How?
28. Depressing the rightmost pedal on a piano causes notes to sound much longer than usual. What quantity changes in Equation 13–28 when the pedal is pressed?
29. Real physical systems often have more than one resonant frequency. How can this come about?
30. What does the collapse of the Tacoma Narrows Bridge (Fig. 13–37) say about the damping forces acting on the bridge?

PROBLEMS

Sections 13.1–13.2   *Oscillations and Simple Harmonic Motion*

1. Show that ω and f in Equations 13–12 and 13–13 have the units of inverse time.
2. Write expressions for simple harmonic motion (a) with amplitude 10 cm, frequency 5.0 Hz, and with maximum displacement at $t=0$ and (b) with amplitude 2.5 cm, angular frequency 5.0 s^{-1}, and with maximum velocity at $t=0$.
3. Determine the amplitude, angular frequency, and phase constant for each of the simple harmonic motions shown in Fig. 13–39.
4. A 200-g mass is attached to a spring of constant $k=5.6$ N/m, and set into oscillation with amplitude $x_0=25$ cm. Determine (a) the frequency in Hz, (b) the

period, (c) the maximum velocity, and (d) the maximum force in the spring.

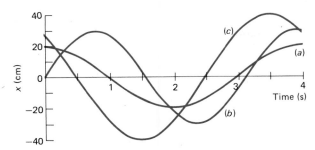

Fig. 13–39 Problem 3

5. A simple model of a carbon dioxide (CO_2) molecule consists of three mass points (the atoms) connected by two springs (electrical forces), as suggested in Fig. 13–40. One way this system can oscillate is if the carbon atom stays fixed and the two oxygens move symmetrically on either side of it. If the frequency of this oscillation is 4.0×10^{13} Hz, what is the effective spring constant? The mass of an oxygen atom is 16 u.

Fig. 13–40 Problem 5

6. Sketch the following simple harmonic motions on the same graph: (a) $x = (15 \text{ cm})[\cos(2.5t + \pi/2)]$; (b) motion with amplitude 30 cm, period 5.0 s, phase constant 0; (c) motion with amplitude 15 cm, frequency 0.40 Hz, phase constant 0.

7. Two identical mass-spring systems consist of 430-g masses on springs of constant $k = 2.2$ N/m. Both are displaced from equilibrium and the first released at time $t = 0$. How much later should the second be released so the two oscillations differ in phase by $\pi/2$?

8. The quartz crystal in a digital quartz watch executes simple harmonic motion at 32,768 Hz. (This frequency is chosen because it is 2^{15} Hz, so that after 15 circuits that divide frequency in half, an electrical signal at 1.00000 Hz is achieved.) If each face of the crystal undergoes a maximum displacement of 100 nm, find the maximum velocity and acceleration of the crystal faces.

9. A mass m slides along a frictionless horizontal surface at speed v_0. It strikes a spring of constant k attached to a rigid wall, as shown in Fig. 13–41. After a completely elastic encounter with the spring, the

Fig. 13–41 Problem 9

mass heads back in the direction it came from. In terms of k, m, and v_0, determine (a) how long the mass is in contact with the spring and (b) the maximum compression of the spring.

10. A 50-g mass is attached to a spring and undergoes simple harmonic motion. Its maximum acceleration is 15 m/s^2 and its maximum speed is 3.5 m/s. Determine (a) the angular frequency, (b) the spring constant, and (c) the amplitude of the motion.

11. Show by substitution that $x = x_0 \sin\omega t$ is a solution to Equation 13–4.

12. Show by substitution that $x = A \cos\omega t - B \sin\omega t$ is a solution to Equation 13–4, and that this form is equivalent to Equation 13–5 with

$$x_0 = \sqrt{A^2 + B^2} \quad \text{and} \quad \phi = \tan^{-1}(B/A).$$

13. Integrating the nonconstant acceleration of a harmonic oscillator over time from the time of maximum displacement to the time of zero displacement should give the velocity at zero displacement. Carry out this integration, using Equation 13–9 for the acceleration, and show that your answer is just the maximum velocity.

14. A 500-g block on a frictionless surface is connected to a rather limp spring of constant $k = 8.7$ N/m. A second block rests on the first, and the whole system executes simple harmonic motion with a period of 1.8 s. When the amplitude of the motion is increased to 35 cm, the upper block just begins to slip. What is the coefficient of static friction between the blocks?

Section 13.3 *Applications of Simple Harmonic Motion*

15. A 640-g hollow ball 21 cm in diameter is suspended by a wire and is undergoing torsional oscillations at a frequency of 0.78 Hz. What is the torsional constant of the wire?

16. A physics student, bored by a lecture on simple harmonic motion, idly picks up his pencil (mass 9.2 g, length 17 cm) by the tip with his frictionless fingers, and allows it to swing back and forth with small amplitude. If it completes 6279 full cycles during the lecture, how long does the lecture last? *Hint:* See Example 13–5.

17. A pendulum of length ℓ is mounted in a rocket. What is its period if the rocket is (a) at rest on its launch pad; (b) accelerating upward with acceleration $a = \frac{1}{2}g$; (c) accelerating downward with acceleration $a = \frac{1}{2}g$; (d) in free fall?

18. While waiting for your plane to leave the airport gate, you take out your keys and suspend them by a thread pulled from your coat. You set the resulting pendulum oscillating and note that it completes 90 full cycles in 1 minute. Finally the plane begins to take off. During the 60 s it takes to become airborne, your pendulum completes 91 cycles. Determine (a) the acceleration (assumed constant) of the plane and (b) its speed as it leaves the ground. *Hint:* Remember that the plane's acceleration and the force of gravity are at right angles.

19. A mass is attached to a vertical spring, which then goes into oscillation. At the high point of the oscillation, the spring is in the original unstretched equilibrium position it had before the mass was attached; the low point is 5.8 cm below this. What is the period of oscillation?

20. Derive the period of a simple pendulum by considering the horizontal displacement x and the force acting on the bob, rather than the angular displacement and torque.

21. A solid disk of radius R is suspended from a spring of linear spring constant k and torsional constant κ, as shown in Fig. 13–42. In terms of k and κ, what value of R will give the same period for the vertical and torsional oscillations of this system?

Fig. 13–42   Problem 21

22. A thin steel beam 8.0 m long is suspended from a crane and is undergoing torsional oscillations. Two 75-kg steelworkers leap onto opposite ends of the beam, as shown in Fig. 13–43. If the frequency of torsional oscillations diminishes by 20%, what is the mass of the beam?

Fig. 13–43   Problem 22

23. Geologists use an instrument called a **gravimeter** to measure the local acceleration of gravity, thereby learning about the variations in density of rocks in earth's crust. A particular gravimeter uses the period of a 1-m-long pendulum to determine g. If g is to be measured to within 1 mgal (1 gal = 1 cm/s^2) and if the period can be measured with arbitrary accuracy, how accurately must the length of the pendulum be known?

24. A pendulum consists of a 320-g solid ball 15.0 cm in diameter, suspended by an essentially massless string

80.0 cm long. Calculate the period of this pendulum, treating it first as a simple pendulum and then as a physical pendulum. How big is the error introduced by the simple pendulum approximation? *Hint:* Remember the parallel axis theorem.

25. A thin, uniform hoop of mass M and radius R is suspended from a thin horizontal rod and set oscillating with small amplitude, as shown in Fig. 13–44. Show that the period of the oscillations is $2\pi\sqrt{2R/g}$. *Hint:* You may find the parallel axis theorem useful.

Fig. 13–44   Problem 25

26. A solid disk of mass M and radius R is mounted on a horizontal axle, as shown in Fig. 13–45. A spring is connected to the disk at a point $\frac{1}{2}R$ above the axle, and in equilibrium runs horizontally to a wall. If the disk is rotated slightly away from equilibrium, what is the angular frequency of the resulting small-amplitude oscillations? *Hint:* For small θ, sinθ≈θ and cosθ≈1.

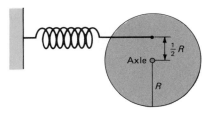

Fig. 13–45   Problem 26

27. A point mass m is attached to the rim of an otherwise uniform solid disk of mass M and radius R (Fig. 13–46). The disk is rolled slightly away from its equilibrium position and released. It rolls back and forth without slipping. Show that the period of this motion is given by

$$T = 2\pi\sqrt{\frac{3MR}{2mg}}.$$

Fig. 13–46   Problem 27

28. Repeat the previous problem for the case when the disk does not contact the ground but is mounted on a frictionless horizontal axle through its center. Why is your answer different?

29. A cyclist turns her bicycle upside down to tinker with it. After she gets it upside down, she notices the front wheel executing a slow, small-amplitude back-and-forth rotational motion with a period of 12 s. Considering the wheel to be a thin ring of mass 600 g and radius 30 cm, whose only irregularity is the presence of the tire valve stem, determine the mass of the valve stem.

30. A mass m is mounted between two springs of constants k_1 and k_2, as shown in Fig. 13–47. Show that the angular frequency of oscillation is given by

$$\omega^2 = \frac{k_1 + k_2}{m}.$$

Fig. 13–47   Problem 30

31. Repeat the previous problem for the case when the springs are connected as in Fig. 13–48.

Fig. 13–48   Problem 31

Section 13.4   *Simple Harmonic Motion in Two Dimensions*

32. Differentiate Equation 13–25 to get the associated velocity vector, and show that the speed is constant.

33. The equation for an ellipse is

$$\frac{x^2}{a^2} + \frac{y^2}{b^2} = 1.$$

Show that two simple harmonic motions of different amplitudes that are at right angles in space and $\pi/2$ out of phase give rise to elliptical motion. How are the constants a and b related to the amplitudes?

34. What is the frequency ratio of the two simple harmonic motions that make the pattern shown in Fig. 13–49?

35. The x- and y-components of motion of a body are harmonic with frequency ratio 1.75:1. How many oscillations must each component undergo before the body returns to its initial position?

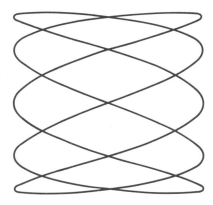

Fig. 13–49   Problem 34

Section 13.5   *Energy in Simple Harmonic Motion*

36. A 1400-kg car with poor shock absorbers is bouncing down the highway at 20 m/s, executing vertical harmonic motion at 0.67 Hz. If the amplitude of the oscillations is 18 cm, what is the total energy in the oscillations? What fraction of the car's total energy is this? Neglect rotational energy of the wheels, and the fact that not all the car's mass participates in the oscillation.

37. A 450-g mass on a spring is oscillating at 1.2 Hz. The total energy of the oscillation is 0.51 J. What is the amplitude of oscillation?

38. The motion of a particle is described by

$$x = (45 \text{ cm})[\sin(\pi t + \pi/6)].$$

At what time is the potential energy twice the kinetic energy? What is the position of the particle at this time?

39. A torsional oscillator of rotational inertia 1.6 kg·m² and torsional constant 3.4 N·m/rad has a total energy of 4.7 J. What are its maximum angular displacement and maximum angular speed?

40. Show that the potential energy of a simple pendulum is proportional to the square of the angular displacement in the small-amplitude limit.

41. Differentiate Equation 13–27 with respect to time and show that the result is Equation 13–4. *Hint:* Remember that $v = dx/dt$, and that total energy is constant.

42. A solid cylinder of mass M and radius R is mounted on an axle through its center. The axle is attached to a horizontal spring of constant k, and the cylinder rolls back and forth without slipping (Fig. 13–50).

Fig. 13–50   Problem 42

Write the statement of energy conservation for this system, and differentiate it to obtain an equation analogous to Equation 13–4 (see previous problem). Comparing your result with Equation 13–4, determine the angular frequency of the motion.

43. A mass m is free to slide on a frictionless slope whose shape is given by $y = ax^2$, where a is a constant with the units of inverse length (Fig. 13–51). The mass is given an initial displacement from the bottom of the track and then released. Find the period of the resulting motion.

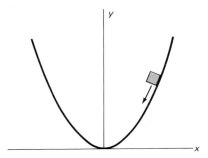

Fig. 13–51   Problem 43

Section 13.6   *Damped Harmonic Motion*

44. A 250-g mass is mounted on a spring of constant $k = 3.3$ N/m. The damping constant for this system is $b = 8.4 \times 10^{-3}$ kg/s. How many oscillations will the system undergo during the time the amplitude decays to $1/e$ of its original value?

45. The vibration of a piano string can be described by an equation analogous to Equation 13–29. If the quantity analogous to $b/2m$ in that equation has the value 2.8 s^{-1}, how long will it take the vibration amplitude to drop to half its original value?

Section 13.7   *Driven Oscillations and Resonance*

46. A mass-spring system has $b/m = \omega_0/5$, where b is the damping constant and ω_0 the natural frequency. How does its amplitude when driven at frequencies 10% above and below ω_0 compare with its amplitude at ω_0?

47. A car's front suspension has a natural frequency of 0.45 Hz. The car's front shock absorbers are worn out, so that they no longer provide critical damping. The car is driving on a bumpy road with bumps 40 m apart. At a certain speed, the driver notices that the car begins to shake violently. What speed?

48. Show by direct substitution that Equation 13–31 satisfies Equation 13–30 with x_0 and ϕ given by Equations 13–32 and 13–33.

49. A harmonic oscillator is underdamped provided that the damping constant b is less than $2m\omega_0$, where ω_0 is the natural frequency of undamped motion. Show that for an underdamped oscillator, Equation 13–32 has a maximum for a driving frequency less than ω_0.

Supplementary Problems

50. Repeat Probem 43 for a small solid ball of mass M and radius R that rolls without slipping on the parabolic track.

51. A child twirls around on a swing, twisting the swing ropes, as shown in Fig. 13–52. As a result, the child and swing rise slightly, with the rise, h, in cm equal to the square of the number of full turns of the swing. When the child stops twisting up the swing, it goes into torsional oscillation. What is the period of this oscillation, assuming that all the potential energy of the system is gravitational? The combined mass of the child and swing is 20 kg, and the rotational inertia of the pair about the appropriate vertical axis is 0.12 kg·m^2.

Fig. 13–52   Problem 51

52. A 1.2-kg block rests on a frictionless surface, and is attached to a horizontal spring of constant $k = 23$ N/m (Fig. 13–53). The block is oscillating with amplitude 10 cm and with phase constant $\phi = -\pi/2$ in Equation 13–5. A block of mass 0.80 kg is moving from the right at 1.7 m/s. It strikes the first block when the latter is at the rightmost point in its oscillation. The collision is completely inelastic, and the two blocks stick together. Determine the frequency, amplitude, and phase constant (relative to the *original* $t = 0$) of the resulting motion.

Fig. 13–53   Problem 52

53. The motion of a two-dimensional simple harmonic oscillator is described by

$$\mathbf{r} = A \sin\omega t \; \mathbf{\hat{i}} + A \sin(\omega t + \pi/4) \, \mathbf{\hat{j}}.$$

The path is an ellipse; find the orientation of its major axis. *Hint:* At what *time* is the magnitude of the displacement a maximum? What are the components of the displacement at this time?

54. A small object of mass m slides without friction in a circular bowl of radius R. Derive an expression for small-amplitude oscillations about equilibrium, and compare with that of a simple pendulum.

55. A more exact expression than Equation 13–24 for the period of a simple pendulum is

$$T = T_0[1 + \tfrac{1}{4}\sin^2(\tfrac{1}{2}\theta_0) + \tfrac{9}{64}\sin^4(\tfrac{1}{2}\theta_0) + \cdots],$$

where $T_0 = 2\pi\sqrt{\ell/g}$ is the period in the limit of arbitrarily small amplitude, and θ_0 is the amplitude. The $\cdots$ indicates that additional terms (in fact, infinitely many more) are needed for an exact expression. For a pendulum with $T_0 = 1.00$ s, plot the period given above versus amplitude for amplitudes from 0 to 45°. By what percentage does the plotted period differ from T_0 for θ_0 of 30° and 45°?

56. A mass m is connected between two springs of length L, as shown in Fig. 13–54. At equilibrium, the tension force in each spring is F_0. Find the period of oscillations *perpendicular* to the springs, assuming sufficiently small amplitude that the magnitude of the spring tension is essentially unchanged.

Fig. 13–54   Problem 56

57. A disk of radius R is suspended from a pivot somewhere between its center and edge (Fig. 13–55). For what pivot point will the period of this physical pendulum be a minimum?

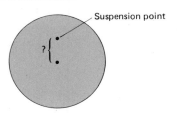

Suspension point

Fig. 13–55   Problem 57

58. A uniform piece of wire is bent into a V-shape with angle θ between two legs of length ℓ. The wire is placed over a pivot, as shown in Fig. 13–56. Show that the angular frequency of small-amplitude oscillations about this equilibrium is given by

$$\omega = \sqrt{\frac{3g\,\cos(\theta/2)}{4\ell}}.$$

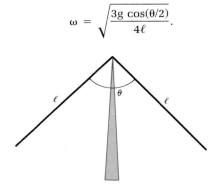

Fig. 13–56   Problem 58

59. An object in *unstable* equilibrium is subject to a force that increases linearly with displacement from equilibrium: $F = kx$. Set up Newton's law as a differential equation for this case, and show that one solution is

$$x = x_0\,e^{t\sqrt{k/m}}.$$

Does this solution represent reasonable physical behavior? Can you find another solution? Is it physically very probable?

60. Imagine a small hole bored directly through the center of the earth and out to the other side. Show that an object dropped into this hole executes simple harmonic motion, and calculate the period of the motion. Assume that the earth has uniform density. *Hint:* Consult Section 8.5.

14

WAVE MOTION

Disturbing the equilibrium of the simple mass-spring system in Fig. 14–1a results in oscillatory motion. In the more complicated system of Fig. 14–1b, the motion of one mass is "felt" by the others—first by those nearby, then by those farther away. The result is a **wave**—a disturbance that moves or **propagates** through the system. Although the individual masses oscillate about their equilibrium positions, neither they nor the entire system move with the wave. What moves, instead, is energy, as evidenced by the temporary motions of the masses and stretching of the springs as the wave goes by. We clarify this point in defining a wave:

wave
propagates

definition of wave

> A wave is a travelling disturbance that transports energy but not matter.

You are familiar with many examples of waves. Information in your professor's lectures is carried in the energy of sound waves that disturb the air and eventually your eardrums. But air from the professor's mouth does not move across the classroom. Similarly, ocean waves bring to shore the energy imparted to the water by distant winds. But the water itself does

Fig. 14–1
(a) Disturbance of the simple mass-spring system results in oscillatory motion about equilibrium. *(b)* The motion of one disturbed mass in the coupled mass-spring system is eventually communicated to adjacent masses. The result is a propagating wave—in this case, regions of compression and elongation that move along the system. The system is shown at two different times to illustrate the motion of the wave.

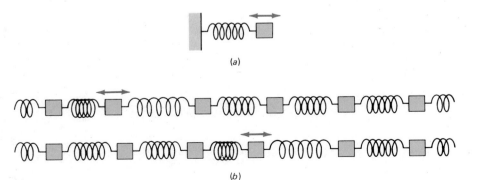

(a)

(b)

Fig. 14–2
A boat bobs up and down as a wave
passes, but does not participate in the
forward motion of the wave.

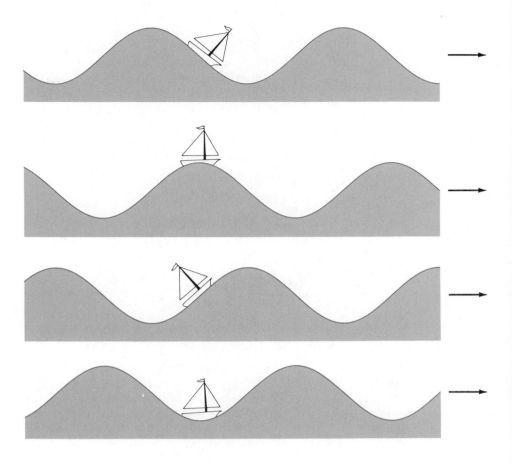

not move with the wave, as you can see by watching a boat bob up and
down (Fig. 14–2). Ultrasound waves—sound waves of much higher pitch
than the human ear can detect—are used to make images of the interior of
the human body (Fig. 14–3). Earthquakes set up wave motion in the earth
itself. Detection of these waves helps determine the location and strength
of the quake (Fig. 14–4).

Fig. 14–3 (left)
Twin fetuses are evident in this image,
produced by ultrasound waves
reflecting within the human body.

Fig. 14–4 (right)
This seismograph at Kilauea Volcano,
Hawaii, records not only tremors
associated with the volcano but also
waves generated by earthquakes
thousands of kilometers distant.

mechanical waves

The waves we have mentioned are **mechanical waves,** so called because they involve the disturbance of some mechanical medium, be it a mass-spring system, air, water, or the solid earth. In this chapter, we will develop a physical understanding of mechanical waves. Many properties of mechanical waves are also shared by electromagnetic waves, which include visible light, radio waves, x-rays, and others. We will explore electromagnetic waves further in Chapters 32 to 35.

14.1
PROPERTIES OF WAVES

Wave Amplitude

amplitude

A wave displaces a medium from its equilibrium state. The maximum displacement is the **amplitude** of the wave. Wave amplitude measures whatever physical quantity is affected by the wave—for example, the height of a water wave, or the pressure of a sound wave.

Longitudinal and Transverse Waves

longitudinal wave

transverse wave

We could set up a wave on the coupled mass-spring system of Fig. 14–1b by displacing a mass either along the direction of the spring or at right angles to it. In the first case we get a **longitudinal wave**—a travelling disturbance consisting of regions of stretched and compressed springs, with masses moving back and forth along the direction that the wave itself travels (Fig. 14–5). Sound waves provide another example of longitudinal waves (Fig. 14–6). Figure 14–7 illustrates a **transverse wave**—a travelling

Fig. 14–5
A longitudinal wave on a coupled mass-spring system. Large arrow indicates direction of wave propagation, small arrows the motions of the individual masses.

Fig. 14–6
A sound wave is a longitudinal disturbance characterized by changes in air pressure.

Fig. 14–7
This transverse wave on a coupled mass-spring system. Large arrow indicates direction of wave propagation, small arrows the motions of the individual masses.

Fig. 14–8
Motion of the water in a water surface wave is approximately circular, giving the wave both transverse and longitudinal components. Colored arrows represent instantaneous velocity of the water: dotted circles are the paths followed by "parcels" of water as the wave passes. The wave is moving to the right.

disturbance in which masses move perpendicularly to the direction that the wave is travelling. Some waves—like those on the surface of water—are neither fully longitudinal nor transverse, but include components of each (Fig. 14–8).

Waveforms

Wave disturbances come in a variety of shapes, called waveforms. An isolated disturbance, travelling through an otherwise undisturbed medium, is a pulse (Fig. 14–9a). A pulse is produced when a medium is disturbed briefly. At the opposite extreme is a continuous wave (Fig. 14–9b), produced when a medium is disturbed at some point in a regular, periodic way. A wave train (Fig. 14–9c) occurs in the more realistic case when a periodic disturbance lasts for a finite time.

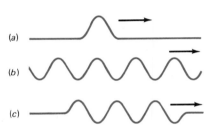

(a)

(b)

(c)

Fig. 14–9
(a) A pulse, (b) a continuous wave, and (c) a wave train.

Wavelength and Period

A continuous wave is further characterized by two quantities that describe the variation of the wave disturbance in space and time. The **wavelength** λ is the distance between one point and the next point where the wave pattern begins to repeat (Fig. 14–10). In a continuous wave, each point in the medium undergoes oscillatory motion (Fig. 14–11). The wave **period** T is the period of this motion. Period is a *temporal* property of a wave, measured most directly by observing the wave at a single point in space. Wavelength, in contrast, is a *spatial* property, measured directly by observing the wave at a single instant of time.

wavelength

period

Fig. 14–10
The wavelength, λ, is the distance in which the wave pattern repeats.

Wave Speed

A wave travels at a characteristic speed through its medium. In air under typical conditions, the speed of sound waves is about 340 m/s. Small ripples on the surface of a pond move at only about 20 cm/s, while earthquake-generated waves in the earth's outer crust move at speeds on the order of 6 km/s. Wave speed, wavelength, and period are related quantities. In one wave period, an observer at a fixed point sees one complete wavelength go by (Fig. 14–12). Since the wave moves a full wavelength in one period, its speed is

$$v = \frac{\lambda}{T}.$$

(14–1)

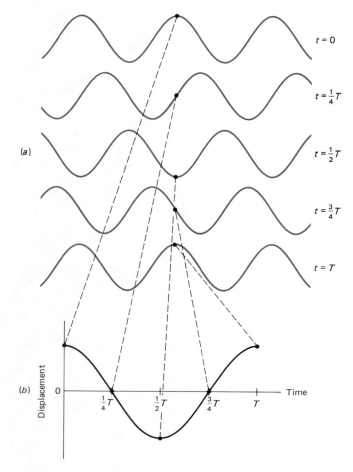

Fig. 14–11
(a) A continuous wave, seen at successive instants of time. A given point in the medium undergoes oscillatory motion *(b)*. The period of this motion is the wave period *T*.

For some kinds of waves, speed is independent of period and wavelength; in that case the ratio λ/T is constant. For other waves, for example, those on the surface of deep water, wave speed depends on wavelength, and the ratio λ/T is not constant (see Problem 30).

Fig. 14–12
One full cycle—occupying a distance of one wavelength—passes a given point in one wave period. The wave speed is therefore $v = \lambda/T$.

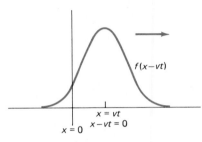

Fig. 14–13
A "snapshot" of a wave pulse at time $t=0$.

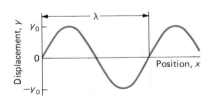

Fig. 14–14
At a later time t, the wave pulse looks the same, but it has moved to the right. It is described by the same function f, but now the argument of the function is $x - vt$, where v is the wave speed.

simple harmonic wave

Fig. 14–15
"Snapshot" of the simple harmonic wave described by Equation 14–2 at time $t=0$.

14.2
MATHEMATICAL DESCRIPTION OF WAVE MOTION

Figure 14–13 shows a "snapshot" of a wave pulse at an instant of time—say, $t=0$. The pulse is moving along the x-axis, and we have chosen $x=0$ to coincide with the position of its peak at time $t=0$. We could describe the pulse at this instant by giving the displacement, y, as a function of position:

$$y = f(x),$$

where the peak of the function $f(x)$ occurs when its argument is zero. The displacement y could be any physical quantity disturbed by the wave. Assuming the wave pulse retains its shape,* Fig. 14–14 shows the situation at arbitrarily later time t. To describe the pulse now, we need a function that gives the same shape as $f(x)$, but moved to the right. How far to the right? The pulse is moving at speed v, and has been doing so for time t, so it has moved a distance vt. A function with the desired effect is $f(x - vt)$. Whatever shape $f(x)$ describes, $f(x - vt)$ describes the same shape. But where the peak of $f(x)$ occurred at $x=0$, the peak of $f(x - vt)$ occurs when $x - vt = 0$, or when $x = vt$. As time increases, the value of x needed to give the peak of the pulse also increases, so that the function $f(x - vt)$ correctly represents the moving pulse.

Although our discussion focused on a single wave pulse, the same considerations apply as well to *any* functions $f(x)$, including continuous waves. Quite generally, any wave moving in the positive x-direction may be described by some function of the quantity $x - vt$, with v the wave speed. You can easily convince yourself that a wave moving in the negative x-direction is described by a function of $x + vt$.

A particularly important case is the **simple harmonic wave,** so called because the wave medium executes simple harmonic motion about its equilibrium. A simple harmonic wave is sinusoidal in shape, with one full cycle occurring in one wavelength λ. At time $t=0$, we can therefore describe such a wave by

$$y = y_0 \cos\left(\frac{2\pi x}{\lambda}\right), \qquad \text{(at } t=0) \qquad (14\text{–}2)$$

where y is the displacement from equilibrium and y_0 the amplitude or maximum displacement (Fig. 14–15). We could also have included a phase constant in this expression; for simplicity we assume a choice of origin $x=0$ that makes the phase constant zero. We choose the argument of the cosine function so that it becomes 2π when $x=\lambda$, thereby ensuring that the function repeats itself in one wavelength. Equation 14–2 describes the wave at time $t=0$; to get a description at all times, we simply replace x by $x \pm vt$, where v is the wave speed, and where our choice of sign depends on which direction the wave is moving:

---

*It may or may not, depending on the medium. See Section 14.5.

$$y = y_0 \cos\left[\frac{2\pi(x \pm vt)}{\lambda}\right] = y_0 \cos\left(\frac{2\pi x}{\lambda} \pm \frac{2\pi vt}{\lambda}\right). \quad (14-3)$$

But Equation 14–1 shows that the wave speed v and wavelength λ are related to the period T by $v = \lambda/T$, so that $v/\lambda = 1/T$. We define the wave **frequency,** in cycles per second or Hz, to be the inverse of the period ($f = 1/T$), so that we have

$$y = y_0 \cos\left(\frac{2\pi x}{\lambda} \pm \frac{2\pi t}{T}\right) = y_0 \cos\left(\frac{2\pi x}{\lambda} \pm 2\pi ft\right). \quad (14-4)$$

Equation 14–4 shows that if we sit at a fixed position—say $x = 0$—then the displacement varies in time as $y = y_0 \cos(2\pi ft)$, which we recognize as simple harmonic motion with angular frequency $\omega = 2\pi f$ (Fig. 14–16). As in the previous chapter, it is usually more convenient mathematically to work with this angular frequency ω, defined by

$$\omega = 2\pi f = \frac{2\pi}{T}. \quad (14-5)$$

Recall that the units of ω are rad/s or simply s^{-1}. Similarly, it is convenient to define the **wave number,** k:

$$k = \frac{2\pi}{\lambda}. \quad (14-6)$$

The wave number is a spatial analog of the angular frequency; the latter describes the number of radians of wave cycle per unit *time*, the former the number of radians of wave cycle per unit *distance*. The definition of k shows that its units are m^{-1}. Using the angular frequency ω and wave number k, we can rewrite Equation 14–4:

$$y = y_0 \cos(kx \pm \omega t). \quad \text{(simple harmonic wave)} \quad (14-7)$$

The simple way in which k and ω enter this description of the wave is the reason these quantities are so often used. If we solve Equations 14–5 and 14–6 for T and λ, respectively, and use the results in Equation 14–1, we can express the wave speed v in terms of ω and k:

$$v = \frac{\lambda}{T} = \frac{2\pi/k}{2\pi/\omega} = \frac{\omega}{k}. \quad (14-8)$$

frequency

Fig. 14–16
Temporal variation of the wave displacement is simple harmonic motion with period T, frequency f, and angular frequency $\omega = 2\pi f$. Note the difference between this figure and the previous one; here we see the *temporal* variation at a *fixed position*, while there we saw the *spatial* variation at a *fixed time*.

wave number

Example 14–1

A Simple Harmonic Wave

A sinusoidal water wave has a maximum height of 7.4 cm above the equilibrium water level, a distance of 55 cm between wave crests, and is propagating in the $-x$-direction at 93 cm/s. Express the wave in the form 14–7, assuming that a wave crest is at $x = 0$ at time $t = 0$.

Solution

To use the form 14–7, we need to know the amplitude y_0, the wave number k, and the angular frequency ω. The 7.4-cm height is the amplitude y_0, and the 55 cm between crests is the wavelength λ. Then the wave number is

$$k = \frac{2\pi}{\lambda} = \frac{2\pi}{55 \text{ cm}} = 0.11 \text{ cm}^{-1}.$$

The angular frequency can then be obtained from Equation 14–8:

$$\omega = vk = (93 \text{ cm/s})(0.11 \text{ cm}^{-1}) = 10 \text{ s}^{-1}.$$

With the wave moving in the $-x$-direction, we choose the plus sign in Equation 14–7, giving

$$y = 7.4 \cos(0.11x + 10t) \text{ cm.}$$

The phase constant is zero since a wave peak is at $x = 0$ at time $t = 0$.

14.3
WAVES ON A STRING: THE WAVE EQUATION

A Stretched String

What determines whether waves can propagate in a given medium, and if so how fast they go? The answer must lie in the physical properties of the medium. To find that answer, we apply Newton's law of motion to the medium. We now illustrate this procedure for transverse waves on a stretched string. Our results are directly applicable to strings and wires on musical instruments, as well as to other elongated structures (Fig. 14–17).

Our string has mass per unit length of μ kg/m, and is stretched to a tension force of F_0 newtons. In equilibrium, the string lies along the x-axis. Suppose the string is distorted slightly, displacing part of it in the y-direction. We want to show that wave motion results when the string is released, and to determine the wave speed.

To do so, we will apply Newton's law to a small mass element dm along the string. To apply Newton's law, we need the net force $d\mathbf{F}$ acting on the mass element. Suppose the string is distorted only slightly, so that the magnitude F_0 of the string tension does not change significantly. Figure 14–18 shows a magnified view of a small portion of the distorted string, including a mass element dm. Although we are assuming that the magnitude F_0 of the tension stays essentially constant, the *direction* of the tension force varies slightly along the mass element because the distorted string is curved. Therefore, the tension forces pulling at opposite ends of the mass element, although of the same magnitude, do not exactly cancel. Because the string is nearly horizontal, the y-components of tension differ more significantly than the x-components. Under our assumption that the distortion is small, then, we consider that the net force on the mass element dm is essentially in the y-direction. From Fig. 14–18, we see that the difference in the y-components of tension between the right and left ends of the mass element is

$$dF_y = F_0 \sin\theta_2 - F_0 \sin\theta_1.$$

But the string is very nearly horizontal, so that the sines of the angles are

Fig. 14–17
A wave pulse on a Slinky is an example of a transverse wave on an elongated structure.

Fig. 14–18
A magnified view of a small portion of the stretched string. There is a nonzero net force on a small mass element dm because the string points in slightly different directions at opposite ends of the mass element. The vertical distortion is exaggerated for clarity: actually, the string remains very nearly horizontal.

Fig. 14–19
When the angle θ is very small, the hypotenuse *h* and longer side *x* are nearly equal. Then sinθ = *y*/*h* and tanθ = *y*/*x* are nearly equal. Both are also essentially equal to the angle itself in radian measure.

very nearly the same as their tangents (Fig. 14–19). But the tangents of the two angles are just the slopes of the string—or the derivatives dy/dx—at the ends of the mass element. Then the y-component of force on the mass element is approximately

$$dF_y \simeq F_0(\tan\theta_2 - \tan\theta_1) = F_0\left(\frac{dy}{dx}\bigg|_{x+dx} - \frac{dy}{dx}\bigg|_x\right).$$

The quantity in parentheses is just the change in the first derivative from one end of the interval dx to the other. Dividing that change by dx would give the rate of change of the first derivative—that is, the second derivative d^2y/dx^2. So we can write our equation more simply if we multiply the right-hand side by one in the form dx/dx, to get

$$dF_y = F_0\frac{d^2y}{dx^2}\,dx. \tag{14–9a}$$

This equation gives the net force on the mass element dm. Before we use this force in Newton's law, we should be a little more careful in expressing derivatives. Figure 14–18, on which Equation 14–9a is based, is a picture of the string *at an instant of time*. Therefore, the derivative in Equation 14–9a is to be taken with *time fixed*. This distinction is important because the displacement of the string is a function not only of position but also of time, and changes if either of these variables changes. We encountered a similar situation in Section 7.5, where we developed the relation between force and potential energy when the latter varies in more than one dimension. Here, as in Chapter 7, we call a derivative taken with respect to one variable while others are held constant a **partial derivative,** and write partial derivatives with the special symbol ∂ in place of the usual d. So Equation 14–9a should be written more correctly as

partial derivative

$$dF_y = F_0\frac{\partial^2 y}{\partial x^2}\,dx. \tag{14–9b}$$

Now we can use Newton's law to equate the force to the mass times acceleration. The mass dm of the tiny piece of string we are considering is given by the mass per unit length, μ, times the length of the piece. Since the string is nearly horizontal, the length is nearly dx. Then

$$dm = \mu dx.$$

Using this mass and the force from Equation 14–9b in Newton's law $F = ma$, we have

$$F_0\frac{\partial^2 y}{\partial x^2}\,dx = \mu\,dx\,\frac{\partial^2 y}{\partial t^2},$$

where we have written the acceleration as the second partial derivative of displacement with respect to time. Cancelling dx on both sides, we can write

$$\frac{\partial^2 y}{\partial x^2} = \frac{\mu}{F_0}\frac{\partial^2 y}{\partial t^2}. \tag{14–10}$$

What is this equation? It is just Newton's law applied to a mass element on our stretched string. Since there is nothing special about the particular mass element we considered, Equation 14–10 must apply along the entire string.

We developed Equation 14–10 to tell us about waves that might propagate on the string. To see what it has to say, let us assume we have a simple harmonic wave propagating on our string. In the previous section, we found that such a wave is described by

$$y = y_0 \cos(kx - \omega t), \tag{14–11}$$

where y is the displacement, y_0 the amplitude, k the wave number, and ω the angular frequency. If this mathematical form is consistent with Newton's law, then such waves are possible. To see if this is the case, we form the second partial derivatives of the wave displacement y in Equation 14–11 and substitute them into Equation 14–10 to see if we get an identity. The derivatives are

$$\frac{\partial^2 y}{\partial x^2} = -y_0 k^2 \cos(kx - \omega t)$$

and

$$\frac{\partial^2 y}{\partial t^2} = -y_0 \omega^2 \cos(kx - \omega t),$$

where in taking the partial derivative with respect to x we treat t as a constant and vice versa. Putting these derivatives into Equation 14–10 then gives

$$-y_0 k^2 \cos(kx - \omega t) = \left(\frac{\mu}{F_0}\right)[-y_0 \omega^2 \cos(kx - \omega t)].$$

Both the amplitude y_0 and the cosine term cancel, leaving

$$k^2 = \frac{\mu}{F_0} \omega^2,$$

or

$$\left(\frac{\omega}{k}\right)^2 = \frac{F_0}{\mu}. \tag{14–12}$$

What is Equation 14–12 telling us? Again, it follows directly from Newton's law applied to the stretched string, under the assumption that a wave described by Equation 14–11 is propagating along the string. So it tells us that such a wave can propagate, provided the wave properties ω and k are related to the properties F_0 and μ of the string in the way Equation 14–12 implies:

$$\frac{\omega}{k} = \sqrt{\frac{F_0}{\mu}}.$$

That is, only waves with ω and k related in this special way can propagate on the string. But ω/k is just the wave speed (see Equation 14–8), so that

$$v = \frac{\omega}{k} = \sqrt{\frac{F_0}{\mu}}. \tag{14–13}$$

Does this make sense? If we stretch the string tighter, increasing the tension F_0, then the restoring force is greater and the disturbance travels faster down the string. If the mass per unit length μ increases, the string's inertia is greater and it responds to the restoring force with less acceleration, resulting in a slower wave. Equation 14–13 also shows that the wave speed on the string is independent of wavelength.

The Wave Equation

Using Equation 14–13, we can write Equation 14–10 in the form

$$\frac{\partial^2 y}{\partial x^2} - \frac{1}{v^2}\frac{\partial^2 y}{\partial t^2} = 0. \qquad (14-14)$$

wave equation   Equation 14–14 is known as the **wave equation.** Whenever analysis of a system results in an equation of the form 14–14, then we know that system supports waves propagating at speed v. The wave equation 14–14 usually holds only for small-amplitude disturbances, typified by our assumption of a stretched string that remains nearly horizontal. Large-amplitude disturbances usually result in a more complicated equation, and in a wave speed that depends on wavelength.

In analyzing waves on a string, we showed that a travelling simple harmonic wave of the form 14–11 is a solution to the wave equation. Is this the only possible kind of wave we can have? No: you can easily show that *any* function of the form $f(x \pm vt)$ also satisfies the wave equation (see Problem 16). Therefore, the shape of a wave that satisfies the wave equation is quite arbitrary; the actual wave shape that propagates depends on the way in which the string or other medium is initially displaced from equilibrium.

Example 14–2 _____
The Wave Equation and Sound Waves

In analyzing the propagation of sound waves in a gas, the following equation arises:

$$\frac{\partial^2 P}{\partial x^2} - \frac{m}{\gamma kT}\frac{\partial^2 P}{\partial t^2} = 0, \qquad (14-15)$$

where P is the gas pressure, x the position in the gas, t the time, T the gas temperature in kelvins (K), m the mass of a gas molecule in kg, γ a constant that depends on the molecular structure of the gas, and $k = 1.38 \times 10^{-23}$ J/K, a constant called Boltzmann's constant. We will encounter k in Chapter 17; note that it is unrelated to the wave number, whose symbol is also k. Obtain an expression for the speed of sound in a gas, and evaluate for air at room temperature (300 K), with $\gamma = 1.4$ and average molecular mass about 29 u.

Solution

Comparing the sound wave equation 14–15 with the general form 14–14, we see that the quantity multiplying the time derivative is the inverse of the wave speed squared:

$$\frac{1}{v^2} = \frac{m}{\gamma kT}.$$

Then the speed of sound is

$$v = \sqrt{\frac{\gamma kT}{m}}. \qquad (14\text{--}16)$$

Evaluating this expression for air, we have

$$v = \left[\frac{(1.4)(1.38 \times 10^{-23} \text{ J/K})(300 \text{ K})}{(29 \text{ u})(1.7 \times 10^{-27} \text{ kg/u})}\right]^{1/2} = 340 \text{ m/s}.$$

This result amounts to about one-fifth of a mile per second, or about 1200 km/h. Problems 3 and 5 explore applications of the sound speed.

14.4
WAVE ENERGY AND INTENSITY

A wave propagates because motion in one part of a medium is communicated to adjacent parts. In the process, energy is passed through the medium.

For a simple harmonic wave on a stretched string, we can determine quantitatively the rate of energy transmission. To do so, we need to know both the kinetic and potential energy associated with a mass element dm on the string. With the displacement y of the string given by Equation 14–11, the speed u of a mass element dm at a point x and time t is

$$u = \frac{\partial y}{\partial t} = \omega y_0 \sin(kx - \omega t).$$

(We use partial derivatives because the displacement y is a function of both x and t, and we want its variation with t alone.) This is the speed of a mass element on the string, and *not* the wave speed v. For our transverse wave, the string motion is in fact at right angles to the wave motion. Since the string has mass μ per unit length, we have $dm = \mu dx$, where dx is the unstretched length of the mass element. Then the kinetic energy dK in the mass element dm becomes

$$dK = \tfrac{1}{2}dm\,u^2 = \tfrac{1}{2}\mu\omega^2 y_0^2\sin^2(kx - \omega t)dx.$$

This expression shows that the kinetic energy oscillates between zero and a maximum of $\tfrac{1}{2}\mu\omega^2 y_0^2$ as the $\sin^2(kx - \omega t)$ term swings between 0 and 1. Over one full cycle, the average of $\sin^2$ is $\tfrac{1}{2}$, as shown in Fig. 14–20, so that the time-average kinetic energy, $\overline{dK}$, in our mass element is

$$\overline{dK} = \tfrac{1}{4}\mu\omega^2 y_0^2 dx.$$

What about the potential energy? In simple harmonic motion, the average kinetic energy and average potential energy are equal,* Therefore, the time-average energy $\overline{dE}$ in the mass element dm is twice its time-average kinetic energy, or

$$\overline{dE} = \tfrac{1}{2}\mu\omega^2 y_0^2 dx.$$

Fig. 14–20
The function $\sin^2$ swings symmetrically between 0 and 1, with average value $\tfrac{1}{2}$.

---

*Although at a given point in a propagating wave, both kinetic and potential energy peak at the same time, rather than being out of phase as in pure simple harmonic motion.

What happens to this energy? As the mass element moves, it does work on the *next* mass element, passing along its energy in the process. But over one cycle, it gains back the same amount of energy from the *previous* mass element. So on the average, the energy in the mass element remains constant (although it does fluctuate over one cycle, something our time-average derivation cannot reveal).

How long does it take the mass element to give up the energy dE? If the wave is moving at speed v, then the energy dE passes the mass element of length dx in time $dt = dx/v$. So the average rate of energy flow, or average power, is

$$\overline{P} = \frac{\overline{dE}}{dt} = \frac{\frac{1}{2}\mu\omega^2 y_0^2 \, dx}{dx/v} = \tfrac{1}{2}\mu\omega^2 y_0^2 v. \qquad (14\text{--}17)$$

Although Equation 14–17 was derived for waves on a string, some aspects of the equation are common to all waves. For example, the power is always proportional to wave speed. Also, all waves share the property that the power is proportional to the *square* of the amplitude.

intensity
plane wave

The total power is a useful quantity in describing a wave confined to a narrow structure like a string for mechanical waves or a coaxial cable or optical fiber for electromagnetic waves. But when waves travel throughout a three-dimensional medium, it makes more sense to speak of the **intensity,** or power per unit area. In a **plane wave**—one whose wavefronts are planes—the intensity remains constant (Fig. 14–21a). With waves from a localized source, however, the wave energy spreads over an ever greater area. When waves emanate in all directions from a small, pointlike source, then the wavefronts are spherical and the area increases as the square of the distance from the source. As a result, intensity decreases as the inverse square of the distance (Fig. 14–21b). Similarly, for a linelike source, intensity decreases as the inverse of the distance (Fig. 14–21c). These decreases

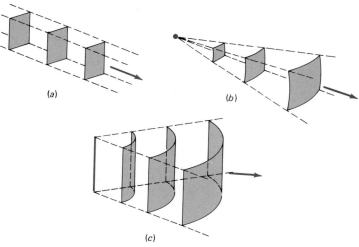

Fig. 14–21
(a) In a plane wave, wave energy remains spread over the same area as the wave propagates, so that the wave intensity remains constant. *(b)* As a wave spreads spherically from a point source, its intensity decreases as the inverse square of distance from the source. *(c)* Wave intensity decreases as the inverse of distance from a line source.

TABLE 14–1 ▬▬▬
Wave Intensities

Wave	Intensity, W/m^2
Sound, 4 m from loud rock band	1
Sound, jet taking off, at 30 m	5
Sound, whisper, intensity at eardrum	10^{-10}
Light, sunlight intensity at earth's orbit	1368
Light, sunlight intensity at Jupiter's orbit	50
Light, 1 m from typical camera flash	4000
Light, at target of laser fusion experiment	10^{18}
TV signal, 5.0 km from 50-kW transmitter	1.6×10^{-4}
Microwaves, inside microwave oven	6000
Microwaves, maximum allowable outside microwave oven	50
Earthquake wave, 5 km from Richter 7.0 quake	4×10^4

do not occur because of any loss of wave energy, but only because the wave energy spreads over greater area. Table 14–1 lists the intensities of various waves. Even though different kinds of waves are listed, it still makes sense to compare intensity, which in each case measures power transmitted per unit area.

Example 14–3 _____
Wave Intensity

Verify the entry in Table 14–1 for the 50-kW TV transmitter.

Solution

At a distance of 5.0 km, the 50-kW transmitter power is spread over the surface of a sphere 5.0 km in radius. The area of a sphere is $4\pi r^2$, so the intensity, or power per unit area, is

$$I = \frac{P}{A} = \frac{50 \times 10^3 \text{ W}}{(4\pi)(5.0 \times 10^3 \text{ m})^2} = 1.6 \times 10^{-4} \text{ W/m}^2.$$

14.5
THE SUPERPOSITION PRINCIPLE AND WAVE INTERFERENCE

The Superposition Principle

Any function of the quantity $x \pm vt$—a wave of any shape—satisfies the wave equation 14–14. Suppose we have two such functions, $f(x \pm vt)$ and $g(x \pm vt)$. Then the function $f(x \pm vt) + g(x \pm vt)$ is also a solution, as you can easily show by substituting it into the wave equation (see Problem 26). Physically, this means that if we have two waves propagating simultaneously in a medium, then the net displacement of the medium is just the sum of the displacements of the two waves. This property—the simple addition of waves to produce a composite wave—is called the **superposition principle.** Waves that obey the superposition principle include all those described by Equation 14–14, and others besides. Some waves—mostly

superposition principle

those in complicated media or those of very large amplitude—do not. We will be concerned primarily with waves that obey the superposition principle.

The superposition principle makes it possible to decompose a complicated wave shape into a sum of simple harmonic waves. Consider the two simple harmonic waves

$$y_1 = y_0 \sin(kx - \omega t)$$

and

$$y_2 = \tfrac{1}{3}y_0 \sin(2kx - 2\omega t)$$

shown in Fig. 14–22. Both have the same speed—the same ratio of angular frequency to wave number. But the second wave has twice the frequency and therefore half the wavelength of the first, along with one-third the amplitude. Their sum, also shown in Fig. 14–22, is a more complicated waveform. Other wave shapes can be built up out of sums of many simple harmonic waves. Figure 14–23 shows how a square wave is constructed from an infinite sum of simple harmonic waves of the form

$$y = \frac{4y_0}{\pi}\left[\frac{\sin(kx - \omega t)}{1} + \frac{\sin(3kx - 3\omega t)}{3} + \frac{\sin(5kx - 5\omega t)}{5} + \cdots\right].$$

Fig. 14–22
Two simple harmonic waves sum to make a more complex waveform.

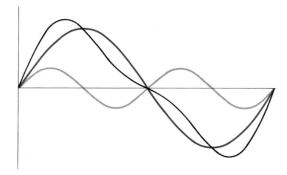

Fig. 14–23
A square wave built up as a sum of simple harmonic waves. Shown are the square wave, the first three harmonic waves in the series, and their sum (black).

(a)   (b)

Fig. 14–24
(a) Waveform produced by a violin. *(b)* Fourier analysis shows the relative strength of the different harmonics whose sum is the complex waveform. To reproduce the waveform faithfully, an audio system must be capable of reproducing not only the fundamental frequency but also the significant harmonics.

Fourier analysis

This decomposition of an arbitrary wave shape into simple harmonic waves is called **Fourier analysis,** after the French mathematician Jean Baptiste Joseph Fourier (1786–1830). Fourier showed that *any* periodic function can be so decomposed. Fourier analysis has many applications, ranging from music to communications, because it allows us to understand how a complex wave shape behaves if we know how its composite simple harmonic waves behave (Fig. 14–24).

When wave speed is independent of wavelength, as it is for waves that satisfy Equation 14–14, then all simple harmonic waves making up a complex waveform travel at the same speed. As a result, the waveform maintains its shape. Other waves, obeying more complicated wave equations, often have speeds that depend on wavelength. Then, individual harmonic waves travel at different speeds, and a complex waveform changes shape as it moves. This phenomenon is called **dispersion,** and is illustrated in Fig. 14–25. Waves on the surface of deep water, for example, have speed given by

dispersion

$$v = \sqrt{\frac{\lambda g}{2\pi}}, \qquad (14\text{–}18)$$

where λ is the wavelength and g the acceleration of gravity. Since v depends on λ, the waves are dispersive. Long-wavelength waves from a storm at sea have the highest speeds and therefore reach shore well in advance of both the storm and the shorter-wavelength waves.

Interference

Figure 14–26*a* shows two identical sinusoidal wave trains travelling in opposite directions on the same string. What happens when they meet? If the waves obey the superposition principle, then their amplitudes simply add at each instant. When they overlap crest-to-crest, that addition results instantaneously in a structure with twice the amplitude of either wave

(a)

(b)

Fig. 14–25
(a) A wave pulse in a nondispersive medium holds its shape as it propagates. *(b)* In a dispersive medium, a pulse changes shape as it propagates.

Fig. 14–26
(a) Sinusoidal wavetrains propagating in opposite directions. *(b)* At this instant, the waves interfere constructively. *(c)* Half a cycle later, they interfere destructively. *(d)* The wavetrains continue on their way, unaffected by their encounter.

(a)

(b)

(c)

(d)

interference
constructive interference
destructive interference

nodal lines

(Fig. 14–26b). Half a wave period later, crests line up with troughs, and the net amplitude is zero (Fig. 14–26c). While they are interacting, the two waves are said to **interfere.** If the composite amplitude is enhanced, the interference is **constructive;** if the amplitude is diminished, then it is **destructive.** Finally, the waves continue on their separate ways, completely unchanged by their interaction.

An important example of wave interference is provided by waves from two point sources (Fig. 14–27). Along curves called **nodal lines,** crests and troughs meet, resulting in diminished amplitude. Between nodal lines are regions of constructive interference, where wave amplitude is enhanced. The same effect can be achieved by passing waves through two small holes or slits (Fig. 14–28). Two-slit interference experiments have considerable importance in optics (Chapter 35) and in modern physics, and are of historical interest because they were first used to demonstrate the wave nature of light (Fig. 14–29). Problem 32 explores the mathematics of two-slit interference.

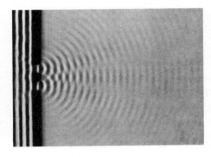

Fig. 14–27
Pattern produced when circular water waves from two point sources interfere. The nodal lines—regions of destructive interference—are clearly evident.

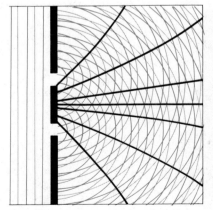

Fig. 14–28
Passing straight waves through two small slits also results in a two-source or double-slit interference pattern.

Fig. 14–29
Interference pattern produced by shining laser light through two narrow slits. The slits were produced by painting a microscope slide black, then scratching the paint with two razor blades held side-by-side.

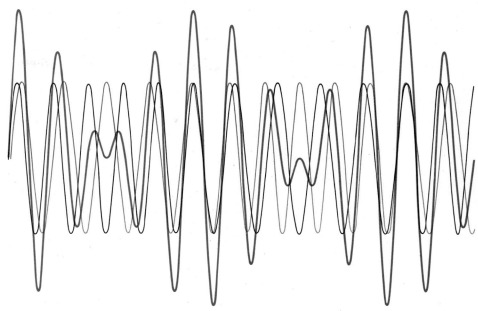

Fig. 14–30
Beats. Two waves of slightly different frequencies and their sum (color). Their sum shows a gradual variation in amplitude. The frequency of this variation is the difference in frequency of the individual waves.

Beats

When waves of two slightly different frequencies are superposed, whether the interference is constructive or destructive at a given point varies with time (Fig. 14–30). The result is a gradual variation in amplitude of the composite waveform at a frequency equal to the difference of the two individual frequencies (see Problem 56). For sound waves, the result is a beats periodic variation in sound intensity called **beats;** the closer the two frequencies, the longer the period of the beats. We hear beats whenever two sound sources operate at slightly different frequencies. In twin-engine propeller-driven aircraft, for example, pilots synchronize engine speeds by reducing the beat frequency toward zero. Beating of two nearby frequencies of electromagnetic waves forms the basis for some very sensitive measurement techniques.

14.6
WAVE REFLECTION

What happens to a wave when the properties of its medium change or the medium ends? Suppose, for example, that we clamp one end of a string tightly to a rigid wall. The wall is incapable of moving, so that none of the wave energy can pass into it. But the wave can't simply stop, for where would its energy go? What happens is that the wave **reflects,** turning reflection around and heading back down the string. For reflection at a rigid wall, the reflected wave is inverted, or turned 180° out of phase from the incident

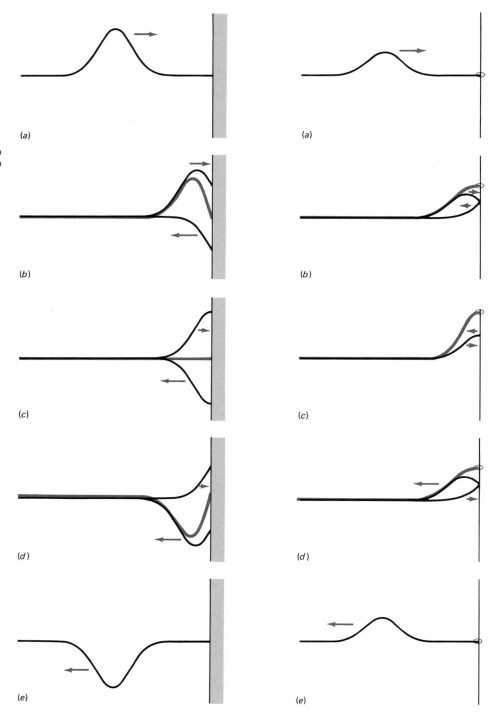

wave (Fig. 14–31). This must happen so the net displacement of the string—the superposition of incident and reflected waves—is zero at the clamped end. At the opposite extreme, our string might terminate in a way that allows its end to move freely up and down. Again, there is no place for the wave energy to go, so reflection must occur. Because the end is free to move, the displacement in this case must be a maximum at the end. Therefore, the incident and reflected waves interfere constructively, so that the two are in phase (Fig. 14–32).

Between the extremes of a rigid wall and a perfectly free end lies the case of a string connected to another string of different mass per unit length. In this case, we find that some wave energy is transmitted into the second string, and some is reflected back along the first (Fig. 14–33). In Problem 57, you can show that the amplitudes of the transmitted and reflected waves are given by

$$A_R = \frac{\sqrt{\mu_1} - \sqrt{\mu_2}}{\sqrt{\mu_1} + \sqrt{\mu_2}} A_I \qquad (14\text{–}19)$$

and

$$A_T = \frac{2\sqrt{\mu_1}}{\sqrt{\mu_1} + \sqrt{\mu_2}} A_I, \qquad (14\text{–}20)$$

where A_I, A_R, and A_T are the incident, reflected, and transmitted wave amplitudes, and μ_1 and μ_2 the mass per unit length of the two strings. Letting μ_2 become indefinitely large gives $A_R = -A_I$ and $A_T = 0$; this corresponds to total reflection at a rigid wall, with the minus sign signifying the phase change. Letting $\mu_2 = 0$ gives $A_R = A_I$, corresponding to reflection with the end of the string perfectly free. Finally, putting $\mu_1 = \mu_2$ gives $A_R = 0$ and $A_T = A_I$, showing that the wave simply continues on if the strings have the same mass per unit length. More generally, when $\mu_2 > \mu_1$, we get reflection with a phase change; otherwise there is no phase change.

Fig. 14–33
Partial reflection at a junction between two different strings.

The phenomenon of partial reflection and transmission at a junction of strings has its analog in the behavior of all sorts of waves at interfaces between two different media. For example, shallow water waves are partially reflected if the water depth changes suddenly. Light incident on even the clearest glass undergoes partial reflection because of the difference in the light-transmitting properties of air and glass. Partial reflection of ultrasound waves at the interfaces of body tissues with different densities makes ultrasound a valuable medical diagnostic (Fig. 14–34).

Fig. 14–34
A tumor is clearly visible in this image formed by reflected ultrasound waves. The waves reflect at the interface of the higher-density tumor tissue.

When waves strike the interface at an oblique angle, the phenomenon of **refraction**—changing of the direction of wave propagation—also occurs. We discuss refraction in Chapter 34.

refraction

14.7
STANDING WAVES

When a string is clamped rigidly at both ends, waves can propagate back and forth, reflecting off the ends. But now, only waves whose amplitude is always zero at the ends can meet the physical conditions imposed by clamping the string. How is this possible? The answer lies in the superposition of waves travelling in opposite directions.

Consider a string of length L lying along the x-axis with one end at $x = 0$ and the other at $x = L$. If a simple harmonic wave is propagating in the $+x$-direction, we may write

$$y_1 = y_0 \cos(kx - \omega t)$$

for the string displacement y_1. When this wave reflects from the rigidly clamped end at $x = L$, it gives rise to a wave propagating in the $-x$-direction:

$$y_2 = -y_0 \cos(kx + \omega t),$$

where the minus sign before the amplitude accounts for the phase change that occurs on reflection at a rigid wall. At the other end, this wave too is reflected. As a result, both waves exist simultaneously on the string, whose net displacement is therefore the superposition of the two waves:

$$y = y_1 + y_2 = y_0[\cos(kx - \omega t) - \cos(kx + \omega t)].$$

Using trigonometric identities for the cosine of a sum and difference of angles (see Appendix A), this becomes

$$y = y_0\{\cos(kx)\cos(\omega t) + \sin(kx)\sin(\omega t)$$

$$- [\cos(kx)\cos(\omega t) - \sin(kx)\sin(\omega t)]\} \qquad (14\text{--}21)$$

$$= 2y_0\sin(kx)\sin(\omega t).$$

What sort of wave does this equation describe? At each position x, the string oscillates up and down with frequency ω and amplitude $2y_0\sin(kx)$. The maximum amplitude always occurs at the same position x, so that the oscillating disturbance does not move along the string. This oscillation is a **standing wave**—a nonpropagating structure that nevertheless can be thought of as a superposition of two waves propagating in opposite directions.

standing wave

nodes

Because the ends of the string are clamped rigidly, they must correspond to points of zero displacement; such points are called **nodes.** In general, nodes lie half a wavelength apart. Therefore, a wave whose wavelength was twice the string length L could form a standing wave. So could a wave with wavelength equal to the string length; in addition to nodes at the clamped ends, this standing wave would have a node at the center of the string. More generally, if the string length L is any multiple of half a wavelength, then a standing wave can fit on the string (Fig. 14–35):

$$L = \frac{n\lambda}{2}, \qquad n = 1, 2, 3, 4, \ldots,$$

or

$$\lambda = \frac{2L}{n}. \qquad (14\text{--}22)$$

Although this result is obvious from Fig. 14–35, we can also derive it using Equation 14–21 for the standing wave. The amplitude $2y_0\sin(kx)$ must be zero at the string ends. This requirement is obviously met at $x = 0$, and at the end $x = L$ it means that

$$2y_0\sin(kL) = 0.$$

This can be true for nonzero amplitude y_0 only when the sine is zero, which occurs at integer multiples of π radians:

$$kL = n\pi, \qquad n = 1, 2, 3, 4, \ldots$$

But $k = 2\pi/\lambda$, so that this condition is

$$\frac{2\pi}{\lambda}L = n\pi,$$

or

$$\lambda = \frac{2L}{n},$$

which is Equation 14–22.

mode number

fundamental

The integer n in Equation 14–22 is called the **mode number.** The $n = 1$ mode is the **fundamental,** and represents the longest wavelength that can exist on the string. The higher modes are called the second harmonic, third harmonic, and so forth.

When a string is fixed rigidly at one end and free to move at the other, a similar analysis applies except that now the string length must be an odd multiple of a quarter wavelength so that the amplitude at the free end is a maximum (Fig. 14–36). In this case, the allowed wavelengths correspond

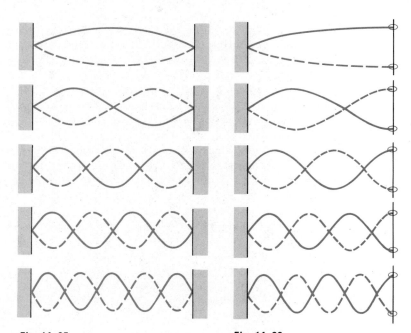

Fig. 14–35
Standing waves on a string. Clamped rigidly at the ends, the string can accommodate only an integer number of half wavelengths. Shown are the fundamental and next four harmonics. The nodes occur at the ends in all cases and in between for the harmonics. Solid line is the string at one instant, dashed line one-half cycle later.

Fig. 14–36
When one end of the string is fixed and the other free, the string can accommodate only an odd number of quarter wavelengths. (Here the string is clamped at the left end, but at the right end is attached to a ring that slides without friction along a vertical pole.)

Fig. 14–37
Waveforms of a clarinet (above) and oboe (below) playing the same note. Although the fundamental frequencies are the same, the waveforms and resulting sounds are quite different, reflecting the different mixtures of standing wave modes in the two instruments.

only to odd harmonics of the fundamental frequency, which is itself half the fundamental frequency of the previous case (see Problem 37).

Our analysis of standing waves on a string applies directly to stringed musical instruments like the violin and piano. Standing waves can also exist in other systems. An organ pipe or woodwind instrument, for example, supports standing sound waves whose allowed modes are determined by the structure of the instrument. In general, a mixture of different modes can exist at once, and it is the particular blend of harmonics that gives an instrument its distinctive sound (Fig. 14–37).

Other examples of standing waves include water waves in a confined space (Fig. 14–38), electromagnetic waves in a closed cavity, and standing waves in mechanical structures. In microwave ovens, a rotating piece of metal is sometimes used to reflect the waves in different directions. Otherwise, standing-wave patterns would be set up and parts of the food at the nodes would receive very little energy.

Fig. 14–38
Oscillations in the thermocline of Lake Ontario. Thermocline is the layer of rapidly changing water temperature separating warmer surface water from cool, deep water. Oscillations represent a standing wave of considerable amplitude, in which the entire lake participates.

Fig. 14–39
Standing-wave patterns on a drum.

Fig. 14–40
Standing wave pattern on a guitar, imaged using holographic interference of laser light.

Standing waves can be started and their amplitude increased by supplying energy at exactly the right frequency—the frequency of an allowed mode. This is just like resonance in a simple harmonic oscillator, except that a standing-wave system can be driven to resonance at any of its many allowed frequencies. The oscillations of the Tacoma Narrows Bridge shown in Fig. 13–37 are actually torsional standing waves, driven in resonance by the wind.

In two- and three-dimensional systems, standing-wave patterns may be quite complex, with different sets of allowed wavelengths in different directions. Figures 14–39 and 14–40 show some standing-wave patterns on a drum head and guitar. Determination of the many resonant frequencies in complicated systems ranging from molecules to stars is an important task for physicists, engineers, and physical chemists (Fig. 14–41).

14.8
THE DOPPLER EFFECT

The intrinsic speed v of a wave is its speed measured relative to the medium through which the wave propagates. A point source that is stationary with respect to the medium produces waves that move outward uniformly in all directions (Fig. 14–42). But when the source moves with respect to the medium, then successive wavefronts originate from different locations (Fig. 14–43). As a result, wave crests moving in the direction of the source occur closer together than if the source were not moving—that is, the wavelength is shorter in this direction. In the opposite direction, source motion makes the wave crests farther apart, resulting in a greater wavelength. Both these effects are evident in Fig. 14–43. The change in wavelength due to relative motion between source and observer is called the **Doppler effect.**

To analyze the Doppler effect, let λ be the wavelength emitted by a stationary source, and λ' that emitted by the same source if it moves with speed u through a medium where the wave speed is v. At some instant, a wave crest is produced at the source. The next crest is emitted one wave period T later. How far does the source move in this time? Simply uT, since u is the source speed. How about the first wave crest? It moves one wavelength, so that the distance between successive crests in the direction of source motion is

$$\lambda' = \lambda - uT.$$

Writing $T = \lambda/v$, this expression becomes

$$\lambda' = \lambda - u\frac{\lambda}{v} = \lambda\left(1 - \frac{u}{v}\right). \quad \text{(source approaching)} \quad (14\text{–}23)$$

In the direction opposite the source motion, the situation is the same except that now the wavelength *increases* by the amount $\lambda u/v$, giving

$$\lambda' = \lambda\left(1 + \frac{u}{v}\right). \quad \text{(source receding)} \quad (14\text{–}24)$$

Doppler effect

Fig. 14–41
Oscillations of the sun form complicated standing-wave patterns that provide a direct probe of conditions deep in the sun's interior. Shown here are computer simulations of four possible oscillation modes.

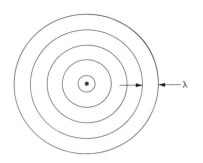

Fig. 14–42
Circular waves produced by a source at rest with respect to the medium.

Because the wave speed in the medium does not change, the relation $v = f\lambda$ still holds. When the wavelength decreases in front of a moving source, therefore, the frequency of the waves at a fixed point in the medium must increase. This is evident from Fig. 14–43, where an observer at point A will see more wave crests per unit time than if the source were not moving. Similarly, an observer at B will see fewer wave crests per unit time, and therefore a decreased frequency associated with the longer wavelength. Using Equations 14–23 and 14–24, and noting that $\lambda = v/f$, we are able to write

$$\frac{v}{f'} = \frac{v}{f}\left(1 \pm \frac{u}{v}\right)$$

or

$$f' = \frac{f}{1 \pm u/v}, \qquad (14–25)$$

where f' is the Doppler-shifted frequency, and where the $+$ and $-$ signs correspond to receding and approaching sources, respectively. A Doppler shift also occurs when an observer moves relative to a source of waves. Problem 49 explores this situation.

You have probably experienced the Doppler effect for sound when standing near a highway. A loud truck approaching you makes a relatively high-pitched sound "aaaaaaaaaaa." As the truck passes you, the pitch drops abruptly, "aaaaaaaaeioooooooooooo," and stays low as the truck recedes. Practical uses of the Doppler effect are numerous. Measuring the Doppler shift in ultrasound reflected from moving body tissues allows measurement of blood flow, fetal heartbeat, and other physiological quantities. Although light and other electromagnetic waves do not require a material medium, they are nevertheless subject to the Doppler effect. Police radar works by measuring the Doppler shift of high-frequency radio waves reflected from

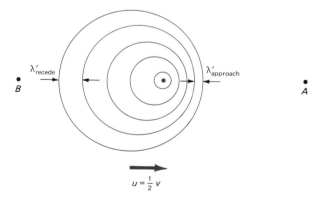

Fig. 14–43
Circular waves produced by a source moving with respect to the medium. The wavelength—the distance between wave crests—is shortened in the direction toward which the source is moving, and lengthened in the opposite direction. In the case shown, the source speed u is half the wave speed v.

Fig. 14–44
The wavelengths of light emitted by hydrogen atoms in a double star system show clearly the presence of one star moving toward the observer, the other away. The pattern changes with time as the stars revolve around one another, so that the motion of the two can be studied in detail even though the individual stars cannot even be resolved in a photographic image.

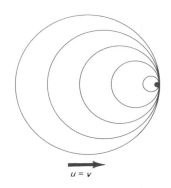

Fig. 14–45
When the source moves at the wave speed, waves pile on top of one another to create a shock wave.

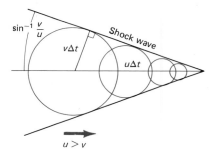

Fig. 14–46
Shock wave formed when source speed u exceeds wave speed v. In a time Δt from the generation of the largest circular wavefront shown, that wavefront moves a distance $v\Delta t$. But at the same time, the source moves a distance $u\Delta t$. As a result, the shock wave forms a cone of half-angle $\theta = \sin^{-1}(v/u)$.

moving cars. The Doppler shift of starlight allows us to study stellar motion (Fig. 14–44). Finally, the Doppler shift of light from distant galaxies is evidence that our entire universe is expanding.

Example 14–4
The Doppler Effect

A car is roaring down the highway with its stereo blasting loudly. An observer with perfect pitch is standing by the roadside and, as the car approaches, notices that a musical note that should be G ($f = 392$ Hz) sounds like A ($f = 440$ Hz). How fast is the car moving? The speed of sound is about 340 m/s.

Solution

Solving Equation 14–25 for the source speed u, we have

$$u = v\left(1 - \frac{f}{f'}\right) = (340 \text{ m/s})\left(1 - \frac{392 \text{ Hz}}{440 \text{ Hz}}\right) = 37.1 \text{ m/s}.$$

14.9
SHOCK WAVES

Equation 14–23 suggests that wavelength goes to zero when a source approaches at the wave speed. What can this mean? When the source moves at exactly the wave speed, wave crests emitted in the forward direction cannot get away from the source, but instead pile up into a very large amplitude wave at the front of the source (Fig. 14–45). This large-amplitude wave is a **shock wave.** When the source moves faster than the wave speed, the waves pile up on a cone whose half-angle is given by $\sin\theta = v/u$, as shown in Fig. 14–46. Shock waves of this sort are formed by supersonic aircraft, and are called sonic booms (Fig. 14–47).

Fig. 14–47
Sonic booms produced by the nose and tail of a supersonic aircraft. If the shock waves are strong enough, they can break glass or do other damage to buildings in their path.

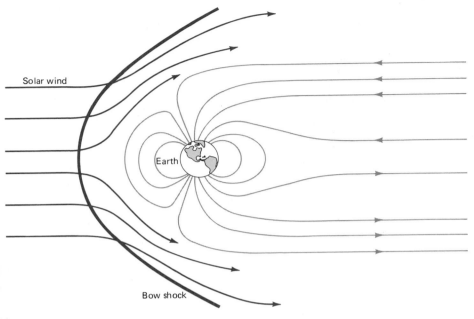

Fig. 14–49
(a) Earth's bow shock, formed as the solar wind encounters earth's magnetic field. Shock actually stands about 20 earth radii on the sunward side of the planet.

Fig. 14–48
The bow wave is a shock wave formed by a boat moving faster than the water wave speed. Note reflections of waves off channel walls.

Shock waves occur in a wide variety of physical situations. The bow wave of a boat is a shock wave on the water surface (Fig. 14–48). On a much larger scale, a huge bow shock forms around the earth as the solar wind—a high-speed outflow of matter from the sun—encounters earth's magnetic field (Fig. 14–49). Other planets exhibit similar bow shocks, and in 1986 a bow shock was discovered sunward of Halley's Comet.

SUMMARY

1. A **wave** is a disturbance that moves through a medium, carrying energy but not matter. Waves have a number of distinguishing properties:
   a. The peak value of the disturbance is the wave **amplitude.**
   b. If the disturbance of the medium is in the direction of wave motion, the wave is **longitudinal.** If the disturbance is at right angles to the wave motion, then the wave is **transverse.** Some waves have both longitudinal and transverse aspects.
   c. A **pulse** is a single, isolated propagating disturbance. A **continuous wave** is a periodic disturbance that repeats indefinitely. A special case of a continuous wave is a **simple harmonic wave,** whose shape is sinusoidal.
   d. A continuous wave is characterized by its **wavelength** λ—the distance between wave crests—and **period**—the time for a full wavelength to pass a given point. Since the wave travels one wavelength in one wave period, the wave speed is

   $$v = \frac{\lambda}{T}.$$

   e. A wave propagating along the x-axis can be described by a function of the quantity $x \pm vt$, where the minus sign signifies propagation in the $+x$-di-

PLATE 1
A computer-aided set of drawings of the skeleton of the Statue of Liberty aided in the statue's reconstruction. [Swanke Hayden Connell Architects]

PLATE 2
The tuned-mass damper in action at the John Hancock Building in Boston. The system oscillates at the same frequency as the building, but out of phase, thus reducing building sway during high winds. (See Example 13–2.) [MTS Systems Corp.]

PLATE 3
Fluid flow at a step, shown by optical
interferometry. [M. Horsmann, Ruhr
University]

PLATE 4
Swirling patterns in Jupiter's atmosphere
reveal complex fluid motion around the
Great Red Spot. [NASA/Jet Propulsion
Laboratory]

rection, and vice versa. In the case of a simple harmonic wave, the function is sinusoidal, and may be written in the form

$$y = y_0\cos(kx \pm \omega t),$$

where y is the displacement of whatever quantity the wave disturbs and y_0 the amplitude. The quantities k and ω are the **wave number** and **angular frequency,** and are related to the wavelength λ and frequency f:

$$k = \frac{2\pi}{\lambda}$$

and

$$\omega = 2\pi f.$$

The wave speed is then given by

$$v = \frac{\omega}{k}.$$

2. Applying Newton's law for small-amplitude displacements of a stretched string results in the **wave equation:**

$$\frac{\partial^2 y}{\partial x^2} - \frac{1}{v^2}\frac{\partial^2 y}{\partial t^2} = 0,$$

where y is the displacement and v the wave speed. For waves on a stretched string, the speed is given by

$$v = \sqrt{F_0/\mu},$$

where F_0 is the string tension and μ the mass per unit length. The wave equation describes not only waves on a string, but also all small-amplitude waves whose speed is independent of wavelength.

3. Waves carry energy. The average rate of energy flow, or average power, is proportional to the wave speed and to the square of the wave amplitude. For waves propagating in three dimensions, a more useful measure is the wave **intensity,** or power per unit area. The intensity of a plane wave remains constant as the wave propagates. But when a wave spreads its energy over an ever-larger area, as in a spherical or circular wave, then the intensity drops with distance from the source. For a spherical wave, this spreading of the energy results in an intensity that is proportional to the inverse square of the distance.

4. Many waves obey the **superposition principle,** meaning that when two waves interact, their amplitudes simply add. The superposition principle allows complex wave shapes to be analyzed as sums of simple harmonic waves. When wave speed is independent of wavelength, the composite waves all travel at the same speed and the complex waveform retains its shape. But when wave speed varies with wavelength, a complex waveform changes shape as it propagates—a phenomenon called **dispersion.**

5. **Interference** occurs when two waves interact. For waves that obey the superposition principle, the overall wave shape is the sum of the displacements of the interfering waves. When the overall amplitude is enhanced, the interference is **constructive;** if the amplitude is decreased, it is **destructive.** The pattern produced by interfering waves may contain regions where destructive interference results in zero displacement of the medium from its equilibrium state; these regions are called **nodes** or **nodal lines.**

6. **Reflection** occurs when a wave encounters a change in the medium. If the new medium permits no displacement whatever—as when a string is clamped rigidly at one end—then the wave is totally reflected with a phase change of 180° or π radians. When the original medium simply ends—as when a string is completely free at one end—then the wave is totally reflected with no phase change. When the new medium differs from the old, but still permits wave propagation, then the wave is partially reflected and partially transmitted at the interface between media.

7. **Standing waves** occur when a medium is bounded at both ends, so that incident and reflected waves interfere to make a nonpropagating disturbance in which each point undergoes an oscillatory displacement from equilibrium. When the system is constrained so that there can be no displacement at either end, then its length must be an integer number of half wavelengths, or

$$L = \frac{n\lambda}{2}.$$

When there can be no displacement at one end of the medium, while the other end is completely free, then an odd integer number of quarter wavelengths must fit in between the ends of the medium. The longest wavelength—lowest frequency—standing wave is the **fundamental mode;** the higher frequencies are **harmonics.** Large-amplitude standing waves may be built up by applying a driving force at a frequency near that of a standing-wave mode—a phenomenon known as **resonance.**

8. The **Doppler effect** is the change in wavelength and/or frequency due to motion of the wave source or observer. For mechanical waves, the Doppler shifted wavelength from a moving source is

$$\lambda' = \lambda\left(1 \pm \frac{u}{v}\right),$$

where λ is the wavelength emitted by a source at rest, v the wave speed, and u the speed of a moving source. The $+$ sign applies to a source receding from the observer, the minus sign to an approaching source.

9. **Shock waves** are formed by sources moving through a medium at speeds greater than the wave speed. In a shock wave, the properties of the medium change abruptly because of the piling up of many wave crests all moving more slowly than the source. The shock wave from a moving source forms a cone of half-angle $\theta = \sin^{-1}(v/u)$, with v the wave speed and u the source speed.

QUESTIONS

1. What distinguishes a wave from an oscillation?
2. Red light has a longer wavelength than blue light. Compare their frequencies.
3. Consider a light wave and a sound wave that have the same wavelength. Which has the higher frequency?
4. A car stops suddenly on a highway. The subsequent stopping of cars behind it can be thought of as a "wave" of "stoppedness" propagating backward through the traffic. In what sense is this a wave? List several factors that determine its speed.
5. Must a wave be either transverse or longitudinal? Explain.
6. As a wave propagates along a stretched string, part of the string moves. Is the speed of this motion related to the wave speed? Explain.
7. The speed of sound in water is about 1500 m/s, compared with 340 m/s in air at room temperature. Yet water is about 1000 times more dense than air. Why might the sound speeds be so much closer than the densities?
8. If the intensity of waves from a point source decreases as the inverse square of the distance, how does the wave amplitude depend on distance?
9. How does the amplitude of circular waves on the surface of water depend on distance from the source? Assume the wave propagates without energy loss.
10. The intensity of light from a point source decreases as the inverse square of the distance from the source. Does this mean that light loses energy travelling great distances? Explain.
11. The wave number k is sometimes called the spatial frequency. Why is this name appropriate?
12. Small-amplitude waves on a stretched string propagate with speed that is independent of wavelength. Do you expect the speed of larger-amplitude waves to depend on wavelength? If so, should the speed increase or decrease with increasing wavelength? Give a physical reason for your answer.
13. An upward and a downward pulse, otherwise of identical shape, are travelling in opposite directions along a stretched string. As they pass through each other, there is an instant when destructive interference is complete and the displacement of the string is everywhere zero. How does this situation differ from true equilibrium? *Hint:* Where is the wave energy?
14. How do the tuning pegs on a guitar or violin work? Do they affect the wavelength of standing waves on the guitar string? The frequency? The wave speed?
15. A lightning flash produces a burst of electromagnetic waves that is heard in a nearby radio as a sudden crash of static. Waves from lightning flashes in the antarctic propagate through the ionosphere (an electrically conducting layer in earth's upper atmosphere) and arrive in the arctic, where a radio receiving them makes a long, whistling sound whose pitch decreases with time. What does this say about the speed of an electromagnetic wave in the ionosphere as a function of frequency? (Only in vacuum is the speed of electromagnetic waves necessarily independent of frequency.)
16. Do the nodal lines of Fig. 14-27 move as the waves propagate? Or does the pattern remain stationary?
17. How does the conservation of energy require that waves reflect when their medium ends abruptly?
18. If you drop a perfectly transparent piece of glass into perfectly clear water, you can still see the glass. Why?
19. Standing waves do not propagate. In what sense, then, are they waves?
20. Can standing waves satisfy the wave equation even though they don't propagate?
21. In the 1920s the astronomer Edwin Hubble observed distant galaxies and found that their light was always red-shifted relative to nearby galaxies. Assuming the red shift is due to the Doppler effect, what does this observation imply about the motion of distant galaxies relative to earth?
22. Why does a boat easily produce a shock wave on the water surface, while it takes very high speed aircraft to produce sonic booms?
23. In Fig. 14-33, which string has the greater mass per unit length? Explain.

PROBLEMS

Section 14.1   *Properties of Waves*

1. The speed of sound waves in air at room temperature is about 340 m/s. Find the wavelength, period, angular frequency, and wave number of a 1.0-kHz sound wave. (The human ear is most sensitive to sound at about this frequency.)
2. Calculate the wavelengths of (a) an AM radio wave (1.0 MHz); (b) a channel 9 TV signal (190 MHz); (c) a police radar (10 GHz; 1 GHz = 10^9 Hz); (d) infrared radiation emitted by a hot stove (4×10^{13} Hz); (e) green light (6.0×10^{14} Hz); and (f) x-rays (1.0×10^{18} Hz). All are electromagnetic waves that propagate at 3.0×10^8 m/s.
3. (a) Determine an approximate value for the normal speed of sound (340 m/s) in miles per second. (b) Suppose you see a lightning flash and, 10 s later, hear the thunder. How many miles from you did the flash occur? Neglect the travel time for the light (why?).
4. Detecting objects by reflecting waves off them is effective only for objects about one wavelength in size or larger. (a) What is the smallest object that can be seen

with visible light (maximum frequency about 8×10^{14} Hz)? (b) What is the smallest object that can be detected by a medical ultrasound device using waves at 5.0 MHz? The speed of sound in body tissue is about 1500 m/s.

5. Short races in a track meet are run over straight courses, and timers at the finish line start their watches when they see smoke from the starting gun, not when they hear the shot. Why? How much error would be introduced by timing a 100-m race at the sound of the shot? The speed of sound in air at normal temperatures is about 340 m/s.

6. Two boats are anchored off shore, and observers on each find themselves bobbing up and down at the rate of 6 complete up-down-up cycles each minute. When one boat is up, the other is down, and vice versa. If the waves causing the bobbing travel at 2.2 m/s, what is the minimum possible distance between the boats?

Section 14.2 *Mathematical Description of Wave Motion*

7. A simple harmonic wave of wavelength 16 cm and amplitude 2.5 cm is propagating along a string in the negative x-direction at 35 cm/s. Write a mathematical expression describing this wave.

8. Figure 14–50 shows a simple harmonic wave at time $t = 0$ and later at $t = 2.6$ s. Write a mathematical expression describing this wave.

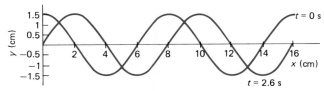

Fig. 14–50 Problem 8

9. What are the amplitude, the frequency in Hz, the wavelength, and the speed of a water wave whose displacement from the equilibrium water level is given by $y = 0.25 \cos(0.52x - 2.3t)$, where y and x are in meters and t in seconds?

Section 14.3 *Waves on a String: The Wave Equation*

10. The main cables supporting the George Washington Bridge in New York City have a mass per unit length of 4100 kg/m, and are under tension of 2.5×10^8 N. At what speed would a transverse wave propagate along these cables?

11. A transverse simple harmonic wave 1.2 cm in amplitude and 85 cm in wavelength propagates along a string. The string is under 21 N tension, and has a mass of 15 g/m. Determine (a) the wave speed and (b) the maximum speed of a point on the string.

12. For a transverse simple harmonic wave on a stretched string, the requirement that the string be nearly horizontal used in deriving Equations 14–10 and 14–14 is met if the wave amplitude is much less than the

wavelength. Why? Show that, under this approximation, the maximum speed u of the string itself must be considerably less than the wave speed v. In particular, if the amplitude is not to exceed 1% of the wavelength, how large can the string speed u be in relation to the wave speed v?

13. A rope is stretched between supports 12 m apart; its tension is 35 N. If one end of the rope is tweaked, the resulting disturbance reaches the other end 0.45 s later. What is the total mass of the rope?

14. A 3.1-kg mass hangs from a 2.7-m-long string whose total mass is 62 g. What is the speed of transverse waves on the string? Hint: You can ignore the string mass in calculating the tension but not in calculating the mass per unit length. Why?

15. A uniform cable hangs vertically under its own weight. Show that the speed of waves on the cable is given by $v = \sqrt{yg}$, where y is the distance from the bottom of the cable. Why is this speed independent of the cable mass and length?

16. Show explicitly that any function of the form $f(x \pm vt)$ satisfies the wave equation (Equation 14–14). Hint: Use the chain rule to express the derivatives with respect to time and space in terms of derivatives with respect to $x \pm vt$.

17. In analyzing the behavior of shallow water, the following equation arises:

$$\frac{\partial^2 y}{\partial x^2} - \frac{1}{gh}\frac{\partial^2 y}{\partial t^2} = 0,$$

where h is the equilibrium depth and y the displacement from equilibrium. What is the speed of waves in shallow water? (Here shallow means water depth much less than wavelength.)

Section 14.4 *Wave Energy and Intensity*

18. A sound wave in air is a pressure disturbance. How does the amplitude of this pressure disturbance drop with distance from a point source of sound?

19. A loudspeaker emits energy at the rate of 50 W, spread uniformly in all directions. What is the intensity of sound 18 m from the speaker?

20. A large boulder drops from a cliff into the ocean, producing a circular wave. A small boat 18 m from the impact point measures the wave amplitude at 130 cm. At what distance will the wave amplitude be 50 cm?

21. Figure 14–51 shows a wave train consisting of two cycles of a sine wave propagating down a string. Obtain an expression for the total energy in this wave train, in terms of the string tension F_0, wave amplitude y_0, and wavelength λ.

Fig. 14–51 Problem 21; the wave amplitude shown is exaggerated.

22. Use the intensity of sunlight from Table 14–1 and radius of earth's orbit from Appendix F to calculate the total power output of the sun.

23. A steel wire has a mass of 5.0 g/m and is under 450 N tension. What is the maximum power that can be carried by transverse waves on this wire if the wave amplitude is not to exceed 10% of the wavelength? How would your answer change if the mass per unit length were doubled?

24. A 1-megaton nuclear explosion produces a shock wave whose amplitude, measured as excess pressure above normal atmospheric pressure, is 1.4×10^5 Pa (1 Pa = 1 N/m²) at a distance of 1.3 km from the explosion. An excess pressure of 3.5×10^4 Pa will totally destroy a typical wood-frame house. At what distance from the explosion will such houses be destroyed? Compare with the size of a typical city. Assume that the wavefront is spherical, and ignore energy losses and reflection from the ground.

25. Use Table 14–1 to determine how close to a rock band you should stand for it to sound as loud as a jet plane at 100 m. Treat the band and the plane as point sources. Is this a reasonable approximation?

Section 14.5   The Superposition Principle and Wave Interference

26. Consider two functions $f(x \pm vt)$ and $g(x \pm vt)$ that both satisfy the wave equation (Equation 14–14). Show by direct substitution into the wave equation that any function of the form $Af(x \pm vt) + Bg(x \pm vt)$ also satisfies the wave equation, where A and B are constants.

27. Two pulses, each consisting of a single sinusoidal cycle, are launched from opposite ends of a taut string at time $t=0$. The total length of the string is four wavelengths, and the pulses propagate at speed v. Sketch the appearance of the string at the following times: λ/v, $5\lambda/4v$, $3\lambda/2v$, and $7\lambda/4v$.

28. The triangular wave of Fig. 14–52 can be described by the following sum of simple harmonic waves:

$$y = \frac{8y_0}{\pi^2}\left[\frac{\sin kx}{1^2} - \frac{\sin 3kx}{3^2} + \frac{\sin 5kx}{5^2} - \cdots\right].$$

where n takes on all integer values. Plot the sum of the first three terms in this series at time $t=0$ for $kx=0$ to $kx=2\pi$, and compare with Fig. 14–52. If you have access to a computer, you may wish to use more terms in your calculation.

29. Figure 14–53 shows a plot of angular frequency ω versus wave number k for waves in some medium. Locate (a) a wavelength range in which a composite wave will retain its shape, (b) a wavelength range in which higher-frequency waves propagate faster than lower-frequency waves, and (c) a wavelength range in which lower-frequency waves propagate faster than higher-frequency waves. The relation between ω and k plotted in Fig. 14–53 is called the dispersion relation for the medium.

Fig. 14–53   Problem 29

30. Graph the dispersion relation (ω versus k, as explained in the previous problem) for surface waves in deep water (see Equation 14–18).

31. Two simple harmonic waves of equal frequency ω and amplitude y_0 differ in phase by ϕ, so that they may be described by

$$y_1 = y_0 \cos(kx - \omega t)$$

and

$$y_2 = y_0 \cos(kx - \omega t + \phi).$$

Show that their superposition is also a simple harmonic wave, and determine its amplitude y_s as a function of the phase difference ϕ.

32. Figure 14–54 shows two wave sources A and B, and a point P a long way from them. Suppose that P is on the innermost nodal line of the interference pattern produced by waves from the two sources. Show that the distance y on the diagram is given by $y=L\lambda/2d$, where λ is the wavelength, d the source spacing, and L the perpendicular distance from a line through the two sources to the point P. Assume that L is much greater than either the wavelength λ or the source spacing d. With this approximation, both lines AP and BP make very nearly the same small angle θ with

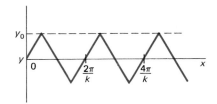

Fig. 14–52   A triangular wave (Problem 28).

Fig. 14–54   Problem 32

the perpendicular bisector of the two sources. *Hint:* Study Figs. 14–28 and 14–54, and recognize that crests and troughs meet along a nodal line, so that one wave must travel half a wavelength farther than the other to reach the point *P. Another hint:* Draw a perpendicular from point *A* to the line *BP,* and think about the previous hint!

Section 14.6   *Wave Reflection*

33. A 3.3-m-long string of total mass 56 g is spliced to a 2.6-m cord of total mass 280 g. The two are under a uniform tension of 110 N. A 2.0-cm-high pulse is launched from the end of the lighter string at time $t = 0$. (*a*) At what time will the pulse reach the far end of the heavier cord? (*b*) What will its amplitude be in the heavier cord? (*c*) At what time will the pulse reflected off the junction return to its starting point? (*d*) What will be the amplitude of this reflected pulse?

34. A wave pulse carrying 0.12 J of energy is propagating down a string with $\mu = 14$ g/m, when it encounters a splice to a heavier string with $\mu = 22$ g/m. How much energy is carried down the heavier string?

35. A rope is made up of a number of identical strands twisted together. At one point, the rope becomes frayed so that only a single strand continues (Fig. 14–55). The rope is held under tension, and a 1.0-cm-high pulse is sent from the single strand. The first pulse reflected back along the single strand has an amplitude of 0.45 cm. How many strands are in the rope?

Fig. 14–55   Problem 35

Section 14.7   *Standing Waves*

36. The A-string (440 Hz) on a piano is 38.9 cm long, and is clamped tightly at both ends. If the string is under 667 N tension, what is its mass?

37. Show that only odd harmonics are allowed on a taut string with one end clamped and the other free.

38. A string is clamped at both ends and tensioned until its fundamental vibration frequency is 85 Hz. If the string is then held rigidly at its midpoint, what is the lowest frequency at which it will vibrate?

39. Show that the standing-wave condition shown in Equation 14–22 is equivalent to the requirement that the time it takes a wave to make one round trip between the ends of the medium be an integer multiple of the wave period.

40. The wave speed on a taut wire is 320 m/s. If the wire is 80 cm long, and is vibrating at 800 Hz, how far apart are the nodes?

41. "Vibrato" in a violin is produced by sliding the finger back and forth along the vibrating string. The G-string on a particular violin measures 30 cm between the bridge and its far end and is clamped tightly at both points. Its fundamental frequency is 297 Hz. (*a*) How far from the end should the violinist place a finger so that the G-string plays the note A (440 Hz)? (*b*) If the violinist executes vibrato by moving the finger 0.50 cm to either side of the position in part *a*, what range of frequencies is played?

42. Estimate the fundamental frequency of the human vocal tract, assuming it to be a cylinder 15 cm long that is closed at one end and open at the other. (These conditions make the tract analogous to a string fixed at one end and free at the other.) Assume that the speed of sound is 340 m/s.

43. A bathtub 1.7 m long contains 13 cm of water. By sloshing water back and forth with your hand, you can build up a large-amplitude oscillation. Determine the lowest frequency possible for such a resonant oscillation. *Hint:* At resonance in this case, the wave has a crest at one end and a trough at the other. The speed of shallow water waves is given by $v = \sqrt{gh}$.

44. Radio and TV antennas are often designed to be about a half wavelength long near the middle of the frequency band in which they operate. This way, weak radio or TV signals can build up relatively strong electrical oscillations in the antenna. What should be the approximate length of an antenna designed to receive FM radio signals ($f = 100$ MHz)? Compare with the length of FM antennas you or fellow students may have connected to FM receivers. The FM band lies near the middle of the channel 2–13 TV band. How does your computed FM antenna length compare with the size of a typical TV antenna?

45. The sun undergoes small-amplitude oscillations in size with a fundamental period of about 160 min. (*a*) Treating the sun like a string clamped at one end (the center) and free at the other end (the surface), estimate the average sound speed in the sun. (*b*) The sound speed in a gas is given by $v_s = \sqrt{\gamma kT/m}$, where T is the temperature in kelvins, γ a constant equal to $\frac{5}{3}$ for the gas composing the sun, k Boltzmann's constant (1.38×10^{-23} J/K), and m the mean molecular mass in kg (for the solar hydrogen/helium mixture, the mean molecular mass is 1.6 u). Use your result from (*a*) to estimate the average temperature of the sun. (The sun's temperature varies from 20×10^6 K at the core to 6000 K near the surface; your answer reflects this range of temperatures.) *Hint:* Consult Appendix F for the sun's radius.

Section 14.8   *The Doppler Effect*

46. A car horn emits 380-Hz sound waves. If the car moves at 18 m/s with its horn blasting, what frequency will a person standing in front of the car hear? The speed of sound is 340 m/s.

47. The Doppler effect in ultrasound is commonly used by obstetricians to detect fetal heartbeat. As the heart muscle pulsates in and out, ultrasound waves reflected off the moving heart are Doppler shifted from the frequency of the incident waves. If the ultrasound

transmitter sends out 5.0-Mhz waves, and the maximum frequency shift of the reflected waves is 100 Hz, how fast does the wall of the heart move? The speed of sound in body tissues is 1500 m/s.

48. Red light emitted by hydrogen atoms in the laboratory has a wavelength of 6563 Å (1 Å = 10^{-10} m). Light emitted in the same process on a distant galaxy is received at earth with a wavelength of 7057 Å. Describe the motion of the galaxy relative to earth.

49. Show that an observer moving toward a source of waves that is stationary with respect to the medium will not detect any shift in wavelength, but will measure a higher frequency given by $f' = f(1 + u/v)$, where f is the unshifted frequency, u the speed of the observer, and v the wave speed. Compare with Equation 14–25 and show that the two give nearly equal results when $u \ll v$.

Section 14.9 *Shock Waves*

50. Figure 14–56 shows a wind-tunnel test of a projectile; shock waves from the nose of the projectile are clearly evident. By making appropriate measurements, determine the speed of the projectile as compared with the sound speed.

Fig. 14–56 Problem 50

51. A supersonic airplane flies directly over you at 2.2 times the speed of sound. You hear its sonic boom 19 s later. What is the plane's altitude? Take the sound speed to be 340 m/s.

Supplementary Problems

52. A steel wire 0.85 mm in diameter propagates transverse waves at 270 m/s. What is the tension in the wire? The density of steel is 7.9 g/cm^3.

53. A rectangular trough is 2.5 m long and is much deeper than its length, so that Equation 14–18 applies to waves propagating in it. Determine the wavelength and frequency of the longest and next-longest standing waves possible in this trough. Why isn't the higher frequency double the lower?

54. A supersonic airplane flies directly over you at an altitude of 6.5 km. 23 s later, you hear its sonic boom. What is the plane's speed? Take the sound speed to be 340 m/s.

55. An astronaut sets a rubber band whirling in a weightless environment, so that it forms a circle. If the ro-

tating circle is disturbed to form a bump (Fig. 14–57), show that the bump remains fixed in space as the rubber band rotates.

Fig. 14–57 Problem 55

56. Beats: consider two waves of the same amplitude but of different frequencies ω_1 and ω_2. Consulting Appendix A for the appropriate trigonometric formulas, show that their superposition at position $x = 0$ may be written

$$y = 2y_0 \sin[\tfrac{1}{2}(\omega_1 + \omega_2)t] \cos[\tfrac{1}{2}(\omega_1 - \omega_2)t].$$

The second term in this expression represents the beats—an overall variation in amplitude at a frequency equal to the difference of the frequencies of the two superposed waves. On a graph, sketch about 10 cycles each of two waves whose frequencies differ by 10%. Add the two to form their superposition, and graph it. The low-frequency variation in amplitude should be quite evident.

57. A string of mass per unit length μ_1 is joined at $x = 0$ to a second string of mass per unit length μ_2. A wave (the incident wave) is propagating from the first string toward the second, and is characterized by a displacement y_I:

$$y_I = A_I \cos(k_1 x - \omega t).$$

At the junction between strings, the wave is partially reflected and partially transmitted. The reflected wave travels in the same medium as the incident wave, and therefore has the same wave number. It can be described by

$$y_R = A_R \cos(k_1 x + \omega t),$$

where the + sign shows that its direction is opposite to that of the incident wave. Finally, there is a transmitted wave in the second string, whose displacement is given by

$$y_T = A_T \cos(k_2 x - \omega t),$$

where k_2 is not the same as k_1 because the media and therefore wave speeds differ. If the string does not break, its total displacement approaching the junction from the left must equal that approaching it from the right, so that $y_I + y_R = y_T$. Furthermore, the derivatives dy/dx must be similarly continuous at the interface, or the acceleration at the junction would be infinite. Use these continuity conditions to derive Equations 14–19 and 14–20 for the reflected and transmitted amplitudes A_R and A_T.

15

FLUID MOTION

A tornado whirls out of a darkened sky, spreading destruction in its path. Over hundreds of millions of years, earth's continents drift about the planet, riding a viscous layer of liquid rock. The interplay of gravitational and magnetic forces shapes complex structures in the sun's outer atmosphere; occasionally the force balance fails, ejecting 10^{12} kg of solar material into space. A jetliner cruises through earth's atmosphere at 1000 km/h, propelled by hot gases spewing from its engines and supported by higher air pressure on the underside of its wings. A stream of gas leaves the surface of a giant star and forms a cosmic whirlpool before it plunges into the star's invisible companion, a black hole. You step on a car's brake pedal; the force of your foot is amplified by the pressure of liquid in the brake lines and cylinders. Your own body is sustained by air moving in and out of your lungs, and by flow of blood throughout your tissues. All these examples (Fig. 15–1) involve fluid motion.

Fig. 15–1
(Left to right) A tornado, a huge prominence in the sun's atmosphere, and the hydraulic brake system of a car all involve fluid motion.

373

fluid

Fluid is matter that cannot maintain its own shape and therefore flows readily under the influence of forces. Liquids and gases are fluids. Unlike solids, where strong intermolecular forces lock atoms into a rigid structure, fluids experience only weak intermolecular forces. In a liquid, these forces are strong enough to maintain molecules in close contact, but are too weak to keep them from moving readily past one another. In a gas, intermolecular forces are almost negligible, and the gas is held together essentially by external forces. These are provided by the walls of a container or, with astronomical-sized systems like stars or planetary atmospheres, by gravity. Plasmas—gases of electrically charged particles—are sometimes contained by magnetic forces.

Fluids are involved in most of the interesting happenings in our universe, whether on earth or in the most remote parts of the cosmos. Think for a minute about a world without fluids! The only motions would be those of rigid, macroscopic objects or the very slow changes in solids resulting from atomic diffusion and other subtle processes. The richness of activity to which we are accustomed would be drastically reduced; indeed, living things as we know them could not exist.

15.1
DESCRIBING FLUIDS

If we could observe a fluid on the molecular scale, we would find large numbers of molecules in continuous motion, colliding frequently with each other and with the walls of their containers. These collisions, and the responses of the individual molecules to external forces like gravity, are governed essentially by the laws of mechanics we developed earlier. In principle, therefore, we could study the behavior of fluids by applying the laws of mechanics to all the individual molecules in a fluid sample. But the number of molecules makes this a practical impossibility. Even a drop of water contains about 10^{21} molecules; to calculate the motions of all the molecules in the drop for one second would take the fastest computers many times the age of the universe!

Because the number of molecules in a typical fluid sample is so large, we approximate the fluid by considering it to be truly continuous rather than being composed ultimately of discrete particles. In this approximation, valid for fluid samples large compared with the spacing between molecules, we describe the fluid by specifying its density and pressure. We define these properties below; in general, each may be a function of both time and position.

Density

density

Density (symbol ρ, the Greek letter rho) measures the mass per unit volume of fluid; its SI units are kg/m^3. The density of water under normal conditions is about 1000 kg/m^3; that of air under normal conditions is

incompressible
compressible

about 1000 times smaller. Liquids are very nearly **incompressible,** meaning that their densities vary only slightly. Gases, in contrast, are **compressible,** meaning that their densities are easily altered.

Pressure

Pressure (symbol P) measures the magnitude of the normal force per unit area that a fluid exerts either on the walls of its container or on an adjacent region of fluid (Fig. 15–2). Accordingly, the SI units of pressure are N/m²; this unit is given the special name **pascal** (Pa), after the French mathematician, scientist, and philosophical writer Blaise Pascal (1623–1662). (Pascal's mathematical contributions are honored through the popular computer language named for him.) Other common units of pressure include the **atmosphere** (1 atm = 1.013×10^5 Pa, or the pressure of earth's atmosphere under normal conditions at sea level), the **bar** (1 bar = 10^5 Pa), the torr (1 torr = 1/760 atm, or the pressure that can support a column of mercury 1 mm high), and, in the English system, the lb/in² or psi.

pascal

atmosphere

bar

Pressure as we have defined it is a scalar quantity. In a static fluid, pressure at a given point is exerted equally in all directions, so that it makes no sense to associate a directionality with pressure (Fig. 15–3). This is because a fluid, by definition, offers no resistance to deformation. Any imbalance in pressure over a small volume element of fluid would result in deformation of the volume element to equalize the pressure.

Fig. 15–2
Pressure describes force per unit area exerted by a fluid, either on its container walls or on adjacent fluid. (According to Newton's third law, container and adjacent fluid exert forces equal but opposite to those shown. These reaction forces are not shown.)

Example 15–1

Pressure in a Basketball

A basketball of radius 12 cm is inflated to a pressure of 5.5×10^4 Pa (8 psi) above atmospheric pressure. What is the force on one hemisphere of the basketball due to this pressure?

Solution

Figure 15–4a shows force vectors associated with the 5.5×10^4-Pa excess pressure inside the ball. Clearly the net force on the right half of the ball points horizontally to the right. To calculate this force, we sum the horizontal components of the force vectors arising from the excess internal pressure. Figure 15–4b shows a small patch of area da on the ball's surface. Calling ΔP the excess of internal over external pressure, and remembering that pressure is force per unit area, we can write the force dF on the area da as $dF = \Delta P\, da$. This force points radially outward; its horizontal component is $dF_x = dF\cos\theta$, where θ is defined in Fig. 15–4b. So we have

$$dF_x = \Delta P\, da\, \cos\theta.$$

But $da\cos\theta$ is just the projection of the infinitesimal area da onto the vertical plane.

Fig. 15–3
A fluid exerts pressure in all directions.

Fig. 15–4
(a) Force vectors associated with the excess pressure inside a basketball. The net pressure force on the right hemisphere of the ball points horizontally to the right. (b) The force on a small surface element of area da is $\Delta P\, da$, where ΔP is the excess internal pressure.

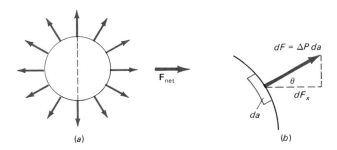

The sum—or integral—of all such projections is just the area πr^2 of a circle through the ball's center, so that the net force on the right half of the ball is

$$F_x = \int dF_x = \pi r^2 \Delta P = (\pi)(0.12 \text{ m})^2(5.5 \times 10^4 \text{ Pa}) = 2.5 \times 10^3 \text{ N},$$

or about 560 pounds! Since there is nothing special about the right hemisphere, this is the magnitude of the net force on any hemisphere of the basketball. (Of course, the net force on the entire ball is zero.) So what keeps the ball from flying apart? The ball itself stretches, and the tension within the rubber of the ball balances the force associated with excess pressure.

Example 15–2
Pressure in a Nuclear Explosion

One of the most destructive effects of a nuclear explosion is the generation of a shock wave consisting of a sudden increase in atmospheric pressure that propagates outward from the site of the explosion. At a distance of 8 km (5 miles) from a 1-megaton nuclear explosion, the shock wave exhibits an abrupt 25 per cent increase in atmospheric pressure. Estimate the net force exerted by the shock wave on a person standing and facing the blast.

Solution

As the wave passes, one side of the person is exposed to natural atmospheric pressure, the other to the excess pressure behind the shock wave. The force on the person is therefore $A\Delta P$, where ΔP is the excess pressure in the shock wave and A the person's area normal to the shock. Estimating that the person has approximately a rectangular cross section, 2 m high and 0.3 m wide, we have $A = 0.6 \text{ m}^2$. The pressure increase ΔP is 25 per cent of atmospheric pressure—that is, 0.25 atm or $2.5 \times 10^4 \text{ N/m}^2$. Then the net force on the person is

$$F = A\Delta P = (0.6 \text{ m}^2)(2.5 \times 10^4 \text{ N/m}^2) = 1.5 \times 10^4 \text{ N},$$

nearly 2 tons! Problem 24 of the preceding chapter also deals with the shock wave from a nuclear explosion.

15.2
FLUIDS AT REST

hydrostatic equilibrium

For a fluid to remain at rest, the net force on every part of the fluid must be zero. When this condition is met, the fluid is said to be in **hydrostatic equilibrium.** In the absence of gravity or other external forces that act throughout the volume of a fluid, hydrostatic equilibrium requires that the pressure be constant throughout the fluid. This is because, in hydrostatic equilibrium, the net force on *any* volume within the fluid must be zero. If the pressure varies with position, then there will be a net force on a fluid volume that extends from a region of lower to higher pressure (Fig. 15–5). As Fig. 15–5 suggests, it is not pressure itself but pressure *differences* that give rise to forces within fluids. In more advanced treatments of fluid behavior, the force per unit volume of fluid arising from pressure differences is shown to be equal to the negative of the pressure gradient, ∇P (we defined the gradient operator ∇ in Chapter 7). What happens at the boundaries of the fluid? The fluid exerts a pressure force on its container. By Newton's third law, the container must exert an equal but opposite force back

Fig. 15–5
(a) If the pressure varies with position, then there is a net pressure force on a volume of fluid. In the absence of other forces acting on the fluid volume, the fluid cannot be in hydrostatic equilibrium. *(b)* If the pressure is constant, the net pressure force on a fluid volume is zero, and the fluid is in hydrostatic equilibrium.

Increasing pressure

(a)

Constant pressure

(b)

F_{net}

Fig. 15–6
This tank burst because of excess pressure; it was propelled over 50 meters before coming to rest.

Pascal's principle

Fig. 15–7
The hydraulic cylinder actuating the power shovel is clearly visible in this photo.

on the fluid. This force is provided by tension associated ultimately with the stretching of interatomic bonds within the container. If the container is incapable of providing a force equal to the pressure force, it will burst (Fig. 15–6).

Suppose we increase the pressure in one part of a fluid—for example, by poking a finger into a balloon. In hydrostatic equilibrium, the pressure must be the same everywhere in the balloon. Therefore, the local pressure increase caused by poking the balloon at one point is transmitted equally throughout the fluid volume. This principle was first articulated by Pascal, and is now known as **Pascal's principle:** an increase in pressure at any point in a fluid is transmitted undiminished throughout the fluid volume and to the walls of the container. Pascal applied this principle in his invention of the hydraulic press; today hydraulic systems, based on Pascal's principle, are used in control of machinery ranging from automobile brake systems to aircraft wings to bulldozers, cranes, and robots (Fig. 15–7).

Application

A Hydraulic Braking System

Figure 15–8 shows a simplified diagram of an automobile braking system. The system includes a "master" cylinder containing a piston actuated by the brake pedal, and "slave" cylinders at each wheel. The cylinders are connected by metal and rubber hoses, and the whole system is filled with an incompressible liquid. When you step on the brake pedal, you force fluid out of the master cylinder. Since the fluid is incompressible, pistons in the slave cylinders move outward to keep the volume of the system constant. These slave pistons push friction pads against the rotating brake disks, thereby dissipating the kinetic energy of the car.

Typically the master cylinder has a much smaller cross-sectional area than the slave cylinders. Applying a given force to the master cylinder piston causes an increase in pressure equal to that force divided by the area of the piston. Pascal's principle tells us that this pressure increase is transmitted undiminished throughout the system. With the same pressure in the slave cylinders, the force—the pressure times the area—on the larger slave pistons is larger than the force on the master cylinder piston. The hydraulic system effectively amplifies the relatively weak force of your foot into the large force that ultimately stops the rotating disks and the wheels attached to them.

Isn't this force amplification giving us something for nothing? No—just as with a mechanical leverage system, the work we do on the master cylinder ends up as

Fig. 15–8
Simplified diagram of an automobile braking system, showing master cylinder and one of the slave cylinders.

Fig. 15–9
Just before landing, the wing flaps on a jetliner are extended enough to expose the hydraulic pistons controlling the flaps.

an equal amount of work done by the slave cylinders. Work—the integral of force over the distance moved by the master piston—is equal to the sum of the four similar integrals for the work done by the slave pistons. Since each slave piston has larger area and therefore larger force, and since there are four of them for one master cylinder, the distance moved by the slave pistons is much less than the distance you move the master piston. The hydraulic system gives a large force applied over a small distance in exchange for a smaller force applied over a larger distance.

Our description gives the essential features of a modern automotive braking system. But a real system is more complicated. Today's cars include two independent hydraulic systems, so that a leak in one system will not leave the car without brakes. And in larger cars, an additional power assist is provided to allow further amplification of the force at the brake pedal.

Hydraulic systems similar to automotive braking systems are used in controlling machinery including aircraft wing and tail flaps (Fig. 15–9). Unlike mechanical linkages, hydraulic hoses may be routed conveniently anywhere, allowing easy control of remote pieces of a machine.

Hydrostatic Equilibrium with Gravity

For a fluid to be in hydrostatic equilibrium in the presence of gravity, the force associated with fluid pressure must counteract the gravitational force. Since a net pressure force arises only when pressure varies with position, we expect that hydrostatic pressure cannot be uniform when gravity is present.

Figure 15–10 shows a fluid element of horizontal cross-sectional area A and small vertical thickness dy in a uniform gravitational field. A gravitational force $g\,dm$ acts on this element, where dm is its mass and where we take the y-direction to be positive downward. In hydrostatic equilibrium this gravitational force must be balanced by an upward pressure force. Therefore, the pressure at the bottom of the fluid element must be greater than at the top. Suppose the pressure at the top of the fluid element is P, and the pressure at the bottom is $P + dP$, where dP is a small pressure increase. The downward force on the top of the fluid element is PA, and

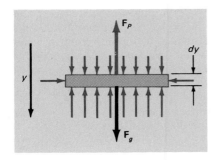

Fig. 15–10
Forces on a fluid element in hydrostatic equilibrium. The net pressure force must balance the gravitational force, requiring a higher pressure at the bottom of the fluid element.

the upward force on the bottom is $(P+dP)A$, so that the net pressure force on the fluid element is

$$dF = PA - (P+dP)A = -A\,dP,$$

where the minus sign indicates that the force is upward, or in the $-y$-direction. In hydrostatic equilibrium the net force—pressure force plus gravitational force—must be zero:

$$g\,dm - A\,dP = 0.$$

But the mass dm is just the density ρ of the fluid element multiplied by its volume, $A\,dy$, so that

$$g\rho A\,dy - A\,dP = 0,$$

or

$$\frac{dP}{dy} = \rho g. \quad \text{(hydrostatic equilibrium)} \tag{15–1}$$

This equation shows that dP/dy is always positive, indicating what we anticipated—that in the presence of a gravitational field pressure increases with depth. The exact form of that increase depends on the nature of the fluid. For a liquid, which is essentially incompressible, ρ is constant and we can multiply through by dy and integrate to get

$$\int_{P_0}^{P} dP = \int_{0}^{y} \rho g\,dy,$$

where P_0 is the pressure at the top of the fluid, where the depth y is zero. Carrying out the integration gives

$$P - P_0 = \rho g y,$$

or

$$P = P_0 + \rho g y. \quad \text{(liquid)} \tag{15–2}$$

Equation 15–2 shows pressure increasing linearly with depth in a liquid.

Example 15–3
Pressure in a Liquid

How far under water would you have to go for water pressure to be twice atmospheric pressure? What is the water pressure at the bottom of the Marianas trench, a 11.3-km-deep valley on the floor of the North Pacific Ocean? Assume in both cases that pressure at the top of the water is 1.0 atm, and that the density of the water is 1.0×10^3 kg/m^3.

Solution

When the water pressure is twice atmospheric pressure, we have $P=2.0$ atm while $P_0=1.0$ atm. Solving Equation 15–2 for the depth y gives

$$y = \frac{P-P_0}{\rho g} = \frac{2.0\times10^5\text{ Pa} - 1.0\times10^5\text{ Pa}}{(1.0\times10^3\text{ kg/m}^3)(9.8\text{ m/s}^2)} = 10\text{ m},$$

where we have converted pressures from atm to Pa for consistency with our other SI units. Our result shows that pressure on a diver would double at a depth of only 10 m or about 30 ft. Since pressure in a liquid increases linearly, water pressure continues to increase by 1 atm for every 10 m of depth. Figure 15–11 shows that

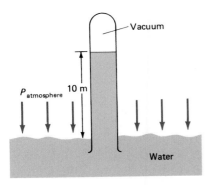

Fig. 15–11
The pressure at the bottom of a 10-m-high column of water is 1 atm higher than at the top. Therefore, normal atmospheric pressure can support a water column 10 m high with vacuum above it.

Fig. 15–12
Oceanographers bring deep ocean water to the surface in this titanium container that maintains the water and any inhabitants at their natural pressure.

our result also has implications for the design of water pumps, for it says that 1 atm of pressure can support a column of water 10 m high. Any water pump that works by suction—that is, by creating a vacuum and allowing air pressure to push water up—can raise water by at most 10 m. Pumping water from greater depths requires a submerged pump or one that somehow increases the pressure at the pumping depth.

To find the pressure in the Marianas Trench, we could solve Equation 15–2 for P. But we have already found that water pressure increases by 1 atm for every 10 m of depth. In the Marianas trench, we therefore have a total increase of

$$\Delta P = \frac{11.3 \times 10^3 \text{ m}}{10 \text{ m/atm}} = 1100 \text{ atm,}$$

or more than 8 tons per square inch! The 1 atm at the top of the ocean is a negligible addition to this huge pressure increase. Creatures living at these depths are in pressure equilibrium with their surroundings; to bring them to the surface for study, scientists must maintain their huge natural pressure or they will explode (Fig. 15–12). A similar plight affects scuba divers who foolishly hold their breath while ascending; air in the lungs expands, bursting the alveoli.

The variation in liquid pressure with depth provides a means of pressure measurement that is used in several practical instruments. Figure 15–13 shows a simple **barometer,** a device commonly used for measuring air pressure. The barometer consists of a tube sealed at its top end and containing the liquid metal mercury. The bottom end is open and immersed in a pool of mercury exposed to atmospheric pressure. Above the top of the mercury column is vacuum (pressure $P = 0$), so that the pressure at the surface of the mercury pool as given by Equation 15–2 is simply $\rho g h$, where ρ is the density of mercury and h the height of the mercury column above the pool surface. In equilibrium, this pressure is exactly balanced by atmospheric pressure, so that the height of the mercury column is directly proportional to atmospheric pressure. Reading the height in mm or inches gives us two commonly used pressure units: torr (mm of mercury) and inches of mercury. Problem 1 explores the conversion of these units to the SI unit Pa, using the density of mercury. In principle, we could make a barometer using water, but then, as Example 15–3 shows, a 10-m-high water column would be needed.

Measurement of pressure differences is accomplished using a **manometer,** a simple U-shaped tube containing a liquid and open at both ends (Fig. 15–14). A difference in pressure between the ends of the tube results in a difference in the heights of the two liquid surfaces; Equation 15–2 shows that this height difference is directly proportional to the pressure difference. A manometer may use mercury, water, or other fluids. Very small pressure differences—associated, for example, with chimney drafts—are often measured in inches of water, a unit arising naturally with water-filled manometers. When one end of a manometer senses atmospheric pressure, the pressure it reads is called **gauge pressure** or **overpressure,** meaning the excess pressure above atmospheric pressure. Tire gauges and inflation specifications for tires, sports equipment, and the like are given in gauge pressure rather than absolute pressure. A tire inflated to 30 psig (pounds per square inch, gauge), for example, has an absolute pressure of

Fig. 15–13
A mercury barometer for measuring air pressure. Note the resemblance to Fig. 15–11, which is essentially a water barometer. Column height in a mercury barometer at 1.0 atm air pressure is 760 mm or 29.92 in.

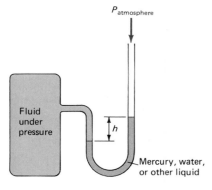

Fig. 15–14
A manometer being used to measure pressure difference between a closed container of fluid and the ambient atmosphere. Difference in height of the two liquid surfaces is a measure of the pressure difference across the ends of the tube.

scale height

about 45 psi because the 15 psi atmospheric pressure is not included in the 30 psig specification.

Although Equation 15–2 applies only to a liquid of constant density, Equation 15–1 is valid for any fluid. In a gas like a planetary atmosphere, it is convenient to measure height h upward from the surface rather than depth y downward. Taking $h = -y$, Equation 15–2 then becomes

$$\frac{dP}{dh} = -\rho g. \qquad (15\text{–}3)$$

In an ideal gas of uniform temperature, pressure and density are directly proportional:

$$P = \rho \frac{kT}{m}, \qquad (15\text{–}4)$$

where T is the temperature in kelvins, k a constant called Boltzmann's constant (equal to 1.38×10^{-23} J/K), and m the mass of a gas molecule in kg. (We will study this relation—called the ideal gas law—in Chapter 17.) Although the temperature of a planetary atmosphere is not exactly uniform, the approximation of uniform temperature allows us to make a rough calculation of the pressure and density structure of an atmosphere. Solving Equation 15–4 for the density ρ and using the result in Equation 15–3, we have

$$\frac{dP}{dh} = -P \frac{mg}{kT}.$$

Multiplying by dh and dividing by P gives

$$\frac{dP}{P} = -\frac{mg}{kT}\, dh.$$

To solve for the pressure P as a function of height h, we integrate both sides from the surface $h = 0$ where the pressure has the value P_0:

$$\int_{P_0}^{P} \frac{dP}{P} = -\frac{mg}{kT} \int_0^h dh.$$

The integral of dP/P is the natural logarithm of P, while the integral of dh is just h, so that

$$\ln P - \ln P_0 = -\frac{mg}{kT}\, h.$$

Recalling that $\ln P - \ln P_0 = \ln(P/P_0)$, and that $e^{\ln x} = x$, we can exponentiate both sides of this equation to get

$$P = P_0 e^{-mgh/kT}. \quad \text{(uniform-temperature atmosphere)} \qquad (15\text{–}5)$$

This equation shows that the pressure in an atmosphere of uniform temperature decreases exponentially with height. The constant kT/mg is called the **scale height**, h_0, and is the height over which atmospheric pressure drops to $1/e$ of its ground-level value. In terms of scale height, Equation 15–5 may be written

$$P = P_0 e^{-h/h_0}. \qquad (15\text{–}6)$$

In deriving Equations 15–5 and 15–6, we assumed that g does not vary significantly with height. For earth's relatively thin atmosphere, this is a good approximation. Problem 38 explores the case of the sun's atmosphere, which extends far enough from the surface that the variation in g is important.

Example 15–4
Pressure Variation in Earth's Atmosphere

Atmospheric pressure at sea level is 1.0 atm. Assuming a uniform temperature of 280 K and an average molecular mass of 28.8 u (4.8×10^{-26} kg; this reflects atmospheric composition of approximately 80 per cent N_2 and 20 per cent O_2), calculate the scale height in earth's atmosphere and from it the pressure atop Mt. Washington in New Hampshire (altitude 1900 m), atop Dhaulagiri in Nepal (altitude 8200 m), and in California's Death Valley, 86 m below sea level.

Solution

The scale height is

$$h_0 = \frac{kT}{mg} = \frac{(1.38 \times 10^{-23} \text{ J/K})(280 \text{ K})}{(4.8 \times 10^{-26} \text{ kg})(9.8 \text{ m/s})} = 8200 \text{ m}.$$

We then have

$$P_{\text{Washington}} = P_0 e^{-h/h_0} = (1.0 \text{ atm})(e^{-1900 \text{ m}/8200 \text{ m}}) = 0.79 \text{ atm}.$$

Similar calculations give $P_{\text{Dhaulagiri}} = 0.37$ atm and $P_{\text{Death Valley}} = 1.01$ atm, where in the last case the altitude h is negative, resulting in a pressure greater than that at sea level. Since gas density is proportional to pressure, these results show that much less air is available on a high mountain like Dhaulagiri, which is why most climbers carry oxygen tanks.

Archimedes' Principle and Buoyancy

Throw a rock into water and it sinks. Throw in a block of wood and it floats. Why the difference?

Consider an arbitrarily shaped volume within a fluid in hydrostatic equilibrium (Fig. 15–15a). We know that equilibrium is maintained by the upward pressure force that exactly balances the weight of the fluid volume. Now imagine replacing the fluid volume by a solid object of identical shape (Fig. 15–15b). The remaining fluid has not changed in any way, so it continues to exert an upward force on the object—a force whose magnitude equals the weight of the *original fluid volume.* This upward force is called the **buoyancy force;** as we have just shown, the buoyancy force on an object is always equal to the weight of the fluid displaced by that object. This principle—called **Archimedes' principle**—was first articulated in the third century B.C. by the Greek inventor and mathematician Archimedes. If the object weighs more than the original fluid volume, the net force on it— downward weight plus upward buoyancy force—is downward, and it sinks. If the object weighs less than the original fluid volume, the buoyancy force is greater than its weight, and it rises. Therefore, an object will float or sink, depending on whether its average density is greater or less than that of the fluid. An object whose density is equal to that of the fluid experiences zero net force, and is said to be in **neutral buoyancy.** Most fish

buoyancy force

Archimedes' principle

neutral buoyancy

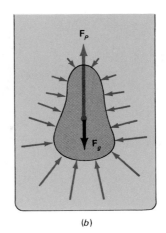

Fig. 15–15
(a) In hydrostatic equilibrium, there is an upward pressure force F_p equal to the weight F_g of any fluid volume. *(b)* If the fluid volume is replaced by a solid object of identical shape, the remaining fluid is not changed in any way, so that there remains an upward force equal to the weight of the fluid displaced by the object. In general, this upward buoyancy force may be more or less than the weight of the object.

Fig. 15–16
Most fish contain a "swim bladder"—a gas-filled bladder whose volume adjusts to keep the fish in neutral buoyancy, with no tendency to float or sink.

Fig. 15–17
A hot-air balloon is in neutral buoyancy when it maintains a constant altitude.

contain a gas-filled bladder whose volume changes to maintain the fish in neutral buoyancy (Fig. 15–16). Submerged submarines, too, take on and discharge sea water as needed to maintain neutral buoyancy. A balloon cruising at constant altitude is another example of an object in neutral buoyancy (Fig. 15–17).

What happens when a buoyant object reaches the surface of the fluid? As the object breaks through the surface, only part of it remains immersed in the fluid. As always, the buoyant force is equal to the weight of the fluid displaced by the object. But now, the volume of fluid displaced is less than the volume of the entire object. So the buoyant force decreases. Eventually an equilibrium is reached in which the buoyant force balances the weight of the entire object. Since the buoyant force is equal to the weight of the fluid displaced by the submerged portion of the object, in equilibrium the object will float at such a level that its submerged portion displaces an amount of water whose weight equals the object's entire weight (Fig. 15–18).

Example 15–5
The Tip of the Iceberg

The average density of a typical arctic iceberg is about 0.86 that of sea water (iceberg density varies depending on the amount of air and rock entrained in the iceberg; for antarctic icebergs the typical density is closer to 0.80 that of sea water). What fraction of an arctic iceberg's volume is submerged?

Solution

In equilibrium, the entire weight of the iceberg is supported by the buoyant force, equal to the weight of the volume of water displaced by the submerged portion of the iceberg. If V_{sub} is the submerged volume, the weight of this volume of water—and therefore the magnitude of the buoyant force—is

$$F_b = W_{water} = m_{water}g = \rho_{water}V_{sub}g.$$

Fig. 15–18
Supertankers (left) empty and (right) fully loaded. In both cases the full weight of the supertanker and cargo is supported by the buoyant force, which is equal to the weight of the water displaced by the ship. The heavily loaded tanker must therefore displace more water, so it rides lower.

The weight of the iceberg is

$$W_{ice} = m_{ice}g = \rho_{ice}V_{ice}g,$$

where V_{ice} is the volume of the entire iceberg. Equating the iceberg weight to the magnitude of the buoyant force, we have

$$\rho_{ice}V_{ice}g = \rho_{water}V_{sub}g,$$

so that

$$\frac{V_{sub}}{V_{ice}} = \frac{\rho_{ice}}{\rho_{water}} = 0.86.$$

Roughly six-sevenths of an arctic iceberg is therefore submerged (Fig. 15–19).

Example 15–6
An Overloaded Boat

A flat-bottomed rowboat has length $\ell = 3.2$ m, width $w = 1.1$ m, and is 28 cm deep. Empty, it has a mass of 130 kg. Its maximum rated load is 450 kg. How much of the boat is submerged (a) when it is empty and (b) when it carries its maximum rated load? (c) What is the total mass it could carry without taking on water?

Fig. 15–19
Because the density of ice is close to that of water, only about one-seventh of an iceberg's volume is above water.

Solution

In equilibrium, the total weight of the boat and its load must be supported by the buoyant force of the water. By Archimedes' principle, this force is equal to the weight of water displaced by the boat. Letting y be the depth to which the boat is submerged, we have

$$\ell w y \rho_w g = Mg.$$

Here ρ_w is the density of water, and $\ell w y$ the submerged volume, so that the term on the left is the weight of displaced water, and is therefore equal to the magnitude of the buoyant force. M is the total mass of the boat plus its load, so that the term on the right is the weight supported by the buoyant force. Solving for y, we have

$$y = \frac{M}{\ell w \rho_w} = \frac{(130 \text{ kg})}{(3.2 \text{ m})(1.1 \text{ m})(1000 \text{ kg/m}^3)} = 3.7 \text{ cm}$$

for the empty boat, and

$$y = \frac{(130 \text{ kg} + 450 \text{ kg})}{(3.2 \text{ m})(1.1 \text{ m})(1000 \text{ kg/m}^3)} = 16 \text{ cm}$$

at maximum rated load. To find the absolute maximum load the boat can hold before water pours over its sides, we set y equal to the boat's 28-cm depth, and solve for M:

$$M = \ell w y \rho_w = (3.2 \text{ m})(1.1 \text{ m})(0.28 \text{ m})(1000 \text{ kg/m}^3) = 986 \text{ kg}.$$

This is the total mass; subtracting the 130-kg boat mass gives 856 kg for the absolute maximum load. In this example we assumed that the load is centered over the boat's center of mass, so that there is no net torque tending to tip the boat.

15.3
FLUID DYNAMICS

In the preceding section, we considered fluids in static equilibrium. We now turn our attention to moving fluids, which are described by giving the flow velocity at each point in the fluid and at each instant of time. Figure 15–20 shows some flow velocity vectors in a river. We can describe flow velocity either with individual vectors, as in Fig. 15–20, or by drawing continuous lines that connect the velocity vectors head-to-tail (Fig. 15–21). streamlines Called **streamlines,** these lines lie along the local direction of flow. Their spacing is a measure of flow speed, with closely spaced streamlines indicating high speed. Small particles, like smoke or dyes, are often introduced

Fig. 15–20
Vectors describing flow velocity in a river. Note the higher velocity where the river is narrower.

into moving fluids because they follow streamlines and therefore give a visual indication of the flow velocity pattern (Fig. 15–22).

steady flow

unsteady flow

Fig. 15–22
In this aerodynamic test of an automobile, smoke particles introduced into the air follow streamlines and therefore allow airflow to be traced.

We distinguish two types of fluid motion. In **steady flow,** the pattern of fluid motion remains the same at each point, even though individual fluid elements are in continual motion. When you look at a river in steady flow, for example, it always looks the same, even though you are not seeing the same water each time you look. At a given point in the river, the water velocity, density, and pressure are always the same. **Unsteady flow,** in contrast, involves fluid motion that changes with time even at a fixed point. The flow of blood in your arteries is an example of unsteady flow; with each contraction of the heart ventricles, the pressure rises, and the flow velocity increases. Figure 15–23 shows other examples of steady and unsteady flow. We will restrict our quantitative description of fluid motion to steady flow. Like all other motion in classical physics, fluid motion is governed by Newton's laws. Indeed, it is possible to write Newton's second law in a form that involves explicitly the fluid velocity as a function of position and time. But the resulting equation is difficult to solve in any but the simplest cases. Instead of applying Newton's law directly, we will approach fluid dynamics from the point of view of energy conservation. In mechanics, we found that energy conservation gave us a "shortcut" in solving mechanics problems where the application of Newton's law would be

Fig. 15–23
(Left) Airflow above a burning cigarette is traced by the smoke. At first the flow is steady but soon becomes unsteady. (Right) Unsteady flows in Jupiter's atmosphere, photographed by a Voyager spacecraft. (See also color plate 2.)

difficult. The price we paid for the simplicity of the energy conservation method was a loss of detailed information about the behavior of a system as a function of time. Similarly, in fluid dynamics, use of energy conservation allows us to solve simply for many features of a moving fluid, but does not give all the details of the motion.

Conservation of Mass: The Continuity Equation

continuity equation

In mechanics problems, we had no trouble keeping track of the individual objects involved. But a fluid is continuous and deformable, so that it is not easy to follow an individual fluid element as it moves. Yet we know that fluid is conserved; as a fluid moves and deforms, new fluid is neither created nor destroyed. The **continuity equation** is a mathematical statement of this fact that fluid (that is, matter itself) is conserved.

flow tube

To develop the continuity equation, consider an arbitrary steady fluid flow represented by streamlines as shown, for example, in Fig. 15–24. Since streamlines are the paths followed by individual fluid elements, fluid flows along streamlines but never across them. In Fig. 15–24 we have shaded a **flow tube**—a small tube-like region bounded on its sides by a set of streamlines and on its ends by areas at right angles to the streamlines. We choose the flow tube to have sufficiently small cross-sectional area that fluid velocity and other fluid properties do not vary significantly over any cross section; however, fluid properties may vary along the flow tube. Although our flow tube has no physical boundaries, it nevertheless acts like a pipe of the same shape, for no fluid crosses the streamlines, just as no fluid crosses the walls of a pipe. With the direction of flow shown, fluid enters the flow tube at its left end and exits at the right. In steady flow, the rate at which fluid enters the flow tube must equal the rate at which it exits; otherwise, fluid would accumulate in or be displaced from the tube, and the fluid properties at each point could not be independent of time.

Figure 15–25 shows our flow tube in more detail, with a small fluid element just about to enter the tube, a process that will take a time Δt.

Fig. 15–24
Streamlines in steady flow. Shaded area outlines a flow tube. In steady flow, the rate at which fluid enters the flow tube equals the rate at which it leaves the tube.

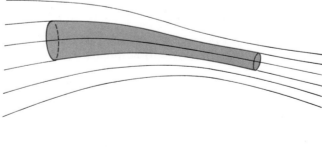

Fig. 15–25
Fluid elements of equal mass entering and leaving the flow tube.

Another fluid element is shown just about to leave the flow tube; suppose that it contains the same amount of fluid as the entering fluid element. In steady flow, its exit from the tube must also take time Δt, so that there is no change in the total amount of fluid in the tube. The entering fluid element is moving at some speed v_1; since it takes time Δt for all of it to enter the tube, its length is $v_1\Delta t$. With cross-sectional area A_1, length $v_1\Delta t$, and density ρ_1, the mass of the entering fluid element is

$$m_1 = \rho_1 A_1 v_1 \Delta t.$$

Similarly, the exiting fluid element has length $v_2\Delta t$, and therefore its mass is

$$m_2 = \rho_2 A_2 v_2 \Delta t.$$

We have argued that, in steady flow, the mass entering in time Δt and that leaving in the same time must be equal. Therefore

$$\rho_1 v_1 A_1 = \rho_2 v_2 A_2. \tag{15–7}$$

Since the endpoints of the tube are arbitrary, we conclude that the quantity $\rho v A$ must have the same value anywhere along the flow tube:

$$\rho v A = \text{constant along a flow tube.} \quad \text{(any fluid)} \tag{15–8}$$

mass flow rate

What is this quantity $\rho v A$ that is constant along a flow tube? Its SI units are $(kg/m^{-3})(m/s)(m^2)$, or simply kg/s. $\rho v A$ is therefore the **mass flow rate** or mass of fluid per unit time passing through the flow tube. Equations 15–7 and 15–8 are equivalent expressions of the continuity equation, both stating that the mass flow rate is constant along a flow tube in steady flow.

For a liquid, the density ρ is essentially constant, and the continuity equation 15–8 becomes simply

$$v A = \text{constant along a flow tube.} \quad \text{(liquid)} \tag{15–9}$$

volume flow rate

Now the constant quantity is just vA, with units of $(m/s)(m^2)$, or m^3/s. vA is therefore the **volume flow rate**; in a fluid of constant density, constancy of mass flow rate (Equations 15–7 and 15–8) also implies constancy of volume flow rate, since a given mass of fluid does not change volume. In the form 15–9, the continuity equation makes obvious physical sense. Where the liquid has a large cross-sectional area, it can flow relatively slowly to transport a given mass of fluid per unit time. But where the area is more constricted, the flow must be faster to carry the same mass per unit time. With a gas, obeying Equation 15–8 but not necessarily 15–9, the situation is slightly more ambiguous, as density variations too play a role in the continuity equation. For flow speeds below the speed of sound in a gas, it turns out that lower area implies a higher flow speed just as for a liquid. But when gas flow speed exceeds the sound speed, density changes become so great that flow speed actually decreases with lower area.

Example 15–7
The Continuity Equation

In the lower part of its valley, the Ausable River in upstate New York is about 40 m wide. Under typical early summer conditions, it is 2.2 m deep and flows at 4.5 m/s. Just before it reaches Lake Champlain, the river enters Ausable Chasm, a

Fig. 15–26
The Ausable River in upstate New York cuts through a narrow chasm. To accommodate the flow, water depth in the chasm is much greater than elsewhere.

deep gorge cut through rock (Fig. 15–26). At its narrowest, the gorge is only 3.7 m wide at the river surface. If the flow rate in the gorge is 6.0 m/s, how deep is the river at this point? Assume that the river has a rectangular cross section, with uniform flow speed over a cross section.

Solution

Writing the cross-sectional area as the product of width w and depth d, Equation 15–9 may be written

$$v_1 w_1 d_1 = v_2 w_2 d_2.$$

Solving for the gorge depth d_2 gives

$$d_2 = \frac{v_1 w_1 d_1}{v_2 w_2} = \frac{(4.5 \text{ m/s})(40 \text{ m})(2.2 \text{ m})}{(6.0 \text{ m/s})(3.7 \text{ m})} = 18 \text{ m},$$

or about 60 feet!

Conservation of Energy: Bernoulli's Equation

Having expressed conservation of matter through the continuity equation, we now turn to conservation of energy. Figure 15–27 again shows a flow tube with fluid elements entering and leaving. In steady flow, the properties of the fluid at a given point are always the same. So it doesn't matter whether we think of Fig. 15–27 as a "snapshot" showing two different fluid elements at the same time or the same fluid element at two different times. In deriving the continuity equation, we took the former viewpoint; here we will find the latter viewpoint more convenient. Our fluid element of mass m enters the flow tube with velocity v_1 and leaves with velocity v_2. Therefore, the change in kinetic energy of the fluid element as it traverses the flow tube is

$$\Delta K = \tfrac{1}{2}m(v_2^2 - v_1^2).$$

The work-energy theorem (Equation 6–19) tells us that the change in ki-

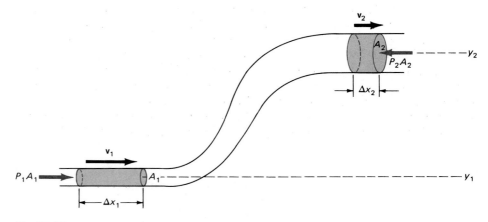

Fig. 15–27
A flow tube showing a fluid element entering and leaving. The work done by pressure and gravitational forces equals the change in the kinetic energy of the fluid element.

netic energy is equal to the net work done on the fluid element. As the fluid element enters the tube, it is subject to a pressure force P_1A_1 from the pressure of adjacent fluid outside the tube. This external force acts over the length Δx_1 of the fluid element as it enters the tube, so that it does work $W_1 = P_1A_1\Delta x_1$ on the fluid element. Similarly, as it leaves the tube, the fluid element is subject to a force P_2A_2 from the pressure of the fluid beyond the right-hand end of the tube. Since the direction of this force is opposite to the flow direction, it does negative work $W_2 = -P_2A_2\Delta x_2$ on the fluid element. Of course there are also forces on the fluid element arising from the pressure of adjacent fluid within the flow tube. But as the fluid element moves through the tube, it experiences such forces first on one end, then on the other, so that no net work is done by these forces internal to the flow tube. Forces from adjacent flow tubes act at right angles to the flow, so that they, too, do no work. Finally, the fluid element rises a distance $y_2 - y_1$ as it traverses the flow tube; the downward gravitational force therefore does negative work $W_g = -mg(y_2 - y_1)$ on the fluid element. Here y measures the vertical distance from an arbitrary reference height to the center of the flow tube; we assume that the flow tube is small enough that we can neglect variations in height and pressure across it. Summing the three contributions to the work done on the fluid element, and applying the work-energy theorem to equate that net work to the change in kinetic energy across the flow tube, we have

$$W_1 + W_2 + W_g = \Delta K,$$

or

$$P_1A_1\Delta x_1 - P_2A_2\Delta x_2 - mg(y_2 - y_1) = \tfrac{1}{2}m(v_2^2 - v_1^2).$$

The quantities $A_{1,2}\Delta x_{1,2}$ are the volumes of the fluid element as it enters and leaves; since density is mass per unit volume, we can write these volumes in the form $m/\rho_{1,2}$. Making this substitution, the mass m cancels from the equation. Rearranging the resulting equation so that all the terms associated with the entering fluid element are on the left side, and those associated with the departing fluid element are on the right, we have

$$\frac{P_1}{\rho_1} + \tfrac{1}{2}v_1^2 + gy_1 = \frac{P_2}{\rho_2} + \tfrac{1}{2}v_2^2 + gy_2. \qquad (15\text{--}10)$$

What do the three terms on each side of this equation mean? The terms $\tfrac{1}{2}v^2$ and gy look like kinetic and potential energy, respectively, but divided by the mass. Therefore, they represent the kinetic energy per unit mass associated with the flow velocity v, and the potential energy per unit mass associated with the fluid height y. What about the terms P/ρ? They, too, have the units of energy per unit mass, and represent energy associated with the compression of the fluid. So Equation 15–10 expresses conservation of energy along the flow tube. Since the endpoints of the tube are arbitrary, we conclude that the quantity $P/\rho + \tfrac{1}{2}v^2 + gy$ is constant along a flow tube.

So far, we have assumed only that our flow tube is narrow and that there is no energy loss or gain from friction or from mechanical devices like pumps and turbines within the flow tube. If we further restrict consideration to liquids, which are essentially incompressible, the quantities ρ_1

and ρ_2 in Equation 15–10 become the constant density ρ, and we can re-write the equation in the form

$$P + \tfrac{1}{2}\rho v^2 + \rho gh = \text{constant along flow tube.} \quad \text{(liquid)} \quad (15\text{–}11)$$

Bernoulli's equation

Equation 15–11—the statement of energy conservation for an ideal incom-pressible fluid with no energy dissipation—is called **Bernoulli's equation,** after the Dutch-born Swiss mathematician Daniel Bernoulli (1700–1782). If we make the further restriction that the flow is irrotational—that a fluid element at any point has no angular momentum about that point—then it turns out that the constant in Bernoulli's equation has the same value for all flow tubes.

Applications of Fluid Dynamics

The laws of mass and energy conservation that we have just written for fluids can be used to explain a wide variety of natural and technological phenomena involving fluid motion.

Example 15–8
The Flow of Liquid from a Tank

A large, open tank is filled to a height h with liquid of density ρ. What is the speed of liquid emerging from a small hole at the base of the tank (Fig. 15–28)?

Solution

Assuming that the flow is steady and irrotational, we can apply Bernoulli's equation to the emerging fluid. Since the hole is open to the atmosphere, the fluid pressure at the hole must be atmospheric pressure, P_a. If we define the height at the tank bottom, where the hole is, to be $y = 0$, then the quantity $P + \tfrac{1}{2}\rho v^2 + \rho gh$ evaluated at the hole has the value $P_a + \tfrac{1}{2}\rho v_{\text{hole}}{}^2$. To solve for v_{hole}, we need to know the value of this quantity at some other point. A suitable point is the top of the tank, where the pressure is also atmospheric pressure since the tank is open. What about the flow velocity? If the area of the tank is large compared with the hole area, the liquid level at the top drops only slowly, and we can take $v_{\text{top}} \approx 0$. Therefore, the quantity $P + \tfrac{1}{2}\rho v^2 + \rho gy$—the constant in Bernoulli's equation—has the value $P_a + \rho gh$ at the top of the tank. Bernoulli's equation states that $P + \tfrac{1}{2}\rho v^2 + \rho gy$ has the same value everywhere; equating our expressions for this quantity at the hole and at the tank top then gives

$$P_a + \tfrac{1}{2}\rho v_{\text{hole}}{}^2 = P_a + \rho gh.$$

Solving for the outflow velocity at the hole, we have

$$v_{\text{hole}} = \sqrt{2gh}.$$

Does this simple result make sense? We would get the same speed by dropping an object through a distance h—and for the same reason: conservation of energy. Draining a gram of water through the hole is energetically the same as removing a gram of water from the top of the tank and dropping it through the distance h. Just as the speed of a falling object is independent of its mass, so is the speed of the emerging liquid independent of its density, or mass per unit volume.

Our use of Bernoulli's equation—an equation derived for *steady* flow—is an approximation in this example, for the liquid level at the tank top must drop as liquid drains through the hole. The approximation is a reasonable one provided the tank area is large compared with the hole area. Problem 32 explores the long-term situation as the tank drains completely.

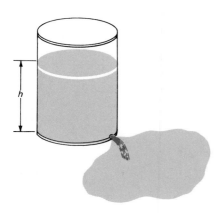

Fig. 15–28
Example 15–8

Example 15–9

Flow from a Faucet

Water leaves a faucet in steady, near-vertical flow (Fig. 15–29 left). Use the continuity equation and Bernoulli's equation to find the diameter of the falling water column as a function of the distance h measured downward from the faucet. Take D_0 to be the outlet diameter of the faucet and v_0 to be the flow velocity at the faucet.

Solution

Since the density of a liquid is constant, we use the continuity equation in the form 15–9:

$$\tfrac{1}{4}\pi D^2 v = \tfrac{1}{4}\pi D_0^2 v_0,$$

where D and v are the diameter and flow speed at any point, and where $\tfrac{1}{4}\pi D^2 = \pi r^2$ is the cross-sectional area of the water column. So the diameter and flow speed are related by

$$D^2 = \frac{D_0^2 v_0}{v}.$$

We want the diameter as a function of position, so we must express flow speed in terms of position. Bernoulli's equation provides the desired link. Since the entire water column is open to the atmosphere, the pressure anywhere is atmospheric pressure, P_a. (Here we neglect variation in atmospheric pressure over the height of the water stream.) So Bernoulli's equation reads

$$P_a + \tfrac{1}{2}\rho v^2 + \rho g y = P_a + \tfrac{1}{2}\rho v_0^2,$$

where the left-hand side applies to an arbitrary point and the right-hand side to the faucet outlet. We have taken $y = 0$ at the faucet, and our y-axis is positive upward for consistency with our derivation of Bernoulli's equation. Then the downward distance from the faucet, h, is given by $h = -y$. Making this substitution and solving for v gives

$$v = \sqrt{v_0^2 + 2gh}.$$

Fig. 15–29
(Left) Steady flow from a faucet. (Right) Theoretical result of Example 15–9 closely matches the observed behavior of the water.

This is just the result we would expect for an object with initial velocity v_0 falling a distance h. Using this result in our expression for the diameter D then gives

$$D = D_0\left(\frac{v_0^2}{v_0^2 + 2gh}\right)^{1/4}.$$

Figure 15–29 (right) shows that this theoretical result matches closely the actual flow. Problem 30 explores this example further.

For horizontal flow, or when changes in gravitational potential energy density are small compared with kinetic energy density and with pressure, we can drop the $\rho g y$ terms in Bernoulli's equation to obtain

$$P + \tfrac{1}{2}\rho v^2 = \text{constant.} \tag{15–12}$$

This equation shows that flow speed is high where pressure is low, and vice versa. You might think that flow speed should be high where pressure is high. But conservation of energy requires the opposite. Both the pressure term P and the flow kinetic energy term $\tfrac{1}{2}\rho v^2$ represent energy per unit volume; if one increases, the other must decrease to conserve energy.

Equation 15–12, like Equation 15–11, applies strictly only to an incompressible fluid—a liquid. With a gas, density can vary with position and we must use Equation 15–10. If the density of a gas decreases sufficiently in a region where pressure increases, flow velocity can actually increase to satisfy energy conservation in the form 15–10. However, it is only with supersonic flows—flow speeds greater than the sound speed in the gas—that such effects occur. Indeed, density variations in a gas are generally insignificant when the flow speed is much less than the speed of sound. (Here we continue to assume that density variations due to gravity are negligible, as we are dealing only with small vertical distances.) For this reason we can treat slowly moving gas as an incompressible fluid, and apply Equation 15–12.

Nature and technology abound with applications of Equation 15–12 to liquids and to gases flowing at well below their sound speeds. Blow across the top of a piece of paper and it extends horizontally (Fig. 15–30). Why? Because you have increased the flow speed above the paper and therefore lowered the pressure. Higher pressure below the paper therefore results in a net upward force on the paper. Airplane wings work in the same way. They are shaped or angled so that air flows at a higher speed over the top surface, again resulting in a lower pressure above the wing and therefore a net upward force (Fig. 15–31). Think about a jumbo jet, and you will agree that this upward force can be substantial (Fig. 15–32). The dirt around a prairie dog's hole is mounded up in a shape that resembles the leading edge of an airplane wing (Fig. 15–33). When the wind blows, this design results in lower air pressure above the hole and therefore in an outflow of air from the burrow. Biologists speculate that prairie dogs have evolved this hole design to provide ventilation. The **Bernoulli effect,** as the occurrence of low pressure with high flow speed is called, can sometimes be strikingly counterintuitive. Figure 15–34 shows a Ping-Pong ball supported by a *downward* blowing column of air in an inverted funnel. Rapid divergence of the airflow in the expanded region of the funnel results in a

High v
low P

Low v
high P

Fig. 15–30
When you blow across the top of a piece of paper, higher flow speed at the top results in lower pressure, and therefore a net upward force.

Bernoulli effect

Fig. 15–31
A model wing being tested in a wind tunnel. Both wing shape and its inclination to the horizontal result in higher flow speed and therefore lower pressure over the top surface, giving a net upward pressure force. Note the slight downward deflection of airflow at upper right. This shows that the wing has exerted a downward force on the air, in reaction to the upward force of air on the wing.

Fig. 15–32
A fully loaded 747 jet can weigh nearly 4×10^6 N (over 400 tons). Its weight is supported by the force associated with the difference in air pressure across its wings.

lower flow speed and therefore higher pressure below the ball, whose weight is thereby supported. A new application of the Bernoulli effect is the so-called "Bernoulli box," a computer disk that combines the high speed of a hard disk with the ruggedness and low cost of floppy disks. In the Bernoulli box disk, pressure differences associated with airflow are used to maintain the otherwise flexible disk in a rigid state, allowing high-speed data access.

A constriction in a pipe carrying incompressible liquid requires that the flow speed increase in order to maintain constant mass flow. Such a constriction is called a **venturi.** Bernoulli's equation requires that the fluid

venturi

Fig. 15–33
Is the entrance of a prairie dog hole shaped to provide ventilation by lowering the pressure over the hole?

Fig. 15–34
A Ping-Pong ball supported by a downward-moving air stream.

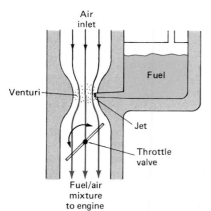

Fig. 15–35
Simplified view of a carburetor, showing the venturi and the jet where fuel enters.

pressure be lower in the venturi. The venturi is put to good use in an automobile carburetor. Air flows into the carburetor because of lower pressure created by the downward motion of the engine's pistons. In the venturi (also called the throat) of the carburetor, the flow speed increases and the pressure drops. A tiny hole, or jet, opens into the venturi and carries gasoline. The lower pressure in the venturi results in a flow of gasoline into the carburetor, where it mixes with the high-speed air stream to form the combustible mixture burned in the engine. A flat disk—the throttle valve—below the venturi is connected to the car's accelerator pedal. The throttle valve pivots to control the rate at which the fuel/air mixture reaches the engine. Figure 15–35 gives a simplified view of a carburetor.

Example 15–10
A Carburetor

With its throttle valve wide open, an automobile carburetor has a throat diameter of 2.4 cm. With each revolution, the car's 2.2-L, 4-cylinder engine sucks in 0.55 L of air through the carburetor. At an engine speed of 3000 revolutions per minute, what are (a) the volume flow rate, (b) the airflow speed, and (c) the difference between atmospheric pressure and air pressure in the carburetor throat? The density of air is 1.3 kg/m³.

Solution:

With 0.55 L of air per revolution, at 3000 rpm the engine takes in air at the volume flow rate $\mathscr{F}$ given by

$$\mathscr{F} = (0.55 \text{ L/rev})(3000 \text{ rev/min}) = 1650 \text{ L/min} = 0.0275 \text{ m}^3/\text{s}.$$

But the volume flow rate is the product of flow speed and area, so that within the carburetor throat we have $\mathscr{F} = vA = \pi r^2 v$. Then

$$v = \frac{\mathscr{F}}{\pi r^2} = \frac{0.0275 \text{ m}^3/\text{s}}{(\pi)(0.012 \text{ m})^2} = 61 \text{ m/s}.$$

Since this is well below the sound speed (approximately 340 m/s), the air acts as though it were incompressible.

We can now use Bernoulli's equation to find the pressure difference, taking as our reference point the ambient atmosphere where the flow speed is essentially zero. Then Bernoulli's equation becomes

$$P_a + 0 = P_c + \tfrac{1}{2}\rho v^2,$$

where P_a is atmospheric pressure and P_c the pressure in the carburetor. Solving for the pressure difference $P_a - P_c$ gives

$$P_a - P_c = \tfrac{1}{2}\rho v^2 = \tfrac{1}{2}(1.3 \text{ kg/m}^3)(61 \text{ m/s})^2 = 2.4 \times 10^3 \text{ N/m}^2,$$

or about 2.4 per cent of atmospheric pressure. It is this pressure difference that drives gasoline through the jet and into the carburetor throat. Problem 33 explores the gasoline flow, which itself can be treated using the equations of fluid dynamics.

Figure 15–36 shows a venturi flowmeter, a device used to measure the rate of fluid flow. With no flow, the fluid is in static equilibrium and there is no pressure difference between the venturi and the main pipe. As the flow rate increases, the pressure in the venturi of the flowmeter decreases,

Fig. 15–36
A venturi flowmeter. According to Bernoulli's equation, the pressure difference across the manometer tube depends on the flow rate through the flowmeter.

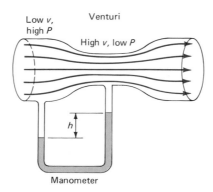

so that the manometer reading provides a measure of flow speed. Known values of the fluid density and venturi area can then be used to calculate the mass flow rate. Problem 29 explores the venturi flowmeter.

Natural examples of venturi flow range from airflow in caves to the exchange of matter in binary star systems (Fig. 15–37).

15.4
OTHER ASPECTS OF FLUID MOTION

viscosity

Our discussion of fluid motion has been limited to the special case of the steady flow of an ideal fluid. By ideal, we mean that fluid friction or **viscosity** is absent. The neglect of viscosity is often a valid approximation, especially in large-volume flows where not much of the fluid is near any boundary like a pipe wall. But when a fluid is confined to a narrow channel, and for any fluid near enough to a solid boundary, viscosity always plays an important role. The importance of viscosity depends not only on the dimensions of the flow but also on the fluid itself; water is relatively inviscid, while molasses is extremely viscous. Viscosity in a flowing fluid results in the conversion of flow kinetic energy into heat, and can also be

Fig. 15–37
This artist's conception of the binary star system Cygnus X-1 shows gas streaming off the large star and into a gaseous disk surrounding its companion black hole (left). A venturi-like constriction in the flow is provided by the effects of gravity and orbital motion. (See also Fig. 32–18.)

Fig. 15–38
(a) In an inviscid fluid, flow velocity in a pipe would be uniform. *(b)* Viscosity reduces the flow velocity, especially near the pipe walls, resulting in a nonuniform velocity profile.

(a)   (b)

important in introducing angular momentum into the flow. At a solid surface bounding a viscous fluid, viscosity results in a drag force that slows the fluid, bringing it to a complete halt right at the wall. The result is a nonuniform flow velocity profile in enclosed structures like pipes (Fig. 15–38). Viscosity is the dominant influence on fluids confined to very small spaces, as, for example, the lubricating oils separating metal surfaces in machinery. And viscosity plays an important role in stabilizing flows that would otherwise become **turbulent,** or chaotically unsteady (Fig. 15–39).

turbulent

Since we have discussed only steady flows, we have not been able to consider the fascinating subject of waves in fluids. Physically, a slight buildup of pressure in an otherwise hydrostatic fluid will propagate through the fluid to form a sound wave. Mathematically, an analysis of this situation shows that common fluids obey, at least approximately, the wave equation we introduced in the last chapter. The sound speed revealed by such a wave equation depends on the properties of the fluid. Other types of waves are possible, too. Waves at the interface of two fluids—like waves on the surface of the ocean—are one example. In electrically conducting fluids, more complicated wave modes exist, often involving the interaction of electrical, magnetic, and pressure forces.

Fig. 15–39
A jet of water quickly becomes turbulent. In a more viscous fluid like molasses, viscosity would delay the onset of turbulence.

SUMMARY

1. **Fluid** is matter in a state that is capable of deforming and flowing in response to forces. Fluids are approximated as continuous distributions of matter, and are characterized by their density and pressure:
   a. **Density** (symbol ρ) measures mass per unit volume of fluid. Liquids are nearly incompressible, meaning that they are capable only of very small changes in density. Gases, on the other hand, can undergo large density changes.
   b. **Pressure** measures the force exerted normal to a unit area by the fluid.
2. In **hydrostatic equilibrium** there is no net force on any element of a fluid.
   a. In the absence of external forces like gravity that act throughout the volume of a fluid, hydrostatic equilibrium requires that pressure be constant through-

out the fluid. With constant pressure, there is no net pressure force on any fluid element; net pressure force arises only when pressure varies with position. An increase in pressure anywhere in the fluid is transmitted throughout the fluid to maintain hydrostatic equilibrium, a fact known as **Pascal's principle.**
   b. In hydrostatic equilibrium in the presence of gravity, pressure increases going downward, so that there is a net upward pressure force to balance the gravitational force on a fluid element. In a liquid, whose density is constant, pressure increases linearly with depth:

$$P = P_0 + \rho g y, \quad \text{(liquid)}$$

where P_0 is the pressure at the liquid surface and y

the depth. In a gas at constant temperature T, pressure decreases exponentially with height h:

$$P = P_0 e^{-h/h_0},$$

where $h_0 = mg/kT$ is the **scale height,** with m the mass of a gas molecule and k Boltzmann's constant $(1.38 \times 10^{-23} \text{ J/K})$.

 c. **Buoyancy force** is an upward force on an object wholly or partly immersed in a fluid. The buoyancy force arises because the pressure force is greater at the bottom of the object than at the top. The buoyancy force is equal to the weight of the fluid displaced by the object—a fact known as **Archimedes' principle.** The net force on an object is the sum of its downward weight and the upward buoyancy force; therefore, objects float if they are less dense than the fluid and sink if they are more dense.

3. A moving fluid is characterized by giving its flow velocity at each point in space and at each instant of time. Flow velocity is conveniently represented by **streamlines,** curves traced out by individual fluid elements. Flow velocity is higher where streamlines are closer together and lower where they are farther apart. In **steady flow,** flow velocity is always the same at a given point; in **unsteady flow,** it varies with time as well as position. A simplified description of a moving fluid is provided by applying laws of conservation of mass and conservation of energy. Both laws are applied to a narrow **flow tube**—a volume bounded by a specific set of streamlines, so that fluid cannot cross the flow tube boundary. Conservation of mass results in the **continuity equation:**

$$\rho v A = \text{constant along a flow tube,}$$

where A is the tube area, which may vary with position along the tube. The quantity $\rho v A$ is the **mass flow rate,** with SI units kg/s. In a liquid, or in a gas flowing without significant density change, the continuity equation becomes

$$vA = \text{constant along a flow tube.}$$

The quantity vA is the **volume flow rate,** with SI units m³/s. With steady flow in the absence of fluid friction (viscosity) or energy addition by heat or mechanical means, energy conservation implies that the energy per unit mass of fluid is constant along a flow tube:

$$\frac{P}{\rho} + \tfrac{1}{2}v^2 + gy = \text{constant along a flow tube,}$$

where y is the vertical height of the flow tube, which may vary along the tube. For an incompressible fluid, the density ρ is constant, and the statement of energy conservation becomes **Bernoulli's equation:**

$$P + \tfrac{1}{2}\rho v^2 + \rho g h = \text{constant along a flow tube.}$$

Bernoulli's equation implies that a fluid in horizontal motion moves fastest where pressure is lowest, and vice versa. This **Bernoulli effect** is crucial in many technological and natural phenomena, including the flight of birds and aircraft.

4. Fluid friction, or **viscosity,** results in a loss of fluid energy to heat. Viscosity is especially significant in narrowly confined flows, or near flow boundaries. Viscosity exerts a stabilizing influence on flows that would otherwise become **turbulent,** or chaotically unsteady.

5. Disturbances in fluid properties can result in waves propagating through fluids at characteristic speeds that depend on the fluid.

QUESTIONS

---

1. What is the difference between hydrostatic equilibrium, steady flow, and unsteady flow?
2. Why do your ears "pop" when you drive up a mountain?
3. The cabins of commercial jet aircraft are usually pressurized to the pressure of the atmosphere at about 2 km (7000 ft) above sea level. Why do you not feel the lower pressure on your entire body?
4. Water pressure at the bottom of the ocean arises from the weight of the overlying water. Does this mean that the water exerts pressure only in the downward direction? Explain.
5. The three containers in Fig. 15–40 are filled to the same level and are open to the atmosphere. How do the pressures at the bottoms of the three containers compare?
6. Municipal water systems often include tanks or reservoirs mounted on hills or towers. Besides water storage, what function might these reservoirs have?

Fig. 15–40 Question 5

7. Why is it easier to float in the ocean than in fresh water?
8. Figure 15–41 shows a cork suspended from the bottom of a beaker of water. The beaker is mounted on a board that is rotating about a vertical axis through its far end. Explain the position of the cork as shown in the figure.
9. An ice cube is floating in a cup of water. Will the water level rise, fall, or remain the same when the cube melts?

Fig. 15–41   Question 8

10. Figure 15–42 shows a hydraulic lift in which a person pushing with one finger lifts a large truck. Is this device really possible? Is it practical? How would the fluid pressure below the truck-supporting piston compare with that below the piston on which the person is pushing?

Fig. 15–42   Hydraulic lift (Question 10); the drawing is *not* to scale.

11. A mountain stream, frothy with entrained air bubbles, presents a serious hazard to hikers who fall into it, for they may sink in the stream where they would float in calm water. Why?
12. Why are dams thicker at the bottom than at the top?
13. It is not possible to breathe through a snorkel-like tube from a depth greater than a meter or so (Fig. 15–43). Why not?

Fig. 15–43   It is not possible to breathe through a snorkel tube from significant depths (Question 13).

14. Most humans float naturally in fresh water. Yet the body of a drowning victim generally sinks, often rising several days later after bodily decomposition has set in. What might explain this sequence of floating, sinking, and floating again?
15. A helium-filled balloon stops rising long before it reaches the "top" of the atmosphere, while a cork released from the bottom of a lake rises all the way to the surface of the water. Explain the difference between these two behaviors.
16. A barge filled with steel beams overturns in a lake, spilling its cargo. Does the water level in the lake rise, fall, or remain the same?
17. Imagine a cylindrical tube filled with water and set rotating about its axis. If pieces of wood and stone are introduced into the cylinder, where will each end up? Assume the cylinder is in the weightless environment of an orbiting spacecraft.
18. When gas in steady, subsonic flow through a tube encounters a constriction, its flow speed increases. When it flows supersonically in the same situation, flow speed decreases in the constriction. What must be happening to the gas density at the constriction in the supersonic case?
19. A ball moves horizontally through the air without spinning. Where on the ball's surface is the air pressure greatest? Explain your answer in terms of Bernoulli's equation.
20. A ball supported by an upward-flowing air column (Fig. 15–44) is essentially in stable equilibrium; if the ball is displaced slightly in any direction, it returns to its original position. Explain. *Hint:* How do you expect the airflow velocity to vary with horizontal position from the center of the air column?

Fig. 15–44   Question 20

21. Under what conditions can a gas be treated as incompressible?
22. As you drive along a highway and are passed by a large truck, your car may experience a force toward the truck. Explain the origin of this force in terms of the Bernoulli effect.
23. A pump is submerged at the bottom of a 200-ft-deep well. Does it take more power to pump water to the surface when the well is full of water or nearly empty? Or doesn't it matter?

PROBLEMS

Section 15.1   *Describing Fluids*

1. Use the densities of water and mercury (1.00×10^3 kg/m^3 and 1.36×10^4 kg/m^3, respectively) to derive the conversion factors from inches of water, inches of mercury, and torr (mm of mercury) to the SI unit Pa.

2. A rubber suction cup 3.2 cm in diameter is used to suspend a hanging plant from a horizontal glass surface (Fig. 15–45). What is the maximum weight that can be so suspended (*a*) at sea level and (*b*) in Denver, where atmospheric pressure is about 0.80 atm?

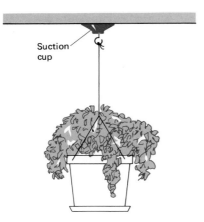

Suction cup

Fig. 15–45   Problem 2

3. 8.8 kg of compressed air is stored in a gas cylinder with a volume of 0.050 m^3. (*a*) What is the density of air in the cylinder? (*b*) How large a volume would the same gas occupy at standard atmospheric density of 1.3 kg/m^3?

4. The fuselage of a 747 jumbo jet can be considered roughly a cylinder 60 m long and 6 m in diameter. If the interior of the aircraft is pressurized at 0.75 atm, what is the force tending to tear any two half-cylinders of the aircraft apart when it is flying at an altitude of 10 km, where air pressure is about 0.25 atm? (The earliest commercial jets of the 1950's suffered structural failure from just such forces. Modern jets are better engineered to accommodate these forces.)

5. The piston of the hydraulic lift used in a garage has a diameter of 40 cm. If the piston supports a total mass of 3100 kg, what is the pressure in the hydraulic fluid supporting the piston? Assume normal atmospheric pressure of 1.0×10^5 Pa.

6. Exhaust hoods in the chemistry labs of the Middlebury College Science Center are kept on constantly for safety reasons. However, many of the ventilation fans supplying replacement air to the building have been shut down to conserve energy. The result is a lower pressure inside the building than outside. On a day when atmospheric pressure is 765.0 torr, a physics student leaving the building notices that a force of 150 N is required to open the door, which measures 90 cm × 210 cm. The door is hinged on one of its 210-cm vertical sides, and the student pulls a door handle at the opposite side. What is the pressure inside the building? *Hint:* What is the torque on the door?

7. Fully loaded, a model 240 Volvo station wagon has a mass of 1950 kg (4300 lb). If each of its four tires is inflated to a gauge pressure of 230 kPa (32 psig), and if each supports one-fourth of the car's weight, how much surface area of each tire is in contact with the road?

8. The emergency escape window over the wing of a DC-9 jetliner measures 50 cm × 90 cm. If the pressure inside the plane is 650 torr when it is flying at an altitude where atmospheric pressure is 320 torr, is there any danger that a passenger could open the emergency window while at that altitude? To answer this question, calculate the force that would be required to pull the escape window open (the window opens inward). For simplicity, assume that the window is pulled straight inward, rather than being pivoted about one edge.

9. The density of earth's atmosphere as a function of height h is given approximately by $\rho = \rho_0 e^{-h/h_0}$, where $\rho_0 = 1.3$ kg/m^3 is the density at the surface and $h_0 = 8.2$ km. Calculate the total mass of atmosphere within the first 150 km of the surface. *Hint:* Since the atmosphere is thin compared with the radius of the earth, you can treat it as a slab whose area is that of earth's surface and whose height is 150 km. But don't forget that the density varies with height! (See Problem 37 for more on the mass of the atmosphere.)

Section 15.2   *Fluids at Rest*

10. Figure 15–46 shows a schematic diagram of a hydraulic lift. The diameter of the large piston is 40 cm, and that of the small tube leaving the pump is 1.7 cm. A total load of 2800 kg (including the piston mass) is raised a distance of 2.3 m with the lift. (*a*) What volume of fluid passes through the pump? (*b*) What is

Pressurized fluid

Pump

Fluid reservoir atmospheric pressure

Fig. 15–46   Problem 10

the pressure at the pump outlet? (*c*) What is the force exerted by the pump on the fluid at its outlet? (*d*) How much work does the pump do? (*e*) If the lifting operation takes 40 s, what is the power output of the pump? In your calculations, neglect changes in pressure associated with varying depth of the hydraulic fluid. Neglect also the mass of the fluid raised in the cylinder.

11. In a properly functioning chimney, the pressure is slightly lower than the pressure in the building housing the fireplace, woodstove, or furnace connected to the chimney. This lower pressure is associated with the rise of hot, buoyant gases in the chimney, and ensures that these gases do not leak into the building. Chimney pressure, also called draft, can be measured with a water manometer, as shown in Fig. 15–47. If the difference in water levels on the two sides of the manometer tube is 0.04 in (typical of an oil furnace), by how much does the chimney pressure differ from atmospheric pressure in the building?

Fig. 15–47 Water manometer used on a chimney (Problem 11).

12. A research submarine can withstand external pressures of 7500 psi when its internal pressure is 1.0 atm. How deep can it dive?

13. Scuba diving equipment supplies the diver with air at the same pressure as the surrounding water, allowing the diver to breathe easily. But at air pressures greater than about 150 psi, nitrogen narcosis becomes a serious problem. (Nitrogen narcosis is an intoxicating effect of high-pressure nitrogen that can result in fatally abnormal behavior, like offering one's air supply to passing fish.) At what depth does nitrogen narcosis become a hazard?

14. The U-shaped tube shown in Fig. 15–48 initially contains only water, and then a quantity of oil occupying a 2.0-cm length of the tube is added, as shown. If the oil has a density 0.82 times that of water, what is the difference in heights of the liquid levels on the two sides of the tube? (Both ends of the tube are open to the atmosphere.)

15. A child attempts to drink water through a 100-cm-long straw, but finds that the water rises only 75 cm. By how much has the child reduced her mouth pressure below that of the atmosphere?

Fig. 15–48 Problem 14

16. The maximum cruising altitude of a DC-9 jetliner is 42,000 ft. Making the approximation that the atmosphere is at a uniform temperature of 280 K, what is the air pressure at this altitude (see Example 15–4)?

17. Barometric pressure in the eye of a typical hurricane is on the order of 0.91 atm (27.2 inches of mercury). How does the level of the ocean surface (assumed calm) under the eye compare with that under a distant fair-weather region where the pressure is 1.0 atm?

18. On land, the most massive concrete block you can carry has a mass of 25 kg. How massive a block could you carry under water? The density of concrete is 2.3×10^3 kg/m^3.

19. A partially full beer bottle with an interior diameter of 52 mm is floating upright in water, as shown in Fig. 15–49. A beer drinker takes a swig and replaces the bottle in the water, where it now floats 28 mm higher than before. How much beer did the beer drinker drink? Assume the density of beer is essentially that of water.

Fig. 15–49 Beer bottle before and after (Problem 19).

20. A glass beaker has a mass of 25 g and measures 10 cm high by 4.0 cm in diameter. Empty, it floats in water with one-third of its height submerged. How many 15-g rocks can be placed in the beaker before it sinks?

21. A typical supertanker has a mass of 2.0×10^8 kg and carries twice that amount of oil. If 9.0 m of the ship is submerged when it is empty, what is the minimum water depth needed for it to navigate when full? Assume the sides of the ship are vertical.

22. A balloon contains gas of density ρ_g, and is to lift a payload of mass *M*, not including the mass of the gas. Show that the minimum mass *m* of gas required is

$$m = \frac{M\rho_g}{\rho_a - \rho_g},$$

where ρ_a is the density of the atmosphere. Evaluate your result for a helium balloon carrying two people and a basket with total mass 230 kg. The density of helium is about one-seventh that of air.

23. A ship's hull has a V-shaped cross section, as shown in Fig. 15–50. The ship has vertical height h_0 from keel to deck, and a total length ℓ perpendicular to the plane of Fig. 15–50. Empty, the hull extends underwater to a depth h_1, as shown. Obtain an expression for the maximum load the ship can carry, in terms of the density ρ of water and the quantities h_0, h_1, ℓ, and θ shown in Fig. 15–50.

Fig. 15–50   Problem 23

Fig. 15–51   Problem 27

Fig. 15–52   Problem 29

Section 15.3   *Fluid Dynamics*

24. A fluid is flowing steadily, roughly from left to right. At the left it is flowing rapidly; then it slows down, and finally speeds up again. Its final speed at the right is not as fast as its initial speed at the left. Sketch some streamlines associated with this flow.

25. Show that pressure has the units of energy density and that the quantity P/ρ has the units of energy per unit mass.

26. A fire hose 10 cm in diameter delivers water at the rate of 15 kg/s. The hose terminates in a nozzle 2.5 cm in diameter. What are the flow speeds (a) in the hose and (b) in the nozzle?

27. A can of height h is full of water. At what distance y from the bottom of the can should a small hole be cut so that initially the water travels the same distance y horizontally as it does vertically? (See Fig. 15–51.)

28. The water in a garden hose is at a gauge pressure of 20 psig, and is moving at negligible speed. The hose terminates in a sprinkler consisting of many small holes. What is the maximum height reached by the jets of water emerging from these holes?

29. The venturi flowmeter shown in Fig. 15–52 is used to measure the flow rate of water in a solar collector system. The flowmeter is inserted in a pipe with internal diameter of $\frac{3}{4}$ in; at the venturi of the flowmeter, the diameter is reduced to $\frac{1}{4}$ in. The manometer tube contains oil with density 0.82 times that of water. If the difference in oil levels between the two sides of the

manometer tube is 0.55 in, what is the flow rate in gallons/minute?

30. You turn on a bathroom sink faucet and notice that the water column has shrunk to about half its original diameter about 15 cm below the faucet outlet. What is the approximate outflow speed? *Hint:* See Example 15–9.

31. A drinking straw 20 cm long and 3.0 mm in diameter stands vertically in a cup of juice 8.0 cm in diameter. 6.5 cm of the straw extends above the surface of the juice. A child sucks on the straw, and the level of juice in the glass begins dropping at the rate of 0.2 cm/s. (a) By how much does the pressure in the child's mouth differ from atmospheric pressure? (b) What is the greatest distance above the liquid surface from which the child could drink, assuming the same mouth pressure? (Note: You are concerned here only with the *initial* rate, before the juice level has dropped appreciably, but after the straw has filled and approximately steady flow has been established.) The density of the juice is approximately that of water.

32. A can of height h and cross-sectional area A_0 is initially full of water. A small hole of area $A_1 \ll A_0$ is cut in the bottom of the can. Find an expression for the time it takes all the water to drain from the can. *Hint:* Call the water depth y, and use the continuity equation to write the rate dy/dt at which the depth decreases in terms of the outflow velocity at the hole. Then integrate.

33. While a car is driving at a steady 55 mph on a level road, the pressure inside the venturi of its carburetor is 4% below atmospheric pressure. (a) What is the speed of the air in the venturi? (b) Gasoline enters the venturi through a hole (the "jet") 0.90 mm in diameter, coming from a bowl within the carburetor that is exposed to atmospheric pressure and that is not significantly higher than the jet. How many miles per gallon of gasoline can the car drive under these conditions? The density of gasoline is 0.67 g/cm^3. See Example 15–10.

34. If the pressure just inside the tip of the firehose nozzle in Problem 26 is 10% greater than atmospheric pressure, what are the speed and diameter of the water column just outside the nozzle tip?

35. Figure 15–53 shows a simplified diagram of a Pitot tube, a device used for measuring flow speeds of fluids not confined in pipes. The Pitot tube arrangement shown here is used to measure airspeed on the underside of an aircraft wing. The device consists of two small tubes, A opening at right angles to the flow and B opening parallel to the flow. The other ends of both tubes are connected to an instrument—for instance, a manometer—that measures the pressure difference between them. Fluid at the entrance of tube A moves past with its normal velocity and pressure. But there is no flow through either tube, so that fluid stops at the entrance of tube B. Bernoulli's equation shows that the pressure in tube B is therefore higher. Show that the flow speed is given by

$$v = \sqrt{\frac{2\Delta P}{\rho}},$$

where ΔP is the pressure difference between the two tubes, and ρ is the density of the moving fluid.

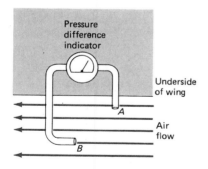

Fig. 15–53 Pitot tube mounted on the underside of an aircraft wing (Problem 35).

Supplementary Problems

36. How massive an object can be supported by a 2-in-diameter suction cup mounted on a vertical wall, if the coefficient of friction between the cup and wall is 0.72? Assume normal atmospheric pressure.

37. Use the information given in Problem 9 to calculate the height below which half of earth's atmosphere lies. Assume a uniform temperature of 280 K, as in Example 15–4. You can consider that the atmosphere ends at about 150 km, or that it extends forever. Why doesn't it make any significant difference which you assume?

38. The sun's atmosphere, or corona, extends far enough from the surface that the variation in gravity with height must be considered in accurate descriptions of the atmosphere. Show that the pressure of a uniform-temperature atmosphere surrounding a spherical star or planet of mass M and radius R is given by

$$P = P_0 \exp\left[\frac{GMm}{kT}\left(\frac{1}{r} - \frac{1}{R}\right)\right],$$

where G is the constant of universal gravitation, r the distance from the sun's center, m the mass of a gas molecule, k Boltzmann's constant (see Section 15.2), and P_0 the pressure at the base of the atmosphere. Using the approximation $e^x \approx 1 + x$ for $|x| \ll 1$, show that this result reduces to Equation 15–5 when $r - R \ll R$ (that is, close to the solar surface). Why does this make sense? (Note: $\exp(x)$ means e^x.)

39. A pencil is weighted at one end so that it floats vertically with length ℓ submerged. The pencil is pushed vertically downward (without being totally submerged), then released. Show that it undergoes simple harmonic motion with period $T = 2\pi\sqrt{\ell/g}$.

16

TEMPERATURE AND HEAT

Fig. 16–1
A bullet travelling supersonically through the heated air above a candle flame. Flame, shock wave, and distortion of the shock by the heated air are all thermal effects.

In the next four chapters, we turn our attention to thermodynamics—the physics of heat, temperature, and related phenomena. Our own bodies provide a qualitative sense of what it means for things to be "hot" or "cold." In our study of thermodynamics, we will quantify this sense and explore the behavior of matter under different thermal conditions (Fig. 16–1). And we will learn something our sense of temperature could never tell us— namely, how thermal phenomena reflect the laws of mechanics operating on a microscopic scale.

16.1
MACROSCOPIC AND MICROSCOPIC DESCRIPTIONS

Some physical quantities—for example, mass—apply equally to microscopic objects like atoms and molecules and to macroscopic objects like cars, gas cylinders, and planets. But other quantities that we use to describe macroscopic objects—for example, temperature and pressure—have no meaning on a microscopic scale. We speak of the temperature and pressure of air, but it makes no sense to ask about the temperature or pressure of an individual air molecule. The study of temperature, heat, and related mac-

thermodynamics

roscopic quantities comprises the branch of physics called **thermodynamics.**

The thermodynamic behavior of matter is determined by the behavior of its constituent atoms and molecules in response to the laws of mechan-

statistical mechanics

ics. **Statistical mechanics** is the branch of physics that relates the macroscopic description of matter to the underlying microscopic processes. Historically, thermodynamics was developed before the atomic theory of matter was well established. The subsequent explanation of thermodynamics in terms of statistical mechanics—the mechanics of atoms and molecules—was a triumph for classical physics. At the same time, the few ther-

404

modynamic phenomena that could not be explained successfully with classical physics helped point the way to the development of the quantum theory. In our study of thermal phenomena, we will interweave the macroscopic and microscopic descriptions to provide the fullest understanding of both viewpoints.

16.2
TEMPERATURE AND THERMODYNAMIC EQUILIBRIUM

Take a bottle of soda from the refrigerator and leave it on the kitchen counter. Eventually, it reaches room temperature. Come back much later and it's still at room temperature. No scientific definition of temperature is involved here. Our own sense of touch is enough to tell us that the bottle of soda is somehow different than when we first removed it from the refrigerator, and that after a long time it is no longer changing. We generalize from this simple experiment to say that when two systems—in this case the bottle and the surrounding air—are allowed to remain in contact until no further change occurs in any macroscopic property of either, then the *thermodynamic equilibrium*   two are in **thermodynamic equilibrium.**

The concept of thermodynamic equilibrium does not require a prior notion of temperature. To determine whether two systems are in equilibrium, we can consider *any* macroscopic properties. Typical properties include length, volume, pressure, electrical resistance, and fluid viscosity as well as temperature. If any macroscopic property changes when two systems are placed in contact, then they were not originally in equilibrium. If no macroscopic changes occur, then the systems were and are in equilibrium.

thermal contact   When we speak of placing systems in contact, we mean specifically **thermal contact.** Two systems are in thermal contact if heating one of them results in macroscopic changes in the other. For example, if we place two metal cups of water in physical contact, and heat one cup with a flame, the water in both cups gets hotter. In this case, the cups are in thermal contact. If we were to separate our cups by a layer of styrofoam, then heating one would have little effect on the other. In this case, the two systems are **ther-**
thermally insulated   **mally insulated.**

Using the concept of thermodynamic equilibrium, we can now define quantitatively what we mean by temperature. We first state what it means for two systems to be at the same temperature:

systems at the same   Two systems are at the same temperature if they are in thermody-
temperature   namic equilibrium.

Conversely, two systems that are not in thermodynamic equilibrium are at different temperatures.

To define temperature more quantitatively, we associate numerical values of temperature with values of some macroscopic property of a system. We might associate temperature with the length of an iron rod so that increasing length corresponds to higher temperature. Or we could use the pressure of gas in a fixed-volume container, assigning increasing values of temperature to increasing pressures.

What makes such a temperature scale useful is a simple experimental fact. Consider two systems A and C that are each in thermal contact with a third system, B, but not with each other (Fig. 16–2a). We wait until system A is in thermodynamic equilibrium with B, and C with B. If we then bring systems A and C into thermal contact (Fig. 16–2b), we find that no further changes occur, showing that A and C had already reached thermodynamic equilibrium with each other. This basic fact—that two systems in thermodynamic equilibrium with a third system are also in equilibrium with each other—is often called the **zeroth law of thermodynamics.** Rephrased in terms of temperature, the zeroth law states that if system A is at the same temperature as system B, and B is at the same temperature as system C, then systems A and C are at the same temperature. The experimental fact embodied in the zeroth law therefore allows us to define temperature in a consistent way that applies equally to all systems.

zeroth law of
thermodynamics

16.3
MEASURING TEMPERATURE

A **thermometer** is a system with a conveniently observed macroscopic property that changes with temperature. In principle, any such system will do, and we can use any monotonic function of the macroscopic variable as our measure of temperature. We might choose an iron rod, whose length increases with temperature and thus serves as a measure of temperature. The length of a mercury column serves as the temperature indicator in a standard mercury thermometer. An approach often used in thermostats involves two different metals bonded together in a thin strip. When heated, the two metals expand at different rates, causing the strip to bend (Fig. 16–3). This bending can turn an indicating needle or open electrical contacts that, for example, control a furnace. Electrical resistance has long been used in scientific and engineering work to measure temperature, and, with the development of microelectronics, is rapidly replacing the mercury thermometer in medical and other applications (Fig. 16–4). Another, and very accurate, electrically based thermometer is the thermocouple, a junction of two different metals that generates a small electrical voltage that depends on the temperature of the junction.

thermometer

To use different thermometers quantitatively, we must make them all consistent with each other. We can get consistent results by choosing a standard thermometer that works over the widest possible range, and then relating actual values of temperature to physical processes that always occur at the same temperature. One class of thermometers—gas thermometers—fits our requirement at all but the most extreme temperatures. Gas thermometers use as their indication of temperature either (1) the volume of a gas kept at constant pressure, or (2) the pressure of a gas kept at constant volume. Figure 16–5 shows a constant-volume gas thermometer, widely used in scientific work or for calibrating other thermometers.

The temperature measured by a constant-volume gas thermometer is taken to be a linear function of the gas pressure. We need two points to define a linear function. The Kelvin scale, which is part of the SI system of

Fig. 16–2
(a) A and C are in thermal contact with B, but not with each other. (b) When they are brought together, A and C are found to be in thermodynamic equilibrium.

Fig. 16–3
The coil shown at the center of this thermostat is a bimetallic strip whose configuration changes with temperature, actuating a switch that controls a furnace.

Fig. 16–4
An electronic digital fever thermometer.

Fig. 16–5
A constant-volume gas thermometer.
As the gas pressure increases with
temperature, the closed tube at right is
raised to keep the mercury at the
reference point R, thus maintaining
constant gas volume. The height
difference h is then a measure of gas
pressure. Temperature is taken to be
directly proportional to h.

measurement, defines the zero of temperature as zero gas pressure in a constant-volume gas thermometer. The second point is established by the **triple point** of water—the unique temperature at which water can exist with solid, liquid, and gas simultaneously in equilibrium.* At the triple point, the temperature is, by definition, 273.16 K. A plot of temperature versus gas pressure for a constant-volume gas thermometer then looks like Fig. 16–6. The linear relation shown in Fig. 16–6 is given algebraically by

$$T = 273.16 \, \frac{P}{P_3}, \tag{16–1}$$

where P_3 is the gas thermometer pressure at the triple point.[†]

The Kelvin temperature scale, with its zero point where a gas thermometer would have zero pressure, is a fundamental scale for dealing with basic thermodynamic phenomena. Since a gas cannot have negative pressure, the zero of the Kelvin scale represents an absolute lower limit of temperature, and is called absolute zero. For this reason the Kelvin scale is also called the absolute temperature scale. We will explore further this sense of "absoluteness," and the meaning of absolute zero, in Chapter 19. Figure 16–7 shows some important physical situations on the Kelvin scale.

Other scales in common use include the Celsius (°C), Fahrenheit (°F), and Rankine (°R) scales, although the latter two are now largely limited to the United States. One degree Celsius represents the same temperature difference as one kelvin (K), but the zero of the Celsius scale occurs at 273.15 K, so that

$$T_C = T - 273.15, \tag{16–2}$$

where T_C is the Celsius temperature and T the absolute temperature in kelvins. Historically, the Celsius scale was defined before the absolute scale, and was chosen so that the melting point of ice at standard atmospheric pressure—the ice point—is at exactly 0°C, while the boiling point of water at standard atmospheric pressure—the steam point—is at exactly 100°C. The triple point of water occurs at 0.01°C, which accounts for the 273.15 difference between the Kelvin and Celsius scales as well as for the difference of 0.01 in the constants of Equations 16–1 and 16–2.

The Fahrenheit scale, which is part of the British system of units, is defined with the ice point at 32°F and the steam point at 212°F. As a result, the relation between the Fahrenheit and Celsius scales is

$$T_F = \tfrac{9}{5}T_C + 32. \tag{16–3}$$

A fourth scale, often used in engineering work in the United States, is the Rankine scale. A Rankine degree is the same size as a Fahrenheit degree, but the zero of the Rankine scale coincides with the zero of the Kelvin scale, so that

$$T_R = \tfrac{9}{5}T = T_F + 459.67. \tag{16–4}$$

Figure 16–8 summarizes the four temperature scales in relation to some important physical processes.

---

*The triple point is discussed in detail in the next chapter.
†This pressure depends on the particular thermometer, and should not be confused with the 610 Pa pressure of the water at its triple point.

Fig. 16–6
Kelvin temperature scale defined using constant-volume gas thermometer.

Example 16–1
Temperature Scales

What is normal body temperature (98.6°F) on the Celsius, Kelvin, and Rankine scales? If you have a fever of 101.6°F, by how much has your temperature risen on each of these scales?

Solution

Solving Equation 16–3 for T_C gives

$$T_C = \tfrac{5}{9}(T_F - 32) = \tfrac{5}{9}(98.6 - 32.0) = 37.0°C.$$

Then Equation 16–2 gives the Kelvin temperature:

$$T = T_C + 273.2 = 310.2 \text{ K.}$$

Finally, from Equation 16–4,

$$T_R = T_F + 459.7 = 558.3°R.$$

A degree Rankine and a degree Fahrenheit are the same size, so that a fever of 101.6°F represents a 3.0° rise on either scale. A kelvin and a degree Celsius are the same size, and are both larger than a degree Fahrenheit by the factor $\tfrac{9}{5}$, so that a rise of 3.0°F is equivalent to a rise of

$$\frac{3.0}{9/5} = 1.7°C = 1.7 \text{ K.}$$

16.4
TEMPERATURE AND HEAT

A lighted match is hot enough to burn your finger, yet it would not provide much heat in a cold room. A large vat of hot water—although much cooler than the match—would do a better job of heating the room. This example illustrates our intuitive sense of the difference between temperature and heat: heat measures an *amount* of "something," while temperature measures the *intensity* of that "something."

caloric   What is that "something"? Before the early 1800's, heat itself was thought to be a substance, called **caloric,** that was transferred from a hot body to a cooler one in much the same way that fluid flows from a region of higher pressure to one of lower pressure. The theory of caloric was invoked to explain a wide variety of thermal phenomena, including heat

Fig. 16–7
Some physical processes on the Kelvin scale. Chart is logarithmic to allow display of a wide temperature range.

Fig. 16–8
Relations among the four temperature scales.

transfer and the thermal expansion of materials. Temperature changes associated with mechanical friction were explained by saying that small pieces of material shaved off in the frictional process released large amounts of caloric.

In the late 1700's, Benjamin Thompson (1753–1814) made observations refuting the caloric theory. Thompson, an American who was hired to direct the Bavarian arsenal and who later became Count Rumford of Bavaria, supervised the boring of cannon. That heat was involved in this process was well known, and water was needed to cool both the cannon and the boring tool. But Thompson noticed that the heating was not associated with the production of metal chips that could release caloric, for a dull tool that did little drilling actually caused more heating. It appeared that caloric could be produced in endless quantities in such a frictional process. This observation was difficult to reconcile with the notion of caloric as a conserved physical substance. Thompson suggested instead that the heating was associated with the mechanical work done on the drill bit.

In the half-century following Thompson's observations, the caloric theory gradually faded in popularity as a series of experiments confirmed the association between heating and the expenditure of mechanical energy. These experiments culminated in the work of the British brewer and physicist James Joule (1818–1889), who explored the relation between heat and mechanical, electrical, and chemical energy. In 1843, Joule quantified the relation between heat and energy, bringing thermal phenomena under the powerful conservation-of-energy law. In recognition of this major synthesis in physics, the SI unit of energy is named after Joule. In Chapter 18 we will explore in detail the relation between heat and energy.

Our everyday experience of heat is nearly always associated with the movement of energy from one body to another. A hot stove burner heats a pot of soup, or a furnace heats water that, in turn, transfers heat to a house. We rarely make statements about the actual amount of "heat" in an object—we are concerned instead that the temperature of the object be appropriate. We want the furnace to transfer energy to our house in the winter, and are satisfied when the house reaches a certain temperature, not when it contains a certain amount of "heat." Our scientific definition of heat reflects this natural inclination to think of heat as energy in transit:

heat   **Heat** is energy that is transferred from one object to another because of temperature differences alone.

internal energy

Strictly speaking, the word heat refers only to energy in transit. Once heat has been transferred to an object, we say that the **internal energy** of the object has increased, but not that it contains more heat. This distinction reflects the fact that other processes than heating—such as transfer of mechanical or electrical energy—can also change the temperature of an object. As a result, heat alone does not uniquely determine the energy contained in a given object. In subsequent chapters, we will explore further this distinction between heat and internal energy.

calorie

We can determine the amount of heat transferred to an object by noting the change in its temperature. Before the equivalence of heat and energy was well established, heat was measured in **calories** (cal). One calorie was defined as the amount of heat needed to raise the temperature of one gram of water from 14.5°C to 15.5°C. Through the work of Joule, we now know that one calorie is equivalent to about 4.18 J of energy. Several slightly different definitions of the calorie have been established, based on different experimental conditions for determining the equivalence. In this book, we use the so-called thermochemical calorie, defined as exactly 4.184 J. The "calorie" used in describing the energy content of foods is actually a kilocalorie. In the British system of units, still widely used in engineering work in the United States, the unit of heat is the **British thermal unit** (Btu). One Btu is the amount of heat needed to raise the temperature of one pound of water from 63°F to 64°F, and is equal to 1055 J.

British thermal unit

Example 16–2
The Calorie

A typical fast-food hamburger contains "300 calories," which means 300 kcal. If the hamburger were consumed by a 50-kg person, and all its energy content released as heat, by how much would the person's body temperature rise? Assume that the person is made essentially of water, and is insulated so that heat from the hamburger cannot be released to the environment.

Solution

Each kcal can raise one kg of water by one degree Celsius. The hamburger releases 300 kcal, but these must be distributed among 50 kg, so that each kg gets 300/50 or 6.0 kcal, and therefore the temperature would rise by 6.0°C. (That this rise doesn't occur is a tribute to our bodies' ability to store excess energy as fat, as well as to the fact that we use food energy to do mechanical work and to keep our bodies warmer than our surroundings.)

16.5
HEAT CAPACITY AND SPECIFIC HEAT

Matter usually gets hotter when we transfer heat to it. How much hotter? That depends on what kind of matter we have and on how much of it there is. We already know the answer for water: if we have 1.0 g of water, and transfer 4.184 J or 1.0 cal of heat to it, then its temperature will rise approximately 1.0°C. The amount of heat needed to produce a unit temperature rise in a unit mass of a substance is the **specific heat** of that substance.

specific heat

Water's specific heat is 1.0 cal/g·°C, or 4184 J/kg·K. (Degrees Celsius and kelvins are interchangeable in describing specific heats, for we are concerned only with temperature *changes*.) More precisely, the specific heat of a substance is defined as the ratio of the heat ΔQ per unit mass required to produce a temperature change ΔT, in the limit of arbitrarily small ΔT:

$$c = \frac{1}{m} \lim_{\Delta T \to 0} \frac{\Delta Q}{\Delta T} = \frac{1}{m} \frac{dQ}{dT}. \tag{16-5}$$

heat capacity

The amount of heat needed to cause a unit temperature rise in a *particular* piece of matter of mass m is called the **heat capacity, C:**

$$C = \frac{dQ}{dT} = mc. \tag{16-6}$$

For many substances under normal conditions, specific heat is nearly independent of temperature, so we can find the total amount of heat needed to bring an object from temperature T_1 to T_2 by multiplying its heat capacity by the temperature difference:

$$Q = C(T_2 - T_1) = mc(T_2 - T_1). \tag{16-7}$$

When the specific heat itself depends on temperature, we write $c(T)$ and consider a series of infinitesimal temperature rises dT, with heat required for each given by $dQ = mc(T)dT$. To find the total heat required to raise the temperature from T_1 and T_2, we then integrate over the temperature interval:

$$Q = \int_{T_1}^{T_2} mc \; dT. \tag{16-8}$$

Table 16–1 lists the specific heats of common substances. Because the British thermal unit is defined as the amount of heat needed to raise one pound of water by one degree Fahrenheit, the specific heat in cal/g·°C is numerically equal to its value in Btu/lb·°F.

TABLE 16–1

Specific Heats (temperature range 0°C to 100°C except as noted)

Substance	Specific Heat (J/kg·K)	Specific Heat (cal/g·°C, kcal/kg·°C, Btu/lb·°F)
Aluminum	900	0.215
Copper	386	0.0923
Iron	447	0.107
Glass	753	0.18
Mercury	140	0.033
Steel	502	0.12
Stone (granite)	840	0.20
Water:		
Liquid	4184	1.00
Ice, −10°C	2050	0.49
Wood	1400	0.33

Example 16–3

Heat Capacity and Specific Heat

A water heater holds 150 kg of water. How much energy does it take to bring the water temperature from 18°C to 50°C? If the energy is supplied by a 5.0-kW electric heating element, how long must the electricity be on?

Solution

The heat required is given by Equation 16–7:

$$Q = mc(T_2 - T_1) = (150 \text{ kg})(4184 \text{ J/kg·K})(50°C - 18°C) = 2.0 \times 10^7 \text{ J}.$$

Note that we are justified in mixing K and °C here because a temperature *difference* is the same whether expressed in degrees Celsius or in kelvins.

The heating element supplies heat at the rate of 5.0 kW, or 5.0×10^3 J/s, so that it must be on for a time t given by

$$t = \frac{2.0 \times 10^7 \text{ J}}{5.0 \times 10^3 \text{ J/s}} = 4000 \text{ s,}$$

or a little over an hour. (At 10¢/kWh, we would pay 56¢ for this energy.)

Example 16–4

A Temperature-Dependent Specific Heat

At very low temperatures, the specific heat of a solid is approximately proportional to the cube of the absolute temperature. For example, the specific heat of copper in the range from a few K to about 50 K is given very nearly by

$$c = 31 \left(\frac{T}{343 \text{ K}} \right)^3 \text{ J/g·K.}$$

How much heat is required to raise the temperature of a 40-g sample of copper from 10 K to 25 K?

Solution

Because the specific heat is temperature-dependent, we must use the integral in Equation 16–8 to calculate the heat:

$$Q = \int_{T_1}^{T_2} mc \, dT$$

$$= \frac{(40 \text{ g})(31 \text{ J/g·K})}{(343 \text{ K})^3} \int_{10\text{K}}^{25\text{K}} T^3 dT = (3.1 \times 10^{-5} \text{ J/K}^4) \frac{T^4}{4} \Big|_{10\text{K}}^{25\text{K}}$$

$$= (3.1 \times 10^{-5} \text{ J/K}^4) \frac{(25 \text{ K})^4 - (10 \text{ K})^4}{4} = 2.9 \text{ J.}$$

In contrast, it takes nearly 100 times as much energy—230 J—to raise the same 40-g piece of copper from 300 to 315 K, as you can confirm by applying Equation 16–7 and the data from Table 16–1.

When two objects at different temperatures are placed in thermal contact, energy is transferred from the hotter object to the cooler one until thermodynamic equilibrium is reached. If the two objects are thermally insulated from their surroundings, then all the energy leaving the hotter object is transferred to the cooler one. Mathematically, this statement may be written

$$m_1 c_1 \Delta T_1 + m_2 c_2 \Delta T_2 = 0, \tag{16–9}$$

where mc is the heat capacity of an object of mass m and specific heat c, and ΔT is the temperature change (final temperature minus initial temperature) of that object. For the hotter object, ΔT is negative, so that the two terms in Equation 16–9 have opposite signs, and can therefore sum to zero. One term represents the outflow of heat from the hotter object, the other inflow into the cooler object.

Example 16–5
The Equilibrium Temperature

An aluminum frying pan with a mass of 1.5 kg is heated on a stove to 180°C, then plunged into a sink containing 8.0 kg of water at room temperature (20°C). Assuming that none of the water boils, and that no heat is lost to the surroundings, what is the equilibrium temperature of the water and pan?

Solution

We write Equation 16–9 in the form

$$m_p c_p (T - T_p) + m_w c_w (T - T_w) = 0,$$

where the subscripts p and w refer to the pan and the water, and where the equilibrium temperature T is the same for both. Solving for T and using the appropriate numerical values then gives

$$
\begin{aligned}
T &= \frac{m_p c_p T_p + m_w c_w T_w}{m_p c_p + m_w c_w} \\[2mm]
&= \frac{(1.5 \text{ kg})(0.215 \text{ kcal/kg·°C})(180°C) + (8.0 \text{ kg})(1.0 \text{ kcal/kg·°C})(20°C)}{(1.5 \text{ kg})(0.215 \text{ kcal/kg·°C}) + (8.0 \text{ kg})(1.0 \text{ kcal/kg·°C})} \\[2mm]
&= 26°C.
\end{aligned}
$$

16.6
HEAT TRANSFER*

So far we have said nothing about the mechanisms whereby energy is transferred between two objects. We have simply assumed that somehow we had the means either to facilitate or to inhibit this transfer. In engineering problems involving heat, we need to know precisely how to achieve a desired degree of energy transfer. In scientific work, knowledge of energy-transfer mechanisms helps us understand a system's thermal behavior.

Three heat-transfer mechanisms commonly occur. These are conduction, a process involving direct physical contact; convection, involving energy transfer by the bulk flow of a fluid; and radiation, or energy transfer by electromagnetic waves. In a given situation, one of the three may dominate, or we may have to take all three into account.

---

*Strictly speaking, the term "heat transfer" is redundant, for heat is energy being transferred from one object to another. But the term is in such widespread use that we will speak of heat transfer when we really mean energy transfer that occurs because of a temperature difference.

Conduction

conduction

Conduction is the transfer of heat through direct physical contact. Microscopically, conduction occurs because molecules in a hotter region transfer energy to those of an adjacent cooler region by colliding with them. The effect of these collisions in a given material is quantified in the material's **thermal conductivity,** k, whose SI units are W/m·K. Common materials exhibit a broad range of thermal conductivities, from about 400 W/m·K for copper—a good conductor of heat—to 0.029 W/m·K for styrofoam, a good thermal insulator.

thermal conductivity

Figure 16–9 shows a slab of material of thickness Δx and cross-sectional area A. Suppose one face of the material is held at temperature T and the other at $T + \Delta T$. Intuitively, we might expect the rate of heat flow through the slab to increase with increasing area A and to decrease with increasing thickness Δx. Of course, the heat-flow rate must also depend on the thermal conductivity of the material. We expect further that heat will flow from the hotter to the cooler face of the slab, with the heat-flow rate dependent also on the temperature difference between the two faces. Our intuition is borne out experimentally: for a rectangular slab of material, the heat-flow rate dQ/dt is given by

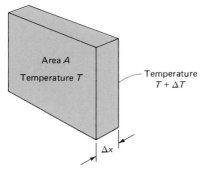

Fig. 16–9
Slab geometry for Equation 16–10.

$$\frac{dQ}{dt} = -kA\frac{\Delta T}{\Delta x}. \tag{16–10}$$

Since dQ/dt is a rate of energy flow, its units are joules/second, or watts. The minus sign in Equation 16–10 shows that heat transfer is opposite to the direction of increasing temperature, that is, from hotter to cooler. Equation 16–10 is strictly correct only when the temperature varies uniformly from one surface to the other, and when the areas of the two surfaces are equal. Because the thermal conductivity k may vary with temperature, or because we may be interested in heat transfer in other geometries (such as through the insulation around a pipe), we often write Equation 16–10 in the limit of arbitrarily small Δx. In this limit we have

$$\frac{dQ}{dt} = -kA\frac{dT}{dx}. \qquad \text{(heat conduction)} \tag{16–11}$$

Many practical problems involve rectangular geometry and an insignificant variation of k with temperature; in those cases we can use Equation 16–10. Table 16–2 lists thermal conductivities of some common materials. Both SI and British units are listed, as the latter are commonly used in calculations involving heat loss in buildings.

Table 16–1 is remarkable for the range of thermal conductivities it contains. Metals are exceptionally good conductors of heat as well as of electricity: they contain free electrons that can move quickly, carrying internal energy and electric charge from one region to another. Gases, on the other hand, are poor conductors because the wide spacing of their molecules makes for infrequent transfers of energy. Good heat insulators, like fiberglass and styrofoam, owe their insulating properties not to their chemical composition but to their physical structure, which traps small volumes of air or other gas.

TABLE 16–2
Thermal Conductivities

Material	k (W/m·K)	k (Btu·in/h·ft²·°F)
Air	0.026	0.18
Aluminum	237	1644
Concrete (varies with mix)	1	7
Copper	401	2780
Fiberglass	0.042	0.29
Glass	0.7–0.9	5–6
Goose down	0.043	0.30
Helium	0.14	0.97
Iron	80.4	558
Steel	46	319
Styrofoam	0.029	0.20
Water	0.61	4.2
Wood (pine)	0.11	0.78

Example 16–6
Heat Conduction

A lake with a flat bottom and steep sides has a surface area of 1.5 km² and is 8.0 m deep. On a summer day, the surface water is at a temperature of 30°C, while the bottom water is at 4.0°C. What is the rate of heat conduction through the lake? Assume that the temperature declines uniformly from surface to bottom.

Solution

Our lake resembles the slab of Fig. 16–9, so that Equation 16–10 applies. Taking the thermal conductivity of water from Table 16–2, we have

$$\frac{dQ}{dt} = -kA\frac{\Delta T}{\Delta x} = -(0.61 \text{ W/m·K})(1.5 \times 10^6 \text{ m}^2)\frac{30°C - 4.0°C}{8.0 \text{ m}} = -3.0 \times 10^6 \text{ W}.$$

The minus sign indicates that heat flows in the direction of decreasing temperature, or downward into the lake. (Unless the surface and bottom temperatures are held fixed, this heat flow will eventually bring the entire lake to a single temperature.)

Example 16–7
Heat Conduction in Cylindrical Geometry

A 10-m-long copper pipe of diameter 2.0 cm carries hot water at 95°C. The pipe passes through an unheated space where the temperature is −20°C. The pipe is insulated with a 1.5-cm-thick layer of styrofoam. What is the rate of heat loss from the pipe?

Solution

Here we do not have rectangular geometry, so we cannot apply Equation 16–10. However, if we consider a very thin cylindrical layer within the insulation (Fig. 16–10), then the areas of the inner and outer surfaces of the layer must be nearly equal. Although the geometry is not rectangular, we could imagine unrolling the thin layer into a rectangular sheet, to make the situation resemble Fig. 16–9. Let dr be the thickness of the layer, and dT the temperature difference across it. The area of either side of the layer is approximately $2\pi rL$, where r is the distance to the layer from the center of the pipe, and L is the length of the pipe. Then Equation 16–11 becomes

$$\frac{dQ}{dt} = -kA\frac{dT}{dr} = -k2\pi rL\frac{dT}{dr}. \qquad (16\text{–}12)$$

Insulation

Fig. 16–10
Cross section of cylindrical, insulated pipe, showing thin layer of insulation of thickness dr used in setting up integration.

We don't know what dQ/dt is—that's what we're trying to determine—but we do know that the heat flowing through our thin layer also flows through any other thin layer of the insulation, since there are no sources of heat in the insulation. Thus the rate at which heat leaves the copper pipe is equal to the rate at which heat flows across any layer of the insulation, and that in turn is equal to the rate of heat loss at the top surface of the insulation.

We can rewrite Equation 16–12 in the form

$$\frac{dQ}{dt}\frac{dr}{r} = -2\pi kL\ dT, \tag{16–13}$$

where our argument of the previous paragraph tells us that the heat-loss rate dQ/dt is a constant, independent of r. We need to relate this loss rate to the temperature difference across the insulation. We do so by integrating Equation 16–13 across the insulation. Letting R_1 be the inner radius of the insulation (equivalently, the pipe's radius), and R_2 the outer radius of the insulation, we have

$$\frac{dQ}{dt}\int_{R_1}^{R_2}\frac{dr}{r} = -2\pi kL\int_{T_1}^{T_2} dT.$$

Here we have pulled constants out of the integral, and have called the temperatures at the inner and outer edges of the insulation T_1 and T_2, respectively. Evaluating the integrals gives

$$\frac{dQ}{dt}\ln r\Big|_{R_1}^{R_2} = -2\pi kL\ T\Big|_{T_1}^{T_2},$$

or

$$\frac{dQ}{dt}\ln\left(\frac{R_2}{R_1}\right) = -2\pi kL(T_2 - T_1).$$

Solving for the heat-loss rate dQ/dt then gives

$$\frac{dQ}{dt} = \frac{2\pi kL(T_1 - T_2)}{\ln(R_2/R_1)}. \tag{16–14}$$

Our particular pipe has a radius of 1.0 cm and 1.5-cm-thick insulation, so that the outer radius of the insulation is $R_2 = 2.5$ cm. Obtaining k for styrofoam from Table 16–2, and inserting values for L, T_1, and T_2, we have

$$\frac{dQ}{dt} = \frac{2\pi(0.029\ \text{W/m·°C})(10\ \text{m})[95°C - (-20°C)]}{\ln(2.5/1.0)} = 230\ \text{W}.$$

Knowing the heat-loss rate, we could integrate Equation 16–13 from the inner edge of the insulation to an arbitrary position r within the insulation, and from this obtain an expression for the temperature as a function of position in the insulation (see Problem 35). Heat-loss calculations in spherical geometry are handled in a similar manner (see Problem 38).

Frequently we have a situation in which heat flows through several different materials. A typical example is the wall of a building, which may contain wood, plaster, fiberglass insulation, and other materials. Figure 16–11 shows such a composite structure, involving two slabs of different materials with a temperature T_1 on one side of the composite and T_3 on the other. The two slabs may have different thicknesses Δx_1 and Δx_2, but they have the same area. The heat-flow rate dQ/dt through each slab must be the same, since energy does not accumulate or disappear at the interface between the two. We then have

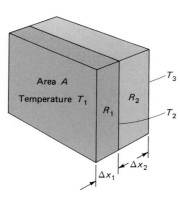

Fig. 16–11
A composite slab.

$$\frac{dQ}{dt} = -k_1 A \frac{T_2 - T_1}{\Delta x_1} = -k_2 A \frac{T_3 - T_2}{\Delta x_2}, \tag{16-15}$$

where k_1 and k_2 are the thermal conductivities of the two materials, and T_2 is the temperature at the interface. We would like to express the heatflow rate in terms of the surface temperatures T_1 and T_3 alone, without having to worry about the intermediate temperature T_2. To do so, it is convenient to define the **thermal resistance,** R, of each slab:

thermal resistance

$$R = \frac{\Delta x}{kA}. \tag{16-16}$$

The SI units of R are K/W. Unlike the thermal conductivity, k, which is a property of a *material*, R is a property of a *particular piece* of material, reflecting both its conductivity and its geometry. In terms of thermal resistance, Equation 16–15 becomes

$$\frac{dQ}{dt} = -\frac{T_2 - T_1}{R_1} = -\frac{T_3 - T_2}{R_2},$$

so that

$$R_1 \frac{dQ}{dt} = T_1 - T_2$$

and

$$R_2 \frac{dQ}{dt} = T_2 - T_3.$$

Adding these two equations gives

$$(R_1 + R_2) \frac{dQ}{dt} = T_1 - T_2 + T_2 - T_3 = T_1 - T_3,$$

or

$$\frac{dQ}{dt} = \frac{T_1 - T_3}{R_1 + R_2}. \tag{16-17}$$

Equation 16–17 shows that the composite slab acts like a single slab whose thermal resistance is the sum of the resistances of the two slabs that compose it. We could easily extend this treatment to show that the thermal resistances of three or more slabs add when the slabs are arranged so that the same heat flows through all of them.

In the United States, the insulating properties of building materials are usually described in terms of the **R-factor,** $\mathcal{R}$, which is the thermal resistance per unit area:

R-factor

$$\mathcal{R} = \frac{R}{A} = \frac{\Delta x}{k}. \tag{16-18}$$

The units of $\mathcal{R}$, although rarely stated, are $\text{ft}^2 \cdot {}^\circ\text{F} \cdot \text{h/Btu}$. This means that $\mathcal{R}$-19 fiberglass insulation, now in common use as a wall insulation in the northern part of the United States, has a heat loss of $\frac{1}{19}$ Btu per hour for each square foot of insulation for each degree Fahrenheit temperature difference across the insulation.

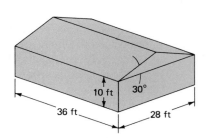

Fig. 16–12
House of Example 16–8.

Example 16–8
Building Insulation and Heat Loss

The rectangular house of Fig. 16–12 measures 36 ft long, 28 ft wide, and has 10-ft-high side walls. The peaked roof is pitched at a 30° angle, and consists of a $\frac{1}{2}$-in plaster ceiling ($k=3.0$ Btu·in/h·ft²·°F for plaster), $9\frac{1}{2}$-in fiberglass insulation ($\mathcal{R}=30$), $\frac{1}{2}$-in plywood ($\mathcal{R}=0.65$), and $\frac{1}{2}$-in cedar shingles ($\mathcal{R}=0.55$). The walls have similar construction, except that they contain only $3\frac{1}{2}$ in of fiberglass insulation ($\mathcal{R}=11$). The average outdoor temperature during a winter month is 20°F, and the house is maintained at 70°F. If the house is heated by an oil furnace that produces 100,000 Btu of heat per gallon of oil, and if oil costs 83¢/gallon, how much does it cost to heat the house for the month? Ignore heat losses through the floor and windows (even though these may be substantial).

Solution

We must first calculate the R-factors for the composite walls and roof. We are given $\mathcal{R}$ for all but the plaster; from Equation 16–18 we have

$$\mathcal{R}_{\text{plaster}} = \frac{\Delta x}{k} = \frac{\frac{1}{2} \text{ in}}{3.0 \text{ Btu·in/h·ft}^2\cdot\text{°F}} = 0.17.$$

Then the R-factors for the walls and roof are

$$\mathcal{R}_{\text{wall}} = \mathcal{R}_{\text{plaster}} + \mathcal{R}_{\text{fiberglass}} + \mathcal{R}_{\text{plywood}} + \mathcal{R}_{\text{shingles}}$$
$$= 0.17 + 11 + 0.65 + 0.55 = 12,$$

and

$$\mathcal{R}_{\text{roof}} = 0.17 + 30 + 0.65 + 0.55 = 31.$$

The total wall area is

$$A_{\text{wall}} = (28 \text{ ft} + 36 \text{ ft} + 28 \text{ ft} + 36 \text{ ft})(10 \text{ ft}) + (28 \text{ ft})(7 \text{ ft}) = 1480 \text{ ft}^2,$$

where the second term in the sum is the area of the two triangular portions of the side walls, whose height is (14 ft)(sin30°), or 7 ft. These $\mathcal{R}$-12 walls lose $\frac{1}{12}$ Btu/h/ft²/°F, and the temperature difference across them is 50°F, so that the total heat-loss rate through the walls is

$$\left(\frac{dQ}{dt}\right)_{\text{walls}} = (\tfrac{1}{12} \text{ Btu/h/ft}^2/\text{°F})(1480 \text{ ft}^2)(50\text{°F}) = 6170 \text{ Btu/h}.$$

The area of the pitched roof is increased over that of a flat roof by the factor 1/cos30°, so that the heat-loss rate through the roof is

$$\left(\frac{dQ}{dt}\right)_{\text{roof}} = (\tfrac{1}{30} \text{ Btu/h/ft}^2/\text{°F})\frac{(36 \text{ ft})(28 \text{ ft})}{\cos 30°}(50\text{°F}) = 1940 \text{ Btu/h}.$$

The total heat-loss rate is then

$$\left(\frac{dQ}{dt}\right) = 6170 \text{ Btu/h} + 1940 \text{ Btu/h} = 8110 \text{ Btu/h}.$$

In a month, this results in a total heat loss of

$$Q = (8110 \text{ Btu/h})(30 \text{ days/month})(24 \text{ h/day}) = 5.8 \times 10^6 \text{ Btu}.$$

With 10^5 Btu per gallon of oil burned, this requires 59 gallons of oil, at a cost of (58)($0.83) = $48.

This estimate is low; losses through windows and doors are substantial, and cold air infiltration results in additional heat loss. A more accurate analysis would also consider heat lost to the ground and solar energy gained through the windows. Problem 31 provides a more realistic look at heat loss in this house.

Fig. 16–13
Convection between two plates at
different temperatures.

Fig. 16–14
Top view of convection cells in a
laboratory experiment.

Convection

convection

Fig. 16–15
Granulation of the sun's surface shown
in this photograph is caused by large-
scale convection cells that carry energy
from the solar interior to the surface.

Convection is the transfer of heat by the bulk motion of a fluid. Convection occurs in the presence of gravity because a fluid usually becomes less dense when heated, so that warmer fluid rises. Figure 16–13 shows two plates held at different temperatures, with fluid between them. If the lower plate is hotter, heat is transferred to the bottom fluid, which becomes less dense and rises. When the heated fluid reaches the top plate, it transfers heat to the plate, thus cooling and again sinking to the bottom. A steady fluid flow results, in which fluid rises, cools, and sinks again, in the process transferring heat from the lower to the upper plate, as suggested in Fig. 16–13. Often the flow pattern acquires a striking regularity. Figure 16–14 shows photographs of convection between two plates in the laboratory, while Fig. 16–15 shows remarkably similar patterns associated with convective motions in the sun.

Convection is an important heat-transfer mechanism in a wide range of technological and natural environments. When you heat water on a stove, convection carries heat from the bottom of the pan to the top. Houses usually rely on convection from heat sources near floor level to circulate warm air throughout a room. Insulating materials like fiberglass and goose down trap air and thereby inhibit convection that would otherwise cause excessive heat loss from our houses and our bodies. Convection associated with solar heating of the earth's surface drives the vast air movements that establish our overall climate. Violent convective movements, such as those in thunderstorms (Fig. 16–16), are associated with localized temperature differences. On a much longer time scale, convection in the earth's mantle, brought about because of earth's hot inner core, is responsible for continental drift (Fig. 16–17). Convection plays a crucial role in many astrophysical processes, including the generation of magnetic fields in stars and planets.

As with conduction, the convective heat-loss rate often is approximately proportional to the temperature difference. But the calculation of convective heat loss is complicated because of the need to understand the details of the associated fluid motion. The study of convection processes is an important research area in many fields of contemporary science and engineering.

Fig. 16–16
Convection cells in a thunderstorm.
Violent up- and downdrafts may exceed
100 km/h.

Fig. 16–17
Slow convection in the earth's mantle is responsible for continental drift. Continents *A* and *B* are on a collision course, while ocean between them is closing as crust from *A* is pulled into the mantle.

Radiation

radiation

When we turn an electric stove burner to "high," it glows a brilliant red-orange color. By virtue of its high temperature, the burner is emitting visible light. Set on "low," the burner does not appear to glow, but we can still tell it is hot by holding a hand near it. Again, the hot burner is emitting something that tells us it is hot. In both cases, that something is **radiation.** In later chapters, we will investigate the nature and origin of radiation in terms of electromagnetic phenomena and atomic theory; our "radiation" is really called "electromagnetic radiation." For now, we simply assert that heated objects lose energy by emitting radiation. Our stove-burner example suggests the amount of radiation emitted increases very rapidly with tem-

luminosity
Stefan-Boltzmann law

perature. Experiment confirms this: the rate of energy loss by radiation— often called the **luminosity,** *L*—is given by the **Stefan-Boltzmann law:**

$$L = e\sigma AT^4, \tag{16-19}$$

Stefan-Boltzmann constant

where *L* is measured in watts, *A* is the surface area of the emitting material, *T* its absolute temperature, and σ a universal constant called the **Stefan-Boltzmann constant.** (In SI, $\sigma = 5.67 \times 10^{-8}$ W/m²·K⁴.)

emissivity

The quantity *e* is called the **emissivity** of the material and measures its effectiveness at radiating energy. The value of *e* ranges between 0 and 1. Emissivity is closely related to a material's ability to absorb radiation; for this reason, materials with emissivity close to 1 appear dark, while light-

black body

colored materials have low emissivity. An object with *e* = 1 is called a **black body** because it absorbs all light and other radiation, and therefore appears black at normal temperatures. High emissivity and correspondingly high absorption is the reason why a dark-colored car gets hotter in bright sunlight, and why solar collector plates are painted black.

Materials not only emit radiation; they also absorb it. In thermodynamic equilibrium, the temperature of an object is the same as that of its surroundings. Therefore, the object must emit the same amount of radiation as it absorbs; otherwise it would gain or lose energy and its temperature would change. This statement must be true at *any* temperature, so in equilibrium the rate of absorption of radiation must also be given by Equation 16–19. When an object is not in equilibrium, there is a net transfer of energy between the object and its surroundings, given by the difference between its emission and absorption.

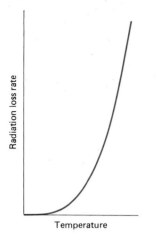

Fig. 16–18
Radiation loss as a function of temperature.

The rate of energy transfer by radiation depends on the fourth power of the temperature. Because of this very steep dependence on temperature (Fig. 16–18), radiation is generally unimportant at low temperatures, but dominates at high temperatures. Houses lose relatively little heat through radiation, while much of the energy transferred from a woodburning stove is through radiation. A hot stove burner with nothing on it glows red and loses energy predominantly by radiation; with a pan on the burner, it stays cooler and loses heat predominantly through conduction to the pan. (From the pan, heat may be lost through convection in a boiling liquid.) Very hot objects, like the surface of the sun or the filament of a light bulb, lose most of their energy through radiation. When an object is surrounded by vacuum, so that conduction and convection cannot occur, then all the energy loss is by radiation.

Example 16–9
The Surface Temperature of the Sun

The sun radiates energy at the rate $L = 3.9 \times 10^{26}$ W, and its radius is 7.0×10^8 m. Assuming the sun to be a black body (emissivity $= 1$), what is the surface temperature of the sun?

Solution

The radiated power is given by the Stefan-Boltzmann law, Equation 16–19. Solving this equation for T and using $4\pi R^2$ for the surface area of the sun gives

$$T = \left(\frac{L}{4\pi R^2 \sigma}\right)^{1/4} = \left[\frac{3.9 \times 10^{26} \text{ W}}{4\pi (7.0 \times 10^8 \text{ m})^2 (5.7 \times 10^{-8} \text{ W/m}^2 \cdot \text{K}^4)}\right]^{1/4} = 5.8 \times 10^3 \text{ K},$$

in agreement with observational measurements.

16.7
THERMAL ENERGY BALANCE

thermal energy balance

When an object is in thermodynamic equilibrium with its surroundings, its temperature remains constant. But an object could also maintain a constant temperature, different from that of its surroundings, by balancing energy gain with energy loss. We call the latter situation **thermal energy balance.** A house in the winter provides a good example. If the house is unheated, it will come to equilibrium at the outdoor temperature. If the house is heated, it will lose heat because of the temperature difference between itself and its environment, but this loss will be balanced by energy input from a furnace, wood stove, solar collector, electricity, or other heat source.

The principle of thermal energy balance is a powerful one, used throughout physics and engineering to determine the temperatures of objects under different conditions. It is also used to calculate the output of heat sources needed to achieve desired temperatures. If we supply heat to an object at a constant rate, its temperature will at first rise. But as it rises, so does the heat-loss rate. Eventually the object reaches a temperature where the heat-loss rate is equal to the rate of heat input. At that point, the object is in thermal energy balance, and its temperature remains constant.

Example 16–10
Thermal Energy Balance

A poorly insulated electric water heater loses heat at the rate of 40 W for each degree Celsius difference between the water temperature and the ambient temperature outside the tank. The heater is located in a basement where the ambient temperature is 15°C. The tank is heated by a 2.5-kW electric heating element. Assuming that no water is drawn from the tank, and that the heating element operates continuously, what is the water temperature in the tank?

Solution

Heat is supplied to the water at the rate $(dQ/dt)_{\text{gain}} = 2.5$ kW; it is lost at a rate given by

$$\left(\frac{dQ}{dt}\right)_{\text{loss}} = (40 \text{ W/°C})(\Delta T),$$

where ΔT is the temperature difference between the water and its surroundings. In thermal energy balance, the heat loss and gain are equal, so that

$$(40 \text{ W/°C})(\Delta T) = 2.5 \text{ kW},$$

or

$$\Delta T = \frac{2.5 \text{ kW}}{40 \text{ W/°C}} = 63°C.$$

With the ambient temperature at 15°C, the water temperature is 15°C + 63°C = 78°C.

Example 16–11
The Temperature of the Earth

The intensity, S, of sunlight at the earth's orbit is about 1.4 kW/m². If the earth had no atmosphere and behaved like a black body, what would be its average temperature? Assume that the entire planet is at the same temperature.*

Solution

Surrounded by the vacuum of space, earth exchanges energy with its environment through radiation.† From Fig. 16–19, we see that our planet presents an effective area of πR_e^2 to the nearly parallel rays of the incident sunlight. But the entire $4\pi R_e^2$ of earth's surface area radiates energy back into space. Thus the condition of energy balance becomes

$$\pi R_e^2 S = \sigma 4\pi R_e^2 T^4,$$

where we have set $e = 1$ for a black body. Then

$$T = \left(\frac{S}{4\sigma}\right)^{1/4} = \left(\frac{1.4 \times 10^3 \text{ W/m}^2}{(4)(5.7 \times 10^{-8} \text{ W/m}^2 \cdot \text{K}^4)}\right)^{1/4} = 280 \text{ K} = 7°C.$$

---

*The fairly rapid rotation of the earth, combined with the effects of atmospheric and oceanic circulation, moderates the extremes of temperature that would otherwise occur between the night and day sides of the planet.

†The earth gains a very small amount of energy from the tides—actually gravitational energy from the earth-moon system—as well as from the decay of radioactive elements in the planet's interior. And a very small fraction of the incident solar energy is not returned to space, but is stored in fossil fuels. Nevertheless, solar energy provides 99.98 per cent of the earth's energy input, and the earth is in nearly perfect energy balance. This nearly perfect balance accounts for our looming shortage of fossil fuels, as we release in a few decades energy that took hundreds of millions of years to accumulate.

Fig. 16–19
Earth presents an effective area πR_e^2 to incident solar energy, but radiates from its entire surface area.

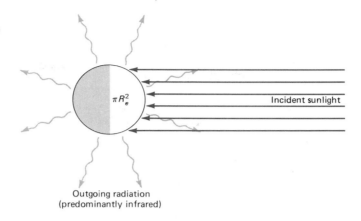

Although this result is only slightly below the 286 K average temperature of our planet, we have ignored several factors that have a substantial influence on that temperature. First, the atmosphere both reflects and absorbs some incident sunlight, so that the peak intensity at the surface is about 30 per cent lower than in space. Second, earth is not a black body. Third, carbon dioxide in the atmosphere, although transparent to the incident visible light, is relatively opaque to the infrared radiation emitted by the earth. The first effect tends to decrease the temperature, while the third increases it because a higher surface temperature is required to ensure that enough radiation escapes the atmosphere.

A change of only a few degrees in the average temperature might bring major changes in climate. The injection of particulate matter into the atmosphere could result in a decrease in sunlight intensity at the surface, thereby lowering the temperature. Air pollution from industrial processes and volcanic eruptions could have this effect. Substantial temperature changes might also occur in the aftermath of a nuclear war (Fig. 16–20). Although the original drastic predictions of a "nuclear winter" have been moderated by more sophisticated computer models, active research on this topic continues in several countries. At the other extreme, burning

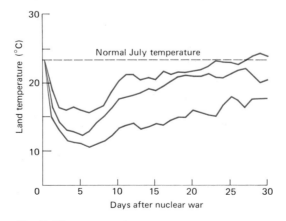

Fig. 16–20
The results of a 1986 study at the National Center for Atmospheric Research predict a maximum temperature drop of 12°C in the aftermath of a nuclear war. The three curves correspond to different amounts of smoke released into the atmosphere, including 18 billion kg (top), 54 billion kg (middle), and 160 billion kg (bottom).

fossil fuels release carbon dioxide that traps infrared radiation, leading to a temperature increase. Such climatic disasters are a major concern of atmospheric scientists, and are explored further in Problems 36 and 37.

Example 16–12
A Solar Greenhouse

Fig. 16–21
Greenhouse for Example 16–12.

Figure 16–21 shows a solar-heated greenhouse. The south-facing diagonal wall is made entirely of double-pane glass ($\mathcal{R} = 1.8$), while the other walls are opaque and have R-factors of 30. Although the glass walls are transparent to sunlight, they are essentially opaque to infrared radiation emitted by the warm greenhouse—just as the earth's atmosphere is transparent to visible light but somewhat opaque to infrared radiation. On a typical winter day, the intensity of sunlight on the glass wall amounts to 120 W/m² when averaged over the 24-hour period. If the greenhouse is maintained at 80°F, what is the lowest the daily average outdoor temperature can get before it is necessary to turn on a backup heat source? The greenhouse is built on a heavy concrete slab with enough heat capacity to store at least a day's energy, so that fluctuations in temperature and sunlight throughout the day are unimportant as long as appropriate daily averages are maintained. The slab is heavily insulated on the bottom, so that heat loss to the ground is negligible.

Solution

We first calculate the heat-loss rate for the greenhouse. The total area of insulated wall is

$$A_w = (10 \text{ ft})(20 \text{ ft}) + 2[\tfrac{1}{2}(10 \text{ ft})^2] = 300 \text{ ft}^2,$$

so that the heat-loss rate through these $\mathcal{R}$-30 walls is

$$\left(\frac{dQ}{dt}\right)_w = \frac{A_w \Delta T}{\mathcal{R}_w} = \frac{300\Delta T}{30} = 10\Delta T \text{ Btu/h·°F}.$$

Similarly, the glass area is

$$A_g = (20 \text{ ft})(10\sqrt{2} \text{ ft}) = 280 \text{ ft}^2,$$

so that the heat-loss rate through the glass is

$$\left(\frac{dQ}{dt}\right)_g = \frac{A_g \Delta T}{\mathcal{R}_g} = \frac{280\Delta T}{1.8} = 160\Delta T \text{ Btu/h·°F}.$$

If the greenhouse is to be in thermal energy balance, the total heat-loss rate of $170\Delta T$ Btu/h·°F must be balanced by the energy gained from the sun. The average solar input is $S = 120$ W/m², or

$$S = (120 \text{ W/m}^2)[3.4 \text{ (Btu/h)/W}](0.093 \text{ m}^2/\text{ft}^2) = 38 \text{ Btu/h·ft}^2,$$

where we have obtained the conversion factors from Appendix D. Then the total solar gain on the 280-ft² glass is

$$(280 \text{ ft}^2)(38 \text{ Btu/h·ft}^2) = 11 \times 10^3 \text{ Btu/h}.$$

Equating the heat loss to the solar gain gives

$$170\Delta T \text{ Btu/h·°F} = 11 \times 10^3 \text{ Btu/h},$$

so that

$$\Delta T = \frac{11 \times 10^3 \text{ Btu/h}}{170 \text{ Btu/h·°F}} = 65°F.$$

With a greenhouse temperature of 80°F, the outdoor temperature can drop as low as 80°F − 65°F = 15°F before a backup heat source is needed.

What happens when a system is not in energy balance? Then it gains or loses heat at a rate given by the difference between the heat input and the heat output. A house, for example, is subject to varying outdoor temperatures, energy input from sunlight, and internal heat supply as the furnace cycles on and off. Energy input to the earth itself varies because of the ellipticity of the planet's orbit, changes in ice and cloud cover, changes in atmospheric and oceanic composition, and possibly very slight changes in the sun's power output. Although the analysis of such time-varying situations is conceptually straightforward, researchers are often hampered by imperfect knowledge of physical processes. For example, we simply do not know how much of the carbon dioxide released into the atmosphere ends up dissolved in the oceans, so that we cannot yet predict the climatic effects of carbon dioxide emission. Even when all factors are known, the complicated functional forms of the varying quantities mandate computer calculations in all but the simplest cases. Example 16–13 and Problems 39 to 41 explore such time-varying situations.

Example 16–13

The Approach to Equilibrium

In deep space, far from any star or planet, an astronaut releases a spherical container filled with 100 kg of water at 300 K. The container has a radius of 29 cm, negligible mass, and is painted black so that its emissivity is 1. Obtain an expression for the temperature of the water as a function of time while it remains in the liquid state, and determine how long it takes to reach the freezing point. The amount of radiation incident on the sphere in deep space is so low (corresponding to a temperature of only 3 K) that you can ignore it for the temperatures of interest here.

Solution

The sphere radiates energy at a rate given by the Stefan-Boltzmann law (Equation 16–19):

$$L = \sigma A T^4,$$

where we have set the emissivity to 1. This energy loss is associated with a temperature drop given by differentiating Equation 16–7:

$$L = -\frac{dQ}{dt} = -mc\,\frac{dT}{dt},$$

where the minus sign indicates a heat loss. Combining these two equations and solving for dT/dt gives

$$\frac{dT}{dt} = -\frac{\sigma A}{mc}T^4.$$

This is a differential equation for T; multiplying through by $T^{-4}dt$ gives

$$T^{-4}dT = -\frac{\sigma A}{mc}dt.$$

To find the temperature as a function of time, we integrate from the initial temperature T_0 and time $t_0 = 0$ to an arbitrary temperature T and time t:

$$\int_{T_0}^{T} T^{-4} dT = -\int_0^t \frac{\sigma A}{mc} dt,$$

or

$$\frac{T^{-3} - T_0^{-3}}{-3} = -\frac{\sigma A}{mc} t.$$

Solving for T gives our desired expression for temperature as a function of time:

$$T = \left(\frac{3\sigma A}{mc} t + T_0^{-3} \right)^{-1/3}.$$

To find when the water reaches the freezing point, we can solve instead for the time t:

$$t = \frac{mc}{3\sigma A} \left(\frac{1}{T^3} - \frac{1}{T_0^3} \right).$$

Using $m = 100$ kg, $c = 4184$ J/kg·K, and noting that $A = 4\pi r^2$, the drop from $T_0 = 300$ K to the freezing point at 273 K then takes 2.8×10^4 s, or about 8 hours.

SUMMARY

1. A system consisting of many atoms or molecules may be described from either a **microscopic** or a **macroscopic** viewpoint. A microscopic description is concerned with the properties of the individual particles—their masses, positions, and velocities. A macroscopic description involves general properties—like temperature, pressure, and volume—that are not associated directly with the individual particles. **Statistical mechanics** is the branch of physics dealing with the microscopic description of many-particle systems, while **thermodynamics** takes the macroscopic viewpoint.

2. Two systems are in **thermodynamic equilibrium** if, when they are brought into contact, none of the macroscopic properties of either system changes. Two systems in thermodynamic equilibrium have the same **temperature.**

3. The **zeroth law of thermodynamics** states that two systems in equilibrium with a third system are in equilibrium with each other. The zeroth law allows us to establish temperature scales.

4. A **thermometer** is a system one of whose macroscopic properties is used as an indicator of temperature. When a thermometer is in thermodynamic equilibrium with another system, then the temperature indicated by the thermometer is equal to the temperature of the other system. Although there are many practical thermometers and several different temperature scales in use, most laboratory standards are set using **gas thermometers,** either the constant-volume or constant-

pressure type. The **kelvin,** or **absolute,** temperature scale is used in the SI system of units.

5. **Heat** is energy being transferred between two objects as a result of a temperature difference alone.

6. The **specific heat** of a material is the ratio of heat to temperature change for a unit mass of the material:

$$c = \frac{1}{m} \frac{dQ}{dT}.$$

The **heat capacity** of a given object is the ratio of heat to temperature change for that object:

$$C = mc = \frac{dQ}{dT}.$$

7. **Heat transfer** can occur through any of three distinct physical mechanisms:

a. **Conduction** is the direct transfer of heat through physical contact between two objects. Microscopically, conduction involves energy exchange through molecular collisions. The rate of conduction depends on the **thermal conductivity** k of the material through which heat flows, on its thickness Δx and area A, and on the temperature difference ΔT across the material:

$$\frac{dQ}{dt} = -kA \frac{\Delta T}{\Delta x}.$$

We often describe heat conduction through a particular piece of material in terms of its **thermal resis-**

tance, $R = \Delta x/kA$, or its **R-factor**, $\mathscr{R} = \Delta x/k$. The resistances or R-factors of a composite material are obtained by adding the individual R's or $\mathscr{R}$'s.

b. **Convection** is the transfer of heat through the bulk motion of material, as when heated air rises and transfers its energy to the ceiling of a room. Convection is difficult to describe quantitatively, but is an important process in the laboratory, in engineering situations, and in nature.

c. **Radiation** is electromagnetic energy that can be transferred across empty space. The net rate at which energy is lost from a hot object of area A through radiation is given by

$$L = e\sigma AT^4,$$

where T is the temperature of the object. The emissivity e is a number between 0 and 1 that describes the effectiveness of the object as an emitter of radiation, while σ is the universal **Stefan-Boltzmann constant**, $\sigma = 5.67 \times 10^{-8}$ W/m²·K⁴.

8. **Thermal energy balance** exists when an object gains and loses energy at the same rate. The temperature of an object in thermal energy balance remains constant as long as the rates of heat loss and gain are constant. If one of these changes, the temperature will rise or fall until heat loss again balances heat gain.

QUESTIONS

1. Two identical-looking physical systems are in the same macroscopic state. Must they be in the same microscopic state? Explain.

2. Two identical-looking physical systems are in the same microscopic state. Must they be in the same macroscopic state? Explain.

3. Given that there are three mechanisms of heat transfer, how would you construct a good insulator?

4. Does a thermometer measure its own temperature, or the temperature of its surroundings? Explain.

5. To get an accurate body temperature measurement, you must hold a standard glass-and-mercury fever thermometer under your tongue for about 3 minutes. Some of the new electronic fever thermometers require less than a minute. What might account for the difference?

6. Why is it better to define temperature scales in terms of a physical state, like the triple point of water, rather than by having an official, standard thermometer stored at the International Bureau of Weights and Measures?

7. Compare the relative sizes of the kelvin, the degree Celsius, the degree Fahrenheit, and the degree Rankine.

8. Does a vacuum have temperature? Explain.

9. If you put a thermometer in direct sunlight, what do you measure? The air temperature? The temperature of the sun? Some other temperature?

10. Why does the temperature in a stone building usually vary less than in a wooden building?

11. Why do large bodies of water exert a temperature-moderating effect on their surroundings?

12. A Thermos bottle (Fig. 16–22) consists of an evacuated, double-wall glass liner. The glass is coated with a thin layer of aluminum. How does a Thermos bottle work?

13. Stainless-steel cookware often has a layer of aluminum or copper embedded in the bottom. Why?

14. What method of energy transfer is involved in baking? In broiling?

Fig. 16–22   Cross section of a Thermos bottle (Question 12).

15. Solar collectors often have a copper absorber surface coated with a black paint, whose emissivity is nearly 1 for visible and infrared radiation. Better results can be achieved, though, with a "selective surface," whose emissivity is high for visible light but low for the infrared radiation associated with lower temperatures than the sun's. Why is this?

16. Glass and fiberglass are made from the same material, yet have dramatically different thermal conductivities. How can this be?

17. A thin layer of glass does not offer much resistance to heat conduction. Yet double-glazed windows provide substantial energy savings. Why?

18. The insulating value of a double-glazed window actually decreases if the spacing is made too great. Can you think of a reason why this might be?

19. To keep your hands warm while skiing, you should wear mittens instead of gloves. Why?

20. Since earth is exposed to solar radiation, why is earth not at the same temperature as the sun?

21. On a clear night, a solar collector will often cool well below the ambient air temperature. Why? Why does this not happen on a cloudy night?

22. Is earth in perfect energy balance? If not, why not?

PROBLEMS

Section 16.1   *Macroscopic and Microscopic Descriptions*

1. Consider a simple system consisting of three shelves, one at ground level, one 0.50 m above the ground, and one 1.0 m above the ground. The system also includes three masses A, B, and C. A and B are each 1.0 kg and C is 2.0 kg. A microscopic state of the system is specified by giving the location (shelf) of each mass. (There may be more than one mass on a shelf.) A macroscopic state of the system is specified by giving the total gravitational potential energy of the system. How many microscopic states correspond to the macroscopic state with energy 20 J? (Take $g = 10$ m/s^2.)

2. The macroscopic state of a carton capable of holding a half-dozen eggs is specified by giving the number of eggs in the carton. The microscopic state is specified by telling where each egg is in the carton. How many microscopic states correspond to the macroscopic state of a full carton?

Section 16.2   *Temperature and Thermodynamic Equilibrium*

3. Systems A and B are in thermodynamic equilibrium. The two systems are then separated by an insulating wall, and system C, not initially in equilibrium with B, is brought into contact with B and allowed to reach equilibrium. Can you reach any conclusion about the final temperatures of A and C?

4. If system A is not in thermodynamic equilibrium with system B, and B is not in equilibrium with C, can you draw any conclusions about the temperatures of the three systems?

Section 16.3   *Measuring Temperature*

5. A constant-volume gas thermometer is filled with air whose pressure is 1.01×10^5 Pa (1.00 atm) at the normal melting point of ice. Assuming ideal behavior, what would the pressure be at (a) the normal boiling point of water? (b) the normal boiling point of oxygen (90.2 K)? (c) the normal boiling point of mercury (630 K)?

6. A thermistor is a device whose electrical resistance, R, decreases exponentially with increasing temperature:

$$R = R_0 e^{-\alpha(T - T_0)},$$

where α is a constant and T_0 is some reference temperature at which the resistance is R_0. The unit of electrical resistance is the ohm (Ω). A particular thermistor has a resistance of 1.1×10^5 Ω at the melting point of ice and 9.0×10^3 Ω at the boiling point of water. What is its resistance at normal human body temperature?

7. At what temperature(s), if any, do the following temperature scales coincide? (a) Fahrenheit and Celsius (b) Celsius and Rankine, (c) Celsius and Kelvin, (d) Kelvin and Rankine, (e) Rankine and Fahrenheit.

8. The normal boiling point of nitrogen is 77 K. Express this temperature in Celsius, Fahrenheit, and Rankine, keeping only two significant figures in your answers.

9. The temperature at the center of the sun is about 16×10^6 K. Express this temperature in Celsius, Fahrenheit, and Rankine, keeping only two significant figures in your answers. Why is this problem easier than the preceding one?

10. The temperature of a constant-pressure gas thermometer is directly proportional to the gas volume. If the volume is 1.00 L at the triple point of water (0.01°C), what is it at the normal boiling point of water?

Sections 16.4–16.5   *Temperature and Heat, Heat Capacity and Specific Heat*

11. The average human diet contains about 2000 kcal per day. If all this food energy is used by the body in producing heat and mechanical energy, what is the average power output of the body?

12. A circular lake 1.0 km in diameter is 10 m deep. Solar energy is incident on the lake at an average rate of 200 W/m^2. Assuming that all this energy is absorbed by the lake, and that the lake does not exchange heat with its immediate surroundings (an unrealistic assumption!), how long will it take for the lake's temperature to rise from 10°C to 20°C?

13. 1700 J of heat is required to raise the temperature of 180 g of a substance by 15°C. (a) What is the heat capacity of this piece of the substance? (b) What is the specific heat of the substance?

14. How much heat is required to raise the temperature of an 800-g copper pan from 15°C to 90°C if (a) the pan is empty? (b) the pan contains 1.0 kg of water? (c) the pan contains 4.0 kg of mercury?

15. 100 g of water and 100 g of another substance from Table 16–1 are initially at 20°C. Both are placed over identical flames that transfer heat to the substances at the same rate. At the end of 1 minute, the water is at 32°C and the other substance at 76°C. (a) What is the other substance? (b) What is the heating rate?

16. Two neighbors return from Florida one winter to find their houses at a frigid 15°F. Each house has a furnace that produces heat at the rate of 100,000 Btu/h. One house is made of stone and weighs 75 tons. The other is made of wood and weighs 15 tons. How long does it take to bring each house to a comfortable 65°F? Neglect heat loss that occurs during the heating process, and assume that the houses are heavily insulated on the outside of the wall structure, so that the entire wall mass must reach 65°F.

17. A child complains that her cocoa is too hot. The temperature of the cocoa is 90°C. Her father pours 2 oz of milk at 3°C into the 6 oz of cocoa. Assuming that milk and cocoa have the same specific heat as water, what is the new temperature of the cocoa?

18. A piece of copper at 300°C is dropped into 1.0 kg of water at 20°C. If the equilibrium temperature is 25°C, what is the mass of the copper?

19. Two 1000-kg cars collide head-on at 90 km/h. If all their kinetic energy ends up as heat, what is the increase in temperature of the wrecks? The specific heat of the cars is essentially that of iron.

20. A 1500-kg car moving at 40 km/h is brought to a sudden stop. What is the increase in temperature of the car's four steel brake disks, each of mass 5.0 kg? Assume that all the kinetic energy of the car goes into heating the brake disks, and that no heat is lost to the environment or to other parts of the car.

21. A thermometer whose mass is 83.0 g is used to measure the temperature of a 150-g sample of water. The thermometer has a specific heat of 0.190 cal/g·°C, and it reads 20.0°C before being immersed in the water. The temperature of the water is 60.0°C. If the thermometer is perfectly accurate, what will it read after it comes to equilibrium with the water?

Section 16.6–16.7   Heat Transfer and Thermal Energy Balance

22. How thick a concrete wall would be required in order to give the same insulating value as $3\frac{1}{2}$ inches of fiberglass?

23. Compute the R-factors for 1-inch thicknesses of air, concrete, fiberglass, glass, styrofoam, and wood.

24. An iron rod is 50 cm long and 2.0 cm in diameter. One end of the rod is in contact with boiling water and the other end is in contact with ice water. If the rod is well insulated so that there is no heat lost out the sides, what is the rate at which the rod transfers heat from the boiling water to the ice water?

25. What is the R-factor for a wall consisting of $\frac{1}{4}$-in pine paneling, $\mathcal{R}$-11 fiberglass insulation, $\frac{3}{4}$-in pine sheathing, and 2.0-mm aluminum siding?

26. A house measures 28 ft × 28 ft × 9 ft high and has $\mathcal{R} = 30$ for its roof and $\mathcal{R} = 20$ for its walls. The house next door has the same height, the same wall and roof construction, and the same square shape, but twice the floor area. Compare the heating bills in the two houses, assuming they are maintained at the same temperature. Neglect heat loss through the floor.

27. A house is insulated so that its total heat loss is 700 Btu/h·°F. On an evening when the outdoor temperature is 55°F, the owner of the house throws a party and 40 people come. If the average power output of the human body is 100 W, and if there are no other heat sources on in the house, what will the house temperature be during the party?

28. The surface area of an electric clothes iron is 300 cm². If the surface temperature of the iron is 450 K and the room temperature is 300 K, at what rate is energy radiated by the iron? If electric power is supplied to the iron at the rate of 1000 W, what does your answer say about the importance of other energy transfer mechanisms in maintaining the iron at a steady temperature? Take the emissivity of the iron to be 0.95.

29. An electric stove burner has a total surface area of 325 cm². If the temperature of the burner is 900 K, and the electric power input to the burner is 1500 W, what fraction of the burner's heat loss is by radiation? The emissivity of the burner is 1.0, and room temperature is 300 K.

30. An electric current is passed through a metal strip that measures 0.50 cm × 5.0 cm × 0.10 mm. As a result, energy is supplied to the strip at the rate of 50 W. The strip is covered with a black coating that gives it an emissivity of 1, and is in a room where the temperature is 300 K. What is the temperature of the strip if (a) the strip is enclosed in a vacuum bottle that is transparent to all radiation? (b) the strip is enclosed in an insulating box with thermal resistance $R = 8.0$ K/W that blocks all radiation?

31. Rework Example 16–8, now assuming that the house has 10 single-glazed windows ($\mathcal{R} = 0.90$), each measuring 2.5 ft × 5.0 ft. Four of the windows are on the south, and supply the house with solar energy at an average rate of 30 Btu/h·ft². The rest of the windows contribute no solar gain but, of course, there is heat loss through *all* the windows. What is the total heating cost for the month? How much is the solar gain worth?

32. The average human body produces heat at the rate of 100 W. What is the coldest outdoor temperature in which a goose-down sleeping bag is usable, if the bag has a loft (thickness) of 5 cm? Make reasonable simplifying assumptions about the shape of the person and sleeping bag, and assume that normal body temperature (37°C) is to be maintained.

33. A steam pipe of 12-cm diameter carries steam at 550 K. How thick a layer of fiberglass insulation should be wrapped around this pipe if the heat loss per meter of pipe is to be 150 W? The air around the pipe is at 300 K.

34. A pipe of $\frac{3}{4}$-in diameter is surrounded by a $\frac{1}{2}$-in-thick layer of insulation. If the insulation thickness is doubled, how is the heat-loss rate changed?

35. Integrate Equation 16–13 from the inner edge of the insulation to an arbitrary point within the insulation, and use your result in conjunction with Equation 16–14 to show that the temperature as a function of position is given by

$$T = T_1 - (T_1 - T_2) \frac{\ln(r/R_1)}{\ln(R_2/R_1)},$$

where r is the position measured from the center of the pipe, and R_1 and R_2 are the inner and outer radii of the insulation. Show that this result reduces to the expected values at R_1 and R_2.

36. Combustion of fossil fuels like coal and oil puts large quantities of carbon dioxide into the atmosphere, effectively reducing the emissivity of the earth for the infrared radiation it emits. If we put enough CO_2 into the atmosphere to reduce the effective emissivity by 10%, what would happen to the average temperature of the earth?

37. In contrast to the previous problem, suppose that air

pollution in the form of soot reduced by 4% the amount of sunlight reaching earth's surface. What would be the average global temperature under these conditions? Use the assumptions of Example 16–11.

Supplementary Problems

38. A sphere of radius R_1 is maintained at a temperature T_1. The sphere is surrounded by insulation of thermal conductivity k and outer radius R_2. Show that the rate of heat loss from the sphere is

$$\frac{dQ}{dt} = \frac{4\pi k R_1 R_2 (T_1 - T_2)}{R_2 - R_1},$$

where T_1 and T_2 are the temperatures at the inner and outer edges of the insulation, respectively.

39. An object of heat capacity C is surrounded by insulation that results in a heat loss at the rate h per unit temperature difference between the object and its surroundings. If the object is at an initial temperature T_1, and its surroundings at a constant temperature T_0, and if there is no energy transferred to or from the object except by conduction through the insulation, show that the temperature of the object as a function of time is described by the equation

$$C\frac{dT}{dt} = -h(T - T_0).$$

Show that the solution to this equation is

$$T = T_0 + (T_1 - T_0)e^{-ht/C},$$

where t is the time. Show that this solution gives reasonable results when $t = 0$ and as $t \to \infty$.

40. A house is being maintained at 20°C on a winter day when the outdoor temperature is $-15°C$. Suddenly, the furnace fails. Determine how long it will take for the house temperature to reach the freezing point. The heat-loss rate for the house is 150 W/°C, and its heat capacity is 6.5×10^6 J/K. (See the result of the preceding problem.)

41. During a week in the summertime, the outdoor temperature fluctuates according to the equation

$$T_0 = 20°C - (5°C)\cos\left(\frac{\pi t}{12}\right),$$

where t is the time measured in hours since midnight. If there is no heat source in the house of the preceding problem, show that the house temperature also varies sinusoidally with time, and find the maximum and minimum house temperature. To do this, you can assume a sinusoidally varying house temperature, and see if it is a solution to the differential equation of Problem 39, when T_0 is varying sinusoidally. Does the house temperature peak at the same time as the outdoor temperature? Physically, why is this so?

17

THE THERMAL BEHAVIOR
OF MATTER

Matter responds in a variety of ways to the transfer of heat. It may get hotter, as we discussed in the preceding chapter, or it may undergo a change of phase, as when ice melts. It may experience changes in size or shape, or in pressure. In this chapter, we seek to understand the thermal behavior of matter. We start with a particularly simple state—the gaseous state—whose behavior can be accounted for by applying Newtonian mechanics at the molecular level. We then move to more complicated situations whose explanation is still grounded in the molecular properties of matter, but whose description is necessarily more empirical.

17.1
THE IDEAL GAS

A gas consists of matter in a rarefied state. Gas, like liquid, is a fluid, capable of deforming and flowing. But unlike liquid, gas is readily compressible, so that the volume of a given sample of gas is easily altered. The rarefied nature of a gas, resulting in weak interactions along its constituent particles, makes the thermal behavior of a gas particularly simple. In studying this behavior, we will develop a clear understanding of the relation between macroscopic properties—like temperature and pressure—and the underlying microscopic properties including the masses and velocities of the constituent particles.

The Equation of State of an Ideal Gas

At the macroscopic level, the state of a given sample of gas in thermodynamic equilibrium is determined completely by its temperature, pressure, and volume. A simple system for studying gas behavior consists of a cylinder sealed by a movable piston (Fig. 17–1). If we maintain the gas at a

Fig. 17–1
A piston-cylinder system.

431

constant temperature—by immersing the cylinder in a large reservoir of water or other substance at a fixed temperature—and push slowly on the piston to decrease the gas volume, we find that the pressure rises approximately in inverse proportion to the volume:

$$P \propto \frac{1}{V}. \qquad \text{(at fixed } T\text{)}$$

Boyle's law

Known as **Boyle's law,** this relation was described by the English scientist Robert Boyle in 1660, a year before Isaac Newton entered college. If we keep the volume constant by holding the piston at a fixed position, and heat the gas, we find that the pressure is approximately proportional to the absolute temperature:

$$P \propto T. \qquad \text{(at fixed } V\text{)}$$

Combining our two proportionalities, we have

$$P \propto \frac{T}{V}.$$

If we now hold T and V constant, but introduce more gas into the cylinder, we find that the pressure increases in proportion to the amount of gas. If N is the actual number of gas molecules, we can then write

$$P = \frac{NkT}{V},$$

or

$$PV = NkT, \qquad (17\text{--}1)$$

where k is a constant.

ideal gas law

Equation 17–1 is called the **ideal gas law.** The constant k is found experimentally to have very nearly the same value for all gases:

$$k = 1.38 \times 10^{-23} \text{ J/K},$$

Boltzmann's constant

and is called **Boltzmann's constant,** after the Austrian physicist Ludwig Boltzmann (1844–1906), who was instrumental in developing the microscopic description of thermal phenomena.

Because the number of molecules, N, in a typical sample of gas is so large, we often express the ideal gas law in terms of the number of moles (mol) of gas. A mole of anything consists of Avogadro's number of that thing, where Avogadro's number is $N_A = 6.022 \times 10^{23}$. ($N_A$ is defined so that 12.0 g of ^{12}C atoms contains exactly one mole of those atoms.) If there are n moles of molecules in a gas, then $N = nN_A$ is the number of molecules, so that the ideal gas law can be written:

$$PV = nN_A kT = nRT, \qquad (17\text{--}2)$$

universal gas constant

where the constant $R = N_A k = 8.314$ J/K·mol is called the **universal gas constant.**

Example 17–1
The Ideal Gas Law

What is the volume occupied by 1.00 mol of an ideal gas at standard temperature and pressure (STP), where $T = 0°C$ and $P = 1.00$ atm?

Solution

Solving the ideal gas law for the volume V, and expressing all quantities in SI units, we have

$$V = \frac{nRT}{P} = \frac{(1.00 \text{ mol})(8.31 \text{ J/K·mol})(273 \text{ K})}{1.01 \times 10^5 \text{ Pa}} = 22.4 \times 10^{-3} \text{ m}^3 = 22.4 \text{ L}.$$

The ideal gas law is remarkably simple. It relates in a straightforward way the quantity of gas and its temperature, pressure, and volume. The form of the law and the numerical values of the constants k and R do not depend on such things as the substance making up the gas or the mass of the individual molecules. Yet the ideal gas law is obeyed very well by most real gases over a wide range of pressures. A plot of PV/nT versus pressure for an ideal gas (Fig. 17–2) gives a horizontal straight line whose vertical coordinate is the gas constant, R. As pressure is lowered, *all* gases converge to the ideal gas value of PV/nT and therefore exhibit ideal gas behavior. This nearly ideal behavior is what gives the gas thermometer its high precision over a wide temperature range.

Kinetic Theory of the Ideal Gas

Why do all gases obey such a simple relation among pressure, temperature, and volume? Studying the macroscopic properties themselves can never answer this question; instead, we must examine physical processes at the molecular level.

The gaseous state of matter is a rarefied state in which individual molecules are relatively far apart and interact only weakly. To understand how matter in this state might behave, we make a number of simplifying assumptions:

1. We assume that our gas consists of a very large number of identical point particles, having no size or internal structure, each of mass m. Of course, this assumption is false for real atoms or molecules, but if the gas is sufficiently rarefied, the size of the particles becomes negligible compared with the distance between them.
2. The particles do not interact with each other. This assumption rules out interactions—involving electrical, gravitational, or nuclear forces—that

Fig. 17–2
A plot of *PV/nT* versus pressure shows that real gases exhibit ideal behavior at low pressures. Even at 10 atm, oxygen deviates from the ideal gas law by less than 2 per cent.

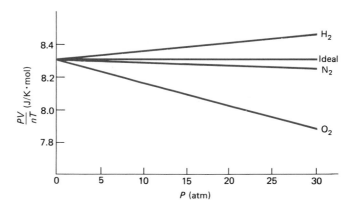

might cause the particles to attract or repel one another. Again, this assumption is not strictly correct for real particles, but normally, the average potential energy associated with such interactions is negligible compared with a particle's kinetic energy.

3. The particles are moving in random directions with a range of speeds. This assumption ensures that the gas has, on the average, no net momentum.

4. The particles undergo collisions with the walls of their container, and these collisions conserve momentum and energy. Here is where our gas model is tied to the laws of Newtonian mechanics. We also assume that the walls are perfectly smooth, so that forces exerted during these collisions are normal to the walls.

Consider a gas confined inside a rectangular container (Fig. 17–3). Each time a gas molecule collides with a container wall, it exerts a force on the wall. There are so many molecules that individual collisions are not evident on the macroscopic scale; instead the wall experiences a force that is essentially constant. The gas pressure is simply a measure of this force on a unit area.

To calculate the pressure, consider one molecule colliding with a wall (Fig. 17–4). Call the direction perpendicular to the wall the x-direction. Since the wall is smooth and the collision elastic, the component of the molecule's velocity in the y-direction remains unchanged during the collision, but the x-component of the velocity changes sign. Thus the molecule undergoes a change in momentum of magnitude $2mv_{xi}$, where v_{xi} is the magnitude of the x-velocity of this particular molecule. Now suppose that there are N_i molecules in the container whose x-components of velocity have the same magnitude v_{xi}. Because the molecules are moving in random directions, on the average half of them have x-components of velocity in the $+x$-direction and half in the $-x$-direction. Then in the time it takes one of these N_i molecules to cross the entire container, all $N_i/2$ of them that are moving toward the wall will hit it. The time in which these $N_i/2$ collisions take place is

$$\Delta t = \frac{\ell}{v_{xi}},$$

where ℓ is the length of the container in the x-direction. The change in momentum of all these molecules during this time is then

$$\Delta p_i = \frac{N_i}{2} 2mv_{xi} = N_i mv_{xi}.$$

By Newton's second law, the wall exerts a force whose average magnitude is equal to the average rate of change of the molecules' momentum:

$$F_i = \frac{\Delta p_i}{\Delta t} = \frac{N_i mv_{xi}}{\ell/v_{xi}} = \frac{N_i mv_{xi}^2}{\ell}.$$

By Newton's third law, this is also the magnitude of the average force exerted on the wall by the molecules whose x-component of velocity is v_{xi}. The total force on the wall is obtained by summing over all values of v_{xi}:

$$F = \sum F_i = \frac{\sum N_i mv_{xi}^2}{\ell}.$$

Fig. 17–3
Gas molecules confined to a rectangular box.

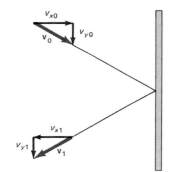

Fig. 17–4
A molecule undergoes an elastic collision with the container wall, reversing its x-component of velocity and transferring momentum $2mv_x$ to the wall. The y-component of velocity remains unchanged.

If the wall has area A, then the pressure, or force per unit area, is

$$P = \frac{F}{A} = \frac{\sum N_i m v_{xi}^2}{\ell A} = \frac{\sum N_i m v_{xi}^2}{V},$$

where $V = \ell A$ is the volume of the container. We can rewrite the pressure in a more meaningful way if we consider the average value of v_x^2 over all the molecules. This average, designated by $\overline{v_x^2}$, is obtained by summing the individual values v_{xi}^2, weighted by the number of molecules N_i with each value, and then dividing by N, the total number of molecules:

$$\overline{v_x^2} = \frac{\sum N_i v_{xi}^2}{N}.$$

Comparing this average with our expression for pressure shows that the pressure can be written

$$P = \frac{Nm\overline{v_x^2}}{V},$$

so that

$$PV = Nm\overline{v_x^2} = 2N(\tfrac{1}{2}m\overline{v_x^2}). \tag{17–3}$$

We recognize the quantity $\tfrac{1}{2}m\overline{v_x^2}$ as the average kinetic energy per molecule associated with the motion of molecules in the x-direction. In Equation 17–3 we have the ideal gas law expressed in microscopic terms! Comparing with the macroscopic expression, $PV = NkT$, shows that

$$kT = 2\,(\tfrac{1}{2}m\overline{v_x^2}),$$

or

$$\tfrac{1}{2}m\overline{v_x^2} = \tfrac{1}{2}kT.$$

Because our molecules are moving in random directions, the average kinetic energy associated with motion in the x-direction is the same as in the y- and z-directions. The average total kinetic energy of a molecule is thus three times the average kinetic energy associated with its motion in any one direction, so that

$$\tfrac{1}{2}m\overline{v^2} = \tfrac{3}{2}kT. \tag{17–4}$$

Our derivation of Equation 17–3 shows us why, in terms of simple Newtonian mechanics, we should expect a gas to obey the ideal gas law. In Equation 17–4 we get an added bonus: a microscopic understanding of the meaning of temperature. Temperature is simply a measure of the average kinetic energy associated with translational motion of the molecules.

Example 17–2
Temperature and Kinetic Energy

What is the average kinetic energy of a molecule in air at room temperature? What would be the speed of a nitrogen molecule with this energy?

Solution

The average kinetic energy is given by Equation 17–4, where room temperature is about 20°C (293 K):

$$\tfrac{1}{2}m\overline{v^2} = \tfrac{3}{2}kT = \tfrac{3}{2}(1.4 \times 10^{-23} \text{ J/K})(293 \text{ K}) = 6.2 \times 10^{-21} \text{ J}.$$

A nitrogen molecule consists of two nitrogen atoms (atomic mass 14 u; see Appendix E), so its mass is

$$m = 2(14 \text{ u})(1.7 \times 10^{-27} \text{ kg/u}) = 4.8 \times 10^{-26} \text{ kg}.$$

The kinetic energy is $K = \tfrac{1}{2}mv^2$, so that

$$v = \sqrt{\frac{2K}{m}} = \sqrt{\frac{2(6.2 \times 10^{-21} \text{ J})}{4.8 \times 10^{-26} \text{ kg}}} = 510 \text{ m/s}.$$

thermal speed   Not surprisingly, this **thermal speed** is of the same order of magnitude as the sound speed in air at room temperature. At the microscopic level, the speed of the individual molecules sets an approximate upper limit on the maximum rate at which information can be transmitted by disturbances—that is, sound waves—propagating through the gas.

The Distribution of Molecular Speeds

Our results 17–3 and 17–4 are fundamentally statistical. The macroscopic pressure is not associated with any one molecular collision, but only with huge numbers of collisions occurring so frequently, and each transferring so little momentum, that we sense only the average force and not the many individual impacts. Similarly, temperature does not tell us much about the energy of any individual molecule, but only about the average over all the molecules. In describing a gas—or any macroscopic system—in terms of temperature and pressure, we have averaged out the details of what is going on at the microscopic level. From this averaging, there emerges a simplicity at the macroscopic level that would be lost in the chaos of 10^{23} or so random molecular motions.

Frequently, though, we want to know more than just these average quantities. For example, is the range of molecular speeds limited to a narrow band about the thermal speed $v_{th} = \sqrt{3kT/m}$ obtained from Equation 17–4? Or are there many molecules moving much faster than the thermal speed? Such fast molecules would be important in determining, for example, the chemical reaction rates in a gas mixture, or the tendency of an atmosphere to escape the gravitational field of its planet.

In the 1860's, the Scottish physicist James Clerk Maxwell considered the sharing of energy that must result from collisions among the molecules of a gas. Although we have neglected such collisions, their presence changes none of our earlier conclusions as long as the collisions are elastic; in fact, collisions are responsible for bringing a gas into thermodynamic equilibrium. Maxwell showed that molecular collisions result in a speed distribution where the number of molecules in a very small speed range Δv about some speed v is given by

$$N(v)\,\Delta v = 4\pi N \left(\frac{m}{2\pi kT}\right)^{3/2} v^2 e^{-mv^2/2kT} \Delta v, \qquad (17\text{–}5)$$

where N is the total number of molecules in the gas, m the molecular mass, k Boltzmann's constant, and T the absolute temperature. The quantity $N(v)$ is the number of molecules per unit speed range; multiplying by a small

Fig. 17–5
Maxwell-Boltzmann distribution of molecular speeds for a sample of 10^{20} nitrogen molecules (N_2) at temperatures of 80 K and 300 K. Also marked is the thermal speed $v_{th} = \sqrt{3kT/m}$. Areas under both curves correspond to the total number of molecules, and are therefore the same.

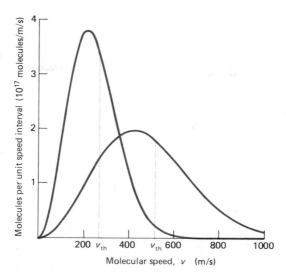

Molecules per unit speed interval (10^{17} molecules/m/s)

Molecular speed, v (m/s)

Maxwell-Boltzmann distribution

speed range Δv gives $N(v)\Delta v$, or the actual number of molecules in that speed range. Equation 17–5 is known as the **Maxwell-Boltzmann distribution.** Figure 17–5 shows plots of this distribution for the same gas sample at two different temperatures. Each curve exhibits a single peak; this is the most probable value for a molecule's speed. Because the curve is not symmetric about the peak, the most probable speed lies below the mean thermal speed (see Problem 16). Figure 17–5 shows what Equation 17–4 already told us: that an increase in temperature corresponds to an increase in mean thermal speed. But it also shows something averages alone could not reveal: that an increase in temperature results in a broader speed distribution, with relatively fewer molecules near the most probable speed.

The Maxwell-Boltzmann distribution shows why the chemical reaction rates of gas mixtures increase dramatically with temperature; it is the excessively energetic molecules, of which there are more at higher temperatures, that are largely responsible for sustaining chemical reactions. A similar distribution holds for molecular speeds in liquids, and explains why a liquid evaporates at temperatures below its boiling point, and why evaporation results in cooling. Even though molecules with speeds near the thermal speed lack sufficient energy to escape the liquid, those in the high-speed "tail" of the Maxwell-Boltzmann distribution can escape. As they leave, the mean speed of the remaining molecules drops, and with it the temperature.

Real Gases

Though the ideal gas law is a good approximation to the behavior of real gases, the assumptions that led to our derivation of the ideal gas law are not entirely realistic. We should, therefore, expect a real gas to exhibit deviations from ideal behavior.

We assumed that our ideal gas molecules were point particles that underwent no intermolecular collisions or other interactions. But real mole-

Fig. 17–6
At closest approach, the centers of two spherical molecules are separated by twice their radius. Each molecule therefore excludes the center of the other from a volume eight times its actual volume, as indicated by the dashed circle. We can regard either molecule as excluding the other, so that in the total sample half the molecules contribute to the excluded volume, which is therefore four times the molecular volume times the total number of molecules.

van der Waals force

van der Waals equation

cules have nonzero size, and therefore collide. During a collision, one molecule can only approach within two molecular radii of another (Fig. 17–6). Some of the total volume of the container is therefore excluded because of the finite molecular size, so that the volume V entering the gas law should be less than the total volume of the container. How much less? As Fig. 17–6 shows, a pair of spherical molecules has associated with it an excluded volume eight times the actual molecular volume. If b is this excluded volume summed over all the molecular pairs in one mole of gas, then we should write

$$P(V - nb) = nRT,$$

or

$$PV\left(1 - \frac{nb}{V}\right) = nRT,$$

where nb is the excluded volume in n moles of gas. In a rarefied gas, where the density of molecules n/V is small, we recover the ideal gas law.

Another deviation from ideal behavior occurs because each molecule exerts a weak attractive force on its neighbors. This force originates in electrical interactions among the particles making up the molecules; in Chapter 22 we will show how it arises.* Called the **van der Waals force,** it has a very short range and is therefore important only when molecules are relatively close. Physically, the van der Waals force reduces gas pressure because molecules slow down as they move apart, therefore lowering the force of molecular collisions with container walls. Mathematically, this results in an additional term in the equation describing gas behavior. Correcting for both finite molecular volume and the van der Waals force gives the **van der Waals equation:**

$$\left(P + \frac{n^2 a}{V^2}\right)(V - nb) = nRT, \tag{17–6}$$

where a and b are constants that depend on the particular gas. For low particle densities n/V, both correction terms in the van der Waals equation become negligible, showing that a rarefied gas closely follows the ideal gas law.

Example 17–3
The van der Waals Equation

The constants a and b in the van der Waals equation for nitrogen have the values $a = 0.14$ Pa·m^6/mol^2, $b = 3.91 \times 10^{-5}$ m^3/mol. If 1.000 mol of nitrogen is confined to a volume of 2.000 L, and is at a pressure of 10.00 atm, by how much does its temperature as predicted by the van der Waals equation differ from the ideal gas prediction?

Solution

Converting to SI units, we have $P = 1.013 \times 10^6$ Pa and $V = 2.000 \times 10^{-3}$ m^3. Then the ideal gas law predicts a temperature of

---

*Of course, there is also a gravitational attraction among the molecules. But this is entirely negligible.

$$T_{ideal} = \frac{PV}{nR} = \frac{(1.013 \times 10^6 \text{ Pa})(2.000 \times 10^{-3} \text{ m}^3)}{(1.000 \text{ mol})(8.314 \text{ J/K·mol})} = 244 \text{ K}.$$

The van der Waals equation predicts a temperature of

$$T_{van} = \frac{(P + n^2 a/V^2)(V - nb)}{nR}$$

$$= [1.013 \times 10^6 \text{ Pa} + (1.000 \text{ mol})^2 (0.14 \text{ Pa·m}^6/\text{mol}^2)/(2.000 \times 10^{-3} \text{ m}^3)^2]$$

$$\times \left(\frac{2.000 \times 10^{-3} \text{ m}^3 - (1.000 \text{ mol})(3.91 \times 10^{-5} \text{ m}^3/\text{mol})}{(1.000 \text{ mol})(8.314 \text{ J/K·mol})} \right) = 247 \text{ K}.$$

Even at 10 atm, nitrogen deviates from ideal gas behavior by only about 1 per cent.

17.2
PHASE CHANGES

For gases at high densities and pressures, the van der Waals equation provides a much better description of gas behavior than the ideal gas law. But even the van der Waals equation is only an approximation. At high enough pressure or low enough temperature, intermolecular forces become dominant, locking molecules so tightly together that the gas condenses into a liquid or even a solid. These different states of matter are called **phases.** A full theoretical description of phases and the **phase changes** that substances undergo is well beyond the scope of this book, but we can gain a qualitative understanding by examining the relation of pressure, volume, and temperature over a wide range of values.

phases
phase changes

PVT Diagrams

Suppose we have a gas at such pressure, temperature, and volume that it behaves very nearly like an ideal gas. Then if we hold the temperature constant but decrease the volume, the pressure rises inversely as the volume:

$$P \propto \frac{1}{V}.$$

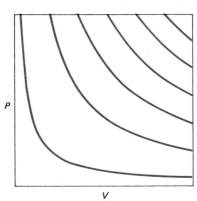

Fig. 17–7
PV diagram for an ideal gas, showing curves of constant temperature (isotherms). For an ideal gas, the isotherms are hyperbolas.

iostherms

The proportionality constant is, from the ideal gas law, just nRT. If we hold our gas at a different temperature, we get a similar inverse proportionality, but with a different proportionality constant. We can describe these different proportionalities by plotting curves of pressure versus volume for a variety of temperatures. Figure 17–7 shows such a *PV* diagram for an ideal gas. These constant-temperature curves are called **isotherms.**

For a real gas, we expect van der Waals deviations from ideal behavior at very low volumes where intermolecular spacing becomes small. As we lower the gas temperature, these deviations become more pronounced. Eventually we reach a **critical temperature** T_C below which even the van der Waals description fails. Here the *PV* diagram exhibits a most unusual behavior: the pressure versus volume curves become flat over a finite range of volumes (Fig. 17–8).

critical temperature

Fig. 17–8
Isotherms in the *PV* diagram for a substance that liquefies. T_C labels isotherm at the critical temperature. Moving along the horizontal line *AB* on the isotherm below T_C, the volume increases as the liquid changes to vapor. Since *AB* is part of an isotherm, temperature remains constant during this process.

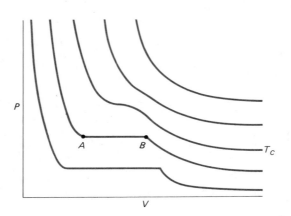

What is going on here? One clue comes from looking on the left side of the *PV* curves for temperatures below T_C. Here the curves are almost vertical, indicating that any change of volume results in a huge pressure change. In other words, the substance is virtually incompressible: it has become a liquid. As we drop steeply down a curve of decreasing pressure, the volume increases only slightly until we reach the point where the *PV* curve suddenly becomes horizontal. For a range of volumes beyond this point, the pressure remains constant as the volume increases. In this region, the liquid and gas phases can coexist, so that as the volume increases, more and more of the liquid evaporates, greatly increasing the volume without any change in pressure. The pressure at which this occurs is called the

saturated vapor pressure   **saturated vapor pressure.**

We entered the horizontal portion of the curve at point *A*, with our substance entirely in the liquid state. As we traverse from *A* to *B*, the liquid evaporates. Finally, at point *B*, the liquid is completely gone and the substance again exhibits the compressibility characteristic of a gas.

If we set a liquid at its vapor pressure and give it a large volume into which to expand, the liquid changes rapidly into a gas. This is just what happens when water boils. The saturated vapor pressure of water at 100°C is 1 atm, so that under these conditions water is on the horizontal portion of its *PV* curve. When exposed to the open air, so that its expansion is uninhibited, the liquid changes vigorously into gas. When we say that the boiling point of water is 100°C, we really mean that at this temperature, the vapor pressure equals atmospheric pressure. Water will boil at *any* temperature if placed in an environment where the pressure is equal to its vapor pressure at that temperature (Figure 17–9). The decrease in boiling point with decreasing pressure is a hazard to astronauts and high-altitude fliers, whose bodily fluids may boil abruptly if their air- or spacecraft lose pressure.

Figure 17–10 again shows the *PV* curves for a substance that liquefies, now with the boundaries between the liquid and gas phases clearly vapor   marked. The term **vapor** is sometimes applied to the gas phase at temperatures below T_C, although the term is sometimes restricted to mean gas in equilibrium with liquid. Notice that there is no really clear-cut distinction

Fig. 17–9
At the 3000-m altitude of Sacramento Peak Observatory in New Mexico, air pressure is sufficiently low that water boils at 92 °C.

between liquid and gas, except in the region of liquid-vapor equilibrium. If we start above the critical temperature and decrease the temperature while holding pressure constant, we move horizontally to the left in the *PV* diagram. As we do so, the volume drops and so the density of the substance rises, and we move smoothly from gas to liquid. In this region of the *PV* diagram, both gas and liquid are extremely dense fluids and are essentially indistinguishable. It is only below the so-called **critical point,** where the *PV* curves begin to exhibit a horizontal portion, that there is a clear distinction between liquid and gas. Most of our experience with liquid-vapor transitions is below the critical point. Water, for example, has its critical point at the high temperature and pressure of 647 K and 218.3 atm. Figure 17–11 shows carbon dioxide in a sealed container being brought to its critical point. At that point the liquid-gas interface simply disappears as the two phases become indistinguishable.

critical point

The *PV* diagram of Fig. 17–10 is still incomplete, for it does not account for the third phase of matter—the solid phase. Modifying our *PV* diagram to include the solid phase would make it extremely complicated. Instead of trying to plot *PV* curves for each different temperature, we resort to a three-dimensional diagram with pressure, volume, and temperature along the three axes. The result is a *PVT* surface—a three-dimensional surface which, at each point, gives the relation between temperature, pressure,

Fig. 17–10
PV diagram showing boundaries between liquid and gas phases.

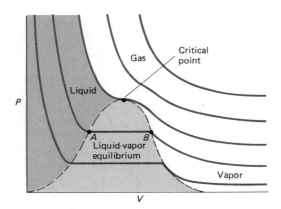

Fig. 17–11
The liquid-gas interface disappears as CO_2 in a glass container is brought to its critical point. Temperature and pressure at the critical point are 304 K and 73 atm.

and volume. Figure 17–12 shows a *PVT* surface for a typical substance that expands when it melts.

The *PVT* surface describes fully the relation among the three variables *P*, *V*, and *T*. If we specify any two of these quantities, the third is determined by the distance to the *PVT* surface from the plane defined by the axes of the two known quantities. If we have a substance at some point on

Fig. 17–12
A *PVT* surface. Also shown are projections of the surface onto the *PV* plane—giving a *PV* diagram analogous to Fig. 17–10—and onto the *PT* plane, giving a *PT* diagram.

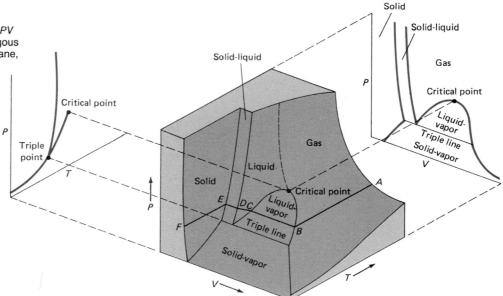

the *PVT* surface, we can perform processes that move it to other points. For example, we might enclose our substance in a tightly sealed cylinder with a movable piston. If we put the cylinder in a large bath of water at constant temperature, we can move along the isotherms—curves of constant temperature—in the *PVT* diagram by moving the piston and thus changing the volume of the substance. Or we might maintain a constant pressure, by exposing the piston to the atmosphere, and then move through the *PVT* surface by changing the temperature. Such a constant-pressure process is termed **isobaric,** and the resulting paths on the *PVT* diagram are **isobars.**

Imagine moving along the isobar marked *ABCDEF* in Fig. 17–12. This path is an isobar because it is at constant height—that is, constant pressure—above the *VT* plane. At point *A* our substance is in the gas phase. As we lower the temperature, the volume drops proportionately, with slight deviations from a straight line because of van der Waals effects. At point *B* we reach the zone where liquid and vapor exist in equilibrium. As we try to cool the substance further, we find it remains at constant temperature while it liquefies. As it liquefies, the volume drops and we move along the liquid-vapor equilibrium curve, section *BC* of the isobar. When we reach point *C*, all the substance is in the liquid phase. Further cooling occurs with very little change in volume—the liquid is virtually incompressible—until we reach point *D*. Here the liquid begins to solidify, and again the substance experiences a significant change in volume without any change in temperature. Finally, at point *E*, the substance is entirely in the solid phase, and continues cooling with only slight changes in volume.

The particular isobar *ABCDEF* encompassed all three phases of the substance. Other isobars would have given different behaviors. At pressures greater than the critical pressure P_C we would have passed smoothly from gas to liquid without having noticed the distinction between the two, but would later have entered a region of solid-liquid equilibrium before the substance was entirely solid. At low enough pressure, we would have missed the liquid phase altogether, passing directly into a region of solid-vapor equilibrium. At the so-called triple-point pressure P_3, we would have moved through a region in which all three phases coexist in equilibrium. The unique values of pressure and temperature in this region define the **triple point** of the substance. We have already seen that the triple point of water is used in establishing the absolute temperature scale. To know that we are at the triple-point temperature, we need not make any measurements; it suffices to observe that all three phases are in equilibrium.

In our everyday experience, we associate heating a solid with eventual transitions to the liquid and then to the gas phase. The occurrence of these transitions, and the notion that the gas phase is always hotter than the liquid and solid phases, is partly an artifact arising because our everyday experience is confined to a pressure of 1 atm. For different pressures, or substances less common than those we deal with every day, rather different things may happen. For example, carbon dioxide at atmospheric pressure never enters the liquid phase—solid CO_2 (dry ice) goes directly from the solid to the vapor phase, giving it the name dry ice (Fig. 17–13). Only at much higher pressures does CO_2 liquefy. Fire extinguishers, for example, often contain liquid CO_2 under pressure. The interior of the earth is under

isobaric
isobars

Fig. 17–13
Carbon dioxide subliming from solid to gas. The gray mist is actually a cloud of water droplets that condensed on contact with the cold CO_2 gas.

triple point

enormous pressure from the weight of the overlying layers, and is hot enough that some of it is liquid. But the central core of the planet, although the hottest part, is solid because the pressure is so high (Fig. 17–14).

The relations among the various phases are summarized in a **phase diagram,** which is the projection of the PVT surface onto the PT plane (Fig. 17–15). In plotting only this two-dimensional picture, we lose information about volume changes, but we show more clearly the regimes of temperature and pressure in which the different phases exist. The solid lines in the phase diagram show where the processes of melting (and its inverse, freezing or fusion), vaporization (and its inverse, liquefying), and sublimation (a change directly from solid to gas) occur. The special status of the triple and critical points shows clearly on the phase diagram.

Our PVT surface and phase diagram are for a particularly simple substance. Many real substances exhibit more complicated diagrams associated with subphases of liquid and solid that reflect changes in crystalline structure and molecular bonding.

phase diagram

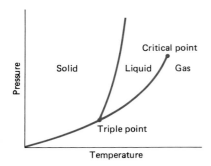

Fig. 17–14
Because of its extreme pressure, the inner core of the earth is solid, even though it is hotter than the surrounding liquid. Core temperatures range from a low around 4300 K in the outer core to a high around 6400 K in the solid inner core.

Heat and Phase Changes

Once we have heated a solid to its melting point, we can continue to add heat without any corresponding change in temperature until the solid has entirely liquefied. The same thing happens at the vaporization point. At a pressure of 1 atm, a pot of boiling water stays at 100°C until all the water is gone. Conversely, if we try to cool water below its freezing point, the temperature stays at 0°C until all the water has frozen. Only then does the temperature decrease again.

What is happening to the heat we add or remove during these phase changes? On a molecular level, the energy goes primarily into breaking the bonds that hold molecules in the tight configurations of solid or liquid. During a phase change, the potential energy of molecular separation changes, rather than the kinetic energy and therefore temperature. Macroscopically, we characterize phase changes by the energy required to melt or vaporize a given amount of material. We call this energy the **heat of fusion,** L_f, or **heat of vaporization,** L_v. Both are **heats of transformation.** If we determine that a mass m of a given substance requires heat Q to change completely from one phase to another with no temperature change, then the heat of transformation is given by:

heat of fusion
heat of vaporization
heats of transformation

$$L = \frac{Q}{m}. \qquad (17\text{–}7)$$

To reverse the phase change—that is, to change water to ice—we must remove the energy implied by Equation 17–7. In addition to the heats of fusion and vaporization, we specify a heat of sublimation when a substance goes directly from the solid to the vapor state. Table 17–1 lists heats of transformation for some common materials at atmospheric pressure.

Heat transfers associated with phase changes are typically quite large. The heat of fusion of water, for example, is 334 kJ/kg or 80 cal/g—meaning that it takes as much energy to melt one gram of ice as it does to raise the resulting water from 0°C to 80°C.

Fig. 17–15
A phase diagram is the projection of a PVT surface onto the PT plane.

TABLE 17–1 ▬▬▬

Heats of Transformation (at atmospheric pressure)

Substance	Melting Point, K	L_f, kJ/kg	Boiling Point, K	L_v, kJ/kg
Alcohol, ethyl	159	109	351	879
Copper	1356	205	2839	4726
Lead	600	24.7	2023	858
Mercury	234	11.3	630	296
Oxygen	54.4	13.8	90.2	213
Sulfur	388	38.5	718	287
Water	273	334	373	2257

Example 17–4

Heat of Transformation

A 500-g block of lead is at its melting point of 600 K. How much heat does it take to melt the lead?

Solution

Solving Equation 17–7 for Q gives the required heat:

$$Q = mL_f = (0.500 \text{ kg})(24.7 \text{ kJ/kg}) = 12.4 \text{ kJ}.$$

The heats of fusion and vaporization measure only the energy associated with phase changes, during which the temperature does not change. To calculate the energy required to change first the temperature and then the phase of a substance, we must use both the specific heat and the heat of transformation.

Example 17–5

Changes of Temperature and Phase

A 50-g ice cube is taken from a freezer at $-10°C$, put in a pan on a hot stove, and heated until it has all turned to steam. How much energy is required?

We break this problem into several parts, each dealing with either a temperature change or a phase change. Equation 16–7, along with the appropriate specific heat from Table 16–1, allows us to calculate the heat associated with temperature changes. Equation 17–7 and Table 17–1 allow us to calculate the heat of transformation, as in Example 17–4.

1. To bring 50 g of ice from $-10°C$ to its melting point of $0°C$, we have

$$Q_1 = mc\Delta T = (0.050 \text{ kg})(2.1 \text{ kJ/kg·K})(10 \text{ K}) = 1.1 \text{ kJ}.$$

2. To melt the 50 g of ice takes

$$Q_2 = mL_f = (0.050 \text{ kg})(330 \text{ kJ/kg}) = 17 \text{ kJ}.$$

3. To raise the water from $0°C$ to its boiling point at $100°C$ takes

$$Q_3 = mc\Delta T = (0.050 \text{ kg})(4.2 \text{ kJ/kg·K})(100 \text{ K}) = 21 \text{ kJ}.$$

4. Finally, to boil the water completely takes

$$Q_4 = mL_v = (0.050 \text{ kg})(2.3 \times 10^3 \text{ kJ/kg}) = 120 \text{ kJ}.$$

Then the total energy required for the process is

$$Q = Q_1 + Q_2 + Q_3 + Q_4 = 160 \text{ kJ.}$$

Note that 75 per cent of this energy is associated with vaporization.

Example 17–6
Equilibrium Temperature Following a Phase Change

200 g of ice at $-10°C$ is added to 1.0 kg of water at 15°C, and the mixture kept in an insulated container. When thermodynamic equilibrium is reached, how much, if any, ice is left? What is the equilibrium temperature?

Solution

To solve this problem we must first find out whether the water is capable of melting all the ice. To bring the ice to its melting point and then melt all of it requires

$$Q_1 = mc\Delta T + mL_f$$

$$= (200 \text{ g})(0.49 \text{ cal/g·°C})(10°C) + (200 \text{ g})(80 \text{ cal/g})$$

$$= 980 \text{ cal} + 16 \times 10^3 \text{ cal} = 17 \text{ kcal.}$$

Here we have chosen to work in calories rather than joules because the specific heat of water is conveniently 1.0 cal/g·°C.

If we cool the water to 0°C, we can extract an amount of heat given by

$$Q_2 = mc\Delta T = (1.0 \times 10^3 \text{ g})(1.0 \text{ cal/g·°C})(15°C) = 15 \text{ kcal.}$$

This is not enough heat to melt all the ice. We know immediately that we will be left with at least some ice, and that the temperature cannot exceed 0°C. On the other hand, the heat we can extract from the water is far more than needed simply to raise the ice to 0°C, so that we will melt some of the ice and thus will have a mixture of ice and water in equilibrium at 0°C. Since our final temperature is 0°C, we will extract all 15 kcal from the water. From our calculation of Q_1, we know that 0.98 kcal is needed to raise the ice to 0°C. The remaining 15 kcal $-$ 0.98 kcal $= 14$ kcal goes into melting ice. We can solve Equation 17–7 for m to find how much ice melts:

$$m = \frac{Q}{L_f} = \frac{14 \text{ kcal}}{80 \text{ kcal/kg}} = 0.18 \text{ kg} = 180 \text{ g.}$$

Therefore, we are left with 20 g of ice in 1180 g of water, with the mixture at 0°C.

17.3
THERMAL EXPANSION

We have explored changes of temperature and phase that occur when matter is heated. But our PVT diagrams show that matter may also change in volume or pressure when heated. When an ideal gas is held at constant pressure, for example, then its volume is directly proportional to its temperature.

The volume and pressure relations in the liquid and solid phases are not quite so simple. Liquids and solids are far less compressible than gases, so that thermal expansion is less pronounced. This low compressibility is reflected in the steepness of the PVT surface in the regions of pure liquid or solid. A large change in pressure or temperature is required for even a small change in volume. On the microscopic level, the molecules in a liquid or solid are closely spaced; to move them requires that we do work against large (electrical) forces.

We can characterize the change in the volume of a substance with temperature in terms of its **coefficient of volume expansion,** β, defined as the fractional change in volume when the substance undergoes a small temperature change ΔT:

$$\beta = \frac{\Delta V/V}{\Delta T}.$$ (17–8)

coefficient of volume expansion

Because β varies with temperature, Equation 17–8 is strictly valid only in the limit as ΔT approaches 0, so that we should write

$$\beta = \lim_{\Delta T \to 0} \frac{\Delta V/V}{\Delta T} = \frac{1}{V}\frac{dV}{dT}.$$ (17–9)

In practice, we can often consider β constant over a finite temperature range, and thus use Equation 17–8. Our definition of β assumes that pressure remains constant. We could entirely inhibit thermal expansion with appropriate pressure increases.

Often we want to know how one linear dimension of a solid changes with temperature. This is especially true with long, rodlike structures where the absolute change is greatest along the long dimension (Fig. 17–16). We then speak of the **coefficient of linear expansion,** α, defined by

coefficient of linear expansion

$$\alpha = \lim_{\Delta T \to 0} \frac{\Delta L/L}{\Delta T} = \frac{1}{L}\frac{dL}{dT}.$$ (17–10)

The volume expansion coefficient and linear expansion coefficient α are related in a simple way:

$$\beta = 3\alpha,$$ (17–11)

Fig. 17–16
As its length increases on a hot summer day, a power line sags noticeably.

as you can show in Problem 40. This relation means that either of these coefficients fully characterizes the thermal expansion of a material. However, the linear expansion coefficient α is really only meaningful with solids, because liquids and gases deform readily and therefore do not generally expand proportionately in all directions (see Question 32). Table 17–2 lists expansion coefficients for some common substances.

TABLE 17–2
Expansion Coefficients*

Solids	α (K^{-1})	Liquids and Gases	β (K^{-1})
Aluminum	24×10^{-6}	Air	3.7×10^{-3}
Brass	19×10^{-6}	Alcohol, ethyl	75×10^{-5}
Copper	17×10^{-6}	Gasoline	95×10^{-5}
Glass (Pyrex)	3.2×10^{-6}	Mercury	18×10^{-5}
Ice	51×10^{-6}	Water, 1°C	-4.8×10^{-5}
Invar†	0.9×10^{-6}	Water, 20°C	20×10^{-5}
Steel	12×10^{-6}	Water, 50°C	50×10^{-5}

*At approximately room temperature unless noted.
†Invar, consisting of 64 per cent iron and 36 per cent nickel, is an alloy designed for use where thermal expansion must be minimized.

Example 17–7
Thermal Expansion

A steel girder is 15 m long at $-20°C$. It is used in the construction of a building where temperature extremes of $-20°C$ to $40°C$ are expected. By how much does the girder length change between these extremes?

Solution

Table 17–2 gives the coefficient of linear expansion for steel: $\alpha = 12 \times 10^{-6}$ K^{-1}. Equation 17–10 then gives

$$\Delta L = \alpha L \Delta T = (12 \times 10^{-6}\ °C^{-1})(15\ m)(60°C) = 1.1\ cm.$$

Fig. 17–17
How does the size of the hole change when the solid expands?

What happens when a hollow object, like that shown in Fig. 17–17, expands? Do you expect that the exterior dimensions of the object would increase, while the hole shrinks in size as the material expands into it? In reality, *every* linear dimension in the solid expands in the same proportion, causing the hole to expand, too (Fig. 17–18).

Example 17–8
Thermal Expansion

A car's gasoline tank is made of steel and has internal dimensions of 60 cm $\times$ 60 cm $\times$ 20 cm at a temperature of 10°C. It is filled with gasoline at 10°C. If the temperature now increases to 30°C, by how much does the volume of the tank increase? How much gasoline spills out of the tank?

Solution

The initial volume of the tank is

$$V = (0.60\ m)(0.60\ m)(0.20\ m) = 0.072\ m^3.$$

Equation 17–8 then gives the volume increases:

$$\Delta V = \beta V \Delta T,$$

so that

$$\Delta V_{tank} = (3)(12 \times 10^{-6}\ °C^{-1})(0.072\ m^3)(20°C) = 5.2 \times 10^{-5}\ m^3,$$

and

$$\Delta V_{gas} = (95 \times 10^{-5}\ °C^{-1})(0.072\ m^3)(20°C) = 1.4 \times 10^{-3}\ m^3.$$

Since Table 17–2 gives the coefficient of linear expansion, α, for solids, we have used $\beta = 3\alpha$ in calculating the volume change of the tank.

The expansion of the steel tank is negligible compared with that of the gasoline, so that we lose $1.4 \times 10^{-3}\ m^3$, or 1.4 L of gasoline. Don't fill your gas tank to the very top!

Fig. 17–18
A hollow solid made of rectangular slabs. As the slabs expand, so does the interior hole.

Fig. 17–19
Volume of one gram of water near its melting point.

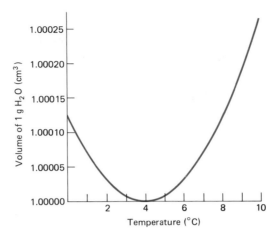

Thermal Expansion of Water

The entry for water at 1°C in Table 17–2 is remarkable, for the negative expansion coefficient shows that water at this temperature actually contracts on heating. Figure 17–19 shows the volume occupied by one gram of water as a function of temperature. From 0°C to 4.0°C, the volume decreases with increasing temperature, indicating a negative expansion coefficient. This curious behavior occurs only near the melting point, and is related to another anomalous property of water—that its solid state is less dense than its liquid state. This unusual situation occurs because the structure of the ice crystal prevents H_2O molecules in the solid state from coming as close as they do in the liquid state (Fig. 17–20). Just above the melting point, the same intermolecular forces that give the ice crystal its structure still influence the molecules strongly enough to cause the liquid to contract with increasing temperature. Finally, above 4.0°C, thermal motion of the molecules becomes more important than these intermolecular forces, and the liquid exhibits normal thermal expansion with increasing temperature.

The anomalous behavior of water has important consequences for aquatic life. Because water occupies the least volume when it is at 4.0°C, water at this temperature sinks to the bottom of freshwater lakes. For lakes deeper than a few meters, sunlight is insufficient to change this temperature, so that the deep water remains at 4.0°C year-round. In winter, the surface waters cool below 4.0°C and eventually freeze, forming an insulating layer of ice that, because of its lower density, floats on the surface. As a result, ice cover in temperate climates rarely exceeds a meter or so, and aquatic life can continue below the ice layer. If water behaved like most other liquids, the coldest water would be at the bottom and lakes would freeze from the bottom up, destroying most aquatic life.

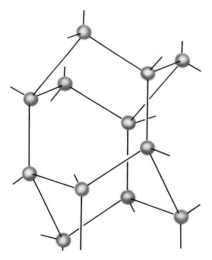

Fig. 17–20
The structure of an ice crystal makes the solid phase less dense than the liquid. Spheres represent individual H_2O molecules.

Example 17–9
Thermal Expansion of Water

The coefficient of volume expansion of liquid water in the temperature range from 0°C to about 20°C is given approximately by

$$\beta = a + bT + cT^2, \tag{17-12}$$

where T is the temperature in degrees Celsius, and where $a = -6.43 \times 10^{-5}°C^{-1}$, $b = 1.70 \times 10^{-5}°C^{-2}$, and $c = -2.02 \times 10^{-7}°C^{-3}$. If a sample of water occupies 1.00000 L at 0°C, what will its volume be at 12°C?

Since the expansion coefficient β is temperature-dependent, we must integrate, using Equation 17–9, to find the new volume. Multiplying that equation by dT, we have

$$\beta dT = \frac{dV}{V}.$$

We now integrate this expression from our initial temperature T_1 and volume V_1 to the final temperature T_2 and unknown final volume V_2, using Equation 17–12 for β:

$$\int_{T_1}^{T_2} (a + bT + cT^2)dT = \int_{V_1}^{V_2} \frac{dV}{V},$$

or

$$a(T_2 - T_1) + \tfrac{1}{2}b(T_2^2 - T_1^2) + \tfrac{1}{3}c(T_2^3 - T_1^3) = \ln\left(\frac{V_2}{V_1}\right).$$

Evaluating the left-hand side of this equation using the appropriate values of a, b, c, T_1, and T_2, we have

$$3.36 \times 10^{-4} = \ln\left(\frac{V_2}{V_1}\right),$$

so that

$$\frac{V_2}{V_1} = e^{3.36 \times 10^{-4}} = 1.00034.$$

With $V_1 = 1.00000$ L, the final volume V_2 is 1.00034 L.

Fig. 17–21
This tank of torch fuel overheated and burst from the resulting pressure increase, injuring the operator of the torch.

Fig. 17–22
Thermal expansion distorted these railroad tracks, causing a derailment.

Thermal Stresses

By enclosing a liquid or gas in a rigid container, or by tightly clamping the ends of a solid in place, we can inhibit thermal expansion. Following its *PVT* diagram, the material must then experience a pressure increase. If a container is unable to withstand this increase, it will burst (Fig. 17–21). If a solid is restrained along only one dimension, it will deform and perhaps crack (Fig. 17–22). Similarly, when a solid is clamped at both ends and cooled, tension forces develop that may cause it to break. Finally, if a solid is heated or cooled unevenly, part of the material expands or contracts at a different rate from the surrounding material. Again, the resulting forces are often sufficient to destroy the material.

SUMMARY

1. An **ideal gas** is described by a the **ideal gas law,** a particularly simple relation among pressure, temperature, and volume:

$$PV = NkT.$$

Here N is the number of molecules in the gas and $k = 1.38 \times 10^{-23}$ J/K is **Boltzmann's constant.** The ideal gas law may also be written

$$PV = nRT,$$

where n is the number of moles of the gas and $R = 8.314$ J/K·mol is the **universal gas constant.**

2. **Kinetic theory** provides a description of the ideal gas in terms of the microscopic physics of large numbers of molecules. Kinetic theory allows us to interpret temperature as a measure of the average kinetic energy of the gas molecules:

$$\tfrac{1}{2}m\overline{v^2} = \tfrac{3}{2}kT.$$

3. **Real gases** deviate from ideal behavior at high densities, where the finite size of the molecules and the intermolecular forces become significant. Real gases are described approximately by the **van der Waals equation:**

$$\left(P + \frac{n^2a}{V^2}\right)(V - nb) = nRT,$$

where a and b are constants describing a particular gas.

4. Most substances can exist in any of several **phases,** including gas, liquid, and one or more solid phases. The relations among temperature, pressure, and volume in these phases are described by a **PVT surface.** Projection of the PVT surface onto the PT plane gives the **phase diagram** for the substance. Important points on this diagram are the **triple point,** where the three phases can coexist in equilibrium, and the **critical point,** where the boundary between liquid and gas phases ceases to be distinct.

5. During a phase change, energy is transferred to or from a substance without an accompanying temperature change. The energy associated with the phase change of a unit mass of the substance is called the **heat of transformation.** The heat of **fusion** describes the solid-liquid transition, the heat of **vaporization** describes the liquid-gas transition, and the heat of **sublimation** describes the solid-gas transition.

6. Most substances expand when heated at constant pressure. The change in volume of a substance is given by

$$\Delta V = \beta V \Delta T,$$

where the quantity β is called the **coefficient of volume expansion.** β is temperature-dependent, so that this equation holds only for relatively small temperature changes. The change in length of a solid is given by a similar expression:

$$\Delta L = \alpha L \Delta T,$$

where $\alpha = \beta/3$ is the **coefficient of linear expansion.** Water provides an important exception to the general rule that substances expand when heated. In the range from 0°C to 4°C, water contracts on heating, a phenomenon with significant implications for ecological systems.

7. If a substance is held rigidly, so that thermal expansion or contraction cannot occur, then **thermal stresses** develop that may destroy either the object or its container.

QUESTIONS

1. If the volume of an ideal gas is increased, must the pressure drop proportionately? Explain.
2. According to the ideal gas law, what should the volume of a gas be at absolute zero? Why is this result absurd?
3. Why are you supposed to check the pressure in a tire when the tire is cold?
4. Figure 17–23 shows a thin, flexible wire draped over an ice cube, with weights tied on either end of the wire. If the weights are heavy enough, the wire will gradually melt its way through the ice cube, nevertheless leaving the cube in one piece. Explain this unusual phenomenon in terms of the phase diagram for water (Fig. 17–24).

Fig. 17–23   Question 4

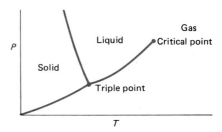

Fig. 17–24   Phase diagram for water.

5. Figure 17–25 shows a phase diagram for carbon dioxide. Could you perform the experiment in Fig. 17–23 on a dry ice cube at atmospheric pressure? At pressures above the triple-point pressure? See preceding question.

Fig. 17–25 Phase diagram for CO_2.

6. Suppose there are only two molecules in a container. Does it make sense to talk about the temperature and pressure of this gas?
7. The average *speed* of the molecules in a gas increases with increasing temperature. What about the average *velocity*?
8. Suppose you start running while holding a jar of air. Do you change the average speed of the air molecules? The average velocity? The temperature?
9. Gas thermometers containing different gases at relatively high pressures do not agree exactly at all temperatures, even if they were all calibrated at the triple point of water. Why not?
10. Do all molecules in a gas have the same speed? If so, how does this come about? If not, how can the notion of temperature be meaningful?
11. The speed of sound in a gas is closely related to the thermal speed of the molecules. Why?
12. Two different gases are at the same temperature, and both are at low enough densities that they behave like ideal gases. Do their molecules have the same thermal speeds? Explain.
13. The atmosphere of a small planet such as earth contains very little of the lighter gases like hydrogen and helium. The massive planet Jupiter has an atmosphere rich in light gases. Why might this be?
14. Is the van der Waals force attractive or repulsive? Justify your answer in terms of the sign of the term n^2a/V^2 appearing in the van der Waals equation, assuming that the parameter a is positive.
15. Some people think that ice and snow must always be at 0°C. Is this always true? Under what circumstances must it be true? Could you paraphrase the same arguments for another substance? Try steel, for example.
16. What is the temperature of water just under the ice layer of a frozen lake? At the bottom of the lake?
17. Deep lakes usually "turn over" twice each year. During the overturn, water from the lake bottom gets mixed with surface water, while at other times deep water and surface water do not mix. Under what conditions should such an overturn occur?
18. How is it possible to have liquid water at 0°C?
19. Some ice and water have been together in a glass for a long time. Is the water hotter than the ice?
20. Does it take more heat to melt a gram of ice at 0°C than to bring the resulting water to the boiling point? Once at the boiling point, does it take more heat to boil all the water than it did to bring it from the melting point to the boiling point?
21. Table 17–1 suggests that substances that are gases at room temperature and atmospheric pressure have relatively low heats of vaporization. Why might this be?
22. Why do we use the triple point of water for thermometer calibration? Why not just use the melting point or boiling point?
23. When the average temperature drops below freezing in winter, regions near large lakes remain warmer for some time. Why?
24. Must all substances exhibit solid, liquid, and gas phases? What might happen before a substance reaches the gas phase? Consider sugar, for example.
25. What would you do to air to liquefy it in such a way that the gas-liquid transition was obvious? In such a way that it was not obvious?
26. How is it possible to have boiling water at a temperature other than 100°C?
27. Why does the water in a car radiator boil explosively when you remove the radiator cap?
28. How does a pressure cooker work?
29. Why does a double boiler prevent food from burning?
30. Why can you boil water in a paper cup without burning the cup?
31. Suppose mercury and glass had the same coefficient of volume expansion. Could you build a mercury thermometer?
32. In calculating the change in length of the column in a mercury thermometer, should you use the coefficient of linear expansion or the coefficient of volume expansion? Explain.
33. Can you think of any circumstance in which you might heat a liquid and have it expand without deforming (that is, with no change in shape)?
34. Why are the coefficients of volume expansion generally greater for liquids than for solids?
35. A bimetallic strip consists of thin pieces of brass and steel bonded together (Fig. 17–26). Such strips are often used in thermostats. What will happen when the strip is heated? *Hint:* Consult Table 17–2.

Fig. 17–26 Bimetallic strip (Question 35).

36. Modern railroad tracks are often welded together, with no gaps for many miles. What do you suppose is done about thermal expansion of such tracks?
37. Why are power lines more likely to break in winter?

PROBLEMS

Section 17.1   The Ideal Gas

1. An ideal gas occupies a volume V at a temperature of 100°C. If the pressure of the gas is held constant, by what factor does the volume change when (a) the Celsius temperature is doubled? (b) the absolute (Kelvin) temperature is doubled?

2. 2.0 mol of an ideal gas are at an initial temperature of 250 K and pressure of 1.5 atm. (a) What is the volume occupied by the gas? (b) The pressure is now increased to 4.0 atm and the volume of the gas is observed to drop to half its original value. What is the new temperature of the gas?

3. The solar corona is an extended atmosphere of hot $(2 \times 10^6$ K) gas surrounding the cooler visible surface of the sun. The gas pressure in the solar corona is about 3×10^{-2} Pa. What is the number density (particles per cubic meter) in the solar corona? Compare with the number density of molecules in earth's atmosphere.

4. In a typical laboratory vacuum apparatus, a pressure of 1.0×10^{-10} Pa is readily achievable. If the residual air in this "vacuum" is at 0°C, how many air molecules are there in one liter?

5. A cubical metal box with thin walls measures 10 cm on each side. It is filled with 0.50 mol of an ideal gas at 180 K, and is surrounded by air at atmospheric pressure. What is the pressure force (magnitude and direction) on each side of the box?

6. A helium balloon occupies a volume of 8.0 L at 1.0 atm pressure and a temperature of 20°C. The balloon rises to an altitude where air pressure is 0.65 atm and where the temperature is −10°C. Assuming that the balloon stays in thermodynamic equilibrium with its surroundings, what is its volume at the new altitude?

7. A cylinder of compressed air stands 100 cm tall and has an internal diameter of 20.0 cm. At room temperature, the pressure in the cylinder is 180 atm. (a) How many moles of air are in the cylinder? (b) What volume would this air occupy at 1.0 atm pressure and room temperature?

8. A 3000-mL flask may be closed tightly by means of a valve. The valve is initially open while the flask is in a room containing air at 1.00 atm and 20°C. The valve is then closed, and the flask immersed in a bath of boiling water at 1.00 atm pressure. When the air in the flask has reached thermodynamic equilibrium, the valve is opened, air is allowed to escape, and the valve then closed. The flask is then cooled to room temperature. (a) What is the maximum pressure reached in the flask? (b) How many moles of gas escape when the air is let out of the flask? (c) What is the final pressure in the flask?

9. A student's dormitory room measures 3.0 m × 3.5 m × 2.6 m. (a) How many air molecules does it contain? (b) What is the total translational kinetic energy of these molecules? (c) How does this energy compare with the kinetic energy of the student's 1200-kg car going at 90 km/h?

10. At what temperature would the thermal speed of nitrogen molecules in air be one per cent of the speed of light? Why might it not be possible to achieve such a temperature in N_2 gas?

11. What is the thermal speed of hydrogen (H_2) molecules at a temperature of 800 K?

12. The principal gas components of earth's atmosphere are N_2, O_2, and Ar, with smaller amounts of CO_2 and H_2O and trace amounts of other gases. In air at 300 K, what are the thermal speeds of these gases?

13. The diameter of the hydrogen molecule (H_2) is on the order of 10^{-10} m. (a) What is the approximate value of the constant b in the van der Waals equation for hydrogen? Hint: Consult Fig. 17–6. (b) For H_2 gas at 273 K, at what pressure does the finite size of the H_2 molecule cause a deviation of one per cent from ideal gas behavior?

14. The van der Waals constants for helium gas (He) are $a = 0.0341$ $L^2 \cdot atm/mol^2$ and $b = 0.0237$ L/mol. What is the temperature of 3.00 mol of helium at 90.0 atm pressure if the gas is confined to a volume of 0.800 L? How does this result differ from the ideal gas prediction?

15. Plot the Maxwell-Boltzmann distribution of molecular speeds for samples of monatomic helium gas (He) containing 10^{18} atoms at temperatures of 50 K and 250 K.

16. (a) Show that Equation 17–4 implies a thermal speed given by $\sqrt{3kT/m}$. (b) By differentiating the Maxwell-Boltzmann distribution (Equation 17–5), show that the most probable molecular speed is lower than this thermal speed by a factor of $\sqrt{2/3}$.

Section 17.2   Phase Changes

17. Carbon dioxide sublimes (changes from solid to gas) at 195 K. The heat of sublimation is 573 kJ/kg. How much heat must be extracted from 250 g of CO_2 vapor at 195 K in order to solidify it?

18. A 100-g block of ice is initially at −20°C. Heat is supplied to it at the rate of 500 W. (a) How long must the heat be applied in order to produce water at 50°C? (b) Make a graph showing temperature versus time from when the heating starts until the water reaches 50°C.

19. Repeat Example 17–6 for the case when the initial mass of ice is 50 g.

20. Water at 300 K is sprinkled onto 200 g of molten copper at its melting point of 1356 K. The water boils away completely, leaving the copper entirely solid but still at 1356 K. How much water was sprinkled on the copper? Assume that water vapor leaves the system and need not come to thermodynamic equilibrium with the copper, and that there is no heat transfer from the copper except to the liquid water.

21. A 50-g ice cube at $-10°C$ is placed in an equal mass of water. What must the initial temperature of the water be in order that there remain 50 g of ice and 50 g of liquid water?

22. The size of industrial air conditioning and refrigeration units is often given in tons, meaning the number of tons of water at its melting point that the unit could freeze in one day. (This unit is a holdover from the days when ice was cut from lakes in winter to use for cooling throughout the year.) What is the rate of heat extraction, in watts, of a 15-ton refrigeration unit?

23. 1.0 kg of ice at $-40°C$ is added to 1.0 kg of water at $5.0°C$. Describe the composition and temperature of the equilibrium mixture.

24. Repeat the preceding problem if the 1.0 kg of ice is initially at $-80°C$ and if there are only 200 g of water at $5.0°C$.

25. A 40-kg block of aluminum is at a temperature of $50°C$. A jet of steam at $100°C$ is directed at the aluminum. Assuming that all the steam hits the block and condenses, and that the resulting liquid water drops off immediately without transferring heat to the aluminum, how much steam must reach the aluminum to heat it to $100°C$?

26. A solar-heated house stores energy in 5.0 tons of Glauber salt ($Na_2SO_4 \cdot 10H_2O$), a substance that melts at $90°F$. The heat of fusion of Glauber salt is 104 Btu/lb, and the specific heats of the solid and liquid are, respectively, 0.46 Btu/lb·°F and 0.68 Btu/lb·°F. After a week of sunny weather, the storage medium is all liquid at $95°F$. Then a cool, cloudy period sets in, during which the house loses heat at a rate averaging 20,000 Btu/h. (a) How long is it before the temperature of the storage medium drops below $60°F$? (b) How much of this time is spent at $90°F$?

Section 17.3   *Thermal Expansion*

27. Show that the coefficient of volume expansion of an ideal gas is just the reciprocal of the absolute temperature.

28. Suppose that a single piece of welded steel railroad track stretched across the continental United States. If the track were free to expand, but not to bend sideways, estimate its length change in going from the coldest winter day ($-25°C$) to the hottest summer day ($+40°C$)?

29. A constant-volume gas thermometer like that of Fig. 16–5 is made from Pyrex glass. If the thermometer is calibrated at the triple point of water and then used to determine the boiling point of water, how much error will be introduced by ignoring the expansion of the glass?

30. A 2000-mL graduated cylinder is filled with liquid at 350 K. When the liquid is cooled to 300 K, the cylinder is full only to the 1925-mL mark. Using Table 17–2, identify the liquid.

31. A steel ball bearing 5.0 mm in radius is encased in a Pyrex glass cube 1.0 cm on a side. At 330 K, the ball bearing fits tightly in its cavity. At what temperature will it have a clearance of 1.0 μm all around?

32. Referring to Example 17–9, calculate the change in volume of 1.00000 L of water in going from (a) $0°C$ to $4.0°C$, (b) $4.0°C$ to $15°C$. Compare your result in part (b) with the answer you would get assuming that the coefficient of volume expansion were constant and equal to its value at $0°C$.

33. Use Equation 17–12 to show that water has its greatest density at very nearly $4.0°C$.

34. A sample of water occupies 5.00000 L at $0°C$. At what other temperature would it have the same volume? (See Example 17–9.)

35. In Equation 17–12, the coefficients appropriate to carbon tetrachloride (CCl_4) are $a = 1.18 \times 10^{-3}°C^{-1}$, $b = 0.396 \times 10^{-6}°C^{-2}$, and $c = 0.390 \times 10^{-7}°C^{-3}$. If a sample of CCl_4 occupies 2.000 L at $10°C$, what is its volume at $50°C$? Compare with the result obtained by assuming that the coefficient of volume expansion is constant and is equal to its value at $0°C$.

36. A glass marble 1.000 cm in diameter is to be dropped through a hole in a steel plate. At room temperature the hole has a diameter of 0.997 cm. By how much must the temperature of the steel be raised so that the marble fits through the hole?

Supplementary Problems

37. Temperatures in the upper atmospheres of earth and Jupiter are about 1000 K and 300 K, respectively. Calculate the thermal speeds of hydrogen (H_2) and oxygen (O_2) at each planet, and compare with the escape speed for that planet. What implications do your results have for the atmospheric composition of the planets? Explain in terms of your numerical results and the shape of the Maxwell-Boltzmann distribution.

38. Ignoring air resistance, find the height from which you must drop an ice cube at $0°C$ so that it completely melts on impact. Assume no heat is exchanged with the environment.

39. The timekeeping of an old pendulum clock is regulated by a brass pendulum 20.0 cm long. If the clock is accurate at $20°C$, but is in a room at $18°C$, how long will it be before the clock is in error by one minute? Will it be too fast or too slow?

40. Prove the relation of Equation 17–11, showing that the volume expansion coefficient β and linear expansion coefficient α are related by $\beta = 3\alpha$. To do so, consider a cube of side L. Use the chain rule to write

$$\frac{dV}{dT} = \frac{dV}{dL}\frac{dL}{dT}.$$

Substitute this expression for dV/dT in Equation 17–9. Express the cube's volume V in terms of its side length L, and from this evaluate the quantity dV/dL. Show that your result then takes the form of Equation 17–10, with $\alpha = \frac{1}{3}\beta$.

18

HEAT, WORK, AND THE FIRST LAW OF THERMODYNAMICS

How do we change the temperature of a substance? One approach, described in detail in Chapter 16, involves heat transfer between substances at different temperatures. Another approach—which you have experienced if you ever pulled a rope too quickly through your hands, or touched a drill bit just after drilling a hole, or smelled your car's brakes burning as you went down a steep hill—involves mechanical energy. In this chapter, we will explore this second approach to temperature change, and in the process come to a deeper understanding of the relation between heat and mechanical energy.

18.1
THE FIRST LAW OF THERMODYNAMICS

We have defined heat as energy that is transferred from one object to another because of a temperature difference alone. As a result of heat transfer, a substance undergoes changes in its thermodynamic state—its temperature, pressure, and volume may change, and it may undergo a change of phase. But we can accomplish these same changes by the transfer of mechanical energy. As Fig. 18–1 suggests, we can raise the temperature of water by heating with a flame or by stirring violently with a spoon. For the flame to heat the water, the flame temperature must exceed the water temperature. But the temperature of the spoon is irrelevant, for it is the transfer of the mechanical energy associated with the spoon's motion that raises the water temperature. We use the term **work** to describe energy transfer that does not require a temperature difference. This sense is consistent with our earlier use of the word work to describe mechanical energy being transferred from one object to another. Sometimes that energy ends up as stored potential energy, but often it results in a temperature change—as when we do work against frictional forces. That both heat and mechanical work can

Fig. 18–1
Water temperature may be raised *(a)* with a flame or *(b)* by mechanical agitation.

work

internal energy

Fig. 18–2
Schematic diagram of Joule's apparatus. Potential energy of the falling weights is converted to kinetic energy of the rotating paddle, which in turn becomes internal energy of the water.

first law of
thermodynamics

Fig. 18–3
Molecular rotation and vibration contribute to the internal energy of a diatomic gas.

have the same effect on a substance—namely, a temperature change—is what made possible Joule's quantitative identification of heat as a form of energy (Fig. 18–2).

What happens to the energy we transfer to a system, either through heat or through mechanical work? It ends up changing the **internal energy** of the system. We discussed internal energy earlier in connection with heat transfer alone. Now, recognizing that heat and mechanical energy can have the same effect on a system, we conclude that both are associated with internal energy changes. What, exactly, is internal energy? It is simply the sum of all the different kinds of energy associated with the individual particles making up a substance. For the ideal gas of the previous chapter, internal energy is the total kinetic energy of the gas molecules. In a more complicated substance, other forms of energy also contribute to the internal energy. In a gas of diatomic molecules, for example, we must consider also the energy of rotation or vibration of the molecules (Fig. 18–3). In a solid or liquid, with molecules close together, the potential energy associated with intermolecular forces also accounts for some internal energy. When energy is released in reactions that rearrange atoms or even atomic nuclei, then we must include the potential energy of atomic and nuclear configurations as internal energy. A fuel—like gasoline or uranium—has considerable internal potential energy.

If we keep track of all energy entering and leaving a system, and monitor corresponding changes in internal energy, we find experimentally that energy is conserved. Given the extent to which we have stressed energy conservation in our study of mechanics, this is hardly surprising. But our statement of energy conservation is now broader, for it applies to heat transfer as well as to mechanical work. This broader statement of energy conservation is known as the **first law of thermodynamics:**

> The change in the internal energy of a system is equal to the heat added to the system minus the work done by the system.

Mathematically, we can state the first law by writing

$$\Delta U = Q - W, \qquad (18\text{–}1)$$

where ΔU $(= U_{\text{final}} - U_{\text{initial}})$ is the change in internal energy of a system, Q the heat added *to* the system, and W the work done *by* the system. Why the minus sign in Equation 18–1? Had we defined W as the work done *on* the system, then positive values of both W and Q would represent energy input to the system, and both would enter the equation with plus signs. Historically, though, the first law was developed in connection with the study of engines, which typically take in energy from a heat source and give out energy in the form of mechanical work. Keeping track of energy transfers in an engine is made simpler by considering both the heat input and work output as positive quantities; their difference is then the change in internal energy.

The first law of thermodynamics shows that there are many ways to change the internal energy of a system. We could heat the system without doing any mechanical work on it. Or we could do only mechanical work, without allowing any heat transfer. Or we could apply some combination of heat and mechanical work. The change in internal energy does not de-

thermodynamic state variable

pend on the details of the process whereby we change it—it depends only on the net amount of energy transferred to the system. Like temperature and pressure, internal energy is a **thermodynamic state variable**—a quantity whose value is independent of how the system got into a particular state.

Frequently we are concerned with the rates of energy flow in a system. By differentiating the first law with respect to time, we obtain a statement about these rates:

$$\frac{dU}{dt} = \frac{dQ}{dt} - \frac{dW}{dt}. \tag{18–2}$$

Here dU/dt is the rate of change of internal energy, dQ/dt the rate at which heat is supplied to the system, and dW/dt the rate at which the system does work in its surroundings.

Example 18–1
A Nuclear Power Plant

In a nuclear power plant, heat produced from nuclear fission boils water that, in turn, drives a steam turbine connected to an electric generator. The steam is then cooled and condensed through thermal contact with water from a river, lake, or ocean, and sent back to the reactor to be reheated and turned to steam again. The nuclear reactor in a certain power plant releases energy at the rate of 1500 MW. (This is the rate at which the internal energy of the nuclear fuel decreases.) The power plant supplies 500 MW of electric power. At what rate is heat transferred to the cooling water used to condense steam?

Solution

Solving Equation 18–2 for the rate of heat transfer gives

$$\frac{dQ}{dt} = \frac{dU}{dt} + \frac{dW}{dt}.$$

Here dU/dt is -1500 MW, since the internal energy is decreasing, while dW/dt, the work done *by* the power plant, is $+500$ MW, so that

$$\frac{dQ}{dt} = -1500 \text{ MW} + 500 \text{ MW} = -1000 \text{ MW}.$$

Since a positive Q represents heat transferred *to* a system, the minus sign in this answer shows that heat is being transferred *from* the power plant *to* the cooling water at the rate of 1000 MW. The numbers in this example are typical of a medium-sized power plant. We will see in the next chapter just why it is that so much of the energy released in the reactor ends up in the cooling water rather than as electricity.

18.2
THERMODYNAMIC PROCESSES

The first law of thermodynamics relates the two kinds of energy transfers—heat and work—that can change the thermodynamic state of a system. Although the law applies to *any* system, we can most readily illustrate its use in application to an ideal gas. The ideal gas law (Equation 17–1 or 17–2) relates the temperature, pressure, and volume of a given sample of gas:

$$PV = nRT.$$

If we know any two of these, the thermodynamic state of the gas is completely determined. One way to specify the thermodynamic state is to use a diagram whose two coordinate axes represent two of the thermodynamic state variables—for example, pressure P and volume V. Each point on such a diagram specifies a unique combination of pressure and volume, and therefore a thermodynamic state of the system. The utility of a PV diagram in specifying thermodynamic states is not limited to ideal gases, but applies to any substance whose thermodynamic state is uniquely specified by giving values of P and V.

Thermodynamic state is a meaningful concept only for a system in thermodynamic equilibrium, for only in equilibrium does the system have uniquely defined values of temperature and pressure. While we are changing the thermodynamic state of a system, we may temporarily find that the system has no uniquely defined state. Suppose we take a sealed container of gas in thermodynamic equilibrium at 100 K and plunge it suddenly into a vat of boiling sulfur at 718 K (Fig. 18–4). Before the gas comes to equilibrium with the sulfur, there will be a period of chaos when gas molecules nearest the container walls have much more energy than those near the center of the container. Only gradually, as the molecules share energy through collisions, will the system come to an equilibrium state in which the average molecular energy is the same throughout the gas and therefore in which temperature is well defined.

A very different approach to heating the same gas sample would be to put it in contact with a heat reservoir whose temperature we can control (Fig. 18–5). If we raise the reservoir temperature very slowly, its temperature will exceed that of our gas sample by only a very small amount, and the gas will be very nearly in equilibrium at all times. In the limit of an arbitrarily slow change in reservoir temperature, we can consider the gas sample to be exactly in equilibrium at all times. Such a slow change, in which a system remains in equilibrium, is called a **quasi-static process.** No real process quite achieves the quasi-static limit, but we can approach it by making the changes in a system occur very slowly. Because a system undergoing quasi-static change is always in thermodynamic equilibrium, it is always describable by a point in a thermodynamic state diagram like a PV diagram. The overall quasi-static change from one state to another is then described by a continuous set of points—a curve—in that diagram (Fig. 18–6).

In the quasi-static heating process we just described, our gas sample is always at very nearly the same temperature as its surroundings. If we make the surroundings infinitesimally cooler rather than warmer than the gas, the process will proceed in the opposite direction. For this reason, such a process is also called a **reversible process.** Once we have heated our gas sample quasi-statically to the boiling point of sulfur, for example, we could quasi-statically cool it to its original state. In the process, the gas would pass in the opposite direction through the same series of equilibrium states that it did while heating, thereby reversing the direction of its travel in the PV plane. A process like the sudden plunging of the gas sample into boiling sulfur is, in contrast, **irreversible.** A system undergoing irreversible change

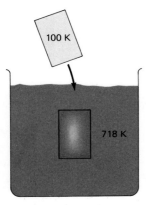

Fig. 18–4
An irreversible process. A gas sample at 100 K is plunged suddenly into boiling sulfur. A period of disequilibrium ensues, in which molecules near the container walls have more energy than those in the center of the sample. Eventually a new equilibrium is established as molecules share energy through collisions.

quasi-static process

reversible process

irreversible

Fig. 18–5
A gas sample in contact with a heat reservoir whose temperature is adjustable. If the reservoir temperature is changed very slowly, the gas remains very nearly in equilibrium at all times.

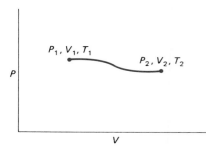

Fig. 18–6
Because a system undergoing a quasi-static change is always in equilibrium, the change may be described by a succession of states—a continuous path—in the PV diagram.

Fig. 18–7
A gas-cylinder system.

has no well-defined thermodynamic state until the process is complete, so it makes no sense to think of a path in the PV diagram. A process may be irreversible even though it returns a system to the same original state it started from. The distinction between reversible and irreversible refers not to the end states but to the process that takes a system between those states.

The terms reversible and irreversible refer to transfers of mechanical energy as well as of heat. For example, we hold a small balloon in our hands and suddenly, violently compress it. Gas molecules near the edges of the balloon are rapidly accelerated, while those at the center do not yet sense the compression. The system is temporarily out of equilibrium; we have performed an irreversible process. Eventually the system reaches equilibrium with constant temperature and pressure throughout, but during the compression these quantities have no well-defined values. If, on the other hand, we compress the balloon so slowly that the entire volume of gas can adjust continuously to the changing conditions, then we perform a reversible compression.

We can imagine many ways to change the thermodynamic state of a system—reversibly, irreversibly, while maintaining a constant pressure, while maintaining a constant temperature, changing both temperature and pressure simultaneously, and so on. We now consider several important special cases of such changes, as they apply to a simple ideal gas system. Although the system we use and the processes to which we subject it may seem artificial, our special cases in fact illustrate the physical principles behind a myriad of technological devices and natural phenomena, from the operation of a gasoline engine to the propagation of a sound wave to the oscillations of a variable star.

Our system consists of an ideal gas confined to a cylinder that is sealed with a movable piston (Fig. 18–7). The piston and the cylinder walls are perfectly insulating—they block all heat transfer—while the bottom of the cylinder is a perfect conductor of heat. By altering the gas temperature and/or the location of the piston, we can change the thermodynamic state of the gas. We will consider only reversible processes, which we can describe by paths in the PV diagram for our gas, and will use the first law of thermodynamics to relate the associated energy transfers by heat and work.

Before examining specific processes, we develop a general relation between volume change and work that holds for all processes. If A is the cross-sectional area of our piston and cylinder, and P the gas pressure, then $F = PA$ is the force exerted by the gas on the piston (Fig. 18–8). If the piston moves a small distance Δx, then the work done by the gas is

$$\Delta W = F\Delta x = PA\Delta x.$$

But $A\Delta x$ is the change in volume of the gas, so that

$$\Delta W = P\Delta V. \qquad (18-3)$$

The work ΔW is positive when the volume increases, indicating that the gas does work on the piston and its surroundings, while the work is negative if ΔV is negative, indicating that work is done on the gas. In general, the pressure may depend on the volume, so that Equation 18–3 is strictly valid only in the limit of arbitrarily small volume changes. To find the

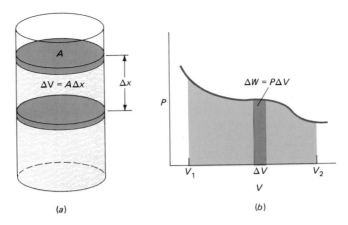

Fig. 18–8
(a) The force on piston of area A is PA, so that the work done in moving the piston a small distance Δx is PAΔx, or PΔV. (b) On the PV diagram, this work corresponds to the area under the PV curve on the volume interval ΔV associated with the change Δx in the position of the piston. The total work to take the system from V_1 to V_2 is the area under the PV curve between V_1 and V_2.

work associated with a larger volume change, we take the limit $\Delta V \rightarrow 0$, and integrate over the volume change:

$$W = \int dW = \int_{V_1}^{V_2} P\,dV, \tag{18–4}$$

where V_1 and V_2 are the initial and final volumes. Figure 18–8b shows the geometrical interpretation of this equation: the work done by the gas is simply the area under the PV curve.

Isothermal Processes

isothermal process

To perform a reversible **isothermal process,** we place the heat-conducting bottom of our gas cylinder in good thermal contact with a substance—a heat reservoir—whose temperature is held constant (Fig. 18–9). We then move the piston to change the volume of the system, doing so slowly enough that the gas remains in equilibrium with the heat reservoir. The system then moves from its initial state to its final state along a curve of constant temperature—an **isotherm**—in the PV diagram (Fig. 18–10). The work done in the process is given by Equation 18–4, and is equal to the area under the isotherm.

isotherm

For an ideal gas, we can relate pressure P and volume V through the ideal gas law:

$$P = \frac{nRT}{V}.$$

Then Equation 18–4 becomes

$$W = \int_{V_1}^{V_2} \frac{nRT}{V}\,dV.$$

Fig. 18–9
During an isothermal process, the system is held in thermal contact with a heat reservoir at fixed temperature.

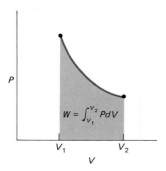

Fig. 18–10
PV diagram for an isothermal process. The work done during the process is the area under the curve.

For an isothermal process, the temperature T is constant, giving

$$W = nRT \int_{V_1}^{V_2} \frac{dV}{V} = nRT \ln V \Big|_{V_1}^{V_2} = nRT \ln\left(\frac{V_2}{V_1}\right). \quad (18\text{–}5)$$

The internal energy of an ideal gas consists only of the kinetic energy of its molecules which, as we saw in the previous chapter, depends only on temperature. Therefore, in an isothermal process, there is no change in the internal energy of the ideal gas. The first law of thermodynamics then gives

$$\Delta U = 0 = Q - W,$$

so that

$$Q = W = nRT \ln\left(\frac{V_2}{V_1}\right). \quad \text{(isothermal process)} \quad (18\text{–}6)$$

What does this result $Q = W$ mean? Recall that Q is the heat transferred *to* the gas, while W is the work done *by* the gas. Therefore, our result says that when an ideal gas does work W on the external world with no change in temperature, it must absorb an equal amount of heat from outside. Similarly, if work is done on the gas, then the gas must reject an equal amount of heat to the outside if its temperature is not to change.

The result 18–6 applies only to an ideal gas, in which the internal energy depends only on the temperature. In a real gas, a change in volume results in a change in the potential energy associated with intermolecular forces. Because these forces are attractive, the potential energy increases as gas volume increases. In an isothermal expansion, in which the *kinetic* energy of the molecules remains constant, the *total* internal energy actually increases, and the gas must absorb an amount of heat Q that exceeds slightly the work W it does on the external world.

Example 18–2 _____

A Diver Exhales

A scuba diver is swimming at a depth of 25 m, where the pressure is 3.5 atm (recall Example 15–3). The air she exhales forms bubbles 8.0 mm in radius. How much work is done by each bubble as it expands on rising to the surface? Assume that, because of their small size and relatively slow rise, the bubbles remain at the uniform 300 K temperature of the surrounding water.

Solution

Since the bubbles remain at constant temperature, the process is isothermal and Equation 18–6 applies. Just before they break the surface, the bubbles are at essentially 1 atm pressure, so that their pressure has decreased by a factor of 3.5. The ideal gas law, $PV = nRT$, shows that when temperature is constant, pressure and volume are inversely related. Therefore, the bubble volume has increased by a factor of 3.5. To apply Equation 18–6, we also need the quantity nRT for a bubble. We can get this from the ideal gas law using the given radius of the bubbles at 3.5 atm pressure:

$$nRT = PV = P(\tfrac{4}{3}\pi r^3),$$

so that Equation 18–6 becomes

$$W = nRT \ln\left(\frac{V_2}{V_1}\right) = \tfrac{4}{3}\pi r^3 P \ln\left(\frac{V_2}{V_1}\right)$$

$$= \tfrac{4}{3}\pi(8.0 \times 10^{-3} \text{ m})^3(3.5 \text{ atm})(1.01 \times 10^5 \text{ Pa/atm}) \ln(3.5)$$

$$= 0.95 \text{ J.}$$

Where does this energy go? As the bubble expands, it pushes water outward and, ultimately, upward. It therefore raises the gravitational potential energy of the ocean. (When the bubble breaks the surface, this excess potential energy becomes kinetic energy, appearing in the form of small waves on the water surface.)

Constant-Volume Processes and Specific Heat

constant-volume process

A **constant-volume process** (also called isometric, isochoric, or isovolumic), occurs in a rigid, closed container whose volume cannot change. In our piston-cylinder arrangement, we could tightly clamp the piston to achieve a constant-volume process. Because the piston does not move, the gas does no work, and the first law becomes simply

$$Q = \Delta U. \tag{18-7}$$

molar specific heat at constant volume

To express this result in terms of a temperature change ΔT, we introduce the **molar specific heat at constant volume,** C_V, defined by the equation

$$Q = nC_V\Delta T, \tag{18-8}$$

where n is the number of moles of gas in our system. This molar specific heat is like the specific heat we defined in Chapter 16, except that with a gas it is more convenient to consider the heat per mole rather than per unit mass. Introducing the definition of C_V into Equation 18–7 gives

$$nC_V\Delta T = \Delta U. \tag{18-9}$$

Solving for C_V, and taking the limit of very small temperature changes, gives

$$C_V = \frac{1}{n}\frac{dU}{dT}. \tag{18-10}$$

For an ideal gas, the internal energy is a function of temperature alone, so that dU/dT has the same value no matter what process the gas may be undergoing. Therefore, Equation 18–9, relating the temperature change ΔT and internal energy change ΔU, applies not only to a constant-volume process, but also to *any* ideal gas process. Why, then, have we been so careful to label C_V the specific heat *at constant volume*? Although the relation $nC_V\Delta T = \Delta U$ holds for any process, it is only when no work is done that the first law allows us to write $Q = \Delta U$, and therefore only for a constant-volume process that Equation 18–8 holds.

Isobaric Processes and Specific Heat

isobaric

Isobaric means constant pressure. In a reversible isobaric process, a system moves along an isobar, or curve of constant pressure, in its *PV* diagram (Fig. 18–11). The isobar is simply a horizontal straight line in the *PV* dia-

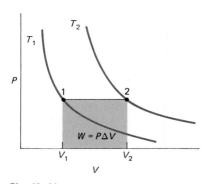

Fig. 18–11
PV diagram for an isobaric process. Also shown are the isotherms for the initial and final temperatures. Work done is the shaded area under the isobar.

gram, and the system moves from an initial state with temperature T_1 and volume V_1 to a final state (T_2, V_2) while its pressure P remains constant. The work done in the process is the area under the isobar, and is given by Equation 18–4:

$$W = \int_{V_1}^{V_2} P\,dV = P \int_{V_1}^{V_2} dV = P(V_2 - V_1) = P\Delta V,$$

since P is constant.

Solving the first law (Equation 18–1) for Q and using our expression for work gives

$$Q = \Delta U + W = \Delta U + P\Delta V.$$

But we found in the previous section that the change in internal energy of an ideal gas is given by $\Delta U = nC_V\Delta T$ for *any* process. Therefore

$$Q = nC_V\Delta T + P\Delta V \qquad (18\text{–}11)$$

molar specific heat at constant pressure

for an isobaric process. We define the **molar specific heat at constant pressure** as the heat required to raise one mole of gas through a unit temperature change when the gas is at constant pressure, so that

$$Q = nC_P\Delta T.$$

Equation 18–11 can then be written

$$nC_P\Delta T = nC_V\Delta T + P\Delta V. \qquad \text{(isobaric process)} \qquad (18\text{–}12)$$

Equation 18–12 is a useful form for calculating temperature changes in an isobaric process, if we know both specific heats C_P and C_V. However, we really need only one of these specific heats, for a simple relation holds between the two. The ideal gas law, $PV = nRT$, allows us to write

$$P\Delta V = nR\Delta T$$

for an isobaric process. Using this expression in Equation 18–12 gives

$$nC_P\Delta T = nC_V\Delta T + nR\Delta T,$$

so that

$$C_P = C_V + R. \qquad (18\text{–}13)$$

Does this result make sense? Specific heat is a measure of the amount of heat needed to cause a given temperature change. In a constant-volume process, no work is done and all the heat goes into raising the internal energy and thus the temperature of an ideal gas. In a constant-pressure process, work is done and some of the added heat ends up as mechanical energy of the external world, leaving less energy available for raising the temperature. Therefore, in a constant-pressure process, *more* heat is needed to achieve a given temperature change, so that the specific heat at constant pressure is larger than that at constant volume, as reflected in Equation 18–13.

Why did we not distinguish specific heats at constant volume and constant pressure much earlier? Because we were concerned mostly with solids and liquids, whose coefficients of expansion are far lower than those of gases. As a result of its relatively small expansion, the work done by a solid or liquid is much less than that done by a gas. Since work is what gives rise to the difference between C_V and C_P, the distinction is less significant for solids and liquids. As a practical matter, measured specific heats are usually at constant pressure, because enormous pressures would be needed to prevent volume changes in solids or liquids.

Adiabatic Processes

adiabatic process

In an **adiabatic process,** we allow no heat transfer between a system and its environment. The easiest way to achieve this is to surround the system with a perfect insulator that prevents conduction, convection, and radiation. Because heat transfer takes time, a rapid process is often adiabatic simply because the time for the process to occur is short compared with the time needed to transfer significant amounts of heat into or out of the system. In a gasoline engine, for example, the compression of the gasoline-air mixture and subsequent expansion of the combustion products are nearly adiabatic because they occur so rapidly that little heat flows through the cylinder walls during the process.

In an adiabatic process, the heat Q is zero, so that the first law becomes

$$0 = \Delta U + W,$$

or

$$\Delta U = -W. \quad \text{(adiabatic process)} \quad (18\text{--}14)$$

This equation says that if a system does work on its surroundings, then its internal energy must decrease by the same amount. This makes sense because, if no heat is added, then any energy transferred out as work must come from the system's internal energy. Microscopically, the decrease in internal energy comes about as gas molecules bounce off the moving piston. Were the piston not moving, the molecules would return to the gas with the same speed and hence kinetic energy. But when the piston is moving, their speed is decreased by that of the piston, so that they return to the gas with less kinetic energy (Fig. 18–12). Conversely, if the piston moves inward, work is done on the gas, and its internal energy increases.

What is the path of a reversible adiabatic process in the PV diagram? Because the internal energy changes, so must the gas temperature. In an adiabatic expansion, for example, the temperature drops and the volume increases. The ideal gas law, $PV = nRT$, then requires that the pressure decrease as well—and by more than it would in an isothermal expansion between the same initial and final volumes. Figure 18–13 depicts such an adiabatic path, called an **adiabat.**

adiabat

Fig. 18–12
Molecules bouncing off a stationary piston rebound with no loss of speed. But molecules bouncing off an outward-moving piston rebound with lower speed, having given energy to the piston.

(a) Stationary piston

(b) Moving piston

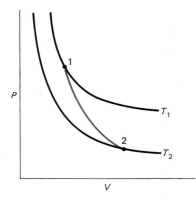

Fig. 18–13
PV diagram for an adiabatic process. Also shown are isotherms for the initial and final temperatures. The adiabatic path is steeper than the isotherms because the gas loses internal energy as it does work.

Because neither temperature nor pressure nor volume remains constant, we can determine the adiabatic path only by considering a sequence of infinitesimal adiabatic changes, and integrating to get a relation between the initial and final states. Earlier we found that for *any* process, the relation between temperature change and internal energy change is given by Equation 18–9, so that the internal energy change during an infinitesimal adiabatic process is

$$dU = nC_V dT.$$

The work done in the process is

$$dW = PdV.$$

Then the first law for an adiabatic process (Equation 18–14) becomes

$$nC_V dT = -PdV. \tag{18-15}$$

To determine the adiabatic path in the *PV* diagram, we must obtain a relation between *P* and *V* alone. To eliminate *dT* in Equation 18–15, we first differentiate the ideal gas law, allowing both *P* and *V* to change:

$$d(PV) = nRdT,$$

or

$$PdV + VdP = nRdT. \tag{18-16}$$

Solving Equation 18–16 for *ndT* and using the result in Equation 18–15 gives

$$C_V \frac{PdV + VdP}{R} = -PdV.$$

Multiplying through by *R* and bringing all terms to the left side of the equation results in

$$(C_V + R)PdV + C_V VdP = 0.$$

But we found earlier that C_P, the specific heat at constant pressure, is given by $C_P = C_V + R$, so that

$$C_P PdV + C_V VdP = 0.$$

Dividing this equation through by $C_V PV$ gives

$$\frac{C_P}{C_V} \frac{dV}{V} + \frac{dP}{P} = 0.$$

The specific heats are essentially constant (see Section 18.3), so that we can integrate this equation to obtain

$$\frac{C_P}{C_V} \ln V + \ln P = \ln(\text{constant}),$$

where we have chosen to call the constant of integration ln(constant). The ratio of specific heats, C_P/C_V, is commonly called γ, so that

$$\gamma \ln V + \ln P = \ln(\text{constant}).$$

Noting that $\gamma \ln V = \ln(V^\gamma)$, it follows by exponentiation that

$$PV^{\gamma} = \text{constant.} \quad \text{(adiabatic process)} \qquad (18\text{--}17)$$

Equation 18–17 is the equation for an adiabatic path in the PV diagram of an ideal gas. For a particular adiabatic process starting from a given state (P_0, V_0), the constant in the equation is determined from the initial conditions:

$$\text{constant} = P_0 V_0^{\gamma}. \qquad (18\text{--}18)$$

Because $C_P = C_V + R$, the ratio $\gamma = C_P / C_V$ is always greater than 1. Therefore, an adiabatic process with a given volume change results in a greater pressure change than would an isothermal process starting from the same initial conditions, for the isothermal process satisfies the condition $PV = \text{constant}$, while the adiabatic process satisfies $PV^{\gamma} = \text{constant}$. In the PV diagram, the adiabatic path is steeper than the isothermal path, as reflected in Fig. 18–13. Physically, the adiabatic path is steeper because the gas loses internal energy as it does work, so that its temperature drops.

It might seem that the equation $PV^{\gamma} = \text{constant}$ contradicts the ideal gas law, $PV = nRT$. But the ideal gas law does not imply $PV = \text{constant}$ except in an isothermal process, where T is constant. Since a reversible process cannot be both adiabatic (no heat addition) and isothermal (no temperature change), there is no contradiction. The adiabatic equation $PV^{\gamma} = \text{constant}$ was derived using the ideal gas law, and describes a situation in which the temperature changes. In fact, we can find the temperature change by using the ideal gas law to eliminate pressure from the adiabatic equation. We may write the adiabatic equation in the form

$$PV \cdot V^{\gamma - 1} = \text{constant.}$$

But the ideal gas law gives $PV = nRT$, so that

$$nRTV^{\gamma - 1} = \text{constant,}$$

or

$$TV^{\gamma - 1} = \text{constant,} \qquad (18\text{--}19)$$

where we have absorbed the constants n and R into a new definition of the constant on the right-hand side. Equation 18–19 shows explicitly that an adiabatic process is not isothermal, for the temperature must drop in an adiabatic expansion and rise in an adiabatic compression. We could have written the adiabatic equation in yet a third way, eliminating V in favor of T and P (see Problem 12).

Example 18–3
A Diesel Engine

Ignition of the fuel in a diesel engine occurs on contact with air heated by compression as the piston moves to the top of its stroke. (In this way a diesel differs from a gasoline engine, in which a spark ignites the fuel.) The compression occurs fast enough that very little heat flows out of the gas, so that the process may be considered adiabatic. If a temperature of 500°C is required for ignition, what must be the compression ratio (ratio of maximum to minimum cylinder volume) of the diesel engine? Air has a specific heat ratio γ of 1.4, and before compression its temperature is 20°C.

Solution

Equation 18–19 gives the relation between temperature and volume in an adiabatic process. Writing T_0 and V_0 for the temperature and volume at the bottom of the piston stroke, and T_1 and V_1 for the top of the stroke, Equation 18–19 becomes

$$T_1 V_1^{\gamma-1} = T_0 V_0^{\gamma-1}.$$

Solving for the compression ratio V_0/V_1 gives

$$\frac{V_0}{V_1} = \left(\frac{T_1}{T_0}\right)^{1/(\gamma-1)} = \left(\frac{773 \text{ K}}{293 \text{ K}}\right)^{1/0.4} = 11.$$

Practical diesel engines have considerably higher compression ratios to ensure reliable ignition. Conversely, compressional heating places an upper limit on the compression ratios of gasoline engines, where ignition by hot air would circumvent the carefully timed spark ignition system (see Problem 22).

Example 18–4
Adiabatic and Isothermal Expansion

Two identical gas-cylinder systems each contain 0.060 mol of ideal gas at 300 K and 2.0 atm pressure. The specific heat ratio γ of the gas is 1.4. The gas samples are allowed to expand, one adiabatically and one isothermally, until both are at 1.0 atm pressure. What are the final temperatures and volumes of each?

Solution

The initial volume V_0 of both samples may be obtained from the ideal gas law, $PV = nRT$. Solving for V gives

$$V_0 = \frac{nRT_0}{P_0} = \frac{(0.060 \text{ mol})(8.3 \text{ J/K·mol})(300 \text{ K})}{(2.0 \text{ atm})(1.0 \times 10^5 \text{ Pa/atm})}$$

$$= 7.5 \times 10^{-4} \text{ m}^3 = 0.75 \text{ L}.$$

For the isothermal sample, T remains constant at 300 K. With constant temperature, $PV = \text{constant}$, so that as the pressure drops in half, the volume doubles, becoming 1.5 L.

For the adiabatic expansion, we have

$$PV^\gamma = \text{constant} = P_0 V_0^\gamma.$$

Solving for V gives

$$V^\gamma = \frac{P_0 V_0^\gamma}{P},$$

or

$$V = \left(\frac{P_0}{P}\right)^{1/\gamma} V_0 = \left(\frac{2.0 \text{ atm}}{1.0 \text{ atm}}\right)^{1/1.4} (0.75 \text{ L}) = 1.2 \text{ L}.$$

We can obtain the temperature from Equation 18–19:

$$TV^{\gamma-1} = \text{constant} = T_0 V_0^{\gamma-1},$$

or

$$T = T_0 \left(\frac{V_0}{V}\right)^{\gamma-1} = (300 \text{ K})\left(\frac{0.75 \text{ L}}{1.2 \text{ L}}\right)^{0.4} = 250 \text{ K}.$$

Since we knew both P and V, we could equally well have determined the temperature from the ideal gas law.

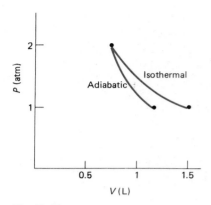

Fig. 18–14
PV diagram showing isothermal and adiabatic processes of Example 18–4.

In this example, both gas samples do work against the outside world as they expand. In the isothermal process, energy leaving the system as work is replaced by energy entering as heat, so that the temperature and internal energy remain constant. But heat cannot flow during the adiabatic process, so that the work done is at the expense of the internal energy of the gas. As a result, the gas temperature drops, and the volume does not increase as much. Figure 18–14 shows both processes on a PV diagram.

How much work is done during a reversible adiabatic process? For an adiabatic process, there is no heat transfer, so that $W = -U$. But earlier we found that $\Delta U = nC_V\Delta T$ for *any* process. Therefore, in an adiabatic process,

$$W = -nC_V\Delta T = nC_V(T_1 - T_2), \qquad (18\text{–}20)$$

where T_1 and T_2 are the initial and final temperatures. We can express this result in terms of pressure and volume changes by solving the ideal gas law, $PV = nRT$, for temperature and using the result in Equation 18–20:

$$W = nC_V \frac{P_1V_1 - P_2V_2}{nR}.$$

But $R = C_P - C_V$, so

$$\frac{C_V}{R} = \frac{C_V}{C_P - C_V} = \frac{1}{(C_P/C_V) - 1} = \frac{1}{\gamma - 1}.$$

Then our expression for the adiabatic work becomes

$$W = \frac{P_1V_1 - P_2V_2}{\gamma - 1}. \qquad (18\text{–}21)$$

We could also have obtained this result by direct integration of Equation 18–4 for an adiabatic process (see Problem 9).

Cyclic Processes

Many systems encountered in nature and in engineering applications undergo cyclic processes, in which the system returns periodically to the same thermodynamic state. Important examples include engines, refrigerators, and air compressors, whose mechanical construction ensures that a gas or fluid sample is eventually returned to the same state. Many natural oscillations, like those of a sound wave or a pulsating star, are very nearly cyclic.

Figure 18–15 shows a cyclic path *ABCDA*, in the *PV* diagram of an ideal gas. Starting from state *A*, we could traverse this path with our gas-cylinder system by

1. Heating the gas at constant pressure P_A until it expands to volume V_B. (We could maintain constant pressure by placing appropriate weights on the piston.)
2. Locking the piston in place and cooling the gas until its pressure drops to P_C.
3. Maintaining constant pressure P_C and continuing to cool until the gas volume drops to $V_D(=V_A)$.

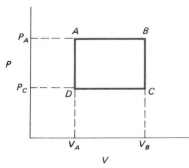

Fig. 18–15
A cyclic process.

4. Locking the piston and heating the system until its pressure again reaches P_A.

How much work does the gas do during the cyclic process ABCDA? During the constant-volume processes BC and DA, the piston is locked so that no work is done. During the isobaric expansion AB, the gas does work

$$W_{AB} = P\Delta V = P_A(V_B - V_A).$$

With a weighted piston, the work goes into raising the gravitational potential energy of the piston. In an engine, the work done by the gas would go into performing some useful task like lifting a weight, accelerating a vehicle, or overcoming friction. During the isobaric compression CD, work is done on the gas. (In our simple example, this work comes at the expense of the piston's gravitational energy.) Equivalently, the gas does negative work:

$$W_{CD} = P_C(V_D - V_C) = P_C(V_A - V_B),$$

where we have used the fact that $V_D = V_A$ and $V_C = V_B$. The net work done by the gas is then

$$W_{ABCDA} = W_{AB} + W_{CD} = P_A(V_B - V_A) + P_C(V_A - V_B) = (P_A - P_C)(V_B - V_A).$$

Geometrically, this result is just the area—measured not in cm^2 but in units of pressure times volume—enclosed by the rectangle ABCD. As we traverse the rectangle in the clockwise direction, the gas does this much work on its surroundings. Had we gone around in the counterclockwise direction, the area enclosed would have been the work done on the gas by the external world. Even when a cyclic path is not a simple rectangle, it remains true that the work done on or by the system is the area enclosed by the path in the PV diagram (Fig. 18–16).

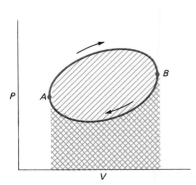

Fig. 18–16
An arbitrary cyclic path, traversed clockwise in the PV diagram. Area between the upper part of the curve and the V-axis (shaded with /////) is the work done by the gas as it goes from state A to state B. Area between the lower part of the curve and the V-axis (shaded also with \\\\\\) is the work done on the gas as it returns from B to A. Net work done by the gas is the area enclosed by the path.

Example 18–5
A Cyclic Process

A sample of ideal gas occupies 4.0 L at 300 K and 1.0 atm pressure. The specific heat ratio of the gas is $\gamma = 1.4$. It is compressed adiabatically until its volume is 1.0 L, and then cooled at constant volume to 300 K. It is then allowed to expand isothermally to its original volume. How much work is done on the gas?

Solution

Figure 18–17 shows the cyclic path ABCA in the PV diagram. The work done on the gas is the area enclosed by this curve, which may be calculated by considering the work done moving along each of the three sections AB, BC, and CA. The adiabatic work W_{AB} is given by Equation 18–21:

$$W_{AB} = \frac{P_A V_A - P_B V_B}{\gamma - 1}.$$

We know P_A, V_A, and V_B. To get P_B, we solve the adiabatic relation $P_B V_B{}^\gamma = P_A V_A{}^\gamma$ to obtain

$$P_B = P_A \left(\frac{V_A}{V_B}\right)^\gamma.$$

Then the adiabatic work is

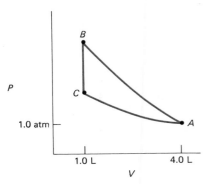

Fig. 18–17
The cyclic process ABCA of Example 18–5 includes adiabatic, constant-volume, and isothermal sections.

$$W_{AB} = \frac{P_A[V_A - (V_A/V_B)^\gamma V_B]}{\gamma - 1}$$

$$= \frac{(1.0 \times 10^5 \text{ Pa})[4.0 \times 10^{-3} \text{ m}^3 - (4.0 \text{ L}/1.0 \text{ L})^{1.4}(1.0 \times 10^{-3} \text{ m}^3)]}{0.4}$$

$$= -7.4 \times 10^2 \text{ J}.$$

The minus sign indicates that work is done *on* the gas during this adiabatic compression.

No work is done during the constant-volume process *BC*, while the isothermal work W_{CA} is given by Equation 18–5:

$$W_{CA} = nRT \ln\left(\frac{V_A}{V_C}\right).$$

The quantity nRT is given by the ideal gas law:

$$nRT = PV,$$

where we can evaluate P and V at any point along the isotherm because it is a curve of constant temperature. We know these values at point A, so that the isothermal work becomes

$$W_{CA} = P_A V_A \ln\left(\frac{V_A}{V_C}\right) = (1.0 \times 10^5 \text{ Pa})(4.0 \times 10^{-3} \text{ m}^3) \ln\left(\frac{4.0 \text{ L}}{1.0 \text{ L}}\right) = 5.5 \times 10^2 \text{ J}.$$

The net work is then

$$W_{ABC} = W_{AB} + W_{BC} + W_{CA}$$

$$= -7.4 \times 10^2 \text{ J} + 0 \text{ J} + 5.5 \times 10^2 \text{ J} = -1.9 \times 10^2 \text{ J}.$$

The minus sign indicates that net work is done *on* the system.

Because the system returns to its original state, there can be no net change in its internal energy. Therefore, it must reject to its surroundings an amount of heat equal to the work done on it. When does this heat rejection occur? The compression *AB* is adiabatic, meaning that no heat flow takes place. During the isothermal expansion *CA*, the gas does work on its surroundings; since its temperature and internal energy do not change, it must therefore absorb heat from its surroundings. So the heat rejection occurs only during the constant-volume cooling period *BC*.

18.3

THE SPECIFIC HEATS OF AN IDEAL GAS

The first law of thermodynamics has given us a relation between the molar specific heats of an ideal gas at constant volume and constant presure:

$$C_P = C_V + R.$$

But what are the actual values of the specific heats? We need to know these in order to calculate the specific heat ratio, γ, that enters the adiabatic equations.

When we modeled an ideal gas in Chapter 17, we assumed that the gas was composed of structureless particles of zero size. The only energy associated with such particles is their kinetic energy of translation (linear motion), so that the internal energy U of the gas is simply the sum of the translational kinetic energies of all the particles. But we found that the average kinetic energy is directly proportional to the temperature:

$$\tfrac{1}{2}m\overline{v^2} = \tfrac{3}{2}kT.$$

If we have n moles of gas, the internal energy is then

$$U = nN_A(\tfrac{1}{2}m\overline{v^2}) = \tfrac{3}{2}nN_AkT,$$

where N_A is Avogadro's number. But $N_Ak = R$, the gas constant, so that

$$U = \tfrac{3}{2}nRT.$$

Using this result in Equation 18–10 for the molar specific heat gives

$$C_V = \frac{1}{n}\frac{dU}{dT} = \tfrac{3}{2}R. \tag{18–22}$$

For this simple gas of structureless particles, the adiabatic exponent γ is then

$$\gamma = \frac{C_P}{C_V} = \frac{C_V + R}{C_V} = \frac{\tfrac{5}{2}R}{\tfrac{3}{2}R} = \frac{5}{3} = 1.67. \tag{18–23}$$

Some gases, notably the inert gases helium (He), neon (Ne), argon (Ar), and others in the last column of the periodic table, behave as though their adiabatic exponents and specific heats were given correctly by Equations 18–23 and 18–22. But other gases do not. At room temperature, for example, hydrogen (H_2), oxygen (O_2), and nitrogen (N_2) obey adiabatic laws with γ very nearly $\tfrac{7}{5}$ ($=1.4$). Solving Equation 18–23 for C_V shows that for these gases

$$C_V = \frac{R}{\gamma - 1} = \frac{R}{\tfrac{7}{5} - 1} = \tfrac{5}{2}R.$$

On the other hand, sulphur dioxide (SO_2) and nitrogen dioxide (NO_2) have specific heat ratios close to 1.3 and therefore volume specific heats of about 3.4R.

What is going on here? Has our ideal gas model failed? Not completely, for all these gases obey the relation $PV = nRT$ to a high degree of accuracy. But something is wrong in our model's assumptions about the internal energy of the gas. A clue lies in the structure of individual gas molecules, which is reflected in their chemical formulas. The inert gas molecules are monatomic—their molecules consist of single atoms. These atoms behave approximately like our model's structureless mass points.* Hydrogen, oxygen, and nitrogen molecules are diatomic. We can model these molecules by considering that they consist of two mass points at slightly different locations, as suggested in Fig. 18–18. Although a gas of such "dumbbell-shaped" molecules should still obey the ideal gas law $PV = nRT$, the molecules differ in one important respect from mass points. In addition to translational kinetic energy, they can have rotational energy as well. We broaden our notion of an ideal gas to include these molecules with internal

Fig. 18–18
"Dumbbell" model of a diatomic molecule.

---

*Of course, atoms do have structure. But that structure is not altered by collisions of gas molecules at normal temperatures, so that no change in internal energy is associated with atomic structure.

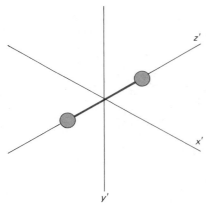

Fig. 18–19
A diatomic molecule can rotate about either of the two mutually perpendicular axes x' and y'.

structure. The "idealness" of the gas then lies not in the nature of the molecules but in the approximation that there is no potential energy of interaction among them.

How might a diatomic molecule rotate? Since the individual atoms behave approximately like mass points, rotation about the axis joining the atoms contributes little to the molecule's energy, for the rotational inertia about this axis is negligible. In a coordinate system x', y', z', whose z'-axis corresponds to the direction of the molecule axis at some instant, we can have energy associated with rotation about either of the other axes x' and y' (Fig. 18–19). Therefore, the total rotational energy of the molecule may be written

$$E_{rot} = \tfrac{1}{2}I_{x'}\omega_{x'}^2 + \tfrac{1}{2}I_{y'}\omega_{y'}^2,$$

where the I's are the rotational inertias about the two axes, and the ω's the corresponding angular velocities. Of course, the center of mass of the molecule may still be moving, so that there is also translational energy associated with each of the three possible directions of motion. Then the total energy of the molecule is

$$E = E_{trans} + E_{rot} = \tfrac{1}{2}mv_x^2 + \tfrac{1}{2}mv_y^2 + \tfrac{1}{2}mv_z^2 + \tfrac{1}{2}I_{x'}\omega_{x'}^2 + \tfrac{1}{2}I_{y'}\omega_{y'}^2.$$

The five terms in this equation correspond to the five independent kinds of motion our dumbbell molecule can have. The number of independent terms needed to describe the state of a system is called the number of **degrees of freedom** of that system. A diatomic molecule has five degrees of freedom. A monatomic molecule, in contrast, has only three degrees of freedom, corresponding to the three independent components of translational motion.

degrees of freedom

The Equipartition Theorem

In Chapter 16, we showed that the average translational kinetic energy associated with the motion of a gas molecule in one direction is equal to $\tfrac{1}{2}kT$. We then argued that all three directions of motion are, on the average, equally likely, so that the total translational energy is, on the average, $\tfrac{3}{2}kT$. The argument from one direction to three is a statistical one, based on the notion that random collisions among the molecules will result in a "sharing" of energy among the three possible degrees of freedom. When a molecule can rotate as well as translate, we expect that collisions will result in energy sharing with the rotational motion as well. The more frequent and more violent the collisions, the more energy we will have in the rotation of molecules. We therefore expect rotational energy, like translational energy, to increase with temperature.

Just how much energy ends up in rotation? If we had a diatomic gas whose molecular motions were initially all translational, collisions would soon transfer energy to molecular rotations. If, on the other hand, the motions were initially nearly all rotational, collisions among the rotating molecules would transfer energy from rotation to translation. So we expect that in equilibrium the total energy will be shared among the various degrees of freedom. This qualitative expectation is expressed quantitatively in the **equipartition theorem,** which states that

equipartition theorem

> When a system is in thermodynamic equilibrium, the average energy per molecule is $\frac{1}{2}kT$ for each degree of freedom.

We will not prove this theorem, which was originally derived by the Scottish physicist James Clerk Maxwell over 100 years ago, although our arguments above certainly suggest that it is reasonable. The equipartition theorem ensures that the internal energy of an ideal gas is still a function of temperature alone, even when the gas molecules have internal structure.

Using the equipartition theorem, we can now calculate the specific heat of a diatomic molecule as described by our dumbbell model. Each molecule has five degrees of freedom, three translational and two rotational. In equilibrium at temperature T, the average energy of a molecule is $5(\frac{1}{2}kT) = \frac{5}{2}kT$. If we have n moles of diatomic gas, the total internal energy is then

$$U = nN_A(\tfrac{5}{2}kT) = \tfrac{5}{2}nRT.$$

Equation 18–10 then gives the specific heat at constant volume:

$$C_V = \frac{1}{n}\frac{dU}{dT} = \tfrac{5}{2}R. \qquad \text{(diatomic molecule)} \qquad (18\text{–}24)$$

Our result $C_P = C_V + R$ still holds, since it was derived from the first law of thermodynamics without regard to molecular structure, so that we have

$$C_P = \tfrac{7}{2}R$$

and

$$\gamma = \frac{C_P}{C_V} = \frac{7}{5} = 1.4.$$

These results describe the observed behavior of diatomic gases like hydrogen, oxygen, and nitrogen at room temperature.

Example 18–6
The Equipartition Theorem

A gas mixture consists of 2.0 mol of oxygen (O_2) and 1.0 mol of argon (Ar). What is the volume specific heat of the mixture?

Solution

Being diatomic, each oxygen molecule has 5 independent components of motion. Then the equipartition theorem gives the total internal energy of all the oxygen molecules:

$$U_{O_2} = nN_A(\tfrac{5}{2}kT) = (2.0\text{ mol})(\tfrac{5}{2}RT) = 5.0RT,$$

where we used $N_A k = R$. Similarly, the internal energy associated with all the monatomic argon molecules is

$$U_{Ar} = nN_A(\tfrac{3}{2}kT) = (1.0\text{ mol})(\tfrac{3}{2}RT) = 1.5RT.$$

Then the total internal energy of the gas is

$$U = U_{O_2} + U_{Ar} = 6.5RT,$$

so that

$$C_V = \frac{1}{n}\frac{dU}{dT} = \frac{6.5R}{3.0\text{ mol}} = 2.2R.$$

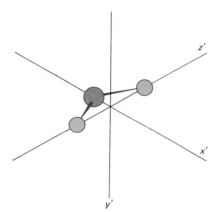

Fig. 18–20
A polyatomic molecule like NO_2 has three rotational degrees of freedom.

A polyatomic molecule like NO_2 (Fig. 18–20) has significant rotational inertias about any three perpendicular axes, and therefore exhibits three independent components of rotational motion. With the three independent components of translational motion, the molecule then has a total of six degrees of freedom. The equipartition theorem then tells us that the internal energy of n moles of such a gas is

$$U = (nN_A)(6)(\tfrac{1}{2}kT) = 3nRT,$$

so that

$$C_V = \frac{1}{n}\frac{dU}{dT} = 3R,$$

$$C_P = C_V + R = 4R,$$

and

$$\gamma = \frac{C_P}{C_V} = \frac{4}{3} = 1.33.$$

These values are reasonably close to the experimental values $\gamma = 1.29$ and $C_V = 3.47R$, although the agreement is noticeably poorer than for the monatomic and diatomic gases that we have considered.

Modifying the notion of an ideal gas to account for molecular structure with its additional degrees of freedom is an example of how remarkably successful the application of Newtonian mechanics can be. But at the molecular level, we are beginning to push the limits of Newtonian mechanics, and are approaching the realm where a quantum-mechanical description is necessary. We can see the breakdown of Newtonian mechanics in Fig. 18–21, which shows the volume specific heat of hydrogen (H_2) as a function of temperature. In the region from about 250 K to 750 K, the volume specific heat is very nearly equal to the value $\tfrac{5}{2}R$ predicted by our rotating dumbbell model. But between its melting point at 20 K and about 100 K, hydrogen shows a volume specific heat close to $\tfrac{3}{2}R$—like that of a mona-

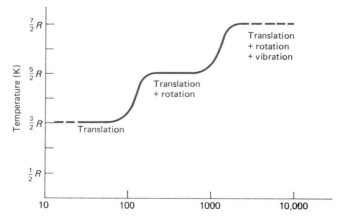

Fig. 18–21
Volume specific heat of H_2 as a function of temperature.

tomic gas. And above 3000 K* the specific heat is about $\frac{7}{2}R$, as though the molecules had somehow acquired two more degrees of freedom.

What is going on here? The molecules act as though they have different degrees of freedom, depending on temperature. In quantum mechanics, the energy associated with a periodic motion like a molecular rotation does not come in arbitrary amounts, but only in discrete multiples of some minimum amount. At low enough temperatures, the average thermal energy $\frac{1}{2}kT$ is less than this minimum, so that a molecule cannot rotate because it cannot acquire the minimum energy needed to do so. At these temperatures, it exhibits only the three translational degrees of freedom, and so the gas behaves as though it were composed of monatomic molecules. As temperature is increased, occasional molecules do acquire enough energy to rotate, and C_V increases. Eventually a plateau is reached, where the temperature and thermal energy are high enough that essentially all the molecules are rotating, and the gas obeys our rotating dumbbell model. That model assumed that the two atoms were joined by a rigid rod; in fact, they are joined by electrical forces and are free to vibrate like a mass-spring system along a line joining the two atoms (Fig. 18–22). At temperatures below about 800 K, the thermal energy is too low to excite these vibrations, but above that temperature more and more molecules are vibrating as well as rotating. There are two degrees of freedom associated with molecular vibrations—one with the kinetic energy of vibration, the other with the potential energy associated with the forces binding the atoms. As a result, each vibrating molecule has two more degrees of freedom. At high enough temperatures, essentially all the molecules are vibrating as well as rotating and translating, and the volume specific heat of $\frac{7}{2}R$ reflects the presence of all seven degrees of freedom. The presence of molecular vibrations is what made our calculation of γ and C_V for NO_2 rather imprecise.

Are you bothered by the strange restrictions quantum mechanics imposes on the rotation and vibration of molecules? You should be! Nothing in the physics you have studied until now, and nothing in your everyday experience, suggests that a rotating object cannot have any amount of energy you care to give it. But quantum mechanics deals with a realm of objects much smaller than those of our diemy experience. The quantization of energy levels is only one of many unusual things that occur in the quantum realm. We will explore more quantum phenomena in Chapter 36.

Fig. 18–22
The atoms of a diatomic molecule are free to vibrate along a line joining their centers.

---

*At 3200 K the H_2 molecule dissociates into two atoms, so that the curve does not continue beyond this temperature.

SUMMARY

1. The **first law of thermodynamics** is a statement of the conservation of energy principle that explicitly includes the internal energy of a system. The first law says that the change in internal energy of a system is equal to the difference between the heat Q added to the system and the work W done by the system:

$$\Delta U = Q - W.$$

2. A **thermodynamic process** takes a system from one thermodynamic state to another. A **quasi-static process** occurs slowly enough that the system remains in thermodynamic equilibrium during the process. Consequently, a quasi-static process may be described by a path in a diagram relating thermodynamic variables of the system, such as pressure and volume. If the system can be made to retrace the same path, then the process

is also **reversible.** In a system like a gas in a cylinder, where work is done only by the expansion of the system, we can write

$$W = \int_{V_1}^{V_2} P\,dV \quad \text{(any process)}$$

for the work done by the system as it undergoes a thermodynamic process during which its volume changes from V_1 to V_2.

a. In an **isothermal process,** temperature does not change. When n moles of an ideal gas undergo a reversible isothermal process, the work done by the gas is

$$W = nRT \ln\left(\frac{V_2}{V_1}\right). \quad \text{(isothermal process)}$$

Since the internal energy of an ideal gas is a function of temperature alone, the internal energy does not change during an isothermal process, and therefore the system absorbs an amount of heat Q equal to the work it does on its environment.

b. In a **constant-volume process,** volume does not change, so the gas does no work, and therefore the change in internal energy is just equal to the heat added. For an ideal gas, the internal energy is a function of temperature alone, so the change in internal energy is

$$\Delta U = nC_V\Delta T, \quad \text{(any process)}$$

where C_V is the molar specific heat at constant volume. This relation between ΔU and ΔT is true for *any* process, whether constant-volume or not. In a constant-volume process, $\Delta U = Q$, so

$$Q = nC_V\Delta T. \quad \text{(constant-volume process)}$$

c. In an **isobaric process,** pressure does not change, and the work done is just

$$W = P\Delta V. \quad \text{(isobaric process)}$$

The heat Q gained by the system in an isobaric process may be calculated from the first law, $Q = \Delta U + W$, or, in terms of the molar specific heats at constant pressure and constant volume,

$$nC_P\Delta T = nC_V\Delta T + P\Delta V. \quad \text{(isobaric process)}$$

d. In an **adiabatic process,** no heat is transferred into or out of the system, so that any work done is at the expense of the system's internal energy:

$$\Delta U = -W. \quad \text{(adiabatic process)}$$

The pressure and volume of a gas undergoing a reversible adiabatic process are related by

$$PV^\gamma = \text{constant}, \quad \text{(adiabatic process)}$$

where $\gamma = C_P/C_V$ is the ratio of specific heats. The work done by the gas during the adiabatic process is

$$W = \frac{P_1V_1 - P_2V_2}{\gamma - 1}. \quad \text{(adiabatic process)}$$

e. In a **cyclic process,** the system returns to its original state, so that there is no change in its internal energy. The work done by the system is equal to the heat transferred to the system, and is given by the area enclosed by the cyclic path in the *PV* diagram.

3. The volume specific heat of an ideal gas is determined by the number of **degrees of freedom** available to the gas molecules. According to the **equipartition theorem,** the average energy associated with each degree of freedom in a gas at temperature T is $\frac{1}{2}kT$. In a gas of monatomic molecules, only the three degrees of freedom corresponding to the three directions of translational motion are present, and the volume specific heat is $C_V = \frac{3}{2}R$. For a gas of diatomic molecules undergoing rotation, there are two additional degrees of freedom associated with the two possible rotation axes, and the volume specific heat is $C_V = \frac{5}{2}R$. In general, the volume specific heat is $\frac{1}{2}R$ times the number of degrees of freedom of a gas molecule. It follows from the first law of thermodynamics that the specific heat at constant pressure, C_P, is given by

$$C_P = C_V + R.$$

4. At lower temperatures, the quantization of energy as described by quantum mechanics may prevent some degrees of freedom from absorbing any energy. As a result, the effective number of degrees of freedom, and with it the specific heats, may vary with temperature.

======================= QUESTIONS =======================

1. In Chapter 7, we wrote the conservation of energy principle in the form $K + U = \text{constant}$. In what way is the first law of thermodynamics a broader statement than that of Chapter 7?

2. The temperature of the water in a jar is raised by violently shaking the jar. Which of the terms Q and W in the first law of thermodynamics is involved in this case?

3. In Example 18–1, we considered the electric power leaving a power plant as part of the work done by the power plant. Why did we include the electric power with the work rather than with the heat?

4. What is the difference between heat and internal energy?

5. Some water is tightly sealed in a perfectly insulated container. Is it possible to change the water temperature? Explain.

6. Is the internal energy of a van der Waals gas a function of temperature alone? Why or why not?

7. Are the initial and final equilibrium states of an irre-

versible process describable by points in a PV diagram? Explain.

8. Why can an irreversible process not be described by a path in a PV diagram?

9. Does the first law of thermodynamics apply to an irreversible process?

10. Is it possible to have a process that is isothermal but irreversible? Explain.

11. A quasi-static process begins and ends at the same temperature. Is the process necessarily isothermal?

12. Figure 18–23 shows two processes connecting the same initial and final states. For which process is more heat added to the system?

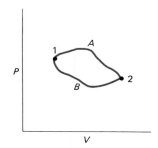

Fig. 18–23   Question 12

13. Two identical gas-cylinder systems are taken from the same initial state to the same final state, but by different processes. Is the work done in each case necessarily the same? The heat added? The change in internal energy?

14. When you let air out of a tire, the air seems cool. Why? What kind of process is occurring?

15. Blow on the back of your hand with your mouth wide open. Your breath will feel hot. Now tighten your lips into a small opening, and blow again. Now your breath feels cool. Why?

16. How is it posssible to have $PV^\gamma =$ constant in an adiabatic process and yet have $PV = nRT$?

17. Water is boiled in an open pan. Of which of the four specific processes we considered is this an example?

18. Is it possible to involve an ideal gas in a process that is simultaneously isothermal and isobaric? Is there any real substance that could undergo such a process? Give an example.

19. Three identical gas-cylinder systems expand from the same initial state to final states that have the same volume. One system expands isothermally, one adiabatically, and one isobarically. Which does the most work? Which does the least work?

20. If the relation $\Delta U = nC_V\Delta T$ holds for any ideal gas process, why do we call C_V the molar specific heat at constant volume?

21. Imagine a gas consisting of very complicated molecules, each with several hundred degrees of freedom. What, approximately, is the adiabatic exponent γ of this gas? Is it easy or hard to change the temperature of the gas?

22. In what sense can we consider a gas of diatomic molecules to be an ideal gas? After all, we must give up our assumption that gas particles are mass points in order to model such a gas successfully.

PROBLEMS

Section 18.1   *The First Law of Thermodynamics*

1. 1.0 kg of water in a closed but uninsulated container is shaken violently until its temperature rises by 2.0°C. The mechanical work required in the process is 14 kJ. How much heat is lost from the water during the process? How much mechanical work would have been required if the water were insulated perfectly in the container?

2. An 8.5-kg rock at 0°C is dropped into a well-insulated vat containing a mixture of ice and water at 0°C. When equilibrium is reached, it is found that there are 6.3 g less of ice in the vat. From what height was the rock dropped?

3. Water flows over Niagara Falls (height 50 m) at the rate of about 10^6 kg/s. Suppose that all the water is passed through a turbine connected to an electric generator, and that the generator supplies 400 MW of electric power. If the water has negligible kinetic energy after leaving the turbine, by how much does the temperature of the water increase between the top of the falls and the outlet of the turbine?

Section 18.2   *Thermodynamic Processes*

4. An ideal gas expands from the state (P_1,V_1) to the state (P_2,V_2), where $P_2 = 2P_1$ and $V_2 = 2V_1$. The expansion is quasi-static, and proceeds along a straight-line path, as shown in Fig. 18–24. How much work is done by the gas during this process?

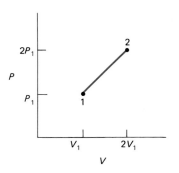

Fig. 18–24   Problem 4

5. Repeat the preceding problem for the case when the gas expands along a path given by

$$P = P_1\left[1 + \left(\frac{V - V_1}{V_1}\right)^2\right].$$

Sketch the path in the PV diagram, and calculate the work done.

6. What is the minimum amount of work needed to take the gas of Problem 4 between its initial and final states, if the gas pressure cannot be less than P_1 or more than P_2? What is the maximum amount of work that could be done under these same restrictions? Sketch the appropriate paths in the PV diagram.

7. A balloon contains 0.30 mol of helium at a temperature of 300 K and pressure of 1.0 atm. It is transported to a region where atmospheric pressure is 0.75 atm but where the temperature is still 300 K. How much work is done by the gas in the balloon? Assume that the process is isothermal.

8. Repeat the preceding problem, now assuming that the process is adiabatic. What should the final air temperature be if the gas is still to be in thermal equilibrium with its surroundings?

9. Show that the application of Equation 18–4 to an adiabatic process leads to Equation 18–21.

10. A gas sample expands isothermally from state A to state B, in the process absorbing 35 J of heat. It is then compressed isobarically to state C, for which its volume is the same as that of state A. During the compression, 22 J of work is done on the gas. The gas is then heated at constant volume until it returns to state A. (a) Draw a PV diagram showing this process. (b) How much work is done by or on the gas as it goes through the whole cyclic process? (c) How much heat is transferred to or from the gas as it goes from state B to state C and on to state A?

11. A piston-cylinder arrangement containing 0.30 mol of nitrogen at high pressure is in thermal equilibrium with an ice-water bath containing 200 g of ice. The pressure of the ambient air is 1.0 atm. The gas is allowed to expand isothermally until it is in pressure balance with its surroundings. After the process is complete, the bath contains 210 g of ice. What was the original pressure of the gas?

12. Derive an equation relating pressure and temperature for an adiabatic process.

13. 2.0 mol of an ideal gas with molar specific heat at constant volume $C_V = \frac{3}{2}R$ is initially at 300 K and 1.0 atm pressure. Determine the final temperature of the gas and the work done by the gas when 1.5 kJ of heat is added to the gas (a) isothermally, (b) isobarically, (c) at constant volume.

14. At any point in the PV diagram of an ideal gas, the slope of the adiabat passing through that point is γ times the slope of the isotherm passing through that point. Prove this.

15. Show that the work done by a van der Waals gas undergoing isothermal expansion from volume V_1 to volume V_2 is given by

$$W = nRT \ln\left(\frac{V_2 - nb}{V_1 - nb}\right) + an^2\left(\frac{1}{V_2} - \frac{1}{V_1}\right).$$

Is the heat gained by the gas equal to the work done? Hint: Consult Section 17.1.

16. A bicycle pump consists of a cylinder whose internal dimensions are 20 cm long by 3.0 cm in diameter when the pump handle is all the way out. The pump contains air ($\gamma = 1.4$) at 20°C and 1.0 atm. If the outlet of the pump is blocked and the handle pushed quickly until the internal length of the pump cylinder is only 10 cm, by how much does the temperature of the air in the pump rise? Assume that no heat is lost during the compression, but that the process is quasi-static.

17. An ideal gas system is taken clockwise around a circular path in its PV diagram, eventually returning to its starting point. The minimum and maximum pressures during the process are 1.5 atm and 5.5 atm; the minimum and maximum volumes are 3.0 L and 11 L. How much work is done in the process?

18. If the system in the preceding problem consists of 1.3 mol of gas, what is the maximum temperature reached in the process? What are the pressure and volume at this hottest point?

19. A tightly sealed glass flask contains 5.0 L of air at 0°C and 1.0 atm pressure. How much heat is required to raise the temperature of the air to 20°C? The molar specific heat at constant volume for air is 2.5R.

20. A balloon contains 5.0 L of air at 0°C and 1.0 atm pressure. How much heat is required to raise the temperature of the air to 20°C, assuming that the gas stays in pressure equilibrium with its surroundings? The molar specific heat at constant volume for air is 2.5R. Ignore any force due to the stretching of the rubber balloon.

21. Figure 18–25 shows an apparatus used to study adiabatic free expansion, an irreversible process in which a gas is allowed to expand into a vacuum. The apparatus consists of two chambers of equal volume V connected by a valve. Both chambers are well insulated so that no heat flows into or out of the system. The left-hand chamber initially contains a gas at pressure P_0 and temperature T_0. The right-hand chamber is initially evacuated. When the valve is opened, the gas expands to fill both chambers. (a) Explain why this process is irreversible. (b) If the gas is ideal, what is its temperature after a new equilibrium has been

Fig. 18–25 Apparatus for adiabatic free expansion (Problem 21).

reached? (c) If the gas obeys the van der Waals equation, is the equilibrium temperature more or less than T_0?

22. A B21F Volvo engine has a compression ratio of 9.3 (ratio of maximum to minimum cylinder volume). If air at 320 K fills an engine cylinder when the piston is at the bottom of its stroke, what is the air temperature when the piston reaches the top of its stroke? The piston rises rapidly enough that there is negligible heat flow into the cylinder, so that the process is essentially adiabatic. The specific heat ratio γ for air is 1.4.

23. A piston-cylinder arrangement has an initial volume of 1.0 L and contains ideal gas at 1.0 atm pressure and a temperature of 300 K. The molar specific heat of the gas at constant volume is $2.5R$. The piston is held fixed and the cylinder is placed in contact with a heat reservoir at 600 K. Once equilibrium is reached, the gas is allowed to expand isothermally. When the pressure reaches 1.0 atm, the gas is allowed to cool at constant pressure to 300 K. This cyclic process is repeated once a second. (a) Draw a PV diagram for the process. (b) What is the net rate at which work is done by the gas?

Section 18.3   *The Specific Heats of an Ideal Gas*

24. You have 2.0 mol of an ideal diatomic gas whose molecules can rotate but not vibrate. Suppose that somehow you arrange to give the gas 8.0 kJ of energy in such a way that it all goes initially into translational motion of the molecules. (a) When equilibrium is reached, what is the temperature of the gas? (b) Why is it not possible to ascribe a temperature to the state of the gas just after you added the energy?

25. A piston-cylinder system contains 0.50 mol of hydrogen (H_2) at 400 K and 3.0 atm pressure. An identical system contains 0.50 mol of helium (He) under the same conditions. Each gas undergoes an expansion that quadruples the system volume. Calculate the work done by each, if the expansion is (a) isothermal, (b) adiabatic.

26. A gas mixture contains 2.5 mol O_2 and 3.0 mol Ar at 350 K and 10 atm pressure. (a) What are the molar specific heats at constant volume and pressure for this mixture? (b) If the mixture expands adiabatically until its temperature is 300 K, what is its final volume?

27. An ideal gas in the apparatus of Problem 21 undergoes an irreversible free expansion that doubles its volume. Once equilibrium has been reached, the gas is compressed slowly back to its original volume. After this compression, the pressure is 1.3 times the original pressure before the free expansion. (a) Is the gas monatomic, diatomic, or polyatomic? (b) By what factor has the internal energy of the gas changed?

28. Figure 28–26 shows a simple model of a CO_2 molecule. Show that this molecule can undergo any of three independent vibrations. Determine the specific heat C_V under the assumption that all these vibrations, plus translation and rotation, are occurring.

Fig. 18–26   Model of a CO_2 molecule (Problem 28).

Supplementary Problems

29. A piston-cylinder arrangement is initially filled with 1.0 g of water at 50°C. The piston, which has negligible mass, is free to move and is exposed to atmospheric pressure (1.0 atm). The system is heated with a bunsen burner until the temperature inside the cylinder is 200°C. Assume that liquid water is incompressible and that steam is an ideal gas with volume specific heat $4.3R$. How much work is done by the system, and how much heat is added to it?

30. A piston-cylinder system containing n moles of ideal gas is surrounded by air at fixed temperature T_0 and fixed pressure P_0. The piston has mass M and cross-sectional area A. If the piston is displaced slightly from its equilibrium position and then released, it will oscillate about its equilibrium position. Determine the angular frequency of oscillation, assumed to be of small amplitude, under the assumption (a) that the gas temperature remains constant at T_0; (b) that no heat flows into or out of the gas during the oscillation.

31. The piston of the preceding problem is connected to a massless spring whose spring constant is k. (a) Show that the angular frequency of adiabatic oscillations is now given by

$$\omega = \left(\frac{\gamma A^2 P_0^2 + knRT}{MnRT} \right)^{1/2}.$$

(b) Obtain an expression for the gas temperature as a function of time.

32. Under normal conditions, the temperature of earth's atmosphere near the ground decreases with altitude. The rate of temperature decrease is called the **lapse rate**. The decrease in pressure with altitude is such that a parcel of air that rises through the atmosphere and expands adiabatically cools at the rate of about 10°C per kilometer of rise. Show that if the lapse rate is less than 10°C/km, a rising parcel of air will end up less dense than its surroundings and thus will continue to rise. (Assume that the air rises adiabatically, so that it does not exchange heat with its surroundings.) In contrast, show that if the lapse rate is greater than 10°C/km, a rising parcel of air will be denser than its surroundings. In the former case, the air is unstable, in that a parcel of air that rises will continue to do so. In the latter case, the air is stable, and a parcel of air that is displaced will return to its original position. Unstable air results in vertical mixing of air, and the formation of typical "fair weather"

clouds. Stable conditions result in the trapping of air in layers, and can be especially serious in cities with significant air pollution.

33. A cylinder of cross-sectional area A is closed by a massless piston. The cylinder contains n mol of air ($\gamma = 1.4$), initially in temperature and pressure equilibrium with the surrounding air at T_0 and P_0. The piston is initially at height h_1 above the bottom of the cylinder. Sand is gradually sprinkled onto the piston, so that it moves downward quasi-statically, reaching a final height h_2. What is the total mass of the sand if (a) the process is isothermal? (b) the process is adiabatic?

19

THE SECOND LAW OF THERMODYNAMICS

Fig. 19–1
Strip mining coal. Much of our electrical energy comes from burning coal—itself a form of chemically stored solar energy.

The first law of thermodynamics tells us that heat and other forms of energy are equivalent. Much of our world works because of this equivalence. A car runs because heat released by burning gasoline gets converted to mechanical work in the car's engine. Most of the electrical energy that operates our lights and motors and computers originates in heat that is released in the burning of coal, oil, or gas, or in the fissioning of uranium nuclei (Fig. 19–1). Our own bodily movements and even our thoughts make use of energy that was once released as heat deep in the core of the sun. But the first law does not tell the whole story. Heat and mechanical energy are not exactly the same thing, and it is the difference between them that makes the conversion of heat to work a more subtle task than the first law alone would imply.

19.1
REVERSIBILITY AND IRREVERSIBILITY

Suppose we make a movie of a ball bouncing off the floor. If we show the movie (Fig. 19–2a), we see the ball coming in from the left, bouncing, and going off to the right at the same angle and nearly the same speed as it came in. If we run the movie backward (Fig. 19–2b), it still makes good sense. Now let's film another simple physical event. Give a block of wood a push along a table. The block slows down and stops, and we find that both the block and the table top are slightly warmer (Fig. 19–3a). Show this movie in reverse (Fig. 19–3b) and it makes no sense. We never see a block at rest on a table suddenly start to move, while the block and table become cooler. Yet energy could be conserved in such a process, so the first law of thermodynamics would be satisfied.

Break an egg into a bowl and start beating; the yolk and white quickly blend into scrambled egg. You would be very surprised if, on reversing the

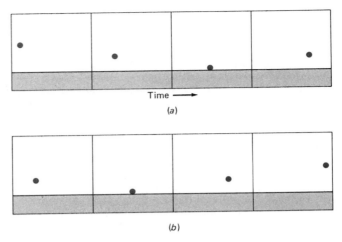

Fig. 19-2
A movie of a bouncing ball makes sense whether it is shown forward or backward.

direction of your beater, the scrambled yolk and white separated—even though there is nothing in the laws of mechanics to prevent it. Or put glasses of hot and cold water in thermal contact. The hot water gets cooler and the cold water gets hotter. The reverse never occurs—even though energy could be conserved if it did.

irreversible   Most happenings in the world are **irreversible,** in the sense of the block, the egg, and the water. Even the bouncing ball is not perfectly reversible, for it rebounds with slightly lower speed, leaving the ball and court warmer. What is the origin of this irreversibility? In each irreversible happening, we start with matter in an organized state. In our sliding block, all the molecules initially have velocity components in the same direction. The egg is initially organized so that all the yolk molecules are in one re-

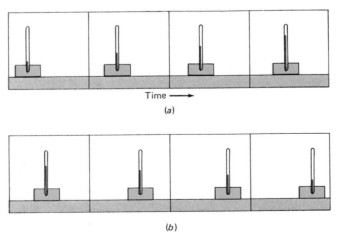

Fig. 19-3
Movie of a block warming as it dissipates kinetic energy through friction. Shown in reverse, it depicts an event that would not happen, even though it does not violate energy conservation.

gion, the white molecules in another. And a greater number of energetic molecules are initially in the hotter glass of water. Of all the possible states into which matter could arrange itself, these *organized* states are very special and relatively rare. There are many more *chaotic* states—for instance, all the possible arrangements of molecules in a scrambled egg—that display less overall organization. If we have a system in a relatively organized state, chances are that it will evolve to a less organized one, simply because there are far more such states available to it. Once a system is in a disorganized state, it is unlikely to assume spontaneously a more organized state. When we are dealing with macroscopic systems of many molecules, the number of less organized states is fantastically larger than the number of more organized states, so that the probability of spontaneously achieving a more organized state is impossibly low.

A key word in this discussion is spontaneous. We could restore some system to its original, organized state—for example, by putting one of our water glasses in the refrigerator and the other on the stove—but to do so we must carry out a rather deliberate and energy-consuming process.

The sense of irreversibility we have been discussing is fully consistent with the notion of an irreversible thermodynamic process that we introduced in the preceding chapter. In an irreversible process, we deliberately force a system into a state of thermodynamic disequilibrium. For example, we push suddenly on the piston of a gas cylinder, temporarily giving the molecules near the piston a common velocity component away from the piston. This temporary state shows more organization than the equilibrium state, for some gas molecules share a common motion. But molecular collisions soon randomize these motions, so that the gas ends up in a new equilibrium state. A spontaneous return to the original state is highly improbable, and in this sense the process is irreversible.

Irreversibility is a probabilistic notion. Events that could occur without violating the principles of Newtonian physics nevertheless do not occur because they are simply too improbable. We cannot make a car move forward by asking all its molecules suddenly to move in the same direction—even though there is more than enough energy in random thermal motion to give the car a substantial velocity. There is a phenomenal amount of energy in the thermal motion of water molecules in the oceans, but we cannot easily extract useful work by cooling the oceans (see Problem 3 and Section 19.3). The extreme improbability that molecules will spontaneously assume an ordered state makes a great deal of the world's energy unavailable to do work.

19.2
THE SECOND LAW OF THERMODYNAMICS

Heat Engines

heat engine   Although we cannot spontaneously convert into useful work *all* the random motion associated with the internal energy of a hot object, we can construct devices, called **heat engines,** that extract at least *some* useful work from internal energy. Examples include gasoline and diesel engines, fossil-fueled and nuclear power plants, and jet aircraft engines.

working fluid

To make a heat engine, we need a source of heat and a **working fluid**— a substance that undergoes changes of thermodynamic state and in the process does work on its surroundings. Conceptually, we can describe a heat engine by a diagram showing how heat flows into the engine and how work emerges. Figure 19–4a shows such an energy flow diagram for a "perfect" heat engine—one that extracts energy as heat from a reservoir and converts it all to work. Such an engine would do exactly what we argued against in the previous section—it would convert the random energy of thermal motion entirely into the ordered motion associated with mechanical work. In fact, a perfect heat engine is impossible, for the same reason that we cannot unscramble an egg or cause a wood block suddenly to accelerate from rest at the expense of its internal energy. This observational fact comprises one statement of the **second law of thermodynamics:**

second law of
thermodynamics,
Kelvin-Planck statement

> It is impossible to construct a heat engine operating in a cycle that extracts heat from a reservoir and delivers an equal amount of work.

This particular form of the second law was formulated by Lord Kelvin and Max Planck. The phase "in a cycle" refers to the fact that an engine must take on a series of mechanical and thermodynamic configurations that repeat themselves if it is to operate continuously. Typical engines have shafts that rotate, or pistons that go back and forth, so that the engine runs in a cyclic fashion.

One way to convert heat to work is to put a gas-cylinder system in contact with a heat reservoir. If the gas pressure is initially higher than the pressure associated with the piston weight and the external atmosphere, then the gas will expand and do work W on the piston. In this isothermal process, the gas simultaneously extracts heat $Q = W$ from the heat reservoir. Eventually the gas expands to reach pressure equilibrium, and the piston must then be returned to its original position if it is to do more work.

To return the piston, we could simply push it back. But this would take as much work as we extracted during the expansion, so that our engine would do no net work. Instead, we can cool the gas to reduce its volume, then complete the cycle by heating at constant volume until the gas is back to its initial state. But to cool the gas, we transfer heat to a reservoir at a lower temperature than our hot reservoir, so that some energy leaves the system as heat rather than work. The energy flow diagram for such a real heat engine is shown in Fig. 19–4b. A real engine extracts heat from a high-temperature reservoir and produces mechanical work. But the amount of work is always less than the heat extracted, and the difference between the two leaves the engine as heat rejected to a lower-temperature reservoir. The radiator in a car (Fig. 19–5) has the specific job of rejecting heat to the environment—heat that comes from burning gasoline but that does not contribute to the motion of the car. A large power plant may use a major river as its low-temperature reservoir, dumping enormous amounts of heat and possibly altering the ecology of the river (Fig. 19–6).

The second law of thermodynamics states that we cannot build a perfect heat engine. But how close can we come? Since we must pay for the fuel that heats our high-temperature reservoir, it is clearly advantageous to minimize the heat rejected to the low-temperature reservoir. We define the

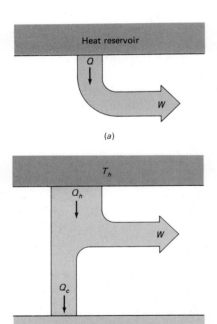

Fig. 19–4
(a) Energy flow diagram for a perfect heat engine. The engine extracts heat Q from a reservoir and delivers an equal amount of work. (b) Energy flow diagram for a real heat engine. Only a fraction of the heat Q_h extracted from the high-temperature reservoir is delivered as work: the remainder is rejected to the low-temperature reservoir.

Fig. 19–5
A car radiator's job is to reject heat to the environment.

Fig. 19–6
Infrared aerial photo shows hot water discharge from a power plant.

efficiency   **efficiency** of an engine as the ratio of work, W, put out by the engine in one cycle to heat, Q_h, extracted from the high-temperature reservoir:

$$e = \frac{W}{Q_h}.$$

Since the process is cyclic, there is no net change in internal energy of the working fluid over one cycle, so that the first law of thermodynamics assures us that the work done is the difference between the heat Q_h extracted from the high-temperature reservoir and the heat Q_c rejected to the low-temperature reservoir. Then the efficiency can be written

$$e = \frac{Q_h - Q_c}{Q_h} = 1 - \frac{Q_c}{Q_h}. \tag{19–1}$$

Figure 19–7 shows a simple heat engine whose efficiency we can readily calculate. The engine consists of a closed cylinder containing an ideal gas. A movable piston is connected to a rod that drives a wheel. The wheel does mechanical work, such as lifting a weight or accelerating a vehicle. To operate the engine, we start with the piston in its most retracted position and place the cylinder in contact with the high-temperature reservoir at T_h. The gas expands isothermally along the path AB in its PV diagram (Fig. 19–8). In the process, the gas extracts heat Q_h from the reservoir and, because its internal energy does not change, delivers an equal amount of work to the wheel. At state B, we remove the cylinder from the reservoir so that the gas continues to expand, but now adiabatically. We design the engine so that, when the piston reaches its maximum displacement, the gas temperature has cooled to T_c, the temperature of the cool reservoir. At this

Fig. 19–7
A simple heat engine.

point the gas is in state C in its PV diagram. We then place the piston in contact with the cool reservoir. The inertia of the wheel causes it to continue turning, and the wheel does work on the gas, compressing it isothermally from state C to state D. This work ends up as heat rejected to the cool reservoir. Finally, at state D, we separate the cylinder from the reservoir and allow the compression to continue adiabatically until the gas temperature has risen to T_h and the piston is once again fully retracted.

The engine we have just described undergoes a cyclic process consisting of four reversible steps, two of them isothermal and two adiabatic. This **Carnot cycle** cycle is called a **Carnot cycle,** and the engine a **Carnot engine,** after the **Carnot engine** French engineer Sadi Carnot (1796–1832), who explored the properties of such an engine even before the first law of thermodynamics was formulated. The particular configuration of our engine is not important, nor is the use of an ideal gas as working fluid necessary. What distinguishes the Carnot cycle from others is the sequence of thermodynamic processes and the fact that these processes are reversible. The Carnot engine is an example of **reversible engine** a **reversible engine**—one in which thermodynamic equilibrium is maintained so that all steps could, in principle, be reversed.

What is the efficiency of a Carnot engine? In the preceding chapter we examined isothermal processes, and found that the heat absorbed during such a process is given by

$$Q = W = nRT \ln\left(\frac{V_B}{V_A}\right),$$

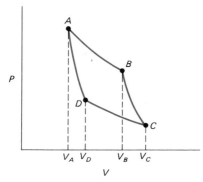

where V_A and V_B are the initial and final volumes. Then the heat Q_h absorbed during the isothermal expansion AB in the Carnot cycle of Fig. 19–8 is

$$Q_h = nRT_h \ln\left(\frac{V_B}{V_A}\right), \qquad (19\text{–}2)$$

Fig. 19–8
PV diagram for the engine of Fig. 19–7.

while the heat Q_c rejected during the isothermal compression CD is

$$Q_c = -nRT_c \ln\left(\frac{V_D}{V_C}\right) = nRT_c \ln\left(\frac{V_C}{V_D}\right). \qquad (19\text{–}3)$$

We put the minus sign in Equation 19–3 because our statement of the first law describes Q as the heat *absorbed*, while Equation 19–1 for the engine efficiency requires that Q_c be the heat *rejected* by the engine. To calculate engine efficiency according to Equation 19–1, we need the ratio Q_c/Q_h:

$$\frac{Q_c}{Q_h} = \frac{T_c \ln(V_C/V_D)}{T_h \ln(V_B/V_A)}. \qquad (19\text{–}4)$$

This expression can be simplified by using Equation 18–19 that relates temperature and volume in an adiabatic process:

$$TV^{\gamma-1} = T_0 V_0{}^{\gamma-1}.$$

Applying this expression to the adiabatic processes BC and DA in the Carnot cycle gives

$$T_h V_B{}^{\gamma-1} = T_c V_C{}^{\gamma-1}$$

and

$$T_h V_A{}^{\gamma-1} = T_c V_D{}^{\gamma-1}.$$

Dividing these two equations, we obtain

$$\left(\frac{V_B}{V_A}\right)^{\gamma-1} = \left(\frac{V_C}{V_D}\right)^{\gamma-1} \quad \text{or} \quad \frac{V_B}{V_A} = \frac{V_C}{V_D}$$

so that Equation 19–4 becomes simply

$$\frac{Q_c}{Q_h} = \frac{T_c}{T_h}.$$

The efficiency of the engine, given by Equation 19–1, is then

$$e = 1 - \frac{Q_c}{Q_h} = 1 - \frac{T_c}{T_h}, \tag{19–5}$$

where the temperatures are measured on an absolute scale (Kelvin or Rankine). Equation 19–5 tells us that the efficiency of a Carnot engine depends only on the highest and lowest temperatures of the working fluid. For a practical engine, the low temperature is usually the ambient temperature of the environment. Then to maximize the efficiency, we must make the high temperature as high as possible. Most real engines represent a compromise between efficiency and the ability of materials to withstand high temperatures and pressures.

Example 19–1
A Carnot Engine

A Carnot engine extracts 240 J of heat from a high-temperature reservoir during each cycle. It rejects 100 J of heat to a reservoir at 15°C. How much work does the engine do in one cycle? What is its efficiency? What is the temperature of the hot reservoir?

Solution

The first law of thermodynamics requires that energy not rejected as heat be delivered as work, so that the engine does

$$W = 240\,J - 100\,J = 140\,J$$

of work. The efficiency is defined by Equation 19–1 as the ratio of work to heat extracted from the hot reservoir:

$$e = \frac{W}{Q_h} = \frac{140\,J}{240\,J} = 0.583 = 58.3\%.$$

Knowing the efficiency, we can solve Equation 19–5 for the high temperature to get

$$T_h = \frac{T_c}{1-e} = \frac{288\,K}{1-0.583} = 691\,K = 418°C.$$

Note that in using Equation 19–5, we must work with absolute temperatures.

Engines, Refrigerators, and the Second Law

What is so special about the Carnot cycle? The efficiency of a Carnot engine is limited by the operating temperatures, but wouldn't it be possible for us to build another kind of engine that would operate at greater efficiency? The answer is no. The Carnot engine is reversible, in that all its thermodynamic steps are reversible. An engine that includes irreversible processes—whether they involve friction or deviations from thermodynamic equilibrium—will be less efficient because organized molecular motion will be lost through the irreversible processes. This idea is elaborated in **Carnot's theorem:**

Carnot's theorem

> All reversible engines operating between the same temperatures have the same efficiency (given by Equation 19–5), and no irreversible engine can be as efficient.

refrigerator

To prove Carnot's theorem, we introduce the notion of a **refrigerator.** A refrigerator is the opposite of an engine: it extracts heat from a cool reservoir and rejects it to a hotter reservoir, taking in work in the process. Figure 19–9 shows an energy flow diagram for a refrigerator. A refrigerator is an unusual device: it forces energy to flow in a way it doesn't spontaneously go. With a refrigerator, we can move heat from a glass of cold water into a glass of hot water, making the cold water colder and the hot water hotter. But to do so, we must do work—a household refrigerator uses electricity. Heat flow from colder to hotter does not happen spontaneously. This observational fact is reflected in another statement of the second law of thermodynamics, this one due to the German physicist Rudolph Clausius (1822–1888):

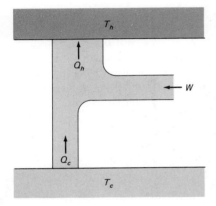

Fig. 19–9
Energy flow diagram for a real refrigerator.

> It is impossible to make a refrigerator, operating in a cycle, whose sole effect is the transfer of heat from a cooler object to a hotter object.

The Clausius statement rules out a "perfect" refrigerator, like that shown conceptually in Fig. 19–10.

How are the Clausius statement of the second law and the Kelvin-Planck statement related? The Clausius statement says that it is impossible to build a perfect refrigerator; the Kelvin-Planck statement says that it is impossible to build a perfect heat engine. Suppose the Clausius statement were false. Then we could build the device of Fig. 19–11, consisting of a real heat engine and a perfect refrigerator. In each cycle the engine would extract, say, 100 J from the hot reservoir, put out 60 J of useful work, and reject 40 J to the cool reservoir. We could arrange for the perfect refrigerator to transfer 40 J from the cool reservoir back to the hot reservoir. The net effect would be to extract 60 J of heat from the hot reservoir and convert it entirely into work. Conceptually, the composite device looks like Fig. 19–12, and would be a perfect heat engine. Therefore, if it is possible to build a perfect refrigerator, it is also possible to build a perfect heat engine. A similar argument can be made to show that if a perfect heat engine is possible, then so is a perfect refrigerator (see Problem 9). Thus the Clausius and Kelvin-Planck statements of the second law of thermodynamics are equivalent, in that if one is false then so is the other.

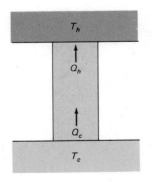

Fig. 19–10
Energy flow diagram for a perfect refrigerator. The Clausius statement of the second law rules out such a device.

How would we build a refrigerator? Because our Carnot engine is reversible, we could do work on the engine, traversing Fig. 19–8 in a counterclockwise direction. All thermodynamic processes would reverse, and the device would transfer heat from the cool reservoir to the hot reservoir.

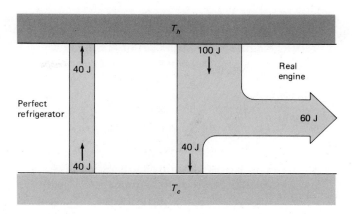

Fig. 19–11
Real engine combined with a perfect refrigerator.

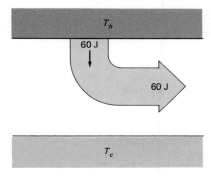

Fig. 19–12
The combination of Fig. 19–11 would be equivalent to a perfect heat engine.

Although real refrigerators are not designed exactly like engines, the two are, in principle, interchangeable.

With our two statements of the second law of thermodynamics, we are now ready to prove Carnot's assertion that the maximum efficiency of a heat engine is given by Equation 19–5. Consider again the reversible engine we showed in Fig. 19–11, which extracts 100 J from its hot reservoir and delivers 60 J of work. This engine is 60 per cent efficient. Since it is reversible, we could equally well run the engine as a refrigerator, supplying 60 J of work and transferring an additional 40 J of heat from the cool reservoir to the hot reservoir. Suppose we had another engine, this one with 70 per cent efficiency, operating between the same two reservoirs. Suppose we run the first engine as a refrigerator and the second as an engine, as suggested in Fig. 19–13. The net result is that we extract 10 J of heat from the cool reservoir and deliver 10 J of work, as shown in Fig. 19–14. The composite device acts like a perfect heat engine, violating the second law of thermodynamics. This same argument could be made for any combination of a

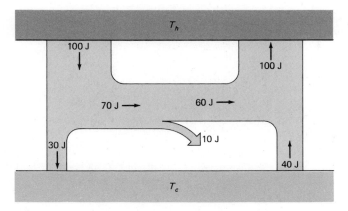

Fig. 19–13
60 per cent efficient reversible engine run as a refrigerator, along with a hypothetical engine of 70 per cent efficiency.

Fig. 19–14
The composite device of Fig. 19–13 would be equivalent to this perfect heat engine.

reversible engine and another, more efficient engine. Therefore, it is impossible to make a heat engine that is more efficient than any reversible heat engine. Since the Carnot engine is reversible, its efficiency is the maximum possible, and must be the same as that of any other reversible engine.

19.3
APPLICATIONS OF THE SECOND LAW OF THERMODYNAMICS

The world abounds with thermal energy, but the second law of thermodynamics imposes a fundamental limitation on our ability to turn that energy to our own uses. Any device we construct that involves the interchange of heat and work is a heat engine or refrigerator, and therefore subject to the second law.

Limitations on Heat Engines

Most of the electricity used in the United States is produced in large power plants that are basically heat engines driven by chemical reactions involving fossil fuels like coal, oil, or natural gas, or by nuclear reactions involving the fissioning of uranium nuclei (Fig. 19–15). Figure 19–16 shows a schematic diagram of such a power plant. The working fluid is water, heated in a boiler and converted to steam at high pressure. The steam expands adiabatically against the blades of a turbine—a fanlike device that spins when struck by the steam. The turbine is coupled mechanically to a generator that converts mechanical work into electrical energy (the principle behind such a generator is described in Chapter 29). Since the flow of electrical energy does not involve a temperature difference, the electrical energy leaving the power plant qualifies as work. Leaving the turbine, the steam is still in the gaseous state, and is usually hotter than

Fig. 19–15
A nuclear power plant showing two reactor containment vessels at left, and large cooling towers in the background.

Fig. 19–16
Schematic diagram of a typical electric power plant.

the water supplied to the boiler. Here is where the second law enters! Had the water returned to its original state, we would have extracted as work all the energy acquired in the boiler, in violation of the second law. To use the steam again, we run it through a **condenser**—a device where pipes carrying the steam are in contact with large volumes of cool water, typically from a river, lake, or ocean. The condensed steam, now cool water, is fed back into the boiler to repeat the cycle.

condenser

The maximum steam temperature in a power plant is limited by the materials used in its construction. For a fossil-fueled plant, current technology permits high temperatures around 650 K. Potential damage to nuclear fuel rods limits the temperature in a nuclear plant to around 570 K. Cooling-water temperature averages about 40°C (310 K), so that maximum possible efficiencies for these power plants, given by Equation 19–5, are

$$e_{fossil} = 1 - \frac{310 \text{ K}}{650 \text{ K}} = 0.52 = 52\%$$

and

$$e_{nuclear} = 1 - \frac{310 \text{ K}}{570 \text{ K}} = 0.46 = 46\%.$$

Any temperature difference between the exhausted steam and the cooling water, mechanical friction, and the need to divert energy for driving pumps and pollution control devices all reduce efficiency further, to about 40 per cent for fossil-fueled plants and 34 per cent for nuclear plants. This means that, when we make electricity, roughly two-thirds of the energy released from our expensive fuels ends up as waste heat.

Where does the waste energy go? Most of it is extracted by the condenser, whose cooling water constitutes the cool reservoir of the heat engine. A typical large power plant produces 1000 MW of electricity, so that another 2000 MW of waste heat is dumped into the cooling water. This rate of energy addition can cause a large temperature rise in even a major river,

Fig. 19–17
Fog forms above the cooling towers of this 1500-MW coal-fired power plant operated by Pennsylvania Power and Light Company.

and can lead to serious ecological problems. The need for power plant cooling water—imposed on us by the second law of thermodynamics—is so great that a substantial fraction of all rainwater falling on the United States eventually finds its way through the condensers of power plants (see Problem 23).

To reduce problems from this "thermal pollution," many modern power plants employ cooling towers—expensive devices in which waste heat is released to the air rather than to water. Environmental effects of the heated air are less serious than with heated water, although the increase in humidity can bring about unfortunate changes in local weather (Fig. 19–17).

Example 19–2
A Power Plant

The Vermont Yankee nuclear power plant at Vernon, Vermont, produces 540 MW of electric power. Within the plant's nuclear reactor, energy from nuclear fission is released as heat at the rate of 1590 MW. Steam produced in the reactor enters the turbine at a temperature of 556 K, and is discharged to the condenser at 313 K. Water from the Connecticut River is pumped through the condenser at the rate of 2.27×10^4 kg/s.

What is the maximum efficiency of the power plant, as limited by the second law of thermodynamics? What is the actual efficiency? How much does the temperature of the cooling water rise? If the minimum flow in the river is 3.40×10^4 kg/s, what is the maximum temperature rise of the entire river? How many houses like that of Example 16–8 could be heated with the waste heat from Vermont Yankee?

Solution

The second-law efficiency is given by Equation 19–5:

$$e = 1 - \frac{T_c}{T_h} = 1 - \frac{313 \text{ K}}{556 \text{ K}} = 0.437 = 43.7\%.$$

The actual efficiency is the ratio of electric power output to the rate of heat extraction at the high temperature:

$$e = \frac{dW/dt}{dQ_h/dt} = \frac{540 \text{ MW}}{1590 \text{ MW}} = 0.340 = 34.0\%.$$

Waste heat is discharged to the river at a rate given by the difference between the thermal power output and the electric power output:

$$\frac{dQ_c}{dt} = \frac{dQ_h}{dt} - \frac{dW}{dt} = 1590 \text{ MW} - 540 \text{ MW} = 1050 \text{ MW}.$$

We can relate the waste power output to the temperature rise of the cooling water by differentiating Equation 16–7 with respect to time:

$$\frac{dQ_c}{dt} = \frac{dm}{dt} c\Delta T,$$

where dm/dt is the mass flow rate and ΔT the fixed temperature rise. Solving for ΔT gives

$$\Delta T = \frac{dQ_c/dt}{c \, dm/dt} = \frac{1050 \times 10^6 \text{ W}}{(4184 \text{ J/kg} \cdot ^\circ\text{C})(2.27 \times 10^4 \text{ kg/s})} = 11.1 ^\circ\text{C}.$$

Eventually, the hot-water discharge mixes with the rest of the river. The result is the same as if the entire river had been used for cooling, so that

$$\Delta T_{\text{river}} = \frac{dQ_c/dt}{c \, (dm/dt)_{\text{river}}} = \frac{1050 \times 10^6 \text{ W}}{(4184 \text{ J/kg·°C})(3.40 \times 10^4 \text{ kg/s})} = 7.4\text{°C}.$$

The house of Example 16–8 uses 8110 Btu/h, or 2.38×10^{-3} MW. Then the waste heat from Vermont Yankee could heat (1050 MW)/(2.38×10^{-3} MW/house), or 440,000 houses. This example is unrealistic because real houses are considerably less energy-efficient than the house of Example 16–8. Nevertheless, waste heat from power plants is a potentially valuable energy source for heating buildings.

Fig. 19–18
Artist's conception of an OTEC power plant.

ocean thermal energy
conversion

solar thermal
power plant

Gasoline and diesel engines used in vehicles provide another pervasive example of heat engines in our society. A typical automobile engine operates at a high temperature of 800 K, and rejects waste heat at the prevailing temperature of the environment, about 300 K. The maximum possible thermodynamic efficiency is then

$$e = 1 - \frac{300 \text{ K}}{800 \text{ K}} = 0.63 = 63\%,$$

but irreversible thermodynamic processes make the actual efficiency much lower. Mechanical friction consumes additional energy, so that less than 20 per cent of the energy released by burning gasoline is available at the driving wheels. When the car is not accelerating or climbing, all of this energy is then converted to heat through friction with air and road.

We would not be quite so concerned with the efficiency of engines if we did not have to pay for fuel. Even a small temperature difference between two regions can drive a heat engine. Surface temperatures in tropical oceans, for example, are about 25°C (298 K). Three hundred meters down, the ocean temperature has dropped to about 5°C (278 K). A heat engine operating between these temperatures would have an efficiency of only 1 − 278 K/298 K = 0.07 or 7 per cent. Nevertheless, there are large amounts of warm water in the ocean, and its energy—ultimately solar in origin—is free. Although the engineering problems of such an **ocean thermal energy conversion** scheme (OTEC) are substantial, research on this method of power generation is currently underway. Figure 19–18 shows one proposal for an OTEC power plant.

Another approach to a fuel-less heat engine is shown in Fig. 19–19. This **solar thermal power plant** uses a large field of computer-controlled mirrors to focus sunlight on a central boiler mounted high on a tower. Pilot plants of this sort are currently operating in the desert southwest of the United States.

Refrigerators and Heat Pumps

Reversing a heat engine gives us a refrigerator. We do mechanical work on the device, and as a result transfer energy from a cooler to a hotter reservoir (Fig. 19–20). Your home refrigerator uses electricity to transfer energy from cool things in the refrigerator to the kitchen environment. If you put your hand near the coils of the refrigerator, you can feel heat rejected to the air. By the first law of thermodynamics, this heat comprises both the energy removed from the refrigerator's contents as well as the en-

Fig. 19–19
10 MW solar thermal power plant at Barstow, California.

ergy that was supplied as work. In designing a refrigerator, we would like to minimize the amount of work needed to extract a given amount of heat.

We characterize a refrigerator by the ratio of total heat extracted at the lower temperature to work input to the refrigerator. This ratio is called the **coefficient of performance** (COP):

coefficient of performance

$$COP = \frac{Q_c}{W} = \frac{Q_c}{Q_h - Q_c}. \qquad (19\text{–}6)$$

For a reversible heat engine, we found in deriving Equation 19–5 that the heat ratio Q_c/Q_h is equal to the temperature ratio T_c/T_h. The best refrigerator we can build is a reversible one, so that for this refrigerator the heat and temperature ratios are also equal. Then Equation 19–6 becomes

$$COP = \frac{T_c}{T_h - T_c}. \qquad (19\text{–}7)$$

As the high and low temperatures encountered in a refrigerator become arbitrarily close, Equation 19–7 shows that the COP becomes large—meaning that the refrigerator requires relatively little work to do its job. But if we wish to effect a transfer of heat between two widely separated temperatures, then the COP drops and the amount of work we must do becomes considerable. In the limit of very large T_h, the COP approaches zero, indicating that we are simply converting mechanical work into a nearly equal amount of heat, and transferring very little additional heat from the cool reservoir. In operating a real refrigerator, we would like to minimize the work needed. But Equation 19–7—like Equation 19–5 for a heat engine—imposes a fundamental limitation on that minimum amount of work.

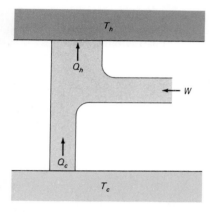

Fig. 19–20
Energy flow diagram for a refrigerator.

Example 19–3

A Refrigerator

A typical home freezer operates between a low temperature of 0°F (−18°C) and a high of 86°F (30°C). What is the maximum possible COP of this refrigerator? With this COP, how much electrical energy would the refrigerator require to freeze 500 g of water, initially at 0°C?

Solution

The COP is given by Equation 19–7:

$$COP = \frac{T_c}{T_h - T_c} = \frac{255 \text{ K}}{303 \text{ K} - 255 \text{ K}} = 5.3.$$

To produce 500 g of ice takes

$$Q_c = mL_f = (0.50 \text{ kg})(334 \text{ kJ/kg}) = 170 \text{ kJ},$$

where we obtained the heat of fusion from Table 17–1. This Q_c is the heat that must be removed from the low-temperature end of the refrigerator. The COP is the ratio of the heat removed to the work done, so that

$$W = \frac{Q_c}{COP} = \frac{170 \text{ kJ}}{5.3} = 32 \text{ kJ}.$$

In a real refrigerator, the COP would be lower, and the work correspondingly higher, because of irreversible processes in the refrigerator cycle.

Fig. 19–21
A heat pump. During the summer, the device acts as a refrigerator that cools the interior of the house and dumps heat into the environment. During the winter, its operation reverses, so that it effectively cools the outdoors and in the process transfers heat into the house. The work, W, is typically in the form of electricity.

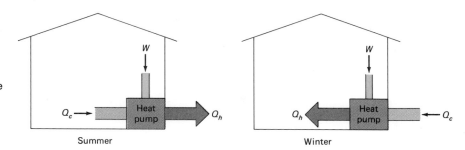

Summer   Winter

Refrigerators are not confined to kitchens. An air conditioner is a refrigerator designed to cool an entire room or building. A heat pump is a refrigerator that cools a building in the summer and heats it in the winter (Fig. 19–21). Heat pumps are widely used in the southern United States, where in winter they pump energy from the cool outside air to the warm house. A heat pump requires electricity, but it supplies more energy as heat than it uses in electricity. The excess energy comes from the outdoor environment, which becomes slightly cooler. Heat pumps operating from the constant 10°C temperatures found two meters below the ground have been used for years in the Scandinavian countries, and are becoming more popular in the northern United States.

Example 19–4
A Heat Pump

A heat pump extracts energy from the ground at 10°C and transfers it to water at 70°C. The water is circulated to heat a building. What is the COP of the heat pump? What is the electrical power consumption of the device if it supplies heat to the building at the rate of 20 kW? Would you be better off with a heat pump or an oil furnace if electricity costs 10 cents/kWh and oil costs 83¢/gallon? (At typical oil burner efficiencies, a gallon of oil releases about 100,000 Btu of useful heat when burned in a home furnace.)

Solution

The COP of the heat pump is given by Equation 19–7:

$$\text{COP} = \frac{T_c}{T_h - T_c} = \frac{283\ \text{K}}{343\ \text{K} - 283\ \text{K}} = 4.7.$$

For every joule of electricity used, the heat pump transfers an additional 4.7 joules from the ground to the house, giving a total of 5.7 joules to the house. If it supplies heat at the rate of 20 kW, the electrical power needed is then

$$P_{\text{electric}} = \frac{20\ \text{kW}}{5.7} = 3.5\ \text{kW}.$$

At 10¢/kWh, it costs 35¢ to run the heat pump for an hour. From Appendix D, we find that 20 kW is equivalent to 68,000 Btu/h, so that we must burn oil at the rate of

$$\frac{68,000\ \text{Btu/h}}{100,000\ \text{Btu/gal}} = 0.68\ \text{gal/h}.$$

At 83¢/gal, the oil costs 56¢/h.

Although the heat pump in this example is far less expensive, two factors make the comparison unrealistic. First, real heat pumps operate at a COP closer to half their theoretical maximum, approximately doubling the cost over that of this example. Second, the initial installation of a heat pump is very expensive, so that economic considerations may still favor oil. As heat pump technology advances, though, these devices will come into wider use.

If we are concerned about energy and not just cost, we should also consider the source of electricity to run the heat pump. If this is a thermal power plant operating at an efficiency of, say, ⅓, then three times as much energy is used at the power plant as is supplied to the heat pump. The overall efficiency of the heat pump and power plant may actually be less than that of the oil furnace (see Problem 22).

19.4
THE THERMODYNAMIC TEMPERATURE SCALE

When we discussed temperature measurement in Chapter 16, we encountered the problem that no single method works at all temperatures. We settled on the gas thermometer as the best laboratory standard, but even a helium gas thermometer becomes useless at temperatures below about 1 K.

The operation of a reversible heat engine provides a way of measuring temperature that is independent of the particular device used and that works at any temperature. We can take such an engine—or any thermodynamic system—through a complete cycle of reversible processes. Measuring the heats Q_c and Q_h, or one of these and the work output, allows us to calculate the efficiency and from it the temperature ratio. If one temperature is known, we can then determine the other. Although this may seem a rather obscure way to measure temperature, it is actually used in certain experiments at very low temperature. And it provides an absolute way of defining temperature that can, in principle, be used at any temperature. The temperature scale so defined is called the **thermodynamic temperature scale.**

thermodynamic
temperature scale

absolute zero

The zero of the thermodynamic scale—**absolute zero**—is absolute in that it represents a state of maximum order. This is reflected in the fact that a heat engine rejecting heat at absolute zero would operate at 100 per cent efficiency, as suggested by Equation 19–5 with $T_c = 0$. Unfortunately, there are no heat reservoirs at absolute zero, and it can be shown that it is impossible to cool anything to this temperature in a finite number of steps. The statement that it is impossible to reach absolute zero in a finite number of steps is called the **third law of thermodynamics.**

third law of
thermodynamics

19.5
ENTROPY AND THE QUALITY OF ENERGY

If offered a joule of energy, would you rather have that joule delivered in the form of mechanical work, heat transferred from an object at 1000 K, or heat transferred from an object at 300 K? Your answer might depend on what you wanted to do with the energy. If you wanted to lift or accelerate a mass, then you would be smart to take your energy as work. But if you want to keep warm, then heat from the 300 K object would be perfectly acceptable.

If, on the other hand, you weren't sure what you wanted to do with the energy, then which should you take? The second law of thermodynamics makes the answer clear: you should take the work. Why? Because you could use it directly to give one joule of mechanical energy—kinetic or potential—to a mass, or you could, through friction or other irreversible processes, use it to raise the temperature of something.

If you chose heat from the 300 K object as the form for your joule of energy, then you could supply a full joule only to objects cooler than 300 K. You could not do mechanical work unless you used your joule of 300 K heat to run a heat engine. With its maximum temperature only a little above ambient, your engine would be very inefficient, and you could only extract a small fraction of a joule of mechanical energy. Nor could you supply your energy to anything hotter than 300 K, unless you ran a refrigerator—and that would take additional work over and above your one joule. You would be better off with one joule of energy in the form of 1000 K heat, for you could transfer it to anything cooler than 1000 K, or could run a heat engine to produce a substantial fraction of a joule of mechanical energy.

Taking your one joule of energy in the form of work gives you the most options. Anything you can do with a joule of energy, you can do with the work. Energy taken as heat is less versatile, with the joule of 300 K energy the least useful of the three. We are not talking here about the quantity of energy—we have exactly one joule in each case—but about the **quality of energy,** indicated by the ability to do a variety of useful tasks. Schematically, we can describe energy quality on a diagram like Fig. 19–22. In Fig. 19–22, we list electricity with mechanical energy because electrical energy flows without requiring a temperature difference, and thus qualifies as work. We can readily convert an entire amount of energy from higher to lower quality, but the second law of thermodynamics prevents us from going in the opposite direction with 100 per cent efficiency.

The notion of energy quality has important implications for our efficient use of energy, suggesting that we try to match the quality of available energy sources to our energy needs. Figure 19–23 shows a breakdown of United States energy use by quality; it makes clear that much of our energy demand is for relatively low-quality heat. Although we can do anything we want with a high-quality energy source like flowing water or electricity, it makes sense to put our high-quality energy to high-quality uses, and use lower-quality sources to meet other needs. For example, we often heat water with electricity—a great convenience to the homeowner, but a thermodynamic folly, for in so doing we convert the highest-quality form of energy into low-grade heat. If our electricity comes from a thermal power plant, we already threw away two-thirds of the energy from fuel as waste heat. It makes little sense to run an elaborate and inefficient heat engine only to have its high-quality output of electricity used for low-temperature heating. On the other hand, if we heat our water by burning a fuel directly at the water heater, then we can, in principle, transfer all the fuel's energy to the water. Another approach to matching energy quality with energy needs is to combine the production of steam for heating with the generation of elec-

Fig. 19–22
Energy quality.

quality of energy

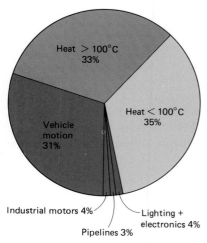

Fig. 19–23
Energy use in the United States, organized by energy quality.

cogeneration

tricity. Popular in Europe for many years, this idea of **cogeneration** is gaining popularity in the United States (Fig. 19–24).

Entropy

How can we make more precise the notion of energy quality? Consider the system shown in Fig. 19–25. It consists of two identical objects, initially at different temperatures and thermally insulated from each other and from the environment. The two objects are then brought into thermal contact, so that they eventually reach equilibrium at the same temperature.

What has changed between the initial and final states of our system? Not the energy, for we did no work on the system, and lost no heat, so that the total energy remained constant. But we have lost the ability to do useful work. In the initial state, we could have run a heat engine between the hot and cool objects. In the final state, there is no temperature difference and therefore no way to run a heat engine. The quality of the energy has decreased. Can we find some system property that reflects this change in energy quality?

Figure 19–26 shows another example of a system whose energy quality deteriorates without any loss of total energy. We start with a gas confined by a removable partition to one side of an insulated container; the other side is evacuated. We then remove the partition and allow the gas to expand freely to fill the whole container. Since the process is adiabatic, and no work is done, the total energy does not change. But we lose the ability to extract some of that energy as useful work. Starting with the initial state, we could have opened a small hole and used the escaping gas to run a turbine (Fig. 19–27). In the final state, there is no way to run the turbine, for there is no pressure difference across which the gas will flow. Again, can we find a quantity that describes this decrease in energy quality?

To find such a quantity, we consider an ideal gas undergoing a Carnot cycle (Fig. 19–28). In deriving the efficiency of such a cycle, we found that

$$\frac{Q_c}{Q_h} = \frac{T_c}{T_h}, \tag{19-8}$$

where Q_c is defined as the heat *rejected from* the system to the low-temperature reservoir at T_c, and Q_h is the heat *added to* the system from the high-temperature reservoir at T_h.

We now change our convention on the meaning of Q_c, taking it also to mean heat *added to* our system. Changing this convention changes the sign of Q_c, for positive heat rejected from our system is the same as negative heat added to it. With this change in convention, Equation 19–8 may be written

Fig. 19–24
This cogenerating unit at Middlebury College provides 600 kW of electricity from high-pressure steam produced in the college's heating plant. After passing through a turbine that drives the electric generator, the steam is used to heat buildings.

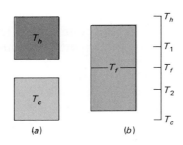

Fig. 19–25
Two identical objects, initially at different temperatures, are allowed to come to thermal equilibrium.

Fig. 19–26
Adiabatic free expansion. No energy leaves the system during the process, but energy quality deteriorates.

Fig. 19–27
A means of extracting useful work from the gas in the initial state of Fig. 19–26.

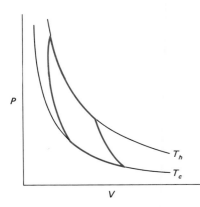

Fig. 19–28
Carnot cycle for an ideal gas.

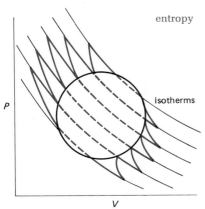

Fig. 19–29
An arbitrary cycle may be approximated by a sequence of adiabatic and isothermal steps.

$$\frac{Q_c}{T_c} + \frac{Q_h}{T_h} = 0,$$

or

$$\sum \frac{Q}{T} = 0. \qquad (19\text{–}9)$$

Although this result follows specifically from consideration of a Carnot cycle consisting of two adiabatic and two isothermal steps, we can generalize it to any reversible cycle. Any such cycle can be approximated arbitrarily closely by a sequence of adiabatic and isothermal steps (Fig. 19–29). One way to move around our reversible cycle is to take in the entire sequence of Carnot cycles shown in Fig. 19–29. But Equation 19–9 holds for each of these Carnot cycles, so that we must have

$$\sum \frac{Q}{T} = 0 \qquad (19\text{–}10)$$

over the entire set of Carnot cycles. Although the Q's in this expression are heats added in the isothermal sections of the individual Carnot cycles, those parts of a Carnot cycle that traverse the interior of our closed path are crossed twice, in opposite directions (Fig. 19–30), so that their heats cancel. Then Equation 19–10 applies equally well to the jagged approximation to our closed path. In the limit as we approximate the smooth curve ever closer by more and more adiabatic and isothermal segments, Equation 19–10 becomes

$$\oint \frac{dQ}{T} = 0, \qquad (19\text{–}11)$$

where the circle on the integral sign indicates that we integrate over all the heat transfers dQ along a *closed* path.

Equation 19–11 tells us that there is some quantity—a small amount of which is given by dQ/T—that does not change when we traverse a closed path, bringing our system back to its original state. We call this quantity the **entropy**, S, and write

$$dS = \frac{dQ}{T} \qquad (19\text{–}12)$$

and

$$S_2 - S_1 = \int_1^2 dS = \int_1^2 \frac{dQ}{T}, \qquad (19\text{–}13)$$

where the limits on the integral refer to two thermodynamic states and S_1 and S_2 are the entropies of those states. Note that we are not concerned with the actual value of the entropy, but only with the *change* in entropy from one state to another. In this way, entropy is like potential energy, for which only changes are meaningful.*

---

*Actually, the zero of entropy is meaningful, in that zero entropy for any system corresponds to a temperature of absolute zero.

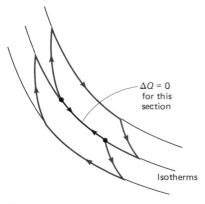

Fig. 19–30
Heat transfers cancel as two adjacent
Carnot cycles are traversed across the
interior of the original cycle.

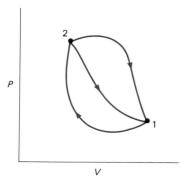

Fig. 19–31
Entropy change is zero when the
system returns to its original state,
so the entropy change from state
2 to state 1 must be independent
of the path taken.

Example 19–5
Entropy

An object of mass m and specific heat c is taken from an initial temperature T_1 to a final temperature T_2. What is the change in its entropy?

Solution

The entropy change is given by Equation 19–13. To evaluate the integral in this equation, we must relate dQ and T. We can do so because we know the specific heat, so that

$$dQ = mcdT.$$

Then Equation 19–13 is

$$\Delta S = \int_{T_1}^{T_2} \frac{dQ}{T} = \int_{T_1}^{T_2} mc\,\frac{dT}{T} = mc\,\ln\!\left(\frac{T_2}{T_1}\right). \qquad (19\text{–}14)$$

What good is this concept of entropy? Equation 19–11 shows that there is no entropy change when we take a system from some initial state and eventually return it to that state. Now suppose we take a system part way around a closed path, from state 1 to state 2 as shown in Fig. 19–31. The entropy change from state 2 back to state 1 must be exactly opposite the change from 1 to 2, so that the change going around the closed path is zero. But this must be true no matter how we get from state 2 to state 1, as suggested by the two possible paths in Fig. 19–31. That is, the entropy change given by Equation 19–13 is independent of path; it is a property only of the initial and final states themselves. Like pressure, temperature, and volume, entropy is a thermodynamic state variable—a quantity that characterizes a given state independently of how a system got into that state.

Equation 19–13 for calculating the entropy difference between two states is meaningful only for reversible processes, for the temperature T is defined only in thermodynamic equilibrium, while an irreversible process takes a system temporarily out of equilibrium. But because entropy is a property of a thermodynamic state, and not of how a system got into that state, entropy changes during an irreversible process can be calculated by finding a reversible process that takes a system between the same two states, then calculating the entropy change for that process using Equation 19–13.

At the beginning of this section, we considered some irreversible processes in which energy quality deteriorated although total energy remained constant. We can come to understand the meaning of entropy by calculating entropy changes for these processes.

Example 19–6
Adiabatic Free Expansion

An ideal gas, initially confined to one side of an insulated container, is allowed to expand freely to fill the entire container (Fig. 19–32). What is the entropy change for this process?

Solution

Since the free expansion is adiabatic and involves no work, the internal energy and temperature of the ideal gas are unchanged. But the gas volume doubles. To

Fig. 19-32
Adiabatic free expansion.

(a)   (b)

find the entropy change for the irreversible free expansion, we can consider a reversible process taking the system between the same two states. Since the initial and final temperatures are the same, such a process is an isothermal expansion. The heat added during such an expansion is given by Equation 18–6:

$$Q = nRT \ln\left(\frac{V_2}{V_1}\right).$$

Since the temperature is constant during the reversible isothermal expansion, the entropy change of Equation 19–13 is given simply by

$$S_2 - S_1 = \frac{Q}{T} = nR \ln\left(\frac{V_2}{V_1}\right). \tag{19–15}$$

Since the final volume V_2 is larger than the initial volume, the entropy change is positive.

In calculating the entropy change, we used the heat Q that would be required during a reversible isothermal process. Of course, no heat is transferred during the actual adiabatic free expansion—but the entropy change is the same as for the reversible isothermal process, which is why we calculated the entropy change as though such a process had occurred.

Example 19–7
Irreversible Heat Transfer

An object at a high temperature T_h is placed in contact with another object at a lower temperature T_c. What is the change in the entropy of the system when the two have reached equilibrium?

Solution

Again, we have an irreversible process. But we can calculate the entropy change by considering any process that takes the two objects from their initial temperatures to the same final temperature T_f. For example, we cool the hot object by placing it in contact with a heat reservoir initially at T_h and gradually lowering its temperature to T_f. The entropy change is given by

$$\Delta S_h = \int_{T_h}^{T_f} \frac{dQ}{T}.$$

Although we could evaluate this integral, let us for the moment note only that there is some average temperature T_1 *that lies between* T_h *and* T_f, for which

$$\Delta S_h = \frac{Q_h}{T_1},$$

where Q_h is the heat absorbed by the hot object. Q_h is, in fact, negative since the hot object loses heat as it cools. Similarly, the entropy change of the cool object is

$$\Delta S_c = \int_{T_c}^{T_f} \frac{dQ}{T} = \frac{Q_c}{T_2},$$

where T_2 is some average temperature *that lies between* T_c *and* T_f, and Q_c is the heat absorbed by the cool object.

The total entropy change of the system is

$$\Delta S = \Delta S_c + \Delta S_h = \frac{Q_c}{T_2} + \frac{Q_h}{T_1}.$$

Because the two objects are insulated from the outside world, any heat lost by the hot object in the actual irreversible process is gained by the cool object. Therefore, $Q_h = -Q_c$, and the total entropy change becomes

$$\Delta S = \frac{Q_c}{T_2} - \frac{Q_c}{T_1} = Q_c\left(\frac{1}{T_2} - \frac{1}{T_1}\right).$$

Now whatever the value of T_1, it lies *above* the equilibrium temperature T_f. Similarly, T_2 lies *below* T_f, so that $T_2 < T_1$. Furthermore, Q_c is positive, since the cool object absorbs heat. Therefore, the first term in our expression for ΔS is greater than the second term, so that the entropy change is positive.

Problem 35 explores this example more quantitatively, but the significant conclusion remains: entropy increases during an irreversible heat transfer.

The systems in Examples 19–6 and 19–7 were closed systems, in that they did not exchange energy or matter with their environments. For each system, entropy increased as the system underwent an irreversible process. At the same time, energy that was originally available to do useful work became unavailable. This correlation between an increase in entropy and a decrease in energy quality can be made more quantitative. Consider the free expansion of Example 19–6. Had we let the gas expand isothermally but reversibly, it could have done an amount of work given by Equation 18–5:

$$W = nRT \ln\left(\frac{V_2}{V_1}\right). \tag{19–16}$$

After the irreversible free expansion, the gas could no longer do this work, even though its energy content was unchanged. During the expansion, its entropy increased by an amount given by Equation 19–15:

$$\Delta S = nR \ln\left(\frac{V_2}{V_1}\right).$$

Comparing this entropy change with the energy that became unavailable to do work (Equation 19–16), we have

$$E_{\text{unavailable}} = T\Delta S. \tag{19–17}$$

Equation 19–17 is an example of a more general relation between entropy and the quality or availability of energy:

entropy and the quality
of energy

> During an irreversible process in which the entropy of a system increases by ΔS, an amount of energy $E = T_{\text{min}}\Delta S$ becomes unavailable to do work. T_{min} is the temperature of the coolest reservoir available to the system.

This statement shows that entropy provides our desired measure of energy quality. Given two systems that are identical in composition and energy content, the system with the lowest entropy contains the highest-quality energy. An increase in entropy always corresponds to a degradation in energy quality, in that some energy becomes unavailable to do work. Problem 36 explores this energy degradation quantitatively.

Entropy and the Second Law

At the beginning of this chapter, we argued that processes in nature always occur irreversibly, going from ordered states to disordered states. It is this loss of order in thermodynamic systems—as when a hot and a cold object eventually reach the same temperature—that is responsible for energy becoming unavailable to do work. Entropy is a measure of this disorder. Given the tendency of systems to evolve toward disordered states, we can make a statement about entropy that is, in fact, a general statement of the second law of thermodynamics:

second law of
thermodynamics

> The entropy of a closed system can never decrease.

At best, the entropy of a closed system remains constant—and this happens only in an ideal, reversible process. If anything irreversible occurs—a slight amount of friction or a deviation from exact thermodynamic equilibrium—then entropy increases. There is no going back. As entropy increases, some energy becomes unavailable to do work, and nothing within the closed system can restore that energy to its original quality. This statement of the second law in terms of entropy is equivalent to our previous statements about the impossibility of perfect heat engines and refrigerators, for the operation of either device would require a decrease in entropy.

What about a system that is not closed? Can't we decrease its entropy? Yes—but only by supplying high-quality energy from outside. When we run a refrigerator, we decrease the entropy of the refrigerator's contents and its surroundings (Fig. 19–33). At the same time, however, we must do work on the refrigerator to effect this entropy decrease—to make heat flow in the direction it doesn't normally go. If we enlarge our closed system to include the power plant or whatever else supplies the refrigerator with work, we would find that the entropy of this new closed system does not decrease. The entropy decrease at the refrigerator is offset by entropy increases elsewhere in the system (Fig. 19–34). If irreversible processes occur anywhere in the system, then there is a net entropy increase.

Fig. 19–33
The entropy decrease of the refrigerator's contents can occur only when work is done on the system from outside.

Fig. 19–34
When the source of work for the refrigerator is included in the system, then entropy of the entire system can at best remain constant.

Whenever we encounter a system whose entropy seems to decrease—that gets more rather than less organized—we do not have a closed system. If we enlarge the boundaries of our system to encompass anything that might exchange energy with it, then we will always find that the enlarged system undergoes an entropy increase. Ultimately, we can enlarge our system to include the entire universe. When we do, we have the ultimate statement of the second law of thermodynamics:

second law of
thermodynamics

> The entropy of the universe can never decrease.

As last examples of this broad statement, consider the growth of a living thing from the random mix of molecules in its environment, or the construction of a skyscraper from materials that were originally dispersed about the earth, or the appearance of ordered symbols on a printed page from what was a uniformly mixed bottle of ink. All these are processes in which matter goes from near chaos to a highly organized state—akin to separating yolk and white from a scrambled egg. They are certainly processes in which entropy decreases. But earth is not a closed system. It gets high-quality energy from the sun, energy that is ultimately responsible for life and all its actions. If we consider the earth-sun system, then the entropy decrease associated with life and civilization on earth is more than balanced by the entropy increase associated with nuclear fusion inside the sun. We living things represent a remarkable phenomenon—the organization of matter in a universe governed by a tendency toward disorder. But we do not escape the second law of thermodynamics. Our highly organized selves and society, and the entropy decreases they represent, come into being only at the expense of greater entropy increases elsewhere in the universe.

SUMMARY

1. Irreversible processes are those that result in a decrease in organization or order. Friction is an irreversible process that converts directed kinetic energy into the random kinetic energy of molecular motions. Thermodynamic processes that take a nonequilibrium state toward equilibrium are similarly irreversible. Because there are many more ways to arrange matter in a disorganized state than in an organized state, the probability that a disorganized state will become spontaneously organized is impossibly small.

2. The **second law of thermodynamics** comprises a set of equivalent statements to the effect that processes never take matter from less organized to more organized states.

   a. A **heat engine** is a device that extracts heat from a reservoir and converts some of the energy to useful work. Applied to heat engines, the second law states that it is impossible to build a perfect heat engine—one that converts heat to work with one hundred per cent efficiency. The most efficient engine is one that includes only reversible processes. The efficiency of such an engine—of which a **Carnot engine** is one example—is

   $$e = 1 - \frac{T_c}{T_h},$$

   where T_c and T_h are the temperatures of cool and hot reservoirs with which the engine exchanges energy. Because of the second law's limitation on efficiency, practical heat engines like automobile engines and electric power plants exhaust a great deal of waste heat to their environments.

   b. A **refrigerator** is a device that extracts heat from a cool object and transfers it to a warmer object. Applied to refrigerators, the second law states that it is impossible to build a perfect refrigerator—one that transfers heat without energy input from outside. Because of this second-law limitation, real refrigerators require a source of outside power. The efficiency of a refrigerator is measured by its **coefficient**

of performance, defined as the ratio of heat extracted from the cool reservoir to the work input to the device:

$$\text{COP} = \frac{Q_c}{W}.$$

A refrigerator could be made by running a reversible engine backward, supplying work instead of producing it. Consideration of the second-law efficiency of such an engine then shows that the maximum COP of a refrigerator is

$$\text{COP} = \frac{T_c}{T_h - T_c}.$$

3. The second-law limit on the efficiency of a heat engine provides a definition of the **thermodynamic temperature scale.** This scale is independent of any particular type of thermometer or material, and coincides with the ideal gas temperature scale in the range where the latter is useful.
4. **Quality of energy** refers to the ability of a given amount of energy to be converted into work. The highest-quality energy is mechanical or electrical; these are associated with the organized motion or potential energy of particles in an object. Next in quality comes the energy associated with large temperature differences, followed by ever smaller temperature differences. The highest-quality energy can be readily converted to lower quality with one hundred per cent efficiency. The reverse process—conversion of lower-quality to higher-quality energy with one hundred per cent efficiency—is prohibited by the second law of thermodynamics.
5. **Entropy** provides a measure of the relative disorder of a system, so that increasing entropy is associated with decreasing energy quality. Entropy is a thermodynamic state variable, so that its value depends only on the state of a system and not on how the system got into that state. The entropy difference between two states may be calculated by evaluating the expression

$$\Delta S = \int_1^2 \frac{dQ}{T}$$

for any reversible process connecting those states.
6. In terms of entropy, the second law of thermodynamics becomes the statement that the entropy of the universe can never decrease. In this form, the second law is a universal statement about the tendency of systems to evolve toward states of higher disorder.

QUESTIONS

1. Which of the following processes is irreversible?
   a. Stirring sugar into coffee
   b. Building a house
   c. Demolishing a house with a wrecking crane
   d. Demolishing a house by taking it apart piece-by-piece
   e. Warming a bottle of milk by transferring it directly from a refrigerator to stove top
   f. Writing a sentence
   g. Harnessing the energy of falling water to drive machinery
2. Could you cool the kitchen by leaving the refrigerator door open? Explain.
3. Could you heat the kitchen by leaving the oven open? Explain.
4. Why don't we simply refrigerate the cooling water of a power plant before it goes to the plant, thereby increasing the plant's efficiency?
5. Should a car get better mileage in the summer or the winter? Explain.
6. Is there a limit to the maximum temperature that can be achieved by focusing sunlight with a lens? If so, what is it?
7. Name some irreversible processes that occur in a real engine.
8. A power company claims that electric heat is one hundred per cent efficient. Discuss this claim.
9. Steam leaves the turbine of a power plant at 150°C, and is condensed to water at the same temperature by contact with a river at 20°C. What temperature should be used as T_c in evaluating the thermodynamic efficiency?
10. A hydroelectric power plant, using the energy of falling water, can operate with an efficiency arbitrarily close to one hundred per cent. Why?
11. Viewed in isolation, a windmill is not a heat engine, for it converts mechanical energy of wind directly into electrical energy. But taking a broader view, the windmill is part of a natural heat engine. Explain.
12. To maximize the COP of a refrigerator, should you strive for a large or a small temperature difference? Explain.
13. The manufacturer of a heat pump claims that the device will heat your home using only energy already available in the ground. Is this true?
14. Proponents of ocean thermal energy conversion do not seem bothered by the extremely low efficiency of this process. Yet comparably low efficiencies would be intolerable in fossil-fueled or nuclear power plants. Why the difference?
15. Could anything useful be done with the waste heat from a power plant? Give two examples.
16. Does sunlight represent high- or low-quality energy? Explain. (See Question 6.)
17. The heat Q added during the process of adiabatic free expansion is zero. Why can't we then argue from

Equation 19–13 that the entropy change during this process is zero?

18. Energy is conserved, so why can't we recycle it like we do materials?

19. Name several systems that undergo entropy decreases. By considering larger systems of which they must be part, argue that the net entropy of the larger systems must increase.

PROBLEMS

Section 19.1   *Reversibility and Irreversibility*

1. An egg carton has places for one dozen eggs, as shown in Fig. 19–35. How many distinct ways are there to arrange six eggs in the carton? Of these, what fraction correspond to all six eggs being in the left half of the carton? Treat the eggs as distinguishable, so that an interchange of any two eggs gives rise to a new state of the system.

Fig. 19–35   Problem 1

2. Consider a gas consisting of only four molecules, all of which have the same speed v in the x-direction, but which can be moving either to the left or to the right. A microscopic state of the gas is specified by telling which molecules are moving in which direction. (a) How many possible microscopic states are there? (b) Of these, how many correspond to all the molecules moving in the same direction? If the system is in some random state, what are the chances that it will be a state with all molecules moving in the same direction? (c) Repeat parts a and b for the case of 10 molecules. (d) Repeat parts a and b for the case of 10^{23} molecules.

3. Estimate the energy that could be extracted by cooling all the oceans 0.1°C. Make reasonable assumptions about the volume of water in the oceans. How does this amount of energy compare with humanity's average yearly energy consumption of 2.5×10^{20} J?

Sections 19.2–19.3   *The Second Law and Applications*

4. What is the efficiency of a reversible engine operating between (a) the normal boiling and freezing points of water? (b) the surface temperature of the sun (5600 K) and the temperature of intergalactic space (3 K)? (c) the normal melting point of helium (1.76 K) and 1.0 K? (d) the temperature of surface water in the tropical oceans (80°F) and deep ocean water (39°F)? (e) a flame at 1000°C and room temperature?

5. The maximum temperature in a nuclear power plant is 570 K. The plant rejects heat to a river where the temperature is 0°C in the winter and 25°C in the summer. What are the maximum possible efficiencies of the power plant in the summer and winter? Why might the plant not achieve these efficiencies?

6. Consider a Carnot engine operating between a high temperature T_h and a low temperature T_c that is still above the ambient environmental temperature T_0. It should then be possible to operate a second Carnot engine between the output of the first engine and the environment, thereby producing more useful work. Show that the maximum overall efficiency of such a two-stage engine is the same as that of a single engine operating between T_h and T_0.

7. What is the COP of a reversible refrigerator operating between a minimum temperature of 0°C and a maximum temperature of 30°C?

8. 4.0 L of water at 9.0°C are put into a refrigerator. The refrigerator's 130-W motor then runs for 4.0 minutes to cool the water to the refrigerator's low temperature of 1.0°C. What is the COP of the refrigerator? How does this compare with the maximum possible COP if the refrigerator exhausts heat at 25°C?

9. In Section 19.2, we showed that the existence of a perfect refrigerator would allow us to construct a perfect heat engine, in violation of the Kelvin-Planck statement of the second law of thermodynamics. Make a similar argument, using appropriate energy flow diagrams, to show that the existence of a perfect heat engine would allow us to construct a perfect refrigerator, thus violating the Clausius statement of the second law.

10. An engine absorbs 900 J of heat each cycle and provides 350 J of work. (a) What is its efficiency? (b) How much heat is rejected each cycle? (c) If the engine is reversible and rejects heat to its environment at 10°C, what is its maximum temperature? (d) If the engine operates at 1000 cycles/minute, what is its mechanical power output?

11. Which would provide the greatest increase in the efficiency of a Carnot engine: an increase of 10°C in the maximum temperature or a decrease of 10°C in the minimum temperature?

12. Which would provide the greatest increase in the COP of a refrigerator: a decrease of 10°C in the maximum temperature or an increase of 10°C in the minimum temperature?

13. What is the maximum efficiency of an OTEC power plant operating between 20°C and 10°C?

14. 0.20 mol of ideal gas are taken through the Carnot cycle of Fig. 19–36. Calculate the heat Q_h absorbed, the heat Q_c rejected, and the work done. Find the maximum and minimum temperature, and show explicitly that the efficiency defined in Equation 19–1 is equal to the Carnot efficiency given by Equation 19–5.

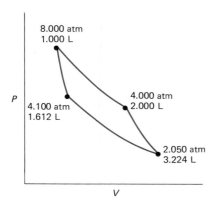

Fig. 19–36   Problem 14 (Diagram is not to scale.)

15. A reversible engine contains 0.20 mol of ideal monatomic gas, initially at 600 K and confined to 2.0 L. The gas is taken through a cycle consisting of the following steps:
    a. Isothermal expansion to a volume of 4.0 L
    b. Isovolumic cooling to 300 K
    c. Isothermal compression to 2.0 L
    d. Isovolumic heating to 600 K
    Calculate heat added during the cycle, and the work done. Determine the engine's efficiency, defined as the ratio of net work done to heat *absorbed* during the cycle. Compare with the efficiency of a Carnot engine operating between the same maximum and minimum temperatures. Why is your result not a violation of Carnot's statement that all reversible engines operating between the same reservoirs must have the same efficiency?

16. Repeat the preceding problem for the cycle of Fig. 19–37.

17. A power plant extracts energy from steam at 250°C and delivers 800 MW of electric power. It discharges waste heat to a river at 30°C. The overall efficiency of the power plant is 28%. (a) How does this efficiency compare with the maximum possible at these operating temperatures? (b) What is the rate of waste heat discharge to the river? (c) How many houses, each requiring 40,000 Btu/h of heat, could be heated with the waste heat from this power plant?

18. Show that it is impossible for two adiabats of any substance to intersect. *Hint:* Connect the two by a suitable isotherm, and show that the resulting cycle represents a heat engine operating at 100% efficiency.

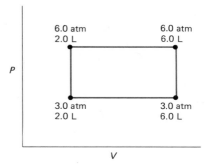

Fig. 19–37   Problem 16

19. Gasoline and diesel engines operate on the **Otto cycle,** shown in Fig. 19–38. In this idealization, we neglect the intake of fuel-air and exhaust of combustion products; the work involved in both is roughly equal but opposite. We also assume that all processes are reversible, which is not true for a real engine. In your calculations, assume that the gas in the cylinder has a fixed specific heat ratio γ. (a) What is the efficiency of this engine? (b) What is the maximum temperature, in terms of the minimum temperature T_c? (c) How does the actual efficiency compare with the efficiency of a Carnot engine operating between the same temperature extremes? (See Problem 15.)

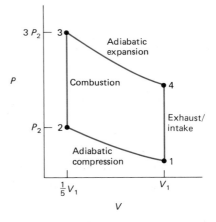

Fig. 19–38   Otto cycle (Problems 19, 20).

20. For the internal-combustion engine of the preceding problem, the **compression ratio** is defined as the ratio of maximum to minimum volume. In the engine of the preceding problem, the compression ratio is 5. What effect does an increase in compression ratio have on engine efficiency? Show by plotting efficiency versus compression ratio. Show also the efficiency of a Carnot engine operating between the same temperature extremes as your internal-combus-

tion engine. Assume that the pressure continues to triple during the combustion phase, as shown in Fig. 19–38.

21. A heat pump designed for use in southern climates extracts heat from the outside air and delivers hot air at 105°F to the inside of a house. (a) If the average outdoor temperature in winter is 40°F, what is the average COP of the heat pump? Assume that the heat pump operates in a reversible Carnot cycle. (b) Suppose the heat pump is used in a northern climate where the average winter temperature is 15°F. Now what is the COP? (c) Two *identical* houses, one in the north and one in the south, are heated by this pump. Both houses maintain indoor temperatures of 65°F. What is the ratio of electric power consumption in the northern house to that in the southern one? *Hint:* Think about heat loss as well as COP!

22. A house is heated by a heat pump with a COP of 2.3. The heat pump is run by electricity generated in a power plant whose efficiency is 28%. What is the overall efficiency of this process, defined as the ratio of heat delivered to the house to heat released from fuel at the power plant? Could the efficiency so defined ever exceed 100%?

23. The electric power output of all the thermal electric power plants in the United States is about 2×10^{11} W. These plants operate with an average efficiency around 33%. What is the rate at which all these plants use cooling water, if the average temperature rise in the water is 5°C? Compare with the average flow at the mouth of the Mississippi River (1.8×10^7 kg/s).

24. A solar "power tower" plant is to be built in a desert location where the only source of cooling water is a small creek with an average flow of 100 kg/s and an average temperature of 30°C. The plant is to cool itself by boiling away the entire creek. If the maximum temperature achieved in the plant is 500 K, what is the maximum electric power output it can sustain without running out of cooling water?

25. The McNeil generating station in Burlington, Vermont, came into operation in 1984 as the largest wood-burning power plant in the United States. Here are some facts about the McNeil power plant:
   a. The electric power output of the plant is 59 MW.
   b. Fuel consumption is 1.2×10^6 kg of wood per day. The wood has an energy content of 1.4×10^7 J/kg, and burns with 85% efficiency, meaning that 85% of this energy is transferred to water in the plant's boiler.
   c. Steam enters the turbine of the power plant at 1000°F, and leaves at 200°F.
   d. Cooling water circulates through the condenser at the rate of 1.8×10^5 kg/min. The temperature of the cooling water increases by 18°F as it extracts heat from steam leaving the turbine.

   Calculate the efficiency of the plant in three ways: (a) Using only fact *c* above to get the maximum possible efficiency; (b) using only facts *a* and *b*; and (c) using only facts *a* and *d*.

Section 19.4   *The Thermodynamic Temperature Scale*

26. A small sample of material is taken through a Carnot cycle between a high-temperature reservoir of boiling helium ($T = 1.76$ K) and an unknown low temperature. During the process, 7.5 mJ of heat is absorbed from the boiling helium, and 0.44 mJ rejected to the low-temperature reservoir. What is the unknown low temperature?

27. A reversible engine operating between a vat of boiling sulfur and a bath of water at its triple point is observed to have an efficiency of 61.4%. What is the boiling point of sulfur?

Section 19.5   *Entropy and the Quality of Energy*

28. Calculate the entropy change associated with melting 1.0 kg of ice at 0°C.

29. The temperature of n moles of ideal gas is changed from T_1 to T_2. Show that the entropy change of the gas is

$$\Delta S = nC_V \ln\left(\frac{T_2}{T_1}\right).$$

30. 5.0 mol of an ideal diatomic gas ($C_V = \frac{5}{2}R$) is initially at 1.0 atm pressure and 300 K. What is the entropy change of the gas if it is heated to 500 K (a) isobarically, (b) isovolumically, and (c) adiabatically?

31. Since entropy and temperature are both state variables, we could describe thermodynamic processes on a TS diagram instead of a PV diagram. Sketch a graph of a Carnot cycle on such a diagram, with absolute temperature on the vertical axis and entropy on the horizontal axis.

32. A 500-g block of copper at 80°C is dropped into 1.0 kg of water at 10°C. (a) What is the final temperature? (b) What is the entropy change of the system?

33. n moles of an ideal monatomic gas are taken around the cycle shown in Fig. 19–39. The process BC is iso-

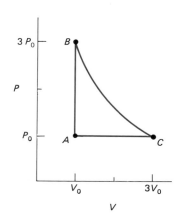

Fig. 19–39   Problem 33

thermal. Calculate the entropy change associated with each of the processes AB, BC, and CA, and show explicitly that there is no net change in entropy on traversing the whole cycle.

34. The interior of a house is maintained at 20°C while the outdoor temperature is −10°C. The house loses heat at the rate of 30 kW. At what rate does the entropy of the universe increase because of this irreversible heat flow?

35. Two identical objects of mass m and specific heat c at initial temperatures T_h and T_c are placed in an insulated box and allowed to come to equilibrium. Show that the entropy increase in the process is

$$\Delta S = mc \ln\frac{(T_h + T_c)^2}{4T_hT_c}.$$

Assume that the specific heat is independent of temperature.

36. You have available 50 kg of steam at 100°C, but no source of heat to maintain it in that condition. You also have a heat reservoir at 0°C. Suppose you operate a heat engine in this system, so that the steam condenses and gradually cools to 0°C as the engine runs. (a) Calculate the total entropy change of the steam and subsequent hot water. (b) Calculate the total entropy change of the reservoir. (c) What is the total amount of work that the engine can do? Hint: Consider the entropy change of the system. This change occurs as a result of a reversible process that supplies useful work. But if it had occurred irreversibly, how much energy would have become unavailable to do work?

37. Arguing by analogy with Example 19–7, show that a perfect refrigerator would reduce the entropy of the universe.

Supplementary Problems

38. In a steam engine, water is boiled under pressure so that its boiling point is above the normal 100°C. The resulting steam expands adiabatically and drives an engine that powers a railroad locomotive with a mass of 3.0×10^4 kg. The engine exhausts 100°C steam at the rate of 3.6 kg/s. If the engine can climb a 200-m-high hill in 45 s, what is the minimum possible temperature of the boiling water?

39. A Carnot engine extracts heat from a block of material of mass m and specific heat c that is initially at temperature T_{ho}. The engine rejects heat to a reservoir at T_c. The cool reservoir is large enough that its temperature never changes, but the hot material has no heat source, so that it cools as the engine runs. The engine is operated in such a way that the mechanical power output is proportional to the temperature difference $T_h - T_c$:

$$P = P_0\frac{T_h - T_c}{T_{ho} - T_c},$$

where T_h is the instantaneous temperature of the hot material and P_0 is the initial power output. Find an expression for T_h as a function of time, and determine how long it takes for the engine's power output to drop to zero. Your expression for T_h should suggest that T_h can drop below T_c. How is this possible?

40. Figure 19–40 shows a cyclic process in the PV diagram of an ideal diatomic gas. The process AB is isovolumic, BC isothermal, CD adiabatic, and DA isobaric. Fill in the blank spaces in the table below:

	P	V	T	$U - U_A$	$S - S_A$
A	P_0	V_0	T_0	0	0
B	$3.4P_0$	V_0			
C					
D	P_0	$3.0V_0$			

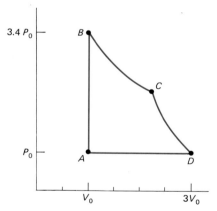

Fig. 19–40   Process for Problem 40. The location of point C is not quantitatively correct.

APPENDIX A
ALGEBRA AND TRIGONOMETRY

Quadratic Formula

If $ax^2 + bx + c = 0$ then $x = \dfrac{-b \pm \sqrt{b^2 - 4ac}}{2a}$

Circumference, Area, Volume

Where $\pi \simeq 3.14159$:

circumference of circle	$2\pi r$
area of circle	πr^2
surface area of sphere	$4\pi r^2$
volume of sphere	$\frac{4}{3}\pi r^3$
area of triangle	$\frac{1}{2}bh$
volume of cylinder	$\pi r^2 \ell$

Trigonometry

definition of angle (in radians): $\theta = \dfrac{s}{r}$

2π radians in complete circle
1 radian $\simeq 57.3°$

Trigonometric Functions

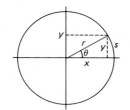

$$\sin\theta = \frac{y}{r}$$

$$\cos\theta = \frac{x}{r}$$

$$\tan\theta = \frac{\sin\theta}{\cos\theta} = \frac{y}{x}$$

Values at Selected Angles

$\theta \rightarrow$	0	$\dfrac{\pi}{6}$ (30°)	$\dfrac{\pi}{4}$ (45°)	$\dfrac{\pi}{3}$ (60°)	$\dfrac{\pi}{2}$ (90°)
$\sin\theta$	0	$\dfrac{1}{2}$	$\dfrac{\sqrt{2}}{2}$	$\dfrac{\sqrt{3}}{2}$	1
$\cos\theta$	1	$\dfrac{\sqrt{3}}{2}$	$\dfrac{\sqrt{2}}{2}$	$\dfrac{1}{2}$	0
$\tan\theta$	0	$\dfrac{\sqrt{3}}{3}$	1	$\sqrt{3}$	∞

Graphs of Trigonometric Functions

  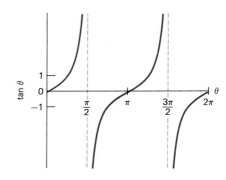

Trigonometric Identities

$$\sin(-\theta) = -\sin\theta$$

$$\cos(-\theta) = \cos\theta$$

$$\sin\left(\theta \pm \frac{\pi}{2}\right) = \pm\cos\theta$$

$$\cos\left(\theta \pm \frac{\pi}{2}\right) = \mp\sin\theta$$

$$\sin^2\theta + \cos^2\theta = 1$$

$$\sin 2\theta = 2\sin\theta\cos\theta$$

$$\cos 2\theta = \cos^2\theta - \sin^2\theta = 1 - 2\sin^2\theta = 2\cos^2\theta - 1$$

$$\sin(\alpha \pm \beta) = \sin\alpha\cos\beta \pm \cos\alpha\sin\beta$$

$$\cos(\alpha \pm \beta) = \cos\alpha\cos\beta \mp \sin\alpha\sin\beta$$

$$\sin\alpha \pm \sin\beta = 2\sin\left[\frac{1}{2}(\alpha \pm \beta)\right]\cos\left[\frac{1}{2}(\alpha \mp \beta)\right]$$

$$\cos\alpha + \cos\beta = 2\cos\left[\frac{1}{2}(\alpha + \beta)\right]\cos\left[\frac{1}{2}(\alpha - \beta)\right]$$

$$\cos\alpha - \cos\beta = -2\sin\left[\frac{1}{2}(\alpha + \beta)\right]\sin\left[\frac{1}{2}(\alpha - \beta)\right]$$

Laws of Cosines and Sines

Where A, B, C are the sides of an arbitrary triangle and α, β, γ the angles opposite those sides:

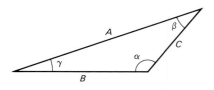

Law of Cosines

$$C^2 = A^2 + B^2 - 2AB\cos\gamma$$

Law of Sines

$$\frac{\sin\alpha}{A} = \frac{\sin\beta}{B} = \frac{\sin\gamma}{C}$$

Exponentials and Logarithms

Graphs

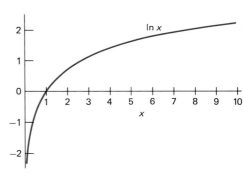

Exponential and Natural Logarithms Are Inverse Functions

$$e^{\ln x} = x, \quad \ln e^x = x \quad e = 2.71828\ldots$$

Exponential and Logarithmic Identities

$$a^x = e^{x\ln a} \qquad \ln(xy) = \ln x + \ln y$$

$$a^x a^y = a^{x+y} \qquad \ln\left(\frac{x}{y}\right) = \ln x - \ln y$$

$$(a^x)^y = a^{xy} \qquad \ln\left(\frac{1}{x}\right) = -\ln x$$

$$\log x \equiv \log_{10} x = \ln(10)\,\ln x \simeq 2.3\,\ln x$$

Expansions and Approximations

Series Expansions of Functions

Note: $n! = n(n - 1)(n - 2)(n - 3) \cdots (3)(2)(1)$

$$e^x = 1 + x + \frac{x^2}{2!} + \frac{x^3}{3!} + \cdots \qquad \text{(exponential)}$$

$$\sin x = x - \frac{x^3}{3!} + \frac{x^5}{5!} - \cdots \qquad \text{(sine)}$$

$$\cos x = 1 - \frac{x^2}{2!} + \frac{x^4}{4!} - \cdots \qquad \text{(cosine)}$$

(x in radians)

$$\ln(1 + x) = x - \frac{x^2}{2} + \frac{x^3}{3} - \cdots \qquad \text{(natural logarithm)}$$

$$(1 + x)^p = 1 + px + \frac{p(p - 1)}{2!}x^2 + \frac{p(p - 1)(p - 2)}{3!}x^3 + \cdots \qquad \text{(binomial, valid for } |x| < 1)$$

Approximations

For $|x| \ll 1$, the first few terms in the series provide a good approximation; that is,

$$
\left.
\begin{aligned}
e^x &\simeq 1 + x \\
\sin x &\simeq x \\
\cos x &\simeq 1 - \tfrac{1}{2}x^2 \\
\ln(1 + x) &\simeq x \\
(1 + x)^p &\simeq 1 + px
\end{aligned}
\right\} \quad \text{for } |x| \ll 1
$$

Expressions that do not have the forms shown may often be put in the appropriate form. For example:

$$\frac{1}{\sqrt{a^2 + y^2}} = \frac{1}{a\sqrt{1 + \dfrac{y^2}{a^2}}} = \frac{1}{a}\left(1 + \frac{y^2}{a^2}\right)^{-1/2}.$$

For $y^2 \ll a^2$, this may be approximated using the binomial expansion $(1 + x)^p \simeq 1 + px$, with $p = -\tfrac{1}{2}$ and $x = y^2/a^2$:

$$\frac{1}{a}\left(1 + \frac{y^2}{a^2}\right)^{-1/2} \simeq \frac{1}{a}\left(1 - \frac{1}{2}\frac{y^2}{a^2}\right).$$

Vector Algebra

Vector Products

$$\mathbf{A} \cdot \mathbf{B} = AB\cos\theta$$

$$|\mathbf{A} \times \mathbf{B}| = AB\sin\theta,$$

with direction of $\mathbf{A} \times \mathbf{B}$ given by right-hand rule:

Unit Vector Notation

An arbitrary vector $\mathbf{A}$ may be written in terms of its components A_x, A_y, A_z and the unit vectors $\hat{\imath}$, $\hat{\jmath}$, $\hat{k}$ that have length 1 and lie along the x, y, z axes:

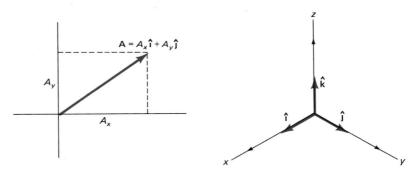

In unit vector notation, vector products become

$$\mathbf{A} \cdot \mathbf{B} = A_x B_x + A_y B_y + A_z B_z$$

$$\mathbf{A} \times \mathbf{B} = (A_y B_z - A_z B_y)\hat{\imath} + (A_z B_x - A_x B_z)\hat{\jmath} + (A_x B_y - A_y B_x)\hat{k}$$

Vector Identities

$$\mathbf{A} \cdot \mathbf{B} = \mathbf{B} \cdot \mathbf{A}$$

$$\mathbf{A} \times \mathbf{B} = -\mathbf{B} \times \mathbf{A}$$

$$\mathbf{A} \cdot (\mathbf{B} \times \mathbf{C}) = \mathbf{B} \cdot (\mathbf{C} \times \mathbf{A}) = \mathbf{C} \cdot (\mathbf{A} \times \mathbf{B})$$

$$\mathbf{A} \times (\mathbf{B} \times \mathbf{C}) = (\mathbf{A} \cdot \mathbf{C})\mathbf{B} - (\mathbf{A} \cdot \mathbf{B})\mathbf{C}$$

APPENDIX B
CALCULUS

Derivatives

Definition of the Derivative

If y is a function of x [$y = f(x)$], then the **derivative of y with respect to x** is the ratio of the change Δy in y to the corresponding change Δx in x, in the limit of arbitrarily small Δx:

$$\frac{dy}{dx} = \lim_{\Delta t \to 0} \frac{\Delta y}{\Delta x}.$$

Algebraically, the derivative is the rate of change of y with respect to x; geometrically, it is the slope of the y versus x graph—that is, of the tangent line to the graph at a given point:

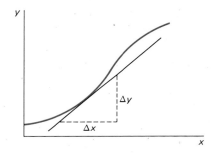

Derivatives of Common Functions

Although the derivative of a function can be evaluated directly using the limiting process that defines the derivative (see Section 2.2 and Example 2–3), standard formulas are available for common functions:

$$\frac{da}{dx} = 0 \qquad (a \text{ is a constant})$$

$$\frac{dx^n}{dx} = nx^{n-1} \qquad (n \text{ need not be an integer})$$

$$\frac{d}{dx} \sin x = \cos x$$

$$\frac{d}{dx} \cos x = -\sin x$$

$$\frac{d}{dx} \tan x = \frac{1}{\cos^2 x}$$

$$\frac{de^x}{dx} = e^x$$

$$\frac{d}{dx} \ln x = \frac{1}{x}$$

Derivatives of Sums, Products, and Functions of Functions

1. Derivative of a constant times a function

$$\frac{d}{dx}[af(x)] = a\frac{df}{dx} \qquad (a \text{ is a constant})$$

2. Derivative of a sum

$$\frac{d}{dx}[f(x) + g(x)] = \frac{df}{dx} + \frac{dg}{dx}$$

3. Derivative of a product

$$\frac{d}{dx}[f(x)\, g(x)] = g\frac{df}{dx} + f\frac{dg}{dx}$$

Examples

$$\frac{d}{dx}(x^2 \cos x) = \cos x \frac{dx^2}{dx} + x^2 \frac{d}{dx}\cos x = 2x \cos x - x^2 \sin x$$

$$\frac{d}{dx}(x \ln x) = \ln x \frac{dx}{dx} + x \frac{d}{dx}\ln x = (\ln x)(1) + x\left(\frac{1}{x}\right) = \ln x + 1$$

4. Derivative of a quotient

$$\frac{d}{dx}\left[\frac{f(x)}{g(x)}\right] = \frac{1}{g^2}\left(g\frac{df}{dx} - f\frac{dg}{dx}\right)$$

Example

$$\frac{d}{dx}\left(\frac{\sin x}{x^2}\right) = \frac{1}{x^4}\left(x^2 \frac{d}{dx}\sin x - \sin x \frac{dx^2}{dx}\right) = \frac{\cos x}{x^2} - \frac{2 \sin x}{x^3}$$

5. Chain rule for derivatives

If f is a function of u and u is a function of x, then

$$\frac{df}{dx} = \frac{df}{du}\frac{du}{dx}.$$

Examples

a. Evaluate $\dfrac{d}{dx}\sin(x^2)$. Here $u = x^2$ and $f(u) = \sin u$, so that

$$\frac{d}{dx}\sin(x^2) = \frac{d}{du}\sin u \frac{du}{dx} = (\cos u)\frac{dx^2}{dx} = 2x \cos(x^2).$$

b. $\dfrac{d}{dt}\sin\omega t = \dfrac{d}{d\omega t}\sin\omega t \dfrac{d}{dt}\omega t = \omega\cos\omega t.$ (ω a constant)

c. Evaluate $\dfrac{d}{dx}\sin^2 5x$. Here $u = \sin 5x$ and $f(u) = u^2$, so that

$$\frac{d}{dx}\sin^2 5x = \frac{d}{du}u^2 \frac{du}{dx} = 2u\frac{du}{dx} = 2 \sin 5x \frac{d}{dx}\sin 5x$$

$$= (2)(\sin 5x)(5)(\cos 5x) = 10 \sin 5x \cos 5x = 5 \sin 2x.$$

Second Derivative

The second derivative of y with respect to x is defined as the derivative of the derivative:

$$\frac{d^2y}{dx^2} = \frac{d}{dx}\left(\frac{dy}{dx}\right).$$

Example

If $y = ax^3$, then $dy/dx = 3ax^2$, so that

$$\frac{d^2y}{dx^2} = \frac{d}{dx}3ax^2 = 6ax.$$

Partial Derivatives

When a function depends on more than one variable, then the partial derivatives of that function are the derivatives with respect to each variable, taken with all other variables held constant. If f is a function of x and y, then the partial derivatives are written

$$\frac{\partial f}{\partial x} \qquad \text{and} \qquad \frac{\partial f}{\partial y}.$$

Example

If $f(x,y) = x^3 \sin y$, then

$$\frac{\partial f}{\partial x} = 3x^2\sin y \qquad \text{and} \qquad \frac{\partial f}{\partial y} = x^3\cos y.$$

Integrals

Indefinite Integrals

Integration is the inverse of differentiation. The **indefinite integral**, $\int f(x)\,dx$, is defined as a function whose derivative is $f(x)$:

$$\frac{d}{dx}[\int f(x)\,dx] = f(x).$$

If $A(x)$ is an indefinite integral of $f(x)$, then because the derivative of a constant is zero, the function $A(x) + C$ is also an indefinite integral of $f(x)$, where C is any constant. Inverting the derivatives of common functions listed in the preceding section gives some common integrals (a more extensive table appears at the end of Appendix B):

$$\int a\,dx = ax + C$$

$$\int x^n\,dx = \frac{x^{n+1}}{n+1} + C, \qquad n \neq -1$$

$$\int \sin x\,dx = -\cos x + C$$

$$\int \cos x\,dx = \sin x + C$$

$$\int e^x\,dx = e^x + C$$

$$\int x^{-1}\,dx = \ln x + C$$

Definite Integrals

In physics we are most often interested in the **definite integral,** defined as the sum of a large number of very small quantities, in the limit as the number of quantities grows arbitrarily large and the size of each arbitrarily small:

$$\int_{x_1}^{x_2} f(x)\,dx \equiv \lim_{\substack{\Delta x \to 0 \\ N \to \infty}} \sum_{i=1}^{N} f(x_i)\Delta x,$$

where the terms in the sum are evaluated at values x_i between the limits of integration x_1 and x_2; in the limit $\Delta x \to 0$, the sum is over all values of x in the interval.

The definite integral is used whenever we need to sum over a quantity that is changing—for example, to calculate the work done by a variable force (Chapter 6), the entropy change in a system whose temperature varies (Chapter 19), or the flux of an electric field that varies with position (Chapter 21).

The key to evaluating the definite integral is provided by the **fundamental theorem of calculus,** which relates the definite and indefinite integrals and which we outlined without naming it in Box 2–1. The theorem states that, if $A(x)$ is an *indefinite* integral of $f(x)$, then the *definite integral* is given by

$$\int_{x_1}^{x_2} f(x)\,dx = A(x_2) - A(x_1) \equiv A(x)\Big|_{x_1}^{x_2}.$$

Geometrically, the definite integral is the area under the graph of $f(x)$ between the limits x_1 and x_2:

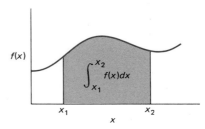

Evaluating Integrals

The first step in evaluating an integral is to express all varying quantities within the integral in terms of a single variable. For example, in evaluating $\int E\,dr$ to calculate an electric potential (Chapter 23), it is necessary first to express E as a function of r. This procedure is illustrated in many examples throughout this text; Example 20–5 provides a typical case.

Once an integral is written in terms of a single variable, it is necessary to manipulate the integrand—the function being integrated—into a form whose integral you know or can look up in tables of integrals. Two common techniques are especially useful:

1. **Change of variables**

   An unfamiliar integral can often be put into familiar form by defining a new variable. For example, it is not obvious how to integrate the expression

   $$\int \frac{x\,dx}{\sqrt{a^2 + x^2}},$$

   where a is a constant. But let $z = a^2 + x^2$. Then

   $$\frac{dz}{dx} = \frac{da^2}{dx} + \frac{dx^2}{dx} = 0 + 2x = 2x,$$

so that $dz = 2x\,dx$. Then the quantity $x\,dx$ in our unfamiliar integral is just $\frac{1}{2}dz$, while the quantity $\sqrt{a^2 + x^2}$ is just $z^{1/2}$. So the integral becomes

$$\int \tfrac{1}{2}z^{-1/2}\,dz = \frac{\tfrac{1}{2}z^{1/2}}{(1/2)} = \sqrt{z},$$

where we have used the standard form for the integral of a power of the independent variable. Substituting back $z = a^2 + x^2$ gives

$$\int \frac{x\,dx}{\sqrt{a^2 + x^2}} = \sqrt{a^2 + x^2}.$$

2. Integration by parts

The quantity $\int u\,dv$ is the area under the curve of u as a function of v between specified limits. In the figure below, that area can also be expressed as the area of the rectangle shown minus the area under the curve of v as a function of u.

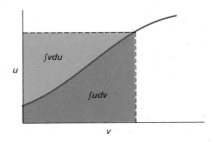

Mathematically, this relation among areas may be expressed as a relation among integrals:

$$\int u\,dv = uv - \int v\,du. \qquad \text{(integration by parts)}$$

This expression may often be used to transform complicated integrals into simpler ones.

Example

Evaluate $\int x\cos x\,dx$. Here let $u = x$, so that $du = dx$. Then $dv = \cos x\,dx$, so that $v = \int dv = \int \cos x\,dx = \sin x$. Integrating by parts then gives

$$\int x\cos x\,dx = (x)(\sin x) - \int \sin x\,dx = x\sin x + \cos x,$$

where the $+$ sign arises because $\int \sin x\,dx = -\cos x$.

Table of Integrals

[More extensive tables are available in many mathematical and scientific handbooks; see, for example, *Handbook of Chemistry and Physics* (Chemical Rubber Co.) or Dwight, *Tables of Integrals and other Mathematical Data* (Macmillan).]

In the expressions below, a and b are constants. An arbitrary constant of integration may be added to the right-hand side.

$$\int e^{ax}dx = \frac{e^{ax}}{a}$$

$$\int \sin ax\,dx = -\frac{\cos ax}{a}$$

$$\int \cos ax\,dx = \frac{\sin ax}{a}$$

$$\int \tan ax\,dx = -\frac{1}{a}\ln(\cos ax)$$

$$\int \sin^2 ax\,dx = \frac{x}{2} - \frac{\sin 2ax}{4a}$$

$$\int \cos^2 ax\,dx = \frac{x}{2} + \frac{\sin 2ax}{4a}$$

$$\int x\sin ax\,dx = \frac{1}{a^2}\sin ax - \frac{1}{a}x\cos ax$$

$$\int x\cos ax\,dx = \frac{1}{a^2}\cos ax + \frac{1}{a}x\sin ax$$

$$\int \frac{dx}{\sqrt{a^2 - x^2}} = \sin^{-1}\left(\frac{x}{a}\right)$$

$$\int \frac{dx}{\sqrt{x^2 \pm a^2}} = \ln\left(x + \sqrt{x^2 \pm a^2}\right)$$

$$\int \frac{dx}{x^2 + a^2} = \frac{1}{a}\tan^{-1}\left(\frac{x}{a}\right)$$

$$\int \frac{x\,dx}{\sqrt{a^2 - x^2}} = -\sqrt{a^2 - x^2}$$

$$\int \frac{x\,dx}{\sqrt{x^2 \pm a^2}} = \sqrt{x^2 \pm a^2}$$

$$\int x e^{ax}\,dx = \frac{e^{ax}}{a^2}(ax - 1)$$

$$\int \frac{dx}{a + bx} = \frac{1}{b}\ln(a + bx)$$

$$\int \frac{dx}{(a + bx)^2} = -\frac{1}{b(a + bx)}$$

$$\int \ln ax\,dx = x\ln ax - x$$

APPENDIX C
THE INTERNATIONAL SYSTEM OF UNITS (SI)

This material is from the United States edition of the English translation of the fifth edition of "Le Système International d'Unités (SI)," the definitive publication in the French language issued in 1985 by the International Bureau of Weights and Measures (BIPM). The year the definition was adopted is given in parentheses.

unit of length (meter): The meter is the length of the path traveled by light in vacuum during a time interval of 1/299 792 458 of a second. (1983)

unit of mass (kilogram): The kilogram is the unit of mass; it is equal to the mass of the international prototype of the kilogram. (1889)

unit of time (second): The second is the duration of 9 192 631 770 periods of the radiation corresponding to the transition between the two hyperfine levels of the ground state of the cesium-133 atom. (1967)

unit of electric current (ampere): The ampere is that constant current which, if maintained in two straight parallel conductors of infinite length, of negligible circular cross section, and placed 1 meter apart in vacuum, would produce between these conductors a force equal to 2×10^{-7} newton per meter of length. (1948)

unit of thermodynamic temperature (kelvin): The kelvin, unit of thermodynamic temperature, is the fraction 1/273.16 of the thermodynamic temperature of the triple point of water. (1957) Also, the unit kelvin and its symbol K should be used to express an interval or a difference of temperature.

unit of amount of substance (mole): (1) The mole is the amount of substance of a system that contains as many elementary entities as there are atoms in 0.012 kilogram of carbon 12. (1971) (2) When the mole is used, the elementary entities must be specified and may be atoms, molecules, ions, electrons, other particles, or specified groups of such particles.

unit of luminous intensity (candela): The candela is the luminous intensity, in a given direction, of a source that emits monochromatic radiation of frequency 540×10^{12} hertz and that has a radiant intensity in that direction of (1/683) watt per steradian. (1979)

SI Base Units

Quantity	SI Unit Name	SI Unit Symbol
length	meter	m
mass	kilogram	kg
time	second	s
electric current	ampere	A
thermodynamic temperature	kelvin	K
amount of substance	mole	mol
luminous intensity	candela	cd

Examples of SI Derived Units Expressed in Terms of Base Units

Quantity	SI Unit	
	Name	**Symbol**
area	square meter	m^2
volume	cubic meter	m^3
speed, velocity	meter per second	m/s
acceleration	meter per second squared	m/s^2
wave number	reciprocal meter	m^{-1}
density, mass density	kilogram per cubic meter	kg/m^3
specific volume	cubic meter per kilogram	m^3/kg
current density	ampere per square meter	A/m^2
luminance	candela per square meter	cd/m^2

SI Derived Units with Special Names

Quantity	SI Unit		Expression in Terms of Other Units	Expression in Terms of SI Base Units
	Name	**Symbol**		
frequency	hertz	Hz		s^{-1}
force	newton	N		$m \cdot kg \cdot s^{-2}$
pressure, stress	pascal	Pa	N/m^2	$m^{-1} \cdot kg \cdot s^{-2}$
energy, work, heat	joule	J	$N \cdot m$	$m^2 \cdot kg \cdot s^{-2}$
power	watt	W	J/s	$m^2 \cdot kg \cdot s^{-3}$
electric charge	coulomb	C		$s \cdot A$
electric potential, potential difference, electromotive force	volt	V	J/C	$m^2 \cdot kg \cdot s^{-3} \cdot A^{-1}$
capacitance	farad	F	C/V	$m^{-2} \cdot kg^{-1} \cdot s^4 \cdot A^2$
electric resistance	ohm	Ω	V/A	$m^2 \cdot kg \cdot s^{-3} \cdot A^{-2}$
electric conductance	siemens	S	A/V	$m^{-2} \cdot kg^{-1} \cdot s^3 \cdot A^2$
magnetic flux	weber	Wb	$V \cdot s$	$m^2 \cdot kg \cdot s^{-2} \cdot A^{-1}$
magnetic field	tesla	T	Wb/m^2	$kg \cdot s^{-2} \cdot A^{-1}$
inductance	henry	H	Wb/A	$m^2 \cdot kg \cdot s^{-2} \cdot A^{-2}$
Celsius temperature	degree Celsius	°C		K
luminous flux	lumen	lm		$cd \cdot sr$
illuminance	lux	lx	lm/m^2	$m^{-2} \cdot cd \cdot sr$

SI Derived Units with Special Names Admitted for Reasons of Safeguarding Human Health

Quantity	SI Unit		Expression in Terms of Other Units	Expression in Terms of SI Base Units
	Name	**Symbol**		
activity (of a radionuclide)	becquerel	Bq	1 decay/s	s^{-1}
absorbed dose	gray	Gy	J/kg, 100 rad	$m^2 \cdot s^{-2}$
dose equivalent	sievert	Sv	J/kg, 100 rem	$m^2 \cdot s^{-2}$

Examples of SI Derived Units Expressed by Means of Special Names

Quantity	SI Unit Name	SI Unit Symbol	Expression in Terms of SI Base Units
dynamic viscosity	pascal second	Pa·s	$m^{-1}\cdot kg\cdot s^{-1}$
torque	newton meter	N·m	$m^{2}\cdot kg\cdot s^{-2}$
surface tension	newton per meter	N/m	$kg\cdot s^{-2}$
heat flux density, irradiance	watt per square meter	W/m²	$kg\cdot s^{-3}$
heat capacity, entropy	joule per kelvin	J/K	$m^{2}\cdot kg\cdot s^{-2}\cdot K^{-1}$
specific heat, specific entropy	joule per kilogram kelvin	J/(kg·K)	$m^{2}\cdot s^{-2}\cdot K^{-1}$
specific energy	joule per kilogram	J/kg	$m^{2}\cdot s^{-2}$
thermal conductivity	watt per meter kelvin	W/(m·K)	$m\cdot kg\cdot s^{-3}\cdot K^{-1}$
energy density	joule per cubic meter	J/m³	$m^{-1}\cdot kg\cdot s^{-2}$
electric field strength	volt per meter	V/m	$m\cdot kg\cdot s^{-3}\cdot A^{-1}$
electric charge density	coulomb per cubic meter	C/m³	$m^{-3}\cdot s\cdot A$
permittivity	farad per meter	F/m	$m^{-3}\cdot kg^{-1}\cdot s^{4}\cdot A^{2}$
permeability	henry per meter	H/m	$m\cdot kg\cdot s^{-2}\cdot A^{-2}$
molar energy	joule per mole	J/mol	$m^{2}\cdot kg\cdot s^{-2}\cdot mol^{-1}$
molar entropy, molar specific heat	joule per mole kelvin	J/(K·mol)	$m^{2}\cdot kg\cdot s^{-2}\cdot K^{-1}\cdot mol^{-1}$
exposure (x and γ rays)	coulomb per kilogram	C/kg	$kg^{-1}\cdot s\cdot A$
absorbed dose rate	gray per second	Gy/s	$m^{2}\cdot s^{-3}$

SI Supplementary Units

Quantity	SI Unit Name	SI Unit Symbol	Expression in Terms of SI Base Units
plane angle	radian	rad	$m\cdot m^{-1}=1$
solid angle	steradian	sr	$m^{2}\cdot m^{-2}=1$

Examples of SI Derived Units Formed by Using Supplementary Units

Quantity	SI Unit Name	SI Unit Symbol
angular velocity	radian per second	rad/s
angular acceleration	radian per second squared	rad/s²
radiant intensity	watt per steradian	W/sr
radiance	watt per square meter steradian	$W\cdot m^{-2}\cdot sr^{-1}$

Rules for Writing and Using SI Unit symbols

1. Roman (upright) type, in general lower case, is used for the unit symbols. If however, the name of the unit is derived from a proper name, the first letter of the symbol is in upper case.
2. Unit symbols are unaltered in the plural.

3. Unit symbols are not followed by a period.
   a. The product of two or more units is indicated as follows, for example:

$$N \cdot m.$$

   b. A solidus (oblique stroke, /), a horizontal line, or negative exponents may be used to express a derived unit formed from two others by division, for example:

$$m/s, \quad \frac{m}{s}, \quad \text{or } m \cdot s^{-1}.$$

   c. The solidus must not be repeated on the same line unless ambiguity is avoided by parentheses. In complicated cases negative exponents or parentheses should be used, for example:

$$m/s^2 \qquad \text{or } m \cdot s^{-2}$$
$$m \cdot kg/(s^3 \cdot A) \quad \text{or } m \cdot kg \cdot s^{-3} \cdot A^{-1}$$

but not:

$$m/s/s$$
$$m \cdot kg/s^3/A.$$

SI Prefixes

Factor	Prefix	Symbol	Factor	Prefix	Symbol
10^{18}	exa	E	10^{-1}	deci	d
10^{15}	peta	P	10^{-2}	centi	c
10^{12}	tera	T	10^{-3}	milli	m
10^{9}	giga	G	10^{-6}	micro	μ
10^{6}	mega	M	10^{-9}	nano	n
10^{3}	kilo	k	10^{-12}	pico	p
10^{2}	hecto	h	10^{-15}	femto	f
10^{1}	deka	da	10^{-18}	atto	a

Non-SI units in Use with the International System

Name	Symbol	Value in SI Units
minute	min	$1 \text{ min} = 60 \text{ s}$
hour	h	$1 \text{ h} = 60 \text{ min} = 3\,600 \text{ s}$
day	d	$1 d = 24 \text{ h} = 86\,400 \text{ s}$
degree	°	$1° = (\pi/180) \text{ rad}$
minute	′	$1' = (1/60)° = (\pi/10\,800) \text{ rad}$
second	″	$1'' = (1/60)' = (\pi/648\,000) \text{ rad}$
liter	L	$1 \text{ L} = 1 \text{ dm}^3 = 10^{-3} \text{ m}^3$
metric ton (tonne)	t	$1 t = 10^3 \text{ kg}$

Units used with the International System Whose Values in SI Units Are Obtained Experimentally

Name	Symbol	Definition
electron volt	eV	(a)
unified atomic mass unit	u	(b)

[a]The electron volt is the kinetic energy acquired by an electron in passing through a potential difference of 1 volt in vacuum; $1 \text{ eV} = 1.602\,19 \times 10^{-19}$ J approximately.

[b]The unified atomic mass unit is equal to $(1/12)$ of the mass of an atom of the nuclide ^{12}C; $1 \text{ u} = 1.660\,57 \times 10^{-27}$ kg approximately.

Units in Use Temporarily with the International System

Name	Symbol	Value in SI Units
nautical mile[a]		1 nautical mile = 1 852 m
knot		1 nautical mile per hour = (1852/3600) m/s
angström	Å	1 Å = 0.1 nm = 10^{-10} m
are[b]	a	1 a = 1 dam^2 = 10^2 m^2
hectare[b]	ha	1 ha = 1 hm^2 = 10^4 m^2
barn[c]	b	1 b = 100 fm^2 = 10^{-28} m^2
bar[d]	bar	1 bar = 0.1 MPa = 100 kPa = 1000 hPa = 10^5 Pa
gal[e]	Gal	1 Gal = 1 cm/s^2 = 10^{-2} m/s^2
curie[f]	Ci	1 Ci = 3.7 × 10^{10} Bq
roentgen[g]	R	1 R = 2.58 × 10^{-4} C/kg
rad[h]	rad	1 rad = 1 cGy = 10^{-2} Gy
rem[i]	rem	1 rem = 1 cSv = 10^{-2} Sv

[a]The nautical mile is a special unit employed for marine and serial navigation to express distances.

[b]This unit and its symbol were adopted in 1879 and are used to express agrarian areas.

[c]The barn is a special unit employed in nuclear physics to express effective cross sections.

[d]Pressure

[e]The gal is a special unit employed in geodesy and geophysics to express the acceleration due to gravity.

[f]The curie is a special unit employed in nuclear physics to express activity of radionuclides.

[g]The roentgen is a special unit employed to express exposure of x or γ radiations.

[h]The rad is a special unit employed to express absorbed dose of ionizing radiations. When there is risk of confusion with the symbol for radian, rd may be used as the symbol for rad.

[i]The rem is a special unit used in radioprotection to express dose equivalent.

The table below lists some specially named units of the centimeter-gram-second (CGS) system. It is in general preferable not to mix these with the units of the International System. (Although the SI system is generally preferred for scientific work, in some specialized fields, there are good reasons for using CGS or other systems.)

CGS Units with Special Names

Name	Symbol	Value in SI Units
erg	erg	1 erg = 10^{-7} J
dyne	dyn	1 dyn = 10^{-5} N
poise	P	1 P = 1 dyn·s/cm^2 = 0.1 Pa·s
stokes	St	1 St = 1 cm^2/s = 10^{-4} m^2/s
gauss[a]	Gs, G	1 Gs corresponds to 10^{-4} T
oersted[a]	Oe	1 Oe corresponds to $(1000/4\pi)$A/m
maxwell[a]	Mx	1 Mx corresponds to 10^{-8} Wb
stilb[a]	sb	1 sb = 1 cd/cm^2 = 10^4 cd/m^2
phot	ph	1 ph = 10^4 lx

[a]This unit is part of the so-called electromagnetic 3-dimensional CGS system and cannot strictly speaking be compared to the corresponding unit of the International System, which has four dimensions when only mechanical and electric quantities are considered.

As regards other units outside the International System, it is in general preferable to avoid them, and to use instead units of the International System. Some of those units are listed in the following table.

Other Units Generally Deprecated

Name	Value in SI units
fermi	1 fermi = 1 fm = 10^{-15} m
metric carat[a]	1 metric carat = 200 mg = 2×10^{-4} kg
torr	1 torr = (101 325/760) Pa
standard atmosphere (atm)[b]	1 atm = 101 325 Pa
kilogram-force (kgf)	1 kgf = 9.806 65 N
calorie (cal)[c]	
micron (μ)[d]	1 μ = 1 μm = 10^{-6} m
x unit[e]	
stere (st)[f]	1 st = 1 m^3
gamma (γ)	1 γ = 1 nT = 10^{-9} T

[a]This name was adopted in 1907 for commercial dealings in diamonds, pearls, and precious stones.

[b]The designation "standard atmosphere" for a reference pressure of 101 325 Pa is still acceptable.

[c]Several "calories" have been in use:
Calorie labeled "at 15°C": 1 cal_{15} = 4.185 5 J (value adopted in 1950)
A calorie labeled "IT" (International Table): 1 cal_{IT} = 4.186 8 J (5th International Conference on the Properties of Steam, London, 1956)
A calorie labeled "thermochemical": 1 cal_{th} = 4.184 J

[d]The name of this unit and its symbol, adopted in 1879, were abolished in 1967.

[e]This special unit was employed to express wavelengths of x rays; 1 x unit = 1.002 $\times$ 10^{-4} nm approximately.

[f]This special unit employed to measure firewood was adopted by the CIPM in 1879 with the symbol "s." The symbol was changed to "st" in 1948.

Source: Extracted from *The International System of Units* (SI), David T. Goldman and R. J. Bell, eds., National Bureau of Standards Special Publication 330, 1986 edition. Only American alternatives are listed. Omitted for this reason are l for liter; litre, metre, and deca as spellings; and N.m or N m as alternate ways of writing N·m.

APPENDIX D
CONVERSION FACTORS

The day of extensive conversion tables has passed, now that we have calculators small enough to carry in a pocket or wear on a wrist. For example, instead of using a table of conversions from square meters to square feet, students need only remember (or look up) 1 m = 39.37 inches (and the definition 1 foot = 12 inches). Then

$$\# \ m^2 = (\# \ ft)^2 (12 \ in/1 \ ft)^2 (1 \ m/39.37 \ in)^2.$$

This method can be followed at any time and anywhere in the world, even when you don't happen to have your physics text along. In any case, following are a few conversions; $\equiv$ signifies a definition.

Length

Based on 1 m = 39.37 in; 1 ft = 12 in; 1 mi = 5280 ft.

Metric	*English System*
1 m = 100 cm = 10^{-3} km	= 39.37 in = 3.281 ft = 6.214×10^{-4} mi

Note: to find conversions from cm, simply divide any term in the preceding row by 100; to find conversions from km, multiply any term by 1000.

1609 m = 1.609×10^5 cm = 1.609 km	= 1 mi
1 cm	= 0.3937 in
2.54 cm	$\equiv$ 1 in

Other Length Conversions

Astronomical
1 light year (ly) = 9.46×10^{15} m
1 astronomical unit (AU) = 1.50×10^{11} m (the average distance from the earth to the sun
1 parsec (pc) = 3.26 ly = 3.09×10^{16} m (The parsec is defined as the distance at which, looking back, 1 AU would subtend 1 second of arc; it is a unit that arises naturally in astronomical measurements.)

Atomic
1 angstrom (Å) $\equiv$ 0.1 nm $\equiv$ 10^{-10} m
1 fermi $\equiv$ 10^{-12} m

Area

Metric	*English System*
1 m^2 = 10^4 cm^2 = 10^{-4} hectares (ha)	= 10.76 ft^2 = 1550 in^2
9.290×10^{-2} m^2	= 1 ft^2
6.452×10^{-4} m^2	= 1 in^2

Other Area Conversions

Normal Scale

1 acre $= 4.356 \times 10^4$ ft^2 $= 4047$ m^2 $= 0.4047$ ha

1 ft^2 $= 144$ in^2

Atomic

1 barn $\equiv 10^{-28}$ m^2

1 shed $\equiv 10^{-2}$ barn

Volume

Metric	English System
1 m^3 $= 10^6$ cm^3 $= 10^3$ L	$= 35.31$ ft^3 $= 6.102 \times 10^4$ in^3 $= 264.2$ gal
2.832×10^{-2} m^3	$= 1$ ft^3
1.639×10^{-5} m^3	$= 1$ in^3
3.786×10^{-3} m^3	$= 1$ gal (U.S.) $= 0.1337$ ft^3 $= 231$ in^3

Other Volume Conversions

1 barrel (oil) $= 42$ gal (U.S.) $= 0.159$ m^3

1 gal (British) $= 277.42$ in^3 (based on volume of 10 pounds of water) $= 4.55$ L

1 fluid ounce (U.S.) $= 1/128$ gal (U.S.) $= 29.6$ mL

Mass

Metric	Atomic	English System
1 kg $=$ 1000 g	$= 6.022 \times 10^{26}$ u	$= 6.852 \times 10^{-2}$ slug
1.661×10^{-27} kg	$= 1$ u	$= 1.38 \times 10^{-28}$
1.459 kg	$= 8.786 \times 10^{27}$	$= 1$ slug

Note: The slug is the unit of mass in the English system. A 1-slug mass has a weight $mg = (1 \text{ slug})(32 \text{ ft/s}^2) = 32$ lb. The pound (lb) is often used (incorrectly) as a mass unit. To say that an object has a mass of 1 lb means that its weight at earth's surface is 1 lb. In this usage,

$$1 \text{ kg} = 2.20462 \text{ lb and } 1 \text{ lb} = 0.454 \text{ kg.}$$

Other Mass Conversions

1 ton $\equiv 2000$ lb $=$ the weight of 907.2 kg

1 tonne (t; metric ton) $\equiv 1000$ kg

1 ounce (oz) $\equiv 1/16$ lb $=$ the weight of 28.35 g

Time

1 year $= 365.2422$ d $= 8766$ h $= 5.259 \times 10^5$ min $= 3.156 \times 10^7$ s

1 day $\equiv 24$ h $\equiv 1440$ min $\equiv 8.640 \times 10^4$ s

1 hour $\equiv 60$ min $\equiv 3600$ s

1 min $\equiv 60$ s

Note: the length of the year (the earth's orbital period) changes slowly. Currently, one tropical year (the time between two successive passages of the sun across the point among the stars known as the vernal equinox, defined as the location where the celestial equator crosses the sun's path) is approximately 365.2422 d $= 3.1557 \times 10^7$ s, conveniently close to $\pi \times 10^7$ s.

Force

Metric	English System
1 newton (N) = 10^5 dyne	= 0.2248 lb
4.448 N	= 1 lb

Note: The gram (g) and kilogram (kg) are sometimes (incorrectly) used as force units. A 1-kg force means the gravitational force on a 1-kg mass where g = 9.80665 N/kg. Thus a 1-kg force corresponds to 9.807 N.

Pressure

1 pascal (Pa) $\equiv$ 1 N·m^{-2} $\equiv$ 10 dyne·cm^{-2} = 7.501×10^{-3} mm Hg (torr) = 9.869×10^{-6} atm = 4.015×10^{-3} in H$_2$O = 1.450×10^{-4} lb/in^2 (psi)

1 atmosphere = 1.013×10^5 Pa

1 in H$_2$O = 249.1 Pa

1 mm Hg (torr) = 133.3 Pa

1 lb/in^2 (psi) = 6.895×10^3 Pa

Energy

Metric	Atomic	English System
1 joule (J) $\equiv 10^7$ erg	= 6.242×10^{18} eV	= 0.2390 cal = 9.85×10^4 Btu
= 2.778×10^{-7} kWh		= 0.7376 ft·lb
1.602×10^{-19} J	= 1 eV	= 1.520×10^{-22} Btu
		= 1.182×10^{19} ft·lb
4.184 J = 1.162×10^{-6} kWh		= 1 cal* = 3.968×10^{-3} Btu
		= 3.086 ft·lb
1054 J		= 1 Btu
1.356 J		= 1 ft·lb
3.6×10^6 J = 1 kWh		

*We have supplied the thermochemical calorie, 4.184 J. The International Table calorie = 4.1868 J.

Other Energy Conversions

1 megaton (explosive yield) = 4×10^{15} J

1 kg (energy equivalence via $E = mc^2$) = 9.0×10^{16} J

Energy Content of Fuels

Energy Source	Energy Content		
coal	2.9×10^7 J/kg	= 7300 kWh/ton	= 25×10^6 Btu/ton
oil	43×10^6 J/kg	= 39 kWh/gal	= 1.3×10^5 Btu/gal
gasoline	44×10^6 J/kg	= 36 kWh/gal	= 1.2×10^5 Btu/gal
natural gas,	55×10^6 J/kg	= 30 kWh/100 ft^3	= 1000 Btu/ft^3
uranium (fission)			
normal abundance	5.8×10^{11} J/kg	= 1.6×10^5 kWh/kg	
pure U-235	8×10^{13} J/kg	= 2×10^7 kWh/kg	
hydrogen (fusion)			
normal abundance	7×10^{11} J/kg	= 3.0×10^4 kWh/kg	
pure deuterium	3.3×10^{14} J/kg	= 9.2×10^7 kWh/kg	
water	1×10^{10} J/kg	= 1×10^4 kWh/gal	= 400 gal gasoline/gal H$_2$O
100% conversion, matter to energy	9.0×10^{16} J/kg	= 931 MeV/u	= 2.5×10^{10} kWh/kg

Power

Metric	English System
1 watt (W) $\equiv 10^7$ erg/s	$= 1.341 \times 10^{-3}$ hp $= 0.7376$ ft·lb/s $= 3.413$ Btu/h
745.7 W	$= 1$ hp $= 550$ ft·lb/s $= 2545$ Btu/h
1.356 W	$= 1.818 \times 10^{-3}$ hp $= 1$ ft·lb/s $= 4.628$ Btu/h
0.2930 W	$= 3.929 \times 10^{-4}$ hp $= 0.2161$ ft·lb/s $= 1$ Btu/h

Note: In engineering, Btu/h is often written Btuh.

Other Power Conversion

solar power, direct sunlight at earth's surface: about 1 kW·m^{-2}

Magnetic Field

1 tesla (T) $\equiv 10^4$ gauss $= 10^9$ γ

10^4 T $= 1$ gauss $= 10$ γ

10^{-9} T $= 10^{-5}$ gauss $= 1$ γ

APPENDIX E
THE ELEMENTS

Periodic Table of the Elements

Key:

Atomic number
Symbol
Atomic mass (u) [a]

1
H
1.008

1	2	3	4	5	6	7	8	9	10	11	12	13	14	15	16	17	18
1 **H** 1.008																	2 **He** 4.003
3 **Li** 6.941	4 **Be** 9.012											5 **B** 10.81	6 **C** 12.01	7 **N** 14.01	8 **O** 16.00	9 **F** 19.00	10 **Ne** 20.18
11 **Na** 22.99	12 **Mg** 24.31											13 **Al** 26.98	14 **Si** 28.09	15 **P** 30.97	16 **S** 32.07	17 **Cl** 35.45	18 **Ar** 39.95
19 **K** 39.10	20 **Ca** 40.08	21 **Sc** 44.96	22 **Ti** 47.88	23 **V** 50.94	24 **Cr** 52.00	25 **Mn** 54.94	26 **Fe** 55.85	27 **Co** 58.93	28 **Ni** 58.69	29 **Cu** 63.55	30 **Zn** 65.39	31 **Ga** 69.72	32 **Ge** 72.61	33 **As** 74.92	34 **Se** 78.96	35 **Br** 79.90	36 **Kr** 83.80
37 **Rb** 85.47	38 **Sr** 87.62	39 **Y** 88.91	40 **Zr** 91.22	41 **Nb** 92.91	42 **Mo** 95.94	43 **Tc** (98)	44 **Ru** 101.07	45 **Rh** 102.91	46 **Pd** 106.42	47 **Ag** 107.87	48 **Cd** 112.41	49 **In** 114.82	50 **Sn** 118.71	51 **Sb** 121.75	52 **Te** 127.60	53 **I** 126.90	54 **Xe** 131.29
55 **Cs** 132.91	56 **Ba** 137.33	57–71 Lanthanide series*	72 **Hf** 178.49	73 **Ta** 180.95	74 **W** 183.85	75 **Re** 186.21	76 **Os** 190.2	77 **Ir** 192.22	78 **Pt** 195.08	79 **Au** 196.97	80 **Hg** 200.59	81 **Tl** 204.38	82 **Pb** 207.2	83 **Bi** 208.98	84 **Po** (209)	85 **At** (210)	86 **Rn** (222)
87 **Fr** (223)	88 **Ra** (226)	89–103 Actinide series†	104 **Unq** (261)	105 **Unp** (252)	106 **Unh** (263)	107 **Uns** (262)	108 **Uno** (265)	109 **Une** (266)									

*Lanthanide Series

57 **La** 138.91	58 **Ce** 140.12	59 **Pr** 140.91	60 **Nd** 144.24	61 **Pm** (145)	62 **Sm** 150.36	63 **Eu** 151.97	64 **Gd** 157.25	65 **Tb** 158.93	66 **Dy** 162.50	67 **Ho** 164.93	68 **Er** 167.26	69 **Tm** 168.93	70 **Yb** 173.04	71 **Lu** 174.97

†Actinide Series

89 **Ac** (227)	90 **Th** 232.04	91 **Pa** (231.04)	92 **U** 238.03	93 **Np** (237)	94 **Pu** (244)	95 **Am** (243)	96 **Cm** (247)	97 **Bk** (247)	98 **Cf** (251)	99 **Es** (252)	100 **Fm** (257)	101 **Md** (258)	102 **No** (259)	103 **Lr** (260)

[a] Atomic mass is average over abundances of stable isotopes. For radioactive elements, mass is in parentheses and is that of the most stable important (in availability, etc.) isotope.

Elements and Isotopes (scaled to $^{12}C = 12$)

The atomic weights of stable elements reflect the abundances of different isotopes, and therefore may vary slightly, depending on the origin and treatment of the material. The values given here apply to elements as they exist naturally on earth. For stable elements, parentheses express uncertainties in the last decimal place given. For elements with no stable isotopes (indicated in boldface), sets of most important isotopes selected by the IUPAC Commission on Atomic Weights and Isotopic Abundances are given.

Atomic Number	Names	Symbol	Atomic Weight
1	Hydrogen	H	1.00794 (7)
2	Helium	He	4.002602 (2)
3	Lithium	Li	6.941 (2)
4	Beryllium	Be	9.012182 (3)
5	Boron	B	10.811 (5)
6	Carbon	C	12.011 (1)
7	Nitrogen	N	14.00674 (7)
8	Oxygen	O	15.9994 (3)
9	Fluorine	F	18.9984032 (9)
10	Neon	Ne	20.1797 (6)
11	Sodium (Natrium)	Na	22.989768 (6)
12	Magnesium	Mg	24.3050 (6)
13	Aluminum	Al	26.981539 (5)
14	Silicon	Si	28.0855 (3)
15	Phosphorus	P	30.973762 (4)
16	Sulfur	S	32.066 (6)
17	Chlorine	Cl	35.4527 (9)
18	Argon	Ar	39.948 (1)
19	Potassium (Kalium)	K	39.0983 (1)
20	Calcium	Ca	40.078 (4)
21	Scandium	Sc	44.955910 (9)
22	Titanium	Ti	47.88 (3)
23	Vanadium	V	50.9415 (1)
24	Chromium	Cr	51.9961 (6)
25	Manganese	Mn	54.93805 (1)
26	Iron	Fe	55.847 (3)
27	Cobalt	Co	58.93320 (1)
28	Nickel	Ni	58.69 (1)
29	Copper	Cu	63.546 (3)
30	Zinc	Zn	65.39 (2)
31	Gallium	Ga	69.723 (4)
32	Germanium	Ge	72.61 (2)
33	Arsenic	As	74.92159 (2)
34	Selenium	Se	78.96 (3)
35	Bromine	Br	79.904 (1)
36	Krypton	Kr	83.80 (1)
37	Rubidium	Rb	85.4678 (3)
38	Strontium	Sr	87.62 (1)
39	Yttrium	Y	88.90585 (2)
40	Zirconium	Zr	91.224 (2)
41	Niobium	Nb	92.90638 (2)
42	Molybdenum	Mo	95.94 (1)
43	**Technetium**	**Tc**	**97, 98, 99**
44	Ruthenium	Ru	101.07 (2)
45	Rhodium	Rh	102.90550 (3)
46	Palladium	Pd	106.42 (1)
47	Silver	Ag	107.8682 (2)
48	Cadmium	Cd	112.411 (8)
49	Indium	In	114.82 (1)
50	Tin	Sn	118.710 (7)
51	Antimony (Stibium)	Sb	121.75 (3)
52	Tellurium	Te	127.60 (3)

53	Iodine	I	126.90447 (3)
54	Xenon	Xe	131.29 (2)
55	Cesium	Cs	132.90543 (5)
56	Barium	Ba	137.327 (7)
57	Lanthanum	La	138.9055 (2)
58	Cerium	Ce	140.115 (4)
59	Praseodymium	Pr	140.90765 (3)
60	Neodymium	Nd	144.24 (3)
61	**Promethium**	**Pm**	**145, 147**
62	Samarium	Sm	150.36 (3)
63	Europium	Eu	151.965 (9)
64	Gadolinium	Gd	157.25 (3)
65	Terbium	Tb	158.92534 (3)
66	Dysprosium	Dy	162.50 (3)
67	Holmium	Ho	164.93032 (3)
68	Erbium	Er	167.26 (3)
69	Thulium	Tm	168.93421 (3)
70	Ytterbium	Yb	173.04 (3)
71	Lutetium	Lu	174.967 (1)
72	Hafnium	Hf	178.49 (2)
73	Tantalum	Ta	180.9479 (1)
74	Tungsten (Wolfram)	W	183.85 (3)
75	Rhenium	Re	186.207 (1)
76	Osmium	Os	190.2 (1)
77	Iridium	Ir	192.22 (3)
78	Platinum	Pt	195.08 (3)
79	Gold	Au	196.96654 (3)
80	Mercury	Hg	200.59 (3)
81	Thallium	Tl	204.3833 (2)
82	Lead	Pb	207.2 (1)
83	Bismuth	Bi	208.98037 (3)
84	**Polonium**	**Po**	**209, 210**
85	**Astatine**	**At**	**210, 211**
86	**Radon**	**Rn**	**211, 220, 222**
87	**Francium**	**Fr**	**223**
88	**Radium**	**Ra**	**223, 224, 226, 228**
89	**Actinium**	**Ac**	**227**
90	Thorium	Th	232.0381 (1)
91	Protactinium	Pa	231.03588 (2)
92	Uranium	U	238.0289 (1)
93	**Neptunium**	**Np**	**237, 239**
94	**Plutonium**	**Pu**	**238, 239, 240, 241, 242, 244**
95	**Americium**	**Am**	**241, 243**
96	**Curium**	**Cm**	**243, 244, 245, 246, 247, 248**
97	**Berkelium**	**Bk**	**247, 249**
98	**Californium**	**Cf**	**249, 250, 251, 252**
99	**Einsteinium**	**Es**	**252**
100	**Fermium**	**Fm**	**257**
101	**Mendelevium**	**Md**	**255, 256, 258, 260**
102	**Nobelium**	**No**	**253, 254, 255, 259**
103	**Lawrencium**	**Lr**	**256, 258, 259, 261**
104	**Unnilquadium**	**Unq**	**257, 259, 260, 261**
105	**Unnilpentium**	**Unp**	**260, 261, 262**
106	**Unnilhexium**	**Unh**	**259, 260, 261, 263**
107	**Unnilseptium**	**Uns**	**261, 262**
108	**Unniloctium**	**Uno**	**264, 265**
109	**Unnilennium**	**Une**	**266**

Note: The systematic names for elements 104–109 use the following code for each digit with an "ium" ending to indicate that they are metals: 1—un; 2—bi; 3—tri; 4—quad; 5—pent; 6—hex; 7—sept; 8—oct; 9—enn; 0—nil. (Element 104 was called Rutherfordium (Rf) by the American discoverers and Kurschatovium (Ku) by the Soviet discoverers. Element 105 was called Hahnium (Ha) by the American discoverers and Nielsbohrium (Ns) by the Soviet discoverers.)

Atomic weights and selected isotopes through element 105 from the IUPAC Commission on Atomic Weights and Isotopic Abundances, 1985 study, courtesy of I. Lynus Barnes, National Bureau of Standards, 1986. Isotopes for elements 106–109 from Peter Armbruster, Gesellschaft für Schwerionenforschung mbH.

APPENDIX F
ASTROPHYSICAL DATA

Sun, Planets, Principal Satellites[a]

Body	Mass $(10^{24}$ kg)	Mean Radius[b] $(10^6$ m except as noted)	Surface Gravity (m/s^2)[c]	Escape Speed (km/s)	Sidereal Rotation Period[d,f] (d)	Mean Distance from Central Body[e] $(10^6$ km)	Orbital Period	Orbital Speed (km/s)
Sun	7.99×10^6	696	274	618	36 at poles 27 at equator	2.6×10^{11}	200 My	250
Mercury	0.330	2.44	3.70	4.25	58.6	57.9	88.0 d	48
Venus	4.87	6.05	8.87	10.4	−243	108	225 d	35
Earth	5.97	6.37	9.81	11.2	0.997	150	365.3 d	30
Moon	0.0735	1.74	1.62	2.38	27.3	0.385	27.3 d	1.0
Mars	0.642	3.38	3.74	5.03	1.03	228	1.88 y	24.1
Phobos	9.6×10^{-9}	9–13 km	0.001	0.008	0.32	9.4×10^{-3}	0.32 d	2.1
Deimos	2×10^{-9}	5–8 km	0.001	0.005	1.3	23×10^{-3}	1.3 d	1.3
Jupiter	1.90×10^3	69.1	26.5	60.6	0.414	778	11.9 y	13.0
Io	0.0889	1.82	1.8	2.6	1.77	0.422	1.77 d	17
Europa	0.478	1.57	1.3	2.0	3.55	0.671	3.55 d	14
Ganymede	0.148	2.63	1.4	2.7	7.15	1.07	7.15 d	11
Callisto	0.107	2.40	1.2	2.4	16.7	1.88	16.7 d	8.2
and at least 13 smaller satellites								
Saturn	569	56.8	11.8	36.6	0.438	1.43×10^3	29.5 y	9.65
Tethys	0.0007	0.53	0.2	0.4	1.89	0.294	1.89 d	11.3
Dione	0.00015	0.56	0.3	0.6	2.74	0.377	2.74 d	10.0
Rhea	0.0025	0.77	0.3	0.5	4.52	0.527	4.52 d	8.5
Titan	0.135	2.58	1.4	2.6	15.9	1.22	15.9 d	5.6
Iapetus	0.0019	0.73	0.2	0.6	79.3	3.56	79.3 d	3.3
and at least 12 smaller satellites								
Uranus	86.6	25.0	9.23	21.5	−0.65	2.87×10^3	84.1 y	6.79
Ariel	0.0013	0.58	0.3	0.4	2.52	0.19	2.52 d	5.5
Umbriel	0.0013	0.59	0.3	0.4	4.14	0.27	4.14 d	4.7
Titania	0.0018	0.81	0.2	0.5	8.70	0.44	8.70 d	3.7
Oberon	0.0017	0.78	0.2	0.5	13.5	0.58	13.5 d	3.1
and at least 11 smaller satellites								
Neptune	103	24.0	11.9	23.9	0.768	4.50×10^3	165 y	5.43
Triton	0.134	1.90	2.5	3.1	5.88	0.354	5.88 d	4.4
and at least 1 other satellite								
Pluto	0.015	1.3	0.4	1.2	−6.39	5.91×10^3	249 y	4.7
and at least 1 satellite								

[a]Except for Mars, principal satellites are those with radii greater than 500 km.

[b]Mean radius is calculated as average of equatorial and polar radii.

[c]Surface gravity is calculated from mean radius and mass as $g = GM/r^2$, except where measured directly.

[d]Rotation period: Minus sign indicates retrograde rotation, in the opposite sense from the orbital motion. Note that all the moons given are in synchronous rotation, with their period of rotation matching their period of revolution.

[e]Central body is galactic center for the sun, sun for the planets, and planet for the satellites.

[f]Periods given are sidereal—that is, the time for the body to return to the same position or orientation relative to the distant stars rather than the sun.

See page 1050 for additional data.

Astrophysical Data

Astronomical Unit, A.U.	$1.495\ 978\ 70 \times 10^{11}$ m
Light year	$9.460\ 530 \times 10^{15}$ m
Tropical year (1900)	$365.242\ 198\ 78$ days
Sidereal (by the stars) year	$365.256\ 366$ days
Mass of sun	$1.989\ 1 \times 10^{30}$ kg
Radius of sun	6.96×10^{5} km
Solar constant	$1368\ \text{W} \cdot \text{m}^{-2}$
Luminosity of sun (from Solar Maximum Mission, 1980–1986 interval)	3.85×10^{26} W
Mass of earth	$5.974\ 2 \times 10^{24}$ kg
Radius of earth (equator)	$6\ 378.140$ km
Hubble constant	$50 - 100$ km/s/megaparsec
	$= 15 - 30$ km/s/Mly
	$= 1.6 - 3.2 \times 10^{-18}\ \text{s}^{-1}$

Parentheses indicate uncertainties in the last decimal places given.

speed of light, c	299 792 458 m/s (exact)
gravitational constant, G	$6.672\ 59(85) \times 10^{-11}\ \text{N} \cdot \text{m}^2 \cdot \text{kg}^{-2}$
Planck's constant, h	$6.626\ 075\ 5(40) \times 10^{-34}\ \text{J} \cdot \text{s}$
Boltzmann constant, k	$1.380\ 658\ (12) \times 10^{-23}\ \text{J} \cdot \text{K}^{-1}$
Stefan-Boltzmann constant, σ	$5.670\ 51(19) \times 10^{-8}\ \text{W} \cdot \text{m}^{-2} \cdot \text{K}^{-4}$
Rydberg constant, R_∞	$1.097\ 373\ 153\ 4(13) \times 10^{7}\ \text{m}^{-1}$
Fine-structure constant, α^{-1}	$137.035\ 989\ 5(61)$
Bohr radius, a_0	$5.291\ 772\ 49(24) \times 10^{-11}\ \text{m}$
Avogadro's number, N_A	$6.022\ 136\ 7(36) \times 10^{23}\ \text{mole}^{-1}$
mass of hydrogen atom, m_H	$1.673\ 534\ 0(10) \times 10^{-27}\ \text{kg}$
mass of neutron, m_n	$1.674\ 928\ 6(10) \times 10^{-27}\ \text{kg}$
	$939.565\ 63(28)\ \text{MeV}$
mass of proton, m_p	$1.672\ 623\ 1(10) \times 10^{-27}\ \text{kg}$
	$938.272\ 31(28)\ \text{MeV}$
mass of electron, m_e	$9.109\ 389\ 7(54) \times 10^{-31}\ \text{kg}$
	$0.510\ 999\ 06(15)\ \text{MeV}$
proton-electron mass ratio, m_p/m_e	$1836.152\ 701(37)$
elementary charge, e	$1.602\ 177\ 33(49) \times 10^{-19}\ \text{C}$
charge to mass, e/m_e	$1.758\ 819\ 62(53) \times 10^{11}\ \text{C} \cdot \text{kg}^{-1}$
permeability of vacuum, $\mu_0 = 4\pi \times 10^{-7}$	$12.566\ 370\ 614 \ldots \times 10^{-7}\ \text{H/m}$
permittivity of vacuum, $\epsilon_0 = 1/\mu_0 c^2$	$8.854\ 187\ 817 \ldots \times 10^{-12}\ \text{F/m}$

Mathematical Constants

$\pi = 3.141\ 592\ 653\ 6$
$e = 2.718\ 281\ 828\ 5$

Values from *The 1986 Adjustment of the Fundamental Physical Constants*, Report of the CODATA Task Group on Fundamental Constants, prepared by E. Richard Cohen and Barry N. Taylor. Committee on Data for Science and Technology CODATA Bulletin No. 63, Pergamon Press.

APPENDIX H
NOBEL PRIZES

All Nobel Prizes in physics are listed (and marked with a P), as well as relevant Nobel Prizes in Chemistry (C) and Physiology or Medicine (M). The key dates for some of the scientific work are supplied; they often antedate the prize considerably.

1901 (P) *Wilhelm Roentgen* for discovering x-rays (1895).

1902 (P) *Hendrik A. Lorentz* for predicting the Zeeman effect and *Pieter Zeeman* for discovering the Zeeman effect, the splitting of spectral lines in magnetic fields.

1903 (P) *Antoine-Henri Becquerel* for discovering radioactivity (1896) and *Pierre and Marie Curie* for studying radioactivity.

1904 (P) *Lord Rayleigh* for studying the density of gases and discovering argon.
(C) *William Ramsay* for discovering the inert gas elements helium, neon, xenon, and krypton, and placing them in the periodic table.

1905 (P) *Philipp Lenard* for studying cathode rays, electrons (1898–1899).

1906 (P) *J. J. Thomson* for studying electrical discharge through gases and discovering the electron (1897).

1907 (P) *Albert A. Michelson* for inventing optical instruments and measuring the speed of light (1880s).

1908 (P) *Gabriel Lippmann* for making the first color photographic plate, using interference methods (1891).
(C) *Ernest Rutherford* for discovering that atoms can be broken apart by alpha rays and for studying radioactivity.

1909 (P) *Guglielmo Marconi* and *Carl Ferdinand Braun* for developing wireless telegraphy.

1910 (P) *Johannes D. van der Waals* for studying the equation of state for gases and liquids (1881).

1911 (P) *Wilhelm Wien* for discovering Wien's law giving the peak of a blackbody spectrum (1893).
(C) *Marie Curie* for discovering radium and polonium (1898) and isolating radium.

1912 (P) *Nils Dalén* for inventing automatic gas regulators for lighthouses.

1913 (P) *Heike Kamerlingh Onnes* for studying materials in low temperatures and liquefying helium (1908).

1914 (P) *Max T. F. von Laue* for studying x-rays from their diffraction by crystals, showing that x-rays are electromagnetic waves (1912).
(C) *Theodore W. Richards* for determining the atomic weights of sixty elements, indicating the existence of isotopes.

1915 (P) *William Henry Bragg* and *William Lawrence Bragg*, his son, for studying the diffraction of x-rays in crystals.

1916 (P) *No prize offered.*

1917 (P) *Charles Barkla* for studying atoms by x-ray scattering (1906).

1918 (P) *Max Planck* for discovering energy quanta (1900).

1919 (P) *Johannes Stark,* for discovering the Stark effect, the splitting of spectral lines in electric fields (1913).

1920 (P) *Charles-Édouard Guillaume* for discovering invar, a nickel-steel alloy of low coefficient of expansion

Five Nobel Prize winners: (left to right) Nernst, Einstein, Planck, Millikan, and von Laue.

(C) *Walther Nernst* for studying heat changes in chemical reactions and formulating the third law of thermodynamics (1918).

1921 (P) *Albert Einstein* for explaining the photoelectric effect (1905).

(C) *Frederick Soddy* for studying the chemistry of radioactive substances and discovering isotopes (1912).

1922 (P) *Niels Bohr* for his model of the atom and its radiation (1913).

(C) *Francis W. Aston* for using the mass spectrograph to study atomic weights, thus discovering 212 of the 287 naturally occurring isotopes.

1923 (P) *Robert A. Millikan* for measuring the charge on an electron (1911) and for studying the photographic effect experimentally (1914).

1924 (P) *Karl M. G. Siegbahn* for his work in x-ray spectroscopy.

1925 (P) *James Franck* and *Gustav Hertz* for discovering the Franck-Hertz effect in electron–atom collisions.

1926 (P) *Jean-Baptiste Perrin* for studying Brownian motion to validate the discontinuous structure of matter and measure the size of atoms.

1927 (P) *Arthur Holly Compton* for discovering the Compton effect on x-rays, their change in wavelength when they collide with matter (1922), and *Charles T. R. Wilson* for inventing the cloud chamber, used to study charged particles (1906).

1928 (P) *Owen W. Richardson* for studying the thermionic effect and electrons emitted by hot metals (1911).

1929 (P) *Louis Victor de Broglie* for discovering the wave nature of electrons (1923).

1930 (P) *Chandrasekhara Venkata Raman* for studying Raman scattering, the scattering of light by atoms and molecules with a change in wavelength (1928).

1931 (P) No prize offered.

1932 (P) *Werner Heisenberg* for starting quantum mechanics (1925).

1933 (P) *Erwin Schrödinger* and *Paul A. M. Dirac* for developing wave mechanics (1925) and relativistic quantum mechanics (1927).

1934 (P) No prize offered.

(C) *Harold Urey* for discovering heavy hydrogen, deuterium (1931).

1935 (P) *James Chadwick* for discovering the neutron (1932).

(C) *Irène* and *Frédéric Joliot-Curie* for synthesizing new radioactive elements.

1936 (P) *Carl D. Anderson* for discovering the positron in particular and antimatter in general (1932) and *Victor F. Hess* for discovering cosmic rays.
(C) *Peter J. W. Debye* for studying dipole moments and diffraction of x-rays and electrons in gases.

1937 (P) *Clinton Davisson* and *George Thomson* for discovering the diffraction of electrons by crystals, confirming de Broglie's hypothesis (1927).

1938 (P) *Enrico Fermi* for producing the transuranic radioactive elements by neutron irradiation (1934–1937).

1939 (P) *Ernest O. Lawrence* for inventing the cyclotron.

1940–1942   No prizes offered.

1943 (P) *Otto Stern* for developing molecular-beam studies (1923), and using them to discover the magnetic moment of the proton (1933).

1944 (P) *Isador I. Rabi* for discovering nuclear magnetic resonance in atomic and molecular beams.
(C) *Otto Hahn* for discovering nuclear fission (1938).

1945 (P) *Wolfgang Pauli* for discovering the exclusion principle (1924).

1946 (P) *Percy W. Bridgman* for studying physics at high pressures.

1947 (P) *Edward V. Appleton* for studying the ionosphere.

1948 (P) *Patrick M. S. Blackett* for studying nuclear physics with cloud-chamber photographs of cosmic-ray interactions.

1949 (P) *Hideki Yukawa* for predicting the existence of mesons (1935).

1950 (P) *Cecil F. Powell* for developing the method of studying cosmic rays with photographic emulsions and discovering new mesons.

1951 (P) *John D. Cockcroft* and *Ernest T. S. Walton* for transmuting nuclei in an accelerator (1932).
(C) *Edwin M. McMillan* for producing neptunium (1940) and *Glenn T. Seaborg* for producing plutonium (1941) and further transuranic elements.

1952 (P) *Felix Bloch* and *Edward Mills Purcell* for discovering nuclear magnetic resonance in liquids and gases (1946).

1953 (P) *Frits Zernike* for inventing the phase-contrast microscope, which uses interference to provide high contrast.

1954 (P) *Max Born* for interpreting the wave function as a probability (1926) and other quantum-mechanical discoveries and *Walther Bothe* for developing the coincidence method to study subatomic particles (1930–1931), producing, in particular, the particle interpreted by Chadwick as the neutron.

1955 (P) *Willis E. Lamb, Jr.* for discovering the Lamb shift in the hydrogen spectrum (1947) and *Polykarp Kusch* for determining the magnetic moment of the electron (1947).

1956 (P) *John Bardeen, Walter H. Brattain,* and *William Shockley* for inventing the transistor (1956).

1957 (P) *T. -D. Lee* and *C. -N. Yang* for predicting that parity is not conserved in beta decay (1956).

1958 (P) *Pavel A. Čerenkov* for discovering Čerenkov radiation (1935) *and Ilya M. Frank* and *Igor Tamm* for interpreting it (1937).

1959 (P) *Emilio G. Segrè* and *Owen Chamberlain* for discovering the antiproton (1955).

1960 (P) *Donald A. Glaser* for inventing the bubble chamber to study elementary particles (1952).
(C) *Willard Libby* for developing radiocarbon dating (1947).

1961 (P) *Robert Hofstadter* for discovering internal structure in protons and neutrons and *Rudolf L. Mössbauer* for discovering the Mössbauer effect of recoilless gamma-ray emission (1957).

1962 (P) *Lev Davidovich Landau* for studying liquid helium and other condensed matter theoretically.

1963 (P) *Eugene P. Wigner* for applying symmetry principles to elementary-particle theory and *Maria Goeppert Mayer* and *J. Hans D. Jensen* for studying the shell model of nuclei (1947).

1964 (P) *Charles H. Townes, Nikolai G. Basov,* and *Alexandr M. Prokhorov* for developing masers (1951–1952) and lasers.

1965 (P) *Sin-itiro Tomonaga, Julian S. Schwinger,* and *Richard P. Feynman* for developing quantum electrodynamics (1948).

1966 (P) *Alfred Kastler* for his optical methods of studying atomic energy levels.

1967 (P) *Hans Albrecht Bethe* for discovering the routes of energy production in stars (1939).

1968 (P) *Luis W. Alvarez* for discovering resonance states of elementary particles.

1969 (P) *Murray Gell-Mann* for classifying elementary particles (1963).

1970 (P) *Hannes Alfvén* for developing magnetohydrodynamic theory and *Louis Eugène Félix Néel* for discovering antiferromagnetism—alternate opposing magnetic domains—and ferrimagnetism—unequally opposing domains (1930s).

1971 (P) *Dennis Gabor* for developing holography (1947).
(C) *Gerhard Herzberg* for studying the structure of molecules spectroscopically.

1972 (P) *John Bardeen, Leon N. Cooper,* and *John Robert Schrieffer* for explaining superconductivity (1957).

1973 (P) *Leo Esaki* for discovering tunneling in semiconductors, *Ivar Giaever* for discovering tunneling in superconductors, and *Brian D. Josephson* for predicting the Josephson effect, which involves tunneling (1958–1962).

1974 (P) *Anthony Hewish* for discovering pulsars (with no mention of Jocelyn Bell, his graduate student, who first noticed the signals in 1967) and *Martin Ryle* for developing radio interferometry.

1975 (P) *Aage N. Bohr, Ben R. Mottelson,* and *James Rainwater* for discovering why some nuclei take asymmetric shapes.

1976 (P) *Burton Richter* and *Samuel C. C. Ting* for discovering the J/psi particle, the first charmed particle (1974).

1977 (P) *John H. Van Vleck, Nevill F. Mott,* and *Philip W. Anderson* for studying solids quantum-mechanically.
(C) *Ilya Prigogine* for extending thermodynamics to show how life could arise in the face of the second law.
(M) *Rosalyn S. Yalow* for developing radioimmunoassay methods.

1978 (P) *Arno A. Penzias* and *Robert W. Wilson* for discovering the cosmic background radiation (1965) and *Pyotr Kapitsa* for his studies of liquid helium.

1979 (P) *Sheldon L. Glashow, Abdus Salam,* and *Steven Weinberg* for developing the theory that unified the weak and electromagnetic forces (1958–1971).
(M) *Allan M. Cormack* and *Godfrey N. Hounsfield* for developing CAT scanners.

1980 (P) *Val Fitch* and *James W. Cronin* for discovering CP (*charge-parity*) *violation* (1964), which possibly explains the cosmological dominance of matter over antimatter.

1981 (P) *Nicolaas Bloembergen* and *Arthur L. Schawlow* for developing laser spectroscopy and *Kai M. Siegbahn* for developing electron spectroscopy (1958).

1982 (P) *Kenneth G. Wilson* for developing a method of constructing theories of phase transitions.

1983 (P) *William A. Fowler* for theoretical studies of astrophysical nucleosynthesis and *Subramanyan Chandrasekhar* for studying physical processes of importance to stellar structure and evolution, including the prediction of white dwarf stars (1930).

1984   (P) *Carlo Rubbia* for discovering the W and Z particles, verifying the electroweak unification, and *Simon van der Meer*, for developing the method of stochastic cooling of the CERN beam that allowed the discovery (1982–1983).

1985   (P) *Klaus von Klitzing* for the quantized Hall effect, relating to conductivity in the presence of a magnetic field (1980).

1986   (P) *Ernst Ruska* for inventing the electron microscope (1931), and *Gerd Binnig* and *Heinrich Rohrer* for inventing the scanning-tunneling electron microscope (1981).

Chapter 1

3. 10^6
5. 8.6 m^2/L
7. yes, by 7 mi/h
9. 10^8
11. 2.5×10^6 m
13. 7.4×10^6 m/s^2
15. (a) 2.5×10^{-4} mm^2; (b) 1.6×10^{-2} mm

Chapter 2

1. 10.14 m/s
3. 12.27 mi/h
5. (a) 24 km north; (b) 9.6 km/h; (c) 16 km/h; (d) 0; (e) 0
7. 13.11 mi/h
9. 48 mi/h
11. 1 m/s = 2.24 mi/h
13. 51 ft/s = 35 mi/h
15. (a) 2d, 17h; (b) 70 km/h
17. 2.6 h later, 1800 km from New York
19. $v_x = 3bt^2$
21. (a) $t = 0$ s, 0.13 s, 2.5 s; (b) $v_x = 3bt^2 - 2ct + d$; (c) $v_{xo} = 1.0$ m/s; (d) $t = 0.065$ s, 1.7 s
23. 0
25. 2×10^{11} m/s^2
27. (a) 28 m/s; (b) 23 m/s^2; (c) 9.4 m/s; (d) 11 m/s^2
29. (a) 2.0 m/s^2; (b) 150 m
31. 27 ft/s^2
33. (a) $t = 2v_0/a$; (b) $v = v_0$
35. 22 m/s
37. (a) 0.42 m/s^2; (b) toward Chicago; (c) 1.1 km
39. $a = 125g = 1200$ m/s^2
41. yes; $a = 370$ m/s^2
43. no collision; they stop 10 m apart
45. 4.6×10^{-3} m/s^2
47. 36 ft/s
49. (a) 27 m; (b) 4.7 s
51. Venus
53. Torey's, by 120 ms
55. 2.7 m/s faster
57. (a) 7.88 m/s and 7.67 m/s, respectively; (b) the upward-jumping diver hits first, by 0.16 s
59. (a) 2.4 m; (b) 47 cm before the chute
61. (b) 3.8 s; (c) 19 m; (d) 100 m
65. (a) 33 m; (b) 8%
67. 1.19 m

Chapter 3

1. 260 m, 7.9° N of W
3. (a) $A_x = 8.7$, $A_y = 5.0$; (b) $A_x = 9.7$, $A_y = -2.6$; (c) $A_x = 10$, $A_y = 0$
5. 18.9 units long, 7.1° E of S
7. $\mathbf{C} = -15\hat{\imath} + 9\hat{\jmath} - 18\hat{k}$
9. $\mathbf{V}_x = -14$ m/s; $v_y = -12$ m/s
11. 13mi/h/min 19° W of S
13. 5.1 m/s^2, 49° W of S
15. (a) $10\hat{\imath} - 21\hat{\jmath}$ m/s; (b) 13 m/s; (c) 89°
17. (a) $v(t = 0) = c\hat{\imath} = 6.7\hat{\imath}$ m/s; (b) $t = \sqrt{c/3b} = 1.7$ s; (c) 8.2 m/s
19. (a) $t = 18$ s; (b) 300 m; (c) 22 m/s at 120° to x-axis
21. (a) 2.6×10^{17} cm/s^2, upward; (b) parabolic
23. (a) 1.4 s; (b) 10 m
25. 1.23 m/s
27. 8.3 m/s at 61°
29. (a) 6640 m/s (14,850 mi/h); (b) 16 min; (c) 8280 m/s
31. 1.1 s
33. 1060 m
37. (a) 8.8 m; (b) 0.5 m
41. 31.2° or 65.7°
43. 2.8×10^{-3} m/s^2
45. 53 min
47. 20 cm
49. 3.44×10^{-10} s
51. $a_t = 3.8$ cm/s^2; $a_r = 95$ cm/s^2
53. (a) 18 km/h, 15 km/h, 10 km/h, 15 km/h; (b) 21 km/h, 17 km/h, 12 km/h, 17 km/h
55. $a = 1000$ m/s^2 in all cases; direction is (a) upward, (b) downward, (c) backward. Velocities in car frame: (a) 19 m/s backward; (b) 19 m/s forward; (c) 19 m/s downward. Velocities in ground frame: (a) 0; (b) 38 m/s forward; (c) 27 m/s at 45° below the forward direction
59. 7.2 m/s at 77° to horizontal
61. 1.2×10^4 m/s^2
65. 26,000 km/h at 26° to equator

Chapter 4

1. 3.8×10^6 N
3. (a) 11 m; (b) 24 m; (c) 43 m; (d) 53 m
5. 2.4×10^5 N
7. 10^{-4} N
9. Uranus
11. $0.75g = 7.4$ m/s^2
13. 98 N in horizontal string; $98\sqrt{2}$ N = 140 N in diagonal string
15. (a) 3.1×10^7 N; (b) 1.6
17. 530 N, 3.6 times the weight
21. (a) 5260 N; (b) 1080 N; (c) 494 N; (d) 589 N
23. 1.3×10^{-21} cm
27. (a) 132 cm; (b) 127 cm; (c) 120 cm; (d) 40 m/s^2
29. 1.9 m/s^2
31. 14 N

35. $\ell + nm(a+g)/k$, where n is the spring number measured from the bottom
37. $Mg + mg(1-y/\ell)$
39. 7.2 m
41. (a) 0.40mg; (b) 2.40mg; (c) 1.40mg
43. (a) 1.6×10^4 N; (b) 850 N
45. (a) 7.1 m/s^2; (b) 48 m/s
47. (a) $a = \dfrac{m_f - m_s}{m_s} g$; (b) $y = \dfrac{a_s h}{(1 + m_s/m_f)(a_s + g)}$

Chapter 5

1. 220 N
3. 880 N
5. (a) 6.3 m/s^2; (b) 0.44 s
7. 43 cm
9. 26 s
11. (a) 13 m/s^2; (b) 3.8 m/s
13. 340 N, 1.6 times the weight
15. (a) 8.0°; (b) 0.50 m/s^2
17. 0.38 s
19. 4.1 m/s^2, 4.7% of accident deceleration
21. (a) 1.6 m/s^2; (b) 3.2 N
23. 4.2 m/s^2
25. 95 km/h
27. 0.12
29. (a) yes; (b) yes
31. $T = mg\left(\dfrac{\mu_s \cos\theta - \sin\theta}{\cos\theta + \mu_s \sin\theta}\right)$
33. (a) 9.6 cm; (b) no
37. 12 cm
39. 3.6 m/s
41. 8.2 m/s
43. $h = \frac{1}{2}\ell$
45. 3.45 rev/min
47. (a) 35°; (b) 22°
49. 37°
51. 0.55
53. (a) 63 km/h (17 m/s); (b) 23 km/h (6.3 m/s)
55. $v = \sqrt{gh}$
57. $\mu_k = \dfrac{v_0^2}{2gx_1} - \dfrac{x_2^2}{4x_1 h}$
63. 28 cm

Chapter 6

1. 1300 J
3. 5.9×10^4 J
5. (a) 400 J; (b) 31 kg
7. 5.9×10^6 N
9. (a) 370 J; (b) 0.26
13. (a) 14; (b) -12; (c) -16
17. (a) 45°; (b) 111°; (c) 66°
19. 25°
21. (a) 360 J; (b) 350 J; (c) 357.5 J; (d) 359.375 J
23. $k_B = 8k_A$
25. 190 J
27. (a) 30 J; (b) 56 J; (c) 72 J
29. $F_0\left(x + \dfrac{x^2}{2\ell_0} + \dfrac{\ell_0^2}{\ell_0 + x} - \ell_0\right)$
33. 90 J

35. (a) 1.4×10^{10} J; (b) 3.3×10^6 J; (c) 28 J
37. 2.3×10^7 m/s, 0.077c
39. 2300 J
41. 7400 J
43. (a) 24 J; (b) 18 m/s
45. 4.1 m
47. 85 cm
49. (a) no work is done
51. (a) 60 kW; (b) 1 kW; (c) 0.04 kW
53. (a) 36 MW; (b) 1.1 MW
59. (a) $P = Mgv \cos(vt/R)$, with the argument of cos in radians
63. (b) 2.0 GJ; (c) 45 GJ; (d) 52 GJ
65. (a) $v = \sqrt{2Pt/M}$; (b) $x = (8P/9m)^{1/2}t^{3/2}$

Chapter 7

1. (a) $2\mu mg\ell$; (b) $\sqrt{2}\,\mu mg\ell$
7. $U = F_0\left(x + \dfrac{x^2}{2\ell} + \dfrac{\ell^2}{\ell + x} - \ell\right)$
9. (a) 1.07 J; (b) 1.12 J
11. no, the force is not conservative
13. $U = -\frac{1}{3}ax^3 - bx$
15. (a) 1.8 J; (b) $+3.6$ J; (c) -1.8 J
17. 50 m/s (180 km/h)
23. 2.6×10^7 N/m
25. 15 km/h
29. 2.6 m/s
31. 10^{10} W, the equivalent of 10 1000-MW nuclear plants
33. (a) 2.53×10^5 m/s; (b) 2.91×10^5 m/s; (c) 2.93×10^5 m/s
37. $F = \left[\dfrac{2ax^3}{c^2} - \left(2a + \dfrac{2b}{c^2}\right)x\right]e^{-x^2/c^2}$
41. (a) 18 m/s; (b) 11.5 m/s
43. (a) 41 cm; (b) 1.3 m/s
45. $v = R\sqrt{2\pi e\dot{B}/m}$
47. 2.6 m/s
49. 0.059
51. 62 cm from left end of frictional zone
53. 1000 MW, or twice the output of the coal-burning plant
59. 75 cm
61. (a) 3.3 cm; (b) 6.2×10^7 m/s; (c) 0.76 cm
63. (a) $v = \left[\dfrac{2}{m}\left(\dfrac{ax^2}{2} - \dfrac{bx^4}{4}\right)\right]^{1/2}$; (c) $v_{max} = \dfrac{a}{\sqrt{2mb}}$
65. $v = [2ax^{b+1}/m(b+1)]^{1/2}$

Chapter 8

1. $R_e/\sqrt{2}$
3. 10^{-7}
5. 443 m
7. 1.87 years
9. 16 million years
11. 1.0 hour
15. 9 s
19. $\sqrt{2}$
21. $\frac{1}{99} R_e = 64$ km; underestimate

23. 6.2 km/s

27. $v = \left[2GM\left(\dfrac{3}{R} + \dfrac{1}{r}\right) \right]^{1/2}$

29. (a) $U = -\dfrac{2GMm}{[(\ell/2)^2 + x^2]^{1/2}}$; (c) $F = -\dfrac{2GMx}{[(\ell/2)^2 + x^2]^{3/2}}$

35. (b) 8.8 mm; (c) 3.0 km

41. 1400 km lower

Chapter 9

1. $X = 50$ cm, $Y = 69$ cm, with origin at lower left
3. $\ell/2\sqrt{3}$ along the perpendicular bisector of any side
5. $X = 44$ cm, $Y = 55$ cm, with origin at lower left corner
7. $0.115a$ above the vertex of the missing triangle
9. 0.065 Å from the oxygen, along the symmetry axis
11. $\mathbf{R} = (t^2 + \frac{10}{3}t + \frac{7}{3})\hat{\imath} + (\frac{2}{3}t + \frac{8}{3})\hat{\jmath}$;
    $\mathbf{V} = (2t + \frac{10}{3})\hat{\imath} + \frac{2}{3}\hat{\jmath}$; $\mathbf{A} = 2\hat{\imath}$
13. about 1 Å (10^{-10} m, or the diameter of a hydrogen atom)
15. $m_{\text{mouse}} = \frac{1}{4}m_{\text{bowl}}$
17. 30 m
19. 8.4 km/h
21. (a) 0.14 N/m^2; (b) 0.014 mm
23. (a) 0.99 m; (b) 3.9 m/s
25. 3.9 km/s
27. (a) 2×10^4 kg·m/s; (b) 2×10^8 J; (c) yes
29. $v_1 = \left(\dfrac{m_2 kx^2}{m_1^2 + m_1 m_2}\right)^{1/2}$; $v_2 = \left(\dfrac{m_1 kx^2}{m_2^2 + m_1 m_2}\right)^{1/2}$
31. $26\hat{\imath} + 16\hat{\jmath}$ m/s
33. 1100 kg
35. (a) 3.3×10^6 N; (b) 3.4×10^5 kg
37. 0.22
39. $K_{\text{cm}} = 67$ keV before and after; $K_{\text{int}} = 0$ before, $K_{\text{int}} = 80$ keV after
41. $K_{\text{cm}} = 8 \times 10^{10}$ J, largely protons; $K_{\text{int}} = 5 \times 10^{10}$ J, all electrons
43. (a) 37.7°; (b) 0.657 m/s
45. 5.8 s after explosion

Chapter 10

1. (a) $I = 150$ N·s, upward; (b) 3000 N, about 5 times the gravitational force
3. about 6.8×10^{-3} N·s
5. (a) 7.3×10^6 N·s; (b) 5.6×10^6 N
7. $\Delta P/P = 2\%$
9. (a) 6.2 mi/h; (b) 12%
11. 19 kg
15. (a) 10^{15} kg; (b) 10^{12} kg
19. 1.3×10^{-6} J
21. 120°
23. 46 m/s
25. $v_A = -\frac{1}{3}v$, $v_B = \frac{2}{9}v$, $v_C = \frac{8}{9}v$
31. 22°
33. $v_m = 0.32$ m/s, $v_{3m} = 1.3$ m/s
    or $v_m = 1.7$ m/s, $v_{3m} = 0.87$ m/s
35. 13 m/s at 27° to the horizontal
37. $v_A = -\frac{1}{5}v_0\hat{\imath}$; $v_B = \frac{3}{5}\hat{\imath} + \frac{1}{5}\sqrt{3}\hat{\jmath}$; $v_C = \frac{3}{5}\hat{\imath} - \frac{1}{5}\sqrt{3}\hat{\jmath}$
39. 0.88

43. 44
45. (b) $v_1 = 0.28v_0$, $v_2 = 0.48v_0$; (c) 3, $0.26v_0$, $0.31v_0$
47. $v_{1200} = 2.2$ km/h, $v_{1800} = 18$ km/h

Chapter 11

1. 1.4 N·m, into page
3. 30 lbs
5. 420 N
7. 0
9. (a) $-7\hat{k}$; (b) $-8\hat{k}$; (c) $10\hat{k}$; (d) $30\hat{\imath} - 20\hat{\jmath}$;
   (e) $14\hat{\imath} - 28\hat{\jmath}$; (f) 0
11. 72 cm from the center, on the side opposite the worker
13. 16 m from wall
15. 480 N
17. vertical forces both 73.5 N, downward horizontal forces both 33.6 N, away from door jamb at top, toward door jamb at bottom
19. 5.0×10^3 N, tension
21. 0.87
23. 500 N
25. 5.0×10^4 N
27. maximum height of CM is at sphere center; lower for clown (b)
29. stable equilibria at $\theta = 0$ and $\theta = 90°$; unstable equilibrium at $\theta = 90° - \tan^{-1}(\frac{1}{2}) = 63°$
31. There are many possible pairs of forces; one such pair is $F_1 = -0.64\hat{\imath} - 1.9\hat{\jmath}$ applied at $r_1 = 1.0\hat{\imath} + 1.53\hat{k}$, and $F_2 = 1.4\hat{\imath} + 1.4\hat{\jmath} - 1.4\hat{k}$ applied at the origin.
35. (a) $0.44mg$, at 12° to earth's polar axis; (b) $0.036mgR^e$, out of the plane of Fig. 11–61; (c) center of mass is midway between pods; center of gravity is $0.084R_e$ to left of center of mass in Fig. 11–61

Chapter 12

1. (a) 7.27×10^{-5} rad/s; (b) 1.75×10^{-3} rad/s;
   (c) 1.45×10^{-4} rad/s; (d) 31.4 rad/s
3. (a) $v = (\pi/30)\,\omega r$; (b) $v = 2\pi\omega r$; (c) $v = (\pi/180)\,\omega r$
5. (a) 66 rpm; (b) 3.7 s
7. (a) 2.0 s; (b) 1.0 rev
9. (a) 15.6 kg·m^2; (b) 0.30 sec
13. (a) $\frac{2}{3}m\ell^2$; (b) $\frac{2}{3}m\ell^2$; (c) $\frac{4}{3}m\ell^2$
15. $m_{\text{pulley}} = 0.49$ kg; $m_1 = 0.41$ kg; $m_2 = 0.58$ kg
17. (a) 430 min; (b) 1900 rev
19. 1900 N·m
21. 170 rpm
23. (a) 15 MW; (b) 41%
25. increases by a factor $\omega_2/\omega_1 = 10^7$
27. 17%
29. hollow
31. $\frac{27}{16}(R - r)$
33. 7.1×10^{33} kg·m^2/s; 2.7×10^{40} kg·m^2/s
35. sun's rotation accounts for 3% of the angular momentum; Jupiter's orbital motion for 62%
37. (a) 45 kg; (b) 22 J
41. $I = mgd/2\omega\Omega$
43. $v = \left[\dfrac{8(m + M)g\ell}{m^2}\left(\frac{1}{4}m + \frac{1}{3}M\right)\right]^{1/2}$

45. Both wheels have stopped rotating about their axes, but the whole contraption is now rotating about the centerline between the two wheels in the same direction as the original disk rotation. The angular speed is

$$\omega_{\text{final}} = \frac{MR^2\omega}{\frac{2}{3}m\ell^2 + 3MR^2}$$

Chapter 13

3. (a) $x_0 = 20$ cm; $\omega = \pi/2$ s^{-1}; $\phi = 0$ (b) $x_0 = 30$ cm; $\omega = 2.0$ s^{-1}; $\phi = -\pi/2$; (c) $x_0 = 40$ cm; $\omega = \pi/2$ s^{-1}; $\phi = \pi/4$
5. 1.7×10^3 N/m
7. 0.69 s
9. (a) $\pi\sqrt{m/k}$; (b) $v_0\sqrt{m/k}$
15. 0.11 N·m/rad
17. (a) $2\pi\sqrt{\ell/g}$; (b) $2\pi\sqrt{2\ell/3g}$; (c) $2\pi\sqrt{2\ell/g}$; (d) infinite
19. 0.34 s
21. $R = \sqrt{2\kappa/k}$
23. within 1 μ (10^{-6} m)
29. 5.0 g
31. $\omega^2 = \dfrac{k_1 k_2}{m(k_1 + k_2)}$
35. 7 oscillations in x and 4 oscillations in y
37. 20 cm
39. 1.7 rad; 2.4 rad/s
43. $2\pi/\sqrt{2ga}$
45. 0.25 s
47. 18 m/s
51. 6.9 s
53. 45° to x-axis
55. 1.7% at 30°; 4.0% at 45°
57. $R/\sqrt{2}$ above center
61. $T = 2\pi\sqrt{R_e^3/GM_e} = 84$ min

Chapter 14

1. $\lambda = 34$ cm; $T = 1.0$ ms; $\omega = 6300$ Hz; $k = 18$ m^{-1}
3. (a) 0.2 mi/s; (b) 2 mi
5. 0.29 s
7. $y = 2.5\cos(0.39x + 14t)$ cm
9. $y_0 = 25$ cm; $f = 0.37$ Hz, $\lambda = 12$ m; $v = 4.4$ m/s
11. (a) 37 m/s; (b) 3.3 m/s
13. 590 g
17. $v = \sqrt{gh}$
19. 0.049 W/m^2
21. $4\pi^2 y_0^2 F_0/\lambda$
23. 2.7×10^4 W; drops by $1/\sqrt{2}$ when μ doubles
25. 6.0 m
31. $y_s = 2y_0\cos(\phi/2)$
33. (a) 0.12 s; (b) 1.1 cm; (c) 0.082 s; (d) 0.86 cm
35. 7
41. (a) 9.75 cm (leaving 20.25 cm of string); (b) 429 Hz − 451 Hz
43. 0.33 Hz
45. (a) 2.9×10^5 m/s; (b) 10^7 K
47. 3.0 cm/s

51. 7.3 km
53. $\lambda_1 = 5.0$ m, $f_1 = 0.56$ Hz; $\lambda_2 = 2.5$ m, $f_2 = 0.79$ Hz

Chapter 15

1. 1 inch $H_2O = 249$ Pa, 1 inch of mercury = 3390 Pa, 1 torr = 133 Pa
3. (a) 176 kg/m^3; (b) 6.8 m^3
5. 3.4×10^5 Pa, or 2.4×10^3 Pa gauge pressure
7. 208 cm^2
9. 5.4×10^{18} kg
11. 10 Pa
13. about 300 ft
15. 7.4×10^3 Pa, or 7%
17. 52 cm higher in hurricane eye
19. 59 g
21. 27 m
23. $\dfrac{\rho\ell}{2}(h_0^2 - h_1^2)\tan\left(\dfrac{\theta}{2}\right)$
27. $y = \frac{4}{5}h$
29. 0.11 gal/min
31. (a) 1650 Pa; (b) 17 cm
33. (a) 79 m/s; (b) 26 mpg
37. $h = h_0\ln 2 = 5.7$ km

Chapter 16

1. 5
3. They are not equal.
5. (a) 1.37 atm; (b) 0.330 atm; (c) 2.31 atm
7. (a) -40; (b) none; (c) none; (d) 0; (e) none
9. 16×10^6°C; 29×10^6°F; 29×10^6°R
11. 100 W
13. (a) 113 J/K; (b) 630 J/kg·K
15. (a) aluminum; (b) 84 W
17. 68°C
19. 0.70 K
21. 56.2°C
23. 5.6, 0.14, 3.4, 0.18, 5.0, 1.3, all in h·ft^2°F/Btu
25. $R = 12.3$ ft^2·h/btu
27. 75°F
29. 0.80
31. monthly heating cost is now $116; solar gain is worth $13/month
33. 3.3 cm
37. 277 K, or 4°C

Chapter 17

1. (a) volume increases by factor of 473/373 = 1.27; (b) volume doubles
3. 1×10^{15} particles/m^3, about 4×10^{-11} of earth's atmospheric particle density
5. 6.5×10^3 N, outward
7. (a) 235 mol; (b) 5.65 m^3
9. (a) 6.8×10^{26} molecules; (b) 4.1×10^6 J; (c) thermal energy is 11 times greater
11. 3.1×10^3 m/s
13. (a) 1.3×10^{-6} m^3/mol; (b) 175 atm
17. 143 kJ
19. mixture is all water (1050 g) at 10°C
21. 4.9°C

23. 1.2 kg of ice, 0.80 kg of water, all at 0°C.
25. 0.80 kg
29. 0.40°C
31. 307 K
35. 2.101 L, compared with 2.094 L using constant-β approximation
37. on earth, 3.5 km/s for H_2; 0.88 km/s for O_2; compared with escape speed of 11 km/s. On Jupiter, 1.9 km/s for H_2; 0.48 km/s for O_2; compared with escape speed of 60 km/s. More particles in the high-energy tail of the Maxwell-Boltzmann distribution will therefore escape earth, leaving earth with less hydrogen.
39. 36 days; too fast

Chapter 18

1. 5.6 kJ, 8.4 kJ
3. 0.02°C
5. $\frac{4}{3}P_1V_1$
7. 220 J
11. 130 atm
13. (a) $T=300$ K, $W=1.5$ kJ; (b) $T=326$ K, $W=430$ J; (c) $T=336$ K, $W=0$
17. 2.5 kJ
19. 93 J
21. (b) T_0; (c) $T_{van} < T_0$
23. (b) 39 W
25. (a) 2.31 kJ for both gases; (b) 1.8 kJ for H_2; 1.5 kJ for He
27. (a) diatomic; (b) 1.3
29. $W=172$ J, $Q=2700$ J

Chapter 19

1. 12!/6!, or 6.7×10^5: of these, 6!, or about one in a thousand correspond to all 6 eggs in the left half
3. assuming oceans cover 75% of earth, with average depth 3 km, energy extracted is 5×10^{23} J, about 2000 times annual use
5. 52% winter, 48% summer
7. 10
11. decrease in minimum temperature
13. 3.4%
15. $W=Q=1216$ J; $e=0.174$
17. (a) maximum efficiency is 42%; (b) 2100 MW; (c) 180,000
19. (a) $1-5^{1-\gamma}$; (b) $3T_C(5^{\gamma-1})$; (c) Carnot efficiency is $1 - \frac{1}{3}(5^{1-\gamma})$
21. (a) 7.7; (b) 5.3; (c) 2.8
23. 2×10^7 kg/s, slightly more than the Mississippi River flow
25. (a) 55%; (b) 36%; (c) 32%
27. 717.75 K
33. $\Delta S_{AB} = 1.5nR\ln 3$, $\Delta S_{BC} = nR\ln 3$, $\Delta S_{CA} = -2.5nR\ln 3$
39. $T_h = T_{h0}e^{-[P_0 t/mc(T_{h0}-T_c)]}$, $P = 0$ at $t = \dfrac{mc(T_{h0}-T_c)}{P_0} \ln\left(\dfrac{T_{h0}}{T_c}\right)$

Chapter 20

1. about 3 C
5. 8×10^8 N, more than 10^6 times your weight

7. electrical force is larger by factor of 2.2×10^{39} at all distances
9. -3.3 μC; $a \gg g$, so okay to ignore gravity; no—acceleration increases
11. 33 μC; 52 μC
15. $\mathbf{F} = 1.6\mathbf{i} - 0.33\hat{\mathbf{j}}$ N; $F=1.7$ N; 11° below x-axis
17. no
19. put $-q$ midway between the others; equilibrium is unstable
21. $\dfrac{a^2}{\ell + 2a}$ from the right end of the rod

Chapter 21

1. 2.0×10^{-4} N
3. (a) 5.5×10^{11} N/C; (b) 8.9×10^{-8} N
5. 1.6×10^{-12} N
7. 4.1 cm to right of 1 μC charge
13. $\dfrac{q}{\pi^2 \epsilon_0 a^2}$, to right
15. $+3.0$ μC
19. $\pi R^2 E$
21. (a) $-q/\epsilon_0$; (b) $-2q/\epsilon_0$; (c) 0; (d) 0
23. 2.9×10^5 N·m²/C; no
25. $40\epsilon_0 = 3.5 \times 10^{-10}$ C/m³
27. -4.5×10^5 C
29. (a) $E = 0$; (b) $E = \dfrac{\rho r}{3\epsilon_0} - \dfrac{\rho a^3}{3\epsilon_0 r^2}$; (c) $E = \dfrac{7\pi a^3 \rho}{3\epsilon_0 r^2}$
31. $E=0$ between sheets; $E=\sigma/\epsilon_0$ outside sheets, directed away from sheets
33. -0.25 C
35. 3.6×10^{-3} C/m³
37. 0.39 μs later
39. (a) 5.1×10^6 N/C; (b) 34 N/C
41. (a) 7.2×10^6 N/C, from positive to negative plate; (b) 0.58 N/C, directed oppositely from the field of part (a)
43. 41 μC
45. $E = 0$ for $r < a$

$E = \dfrac{ac}{\epsilon_0 r^2}(e^{-1} - e^{-r})$ for $a < r < b$

$E = \dfrac{ac}{\epsilon_0 r^2}(e^{-1} - e^{-b})$ for $r > b$

Chapter 22

1. electric force is about 2×10^{12} times stronger
3. $v_{min} = \ell\sqrt{\dfrac{eE}{md}}$
5. (a) 2.8×10^6 m/s; (b) helical
9. (a) zero; (b) 4.0×10^{-3} C/m²; (c) other charges could destroy the spherical symmetry, making the surface charge density nonuniform
11. (b) $-Q$; (c) no
15. (a) 14 μC; (b) -0.18 μC/cm²
17. (a) 3.0×10^{-3} N·m; (b) 1.1×10^{-2} J
19. 1.5×10^{-27} N·m
21. (a) $F=0$, $\tau=0.036$ N·m; (b) $F=1.3$ N, $\tau=0$; (c) 0.036 J
25. 7.8×10^3 N/C

Chapter 23

3. (a) 1.3×10^{-7} J, about the same kinetic energy as a raisin moving at 1 cm/s!; (b) 2.1×10^{4} W

5. 9.4×10^{7} m/s

7. $6.1\ \mu$C

9. (a) $V = -E_0 x^2/2x_0$; (b) $4eE_0 x_0$

11. 0 for all three paths

13. 40 V/m

17. (a) $\mathbf{E} = -ay\hat{\mathbf{i}} - ax\hat{\mathbf{j}}$; (b) V/m^2

21. (a) $V(r) = \dfrac{\rho R^3}{3\epsilon_0 r}$; (b) $V(0) - V(R) = \dfrac{\rho R^2}{6\epsilon_0}$;

   (c) $V(r) = \dfrac{\rho}{6\epsilon_0}(3R^2 - r^2)$

23. $Q/2\pi\epsilon_0 R$

25. (a) $d/(\sqrt{2}-1)$ to right of $-q$; (b) d to right of $-q$ and $d/3$ to left of $-q$

27. 1.2×10^{-3} m

29. (b) $V = \dfrac{1}{4\pi\epsilon_0}\dfrac{Q}{R}$

31. 3 kV

35. (a) 2.9×10^5 V; (b) $0.11\ \mu$C from smaller to larger sphere

39. 5.8×10^5 V

41. 1.7 cm

43. $y = \sqrt{\frac{1}{3}(d^2 + 2xd - 3x^2)}$

Chapter 24

1. $\dfrac{3}{4\pi\epsilon_0}\dfrac{q^2}{a}$

3. $v = q/\sqrt{\pi\epsilon_0 ma}$

5. $U = -7.8 \times 10^{18}$ J or -49 eV; energy released during formation is $-U$

7. $W = \dfrac{Q^2}{8\pi\epsilon_0}\left(\dfrac{1}{a} - \dfrac{1}{b}\right)$

11. 2×10^{11} m^3

13. 2.4×10^{-5} J

15. $Q^2/40\pi\epsilon_0 a$, or 20% more

17. $\dfrac{Q^2}{4\pi\epsilon_0 R}(2^{2/3} - 1) = 3.0 \times 10^{-4}$ J

21. (a) 7600 pF; (b) 1000 V

23. 64 V on each

25. increases by 31 J (doubles)

27. $2\pi\epsilon_0 a$

29. 0.0051 to 0.0082 μF, or 0.0067 μF $\pm$ 24%

31. 0.55 μF, 0.83 μF, 1.3 μF, 1.5 μF, 6.0 μF

33. 75 V

37. (a) 7.5×10^{-2} F; (b) 3.4×10^9 J

41. (a) 15 kJ; (b) 20 kV

43. (a) $C = \dfrac{\kappa + 1}{2}C_0$; (b) $U = \dfrac{C_0 V_0^2}{1 + \kappa}$;

   (c) $F = \dfrac{2C_0 V_0^2}{\ell}\dfrac{\kappa - 1}{(\kappa + 1)^2}$, into capacitor

51. 7.2 pF/m

Chapter 25

1. 4.8 mA, toward back of tube

3. 2.9×10^5 C

5. (a) 480 m; (b) 50 mA; (c) 14 μA

7. v_d is 8.6 times greater in the copper

9. (a) 4.2×10^6 A/m^2; (b) 3.3 A

11. 7.0×10^{-15} s

13. 2.0×10^{-10}

15. diameter of aluminum should be 1.3 times greater

17. (a) 2.1 cm; (b) 2.7 cm; (c) copper \$4.72/m, aluminum \$2.07/m

19. $4.0 \times 10^{-4}\ \Omega$, $1.0 \times 10^{-6}\ \Omega$, $2.5 \times 10^{-7}\ \Omega$

21. (a) 69 μA; (b) 82 A

23. 96 W

25. about 10^{12} W, approximately equal to earth's electric power consumption

27. the resistor that dissipates most power has $\sqrt{2}$ times greater diameter

29. (a) 150 A; (b) 1.7 km (remember that there are 2 wires!)

33. 2700 m/s, significantly different from the empirical result

35. 0.63 A

Chapter 26

5. 6.0 V

7. 0.02 Ω

9. 45 Ω

11. 30 A

13. $\mathcal{E} = 1.4$ V; $R_{\text{int}} = 3.7\ \Omega$

15. 24

19. $R_1\mathcal{E}/(2R_1 + R)$

21. $I_2 = \dfrac{\mathcal{E}_1 R_3 - \mathcal{E}_3 R_1 - \mathcal{E}_2 R_3}{R_2 R_3 + R_1 R_2 + R_1 R_3}$

23. R_1 in all three cases

25. $\mathcal{E}_3 = \dfrac{\mathcal{E}_2 R_1 - \mathcal{E}_1 R_2}{R_1 + R_2}$

27. 1.7% low

29. (a) 13 V; (b) 2.2 mA; (c) 12 V; (d) 2.2 mA

31. 1200 W

33. 0.050 Ω, in parallel

39. (a) $I_1 = \mathcal{E}/R$; $I_2 = 0$; $I_3 = 0$; (b) $I_1 = \mathcal{E}/2R$; $I_2 = \mathcal{E}/2R$; $I_3 = 0$

41. 7.6 s

43. (a) 10 W; (b) 7.5×10^{-3} J

45. (a) $I_1 = 25$ mA; $I_2 = 0$; $V_C = 0$; (b) $I_1 = I_2 = 10$ mA; $V_C = 60$ V; (c) $I_1 = 0$; $I_2 = 10$ mA; $V_C = 60$ V; (d) $I_1 = I_2 = 0$; $V_C = 0$

49. 100 V

51. 83 μs

53. (a) 0; (b) 1.0 A; (c) 0.75 A; (d) 0; (e) 1.0 A; (f) 3.0 A; (g) 3.0 A; (h) 1.0 A

Chapter 27

1. (a) 16 G; (b) 23 G

3. (a) 2.0×10^{-14} N; (b) 1.0×10^{-14} N; (c) 0

5. (a) $(-1.1\hat{\mathbf{i}} + 1.5\hat{\mathbf{j}} + 1.7\hat{\mathbf{k}}) \times 10^{-3}$ N

7. $\mathbf{B} = 0.13\hat{\mathbf{k}}$ T; $\mathbf{v}_2 = -1.4 \times 10^4\hat{\mathbf{i}}$ m/s

11. 15 G

13. (a) 8.7 km; (b) no change

17. 300 G; yes

19. 0.65 μs

21. (a) double the frequency to 30 MHz; (b) no change; (c) 38 MeV; (d) 38 MeV
23. Ne, CO, NO_2
25. 0.38 N
27. 0.12 T
29. $IA \ln(r_2/r_1)$, out of page for I flowing radially outward
33. (a) 0.35 A·m²: (b) 4.2×10^{-2} N·m
35. 24 A
37. 5.6×10^{-27} J $= 3.5 \times 10^{-8}$ eV
39. $\mu = I\ell^2/4\pi N$
41. 501.8 G
43. $\mathbf{E} = 3.0 \times 10^4 \hat{\mathbf{j}}$ V/m; $\mathbf{B} = 0.71(\hat{\mathbf{j}} + \hat{\mathbf{k}})$ T
45. if bottom of magnet is N then $\boldsymbol{\mu}$ points down; if bottom is S then $\boldsymbol{\mu}$ points up

Chapter 28

1. q/ϵ_0, $-q/\epsilon_0$, 0, 0, 0, 0
3. $\mu_0 I/4a$, into page
5. (a) $2\sqrt{2}\mu_0 I/\pi a$; (b) $\mu_0 Ia^2/2\pi x^3$
7. 0.62 G
9. 2.8×10^9 A
11. 5.0×10^{-6} N
13. forces are attractive
19. (a) 0; (b) 3.6 G; (c) 19 G; (d) 5 G
21. $B = \mu_0 I/\ell$ parallel to pipe axis on inside; $B = 0$ outside
23. $(\sqrt{2}/2)\mu_0 i$ both inside and outside (but internal and external fields are mutually perpendicular)
25. (a) $B = \mu_0 J|z|$; (b) $B = \frac{1}{2}\mu_0 Jh$
27. (a) 2300; (b) 3.3 kW; (c) 0
29. (a) 0.016 T; (b) 0.014 T
33. (a) $B = \mu_0 I/2w$; (b) $B = \mu_0 I/2\pi r$
37. (a) $I = \frac{1}{3}\pi J_0 R^2$; (b) $B = \mu_0 J_0 R^2/6r$; (c) $B = J_0\left(\dfrac{r}{2} - \dfrac{r^2}{3R}\right)$

Chapter 29

3. (a) 0.20 mA; (b) increases to 0.44 mA
5. 1.5×10^{-2} T
7. 3.0 s
11. (a) top to bottom; (b) $B\ell v/R$; (c) $B^2\ell^2 v^2/R$
13. (c) $v = \mathscr{E}/B\ell$; R affects time to reach final speed
15. (a) 6.7 mA, counterclockwise; (b) 6.7 mA, counterclockwise; (c) 0.44 mW, both cases
17. (a) $v = \mathscr{E}/2B\ell$; (b) 0
19. (a) $\phi = a^2(B_0 + \frac{1}{2}ba + bx)$; (b) counterclockwise; (c) a^2bv/R; (d) $a^4b^2v^2/R$
21. mgv
23. (a) $\dfrac{-B\ell^2\omega \sin\omega t}{R}$; (b) $\dfrac{B^2\ell^4\omega^2 \sin^2\omega t}{R}$; (c) $\dfrac{-B^2\ell^4\omega \sin^2\omega t}{R}$
25. $E = -bR^2/2r$
27. (a) 140 mV; (b) 0.14 eV; (c) 150 mV/m
29. (a) 530 V/m; (b) 8.0 keV
31. $v = mgR \cos\theta/B^2\ell^2 \sin^2\theta$
33. (a) 2.4 km; (b) 1.6×10^{-5}; (c) \$6.90
35. (a) $J = \dfrac{r}{2\rho}\dfrac{dB}{dt}$; (b) $P = \dfrac{\pi a^4 h}{8\rho}\left(\dfrac{dB}{dt}\right)^2$; (c) 7.0 W

Chapter 30

1. 120 V
3. (a) $2\pi fMI_0 \cos(2\pi ft)$; (b) 130 mH
5. $\dfrac{\mu_0\ell}{2\pi} \ln\left(\dfrac{a+w}{a}\right)$
7. 400 mH
9. $\mathscr{E} = -(12t + 30)$ V
15. (a) 76 mA; (b) 4.4 V; (c) 7.6 V; (d) 2.2 A/s; (e) 0.58 W
17. about 25 s
19. (a) $I_1 = I_2 = 1.0$ A; $I_3 = 0$; (b) $I_1 = 2.1$ A; $I_2 = 0.43$ A; $I_3 = 1.7$ A; (c) $I_1 = 0$; $I_2 = I_3 = 1.7$ A, flowing clockwise through R_3, L, and R_2; (d) $I_1 = I_2 = I_3 = 0$
21. 3.1 kJ
23. (a) 0.82 A; (b) 3.0 s
25. 2500 W; no—the current decreases steadily, but the energy is proportional to the square of the current, so the power is greatest at first
29. smaller by factor $1/4n^2R^2$
31. (a) 10^{24} J; (b) no; effect is one part in 10^6
33. (a) $u = \mu_0 I^2/8\pi^2 r^2$; (b) $\dfrac{\mu_0\ell I^2}{4\pi r} dr$
35. (a) $\mu_0 I/w$; (b) $\frac{1}{2}\mu_0 I^2 d/w$; (c) $\mu_0 d/w$
37. (a) 6.7×10^{-10} J/m³; (b) $u_B = \mu_0\mu^2/32\pi^2 r^6$; (c) 5.8×10^7 m $= 9.1$ R_e

Chapter 31

1. 380 s⁻¹, 170 V → 380 s^{-1}, 170 V
5. $V_{rms} = V_0$
7. $I_1 = I_0 \cos\phi$; $I_2 = I_0 \sin\phi$
9. 45 mA
11. (a) $\omega = 500$ s^{-1} or $f = 80$ Hz; (b) 2.0 H; (c) $X_L = 4X_C$
13. 4.9pF to 42 pF
15. 0.20 μH
19. (a) 32 mH; (b) 1.0 V
21. 0.22 μF
23. 20 V
25. (a) 43 μH; (b) $R > 16$ Ω
29. (a) above; (b) $\phi = \tan^{-1}\left(\dfrac{V_{C0} - V_{L0}}{V_{R0}}\right)$
31. (a) $\frac{1}{3}$; (b) 4.0 W
33. (a) 5.5%; (b) 9.1%; (c) large
35. (a) 140 W; (b) 1.2 A; (c) 1.1 kWh; (d) 13¢
37. (a) 280 Ω; (b) 5900 μF
45. (a) $\epsilon_0 w/d$; (b) 3.0×10^8 rad/sec
47. $\dfrac{k}{m} = \dfrac{1}{LC}$

Chapter 32

5. $-x$
11. 2.6 s
13. 5 km
15. (a) 300 m; (b) 6.3×10^6 s^{-1}; (c) 0.021 m^{-1}; (d) 0.39 V/m; (e) 1.3×10^{-9} T
17. 5000 km
19. x-direction
23. 2700 W/m²
25. 3.0×10^{-6} W/m²

27. (a) 1.4×10^{-17} W/m^2; (b) 4.6×10^{-34} W/m^2;
    (c) to within 6.7×10^{-7} s
29. fields drop like $1/r$, compared with $1/r^2$ for stationary
    point charge
31. (a) 1600 W/m^2; (b) 770 V/m; (c) 2.6×10^{-6} T
33. 1.1×10^8 m^2 if sail is perfect reflector; 2.2×10^8 m^2 if
    perfect absorber
35. 6.7×10^{-6} N
39. 1 μm

Chapter 33

1. (a) 4.50 h; (b) 4.56 h; (c) 4.62 h
3. (a) $v/c = \tan\theta$, where θ is the amplitude of the
   sine curve. Here $\theta = 20''$ (20/3600 degree), giving
   $v = 29$ km/s. (b) The orbit is nearly circular.
5. (a) $v = (1 - 6 \times 10^{-10})c \approx 0.999999999c$; (b) no; they
   would be 4 My old
7. 0.14c
9. A is 83 years old; B is 40 years old
11. C judges civilization B first, by 350,000 years
13. Problem 11: An observer moving from A to B at 0.5c
    will judge the events to be simultaneous. Problem 12:
    There is no such observer because the events could
    be causally related.
17. 0.80c
19. 0.996c
21. 9.6×10^{-31} kg
23. (a) 0.26 eV; (b) 130 keV; (c) 3.1 MeV
25. 1 day

Chapter 34

3. 1.41 m
5. $\theta = 40.5°$
7. 3.0 mm
9. air $\theta_c = 43.2°$; water $\theta_c = 65.6°$
11. $d = 1.14 h$
13. deviations are red 38.2°, blue 41.3°
15. 6.1 m
17. for thickness of 3 mm, $n = 1.6$, appears 1.0001 m
    tall $\approx 0.01\%$
19. 0.33 m
21. 0.5°
23. 0.81 m tall, top is 0.06 m below top of your head
25. 1.2 m tall, bottom is 0.6 m off the floor less $\frac{1}{2}$ distance
    from eyes to top of head
27. 2×10^{-5} rad $= 0.001°$, 1.3×10^{-14} rad $= 7.6 \times 10^{-13°}$
29. (a) -1.2 cm; (b) -1.7 cm; (c) -2.2 cm
33. convex, $R \approx 0.18$ m
35. (a) 107 mm, 42 times; (b) 79 mm, 57 times
37. virtual image 14.6 cm to left of convex lens
39. 2 times
41. 0.15 m back
43. (a) -7.5 cm; (b) 11 cm
45. magnification $= i/o < 0$, so image is virtual
47. 2
49. 23.6 cm
51. $\dfrac{1}{f} = \dfrac{1}{f_1} + \dfrac{1}{f_2}$
57. -4.5 diopters, nearsighted
59. $\frac{1}{4}$

61. 3.0 m, 8.1 m
63. 6.4 cm; 7.5 times, 170 times, 1300 times
65. 110 cm from the objective mirror, flat and elliptical
71. derive 42.53° for red, 40.78° for violet

Chapter 35

1. maxima: 0°, 0.096°, 0.193°. . . ; minima: 0°, 0.048°,
   0.144°. . .
5. yes, since spacing is 1.8 μm
7. 2.484 mm $-$ 0.828 mm $=$ 1.656 mm; 1.657 mm; 0.06%
9. 0.034°
11. 103°
13. 9.8×10^{-8} rad $= 6 \times 10^{-6°}$
15. 0.75 m
17. maxima at $\theta = 0.000°$, 0.084°, 0.169° . . .
19. problem 17 plus secondary maxima at 0.028°, 0.056°,
    0.113°, 0.141° . . .
21. 8 slits, 0.044 mm
23. 1058 nm, 142 nm
25. $\Delta\lambda = 0.006$ nm
27. 415 nm, 484 nm, 581 nm
29. 0.156 mm
31. 545 nm
33. 1.324
35. 105 nm
37. 240 nm, 720 nm. . .
39. 1500 nm; $m = 6, 7, 8, 9$
41. 59
43. 0.056°, 0.111°, 0.167°
45. 0.00074 rad $= 0.034''$
47. 35.4 m
49. 0.16 m, 6×10^{-5} ly
51. 0.7 mm
53. 6'', yes, 1.7
55. 19,000 km
57. $\frac{1}{8}$
59. $n = 1.43$, fluorite
61. 920 times
63. 3 μm
65. 70th: 202.7–204.5 nm; 94th: 150.3–152.8 nm; 95th:
    148.7–151.2 nm; 96th: 147.1–149.6 nm; 120th: 117.2–
    120.4 nm; no gap
67. $0.017(m + \frac{1}{2})$ mm, $m = 0, 1, 2$. . .
69. 4166
71. $\delta = D\lambda/2d$

Chapter 36

1. 122 nm, 103 nm, 97.2 nm
3. 0.17 MHz
5. 10^{-24} kg·m/s
7. 10^{-11} m $= 10$ pm
9. $1s^2 2s^2 2p^3$
11. 74,000 years
13. 20; $+2e$, $+e$, 0, $-e$
15. 3.6×10^9 cm^3
17. 10^{11} ly $= 10^5$ Mly
19. 2.8 Gly
21. 0.097 cm
25. 0.67

CREDITS

We thank Elizabeth Stell and Kimberly S. Levin for their help in obtaining photographs. We thank Hugh Kirkpatrick, Adam Witten, and Crispin Butler for setting up laboratory demonstrations to be photographed. We thank Ernest and John LeClaire of LeClaire Custom Color, as well as Erik Borg, for their expert and expeditious photographic developing and printing. We thank Nikon, Inc., for the loan of photographic equipment.

Cover

Sandia National Laboratories photograph

Color Plates

Plate 1 Swanke Hayden Connell Architects
Plate 2 MTS Systems Corp.
Plate 3 M. Horsmann
Plate 4 NASA/Jet Propulsion Laboratory
Plate 5 Sandia National Laboratories
Plate 6 Jay M. Pasachoff
Plate 7 Dennis di Cicco
Plate 8 Alfred Leitner, Rensselaer Polytechnic Institute
Plate 9 R. Giovanelli and H. R. Gillett, CSIRO National Measurement Laboratory, Australia

Chapter 1

Fig. 1–1 Underlying photo by Alan Dressler and Roger Windhorst, Mt. Wilson and Las Campanas Observatories, Carnegie Institution of Washington
Fig. 1–2 Sprague Electric/Worcester, R. Morrison
Fig. 1–3 Courtesy of Lotte Jacobi
Fig. 1–4 Perkin-Elmer Corporation and Lockheed Missiles & Space Company, Inc.
Fig. 1–5 Heather Couper
Fig. 1–6 National Bureau of Standards
Fig. 1–8 National Bureau of Standards
Fig. 1–9 International Bureau of Weights and Measures
Fig. 1–10 California Association for Research in Astronomy
Fig. 1–11 National Optical Astronomy Observatories
Fig. 1–12 Dale C. Flanders, MIT Lincoln Laboratory, Lexington, MA
Fig. 1–13 Boeing Commercial Airplane Co.
Fig. 1–14 NASA/JSC, Cosmic Dust Program

Chapter 2

Fig. 2–12 Dr. Harold E. Edgerton, Massachusetts Institute of Technology
Fig. 2–13 NASA/JSC
Fig. 2–15 Jay M. Pasachoff
Fig. 2–16 Jay M. Pasachoff

Chapter 3

Fig. 3–1 National Center for Atmospheric Research
Fig. 3–17 *PSSC Physics*, 3rd ed. © 1971 by D. C. Heath & Company, with Educational Development Center, Inc.
Fig. 3–18 Hanon Isachar/Sygma
Fig. 3–19 Laffont and Pierce/Sygma

Chapter 4

Fig. 4–1 NASA
Fig. 4–2 Courtesy of Fletcher Watson, *Project Physics*
Fig. 4–4 Courtesy of Lord Portsmouth and the Trustees of the Portsmouth Estates
Fig. 4–5 Owen Gingerich
Fig. 4–6 From the collection of David Park
Fig. 4–7 Copyright © 1984 by The New York Times Company. Reprinted by permission
Fig. 4–8 Photo by Ralph Crane
Fig. 4–12 NASA/JSC
Fig. 4–14 NASA/JSC
Fig. 4–30 Jay M. Pasachoff

Chapter 5

Fig. 5–1 European Space Agency
Fig. 5–9 Copyright © David Scharf 1977, from *Magnifications* (Schocken Books, Inc.)
Fig. 5–20 By permission of Johnny Hart and News America Syndicate
Fig. 5–28 Michelin Tire Corp.
Fig. 5–31 Jay M. Pasachoff

Chapter 6

Fig. 6–2 American Institute of Physics, Niels Bohr Library
Fig. 6–5 Jay M. Pasachoff
Fig. 6–6 Jay M. Pasachoff
Fig. 6–25 © Lucasfilm Ltd. (LFL) 1981. All rights reserved. From the motion picture *Raiders of the Lost Ark*, courtesy of Lucasfilm Ltd.

Chapter 7

Fig. 7–23 William Kirk, Stanford University
Fig. 7–25 Photo by Erik Borg

Chapter 8

Fig. 8–1 AIP Niels Bohr Library
Fig. 8–2 Chapin Library, Williams College
Fig. 8–3 Jay M. Pasachoff
Fig. 8–4 Chapin Library, Williams College
Fig. 8–7 New Mexico State University Observatory
Fig. 8–9 (above) Courtesy Robert Burger and Marshall Schalk, Smith College

Fig. 8–9 (below) Christopher Duncan, Middlebury College
Fig. 8–11 From the collection of John E. Gaustad
Fig. 8–14 NASA
Fig. 8–15 METEOSAT image supplied by the European Space Agency
Fig. 8–16 Jay M. Pasachoff
Fig. 8–19 © 1986 Max-Planck-Institut für Aeronomie, Lindau/Harz, FRG, taken by the Halley Multicolour Camera on board ESA's spacecraft Giotto, courtesy H. U. Keller
Fig. 8–26 NASA
Fig. 8–29 Royal Greenwich Observatory ; from A. Eddington, *Nature*, vol. 83, May 26, 1910, pp. 372–373; courtesy of Ruth Freitag, Library of Congress
Fig. 8–42 NASA/JPL
Fig. 8–44 (left) Mark R. Showalter
Fig. 8–44 (center and right) NASA/JPL
Fig. 8–47 John F. Hawley and Larry Smarr, University of Illinois at Urbana-Champaign
Fig. 8–49 Courtesy of AT&T Bell Laboratories

Chapter 9

Fig. 9–1 From *Physics* by Edward R. McCliment, © 1984 by Harcourt Brace Jovanovich, Inc. Reproduced by permission of the publisher
Fig. 9–9 BfG: Hauptverwaltung
Fig. 9–10 Jennifer Davis, Pittsburgh Ballet Theater; photo by Michael Friedlander
Fig. 9–13 Jay M. Pasachoff
Fig. 9–14 National Optical Astronomy Observatories/Cerro Tololo Inter-American Observatory
Fig. 9–17 Copyright © 1920 by The New York Times Company. Reprinted by permission
Fig. 9–19 NASA

Chapter 10

Fig. 10–1 Reproduced by permission of Encyclopaedia Britannica, Inc.; illustration by Mark Paternostro
Fig. 10–2 Lick Observatory
Fig. 10–3 Dr. Harold E. Edgerton, Massachusetts Institute of Technology
Fig. 10–5 U.S. Dept. of Transportation
Fig. 10–6 Dr. Harold E. Edgerton, Massachusetts Institute of Technology
Fig. 10–7 (left and right) Jay M. Pasachoff

Chapter 11

Fig. 11–29 Swanke Hayden Connell Architects
Fig. 11–30 After Swanke Hayden Connell Architects
Fig. 11–40 Jay M. Pasachoff

Chapter 12

Fig. 12–29 Palomar Observatory Photograph
Fig. 12–30 Jay M. Pasachoff
Fig. 12–31 Palomar Observatory Photograph
Fig. 12–33 © 1978 Anglo-Australian Telescope Board
Fig. 12–42 NASA/JSC
Fig. 12–43 NASA/Goddard Space Flight Center

Chapter 13

Fig. 13–2 AP/Wide World Photographs
Fig. 13–3 After Bart J. Bok and Priscilla F. Bok, *The Milky Way*, courtesy Harvard University Press. Reprinted by permission
Fig. 13–11 (left) Jay M. Pasachoff
Fig. 13–11 (center and right) MTS Systems Corp.
Fig. 13–13 Jay M. Pasachoff
Fig. 13–14 Photo by Erik Borg
Fig. 13–33 Jay M. Pasachoff
Fig. 13–34 Photos by Erik Borg
Fig. 13–36 Jay M. Pasachoff
Fig. 13–37 (left and center) AP/Wide World Photos
Fig. 13–37 (right) Nathan A. Unterman

Chapter 14

Fig. 14–3 Courtesy of Caroll and Nancy Taylor
Fig. 14–4 Jay M. Pasachoff
Fig. 14–17 Jay M. Pasachoff
Fig. 14–27 *PSSC Physics*, 3rd ed. © 1971 by D. C. Heath & Company with Educational Development Center, Inc., Newton, MA
Fig. 14–29 Jay M. Pasachoff
Fig. 14–34 Dr. Daniel I. Becker, North Adams Regional Hospital
Fig. 14–37 Redrawn with permission of Macmillan Publishing Company from *Sound Waves: Their Shape and Speed*, Dayton C. Miller. Copyright © 1937 by Macmillan Publishing Company, renewed 1965 by Cleveland Trust Co.
Fig. 14–38 Adapted from Boyce, *Journal of the Fisheries Research Board of Canada*, 31, 1974.
Fig. 14–39 SSC-Photocentre-ASC, © 1968 Harvard *Project Physics*
Fig. 14–40 Courtesy of N. –E. Molin, K. Stetson, and E. V. Jansson, with the assistance of Donald White
Fig. 14–41 From Jørgen Christensen-Dalsgaard (1982). Proceedings of Conference on Pulsations in Classical and Cataclysmic Variables, pp. 99–116 (ed. J. P. Cox and C. J. Hansen, JILA, Boulder)
Fig. 14–48 Jay M. Pasachoff
Fig. 14–56 Photograph from Transonic Range, U.S. Army Ballistic Research Laboratory; courtesy of Milton Van Dyke, *An Atlas of Fluid Motion*

Chapter 15

Fig. 15–1 (left) Photo by J. Demmer, National Severe Storms Laboratory, National Oceanic and Atmospheric Administration

Fig. 15–1 (center) Big Bear Solar Observatory, California Institute of Technology
Fig. 15–1 (right) Jay M. Pasachoff
Fig. 15–6 Sandia National Laboratories
Fig. 15–7 Jay M. Pasachoff
Fig. 15–9 AP/Wide World Photos
Fig. 15–12 Courtesy of H. W. Jannasch, Woods Hole Oceanographic Institution
Fig. 15–16 After Karen Arms and Pamela S. Camp, *Biology*, Saunders College Publishing
Fig. 15–17 Tony Korody/Sygma
Fig. 15–18 (left) American Petroleum Institute
Fig. 15–18 (right) Mobil Oil Corp.
Fig. 15–19 J. Guichard/Sygma
Fig. 15–22 Volkswagen of America
Fig. 15–23 (left) A. E. Perry & T. T. Lim 1978, from Milton Van Dyke, *An Atlas of Fluid Motion*
Fig. 15–23 (right) NASA/JPL
Fig. 15–26 Courtesy of Ausable Chasm Company
Fig. 15–29 Jay M. Pasachoff
Fig. 15–31 ONERA photograph, H. Werlé 1974, from Milton Van Dyke, *An Atlas of Fluid Motion*
Fig. 15–32 Boeing Commercial Airplane Co.
Fig. 15–33 Arizona Sonora Desert Museum
Fig. 15–34 Jay M. Pasachoff
Fig. 15–37 Painting by Lois Cohen, Griffith Observatory
Fig. 15–39 Paul E. Dimotakis, R. C. Lye & D. Z. Papantoniou 1981, from Milton Van Dyke, *An Atlas of Fluid Motion*
Fig. 15–44 Jay M. Pasachoff

Chapter 16

Fig. 16–1 Kim Vandiver and Dr. Harold E. Edgerton, Massachusetts Institute of Technology
Fig. 16–3 Jay M. Pasachoff
Fig. 16–4 Photo by Erik Borg
Fig. 16–14 Courtesy of E. L. Koschmieder 1974, from Milton Van Dyke, *An Atlas of Fluid Motion*
Fig. 16–15 Photograph obtained by Gören Scharmer at the La Palma Astrophysics Research Station of the Royal Swedish Academy of Sciences
Fig. 16–20 Courtesy of Stephen H. Schneider, after Starley L. Thompson and Stephen H. Schneider, "Nuclear Winter Reappraised," *Foreign Affairs*, Summer, 1986

Chapter 17

Fig. 17–9 Lou Gilliam, National Optical Astronomy Observatories/National Solar Observatory
Fig. 17–11 The Open University, S272, *The Physics of Matter*, courtesy Oxford University Press
Fig. 17–13 Ken Karp
Fig. 17–16 Jay M. Pasachoff
Fig. 17–21 National Bureau of Standards, courtesy of Charles Tilford
Fig. 17–22 AP/Wide World Photos

Chapter 19

Fig. 19–1 American Electric Power System
Fig. 19–5 Jay M. Pasachoff
Fig. 19–6 Environmental Protection Agency, courtesy of Scott, Foresman and Co.
Fig. 19–15 Tennessee Valley Authority
Fig. 19–17 Pennsylvania Power & Light Company
Fig. 19–18 Lockheed Missiles and Space Company, Inc.
Fig. 19–19 Southern California Edison Company
Fig. 19–23 Data from A. Lovins, *Soft Energy Paths*, Ballinger Publishing Co., Cambridge, MA, 1977
Fig. 19–24 Photo by Erik Borg

Chapter 20

Fig. 20–6 University of California, Lawrence Berkeley Laboratory

Chapter 21

Fig. 21–3 Jay M. Pasachoff
Fig. 21–16 *PSSC Physics*, 3rd ed. © 1971 by D. C. Heath & Company, with Educational Development Center, Inc., Newton, MA
Fig. 21–17 The Franklin Institute, Philadelphia, PA, photo by ©. Richard Dunhoff, courtesy of Donald A. Cooke

Chapter 22

Fig. 22–1 Jay M. Pasachoff
Fig. 22–2 Courtesy of Research-Cottrell, Inc.
Fig. 22–18 Photo by Erik Borg
Fig. 22–24 Jay M. Pasachoff
Fig. 22–27 Object courtesy of SLAC and Sidney Drell; photo by Oscar Kapp, University of Chicago

Chapter 23

Fig. 23–25 Jay M. Pasachoff
Fig. 23–27 Jay M. Pasachoff

Chapter 24

Fig. 24–6 National Center for Atmospheric Research
Fig. 24–10 Photo by Erik Borg
Fig. 24–12 Photo by Erik Borg
Fig. 24–13 Photo by Erik Borg
Fig. 24–14 (left) Jay M. Pasachoff
Fig. 24–14 (right) Los Alamos Scientific Laboratory

Chapter 25

Fig. 25–1 From a painting by Edgard Maxence, Institution of Electrical Engineers, courtesy of American Institute of Physics, Niels Bohr Library
Fig. 25–3 High Altitude Observatory and NASA
Fig. 25–11 Jay M. Pasachoff
Fig. 25–16 (left) Smithsonian Institution
Fig. 25–16 (right) Jay M. Pasachoff

Fig. 25–19   Jay M. Pasachoff
Fig. 25–20   Courtesy of AT&T Bell Laboratories
Fig. 25–22   Fermi National Accelerator Laboratory

Chapter 26

Fig. 26–1   Adapted with permission from R. Markson, *Nature*, vol. 273, No. 5658, p. 104, copyright © 1978 Macmillan Journals Limited
Fig. 26–7   Photo by Erik Borg
Fig. 26–17   (left and right) Jay M. Pasachoff
Fig. 26–21   Jay M. Pasachoff
Fig. 26–28   (left) Jay M. Pasachoff
Fig. 26–28   (right) Jay M. Pasachoff
Fig. 26–35   Photo by Erik Borg
Fig. 26–36   Photo by Erik Borg

Chapter 27

Fig. 27–1   Jay M. Pasachoff
Fig. 27–2   (left) D. Balkwill, D. Maratea, and R. Blakemore
Fig. 27–2   (right) R. Blakemore
Fig. 27–4   (right) From *PSSC Physics*, 3rd ed., copyright © 1971 by D. C. Heath and Co., with Educational Development Center, Inc., Newton, MA
Fig. 27–6   Stanford University
Fig. 27–10   Courtesy of the Francis Bitter National Magnet Laboratory, supported at the Massachusetts Institute of Technology by the National Science Foundation
Fig. 27–14   Palomar Observatory Photograph
Fig. 27–18   High Altitude Observatory and NASA
Fig. 27–20   (center) Photo by Joseph L. Montani © 1978
Fig. 27–20   (right) L. A. Frank, University of Iowa
Fig. 27–21   After "The Origin of the Oceanic Ridges," E. Orowan. Copyright © 1969 by Scientific American, Inc. All rights reserved.
Fig. 27–23   Central Design Group, Superconducting Super Collider, Lawrence Berkeley Laboratory, University of California
Fig. 27–24   Taken for *Fortune* by Ivan Masaar, Black Star
Fig. 27–25   Fermi National Accelerator Laboratory
Fig. 27–27   Courtesy of Princeton Plasma Physics Laboratory
Fig. 27–30   Jay M. Pasachoff
Fig. 27–32   Walker Scientific, Inc.
Fig. 27–43   (left, center, and right) Jay M. Pasachoff
Fig. 27–45   General Electric Research and Development Center
Fig. 27–47   Photo by William L. Masterton, from Masterton/Slowinski/Stanitski: *Chemical Principles*, Sixth Edition, courtesy of Saunders College Publishing
Fig. 27–50   William Kirk, Stanford University

Chapter 28

Fig. 28–2   Courtesy of American Association of Physics Teachers

Fig. 28–8   (left) Big Bear Solar Observatory, California Institute of Technology
Fig. 28–8   (right) National Geophysical Data Center, NOAA, D. C. Wilkinson
Fig. 28–9   (left and right) High Altitude Observatory
Fig. 28–14   From *PSSC Physics*, 3rd ed. © 1971 by D. C. Heath & Company, with Educational Development Center, Inc., Newton, MA
Fig. 28–24   (left) High Altitude Observatory and NASA
Fig. 28–24   (right) Adapted from R. Wolfson, *Astrophysical Journal*, v 288, 1985, p. 776, published by the University of Chicago Press; © 1985 The American Astronomical Society
Fig. 28–33   From *PSSC Physics*, 3rd ed. © 1971 by D. C. Heath & Company, with Educational Development Center, Inc., Newton, MA
Fig. 28–36   (left and right) Jay M. Pasachoff

Chapter 29

Fig. 29–19   Con Edison
Fig. 29–20   Jay M. Pasachoff
Fig. 29–21   Earl Richardson, *Topeka Capital-Journal*
Fig. 29–22   Photos by Erik Borg
Fig. 29–23   Jay M. Pasachoff
Fig. 29–24   Jay M. Pasachoff
Fig. 29–25   Photo by Erik Borg
Fig. 29–30   Courtesy of the Princeton Plasma Physics Laboratory
Fig. 29–38   Jay M. Pasachoff

Chapter 30

Fig. 30–3   Jay M. Pasachoff
Fig. 30–6   Photo by Erik Borg
Fig. 30–12   Jay M. Pasachoff
Fig. 30–14   High Altitude Observatory

Chapter 31

Fig. 31–12   Electronics Associates, Inc.
Fig. 31–15   Jay M. Pasachoff
Fig. 31–16   (below) Photo by Erik Borg
Fig. 31–30   Jay M. Pasachoff

Chapter 32

Fig. 32–4   (left) AIP Niels Bohr Library
Fig. 32–4   (right) U.S. Geological Survey
Fig. 32–11   Deutsches Museum, Munich
Fig. 32–12   Jay M. Pasachoff
Fig. 32–13   Vanscan™ thermogram by Daedalus Enterprises, Inc.
Fig. 32–16   (left and right) National Radio Astronomy Observatory, operated by Associated Universities, Inc. under contract with the National Science Foundation
Fig. 32–17   (left and left center) NASA/JPL
Fig. 32–17   (right center) TRW, Inc.
Fig. 32–17   (right) F. R. Harnden, Jr., and colleagues at the Harvard–Smithsonian Center for Astrophysics

Fig. 32—18   Painting by Lois Cohen, Griffith Observatory
Fig. 32—19   Courtesy of American Science and Engineering, Inc./NASA
Fig. 32—20   NASA Landsat/4 Thematic Mapper, processed by the IBM Palo Alto Scientific Laboratory/Ralph Bernstein
Fig. 32—33   Jay M. Pasachoff
Fig. 32—24   Palomar Observatory Photograph
Fig. 32—25   Jay M. Pasachoff
Fig. 32—26   Robert Mark, Princeton University
Fig. 32—31   Courtesy of AT&T Bell Laboratories
Fig. 32—32   NASA
Fig. 32—35   William Miller and Museum of Northern Arizona

Chapter 33

Fig. 33—6   Jay M. Pasachoff
Fig. 33—11   From *Conceptual Physics*, 5th ed., by Paul G. Hewitt, Little, Brown and Co., © 1985 Paul G. Hewitt
Fig. 33—13   From *Conceptual Physics*, 5th ed., by Paul G. Hewitt, Little, Brown and Co., © 1985 Paul G. Hewitt
Fig. 33—15   Stanford University
Fig. 33—23   Based on data of Kaufmann (1910), Bucherer (1909), and Guye and Lavanchy (1915), after R. S. Shankland, *Atomic and Nuclear Physics* (Macmillan, New York, NY, 1961), from Anthony J. French, *Special Relativity*, W. W. Norton & Co., New York, NY, copyright © 1968, 1966 Massachusetts Institute of Technology
Fig. 33—26   (left) William Kirk, Stanford University
Fig. 33—26   (right) University of California, Lawrence Berkeley Laboratory
Fig. 33—32   Courtesy of Anthony J. French, Massachusetts Institute of Technology

Chapter 34

Fig. 34—1   Jay M. Pasachoff
Fig. 34—2   From *PSSC Physics*, 3rd ed. © 1971 by D. C. Heath & Company, with Educational Development Center, Inc., Newton, MA
Fig. 34—3   From *PSSC Physics*, 3rd ed. © 1971 by D. C. Heath & Company, with Educational Development Center, Inc., Newton, MA
Fig. 34—9   (lower left) Carl Zeiss, Inc.
Fig. 34—9   (center) Perkin-Elmer Corp., E. O. Division
Fig. 34—10   (left) Chris D. Zafiratos, from *Physics*, 2nd ed. Copyright © 1985 John Wiley & Sons, Inc. Reprinted by permission of John Wiley & Sons, Inc.
Fig. 34—11   (left and right) Courtesy of AT&T Bell Laboratories
Fig. 34—14   (right) Courtesy of the Warden and Fellows of New College, Oxford
Fig. 34—15   Jay M. Pasachoff, from Newton's *Optics*
Fig. 34—18   (top) Jay M. Pasachoff and Donald H. Menzel

Fig. 34—18   (center) Courtesy of ARU Culham Laboratory, Berkshire, England; York University, Toronto, Canada; Imperial College, London, England; and Harvard College Observatory, Cambridge, Mass.
Fig. 34—24   Drawing by Charles Addams; © 1957, 1985 The New Yorker Magazine, Inc.
Fig. 34—27   Jay M. Pasachoff
Fig. 34—28   (right) Jay M. Pasachoff
Fig. 34—30   (left) NASA
Fig. 34—30   (center) Jay M. Pasachoff
Fig. 34—30   (right) NASA
Fig. 34—32   Jay M. Pasachoff
Fig. 34—33   (right) New York Times Pictures
Fig. 34—34   Jay M. Pasachoff
Fig. 34—41   Jay M. Pasachoff
Fig. 34—42   (left and right) Jay M. Pasachoff
Fig. 34—48   Irving Baras, Miles Agalin, Kenneth R. Barasch, and Stephen A. Obstbaum
Fig. 34—49   (right) Y. L. Lai and A. Pooley, Peabody Museum, Yale University
Fig. 34—50   Lennart Nilsson, from *Behold Man*, Little, Brown & Co., Boston, MA, 1974.
Fig. 34—51   Jay M. Pasachoff
Fig. 34—52   Reprinted courtesy of Eastman Kodak Co.
Fig. 34—54   (left) After a drawing by Tamron Division, Berkey Marketing Co.
Fig. 34—54   (right) Nikon, Inc.
Fig. 34—55   Jay M. Pasachoff
Fig. 34—56   Jay M. Pasachoff
Fig. 34—57   Jay M. Pasachoff
Fig. 34—58   Photographs by Ansel Adams. Courtesy of the Trustees of the Ansel Adams Publishing Rights Trust. All rights reserved.
Fig. 34—59   AIP Niels Bohr Library
Fig. 34—61   (top) Institute for Astronomy, University of Hawaii, photo by Jay M. Pasachoff
Fig. 34—61   (bottom) California Association for Research in Astronomy
Fig. 34—62   Perkin-Elmer Corp.
Fig. 34—63   (left) Jay M. Pasachoff
Fig. 34—64   Jay M. Pasachoff
Fig. 34—68   Jay M. Pasachoff
Fig. 34—69   (top) Photo Musées de Narbonne, photo by J. Lepage
Fig. 34—71   Jay M. Pasachoff
Fig. 34—72   NASA
Fig. 34—73   James E. Kettler
Fig. 34—78   Kunsthistorisches Museum, Vienna

Chapter 35

Fig. 35—1   From *PSSC Physics*, 3rd ed. © 1971 by D. C. Heath & Company, with Educational Development Center, Inc., Newton, MA
Fig. 35—5   Christopher C. Jones, Union College
Fig. 35—9   The Arecibo Observatory is part of the National Astronomy and Ionosphere Center which is operated by Cornell University under contract with the National Science Foundation

Fig. 35–10   (left) National Radio Astronomy Observatory, operated by Associated Universities, Inc., under contract with the National Science Foundation

Fig. 35–12   National Radio Astronomy Observatory, operated by Associated Universities, Inc., under contract with the National Science Foundation; (lower right) photo by Frazer N. Owen, Jack O. Burns, and Lawrence Rudnick

Fig. 35–16   (top) Christopher C. Jones, Union College

Fig. 35–18   (top) Christopher C. Jones, Union College

Fig. 35–23   (center and bottom) Michelson Museum, U.S. Naval Weapons Center, China Lake, California/U.S. Naval Academy, Nimitz Library, Special Collections

Fig. 35–24   Christopher C. Jones, Union College

Fig. 35–26   Jay M. Pasachoff

Fig. 35–27   Jay M. Pasachoff

Fig. 35–28   Christopher C. Jones, Union College

Fig. 35–29   From PSSC Physics, 3rd ed. © 1971 by D. C. Heath & Company, with Educational Development Center, Inc., Newton, MA

Fig. 35–30   High Altitude Observatory and NASA

Fig. 35–31   (left) G. B. Bianchetti and Salvatore Ganci

Fig. 35–31   (right) Christopher C. Jones, Union College

Fig. 35–32   (top) G. B. Bianchetti and Salvatore Ganci

Fig. 35–32   (bottom) Christopher C. Jones, Union College

Fig. 35–33   (top) Christopher C. Jones, Union College

Fig. 35–34   (top) Christopher C. Jones, Union College

Fig. 35–34   (center) David Stolzman

Fig. 35–35   Perkin-Elmer Corp.

Fig. 35–36   Jay M. Pasachoff

Fig. 35–37   Christopher C. Jones, Union College

Fig. 35–43   Christopher C. Jones, Union College

Fig. 35–48   Jay M. Pasachoff

Fig. 35–49   Jay M. Pasachoff

Fig. 35–50   Jay M. Pasachoff

Fig. 35–51   Jay M. Pasachoff

Fig. 35–54   Jay M. Pasachoff

Fig. 35–57   Jay M. Pasachoff

Fig. 35–58   Jay M. Pasachoff

Chapter 36

Fig. 36–1   Deutsches Museum, Munich

Fig. 36–2   Photo by Paul Ehrenfest; restoration of the negatives and production of the prints by William R. Whipple; AIP Niels Bohr Library

Fig. 36–3   AIP Niels Bohr Library, W. F. Meggers Collection

Fig. 36–5   (top and bottom) From PSSC Physics, 3rd ed., © 1971 by D. C. Heath & Co., with Educational Development Center, Inc., Newton, MA

Fig. 36–7   AIP Niels Bohr Library, Landé Collection

Fig. 36–8   A. F. Burrand and Robert Fisher, New Mexico State University, and American Association of Physics Teachers

Fig. 36–9   AIP Niels Bohr Library, Bainbridge Collection

Fig. 36–10   (left) Courtesy of the Department of Theoretical Physics. Lunds Universitet, Sweden

Fig. 36–10   (right) AIP Niels Bohr Library, Goudsmit Collection

Fig. 36–11   A. F. Burr and Robert Fisher, New Mexico State University, and American Association of Physics Teachers

Fig. 36–13   Tokyo Astronomical Observatory

Fig. 36–14   AIP Niels Bohr Library; Fankuchen Collection

Fig. 36–15   C. D. Anderson, California Institute of Technology

Fig. 36–17   Courtesy of Hughes Aircraft Company

Fig. 36–18   Jay M. Pasachoff

Fig. 36–19   (left) AIP Niels Bohr Library, Physics Today Collection

Fig. 36–19   (center) Photo CERN

Fig. 36–19   (right) Courtesy of the Harvard University Archives

Fig. 36–20   (right) Courtesy of Richard P. Feynman, inscription for Jay M. Pasachoff

Fig. 36–21   Irving Lindenblad, U.S. Naval Observatory Photograph

Fig. 36–22   AIP Niels Bohr Library

Fig. 36–23   AIP Niels Bohr Library, Stein Collection

Fig. 36–24   Jef A. Poskanzer, University of California, Lawrence Berkeley Laboratory

Fig. 36–25   Courtesy National Archives

Fig. 36–26   From Otto Hahn, A Scientific Biography, Charles Scribner's Sons, New York, NY, 1966. Courtesy AIP Neils Bohr Library.

Fig. 36–27   Rosalyn S. Yalow/Medical Media, VA Medical Center, Bronx, NY

Fig. 36–28   (top) AIP Niels Bohr Library, Meggers Gallery of Nobel Laureates

Fig. 36–28   (bottom) AIP Niels Bohr Library

Fig. 36–29   Chien Shiung Wu, Columbia University

Fig. 36–32   (left) Brookhaven National Laboratory

Fig. 36–32   (center) Chuck Painter, Stanford News Center

Fig. 36–32   (right) Brookhaven National Laboratory

Fig. 36–33   Fermi National Accelerator Laboratory

Fig. 36–34   (left) Photo CERN

Fig. 36–34   (center) Photo CERN

Fig. 36–34   (right) Photo CERN

Fig. 36–35   (left and right) Photo CERN

Fig. 36–36   Brookhaven National Laboratory

Fig. 36–38   Mt. Wilson and Las Campanas Observatories, Carnegie Institution of Washington

Fig. 36–40   Courtesy of David Wilkinson and R. Bruce Partridge

Fig. 36–42   National Optical Astronomy Observatories/Cerro Tololo Inter-American Observatory

INDEX

Volume 1 contains pages 1–509 and all Appendices.

References to illustrations, either drawings or photographs, are identified by i; references to tables by t. Page numbers marked s refer to an entry in the chapter summary. Page numbers marked b (for "basic") identify a definition.

aberration of starlight, 875–876, 904s, 906
aberrations, 940–941
absolute temperature scale, 426s
absolute zero, 407, 496
absorption lines, 922, 998
AC circuits, see alternating current circuits
AC current, see alternating current
accelerating frame, 90
acceleration, 22b–24, 34s, 46b–49, 63s
    angular, 276b–277, 278–279, 300s
    angular and linear, 277t
    average, 34s
    constant, 24–29, 25b, 34s, 49–50, 63s
        equations of motion, 27t
    gravity, of, 179, 181i
    radial, 60
    tangential, 60
accelerometer, 92
achromats, 940, 953s
action at a distance, 198, 200i
action-reaction pair, 86
Adams, Ansel, 945
addition,
    of forces, 83–86
    vector, 40–44, 41i, 42i, 63s, 64i
adiabat, 464
adiabatic processes, 464–468, 476s
air track, 100–101
Albrecht, Andreas, 1020
algebra, Appendix A
allowed transitions, 1007
alternating current, 810–812, 837s
alternating current circuits, 810–838
    power in, 831–833, 837s
ammeters, 679–680, 689s
ampere, 5, 639
Ampère, André Marie, 639, 640i
Ampère's law, 740–748, 742b, 744b, 754s, 843–847, 843t, 869s
    using, 744–748
amplitude, 309b, 333s, 342b, 366s
    peak-to-peak, 310b
analog computer, 820, 820i
analyzer, 986
Anderson, C. D., 1009i
Andromeda galaxy, 294i
angle of incidence, 911, 926
angle of reflection, 926

angle of refraction, 911
angular acceleration, 276b–277, 278–279, 300s
angular acceleration vector, 300s
angular displacement, 300s
angular frequency, 312b, 333s, 367s, 811
angular and linear quantities, 301t
angular magnification, 947–948
angular momentum, 291b–300, 301s
    conservation of, 294–297
        three dimensions, 299–300
    vector, 297
angular speed, 274b–276, 300s
    average, 275b
    instantaneous, 275b
angular velocity, 278b–279, 300s
antimatter, 167, 898, 1008
antisolar point, 949
aphelion, 185
apochromats, 940, 953s
apogee, 185
applied torque vector, 297
approximations, Appendix A
Archimedes, 382
Archimedes' principle, 382, 398s
Arecibo radio telescope, 963i, 981i
Aristotle, 73, 177
astigmatism, 940–941, 953s
astronomy, new, 858–860
astrophysical data, Appendix F
atmosphere, 375
atomic masses, Appendix E
aurora, 707i
automotive safety, 110
average acceleration, 34s
average angular speed, 275b
average impulsive force, 233b
average power, 138, 141s
average speed, 15
average velocity, 16, 33s
Avogadro's number, 432

back emf, 793–794, 795
background radiation, 1019–1020, 1023s
ballistic pendulum, 236–237, 236i
Balmer, Johann, 998, 1022s
Balmer series, 1000, 1022s, Plate 8
bar, 375
Bardeen, John, 655
bar magnet, 698–699

barometer, 380
batteries, 670–671
beats, 357b
Becquerel, Henri, 1012, 1022s
Bernoulli, Daniel, 391
Bernoulli effect, 393
Bernoulli's equation, 391, 398s
"big bang," 1019, 1023s
binding energy, 1012
Biot, Jean Baptiste, 732
Biot-Savart law, 732b–740, 754s
    Coulomb's law, comparison to, 733
birefringence, 988–989
black-body radiation, 999
black holes, 204i, 205, 860i
Bohr, Niels, 998, 999i, 1006i, 1008, 1022s
Bohr atom, 998–999
Bohr's theory, 1001–1002
boiling points, 445t
Boltzmann, Ludwig, 432
Boltzmann's constant, 381, 432b, 451s
Born, M., 1022s
Boyle, Robert, 432
Boyle's law, 432b
Bradley, James, 854, 876, 906
Brewster, Sir David, 988
Brewster's angle, 988, 992s
British thermal unit (Btu), 410
bubble chamber, 167i
buoyancy force, 382–383, 398s

Cabrera, Blas, 700i
calcite, 988
calculus, 71, 130, Appendix B
caloric, 408
calories, 410
cameras, 942–945
    pinhole, 944–945, 954s
candela, 5
capacitance, 621, 633s
    calculating, 622
    parallel plate capacitor, 622
capacitive reactance, 814, 837s
capacitors, 620b–633, 633s, 812–814, 837s
    circuits, in, 681–686
    connecting, 626–630
    dielectrics and, 630–633
    energy storage, 624–626
    inductors, comparison to, 818, 818t

capacitors (*continued*)
  parallel connection, 627, 628, 633s
  phase and amplitude relations, 816t
  series connection, 627, 628–630, 633s
  working voltage, 627, 633s
carburetor, 395, 395i
Carnot, Sadi, 486
Carnot cycle, 486, 498–499
Carnot engine, 486–490, 504s
Carnot's theorem, 488b–489
Carpenter's prism, 972–973
Cavendish, Henry, 182, 205s
Cavendish experiment, 181–182
Cavendish Laboratory, 182, 1011
Celsius temperature scale, 407
center of gravity, 211, 257b–258, 266s
center of mass, 211–218, 212b, 214i,
    216i, 217i, 227s, 264i, 289–290
  kinetic energy of, 226
  motion of, 216
  velocity, 227s
center of symmetry, 544
Centre Européen de Recherche
    Nucléaire (CERN), 1016, 1018i
CERN, 1016, 1018i
Chadwick, James, 1011
Chandrasekhar, S., 1010
charge, *see* electric charge
charge distributions, 520–521, 522s
chips, 654
chromatic aberration, 940, 953s
circuit elements, 665, 666i
  series, 674
circuits
  alternating current, 810–838
    power in, 831–833, 837s
  capacitors with, 681–686
  complex, 673–676
  elements
    parallel, 674
  high-Q, 828
  LC, 818–824
    damping, 823–824
    mass-spring system, comparison to,
      820t
    resistance, 823–824
  LR, 794–799
  open, 658
  RC, 685, 820i
  RLC, 823–830, 837s
    driven and resonance, 824–830
  series, 668
  short, 658
  simple, 667–673
circular motion, 56–63, 112–117
  and simple harmonic motion, 322–323
  work and, 134
circular orbits, 182–185, 183, 187i, 205s
  energy and, 191–192, 192i
circular polarization, 862–864, 869s,
    990–991

circulation, 741
Citicorp Tower, 315i
classical electron radius, 637
Clausius, Rudolph, 488
coefficient of kinetic friction, 103, 108,
    117s
coefficient of linear expansion, 447b,
    447t, 451s
coefficient of performance (COP), 494,
    504s
coefficient of restitution, 246b
coefficient of static friction, 107, 117s
coefficient of volume expansion, 447b,
    447t, 451s
cogeneration, 498
coherent beam, 961
collision time, 647–648
collisions, 232–244, 244s
  conservation laws, and, 234–236
  elastic, 235b, 238–244, 244s
    one dimension, 238–242
    two dimensions, 242–244
  impulse, and, 232–234
  inelastic, 235b, 236–238, 244s
    totally, 235b–236, 244s
color force, 76i, 1016
coma, 940, 953s
Comet Biela, 202, 216
compactification, 1018
complementarity, principle of, 1008,
    1022s
components of vector, 16, 33s
compressible fluid, 374
compression forces, 89, 89i
compression ratio, 507
computer, analog, 820, 820i
concave lenses, 930, 953s
condensers, *see* capacitors, 491
conditionally stable equilibrium, 263b
conduction, heat, 414–419, 426s
conductivity, *see* conductors, 644b, 660s
conductors, 565–571, 566b, 579s
  curved, 713–715
  force between two, 739–740
  Gauss's law and, 568–571
  ionic solutions, 649, 660s
  metals, 645–648
  methods of conduction, 644–656
  ohmic, 660s
  plasmas, 649, 660s
  stored energy, 616
  superconductors, 655–656
  two isolated, 613–616
conservation
  of angular momentum, 294–297
  of charge, 514
  of energy, 148–169, 159, 166–168,
    169s, 240–241, 244s, 389–391,
    766–774
  of kinetic energy, 238, 240–241
  of mass, 387–389

  of mass-energy, 166–168
  of mechanical energy, 154–159, 168s
  of momentum, 219b–220, 240–241,
    242, 244s
    law of, 219, 227s
conservation laws
  and collisions, 234–236
conservative field, 585
conservative forces, 148–151, 168s
constant acceleration, 24–29, 25b, 34s,
    49–50, 63s
  equations of motion, 27t
constant of universal gravitation, 178,
    205s
constants, inside front cover
  mathematical, Appendix G
  physical, Appendix G
constant-volume process, 462, 476s
constructive interference, 356, 367s, 961i
continuity equation, 387–389, 398s
continuous wave, 343b, 366s
contour map, 164i
convection, 419, 427s
conversion factors, Appendix D
convex lenses, 930, 953s
Cooper, Leon, 655
Copernican system, 178i
Copernicus, Nicolaus, 177
corner reflector, 927
corona discharge, 604, 605s
cosines, law of, Appendix A
cosmic strings, 1021
coulomb, 513–514, 522s
Coulomb, Charles Augustin de, 513, 515
Coulomb's law, 514–517, 515b, 522s, 528
  Biot-Savart law, comparison to, 733
Crab Nebula, 295i, 704i
Crick, Francis, 182
critical angle, 915–920, 953s
critical damping, 328, 333s, 823–824
critical point, 441b, 451s
critical temperature, 439b
cross-product, 253b–254, 254i, 255i, 266s
Curie, Marie, 1012, 1013i, 1022s
Curie, Pierre, 1012, 1013i, 1022s
Curie temperature, 720
current density, 660s
current loop
  field of, 733–736
  in magnetic field, 715–718, 733–736
  torque on, 717
currents, induced, 760–761
current sheet, 746–748
curved mirrors, 935–938
cyclic processes, 468–470, 476s
cyclotron, 708–709, 708i, 709i
cyclotron frequency, 704

Dalton, John, 1011
damped harmonic motion, 327b–330,
    333s

DC power supplies, 835–837, 838s
de Broglie, Louis, 1002, 1022s
definite integral, 129
degenerate matter, 1010
degrees of freedom, 472, 476s
De Moto Corporum in Gyrum, 176
density, 374b, 397s
dependent variable, 311
derivatives, Appendix B, 20b–21, 130
   partial, Appendix B, 164, 169s, 348
   second, Appendix B, 24
Descartes, René, 71, 912, 949
Descartes' law, 912
destructive interference, 356, 367s, 961i
diamagnetism, 721, 780–781, 782s
dichroic crystals, 989
dielectric breakdown, Plate 5, Plate 6,
   579, 626–627, 631t
dielectric constant, 578b, 580s, 631t,
   632
dielectrics, 577–579, 578b, 580s, 919
   capacitors and, 630–633
   energy density inside, 632
   properties of common, 631t
differential equation, 311
differential force, 200–201
diffraction, 971, 977–981, 992s
   single-slit, 978–980, 982, 992s
diffraction fringes, 978
diffraction gratings, 992s
diffraction ring, 980
diffuse reflection, 953s
Digges, Thomas, 178i
dimensional analysis, 33, 34s
diode, 835, 836i, 838s
diopters, 942, 953s
   induced, 577
dipole-dipole interactions, 576–577
dipole moment
   electric, 531
   magnetic, 717
dipole, 580s
   electric, 530
     in electric fields, 571–595
   magnetic, 699, 717, 735
Dirac, Paul A. M., 699, 1008, 1008i,
   1022s
dispersion, 355b, 367s, 920–924, 953s,
   970
displacement, 16, 33s
displacement current, 846, 869s
doping, 650
Doppler effect, 363–365, 367s
dot product, *see* scalar product
double-slit interference, 961–968, 992s
drift velocity, 640, 660s
driven harmonic motion, 331b
driven oscillations, 330–331
driving frequency, 331b
dynamics, 70–92
   fluid, 385–387

rotational, 285–287
   in three dimensions, 297–300
dyne-centimeter, 136

earth
   atmosphere, 859i
   magnetic field, 736, 804
   magnetosphere, 706–708
   weighing the, 181–182
eddy currents, 773–774
efficiency, 485, 487
Einstein, Albert, 2, 167, 204, 878, 878i,
   945i, 999–1000, 999i, 1003, 1008
   equation, 896–898, 905s
Einstein X-Ray Observatory, 916, 917i
elastic collisions, 235b, 238–244, 244s
   one dimension, 238–242
   two dimensions, 242–244
electric charge, 510–522, 522s, 529, 899
   conservation, 514, 522s
   distributions, 520–521, 522s
   elementary, 513
   magnetic fields and, 700–702
   net, 514
   point, 515
electric circuits, *see* circuits
electric current, 639–661, 639b, 660s
   effect on humans, 687t
   magnetic force on, 711–715, 711b
electric current density, 641–643
electric dipole, 530–532
   force on, 574–575
   torque on, 571–573
electric energy density, 617
electric field, 526–554, 526b, 553s
   calculating, 528–534
   dipoles in a nonuniform electric field,
     574–575
   dipoles in a uniform electric field,
     571–573
   energy and, 616–620
   energy density, 617, 633s
   equipotentials and, 591–594
   force on charged particle, 579s
   induced, 774–780
   infinite line of charge, 533–534
   line symmetry, 547–549
   matter in, 560–580
   nonconservative, 776–777, 781s
   plane symmetry, 549–551
   point charge, 528
   simple charge distributions, 749t
   single charge in, 561–565
   spherical symmetry, 544–547
   strength, 593
   thin spherical shell, 546–547
   uniformly charged sphere, 545–546
electric field lines, 535–542, 535b, 553s
   counting, 538–540
   electric flux, 540–542, 541b, 553s–554s
electric flux, 540–542, 541b, 553s–554s

electric forces, 181, 522s
electric generator, 770–773
electric motors, 718
electric potential, 153, 585–605, 586b,
   605s
   arbitrary charge distribution, 596–601
   dipole, 598–599
   isolated conductor, 602–605
   point charge, 594–596, 595b, 605s
electric potential difference, *see* electric
   potential
electric power, 658–660, 661s
electrical energy conversion, 661s
electrical measuring instruments,
   676–681
electrical safety, 686–689, 687t, 820i
electromagnetic forces, 510
electromagnetic induction, 760–782, 781s
electromagnetic spectrum, 856–860, 858i,
   869s
electromagnetic waves, 848–869, 869s
   energy in, 864–868
   generating, 861
   momentum in, 868
   properties, 855–868
   speed of, 854–855
electromagnetism
   four laws, 843–844, 843t
   relation to fundamental forces, 511
   relativity, and, 901–903
electromotive force, *see also* emf,
   666–667, 666b, 689s
electron
   charge of, 513
   discovery of, 1011
electron shell, 1007
electron spin, 1005–1008
electron volt (eV), 136, 587
electro-optics, 918
electrostatic analyzer, 564–565, 565i
electrostatic energy, 611–620
electrostatic equilibrium, 566–568, 566b,
   579s
electrostatic potential energy, 612b, 633s
electrostatic precipitator, 562–563, 562i
electroweak force, 75
elementary charge, 513
elementary particles, 1014–1015
elliptical orbits, 185–187, 185i, 205s
emf, 666–667, 666b, 689s
   back, 793–794, 795
emission lines, 922, 998
emissivity, 420b
energy, 134, 235
   conservation of, 148–169, 159,
     166–168, 169s, 240–241, 244s,
     389–391
     and induction, 766–774
   electromagnetic waves, in, 864–868
   gravitational potential, 168s, 187–193,
     188b

energy (*continued*)
  internal, 410, 456
  kinetic, 134–136, 141s, 225–226, 287,
      289–290, 324, 351, 390
    of center of mass, 226
    internal, 226, 227s
    in many-particle systems, 225–226
    relativistic, 899
    rotational, 287b–289
    total, 227s
  mechanical, 155b, 168s, 235
    conservation of, 154–159, 168s
  potential, 151b–154, 168s, 324–325,
      351, 390, 717, 723s
    curves, 159–162, 161i
    electric, 153
    and equilibrium 264
    force and, 162–165
    potential energy curves, 168s, 264, 266,
        266i
  relativistic kinetic, 899
  relativity, in, 896–899
  rest, 898
  rotational kinetic, 300s
  waves, 351
energy units, 136–137
English units, 4
ENIAC, 653i
entropy, 496–504, 499b, 505s
  and second law of thermodynamics,
      503–504
equal-area law, *see* Kepler's second law
equation of state, 431–432
equilibrium
  metastable, 267s
  neutrally stable, 264–265
  stable, 264–265, 267s
  static, 266s
  unstable, 264–265, 267s
equilibrium points, 162
equipartition theorem, 472–475, 473b,
    476s
equipotential surfaces, 591–594, 591b,
    605s
erg, 136
escape speed, 190b–191, 205s
estimation, 10–12, 12s
ether, 874–878, 904s
European Southern Observatory, 964
European Space Agency, 98i
exclusion principle, 1005–1008, 1011,
    1016, 1022s
expansions, Appendix A
exponential notation, 7–9
exponentials, Appendix A
external forces, 212, 221–222
eye, 941–942, 941i

Fabry-Perot interferometer, 977, 977i
Fahrenheit temperature scale, 407

farad, 621
Faraday, Michael, 621, 760
Faraday's law, 761–766, 777b, 781s, 805s,
    843–844, 843t, 850–852
Fermat, Pierre de, 950
Fermat's principle, 950–952, 950b
Fermi National Accelerator Laboratory
    (Fermilab), 710i, 1016
ferromagnetic materials, 720, 724s
ferromagnetism, 719–720
FET, 653–654
Feynman, Richard P., 1009, 1010i, 1022s
Feynman diagram, 1009
fiber optics, 917–918
field-effect transistor (FET), 653–654
field emission, 568
field point, 732
filters, 836, 838s
fission, 1013
Fitzgerald, George F., 885
flow tube, 387–388, 398s
fluid motion, 373–398
fluids, Plate 3, 374b, 397s
  describing, 374–376
  dynamics, 385–387
    applications, 391–396
focal point, 930, 953s
focal ratio, 943
focus, 929, 953s
foot-pound, 125, 136
forbidden transitions, 1007
forces, 71, 73, 74–76, 75i
  adding, 83–86
  buoyancy, 382–383, 398s
  color, 76i
  compression, 89, 89i
  conservative, 148–151, 168s
  differential, 200–201
  electric, 181, 522s
  electromagnetic, 510
  electroweak, 75
  external, 212, 221–222
  fundamental, 74–76
  grand unified, 76, 511i
  gravitational, 74–75, 257
  impulsive, 232b, 244s
  internal, 212, 221–222
  magnetic, 697–718
    on moving electric charges, 701
    on currents, 711
  net, 84
  nonconservative, 148–151, 165–166,
      168s
  normal, 88, 88i
  potential energy, and, 162–165
  restoring, 311, 314
  strong, 76, 1012
  super unified, 76
  tension, 89, 89i
  three dimensions, in, 132–134

  tidal, 201, 201i, 202i, 206s
  van der Waals, 438b, 576–577
  varying, 128–132
Fourier, Jean Baptiste Joseph, 355
Fourier analysis, 355
four-vectors, 900, 905s
frame of reference, 60–63
  accelerating, 90
  freely falling, 91, 92s
  inertial, 73
Franck, James, 1001
Franklin, Benjamin, 513, 640
f-ratio, 943–944
f-stops, 943–944
Fraunhofer, Josef von, 978, 998, 1022s
Fraunhofer diffraction, 978, 992s
Fraunhofer lines, 998
free fall, 29, 80
freely falling reference frame, 91, 92s
frequency, 309b
  angular, 312b, 333s, 811
  driving, 331b
frequency (wave), 346b
Fresnel, Augustin, 978
Fresnel diffraction, 978, 992s
friction, 102–112, 103i, 117s
  kinetic, 103b–107, 103i, 110, 117s
  sliding, *see* kinetic
  static, 107–112, 108b, 110, 117s
Friedmann, Alexander, 1019
fringing field, 614
Frisch, Otto, 1013, 1022s
full-wave signal, 837
fundamental mode, 361b, 367s
fusion reactors, 710–711, 779

Galilean relativity, 62, 64s, 875
Galileo, 71, 71i, 177–178, 854
gamma (unit), 702
gas
  ideal, 431–439, 451s
  real, 437–439, 451s
gas thermometer, 406, 426s
gauge pressure, 380
gauss, 701
Gauss's law, 542–553, 543b, 554s
  conductors, and, 568–571
  electricity, 843–844, 843t, 850
  magnetism, 731, 754s, 843–844, 843t,
      850
  spherical symmetry, 544–547
gaussian surface, 544, 554s
Geiger, Hans, 1011
Gell-Mann, Murray, 1014, 1023s
general theory of relativity, 204, 206s,
    903–904, 905s, 952
  gravity and, 203–205
geometrical optics, 909–954
geosynchronous orbit, 185, 185i, 205s
Giotto spacecraft, 1, 98i

Glashow, Sheldon, 75, 1015, 1017, 1017i, 1023s
gluons, 1016
Goddard, Robert, 222, 222i
Goeppert Mayer, Maria, 1012, 1012i, 1022s
Goudsmit, Samuel, 1006, 1022s
gradient, 164, 169s
grand unified force, 76, 511i
grand-unified theories (GUTs), 1017, 1023s
gratings, 971–973
  resolving power, 972
gravimeter, 336
gravitation, 176–204
gravitational field, 198–200, 199b, 199i, 201i, 205s
gravitational force, 74–75, 199i, 257
gravitational potential energy, 168s, 187–193, 188b, 205s
gravitational waves, 204i, 205
gravity, 29, 34s, 80–83
  acceleration of, 179, 181i
  center of, 257b–258
  constant acceleration of, 29–33
  effect on spherical mass, 195–198
    mass inside shell, 197–198, 197i, 198i, 199i
    mass outside shell, 197
  general theory of relativity, and, 203–205
grazing incidence, 916–917
Great Red Spot, Plate 4
Greek alphabet, inside back cover
"green flash," 924, 924i
grism, 972–973
ground, 591
Guth, Alan, 1020
GUTs (grand-unified theories), 1017, 1023s

Hahn, Otto, 1013, 1013i
Hall, Edwin H., 882
Hall effect, 713
Halley, Edmond, 176, 194i
Halley's Comet, 1, 46i, 47, 47i, 98i, 186, 186i, 189–190, 194i
H-alpha line, Plate 8, Plate 9
harmonic motion
  damped, 327b–330
  driven, 331b
  simple, 310b–327, 323i, 333s
    applications, 316–322
    energy in, 324–327
    two dimensions, 322–324
harmonics, 361b, 367s
heat, 404–427, 426s
  and phase changes, 444–446
heat capacity, 411b–412, 426s
heat engines, 483–490, 490–492, 504s

heat of fusion, 444b, 445t, 451s
heat pumps, 493–496
heat of sublimation, 451s
heat transfer, 413–421, 426s
  conduction, 414–419, 426s
  convection, 419, 427s
  radiation, 420–421, 427s
heat of transformation, 451s
heat of vaporization, 444b, 445t, 451s
heats of transformation, 444b
Heisenberg, Werner, 1003, 1004i, 1022s
Heisenberg's uncertainty principle, 1003–1005, 1004b, 1022s
henry, 790
Henry, Joseph, 760, 790
hertz, 309b
Hertz, Gustav, 1001
Hertz, Heinrich, 309, 856
high-Q circuit, 828
Hooke's law, 89, 92s
horsepower, 138
Hubble, Edwin, 1019, 1019i, 1023s
Hubble constant, 1019
Hubble's law, 1019, 1023s
Hubble Space Telescope, 947, 947i, 955i, 980, 981i
Hull, G. F., 868
Huygens, Christian, 854, 912, 982
Huygens' principle, 982–985, 982b, 992s
hydraulic braking system, 377–378
hydrogen
  Balmer series, 1000, 1022s, Plate 8
  Lyman series, 1000
hydrostatic equilibrium, 376, 397s
  with gravity, 378–382
hyperbolic orbits, 187i, 205s
hysteresis, 722

ideal gas, 431–439, 451s
  kinetic theory, 433–436
  specific heats of, 470–475
ideal gas law, 432b–433, 451s
ideal spring, 89, 168s
ignition coil, 790–791
images, 926, 953s
  real, 930–932
  virtual, 926, 953s
impact parameter, 242b, 243i
impedance, 828, 837s
impulse, 233b, 244s
  and collisions, 232–234
impulsive force, 232b, 244s
  average, 233b
inches of mercury, 380
incoherent beam, 961
incompressible liquid, 374
independent variable, 311
index of refraction, 912, 913t, 919, 953s
  vs. wavelength, 920i
induced currents, 760–761, 782s

induced dipole moments, 577
induced electric fields, 774–780
induced emf, 761, 782s
  and magnetic flux, 763–766
inductance, 789–805, 789b
  mutual, 789–791, 789b
  self-, 791–794, 792b, 805s
induction
  and conservation of energy, 766–774
  mutual, 805s
inductive reactance, 816, 837s
inductive time constant, 797, 805s
inductors, 792b, 805s, 814–817
  capacitors, comparison to, 818, 818t
  in circuits, 794–799
  magnetic energy in, 801–802
  phase and amplitude relations, 816t
inelastic collisions, 235b, 236–238, 244s
  totally, 235b–236, 244s
inertia, 72–73
  rotational, 279–285, 280b, 289–290, 300s
    of a disk, 282–283
    of objects, 283–284t
    of a ring, 282
    of a rod, 281–282
inertial frames, 73
infinitesimals, 20
inflationary universe, 1020–1021, 1023s
instantaneous acceleration, 20
instantaneous angular speed, 275b
instantaneous power, 138, 142s
instantaneous speed, 18
instantaneous velocity, 18, 34s, 63s
insulators, 566b
integrals, 130, Appendix B
  definite, Appendix B
  indefinite, Appendix B
  table of, Appendix B
integrated circuits, 654
interference, 355–356, 367s, 960–977
  constructive, 356, 367s, 961i
  destructive, 356, 367s, 961i
  multiple-slit, 968–970, 992s
  thin films, in, 975–977
  two-slit, 961–968, 992s
interference fringes, 961, Plate 3
internal energy, 410, 456
internal forces, 212, 221–222
internal kinetic energy, 227s
internal resistance, 670
International System of Units (SI), Appendix C, 4, 5i, 5t, 6i, 12s, 513
International Ultraviolet Explorer, 996i
Io, 202i
ionic solutions, 660s
irreversibility, 481–483, 504s
irreversible process, 458–459
isobaric, 443b, 462
isobaric process, 476s
isobars, 443b

isothermal processes, 460–461, 476s
isotherms, 439b, 460
isotopes, Appendix E

Jansky, Karl, 858
Jensen, Hans, 1012
Jensen, J. Hans, 1022s
John Hancock building, Plate 2
joule, 125, 141s
Joule, James, 125, 125i, 409, 410
Jupiter, Plate 4, 203i

Kamerlingh Onnes, H., 655
Keck Ten-Meter Telescope, 946i
kelvin, 5
Kelvin, Lord, 484
Kelvin-Planck statement, 488
Kelvin temperature scale, 406–407, 408i,
    426s
Kepler, Johannes, 176–177, 307
Kepler's laws, 177b
    equal-area law, see second law
    first law, 177, 179i, 185
    second law, 177, 179i, 307
    third law, 177, 205s
kilogram, 5, 6, 12s
kilowatt-hours, 136
kinematics, 15, 33s
kinetic energy, 134–136, 141s, 225–226,
    287, 289–290, 324, 351, 390
    of center of mass, 226
    conservation of, 238, 240–241
    internal, 226, 227s
    in many-particle systems, 225–226
    relativistic, 899
    rotational, 287b–289, 300s
    total, 227s
kinetic friction, 103b–107, 103i, 110,
    117s
kinetic theory, 451s
Kirchhoff, Gustav, 669, 998
Kirchhoff's current law, 672b
Kirchhoff's voltage law, 669b

Lageos satellite, 928i
Land, Edwin H., 862, 986
Landsat satellite, 860i
lasers, 1008–1009
Lawrence, E. O., 709i
Lawrence Livermore National Laboratory,
    626i, 1009i
LC circuits, 818–824
    damping, 823–824
    mass-spring system, comparison, 820t
    resistance, 823–824
LC oscillations, 818–820
Lee, T. D., 1014, 1014i, 1022s
Lennard-Jones potential, 161
lens equation, 933b
lenses, 929–935
    concave, 930, 953s

convex, 930, 953s
    thin, 930–935, 953s
lensmaker's formula, 938b–939, 953s
Lenz's law, 767b, 769, 771–772, 781s
leptons, 1015, 1016t, 1023s
lever arm, 250b, 251i, 266s
light
    parallel, 929
    speed of, 4, 854, 910
        in vacuum, 919
    visible, 856
"light box," 880–882, 880i
Linde, Andrei, 1020
linear and angular quantities, 301t
linear polarization, 862, 869s
line charge density, 520
line integrals, 133, 589, 743–744
liquid crystals, 575–576
liquid-drop model, 1012
lissajous figures, 324b, 324i
Livingston, M. S., 709i
load resistor, 670
logarithms, Appendix A
longitudinal wave, 342b, 366s
loop law, 669b, 689s, 796
Lorentz, H. A., 885
Lorentz contraction, 885–887, 904s
Lorentz-Fitzgerald contraction, see
    Lorentz contraction
Lorentz transformations, 889–892, 891t,
    904s
Lousma, Jack, 80
low-Q circuit, 828
LR circuit, 797–799, 805s
Lucid, Shannon, 955i
Lucretius, 1011
luminosity, 420
Lyman series, 1000
Lyman, Theodore, 1000

McDivitt, Jim, 192
macroscopic viewpoint, 426s
magnet, 698
magnetic dipole moment, 717b, 723s
magnetic dipole, 699–700, 723s
magnetic domains, 719
magnetic energy, 789–805
    density, 802–803, 805s
    in inductor, 801–802
magnetic field lines, 698–699
magnetic fields, 697–724, 698b, 723s
    current loop in, 715–718, 733–736
    earth, 736, 804
    electric charge and, 700–702
    energy, 799–805
    inside a wire, 745–746
    motion of charged particles in,
        703–711
    simple current distributions, 748, 749t
    sources of, 731–754

straight wire, 738–739, 744–746
    sun, 737
magnetic flux, 731, 761–764, 762b
    and induced emf, 763–766
magnetic forces
    on a current, 711b–715
    on a moving charged particle, 701
    on a straight wire, 711–713
magnetic levitation, 712
magnetic matter, 718–723
magnetic monopoles, 699–700, 699b,
    723s, 844
magnetic susceptibility, 721–723, 722b,
    723t, 724s
magnetism, 723s
magnification, 934–935, 954s
magnifier, 947–948, 954s
Maiman, Theodore, 1009i
Malus, law of, 862, 987, 992s
manometer, 380, 396
Marconi, Guglielmo, 856–857
Marsden, Ernest, 1011
mascons, 180
masers, 1008–1009
mass, 71, 80–83
    conservation of, 387–389
    relativistic, 894–895b
mass elements, 214–215, 215i
mass-energy, conservation of, 166–168
mass flow rate, 388, 398s
mass on a string, 112–114
mathematical constants, Appendix G
Mathematical Principles of Natural
    Philosophy, The, 72, 73i, 176,
    176i
matrix mechanics, 1003
matter, structure of, 1011–1014
    Nobel Prizes, 1022t
Max-Planck-Institut für Radioastronomie,
    980
Maxwell, James Clerk, 2, 76, 436, 845,
    846i, 855, 869s
Maxwell-Boltzmann distribution, 437b
Maxwell's equations, 845b, 847–848,
    848t, 850
    relativity, and, 901, 905s
    vacuum, in, 848
measurement systems, 4–7
mechanical energy, 155b, 168s, 235
    conservation of, 154–159, 168s
    law of, 155
mechanical wave, 342
mechanics, classical, 1b–403
Meitner, Lise, 1013, 1013i, 1022s
melting, 444
melting points, 445t
mercury, inches of, 380
Mercury, perihelion of, 203i, 204
mesons, 1014
metastable equilibrium, 263b, 267s
meter, 4, 5, 12s

metric system, 4
Michelson, Albert A., 877, 973
Michelson Interferometer, 973–975, 974i
Michelson-Morley experiment, 876–878,
    877i, 904s
microscope, 948
microscopic viewpoint, 426s
milligal, 181i
Millikan, Robert A., 513, 999
mirrors, 925
    curved, 935–938
    plane, 926–928, 953s
mode number, 361b
molar specific heat
    at constant pressure, 463
    at constant volume, 462
mole, 5, 432
molecules
    nonpolar, 577, 578
    polar, 577
moment of inertia, see rotational inertia
momentum, 71–72, 218–225, 219i, 220i,
    227s, 235
    angular, 291b–300, 301s
        conservation of, 294–297
        three dimensions, 299–300
        vector, 297
    conservation of, 219b–220, 240–241,
        242, 244s
    law of, 219, 227s
    relativity, in, 894–895
moon, 928i
    net force on, 193i
moons, planetary, Appendix F
Morley, Edward W., 877
MOSFET, 653
motion
    circular, 112–117
    damped harmonic, 327b–330
    driven harmonic, 331b
    laws of, 71–74
    in more than one dimension, 40–63
    orbital, 182–187
    relative, 64s
    simple harmonic, 310b–327, 323i, 333s
        applications, 316–322
        energy in, 324–327
        two dimensions, 322–324
    straight line, in a, 15–33
    uniform circular, 56–63, 56i, 57b, 63s,
        134, 322–323, 564
        acceleration, 59i
motional emf, 775
multimeter, 681, 689s
multiple-slit interference, 992s, 968–970
multiplication
    cross product, 253b–254, 254i, 255i,
        266s
    scalar product, 126–132, 253b
    vector by a scalar, 44i, 63s
multipole expansion, 552

muons, 882
mutual inductance, 789–791, 789b, 805s

National Magnet Laboratory, 702
negative charge, 513
negative feedback, 696
net charge, 514
net force, 84, 134
neutral buoyancy, 382
neutrally stable equilibrium, 263b,
    264–265
neutral stability, 267s
neutrino, 1011
neutrons, 1011, 1022s
neutron star, 295b
newton, 77, 92s
Newton, Isaac, 71, 72i, 176–178, 180i,
    182, 182i, 185, 187, 920, 949–950,
    960, 975
    Optics, 920i, 951i
    Principia, 72, 73i, 176, 176i
    theory of gravity, 203
newton-meter, 125
Newton's law of gravity, 203, 516
Newton's laws of motion, 72b, 92s, 274,
    347–349, 561
    first law, 72, 183
        and inertia, 72–73
    second law, 72, 76–80, 98–102,
        112–117, 117s, 134, 183, 193, 212,
        218, 227s, 233, 244s, 279–280, 311,
        317, 386, 434
    third law, 72, 86–89, 135, 222, 227s,
        285, 376, 434
        strong form, 285
    using, 98–117
Newton's rings, 975
Nichols, E. F., 868
Nicol prism, 989
Nimbus weather satellite, 185i
Nobel Prizes, 1004t, 1022t, Appendix H
nodal lines, 356, 367s
node, 360b, 367s, 672
node law, 672b, 689s
nonconservative electric fields, 776–777,
    781s
nonconservative forces, 148–151,
    165–166, 168s
nonohmic materials, 644
nonpolar molecules, 577, 578
nonuniform magnetic fields, 713–715
normal forces, 88, 88i
NOVA laser system, 626i, 1009i
N-type semiconductors, 651, 653, 660s
nuclear magnetic resonance (NMR), 332
nuclear model, 1011
nucleus, 1011
nutation, 299b

observables, 1004
ocean thermal energy conversion, 493

Oersted, Hans Christian, 732
ohm, 644
Ohm, Georg, 644
ohmic conductors, 660s
ohmic materials, 644
ohmmeters, 680–681, 689s
Ohm's law, 657b, 661s
    resistance and, 656–658
On the Motion of Bodies in an Orbit, 176
Onnes, see Kamerlingh Onnes
open circuit, 658
open orbits, 187
optical fiber, 917–918, 919i, 953s
optics, 909–992, 953s
    geometrical, 909–954, 953s
    physical, 909, 960–992, 992s
orbital motion, 182–187
orbital period, 184
orbits, 182i, 205s
    circular, 182–185, 183, 187i, 205s
        energy and, 191–192, 192i
    elliptical, 185–187, 185i, 205s
    geosynchronous, 185, 185i, 205s
    hyperbolic, 187i, 205s
    open, 187
order, 970
oscillatory motion, 308b–333, 333s,
    Plate 2
    properties, 309–310
OTEC, 493
overdamped circuit, 824
overdamped motion, 329b, 333s
overpressure, 380

pair creation, 167i, 898
    and charge conservation, 514
parallel axis theorem, 285b
parallel circuit elements, 674
parallel light, 929, 953s
parallel resistors, 671–673
paramagnetic materials, 724s
paramagnetism, 720
parity, 1014
partial derivative, 164, 169s, 348,
    Appendix B
particle, 15
particle accelerators, 1016, see also
    CERN, SLAC, Fermilab, cyclotron,
    synchrotron
Particle Beam Fusion Accelerator (PBFA),
    Plate 5
pascal, 375
Pascal, Blaise, 375, 377
Pascal's principle, 377, 397s
Pauli, Wolfgang, 1005, 1006i, 1011, 1022s
Pauli's exclusion principle, 1005–1008,
    1011, 1016, 1022s
peak-to-peak amplitude, 310b
pendulum
    ballistic, 236–237, 236i

pendulum (*continued*)
  physical, 321b, 333s
  simple, 319b–322, 319i, 333s
perigee, 185
perihelion, 185
period, 309b
  wave, 343b
Periodic Table, Appendix E
permittivity constant, 516
phase changes, 439–446
  and heat, 444–446
phase constant, 312b, 333s, 811
phase diagram, 444b, 451s
phases, 439b, 451s
phasor diagrams, 817, 817i, 827, 827i,
    837s, 983
*Philosophiae Naturalis Principia
    Mathematica*, 72, 73i, 176, 176i
photoelectric effect, 999
photon, 999
physical constants, inside front cover,
    Appendix G
physical optics, 909, 960–992, 992s
physical pendulum, 321b
physics, 12s
  classical, 12s
pinhole cameras, 944–945, 954s
Pioneer spacecraft, 191i
Planck, Max, 484, 999–1000, 999i
Planck's constant, 999
plane polarization, 986
planets, Appendix F
plane wave, 352, 849
Plasma Physics Laboratory (Princeton),
    779i
plasmas, 660s
plum-pudding model, 1011
PN junction, 835
point charge, 515
point dipole, 531
polarization, 861–864, 863i, 869s,
    986–991
  circular, 862–864, 869s, 990–991
  linear, 862, 869s
  plane, 986
  scattering, by, 991
polarization surface charge density, 583
polarizer, 986
polarizing angle, 988
polar molecules, 577
Polaroid (plastic), 861–862, 986
poles, 698
position, angular and linear, 277t
positive charge, 513
positrons, 1008, 1009i, 1022s
potential, *see* electric potential
potential barrier, 160, 168s
potential difference, 776–777
  measuring, 676
potential energy, 151b–154, 168s,

324–325, 351, 390, 717, 723s
  electric, 153
  equilibrium and, 264
  force and, 162–165
  gravitational, 168s, 187–193, 188b,
    205s
potential energy curves, 159–162, 161i,
    168s, 188i, 264, 266, 266i
potential well, 160, 168s
potentiometric voltage measurement, 696
pound, 83
power, 138b–141, 141s
  average, 138, 141s
  electric, 658–660, 661s
  instantaneous, 138, 142s
power factor, 833, 838s
power (wave), 352
Poynting, J. H., 865
Poynting vector, 865, 869s
precession, 297b–299, 301s
pressure, 375b
  fluid, 397s
primary coil, 833–834
Princeton University, 779i
*Principia, see Philosophiae Naturalis
    Principia Mathematica*
principle of complementarity, 1008,
    1022s
principle of Galilean relativity, 62, 64s,
    875
prism, Plate 7, 920i, 921i, 953s
probability amplitude, 1003
projectile motion, 51–56b, 63s
projectiles, 51, 182i
propagation, 340
proton, 76i
Ptolemaic scheme, 177i
P-type semiconductors, 651, 653, 660s
Ptolemy, 177
pulsars, 296b, 702
pulse, 343b, 366s
PVT diagrams, 439–444
PVT surface, 451s
Pyrex glass, 579

QCD (quantum chromodynamics), 1016
QED (quantum electrodynamics),
    1009–1010, 1022s
quadratic formula, Appendix A
quadrupole, 531
quality of energy, 496–504, 505s
quantized, 522s
quantum, 999
  energy of, 999
quantum chromodynamics (QCD), 1016
quantum electrodynamics (QED),
    1009–1010, 1022s
quantum mechanics, 3, 12s, 997–1023
  important dates, 1004t
quantum number, 999, 1005

quarks, 76, 76i, 513, 1014–1016, 1016t,
    1023s
quarter-wave plate, 990–991
quasi-static process, 458, 475s

radial acceleration, 60
radian, 5, 5i
radiation, 420–421, 427s
radiation pressure, 868, 869s
radio, 829i
  tuning, 829
radioactivity, 1012–1014, 1022s
radio telescopes, 963–964, 963i, 980–981,
    981i
rainbows, 948–950, 954s
Rankine temperature scale, 407
Rayleigh, Lord, 924, 981, 991
Rayleigh criterion, 981, 981i, 992s
Rayleigh scattering, 991
ray tracing, 930, 953s
real gases, 437–439, 451s
real images, 930–932
rectifiers, 835
reflection, 357–359, 367s, 910, 925–928
  diffuse, 925, 953s
  law of, 926b, 953s
  specular, 925–928, 953s
reflection grating, 971
refracting telescopes, 945, 945i
refraction, Plate 7, 359, 910–924, 953s
refrigerators, 488–489, 493–496, 504s
relative motion, 64s
relative permeability, 722b, 724s
relativistic invariants, 899–901
relativity, 12s
  electromagnetism and, 901–903
  energy in, 896–899
  general theory of, 204, 206s, 903–904,
    905s, 952
    gravity and, 203–205
  Lorentz contraction, 885–887, 904s
  Lorentz transformations, 889–892, 891t,
    904s
  mass and momentum in, 894–895
  Maxwell's equations and, 901, 905s
  relativistic invariants, 899–901
  relativistic mass, 895b
  simultaneity, 887–889
  space and time in, 879–880
  spacetime interval, 899–900
  special theory of, 2, 167, 200, 873–903,
    878b, 904s
  time dilation, 880–883, 886–887, 904s
  twin paradox, 883–885, 883i, 884i
  velocity addition, 892–894
resistance, 657b, 661s, 667
  Ohm's law, and, 656–658
resistivity, 644b, 645t, 660s
resistors, 812, 837s
  parallel, 671–673

resistors (*continued*)
  phase and amplitude relations, 816t
  series, 668–670
resolution, 963, 992s
resolving power (of grating), 972, 992s
resonance, 330–332, 333s, 367s, 825
resonance curve, 331b
resonant frequency, 837s
rest energy, 898
rest mass, 905s
restoring force, 311, 314
reversibility, 481–483
reversible engine, 486
reversible process, 458–459, 476s
R-factor, 417b, 427s
Richter, Burton, 1015, 1015i
right-handed coordinate system, 254
right-hand rule, 252, 252i, 253i, 266s,
    278, 278i, 701i
rigid bodies, 211
rings, planetary, 203i
ripples, 836–837
Ritchey-Chrétien design, 947
RLC circuits, 823–830, 837s
  driven and resonance, 824–830
rms (root mean square), 810–811
Roche, Edouard, 203
Roche limit, 203, 203i, 206s
rockets, 227s
  terminal speed, 224
  thrust, 223, 224i
rolling objects, 289–291
root mean square (rms), 810–811
Rossi, B., 882
rotational dynamics, 285–287
  in three dimensions, 297–300
rotational inertia, 279–285, 280b,
    289–290, 300s
  of a disk, 282–283
  of objects, 284t
  of a ring, 282
  of a rod, 281–282
rotational kinetic energy, 287b–289, 300s
Rubbia, Carlo, 76, 1017, 1018i, 1023s
Rutherford, Ernest, 998, 1011, 1011i,
    1022s
Rydberg constant, 1000

Salam, Abdus, 75, 1017, 1017i, 1023s
Sandia National Laboratories, Plate 5
saturated vapor pressure, 440b
Saturn, 203i
Savart, Félix, 732
scalar, 16, 126
scalar product, 141s, 253b
  work and, 126–132
scale height, 381, 398s
Schawlow, Arthur, 1008
Schrieffer, J. Robert, 655
Schrödinger, Erwin, 1003, 1003i, 1022s

Schrödinger equation, 1003
Schwinger, Julian, 1009, 1010i, 1022s
scientific notation, 7–9
second, 5, 6, 6i, 12s
secondary coil, 833–834
second derivative, Appendix B, 24
selection rules, 1007
self-inductance, 791–794, 792b, 805s
semiconductors, 566b, 649–655, 660s
  N-type, 651, 653, 660s
  P-type, 651, 653, 660s
series circuit, 668
series circuit elements, 674
series resistors, 668–670
shell model, 1012
shielding, 566
shock waves, 365b–366, 367s
short circuit, 658
SI units, 4, 5, 6i, 12s, 513, Appendix C
  conversions, inside front cover,
    Appendix D
  prefixes, 5t
significant figures, 9, 12s
silicon crystal, 650
simple harmonic motion, 310b–327, 323i,
    333s
  applications, 316–322
  energy in, 324–327
  two dimensions, 322–324
simple harmonic wave, 345b–347,
    354–355, 366s
simultaneity, 887–889
sines, laws of, Appendix A
single-slit diffraction, 978–980, 982, 992s
Skylab, 80i
SLAC, 167i, 886, 886i, 895
sliding friction, *see* kinetic friction
slug, 83
Snell, Willebrord van Roijen, 912
Snell's law, 912
sodium D lines, Plate 9
Solar Maximum Mission, 300i, 978i
solar thermal power plant, 493
solenoid, 750–753, 762–763, 790,
    792–793, 802–803
  inductance of, 792
  uses, 752
spacetime, 900, 905s
spacetime interval, 899–900
special theory of relativity, 2, 167, 200,
    873–903, 878b, 904s
specific heat, 410b–412, 411t, 426s,
    463–464
  of ideal gas, 470–475
spectral analysis, 921, 953s
spectral lines, 922, 953s
spectrograph, 922i, 923, 953s, 970
spectrometer, 923, 953s, 970
spectroscope, 970
specular reflection, 953s

speed
  angular, 274b–276, 300s
    average, 275b
    instantaneous, 275b
  angular and linear, 277t
  average, 15
  instantaneous, 18
spherical aberration, 929, 940, 953s
spherical mass
  gravitational effect of, 195–198
    mass inside shell, 197–198, 197i,
      198i, 199i
    mass outside shell, 197
spring, ideal, 89, 168s
spring constant, 89
spring scale, 89–91, 90i, 91i
stable equilibrium, 263b, 264–265, 267s
standing waves, 359–363, 360b, 367s
Stanford Linear Accelerator Center
    (SLAC), 167i, 886, 886i, 895
starlight, aberration of, 875–876, 904s,
    906
static equilibrium, 249, 254–257, 266s
  stability of, 263–266
static friction, 107–112, 108b, 110, 117s
statistical mechanics, 404, 426s
Statue of Liberty, reconstruction, Plate 1,
    262–263, 262i
steady flow, 386, 398s
steady-state motion, 331b
Stefan-Boltzmann constant, 420b, 427s
Stefan-Boltzmann law, 420b
Steinhardt, Paul, 1020
step-down transformer, 834
step-up transformer, 834
steradian, 5
stimulated emission, 1008
strangeness, 1014
Strassmann, Fritz, 1013
streamlines, 385, 398s
string, mass on a, 112–114
strong force, 76, 1012
sublimation, 444
subnuclear particles, 1014–1017
sun, Appendix F, 978i
  corona, 641i, 706i, 737i, 860i
  coronal streamer, 746i
  eclipses, 737i
  magnetic field, 737
  solar flare, 800i
  spectrum, Plate 9, 922i
  sunspots, 737i
superconductors, 655–656, 661s, 781
supergravity, 76
superposition principle, 193–198, 205s,
    353b–355, 517–520, 518b, 522s,
    529, 553s, 597
superstrings, 1018
supersymmetry theories, 511i
super unified force, 76

surface charge density, 520
symmetry axis, 547
synchrotron, 708, 710i
Système International d'Unités, inside
    front cover, 4, 5i, 6i, 12s, 513,
    Appendix C
systems of particles, 211–227

Tacoma Narrows Bridge, 332, 332i, 363
tangential acceleration, 60
telescopes, 945–947, 946i, 947i, 1019i
    radio, 963–964, 963i, 980–981, 981i
    reflecting, 954s
    refracting, 945, 945i, 954s
temperature, 404–427, 426s
    measuring, 406–408
    scales, 406–408, 409i
tension forces, 89, 89i
terminals, 666
terminal speed, 224
tesla, 701
Tesla, Nikola, 701
thermal behavior of matter, 431–451
thermal conductivity, 414b, 415t, 426s
thermal contact, 405
thermal energy balance, 421b–426, 427s
thermal expansion, 446–450
    water, 449
thermal resistance, 417b, 426s
thermal stresses, 450, 451s
thermally insulated, 405
thermocouple, 406
thermodynamic equilibrium, 405, 426s,
    458
thermodynamic processes, 457–470, 475s
thermodynamic state, 457–458
thermodynamic state variable, 457
thermodynamic temperature scale, 496,
    505s
thermodynamics, 404b–509, 426s,
    455–505
    first law, 455–457, 456b, 475s
    second law, 481–505, 484b, 504s
        and entropy, 503–504
        applications, 490–496
    third law, 496
    zeroth law, 406, 426s
thermometer, 426s
thin film
    interference in, 975–977
thin lenses, 930–935, 953s
Thompson, Benjamin, 409
Thomson, J. J., 1011, 1022s
thrust, 223, 224i
tidal forces, 201, 201i, 202i, 206s
time constant
    capacitive, 684, 689s
    inductive, 797, 805s
time dilation, 880–883, 886–887, 904s
Ting, Samuel C. C., 1015, 1015i

tokamak, 710i, 711, 711i, 779
Tokamak Fusion Test Reactor (TFTR),
    779i
Tomonaga, Sin-Itiro, 1009, 1010i, 1022s
toroids, 753, 803–804
torque, 249–254, 250i, 253, 266s, 300s,
    580s
    current loop, on, 717
    dipole, on, 572
    vector, 297
torr, 380
torsional constant, 318b
torsional oscillator, 317–318, 333s
total internal reflection, 915, 953s
totally inelastic collisions, 235b–236,
    244s
Townes, Charles, 1008
trajectory of projectile, 52–55, 52i
transformers, 833–835, 833i, 834i, 835i,
    836i, 838s
transient solution, 331b
transistors, 652–655
transmission axis, 861
transmission gratings, 971
transverse wave, 342b, 366s
trigonometric functions, Appendix A
trigonometric identities, Appendix A
trigonometry, Appendix A
triple point, 443b, 451s
    of water, 407b
tuned-mass damper, 315–316, Plate 2
turbulence, 397, 398s
turning points, 159, 168s
twin paradox, 883–885, 883i, 884i
two-slit interference, 961–968, 992s
Tycho Brahe, 177, 179i

Uhlenbeck, George, 1006, 1022s
uncertainty principle, 1003–1005, 1004b,
    1022s
underdamped motion, 328, 333s
unification, 1023s
uniform circular motion, 56–63, 56i, 57b,
    63s, 112–116, 322–323, 564
    acceleration, 59i
units, Appendix C
    conversion factors, Appendix D
units, changing, 6–7
unit vector, 43
universal gas constant, 432, 451s
universal gravitation, 177–182, 205s
    constant of, 178, 205s
    law of, 178b–182, 205s
universe
    expansion of, 1019
    inflationary, 1020–1021
unpolarized light, 861
unpolarized wave, 986
unstable equilibrium, 263b, 264–265,
    267s

unsteady flow, 386, 398s
Uranus, 203i

van der Meer, Simon, 76, 1017, 1023s
van der Waals equation, 438b–439, 451s
van der Waals force, 438b, 576–577
vapor, 440b
vaporization, 444
vector product, Appendix A
vectors, 16, 63s
    addition, 40–44, 41i, 42i, 63s, 64i
    algebra, Appendix A
    multiplication by a scalar, 44i, 63s
    subtraction, 63s
    unit, 43
velocity, 16–17b, 33s, 44b–46, 63s
    angular, 278b–279, 300s
    average, 16, 33s
    center of mass, of, 227s
    instantaneous, 18, 34s, 63s
    relativistic addition, 892–894
venturi, 394
Venus, phases of, 180i
vertical mass-spring system, 316–317
Very Large Array (VLA), 859i, 964, 965i
virtual images, 926
virtual photon, 1010
viscosity, 396, 398s
visible light, 856
volt, 587
Volta, Alessandro, 2
voltage, 587, 676
voltage divider, 670
voltmeter, 676–679, 689s
volume charge density, 520
volume flow rate, 388, 398s

water, thermal expansion, 449
Watson, James, 182
watt, 138, 141s
Watt, James, 138
wave equation, 350–351, 367s, 849b,
    1022s
waveforms, 343b
wavefront, 910
wave function, 1003
wave intensity, 864–868, 869s
wavelength, 343b, 366s
wave mechanics, 1003, 1022s
wave motion, 340–367
wave number, 346b, 367s
wave-particle duality, 1008
waves, 340b, 366s
    amplitude, 342b
    continuous, 343b, 366s
    energy and intensity, 351–353
    frequency, 346b
    intensity, 352, 353t, 367s
    interference, 355–356, 367s
    longitudinal, 342b, 366s

waves (*continued*)
  mathematical description of motion, 345–347
  mechanical, 342
  period, 343b
  plane, 352
  power, 352
  properties, 342–344
  reflection, 357–359, 367s
  refraction, 359
  shock, 365b–366, 367s
  simple harmonic, 345b–347
  speed, 343–344
  standing, 359–363, 360b, 367s
  transverse, 342b, 366s

wavelength, 366s
wave train, 343b
weight, 80–83, 92s
weightless, 81–83, 82i, 83i, 92s
Weinberg, Steven, 75, 1017, 1017i, 1023s
white dwarf stars, 1010
white light, Plate 7
White, Ed, 192
Wollaston, William, 998
Wollaston prism, 989
work, 124b–134, 141s, 455, 585–586
  electrostatic field, 775
  scalar product, and the, 126–132
  in three dimensions, 132–134
  total, 134

work-energy theorem, 135–136, 141s, 390
working fluid, 484
W-particles, 1017, 1023s
Wu, Chien Shiung, 1014, 1015i, 1023s

Yalow, Rosalyn, 1013i, 1014
Yang, C. N., 1014, 1014i, 1022s
Yerkes Observatory, 945, 945i
Young, Thomas, 960
Young's experiment, 960–961, 992s
Yukawa, Hideki, 1010i, 1014

Z-particles, 1017, 1023s
zeroth law of thermodynamics, 406, 426s
Zweig, George, 1014, 1023s

INDEX OF SYMBOLS

α angular acceleration, 276
α coefficient of linear expansion, 447
β coefficient of volume expansion, 447
γ specific heat ratio, 465
ϵ_0 permittivity constant, 516
κ dielectric constant, 578
κ_M relative permeability, 722
λ wavelength, 343
μ mass per unit length, 348
$\boldsymbol{\mu}$ magnetic dipole moment, 717
μ_k coefficient of kinetic friction, 103
μ_s coefficient of static friction, 107
μ_0 permeability constant, 732
ρ density, 374
ρ resistivity, 644
σ conductivity, 644
σ Stefan-Boltzmann constant, 420
σ surface charge density, 520
τ torque, 250
ϕ phase constant, 312
ϕ_B magnetic flux
ϕ_E electric flux, 541
χ_M magnetic susceptibility, 722
ω angular frequency, 811
ω angular speed, 275
$\boldsymbol{\omega}$ angular velocity, 278
Ω angular speed of precession, 298

∂ partial differentiation, 164
∇ gradient, 164
$\mathbf{a}$ acceleration, 22
$\mathbf{B}$ magnetic field, 698
c specific heat, 411
c speed of light, 855
C capacitance, 621
C heat capacity, 411
C_P molar specific heat at constant pressure, 463
C_V molar specific heat at constant volume, 462
e elementary charge, 513
$\mathbf{E}$ electric field, 527
f frequency, 309
$\mathbf{F}$ force, 72
g acceleration of gravity, 181
G constant of universal gravitation, 178
$\mathbf{I}$ impulse, 233
I rotational inertia, 280
k wave number, 346
k Boltzmann's constant, 432
k Coulomb constant, 516
K kinetic energy, 135
$\mathbf{L}$ angular momentum, 291
L luminosity, 420
m mass, 72

M mutual inductance, 789
p dipole moment, 531
$\mathbf{p}$ dipole moment vector, 532
$\mathbf{p}$ momentum, 72
P pressure, 375
q, Q electric charge, 515
Q heat, 411
$\mathbf{r}$ displacement vector, 17
$r_{\perp}$ lever arm, 250
$\mathbf{R}$ center of mass, 213
R thermal resistance, 417
$\mathscr{R}$ R-factor, 417
S entropy, 499
$\mathbf{S}$ Poynting vector (electromagnetic wave intensity), 865
t time, 17
T temperature, 407
$\mathbf{T}$ tension, 85
u electric energy density, 617
u unified mass unit, Appendix D
u_B magnetic energy density, 803
U potential energy, 151
$\mathbf{v}$ velocity, 18
V voltage, 678
W work, 124
X_C capacitive reactance, 814
X_L inductive reactance, 816
Z impedance, 828

PHYSICAL CONSTANTS

Speed of light	c	3.00×10^8 m/s
Elementary charge	e	1.60×10^{-19} C
Electron mass	m_e	9.11×10^{-31} kg
Proton mass	m_p	1.67×10^{-27} kg
Gravitational constant	G	6.67×10^{-11} N·m²/kg²
Permittivity constant	ϵ_0	8.85×10^{-12} F/m
Permeability constant	μ_0	1.26×10^{-6} H/m
Boltzmann's constant	k	1.38×10^{-23} J/K
Universal gas constant	R	8.31 J/K·mol
Stefan-Boltzmann constant	σ	5.67×10^{-8} W/m²·K⁴
Planck's constant	h	6.63×10^{-34} J·s
Avogadro's number	N_A	6.02×10^{23} mol⁻¹

SI DERIVED UNITS

newton	$1 \text{ N} \equiv 1 \text{ kg·m/s}^2$
joule	$1 \text{ J} \equiv 1 \text{ N·m}$
watt	$1 \text{ W} \equiv 1 \text{ J/s}$
pascal	$1 \text{ Pa} \equiv 1 \text{ N/m}^2$
volt	$1 \text{ V} \equiv 1 \text{ J/C}$
ampere	$1 \text{ A} \equiv 1 \text{ C/s}$
ohm	$1 \text{ }\Omega \equiv 1 \text{ V/A}$
farad	$1 \text{ F} \equiv 1 \text{ C/V}$
tesla	$1 \text{ T} \equiv 1 \text{ N·s/C·m}$
henry	$1 \text{ H} \equiv 1 \text{ V·s/A}$

For more extensive tables of physical constants and conversion factors, see the Appendices at the back of this book.